The Best Book of:
WordPerfect®
Version 5.0

Rose
Archie-Hillsman

HOWARD W. SAMS & COMPANY
HAYDEN BOOKS

Related Titles

Best Book of: Lotus® 1-2-3®, Second Edition
Alan Simpson

Lotus® 1-2-3® Financial Models
Elna Tymes and Tony Dowden with Charles E. Prael

Best Book of: WordStar® (Features Release 4)
Vincent Alfieri

Best Book of: WordPerfect®, Version 4.2
Vincent Alfieri

Best Book of: dBASE II®/III®
Ken Knecht

Best Book of: Framework™
Alan Simpson

Best Book of: Multiplan™
Alan Simpson

Best Book of: Symphony™
Alan Simpson

Best Book of: Microsoft Works for the PC
Ruth Witkin

Hard Disk Management Techniques for the IBM®
Joseph-David Carrabis

IBM® PC AT User's Reference Manual
Gilbert Held

IBM® PC & PC XT User's Reference Manual, Second Edition
Gilbert Held

The Waite Group's Desktop Publishing Bible
James Stockford, Editor, The Waite Group

The Waite Group's Modem Connections Bible
Carolyn Curtis, Daniel Majhor, The Waite Group

The Waite Group's Printer Connections Bible
Kim G. House, Jeff Marble, The Waite Group

Microsoft® WORD™ for the IBM® PC
Philip Lieberman, Phillip J. Gioe

Personal Publishing with PC PageMaker®
Terry Ulick

For the retailer nearest you, or to order directly from the publisher, call 800-428-SAMS. In Indiana, Alaska, and Hawaii call 317-298-5699.

The Best Book of:

WordPerfect®
Version 5.0

Vincent Alfieri

HAYDEN BOOKS

A Division of Howard W. Sams & Company
4300 West 62nd Street
Indianapolis, Indiana 46268 USA

International Standard Book Number: 0-672-48423-4
Library of Congress Catalog Card Number: 88-61225

Acquisitions Editor: James S. Hill
Development Editor: Jennifer Ackley
Production Editor: Sara Bernhardt Black
Coordinating Editor: Katherine Stuart Ewing
Cover Concept: DGS & D Advertising, Inc.
Cover Photography: Cassell Productions, Inc.
Indexer: Brown Editorial Service
Compositor: Impressions, Inc.

Printed in the United States of America

Trademark Acknowledgments

To My Mother, Alda Alfieri:
A Great Cook!

Contents

Part 1
Absolute Beginners

Part 2
Beyond the Basics

The Best Book of: WordPerfect 5.0

Part 3
The Nitty-Gritty

Part 4
Dedicated to Bibliophiles

Part 6
For Power Users

Appendixes

Preface

Dear Reader, it was inevitable. I had just finished learning all the many features in the *last* version of WordPerfect (version 4.2) when those busy folks at WordPerfect Corporation came out with a major upgrade. As you'll soon see, WordPerfect 5.0 has scads of useful enhancements. If you haven't purchased 5.0, by all means do so!

Some philosophers say that everything in life is a compromise. I wanted to include complete coverage of both versions 4.2 and 5.0, but you can see that the book is big enough as it is. Besides, the WordPerfect 4.2 book upon which this one is based is still available. So, forewarned is forearmed:

> This book discusses WordPerfect 5.0 on computers that use the MS-DOS or PC-DOS operating system. This book will not work with other versions of WordPerfect.

If you're new to WordPerfect, you'll learn version 5.0 quickly. If you're a 4.2 user, you have some adjusting to do. In either case, this book is for you. It takes you on an extended journey through the entire WordPerfect 5.0 realm and even helps 4.2 users get through the new relearning curve. I'll note where differences between 4.2 and 5.0 occur.

Perhaps a friend, associate, or "significant other" has recommended this book to you. Please thank that person for me, but be aware that the book is substantially different from its predecessor. Need I say (ahem) that it's better? For example, I've rearranged virtually everything to make it easier for you to find the information you need. I hope you enjoy the results!

Introduction

This book is a comprehensive exploration of WordPerfect 5.0 that offers new and experienced users valuable insights for the software, including:

- Clear explanations of *all* WordPerfect 5.0 features, with practical examples that illustrate each feature.
- Guided, step-by-step, "hands-on" instructions so you can learn WordPerfect at your own pace.
- Many humorous examples to make learning WordPerfect fun!
- A host of "tricks-of-the-trade" that professional word processors use to help you get the most out of word processing with WordPerfect.
- A command summary and cross-referenced index to help you locate information quickly.
- A concise and useful introduction to computers and word processing for beginners.
- Tips on using WordPerfect with laser printers.
- Information on how to work with WordPerfect from the WordPerfect Library program.

WordPerfect is an exciting and powerful program that offers virtually every word processing feature you'd ever want or need—and then some! Yet, it's surprisingly easy to start using WordPerfect right away. When you're comfortable with the basics of the program, you can explore WordPerfect's more advanced features at your own pace.

Please don't be intimidated by the size of this book. I wanted to make it as complete as possible. WordPerfect has so much to offer that it begs to be studied thoroughly. You don't have to learn everything at once, and there won't be any quizzes—I promise! By the time you've finished the book, you'll be a WordPerfect expert, or at the very least tired of my weak attempts at humor.

It's difficult to "lose your way" in WordPerfect. You can get help at any time by pressing the **F3 Help** key. You don't have to memorize too many program instructions, known as *commands*, because most commands are readily available from the function keys on the left side or top of your keyboard. A keyboard template reminds you which keys to use.

Whenever the program requires a further selection for the completion of a command, it presents a *menu*. As in a restaurant, the menu is a list of choices available to you. If you make a mistake, you can cancel and start again. Fortunately, unlike some waiters I've known, WordPerfect won't insult you. It will patiently let you make another choice.

You'll study a series of graduated lessons in your exploration of WordPerfect. If you're just starting out, you won't be confused or put off by all the advanced features. If you're a more experienced user, you can concentrate on only those features that you need. In any case, you'll work with WordPerfect just as you would in real life.

I strongly recommend that you go through the chapters in order, because some examples build on and revise earlier ones (see Appendix B, The Documents Used in This Book). Novice and experienced users alike will find a variety of useful tips for working with WordPerfect, "tricks-of-the-trade" that I learned in a real word processing center.

At the beginning of each chapter is a listing of the new commands and features that I discuss in the chapter. Appendix C summarizes the WordPerfect commands and notes where I introduce them in the book. Appendix D lists all the WordPerfect codes. Finally, there's a complete index. As a bonus, Appendix E shows you how to use the *WordPerfect Library* program, a companion to WordPerfect.

Although I would be flattered if you curled up with this book in front of a warm fire or glanced at it once or twice during television commercials, my real intention in writing it was quite different. To get the most out of this book, you should work your way through the examples at your computer and *learn by doing*. That way, you'll develop a solid set of good habits and reusable patterns that will pay you back continually in your real work.

After all, you didn't learn how to drive a car by sitting in front of the "tube," did you? You need practice before you'll develop the patterns to use WordPerfect effectively. Of course you will make mistakes! But you will learn from them and maybe even have some fun along the way. At least I hope you'll get a kick out of some of the examples that I have chosen.

Dear Reader, thanks a million for buying this book! I hope you enjoy reading and using it as much as I've enjoyed writing it. Please drop me a line, care of the publisher, to tell me what you think.

Acknowledgments

This book incorporates many helpful suggestions from readers of *The Best Book of: WordPerfect 4.2*. I am deeply gratified by all the kind letters that I've received from WordPerfect users across the country and in Canada. Keep those letters coming, and thanks for making the first edition such a great success!

Unlike my readers, the students in my word processing classes at the University of Southern California were a captive audience and subjected to the slings and arrows of my many outrageous puns. I salute their good nature, and from their problems and questions I learned a great deal about how to teach word processing.

I would especially like to acknowledge the folks at WordPerfect Corporation for their support throughout this project. Rebecca Mortensen had to put up with numerous questions and concerns, but she always came through with flying colors.

A tip of the writer's cap to: my friends at the law firm of Musick, Peeler & Garrett in Los Angeles, who taught me word processing; the staff of Hewlett-Packard's Boise, Idaho, Division, for providing the LaserJet soft fonts; Louis Hirsch; Jackie Burhans at USC's Office of Student Affairs and spouse James Howald at Hewlett-Packard's North Hollywood Division, for being there; the programmers at Inset Systems, for Inset the "screen dumper"; Bill Grout, who started the ball rolling; Lynn Brown for her stunning index; Jennifer Ackley, Kathy Ewing, and Wendy Ford at Howard W. Sams, for putting up with me; and my latest editor, Sara Black, who has endured countless tirades and a lot of gentle ribbing about her "heart condition" (it's improved considerably since I've finished this book).

Finally, thanks to all my friends who intuited without fail when a certain grouchy person was best left to himself and his deadline. Especially fond regards go to Ramón Ramos for his cheer, thoughtfulness, and continual understanding.

Vincent Alfieri
Los Angeles, California

Some Basic Concepts

If you're new to personal computing, please take the time to read through these next pages. If you are already "computer literate," you might want to skim the next few sections. But by all means, read the next section, Prelude: How to Use This Book, before you start Chapter 1.

Word Processing in a Nutshell

If someone were to ask me to describe *word processing* in 25 words or less, I would say: Word processing means that you *never have to retype*. This is, of course, a rash generalization, but it does get to the kernel of what word processing can do for you.

The implications of the above words are tremendous. Anyone who has spent a great deal of time in front of a typewriter—and one can spend a *great deal* of time there—knows that word processing is a new ball game. Sure, you can still apply the basics of typing to word processing. Entering text is "typing," when you think about it. But not having to *re*type your work is an amazing breakthrough for the person. Add to that the other things that word processing can do, and you've got a very powerful friend and co-worker.

When you type, you automatically get a "hard copy" version of your work. With word processing, you print your work as a separate step, but you don't have to print after every editing session. This alone can save you a lot of time.

Computers and the Perils of Adulthood

Why do kids have so little trouble adjusting to computers? Kids think that computers are fun. We adults, regrettably, are often saddled with maturity, which brings with it a variety of hang-ups. For instance: "The computer is smarter than we are"; "A computer can think"; "If we press the wrong key we'll break the machine"; "The computer is taking our jobs away from us"; "The computer will laugh at our mistakes."

Pick a hang-up; pick two, if you wish. Then forget about them because they're just not true! A computer is just a *machine* like a hair dryer or toaster, and the term *personal computer* (or "PC") should also remind you that this is *your* machine and that *you* are the person who is in control. It won't run itself, and a computer is definitely not as smart as you are. It's not even as smart as your cat!

Many people have *computer phobia:* They're afraid to touch a computer for fear that they'll make a horrendous mistake. Yet they do something every day that is far more dangerous: They get into their automobiles and drive to the grocery store. Ironically, if you make a mistake on a computer, you can generally correct it, and there's an end to the matter. What happens if you make even the slightest error of judgment on the road?

I haven't the foggiest notion how the internal combustion engine works, and yet I can operate one. You, in turn, need not trouble yourself with exactly how a computer works, but you can still use this new contraption, because, like all machines, it's there to help you. What's more, a computer cannot think, reason, intuit or even talk back to you. It is a perfect slave! You, however, must know how to harness its power and keep it under control, because, just like Goethe's "Sorcerer's Apprentice," it can't control itself.

So many new users of computers start off on the wrong foot. They read the documentation that comes with their new machines and wonder if they'll ever figure out what *bits* and *bytes* are. They are the victims of what I call the *terminology hassle.* I have tried throughout this book to avoid "computerese" as much as possible. When I introduce a new term, I explain it in everyday language.

What You Really Must Know About Computers

Even though you may not know how a car operates, it's still a good idea to have at least an inkling about certain things, such as keeping the gas tank full or making sure that you have antifreeze in the radiator. And if you know a little more about your car, chances are you won't get stiffed by a heavy repair bill. Similarly, there are only a few things that you really must know about your PC, but they can make working with it that much easier and save you a great deal of potential frustration.

First, a computer is a worthless piece of junk without two things: (1) electricity and (2) the instructions to run it. A computer must have its instructions "fed" into it whenever you use it. The instructions are known as the *program* (in this case, WordPerfect), and when you give the machine its instructions you're *loading the program*.

WordPerfect is actually a *sub*program that runs under another (the main) program of the computer. This main program is the *disk operating system*, *PC-DOS* or *MS-DOS*, different names for essentially the same product.

Note: A new operating system, *OS/2*, has not yet achieved currency. In this book, all references to DOS are to PC-DOS or MS-DOS.

The operating system, DOS, controls the flow of information between the various parts of the computer—the keyboard, central processing unit, disk drives, video display, printer, and so on. It acts very much like the hall monitor when you were in school, making sure that everyone moves along in the proper fashion and that order and decorum reign.

DOS is usually "invisible" to you, because you will spend most of your time working within WordPerfect. But, as parts of this book illustrate, learning how to use DOS in tandem with WordPerfect can be a great time-saver. I strongly urge you to be familiar with at least the basic DOS operations before you get too far along in your apprenticeship.

Formatting Disks

Make sure you understand how to *format*, or *initialize*, floppy disks before you start working. Unlike blank recording tapes, floppy disks can't be used right out of the box. Each computer has its own disk formatting command. On the IBM PC, this command is FORMAT.COM, and it's on the DOS disk.

It's always a good idea to format all new disks when you get them. That way, you won't be caught without a prepared disk when you need one. Fortunately, you can format a disk on the fly from within WordPerfect, but you'll save yourself needless hassle if you prepare all disks before using them.

You can also append a *volume label* to a disk if you use the /V switch with the FORMAT command (for example, FORMAT B: /V). A volume label can be up to 11 characters long, but should include only alphanumeric characters. DOS versions beginning with 3.0 have a separate utility to change volume labels. In DOS 2.0, you must reformat a disk to add a label.

Caution: When you reformat a disk, make sure you've copied any work that you want to keep to another disk first!

The Computer's Work Space

How exactly do you "load the program"? Where does it go? And why? Again, allow me to use an analogy to explain what is happening when you work with your computer. Normally, you work at a desk or other "workplace." This area contains not only the room for you to do your work but also the tools that you need. On your desk are a telephone, books, pencils, papers, and maybe even (heaven forbid!) a typewriter.

The computer has a workplace, too: *memory*. (Officially, it's called *random access memory*, or *RAM*.) All the work that you do in your computer is actually done in memory, although you will see your text on the monitor in front of you. (The monitor is only a convenience to you. The monitor is not necessary for the computer itself to function.)

The computer's memory is a tiny silicon chip that contains millions of little switches. Your words, and the program's instructions, are there in the form of *electrical impulses*, stored in certain locations and readily accessible at all times. That's why it's called *random access memory*. The computer would not know what to do when you give it an instruction (a *command*), or when you type in text from the keyboard if the program were not also in the memory workplace.

You probably work best when all your materials and tools are handy. The computer works only when all *its* materials and tools are in memory. It must have both its instructions (the program) and the specific work to be done (that is, the *file* containing your work) in memory at the same time. So, when you load the program the instructions that allow the computer to do word processing are copied into memory from the disk. This copy of the program's instructions stays in memory as long as you use the program, or until you turn off or reset your computer. The program itself is still on the disk, so you can use it again.

Normally, there are two programs in memory: DOS and WordPerfect. You'd have to exit WordPerfect and load another program from DOS, for instance, PlanPerfect. The WordPerfect Library is a special case. It, too, stays in memory so that it can work with the other programs. That is, the Library keeps track of WordPerfect and other programs and lets you switch between them easily.

Documents, Files, and File Names

WordPerfect refers to your work as *documents*. A document can be a letter, the chapter of a book, or a report, among other things. Think of a document as a collection of related text that will be printed eventually. A *file* is a container in which to store a document on the disk. (Actually, many computerists refer to documents and files interchangeably.) The *disk*, either floppy or hard, is the storage location.

Offices have filing cabinets with manila folders. On a computer, the file is the "folder," the document is the information in the folder, and the disk is the "filing cabinet." The folders in your filing cabinet are generally arranged in some kind of order, usually alphabetic. When you want to "pull" a file, you can find it quickly by locating the correct drawer and looking at the little descriptive tags on the folders.

Because it makes finding documents easier, you should set up a different file for each document. DOS, the computer's filing system, requires that each file be given a name, just like the little tag that is on manila folders. Because you can't physically *see* the files on the disk, you would ask the computer to retrieve the file and show its contents on the monitor. (At the same time, it's loading this file into memory.)

A computer can't read, so it can only look for a file by matching the letters of the name of the file, in the order that you type them, with the names of all the files on the diskette. No two files can have the same name, because if this were possible the computer would not be able to distinguish the two.

Computers are strictly *literal* beasts. As many others have pointed out, computers only do exactly what you tell them to do, not what you *mean*. They have no facility at guessing a file name. If you ask the computer to find and open a file named, say, TEST, but you type TEXT instead, the computer cannot intuit what you want. All it would do would be to match the letters T-E-X-T in that order and see if these four letters occur in the file directory on the disk.

DOS sees to it that each file has a distinct name, even if the names are as similar as CHAPTER.1 and CHAPTER1. Throughout this book, I give examples of naming files, but the ultimate decision rests with you. Develop your own system and then *stick to it*. The DOS documentation covers in detail the few and easy rules for file names. These rules are, in brief:

- A file name can have from one to eight characters, but no spaces.
- You don't have to use all eight characters.
- You can append a period and up to three more characters to any file name (the *file extension*).
- You need not use the file extension.
- Don't include nonalphanumeric characters (such as # or ?) in file names.

A few typical file names, all of which are "legal," would be: VERSION.1, SS.436, A, EXAMPLE, TT.A. A few "illegal" names would be: WP.##, SS.5437, LOSANGELES, TWO BITS.

Question: Why are these names "illegal"? *Answer:* The first contains unacceptable characters (##); the second has an extension that's too long; the third is longer than eight characters; the fourth contains a space. The operating system won't allow you to use these file names.

Saving Your Work

When you *reopen*, or *retrieve*, a document, you're actually instructing DOS to make a copy of it from the disk where it is stored and put the copy into memory. The original document *stays* on the disk, while the copy in memory is the one you edit. After you've made your changes, you instruct WordPerfect to *save* the edited document back to the disk, and in the process replace the original document with the revised version. If you wish, you can have WordPerfect keep the original in a separate backup file (Appendix A).

Caution: Never remove a disk from the drive until the current document is safely saved and the drive door light is no longer red.

Under normal conditions you don't have to worry about losing your work, because the original is always on the disk. But that presupposes that you've stored it there in the first place. When you start a new writing project, the new work is not yet stored at all. Any new typing is done in memory and stays there until you save it to disk, you turn off or reset your computer, or the power accidentally goes off. It is therefore important for you to take the necessary precautions to save your work.

My friend, James Howald, uses an interesting analogy to describe the difference between the work in memory and the document that has been saved on the disk. All work in memory is "cash," and all documents saved on the disk are "traveler's checks." If you're on a trip and you lose cash, it's gone forever. But if you lose traveler's checks, you can get a refund. Save your work to disk, and "don't leave your machine without doing it!"

If you wish, you can have WordPerfect save your text automatically at periodic intervals (say, every 10 minutes) so that even if you fall victim to Murphy's Laws unexpectedly, you won't be thrown off guard. But you must still save the entire document when you've completed the editing session and before you exit WordPerfect.

File Management and Disk Space

Keeping track of your computer files is just as important as keeping track of the files in your filing cabinets. If you have a hard disk, you're well advised to learn how to divide your hard disk into *directories* to keep track of different programs and work files. (If you work only with floppy disks, you don't normally take advantage of DOS directories.)

If the hard disk is your filing cabinet, then directories are like drawers, with the added plus that you can have drawers within drawers! A directory that contains the WordPerfect program can have many *sub*directories, each holding different work files—one for letters, one for reports, and so on. The WordPerfect directory is the "parent," and the subdirectories are "children." The main directory on the disk—the "grandparent" of them all—is the *root* directory.

Figure 1 presents a graphic representation of a typical hard disk directory structure, with several children directories below the parent WordPerfect (WP50) and Lotus 1-2-3 (LOTUS) directories. See your DOS manual for more information about setting up directories.

Because no disk has an infinite storage capability, you should also keep daily tabs on the amount of *available disk space.* You can check the amount of free disk space from within WordPerfect. This and other file management topics are in Chapter 9.

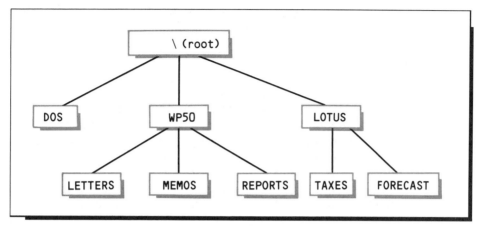

Figure 1   A Typical Hard Disk Directory Structure

DOS measures disk space in bytes, one of those nasty words that humbles beginners. A *byte* is merely the amount of space that the computer needs to store one character of information. Every letter you type thus takes up one byte of storage. That includes spaces and carriage returns, too, by the way. I recommend that you start a new disk if there is less than 10% of space available on the old disk. Hard disk users should periodically delete unused files or archive them onto floppies to free up disk space.

The Modular Approach

Use the *modular approach* to storing documents in files. WordPerfect works better and faster with smaller documents. Most computer users learn from experience that the most efficient way to maintain large documents is to break them down into smaller, modular files. For example, if you're writing a book, keep each chapter in a separate file. Develop a naming scheme that relates the files by name, such as CHAPTER.1, CHAPTER.2, and so forth. Again, see Chapter 9 for more tips on organizing your files.

A Word to the Wise About Backups

There is one *extremely important* procedure that you should know about before you work with any microcomputer: how to back up your work and program disks. Every computer book, every manual, stresses this operation, sometimes *ad nauseam*. But it really *is* important! I'll bet dollars to donuts that each one of you out there has (or will have) a horror story to tell about backups, or what happened when there *weren't* any backups.

This is a sad but true story. I once knew an administrative assistant at a large urban university who was in charge the word processing for all the professors in the department. She stored all the scholarly writing on a hard disk. Now, hard disks are great, but you have to treat them with kid gloves. And when they "expire," disappear, or are accidentally erased, trouble could develop if there are no backups. Although repeatedly admonished to make backups of the files on the hard disk, the administrative assistant either forgot or never got around to doing it. One day the computer was stolen! All that work may just as well have disappeared into thin air.

Dear Reader, please don't let this happen to you. You're too young to be in the loony bin or without a job. Determine from your work volume how often you should make backups, then schedule them as part of your normal routine. Think of it this way: *How much work would you care to lose?* Probably not too much! I always recommend that people do backups at least once a day. This is the rule that I myself follow. You may find, however, that you may only need to back up files perhaps once a week or once every two weeks.

If you use floppies, why not copy the DOS DISKCOPY.COM file, which lets you copy an entire disk easily, to the second WordPerfect program disk? Whenever you want to make backups, you can issue the Go to DOS command from WordPerfect's CTRL-F1 Shell key (Chapter 9), and you're ready to go. Or use WordPerfect's built-in file management feature, the F5 List Files key (also in Chapter 9), to copy individual files or groups of files quickly.

Hard disk users should make backups even more often than people with floppy disk-based systems. But they also have an easy way to do them with the special BACKUP utility. The first backup session will take some time, because you will be copying your programs, too. But then the BACKUP command allows you to back up only those files that have been edited since the last backup session, provided that you give the command correctly (the DOS manual tells you how). Note that this command has nothing to do with DISKCOPY, which can be used only to back up floppies.

Ben Franklin to the Rescue

Now for a bit of *elementary horse sense.* The personal computer is a new tool that is designed for a very old beast, homo sapiens. It did not drop down from the sky, so you can still rely on the age-old, common-sense rules that you've undoubtedly applied throughout your life. When people ask me the best way to learn how to use a computer, I tell them to follow Ben Franklin's advice. Try: "An ounce of prevention is worth a pound of cure." Or: "A stitch in time saves nine."

And remember the most common-sensical adage of all: "Practice makes perfect." The more you work with your computer, the more you will appreciate its tremendous power as your new productivity tool.

Prelude:
How to Use This Book

Before you begin, read through this section to familiarize yourself with how to get the most out of this book. I know you're eager to learn WordPerfect, but this'll only take a few minutes! Version 4.2 users should look this section over, too.

Icons

You'll see some funny things known as icons throughout the book. An *icon* is a pictorial representation of an important section or a point that I want to make. Here's a list of what these icons mean:

 This icon represents a *new* feature available only in WordPerfect 5.0, or a change to the same feature that was already in previous WordPerfect versions.

 This icon marks the beginning of an *example* that you are to type.

 This is a *tip* to help you.

 This is a *question*—no, it's not a quiz! It's just something for you to ponder, for which I *usually* supply an answer.

 This is a *caution* about something that could alter or damage your document.

 This icon shows a *hint* to steer you toward a solution to something.

 And this *note* indicates a feature or situation you should keep in mind.

The Keyboard

WordPerfect relies heavily on the *function keys*. These keys, labeled F1, F2, and so on, are either to the left of the typewriter keyboard or above it. Some computers have ten function keys; others have twelve. WordPerfect uses the function keys alone or with the *SHIFT, CTRL* ("control"), or *ALT* ("alternate") keys. Function keys F11 and F12 on the "extended" keyboard are helpful, but not necessary in WordPerfect.

Tip: If you don't like the function key setup, you can create your own keyboard layout (Appendix A). However, so that the examples work correctly, don't change the keyboard until you're finished studying this book.

The *numeric keypad* on the right side of the keyboard serves both as a cursor movement pad and, under certain conditions, for deleting text. (How WordPerfect uses these keys will be explained in the first few chapters.) The *cursor* is the little blinking line that runs along as you type and shows your position in the document. (The word cursor comes from the Latin word "to run.")

The ARROW keys move the cursor in the directions listed on the 2 (DOWN ARROW), 4 (LEFT ARROW), 6 (RIGHT ARROW), and 8 (UP ARROW) keys. If you see *numbers* on the screen when you press a keypad key, press the NUM LOCK key once to toggle back to cursor mode.

Watch out for the *CAPS LOCK* key. Not only is this key in the worst possible spot on some keyboards, but it doesn't allow you to access the characters above the numbers or punctuation marks. You must still use the SHIFT key for this. The CAPS LOCK key only enters uppercase *letters*. After you depress the CAPS LOCK key, every letter you then type will be in uppercase, except when you press the regular SHIFT key. With the CAPS LOCK key on, the SHIFT key works in reverse!

One final caveat: Touch typists who have for years used the lowercase *L* for the number *1* or the uppercase *O* for zero (0), had better mend their ways! Computers are finicky about such things.

Conventions Used in This Book

To make your journey through the world of WordPerfect as easy as possible, I have limited my basic instruction set to a few words, notably, *Press* and *Type*. Each instruction is listed on a separate line.

The Press Instructions

Press means to hit the key or key combination shown. For example:

Press   **RETURN**

means to press the RETURN key once. (WordPerfect prefers to call the RE-TURN key the *Enter* key.) Keys you should press right now are in **boldface** type, and I tell you when to press a key more than once. *Press* is thus always used to *issue a command.*

Often you'll have to hold down the ALT, SHIFT, or CTRL key as you press another key. Following the WordPerfect nomenclature, I indicate this type of command with a hyphen joining the two keys. Do *not* try to type the hyphen! For instance:

Press   **SHIFT-F8 Format**

You would hold down the SHIFT key and then press the F8 key, which WordPerfect calls the Format key. *Do not type these instructions.* I give you both the key name (here, SHIFT-F8) and its label (Format).

The only important exception to this general practice of holding down one key as you press another is when you use the HOME key on the numeric keypad. Most of the time, you press *and immediately release* the HOME key, then press the other listed key or keys. A comma in the instruction indicates that you should release the HOME key. For example,

Press   **HOME,DOWN ARROW**

means to *press and release* the HOME key and then press the DOWN AR-ROW key. This command:

Press   **CTRL-HOME,UP ARROW**

means to hold down the CTRL key as you press the HOME key. Then release both keys and press the UP ARROW key. Do *not* type the hyphen or comma in any "Press" lines! At times, WordPerfect uses a *caret* (^) to show the CTRL key, as in ^B.

The Type Instructions

WordPerfect often asks you to type a number or letter selection from a menu of choices to complete a command. I use the instruction *Type* and show in brackets the menu choice's name.

You can type the number or the *highlighted mnemonic letter* in the name. The highlight may be underlined or in a different color, depending on your monitor. This book always shows it as an underline. For example,

Type   **2** or **p** [Paragraph]

means to type the number **2** *or* the letter **p**. You don't have to use the SHIFT key.

Note: There are no mnemonic choices in WordPerfect 4.2, and a few 5.0 menus don't have mnemonics. When you type a number, use the normal number keys on the top row of the typewriter keyboard. At times WordPerfect Corporation may change a mnemonic letter in response to user suggestions. Always check the screen to make sure that the mnemonics I list in this book correspond to what WordPerfect displays.

Because there may be two menu items that begin with the same mnemonic letter, WordPerfect highlights another letter. Using the same menu that includes the previous menu choice, here's how I'd tell you to select Page:

Type   **3** or **a** [P<u>a</u>ge]

The *a* represents P<u>a</u>ge, because the *p* mnemonic already stands for <u>P</u>aragraph. When WordPerfect requests a "yes" or "no" answer, you need only type **y** or **n**. The entries you should type are shown in a boldfaced computer font, like the **1** here. And WordPerfect's messages or examples that you don't have to type appear in a nonbold computer font, such as this.

I also use the word *Type* when I'd like you to type in text from the keyboard. Thus:

Type   **Hello 'dere!**

means to type the phrase **Hello 'dere!** exactly as you see it. Make sure you type one space between each word.

Versions and Defaults

This book features the latest version, WordPerfect 5.0. The last version was 4.2. There are substantial differences between the two versions. I'm working with version 1.1 of the WordPerfect Library, but a new version 2.0 will probably be out by the time you read this.

Dear Reader, continual software upgrades are the boon and bane of computer book writers! Because of the inherent delays in the publishing world, this book might not include a discussion of every new feature as soon as it appears, and the messages and menus that you see here might not be exactly what's on your screen. When in doubt, consult the WordPerfect documentation for more help. Believe me, I'm trying to keep the book up to date, but it isn't easy!

Like all word processing programs, WordPerfect provides certain initial settings, also known as *defaults*, so that you don't have to think about margins, tab stops, line spacing, and such matters when you learn the program. At first you'll use the defaults, and then gradually learn how to change them as necessary. Later, you might want to configure the initial settings for your own work (Appendix A).

HOWARD W. SAMS & COMPANY

* fff*

Bookmark

DEAR VALUED CUSTOMER:

Howard W. Sams & Company is dedicated to bringing you timely and authoritative books for your personal and professional library. Our goal is to provide you with excellent technical books written by the most qualified authors. You can assist us in this endeavor by checking the box next to your particular areas of interest.

We appreciate your comments and will use the information to provide you with a more comprehensive selection of titles.

Thank you,

Vice President, Book Publishing
Howard W. Sams & Company

COMPUTER TITLES:

Hardware
- ☐ Apple 140
- ☐ Macintosh I01
- ☐ Commodore I10
- ☐ IBM & Compatibles I14

Business Applications
- ☐ Word Processing J01
- ☐ Data Base J04
- ☐ Spreadsheets J02

Operating Systems
- ☐ MS-DOS K05
- ☐ OS/2 K10
- ☐ CP/M K01
- ☐ UNIX K03

Programming Languages
- ☐ C L03
- ☐ Pascal L05
- ☐ Prolog L12
- ☐ Assembly L01
- ☐ BASIC L02
- ☐ HyperTalk L14

Troubleshooting & Repair
- ☐ Computers S05
- ☐ Peripherals S10

Other
- ☐ Communications/Networking M03
- ☐ AI/Expert Systems T18

ELECTRONICS TITLES:
- ☐ Amateur Radio T01
- ☐ Audio T03
- ☐ Basic Electronics T20
- ☐ Basic Electricity T21
- ☐ Electronics Design T12
- ☐ Electronics Projects T04
- ☐ Satellites T09

- ☐ Instrumentation T05
- ☐ Digital Electronics T11

Troubleshooting & Repair
- ☐ Audio S11
- ☐ Television S04
- ☐ VCR S01
- ☐ Compact Disc S02
- ☐ Automotive S06
- ☐ Microwave Oven S03

Other interests or comments: _____

_____

Name_____

Title _____

Company _____

Address _____

City _____

State/Zip _____

Daytime Telephone No. _____

A Division of Macmillan, Inc.

4300 West 62nd Street   Indianapolis, Indiana 46268   **48423**

Bookmark

HOWARD W. SAMS
& COMPANY

BUSINESS REPLY CARD

FIRST CLASS   PERMIT NO. 1076   INDIANAPOLIS, IN

POSTAGE WILL BE PAID BY ADDRESSEE

HOWARD W. SAMS & COMPANY
ATTN: Public Relations Department
P.O. Box 7092
Indianapolis, IN 46209-9921

Intelligent Printing and Forms

 WordPerfect 5.0 is very "printer-oriented." Not only does it take advantage of all your printer's features, but it also formats your document according to the printer you're using when you create the document (Chapter 5). This is part of what WordPerfect calls *intelligent printing*.

WordPerfect also wants you to learn a little more about *forms*. Forms are types of paper with specific characteristics, such as size and location. For example, the "standard form" is an 8½ by 11 inch page that you insert vertically into the printer. You may also want to create a smaller form for envelopes that you insert horizontally into the printer. For every printer you use, you can have different form settings. WordPerfect attempts to match paper size and type changes to the forms in your printer, but it will use the closest match if it can't find a form. To be on the safe side, however, you should "trip the forms fandango" and explicitly set up all the forms you need (Chapter 13).

File Format Changes

 There is good news and bad news for users of previous WordPerfect versions. The good news is that when you retrieve a document from an earlier WordPerfect into WordPerfect 5.0, the program automatically converts as much of the document as it can to the new format. That means all the text and most of the codes. You can also convert a 5.0 format back to 4.2 format (Chapter 36).

The bad news is that you'll have to make some conversions yourself. As a nice gesture, WordPerfect supplies a comment at the point where it can't make a conversion and tells you to convert the code manually. Here are some other important points about file conversions:

■ Pitch and font changes have been radically altered, so you'll have to amend all pitch and font codes. You can set up a *conversion template* in a special file (it ends in the extension .CRS) to help you convert codes that WordPerfect doesn't convert automatically. This is a complicated procedure, so it might be easier just to insert new codes directly into your documents (Chapter 4). See the appendix of the WordPerfect documentation.

■ You'll have to rethink how you've worked with different forms and page sizes, such as envelopes, and make some changes in this regard (Chapter 13).

■ You must redefine all 4.2 macros or use the MACROCNV.EXE program to convert them to 5.0 macro format (Chapter 7).

- You must select new printer definitions. The old ones won't work (Chapter 5). You can convert some font tables that might not be in 5.0 with the FC utility (Chapter 36).

- You can't use version 4.2 supplemental dictionaries in 5.0. Convert them first to 5.0 format with the Speller utility (Chapter 36).

- You should retrieve and save *all* primary and secondary merge documents at least once in 5.0 before you perform a merge.

- You might want to retain your 4.2 files and directories for a while during the time that you're learning WordPerfect 5.0.

Additionally, the CTRL/ALT key feature originally on the CTRL-F3 Screen key is no longer in the product, but you can still access the extended character set (Chapter 15) and even create your own keyboard layout for CTRL keys (Appendix A).

Installing WordPerfect

Follow the instructions in the WordPerfect documentation to set up the working program disks if you have a floppy disk system, or to install WordPerfect on a directory of your hard disk. In the former case, you'll format several floppies as work disks and copy the WordPerfect program, dictionary, and thesaurus files from the master disks to the work disks. In the latter case, you'll create a new directory (probably \WP50) on your hard disks and then copy the WordPerfect program files to that directory. WordPerfect 5.0 runs best if your computer has at least 512 kilobytes of memory.

 Caution: The CONFIG.SYS file, a special DOS startup file, *must* contain the line FILES=20 for WordPerfect to run correctly (or FILES=40 if you plan to run WordPerfect with the WordPerfect Library). CONFIG.SYS must also reside on your startup floppy disk or in the root directory of your hard disk. Because many other programs require this FILES setting, chances are it's already there! Here's how to find out.

First, make sure you're on the disk or in the directory that contains CONFIG.SYS. To view the contents of this file, type at the DOS prompt **type config.sys** and press **RETURN**. To add the FILES=20 line to the CONFIG.SYS file if it isn't there, type at the DOS prompt **copy config.sys + con: config.sys** (note the spaces!), press **RETURN**, type **files=20**, press **CTRL-Z** or **F6**, and press **RETURN**. Then restart your computer.

Installing the WordPerfect Library

Installing the WordPerfect Library, if you have it, also involves creating a new directory (probably \LIBRARY) on your hard disk and copying the Library files to that directory. The Library has to "know" in which directory the WordPerfect program files reside. After you start the library (see the Daily Warm-Up), make sure there isn't an asterisk (*) next to WordPerfect on the Shell menu. Type 4 [Setup] to access the Shell's Setup menu. Type the letter next to WordPerfect on the Shell menu—it's usually W. Type 1 [Edit] to bring up the Program Information screen.

Then press the **DOWN ARROW** key twice to reach the Default directory: line. Type the correct WordPerfect directory, for example, \wp50. Make any other necessary changes to the program information. When you're finished, press **F7 Exit** to return to the Setup menu, then change the program information for the other Library programs. When you're completely finished changing all program information, press **F7 Exit** to leave the Setup menu and return to the Library's main menu.

WordPerfect and Your Monitor

WordPerfect automatically detects what kind of monitor you have and will use the full capabilities of that device. Not all monitors can display the same special effects, such as underlining or boldface, so some of the WordPerfect screens shown in this book may look slightly different on your computer.

WordPerfect and Your Printers

Once you've installed WordPerfect, you must select the printer or printers you plan to use. To do that, you set up a *printer resource file* for each printer you have. Printer resource files end in the extension .PRS. See Selecting and Editing Printer Resource Files in Chapter 5.

Note: One of the most basic printers is the *standard printer*. It prints your text, but it can't do anything fancy with fonts or graphics. I used the standard printer when I was creating the typed examples in this book, except for a few examples in later chapters that demonstrate laser printer capabilities. *Depending on the printer you're using, the line endings of the examples may be different on your screen.* The keystroke instructions, however, will work correctly no matter what printer you have. If you want your examples to look exactly like mine, then select the standard printer.

During the beta test stage of WordPerfect 5.0, the new *fast save* feature was set to on by default, but now the default is probably off—a good choice. Fast save doesn't save all formatting with a document, so you normally can't print a document from the disk (Chapter 5).

So, follow the instructions in Chapter 5 to set up your printer or select the standard printer until you're finished studying this book. (You can still print to your printer with the standard printer resource file.) To explain in detail the ins and outs of printers would, alas, be beyond the scope of this book. However, here are a few points to consider before you begin.

There are essentially two types of printers, *parallel* and *serial*, depending on how they're connected to your computer. DOS "assumes" that you're working with a parallel printer connected to what it calls LPT1. This is a *port*, a connection in the back of your PC. If—and *only* if—you're using a serial printer, you must tell DOS about your serial printer with the MODE command. Do this before you work with WordPerfect to instruct DOS (1) where the printer is connected (for instance, COM1 or COM2) and (2) the printer's settings.

For example, to redirect the printed output from the assumed parallel printer port to the first serial port (COM1) and set up the settings for the laser printer used in Chapter 35, here are the instructions you'd issue from DOS *before* you load WordPerfect (a copy of MODE.COM must be on the disk):

```
MODE LPT1:=COM1:
MODE COM1:9600,N,8,1,P
```

The first line redirects the printed output, while the second line tells DOS that COM1 is a printer (p) running at 9600 bits per second, with no parity (n), 8 data bits, and 1 stop bit. You're probably confused already by the terminology! See the WordPerfect documentation, your serial printer manual, and your DOS manual for more information about what these terms mean. You must also tell WordPerfect what serial port you're using when you set up your printer.

It may take you a while to determine the exact paper position in the printer that works for you. Use trial and error to determine where you'll put the paper (forms) in the printer and what the top-of-form setting should be. Then rely on this setting consistently. The top-of-form is where the printer advances the top edge of the paper to align with the print head. Change the document formats or form specifications *within* WordPerfect when you need a different layout. As much as possible, let WordPerfect handle the actual formatting. Don't change your printer switches willy-nilly.

The Documents You'll Create

To save some typing work, you'll reuse documents from previous chapters. That's why it's best to study the chapters in order. However, if you intend to skip around, take a look at Appendix B. There you'll find a listing of all documents created in this book, including in what chapter the document was first created and in what further chapters it was used or changed. Make sure you complete all the examples relating to a particular document in their correct order.

What Else You'll Need to Begin

If you have a hard disk computer, you can save all documents in the same directory as your WordPerfect program files. If you're using a floppy disk system, you'll need one blank, *formatted* disk to store the examples. Label it *Book Work Disk*. At times I refer to the WordPerfect documentation, so keep it handy, too.

Two Good Tips

This is a step-by-step, "hands-on" book. I've tested it thoroughly to ensure that if you do all the steps in order, everything will work. However, if you have problems keeping track of where you are in the instructions, here's a simple solution. Keep a *place marker*—a piece of paper or a bookmark—at the current instruction so you never miss a step. I also recommend that you save all scrap paper and use it instead of good paper whenever you want to print. Do your part to conserve precious resources!

The Daily Warm-Up

You should be ready to go with working program and works disks before you begin using this book. I'm assuming that you have either a hard disk or two floppy drives and that in the latter case you're using the B (right or lower) drive for your work disk. The instructions in this book work with either floppy disk or hard disk systems. When there is a difference between the two types of computers—for example, when you have to switch floppy disks—I'll instruct you accordingly.

At the beginning of each chapter, you'll see the following little sign:

> **DO WARM-UP**

The warm-up includes the steps to load the program and to begin using WordPerfect. Because you'll do this every day, I've put the steps here to avoid repeating them at the start of each chapter. Of course, if you continue from one chapter to the next, you don't have to warm up. *But always make sure that you start each chapter with a blank screen.* In Chapter 1, you'll learn how to clear the screen in WordPerfect.

The warm-up is slightly different for floppy disk and hard disk computers, or if you're using the WordPerfect Library, so I've listed them separately next.

If You Have a Dual Floppy System

Insert your DOS disk in the A (left or top) drive and close the drive door. If your computer isn't already on, turn it on now and supply the date and time at the DOS prompts, pressing **RETURN** after each. Remember to use the 24-hour clock for the time. For instance, 1:30 p.m. is 13:30.

Remove the DOS disk and insert the first WordPerfect program disk in the A (left or top) drive and close the drive door. Insert the book work disk in the B (right or bottom) drive. Close the door for drive B. Now, switch over to the B drive and load the program from the A drive, like so:

Type   **b:**

(Don't forget the colon!)

Press   **RETURN**

Type   **a:wp**

Press   **RETURN**

In a few moments WordPerfect requests its second program disk:

```
Insert diskette labeled "WordPerfect 2" and press any key
```

Do as you're told! You'll see a brief sign-on screen, then an almost blank edit screen. You're ready to begin.

If You Have a Hard Disk System Without the WordPerfect Library

Turn your computer on, if it isn't on already, and supply the time and date at the DOS prompts. Make sure you use the 24-hour clock for the correct time. Then, move to the directory containing the WordPerfect files. For example, if the WordPerfect subdirectory is called \WP50, do this:

Type   **cd \wp50**

Press   **RETURN**

Now, load the program:

Type   **wp**

Press   **RETURN**

You'll see the sign-on screen. When the almost blank edit screen appears, you're ready to begin.

If You Have a Hard Disk with the WordPerfect Library

Turn your computer on, if it isn't on already, and supply the time and date at the DOS prompts. Make sure you use the 24-hour clock for the correct time. Then, move to the directory that contains the WordPerfect Library files. For example, if the Library subdirectory is called \LIBRARY, do this:

Type   **cd \library**

Press   **RETURN**

Now, load the WordPerfect Library program:

Type   **shell**

Press   **RETURN**

The shell, or *main*, menu of the Library appears. To start WordPerfect, type the letter next to its name on the menu (it's probably **W**):

Type   **w** [WordPerfect]

to load WordPerfect.

Later, when you return to the main menu, you'll see an asterisk (*) next to WordPerfect to indicate that WordPerfect is still in memory.

Automatic Warm-Up!

You can set up the entire warm-up steps in an *automatic executing file,* named AUTOEXEC.BAT, that will enter the commands for you. You don't have to type them yourself again! See your DOS manual for information about the AUTOEXEC.BAT file. Then consult Chapter 36 to learn how to create this file in WordPerfect and to discover the useful DOS PATH command.

If you're using the WordPerfect Library, you can change the program setup information to have the Library load WordPerfect automatically when you start the Library. Go into the Setup menu, select WordPerfect, and type a plus sign (+). You'll see the plus sign next to WordPerfect on the menu. If you put a plus sign next to the wrong menu item, just type + again to "unmark." You can have the Library load several programs at once, but you must mark each in the same fashion. Press **F7 Exit** to leave the Setup menu when you're finished. The Library will then load the marked programs for you the next time you start the Library.

Special Startup Options

You can include optional startup switches when you load WordPerfect. A *switch* alters the way a program normally works. For instance, the /R switch tells WordPerfect that there is expanded memory, while the /NE switch tells WordPerfect *not* to use expanded memory. To include the /R switch, type **a:wp/r** (floppy disk systems) or **wp/r** (hard disk systems) when you load WordPerfect. You can set up this and other switches in the WordPerfect Library's Program Information screen or in the AUTOEXEC.BAT file, too. That way, you don't have to type it each time.

Table 1 lists some important startup options and what they do. A complete list is in the WordPerfect documentation. You can combine switches. For example, WP/R/B-10/M-BEGIN tells WordPerfect to use expanded memory, set the timed backup feature to save your work every 10 minutes, and run the macro that's in the file BEGIN.WPM.

Note: The /S switch has disappeared, because you now change setup information with the **SHIFT-F1 Setup** key (Appendix A).

Finally, WordPerfect Corporation often supplies a special "read me" file with the product. (The last time I looked, it was on the Conversion disk.) This file, README.WP, contains late-breaking information about changes to WordPerfect and the documentation. Look at it sometime! See Chapter 2 for information about how to retrieve a file.

Table 1   Important Startup Options

Note: Substitute a correct choice for the items shown in italics		
Switch	*Meaning*	*Notes*
WP/B-*minutes*	Set the timed backup for *minutes*	See Appendix A for more information about the backup options
	Example: WP/B-5 for 5 minutes	
WP/D-*directory*	Set the drive and/or directory path for overflow files to *directory* (the directory must already exist)	See Chapter 2 for discussion of the overflow files, and Chapter 9 for more information about drives and directories
	Example: WP/D-C:\TEMP	
WP *filename*	Open *filename* when you load WordPerfect	
	Example: WP MYFILE	
WP/M-*macroname*	Run *macroname* when you load WordPerfect	See Chapters 7 and 32 for more information about macros
	Example: WP/M-START runs the macro in the file START.WPM	
WP/NE	Do not use expanded memory even if it's available	
WP/R	Use expanded memory to make WordPerfect run faster	You must have an expanded memory board or memory above 640 kb
WP/X	Restore the default setup values	See Appendix A to learn more about the setup defaults

Absolute Beginners

1

The Basics, Part 1

In this chapter you'll learn the following new commands:

Function Key Commands

F1 Cancel	Cancel a command
F3 Help	Help
F7 Exit	(1) Exit WordPerfect, (2) clear the screen, with or without saving the current document
F10 Save	Save the current document

Typewriter Keyboard and Numeric Keypad Commands

BACKSPACE	Delete the previous character
CTRL-BACKSPACE	Delete the word at the cursor
CTRL-LEFT ARROW	Cursor to the beginning of the previous word
CTRL-RIGHT ARROW	Cursor to the beginning of the next word
DEL	Delete the character at the cursor
DOWN ARROW	Cursor down one line
END	Cursor to the end of the line
ESC	Cancel most commands

more . . .

GRAY − *or* **HOME,UP ARROW**	Cursor to the top of the current screen or up one screenful ("screen up")
GRAY + *or* **HOME,DOWN ARROW**	Cursor to the bottom of the current screen or down one screenful ("screen down")
HOME,BACKSPACE	Delete from the cursor left to the previous word boundary
HOME,DEL	Delete from the cursor right to the next word boundary
HOME,LEFT ARROW	Cursor to the left side of the screen
HOME,HOME,DOWN ARROW	Cursor to the end of the document
HOME,HOME,UP ARROW	Cursor to the beginning of the document
HOME,RIGHT ARROW	Cursor to the right side of the screen
INS	Turn typeover mode on/off
LEFT ARROW	Cursor left one character
RETURN	(1) End a paragraph, (2) insert a blank line, (3) complete some commands
RIGHT ARROW	Cursor right one character
TAB	(1) Insert a tab (insert mode), (2) move the cursor to the next tab stop (typeover mode)
UP ARROW	Cursor up one line

Dear Reader, before you close this book and decide *not* to learn WordPerfect, relax! The list of new commands is long, but these commands are the most common ones. You'll use them every day. Soon they'll all be second nature to you. If it's any consolation, most of the other chapters don't introduce so many commands at once! Here's another reassuring point: The first part of this book presents a quick tour of the basic WordPerfect features. You'll be "up and running" with WordPerfect in no time.

Experienced computer or WordPerfect users: The chapters in Part 1 go slowly, but the pace picks up quickly. Take the time to do the examples. They illustrate many of Wordperfect 5.0's features and provide a good review. What's more, you'll be working with them again in later chapters. If you don't have the time, skim through the chapters and find the "new" icons to familiarize yourself with WordPerfect 5.0's new features.

DO WARM-UP

Did you overlook the daily warm-up instructions in the Prelude? If so, read them now and perform a warm-up before you continue with this chapter.

What You See on the Screen . . . Not Much!

Don't be upset by the almost blank screen, shown in Figure 1-1, that first confronts you. WordPerfect is programmed to stay out of your way as much as possible so that you aren't distracted from your work. The folks at WordPerfect Corporation call this the *clean screen* approach. Help is always just a keystroke away, but for the most part the screen displays only the text you type.

Because you aren't typing on an actual piece of paper, however, WordPerfect does remind you of your current position in a document. Look

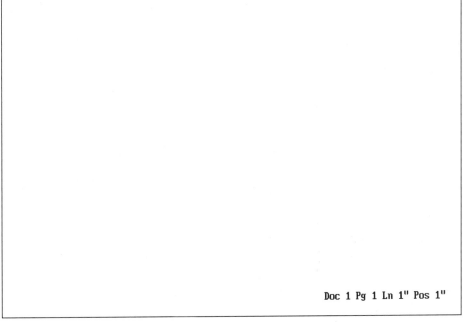

Doc 1 Pg 1 Ln 1" Pos 1"

Figure 1-1   Starting a New Document

at the *status line* at the bottom of the screen. This line doesn't print; it's just there for your convenience.

The status line tells you several things: (1) which document you're working on: you can have two documents in use at one time—Doc 1 and Doc 2 (Chapter 11); (2) the document's file name; (3) the current page number of the document—here displayed as Pg 1; (4) the current line where the cursor is located relative to the top edge of the page—Ln 1"; and (5) the cursor column position relative to the left edge of the paper—Pos 1". See also Units of Measure later in the chapter. Because you haven't typed anything yet, the cursor is at the beginning of a blank document and no file name appears on the left side of the status line.

The Pos indicator changes depending on certain conditions. For instance, if you press the CAPS LOCK key, Pos changes to POS . If you press the NUM LOCK key, Pos flashes as long as the NUM LOCK key is on. Make sure that *both* keys are off now. Later, you'll learn that the status line changes depending on other editing factors, for example, if you've turned on underlining.

The Default Settings

WordPerfect "assumes" that you want 1-inch blank margins on the left and right edges of the paper. This aspect of the page's *white space* is one of the program's formatting defaults. A *format* governs how the document will print. WordPerfect shows most, but not all, formats on the screen.

In due time you'll learn how to change the margins and all other format settings within a document. If the default settings aren't to your liking, you can change them to new defaults, too (Appendix A). That way, whenever you start a new document, WordPerfect will use your default settings.

Caution: So that all the examples in this book work correctly, please do not change the default settings until you're finished studying the book. Thanks!

There are other preset formatting defaults that you should know about, but you don't have to worry about them until future chapters:

- The length of a horizontal text line is 6½ inches for a standard form of 8½ by 11 inches. That's because WordPerfect uses a 1-inch white space for the left and right sides of the page, so $8\frac{1}{2} - 2 = 6\frac{1}{2}$.

- The number of characters that print per horizontal inch depends on your printer, but the *printed* line length is still 6½ inches. That's because WordPerfect formats your documents depending on the printer and typestyle you're currently using.

- When you print the document, there will be a 1-inch top and bottom margin. You don't see these margins on the screen.

- Tab stops occur every 0.5 (half) inch, starting at position 0.0 and extending to position 8.5.

- The document is single spaced.

- WordPerfect does not print page numbers by default.

- Documents normally have justified (even) right margins. When it prints the document, WordPerfect adds the necessary spaces between words so that each line is the same length. You won't see the justified right margin until you print the document or view the printed document on the screen (Chapter 5).

- WordPerfect automatically rewrites the screen when you make changes to your text or to the format settings.

Note: Some people feel more comfortable when they can *see* the left and right margin and tab settings as they work. When you learn how to change these settings, you'll discover how to display them on the screen (Chapter 6).

Units of Measure

Traditional word processing programs, including WordPerfect 4.2, worked with the old typewriter standard of pica-style type. That is, there were ten characters printed per horizontal inch and six printed lines per vertical inch. All that has changed in WordPerfect 5.0.

WordPerfect now uses *inches* as the standard unit of measure for format settings like margins and tabs. Notice that the status line shows the cursor position in inches from the top and left edges of the page. There are other ways to determine measurement: in WordPerfect 4.2 units, centimeters, or points. The term *points* comes from the typesetting world (Chapter 4). If you would like to revert to the older method of measurement, you can (Appendix A). For the time being, however, don't fret! Until you become more comfortable with WordPerfect, just think inches.

Insert Mode and Typeover Mode

Normally, WordPerfect operates in *insert mode:* Everything you type is inserted into the document at the cursor position. If the cursor is under existing text, the new text pushes the cursor and existing text forward on the line. When you move the cursor or reach the right margin, WordPerfect automatically adjusts the lines to fit within the margins. The opposite of insert mode is *typeover mode:* Anything you type replaces the text at the cursor position. To switch to typeover mode, press the **INS** key. You'll see this message on the status line:

Typeover

The message is visible as long as you use this mode. Although at times it's beneficial to be in typeover mode, you can overwrite text by mistake. What's more, on the PC keyboard, the INS key is easy to press when you don't mean to. Always use insert mode when you work with the examples in this book, except in the rare instances when the instructions tell you to switch to typeover mode. To return to insert mode if you are not using it now, press the **INS** key again. The Typeover message disappears from the status line.

Canceling a Command or Menu

Suppose your fingers do some walking over the keyboard while you're not looking and you press a key that starts a command or brings up a menu. You can cancel any command: just press **F1 Cancel**.

Tips: The **ESC** key lets you escape out of most commands. Sometimes a menu choice takes you to another menu. You can press F1 Cancel, ESC, or one of the four ARROW keys to cancel a menu or return to the previous menu.

No Document Yet

When you begin working with WordPerfect, you either type new text, or you *retrieve*, that is, open, an existing document to make editing changes to it. Because you haven't created any documents yet, that will be one of the first goals of this chapter. Many users, experienced and inexperienced alike, are befuddled by WordPerfect's simplicity. Do you have to open a new file before you begin typing? No! Just start typing on the blank screen. Soon you'll see how to save your typing.

Entering Text and Correcting Mistakes

So much for the preliminaries. It's finally time to do some real work. You'll type a standard paragraph.

Press   **TAB**

You would normally start a paragraph with a tab, wouldn't you? There's no difference on a word processor.

Type   **The biggess**

Oops! Your first mistake. No problem!

Press   **BACKSPACE**

The BACKSPACE key lets you correct typing mistakes as you go along. It *rubs out* the previous character and moves the cursor back, as if it contained a built-in eraser. If you hold it down, it will continue to delete backward.

(An aside: In typeover mode, the BACKSPACE key replaces the character to the left with a *space*. In typeover mode, the TAB key just moves the cursor along the line but doesn't insert a tab unless the cursor is at the end of the line.)

Go slowly through these examples and try to catch your typing mistakes as you proceed. Then what appears on your screen will be the same as the examples. However, if you don't catch all your typos, don't worry. You can correct them later. Type as you would normally: *one* space between words, *two* spaces at the end of a sentence. After you've typed the rest of the first line, the cursor should be two spaces after the period at the end of the sentence:

```
The biggest news for this month is the company picnic.
```

You are almost at the end of the line. Will a bell sound, as on your typewriter? No, WordPerfect automatically forms the lines as you type by wrapping the last word that doesn't fit on the current line down to the next line. This is called *wordwrap*. Thus, you don't have to press the RETURN key, sometimes called entering a *carriage return*, at the end of each line. In fact, it's *very* important that you *don't* press the RETURN key until the instructions tell you to. Here is one important new word processing habit to learn. As soon as you see how much time and work it will save you, you'll wonder how you ever got along without it.

If you are too much a creature of habit and you press the RETURN key at the end of a line, do this. Merely press the BACKSPACE key to rub out the carriage return and move the cursor back to the previous line. Then continue typing.

It's time to type the rest of the paragraph. Make sure that you have one, and only one, space between words and two spaces at the end of each sentence. *Watch the screen.* Later, when you are a whiz kid, you won't have to watch the screen very much. Here is the result of your efforts:

```
    The biggest news for this month is the company picnic.  That's
right!  Consolidated Toupee is giving us a real, honest-to-goodness
picnic.  After all, don't we deserve it?  So come one, come all to
Founder's Park on August 21st and join in the fun.  Bring the kids,
bring your friends, bring food and drink.
```

> **Note:** I used the standard printer when I was creating most of the typed examples in this book. The line endings may be different on your screen. That depends on the printer you're using. The keystroke instructions will work correctly no matter what printer you have, but you may want to select the standard printer while you're using this book. See Selecting a Different Printer in Chapter 5.

An Experienced Word Processor's Trick

The cursor should be directly after the period at the end of the last sentence of the paragraph. If it isn't, use the BACKSPACE key to move the cursor back. Now for your first trick.

Experienced word processors know that they often have to add more text to the ends of paragraphs when they edit a document. If they include the required two spaces after the last sentence in the paragraph, they can quickly move the cursor to the end of the line, past the two spaces, and start typing new text later. I call this the *end of paragraph trick*. If you wish, press the **SPACEBAR** twice now to add the extra two spaces to the end of the paragraph. It's up to you whether you do this at the end of every paragraph!

Finishing the Paragraph

WordPerfect would wrap the lines continuously if you didn't tell it where to stop. Because you want to end the paragraph now, do this:

Press   **RETURN** twice

Use the RETURN key when you want to create a short line, such as at the end of a paragraph, that is, when you don't want WordPerfect to wrap the line. When you press RETURN you move down to the next line and position the cursor at the left margin. You've added one blank line between paragraphs by pressing RETURN twice, once to end the paragraph and once for spacing. The cursor should now be at the left margin.

An Important Note About Tabs

On some screens the tab stop may be farther to the right. Because WordPerfect now measures the line in inches, it shows the tab stop farther over. What's more, the appearance of tab stops may differ depending on the printer you're using. The document will still print correctly.

It's important that you understand what a tab really means to Word-Perfect and your printer. A tab is an *exact* measurement that moves the print head a certain distance to the right. If you use spaces instead of tabs, the paragraphs won't align correctly because a space is an *inexact* measurement. That is, the width of a space can change from printer to printer and from line to line, depending on the other characters in the line. The width of the tab doesn't change unless or until you set other tab stops (Chapter 6).

Two Types of Carriage Returns

WordPerfect distinguishes between the carriage returns that it places at the ends of lines during wordwrap and the ones that you put in to end paragraphs or blank lines. The former are called *soft returns* and the latter, *hard returns.* Hard returns remain in a document unless you delete them, while WordPerfect adjusts the soft returns when you edit the wrapped lines. You'll see this happen shortly.

As Chapter 2 shows, everything has a special *formatting code* associated with it. Soft and hard returns have separate codes, and there's a separate tab code, too.

When they begin using a word processing program, many former typists make the mistake of pressing the RETURN key to move down the page, when all they really wanted to do was to move the cursor. Whenever you press RETURN, you insert a hard return in the document. If you use the RETURN key indiscriminately, you will have some very "spaced-out" documents. You must delete superfluous hard returns yourself, either as you type or later (see Deleting Hard Returns).

More Work

Type the second paragraph. Remember to press **TAB** once to begin the paragraph:

```
        As a special feature, President Glatzkopf will be there to
present the annual Employee of the Year award.  As you probably
know, this handsome gift will go to the Consolidated Toupee
```

employee who best typifies the CT spirit: "Consolidated Toupee Is Tops!"

When you reach the end of the paragraph:

Press   **RETURN** twice

Time to do the third paragraph:

The "Permanent Wave" staff will also present its annual awards, which will include the "Best Dressed Woman and Man," "The Person Most Likely to Succeed," and, well, we'll keep you guessing about the others. Come and find out!

Press   **RETURN** twice

Save Your Work!

Remember that you haven't yet saved this new document to a file on the disk. For the sake of getting used to an important new pattern, even though you've typed only three paragraphs, save your work now and continue. Floppy disk users: Make sure there's a disk in the B drive and that the drive door is closed.

Press   **F10 Save**

On the status line, WordPerfect prompts:

Document to be saved:

Type   news

for the file name.

Press   **RETURN**

Now that you've given the new document a file name, NEWS, WordPerfect displays the file name at the left corner of the status line. The file name reminds you that this is the newsletter that you're working on.

The **F10 Save** key saves the document as the file NEWS on the current drive and, if you have a hard disk, in the current subdirectory. If you want to save the document to a *different* drive or subdirectory, append the drive or subdirectory name to the file name, for instance, **a:news** or **\wp\articles\ news**. WordPerfect then returns you to where you left off in the document.

A Note on Your Printer

WordPerfect formats a document according to the printer you're currently using (the "selected" printer) when you create the document. For each printer you plan to use, you set up a *printer resource file* (with the extension .PRS) that contains specific information about the printer. WordPerfect also saves the name of the printer resource file with the document in a special *document header* or *prefix* that you don't see.

Suppose you work with more than one printer and you've selected another printer in the interim. WordPerfect still selects and uses the original printer whenever you retrieve a document (provided it can find the printer resource file), then reverts to the currently selected printer when you save the document. See The Document and Your Printers in Chapter 5 for more information.

Moving the Cursor

Pretend that you have done a lot more typing than just three paragraphs and that now you want to make some editing changes to this document. The cursor always shows you your current position in the document. If that's not where you want to be, you must move the cursor to where you want to make additions or changes.

Caution: Never use the RETURN key to move the cursor unless you do indeed want to insert blank lines in the document. This is a major trap into which many typists have fallen when they first work with a word processing program like WordPerfect.

You already know that the four ARROW keys on the numeric keypad move the cursor one character at a time in their respective directions: up, down, left, and right. Although these keys repeat if you hold them down, sometimes you'll want to make more wholesale moves to save time and keystroking. In general, you use the CTRL or HOME key together with an ARROW key to jump around in a document. Two of the most frequently used jumps are to the *beginning* and the *end* of the document.

In addition, the HOME key is an extender. That is, it extends the direction of the ARROW key. So, LEFT ARROW moves the cursor one character to the left, while HOME,LEFT ARROW moves the cursor to the left side of the screen, and HOME,HOME,LEFT ARROW moves the cursor to the left side of the entire line. There's even a HOME,HOME,HOME,LEFT ARROW command, but I don't want to get too carried away yet!

Before you issue the next command, I'd like to remind you how to press the keys. Whenever you see the HOME key and other keys together, press and release HOME the stated number of times, then press the other key.

Notice in the instruction that commas separate the HOME key from the other key(s). So:

Press **HOME,HOME,UP ARROW**

(If you see numbers on the screen, you've accidentally pressed the NUM LOCK key, which changes the cursor keypad to an accounting keypad. Press NUM LOCK once to get back to cursor mode, then use the BACKSPACE key to delete the numbers from the screen.)

WordPerfect displays this briefly:

`Repositioning`

and the cursor jumps to the beginning of the document.

Press **HOME,HOME,DOWN ARROW**

Now the cursor is at the end of the document, which should be two lines below the last paragraph. So, the pattern is to press the HOME key *twice*, followed by the UP ARROW or DOWN ARROW key, to go to the beginning or end of the document, respectively.

Press **HOME,UP ARROW**

This command moves the cursor to the top of the screen. When it's at the top of the screen and you press the command again, WordPerfect moves up by screenful (24 lines). However, WordPerfect can't move the cursor past the beginning of the document.

The key combination **HOME,DOWN ARROW** moves the cursor to the bottom of the screen. Again, if the cursor is already at the bottom, the cursor moves down by screenful (24 lines). There are even shortcuts for these two commands: Try pressing the GRAY − key and the GRAY + key on the far right side of the keyboard. Why press two keys when you need press only one? WordPerfect calls the GRAY − and GRAY + keys the screen up and screen down keys.

When you're comfortable with the screen keys, use the ARROW keys to position the cursor in the middle of any typed line in any paragraph. Then:

Press **CTRL-LEFT ARROW**

A reminder about *this* type of command: Whenever you see two keys connected by a hyphen, hold down the first key as you press the second. Then release both keys. The cursor jumps to the beginning of the previous word.

Press **CTRL-RIGHT ARROW**

The cursor jumps to the beginning of the next word. Repeat the commands to become comfortable with them. Often, you'll want to move either to the beginning of the line or the end of the line. With the cursor positioned in the middle of any line of text:

Press   **HOME,LEFT ARROW**

The cursor moves to the beginning text of the line. (Later, you'll see that codes sometimes appear at the beginning of the line, so WordPerfect includes a way to move the cursor in front of these codes.) Actually, this command moves the cursor to the left side of the line on the current screen. Most of the time that will be the left margin, but there are ways to move the cursor when you're working with long lines that don't fit entirely on one screen (Chapter 2).

Press   **HOME,RIGHT ARROW**

The cursor moves to the end of the line. There's a nifty shortcut for this command: Just press the **END** key once. Actually, HOME,RIGHT ARROW moves the cursor only to the right side of the currently visible line, while END always moves the cursor to the actual end of the line.

Tip: These two commands are useful because they can help you correct typing mistakes at the other side of the line. Just move back to the mistake with HOME,LEFT ARROW, use the RIGHT ARROW to move the cursor to the mistake, and correct it. Then press END to return to where you left off. The END key always takes you to the *last entered character* on the line.

Those are the basic cursor movement commands in WordPerfect. Figure 1-2 illustrates these keys on your computer's numeric keypad.

Inserting and Deleting Text

Because WordPerfect is normally in insert mode, all you have to do is position the cursor exactly where you want to insert any word or words. Then type the insertion. Do this:

Press   **HOME,HOME,UP ARROW**

to position the cursor at the beginning of the document.

Press   **DOWN ARROW** enough times

to position the cursor at the beginning of the second line of the second paragraph.

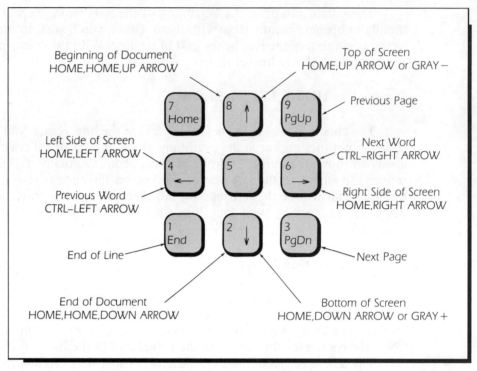

Figure 1-2   Basic Cursor Movement Commands

Press   **CTRL-RIGHT ARROW**

to position the cursor under the *t* of the word *the*.

   Note: Always make sure the cursor is under the correct word before you continue the example.

Type   **to some lucky person**

   Remember to type the *space* after the word *person* so that it is separated from *the*. When you edit text, always make sure you type the correct spaces between words. If your text *looks* wrong on the screen, it will *print* wrong. You have inserted words and pushed the rest of the line to the right. As soon as you move the cursor up or down a line, WordPerfect automatically adjusts the lines.

Press   **DOWN ARROW**

   The lines are brought correctly back into the margins. Position the cursor under the letter *h* of *handsome* on the line. Now you decide that you don't like this word, so delete it.

Press   **DEL** eight times

You've deleted the entire word *handsome* by deleting each individual character; the rest of the line moves back to fill in the space. You did not delete the space after *handsome* because now you'll type in another word. Without moving the cursor:

Type   **beautiful**

How does the line look? Is there one space between each word? There are two ways to delete individual characters: either by rubbing out the *previous* character with the BACKSPACE key or by deleting the character when the cursor is directly *under* it with the DEL key. When you use the BACKSPACE key, you don't delete the character at the cursor location. You merely bring this character back with the cursor as you delete the previous character. Figure 1-3 illustrates how BACKSPACE works.

Tip: You'll use the BACKSPACE key most often when you're typing new text and wish to correct your mistakes as you go, and you'll use the DEL key when you make corrections or changes later. Either key does the same thing, but in a slightly different fashion.

Deleting Hard Returns

Just read this section; don't do any steps. You can delete a hard carriage return with the cursor directly on the return by pressing the DEL key. How do you get to the return? With the cursor anywhere on the line that ends in the hard return, press END to go to the end of the line. If you mistakenly press the RETURN key when you're adding text, remember to press BACKSPACE to delete the hard return.

Tip: As a way of reminding you where hard returns appear in a document, you can set up WordPerfect to display a hard return as a visible character on the screen (Appendix A). For instance, you might want hard returns to appear as < or >.

In this example, the cursor is under the space:

> **If you think I'm going to that stupid picnick_**

When you press **BACKSPACE** once, the space moves back as the *k* is deleted:

> **If you think I'm going to that stupid picnic_**

The space itself is not deleted.

Figure 1-3   How the BACKSPACE Key Works

Deleting a Word

To learn how to delete a word, position the cursor under the space between the words *beautiful* and *gift*. It should be there now.

Press   **CTRL-BACKSPACE**

Instead of pressing the BACKSPACE key nine times—a waste of key-strokes—you deleted the entire word quickly with the Word Delete command, CTRL-BACKSPACE. You also rubbed out the space between *beautiful* and *gift*.

Type   `fabulous`

Make sure there's a space after *fabulous*.

Press   **HOME,HOME,UP ARROW**

to position the cursor at the beginning of the document.

Press   **CTRL-RIGHT ARROW** twice

to position the cursor under the *b* of *biggest*.
You want to delete the words *biggest news for this:*

Press   **CTRL-BACKSPACE** four times

WordPerfect deletes the four words. CTRL-BACKSPACE deletes an entire word up to, but not including, the previous space. The cursor can be anywhere under the word.
Two other commands—HOME,BACKSPACE and HOME,DEL—let you delete *parts* of a word. HOME,BACKSPACE deletes from the cursor *left* to the previous space character, which WordPerfect calls the *word boundary*. This command doesn't delete the space if the cursor is not on the first letter of the word. HOME,DEL deletes from the cursor *right* to the next space character (again, a word boundary), but it does delete the space. Figure 1-4 illustrates these commands.
Regrettably, computers are not magical devices that can understand what you type. The first sentence of the paragraph now doesn't make *grammatical* sense. The computer will not catch this mistake. Insert the following new text:

Type   `most important news of the`

In this example, the cursor is under the *p* of *stupid*:

```
If you think I'm going to that stupid picnic
```

When you press **HOME,BACKSPACE**, WordPerfect deletes to the previous word boundary, the letters *stu*, but does not delete the space before the word:

```
If you think I'm going to that pid picnic
```

Using the same first sentence and cursor position, when you press **HOME,DEL**, WordPerfect deletes to the next word boundary the letters *pid* including the space. This is what you see:

```
If you think I'm going to that stupicnic
```

Figure 1-4   Deleting Parts of Words

Remember to type a space after *the*. When you move the cursor **again**, WordPerfect adjusts the paragraph:

Press   **DOWN ARROW**

to adjust the lines.

Save Again!

You've made some important editing changes to the document, so get into the habit of saving your work often.

Press   **F10 Save**

This time, because you've already saved the document once, Word-Perfect presents the document's file name in its message, `Document to be saved:` . On a floppy disk system, this is `B:\NEWS` . On a hard disk, WordPerfect also supplies the directory path, for instance, `C:\WP50\NEWS`. You could supply another file name, but usually you'll want to save to the same file.

Press   **RETURN**

WordPerfect makes sure that you want to replace the old version with the new version:

```
Replace B:\NEWS? (Y/N) No
```

Type   y

If you want WordPerfect to save your work automatically at periodic intervals, see Appendix A for information on how to set this up as part of the program's defaults.

Getting Help

If you get stuck at any time, press **F3 Help**. You can get three kinds of help:

1. Press **F3 Help** a second time to see a screen version of the keyboard template.
2. Press the command for which you need help to see specific information about that command.
3. Type a letter to view an alphabetical listing of commands and features that begin with that letter or with the next letter for which there are listings.

As an introduction to the next section, get help about the F7 Exit key:

Press   **F3 Help**

The information shown in Figure 1-5 appears. (You may have a different version number and date of issue at the top right of the screen.)

Press   **F7 Exit**

WordPerfect displays information about this command.

Press   **F3 Help**

There's the keyboard template. To cancel and leave help:

Press   **RETURN** or **SPACEBAR**

Clearing the Screen or Exiting WordPerfect

If you're finished working with a document and you want to work on another, save the document and clear the screen with the F7 Exit key.

Press   **F7 Exit**

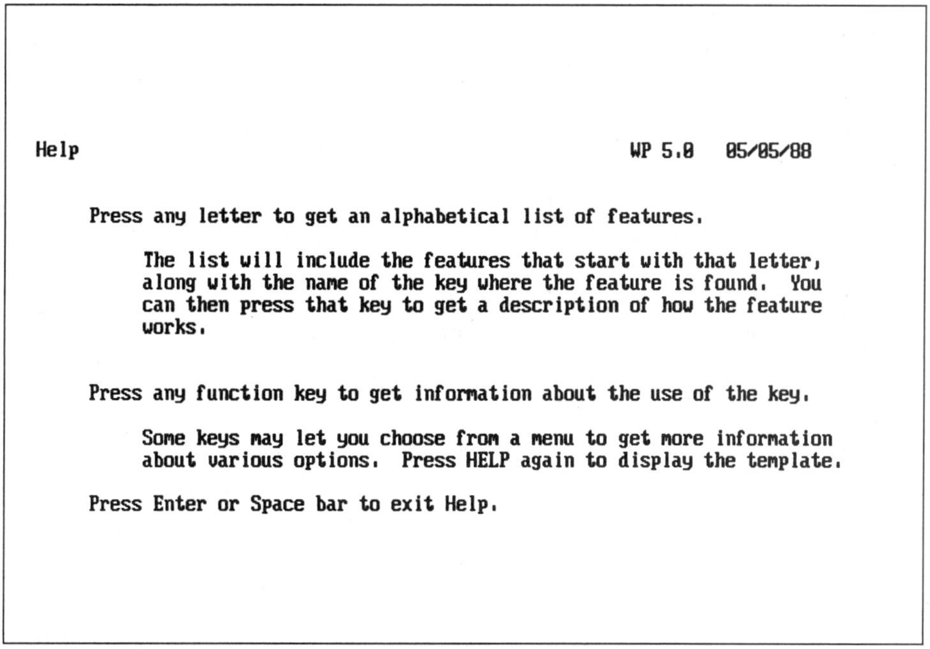

```
Help                                          WP 5.0   05/05/88


    Press any letter to get an alphabetical list of features.

        The list will include the features that start with that letter,
        along with the name of the key where the feature is found.  You
        can then press that key to get a description of how the feature
        works.


    Press any function key to get information about the use of the key.

        Some keys may let you choose from a menu to get more information
        about various options.  Press HELP again to display the template.

    Press Enter or Space bar to exit Help.
```

Figure 1-5   Using the F3 Help Command

WordPerfect asks:

```
Save document? (Y/N) Yes
```

If you have made no changes to the document since the last time you saved it, WordPerfect displays this message instead:

```
Save document? (Y/N) Yes                        (Text was not modified)
```

Normally, you'd *want* to save the edited document, but you just saved it anyway, so you can:

Type   n

If you type y to save the document, follow the save procedure to accept the file name and overwrite the previous version of the document. After you decide whether to save the document, WordPerfect prompts:

```
Exit WP? (Y/N) No                           (Cancel to return to document)
```

You have three choices:

1. Type n (or press **RETURN**) to stay in WordPerfect. The program clears the previous document from the screen so you can work on another document.

2. Type y to exit WordPerfect and return to DOS or to the WordPerfect Library if you're using it.

3. Press **F1 Cancel** to keep the previous document on the screen so you can continue working with it. (This is like the F10 Save command.)

Table 1-1 summarizes the various ways you can use the F7 Exit key. Now, try your hand at exiting WordPerfect:

Press   **F7 Exit**

Type   n

Type   y

to exit WordPerfect.

Table 1-1   Ways to Use the F7 Exit Key

Action	Keystrokes
Save the document and clear the screen	Press **F7 Exit** Type y Press **RETURN** Type y Type n
Save the document and exit WordPerfect	Press **F7 Exit** Type y Press **RETURN** Type y Type y
Save the document and continue working (same as the F10 Save key)	Press **F7 Exit** Type y Press **RETURN** Type y Press **F1 Cancel**
Clear the screen without saving the document	Press **F7 Exit** Type n Type n
Exit WordPerfect without saving the document	Press **F7 Exit** Type n Type y

Finished?

Remember to save an edited document to a file before you turn off your computer. A good pattern to follow is always to *exit* WordPerfect (press **F7 Exit**), because WordPerfect then reminds you to save your work. As Chapter 2 discusses, if you turn off your computer without properly exiting Word-Perfect, you'll see a strange message the next time you load the program. If you are finished for the day, you can remove the diskettes and turn the machine off, or you can use your computer with another program.

A full 90% of all word processing comprises the activities covered in this chapter: entering text, moving the cursor, making additions and corrections by inserting and deleting text, and saving your work. In Chapter 2, you'll learn about the other basic word processing tasks, such as retrieving files and how to use other useful WordPerfect commands.

If you'd like more practice with the commands and operations covered in this chapter, by all means do some word processing on your own. Start a new document, enter text, move the cursor, insert and delete text, and use the F3 Help key. Or repeat the steps in this chapter but supply a different file name when you save the document. The sooner you learn the basic patterns, the quicker you'll become an experienced WordPerfect user.

2

The Basics, Part 2

In this chapter you'll learn the following new commands . . .

Function Key Commands

ALT-F3 Reveal Codes or **F11 Reveal Codes**	Show all formatting codes and the tab ruler
ALT-F4 Block or **F12 Block**	Turn a block on
SHIFT-F6 Center	Center a line between the margins
SHIFT-F10 Retrieve	Retrieve a document

Typewriter Keyboard and Numeric Keypad Commands

CTRL-END	Delete from the cursor to the end of the line
CTRL-HOME	Cursor to a page number or forward to a specific character ("Go to")
CTRL-HOME, DOWN ARROW	Cursor to the bottom of the current page
CTRL-HOME, UP ARROW	Cursor to the top of the current page
CTRL-PG DN	Delete from the cursor to the end of the current page
HOME,HOME, LEFT ARROW	Cursor to the beginning of the line
HOME,HOME,HOME, LEFT ARROW	Cursor to the beginning of the line in front of any codes

more . . .

HOME,HOME, RIGHT ARROW	Cursor to the end of the line
PG DN	Cursor to the beginning of the next page
PG UP	Cursor to the beginning of the previous page

. . . you'll discover other uses for these commands . . .

BACKSPACE	Delete a block
DEL	Delete a block
ESC	Repeat the next command or character
F1 Cancel	(1) Cancel a block, (2) restore ("undelete") previously deleted text

. . . and you'll learn about these codes:

[Block]	Beginning of the block when codes are revealed
[Cntr] and **[C/A/Flrt]**	Begin and end centering
[HRt]	Hard return
[SRt]	Soft return
[Tab]	Tab

Dear Reader, as a novice word processor, you may feel like a *klutz* now. In no time, you'll be a WordPerfect nonklutz! This chapter continues discussion of the basics from Chapter 1. Besides helping you overcome your fear of remaining a word processing klutz forever, it presents some of the most typical word processing situations and how you can master them.

You'll learn more useful patterns for entering text into an existing document and other standard WordPerfect commands and conveniences. At the end of the chapter is important information about disk full errors and other WordPerfect ways.

> **DO WARM-UP**

Retrieving a Document

It's time to continue work on your latest writing project: the company newsletter that you started in Chapter 1. First, *retrieve*, or open, the document by its file name and make a copy of it in the computer's memory.

Caution: If you're finished working on one document and you want to work on another, always save the first document and *clear the screen* with the **F7 Exit** key before you retrieve another document. If you don't, you'll *join* the two documents.

Dear Reader, if there is a "gotcha" in WordPerfect, it's here, and it can be the bane of klutzes and nonklutzes alike. WordPerfect doesn't distinguish between the act of retrieving a document to a blank screen and retrieving—and hence joining—a document *into* another document that may already be on the screen. In both operations you're still retrieving the document and putting a copy of it into memory. If there's a document already on the screen, WordPerfect *inserts* the second document at the current cursor location of the first.

In Chapter 3 you'll learn how to join documents. Right now and for the sake of your sanity, follow this simple rule of thumb to make sure that you aren't joining documents. If the status line doesn't say Pg 1 Ln 1" before you retrieve a document, then you haven't properly cleared the screen. Assuming then that you *have* cleared the screen, you're ready to retrieve a document.

Press   **SHIFT-F10 Retrieve**

WordPerfect prompts:

Document to be retrieved:

Type   **news**

Press   **RETURN**

There's your newsletter. WordPerfect positions the cursor at the beginning of the document after you've retrieved it. If you want to work with a document on another drive or in another directory, supply the drive name or directory path, as in these two examples:

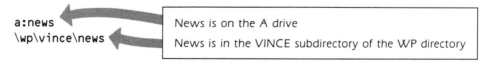

a:news   News is on the A drive

\wp\vince\news   News is in the VINCE subdirectory of the WP directory

The File Edit Line

If you type the document's file name incorrectly, WordPerfect won't be able to locate the file. It then tells you, in no uncertain terms:

```
ERROR: File not found -- <filename>
```

where <filename> is the name you typed.

Sometimes your fingers will slip and you'll type the directory path name incorrectly. WordPerfect honors you with the following cybernetic Bronx cheer:

```
ERROR: Invalid drive/path specification -- <path>
```

where <path> is the incorrect directory path name.

In either case, you have another chance to supply a new path or file name on the *file edit line* at the bottom of the screen. Use the cursor movement keys to move to the mistake, press DEL or BACKSPACE to delete the incorrect characters, then type in the correction. Press RETURN or F7 Exit to continue the command (here, Retrieve) or F1 Cancel to remove the file name from the edit line and cancel the operation.

You can also type a character instead of moving the cursor. WordPerfect deletes the incorrect file name to let you type a new name. This editing feature works whenever WordPerfect requests a file name to complete any command. Soon you'll learn that there is a way to *choose* a file from the directory to avoid this problem.

Version 4.2 users: When you retrieve a 4.2 document in 5.0, WordPerfect tells you this briefly:

```
Document conversion in progress
```

WordPerfect automatically converts 4.2 documents to 5.0 format. You can also convert a document *back* to 4.2 format (Chapter 36).

Note: Some format changes are not converted. See File Format Changes in the Prelude.

Using Blocks to Make Major Deletions

One of the themes of this book is: Saving keystrokes means saving work. WordPerfect offers you other ways to make wholesale deletions with only a few keystrokes. You *block out* the text and then delete it.

A *block* is any continuous section of text, whether a word, a phrase, a line, a sentence, a paragraph, an entire page, or even the whole document. Before you can use a block, WordPerfect has to know the limits of the block. To *delimit* or mark off a block, first position the cursor at the beginning character in the block and then *extend* the block to encompass the remaining text in the block. That is, you "anchor" the beginning of the block as you highlight the rest of the block.

Normally a block extends horizontally to include all characters on each line in the block. That means that a soft or hard return at the end of a line is also part of the block. When you then move or copy a block, the block retains its shape. Sometimes, however, you might want to block out only a rectangular section of text. Because that's an advanced technique, you won't learn about it until later (Chapter 15).

Although you'll learn only how to delete blocks in this chapter, there are many other things you can do with blocks. For all block operations you must first delimit the block as outlined here.

Suppose you want to delete the first paragraph. The cursor should be at the beginning of the line in front of the tab, which you want to include it in the paragraph. To turn block on:

Press   **ALT-F4 Block** or **F12 Block**

WordPerfect tells you:

`Block on`

and continues to flash this message until you finish working with the block.

That is, after you've extended the block to the last character in the block, you leave block mode on while you perform whatever operation you want. Here, because you're deleting a paragraph, you can quickly extend the block to include the entire paragraph:

Press   **RETURN**

Because every paragraph ends with a hard return, WordPerfect looks for the next occurrence of a hard return and then highlights the entire block between the original cursor location and the return. You also want to include the extra hard return that you added for spacing between paragraphs:

Press   **DOWN ARROW** once

but notice that there's no highlighting in the blank lines.

Press   **DEL** or **BACKSPACE**

to delete the block.

WordPerfect asks you to confirm what you're doing:

`Delete Block? (Y/N) No`

Type   `y`

to complete the deletion.

The "Undelete" Feature

Oops! You didn't want to delete that block! WordPerfect offers a feature you can use to "undelete" a previous deletion if you find that you really want to keep the deleted material. How does WordPerfect do it? It keeps deletions in a *buffer*, which is a holding zone.

Press   **F1 Cancel**

WordPerfect brings the last deletion back and highlights it. It also presents the undelete menu:

Undelete 1 Restore; 2 Previous Deletion: 0

To accept the undelete:

Type   1 or r [Restore]

to bring back the paragraph.

Tip: WordPerfect can restore the previous *three* deletions only, so it's always a good idea to undelete as soon as you can.

Here's how WordPerfect keeps track of deletions. Every time you delete text or codes (explained later), that counts as one deletion. Fortunately, WordPerfect is "smart" enough to bunch several deletions together as long as you issue the deletions consecutively.

For example, if you press BACKSPACE three times to delete the previous three characters, that counts as just one deletion. If you delete three words in a row without doing anything else, that's another deletion. If, however, you press DEL once to delete a character, move the cursor, and continue typing, that's one deletion, too. Whatever is the fourth deletion goes into the buffer and pushes the first one out.

You can look at the last three deletions with the **2** [Previous Deletion] choice. You can also press the **UP ARROW** or **DOWN ARROW** keys to circle through the previous three deletions, then type **1** or **r** [Restore] to recall the highlighted deletion. Type **0**, press **F1 Cancel** a second time, or press **RETURN** to cancel the restore operation.

Another Block Example

After you turn the block on, you can use any cursor movement command or type any character to extend the block in a forward direction. The cursor should be at the left margin of the second paragraph. If it isn't, move it there. Then:

Press   **ALT-F4 Block** or **F12 Block**

Type   .

(That's a period.)

    You've asked WordPerfect to find the first period character, which sets up the first sentence as the block. If you want to delete this sentence, you should also delete the two spaces after the sentence:

Type   **SPACEBAR** twice

Because this was just practice:

Press   **F1 Cancel**

to turn off the block.

    Press the F1 Cancel key to stop a block operation. Note that this key works differently when the block is highlighted. Many WordPerfect commands have "dual personalities" depending on whether you use them alone or with a block. Here's another block example.

Press   **ALT-F4 Block** or **F12 Block**

Press   **SPACEBAR**

    This time, you've delimited the block as one word. Continue pressing the SPACEBAR to delimit a *phrase* of several words.

Press   **F1 Cancel**

to turn off the block.

Press   **ALT-F4 Block** or **F12 Block**

Type   T

    Be sure the *T* is uppercase. The block extends to the next occurrence of *T*, which is in the word *Toupee.*

Press   **F1 Cancel**

Press   **ALT-F4 Block** or **F12 Block**

Press   **HOME,HOME,DOWN ARROW**

    Now you've delimited the block from the cursor position to the end of the document.

Press   **F1 Cancel**

You can delimit a block from the cursor position *backward*, but you can only use a cursor movement command to highlight the block. When you type a character while block is on, WordPerfect looks *forward* for that character. Experiment with delimiting blocks using the techniques outlined earlier. In Chapter 3 you'll learn yet another way to delete with the move command.

Two Other Useful Ways to Delete Characters

There are two other deleting commands that you can often use instead of a block operation: (1) delete to the end of the line and (2) delete to the end of the page. Both work from the *current* cursor position.

First, position the cursor on the last line of the third paragraph. Then:

Press   **CTRL-END**

This is the Delete EOL ("end of line") command that deletes text from the current cursor position to the end of the line. It deletes a soft return at the end of a line, but it does not delete a hard return, as here. There is no full line delete command in WordPerfect, but you can set up one on your own (Chapter 7).

Press   **F1 Cancel**

Type   1 or r [Restore]

to restore the deletion.

Press   **HOME,HOME,UP ARROW**

to position the cursor at the beginning of the document.

Press   **CTRL-PG DN**

This command deletes from the cursor position to the end of the page. You're taking out potentially a lot of text, so WordPerfect asks you to confirm your choice:

Delete Remainder of page? (Y/N) No

Type   n

To delete a one-page document, go to the top of the document and press CTRL-PG DN. To delete more text than just to the bottom of the current page, use the block technique. You can always restore a major deletion with the F1 Cancel key as soon as you make it, if necessary. Table 2-1 lists the WordPerfect keys for deleting characters.

More About the F1 Cancel Key

The F1 Cancel key has two functions in WordPerfect. When you issue a command, use F1 Cancel to cancel the command immediately. You can cancel any command except F3 Help with this key. When you press F1 Cancel without first entering a command, WordPerfect presents the undelete feature if you've deleted any text. If there's no text in the undelete buffer, WordPerfect does nothing.

Table 2-1   WordPerfect Commands for Deleting Characters

Key	Action
DEL	Deletes the character at the cursor or the highlighted block
BACKSPACE	Deletes the character to the left of the cursor
CTRL-BACKSPACE	Deletes the word at the cursor
HOME,BACKSPACE	Deletes part of a word from the cursor position to the previous space character ("word boundary")
HOME,DEL	Deletes part of a word from the cursor position to and including the next space character ("word boundary")
CTRL-END	Deletes all characters from the cursor to the end of the line, except a hard return
CTRL-PG DN	Deletes all characters from the cursor to the end of the current page (asks for confirmation)

Clear the Screen and Start Over!

Because you may have made deletions to this document that you really wanted to keep, return to the previous version of the document before you continue. That is, clear the document from the screen and retrieve it again:

Press   **F7 Exit**

Type   n twice

Press   **SHIFT-F10 Retrieve**

Type   news

Press   **RETURN**

An Editing Session

Now you want to add more "copy" to the newsletter, so go to the end of the document quickly:

Press   **HOME,HOME,DOWN ARROW**

There should be two blank lines between the last paragraph and the new one you'll type now.
Type the following new paragraph but make sure it starts with a tab.

        The picnic starts at 9 a.m. and continues until, as Joe Tetrazzini down in Tinting and Dyeing remarked, "the suds are gone." With any luck, that won't be until much later. Founder's Park is located on Route 22 at the Big Sneeze exit. Keep your eyes peeled for our signs.

Press   **RETURN** twice

to end the paragraph and add a blank line.
Type the next paragraph:

        Caution! If you're driving in from the south, try to avoid the construction at the Impromptu interchange. It's a real mess right now!

Press   **RETURN** twice

to end the paragraph and add a blank line.

Combining and Splitting Paragraphs

Taking a look at this wonderful prose on the screen, you decide to rearrange the contents of the last two paragraphs. You'll combine them into one paragraph and then split the paragraph at another spot.

Press   **UP ARROW** six times

to position the cursor on Ln 5" (the last line in the paragraph).

Press   **END**

The cursor is at the end of the paragraph. It should be two spaces past the period. If it isn't there, type the two spaces now. Then:

Press   **DEL** three times

You've deleted the hard return at the end of the paragraph, the second RETURN, and the tab that began the paragraph. The text of the last paragraph is now joined to the previous paragraph. You can combine paragraphs by deleting whatever is between them.

Question: Is there another way to combine the two paragraphs? *Answer:* Yes! Position the cursor on the first word of the second paragraph, then use the BACKSPACE key to delete the intervening tab and hard returns.

Press   **UP ARROW** twice

Press   **CTRL-RIGHT ARROW** enough times

to position the cursor under the *F* of *Founder's.*
This is where you want to begin a new paragraph.

Press   **RETURN** twice

You've split the paragraph at this spot. But is it correct yet? No! Look at the screen. You must insert another tab to indent the paragraph:

Press   **TAB**

Press   **DOWN ARROW**

WordPerfect adjusts the text of the new paragraph to fit within the margins.

Press   **HOME,HOME,DOWN ARROW**

More Work!

Type the following two paragraphs. Make sure you press **RETURN** twice at the end of each. You're on your own this time!

      The other major news of the month is that CT has come out with an entirely new line of men's and ladies' hairpieces, all designed to accentuate today's more lively and carefree lifestyles. These new products reflect the company's rapid growth as one of the major suppliers of quality wigs.

      Among the new arrivals to the CT family this month are a whole bunch of fuzzy little kittens. It turns out that St. Sebastian, the Shipping Department's mascot, is really a she! Such are the ways of the world--you just never know. In any case, these kittens need a home. Any takers?

Time to save your work:

Press   **F10 Save**

Press   **RETURN**

to accept the file name.

Type   **y**

to replace the original file with the new version.

Scrolling Around

Did you remember to press RETURN twice at the end of the last paragraph? Did you also notice that the document has grown too large to fit entirely on the screen? As you added text, WordPerfect *scrolled* the beginning of the document up and out of sight. But you can always bring the unseen parts back into view. One way to scroll is to hold down the **UP ARROW** key to scroll up or the **DOWN ARROW** key to scroll down, but there are other scrolling methods.

Even though this document is still not very long, experiment with the following keys: GRAY +, GRAY −, **PG UP**, and **PG DN**. As I mentioned in Chapter 1, the first two keys scroll the document up or down by screenful. The PG UP and PG DN keys scroll the document by entire pages. If the document is only one page long, or if the cursor is on the last page, the PG DN key moves the cursor to the end of the document. Conversely, PG UP moves the cursor to the beginning of the document if the cursor is anywhere else on the first page.

If you're using a printer other than the standard printer, WordPerfect may format the text in longer lines. The formatting depends on the *initial* or *base font* that you or WordPerfect sets up for the printer (Chapter 4). Part of a long line may not appear on your monitor. You can scroll the rest of a long line into view. Press **HOME,RIGHT ARROW** to scroll right in sections, and **HOME,LEFT ARROW** to scroll left. You may have to repeat these commands depending on the line length.

To scroll quickly to the right side or left side of a long line, press **HOME,HOME,RIGHT ARROW** or **HOME,HOME,LEFT ARROW**.

Tip: To position the cursor at the end of a line of whatever length, press **END**. Chapter 13 also discusses long text lines.

When you're finished:

Press   **HOME,HOME,DOWN ARROW**

to position the cursor at the end of the document.

The ESC Key for Repetitions

Besides letting you cancel a command, the ESC key has another function that can be a real time and keystroke saver. You can use ESC to *repeat* many commands. Use this feature just before you issuc the command. For example, assume you don't want to scroll by screenful, but rather in smaller increments.

Press   **ESC**

WordPerfect displays this on the status line:

`Repeat Value = 8`

The ESC key is thus preset to repeat the next command or character eight times. (Version 4.2 displays n = 8 .)

Press   **UP ARROW**

The cursor has moved up eight lines. Repeat the same steps a few times and watch the document scroll up. Now, with the cursor on any line of text, do this:

Press　　　**ESC,RIGHT ARROW**

to move the cursor eight positions to the right.

You can change the number of repetitions. For instance, you want it to be 20 instead of 8.

Press　　　**ESC**

Type　　　**20**

Press　　　**RETURN**

The ESC key is now set to repeat the next command 20 times. The number of repetitions remains at 20 until you change it again, or until you exit WordPerfect. Try using the ESC key and the UP ARROW or DOWN ARROW keys to scroll now. You can set a permanently different repetition number by changing the WordPerfect defaults (Appendix A).

Press　　　**HOME,HOME,DOWN ARROW**

to position the cursor at the end of the document.

Press　　　**ESC**

Type　　　**64**

Type　　　**–**

(That's a hyphen.)

You just drew a line across the screen quickly! To delete the line quickly, block it out:

Press　　　**ALT-F4 Block** or **F12 Block**

Press　　　**HOME,LEFT ARROW**

Press　　　**DEL** or **BACKSPACE**

Type　　　**y**

to delete the block.

Tip: Although the ESC key won't work with the BACKSPACE key alone, it will work with the Word Delete command, CTRL-BACKSPACE. Normally CTRL-END won't delete a hard return, but when it's used with the ESC key, it *will*. There are many uses for the ESC key. For instance, to delete several lines in one fell swoop, press ESC, type the number of lines, and then press CTRL-END. To cancel the ESC command, press ESC again or F1 Cancel. When you're finished experimenting with this feature:

Press **HOME,HOME,UP ARROW**

to position the cursor at the beginning of the document.

The Screen Codes and Tab Ruler

When it wraps the lines for you, WordPerfect inserts soft return codes in the document. You have manually inserted codes for hard returns at the ends of paragraphs. Every time to make a decision regarding the *format* of the document—including line spacing and special printing effects, for instance—you insert a code for that decision.

WordPerfect uses these codes as *instructions* to show your document correctly on the screen and later to print the document the way you want it. Every special instruction has a code—*every* one! Normally, you don't see the codes, but they're always there. One of WordPerfect's best features is the way it handles the codes. Instead of showing the codes mixed with your typing, WordPerfect hides the codes. That way, you aren't distracted from your work. The codes don't appear unless you decide to look at them:

Press **ALT-F3 Reveal Codes** or **F11 Reveal Codes**

WordPerfect splits the screen and shows part of your document at the top and the same lines together with the codes at the bottom, separated by a *tab ruler* line. WordPerfect presents the codes in intense video or another color to distinguish them visually from your text. The cursor is a large block. Figure 2-1 shows an example of the split screen.

 Notice the message at the bottom of the code display:

`Press Reveal Codes to restore screen`

In previous versions of WordPerfect you couldn't edit the document while the code display was on. Now you can! This means you *can't* use the RETURN key, SPACEBAR, or F1 Cancel to turn off the codes. *You must press ALT-F3 Reveal Codes or F11 Reveal Codes to turn the codes off.* Don't do this yet, though. Take a brief look at the tab ruler.

```
                    "Permanent Wave" - August Issue

       The most important news of the month is the company picnic.
   That's right!  Consolidated Toupee is giving us a real, honest-
   to-goodness picnic.  After all, don't we deserve it?  So come
   one, come all to Founder's Park on August 21st and join in the
   fun.  Bring the kids, bring your friends, bring food and drink.

       As a special feature, President Glatzkopf will be there to
   present to some lucky person the annual Employee of the Year
   C:\WP\NEWS                                     Doc 1 Pg 1 Ln 1" Pos 1"
   {     ▲     ▲     ▲     ▲     ▲     ▲     ▲     ▲     ▲     } ▲     ▲
   [Cntr]"Permanent Wave" [-] August Issue[C/A/Flrt][HRt]
   [HRt]
   [HRt]
   [Tab]The most important news of the month is the company picnic. [SRt]
   That's right!  Consolidated Toupee is giving us a real, honest[-]
   to[-]goodness picnic.  After all, don't we deserve it?  So come[SRt]
   one, come all to Founder's Park on August 21st and join in the[SRt]
   fun.  Bring the kids, bring your friends, bring food and drink.[HRt]
   [HRt]
   [Tab]As a special feature, President Glatzkopf will be there to[SRt]

   Press Reveal Codes to restore screen
```

Figure 2-1   Revealing the Screen Codes and Tab Ruler

The tab ruler shows the current left margin ([), right margin (]), and tab stops (▲). If there is a tab stop at the same position as a margin setting, WordPerfect displays a brace ({ for left or } for right) on the tab ruler. You thus can quickly check the current margin and tab settings by revealing the codes.

With the codes revealed, you can move the cursor around and even edit your text! You can use any cursor movement command. For the moment, leave the cursor where it is and notice that WordPerfect encloses all codes in square brackets. The soft return code is [SRt], the hard return code is [HRt], and the tab code is [Tab].

Note: If you had turned on a block with the codes revealed, you'd see a [Block] code to indicate the beginning of the block.

Why did WordPerfect make the hyphens that you typed in the word *honest-to-goodness* special codes? You'll understand more when you learn about hyphenation (Chapter 20).

Note: In typeover mode, WordPerfect won't let you type over codes. It will just push the codes ahead as you type. Leave the codes on.

"Garbage" and What to Do About It

Klutzes and nonklutzes alike often experience a problem known as *garbage*, which usually doesn't appear until a document prints. Garbage is the result of a heavy hand and the insert mode. You might issue a command inadvertently and thus insert a code in the document without realizing it. This code stays in the document until you delete it. If you get some strange printouts, check the codes in your document around where the garbage has appeared. More than likely, the gremlin at work is a stray code.

Suppose, however, you retrieve a document and you see strange characters that you didn't type. Even worse, WordPerfect won't let you edit the file or move the cursor. You may have a disk problem. See Trashing Disks in Chapter 9.

Deleting Codes

You can delete the codes with the BACKSPACE or DEL key, depending on the cursor position. If the cursor is directly *under* the code, use **DEL**. If the cursor is directly *following* the code, use the **BACKSPACE** key. As an example, try deleting the [Tab] code (the cursor should be under this code right now):

Press   **DEL**

You've deleted the [Tab] code, and the text of the line moves back to the left margin. If at any time you aren't exactly sure where the codes are—for example, when you want to delete a hard return code—turn the codes on as a guide. You can also have WordPerfect *search* for a code (Chapter 8).

Press   **ALT-F3 Reveal Codes** or **F11 Reveal Codes**

to turn off the codes.

Remember to put the tab back in the document:

Press   **TAB**

If you attempt to delete a code (except the most common ones, like a tab) when the codes are not revealed, WordPerfect first asks you to confirm that you really want to get rid of the code.

Moving the Cursor in Front of the Codes

You already know that you can press HOME,LEFT ARROW to move the cursor to the beginning text of the line and HOME,HOME,LEFT ARROW to position the cursor to the left margin when the left margin isn't visible on the screen. These commands do *not* position the cursor in front of any codes that may be in front of the text on the line. To do that, use **HOME,HOME,HOME,LEFT ARROW**. That's right: *three* presses of the HOME key!

Never-Never Land

There's one more thing you should discover now about the screen display. Even though the screen may show you a lot of empty space at times, some parts of the screen are not available for your text. Or, to put it another way, if you try to move the cursor into these areas, WordPerfect won't let you. To see this computer never-never land, move the cursor to any text line. Then:

Press   **END**

Press   **RIGHT ARROW**

The cursor jumped to the beginning of the next line. It can't move into the never-never land past a soft or hard return at the end of a line.

Press   **HOME,HOME,UP ARROW**

to position the cursor at the beginning of the document.

Making Space for Titles and Headings

This month's issue of "Permanent Wave," the newsletter for the employees of Consolidated Toupee, is slowly taking shape. You realize that you haven't inserted a title, but you don't see any room at the top of the document for a title. That's because you *make* the room when you want to insert a new line.

Press   **RETURN** four times

The cursor moves down the page along with the text as you add hard returns. Oops! You only wanted three blank lines:

Press   **BACKSPACE**

to delete one hard return code.

To type the title on the first blank line, position the cursor on the top line again:

Press   **HOME,HOME,UP ARROW**

Centering a Line

To center a line on a typewriter, you have to find the approximate center of the page, then press BACKSPACE once for every *two* characters in the line. WordPerfect has a much better way to center a line between the margins. First, make sure the cursor is at the *left margin* when you want to center a line to the current margins. It should be there now. Then:

Press   **SHIFT-F6 Center**

WordPerfect inserts a begin center code (although you don't see it) and moves the cursor to the center of the line. Watch what happens as you type the title:

Type   `"Permanent Wave" - August Issue`

Caution: Don't press RETURN at the end of this line because you've already added enough blank lines to separate the title from the body of the newsletter. Now take a look at the center codes:

Press   **ALT-F3 Reveal Codes** or **F11 Reveal Codes**

Note that there are *two* codes: a `[Cntr]` before the title and an inexplicable `[C/A/Flrt]` after the title. These codes delimit the centered text. Version 4.2 users are probably flustered already, because many of the codes have changed! (Don't look at me—*I* didn't do it!) Here's what all this means.

Whenever two codes enclose text, the begin code will be in initial caps and the end code in lowercase. When you work with boldface, underlining, and other print effects (Chapter 4), you'll learn similar begin and end codes. The `[C/A/Flrt]` code indicates that the center operation is akin to the *align* and *flush right* operations (Chapter 14). Dear Reader, WordPerfect has many features!

Caution: Don't use the TAB key or SPACEBAR before you press the SHIFT-F6 Center key unless you want WordPerfect to center the text over the tab stop or current column (Chapter 10).

Uncentering and Recentering a Line

If you want to *uncenter* a line, you have to delete just one of the center codes—it doesn't matter which one. With the codes still on, move the cursor under the [C/A/Flrt] code, if it isn't there now. Then:

Press   **DEL**

WordPerfect deletes both center codes and moves the line back to the left margin. If you attempt to delete a center code when the codes are not revealed, WordPerfect will first ask you to confirm your intentions.

To *recenter* a line, you have two options:

1. With the cursor at the end of the line directly past the last character, press **ALT-F4 Block**. Now for a nifty trick. You *don't* have to extend the block! Just press **SHIFT-F6 Center**. WordPerfect prompts:

   [Cntr] (Y/N)? No

   Type **y** to center the line. Try it with the codes revealed right now!

2. Move the cursor to the beginning text on the line, press **SHIFT-F6 Center**. When you move the cursor out of the line, WordPerfect centers the line correctly.

Make sure that you've recentered the title line before you continue. Then:

Press   **ALT-F3 Reveal Codes** or **F11 Reveal Codes**

to turn the codes off.

Carry On . . .

You've covered a lot of ground, but there's still more to learn. First, however, you must do some more typing.

Press   **HOME,HOME,DOWN ARROW**

to position the cursor at the end of the document.

Press   **SHIFT-F6 Center**

Type   Corporate News

Press   **RETURN** twice

Type the following paragraph and press **RETURN** twice when you're done:

The Board of Directors of Consolidated Toupee has released to "Permanent Wave" the sales figures for the previous fiscal year, which ended on June 30th. As usual, CT is right up there in the world of hairpieces and even managed to post a 15 percent increase in sales alone. Added to this substantial profit are the revenues from CT's wholly-owned subsidiaries, Foundations Unlimited, Inc. and the Acme Elevator Shoe Company.

Now for Page Two

As you can imagine, eventually you'll fill up one page. What happens then? Watch the screen as you type the next paragraph. I assume here that you're using the standard printer. If you've selected a printer that prints 12 characters per horizontal inch, you won't see page two yet. So, just pretend! In any case, type this:

President Glatzkopf announced at a recent press conference the appointment of Assistant Vice President Walter de Bellegorge as Executive Vice President in Charge of New Products. He succeeds Jane R. Pomegranate, who moves over to become the Assistant Executive Vice President for Marketing.

(Did you press **RETURN** twice at the end? Make sure you do!) As you typed, WordPerfect began a new page for you. It shows the page break as a line of dashes. This line doesn't print, of course. Figure 2-2 displays how the document looks on your screen if page two has arrived.

How does WordPerfect "know" where the end of the page is? It keeps track of the other page requirements. That is, by default there are 1-inch top and bottom margins. WordPerfect also "assumes" that you're using a standard, 11-inch page. In addition, it has to take into account the *vertical height* of the typestyle you're using. Although you don't have to think about these defaults yet, remember that you can change them to suit your needs.

Save your work before you continue:

Press   **F10 Save**

Press   **RETURN**

Type   y

to overwrite the previous version of the document.

```
Sebastian, the Shipping Department's mascot, is really a she!
Such are the ways of the world -- you just never know.  In any
case, these kittens need a home.  Any takers?

                    Corporate News

    President Glatzkopf announced at a recent press conference
the appointment of Assistant Vice President Walter de Bellegorge
as Executive Vice President in Charge of New Products.  He
succeeds Jane R. Pomegranate, who moves over to become the
Assistant Executive Vice President for Marketing.

    The Board of Directors of Consolidated Toupee has released
to "Permanent Wave" the sales figures for the previous fiscal
year, which ended on June 30th.  As usual, CT is right up there
in the world of hairpieces and even managed to post a 15 percent
increase in sales alone.  Added to this substantial profit are
------------------------------------------------------------------
the revenues from CT's wholly-owned subsidiaries, Foundations
Unlimited, Inc. and the Acme Elevator Shoe Company.



C:\WP\NEWS                              Doc 1 Pg 2 Ln 1.5" Pos 1"
```

Figure 2-2   How WordPerfect Displays a Page Break

Moving the Cursor by Page or Character

It may sound a little silly to discuss multiple page documents when yours is just over one page long, but you might as well learn right now how to move the cursor quickly to a specific page. Use **CTRL-HOME**, the Go To command. WordPerfect prompts you:

```
Go to
```

Type the page number you want to display and press RETURN. WordPerfect takes the cursor to the top of that page. If the page number doesn't exist, WordPerfect goes to the top of the last page, whatever its number may be.

Here are other useful time-savers. To go to the top of the *current* page, use **CTRL-HOME,UP ARROW**; to go to the bottom of the current page, use **CTRL-HOME,DOWN ARROW**. You can also go forward to a specific character if this character is within the next page or so. Just press CTRL-HOME and then type the character you want. For example, press **CTRL-HOME** and then type **G** to move the cursor to the next *G* character, as long as it appears within the next 2000 characters.

To issue the commands CTRL-HOME,UP ARROW and CTRL-HOME,DOWN ARROW, *first* press CTRL-HOME, *then* release both keys before you press the UP ARROW or DOWN ARROW key. That's why the comma is included in the command.

Tip: To scroll quickly page by page, use the PG DN key to move forward through the document and the PG UP key to move backward. You can also use the ESC key, a number, and the PG UP or PG DN keys to move forward or backward a certain number of pages in the document.

The rest of the chapter discusses other important issues that don't relate to editing, so you can clear the screen now if you wish.

Note: I won't step you through exiting WordPerfect at the end of each session, but always exit WordPerfect properly. If you plan to continue to the next lesson, make sure you clear the screen.

The Disk Full Dilemma

If there isn't enough room in the disk on the current drive when you try to save a document, WordPerfect tells you:

```
ERROR: Disk full--Strike any key to continue
```

You can safely get out of this dilemma in three ways:

1. Delete some unnecessary files from the disk and try again.
2. Change to another drive that has room and save the document there.
3. Put another formatted disk in the drive and save the document to the new disk. If you don't have a formatted disk ready, you can format on the fly from within WordPerfect.

Would that this situation doesn't occur too often. If it does, refer to Chapter 9, which shows you how to handle all three options.

The Floppy Disk Flip-Flop

If you do have to remove the second program disk from the drive and insert another, say, to save a file, eventually WordPerfect will tell you this:

```
Put "WordPerfect 2" disk back in drive and press any key
```

You might also see this prompt if you've removed the second program disk to insert the speller's dictionary disk (Chapter 12). Before it can exit,

WordPerfect has to have access to the second program disk. Insert this disk in the proper drive and press a key to continue. (I won't mention this again.)

Overflow Files

As you work, WordPerfect maintains certain *overflow* files on the disk but deletes these overflow files when you save your work and properly exit the program. There are several overflow files, each beginning with {WP}. What they contain is explained in the WordPerfect documentation.

If you turn off or reset your computer without properly exiting WordPerfect, or if the power fails and the computer goes "down," WordPerfect can't delete the overflow files. When you load WordPerfect the next time, the program sees the previous overflow files and you'll see this message:

```
Are other copies of WordPerfect currently running? (Y/N)
```

Because overflow files exist from the previous session, WordPerfect is a bit confused. It "assumes" that another copy of the program is working elsewhere. Normally this isn't the case, so it's safe to do this:

Type   n

WordPerfect deletes the previous overflow files and opens new ones. If you type y, however, WordPerfect requests another directory name and supplies the current directory (for instance, C:\WP as here):

```
Directory is in use. New WP Directory:C:\WP\
```

You can't run two copies of WordPerfect in the same directory, because there can be only one set of overflow files per directory. You must type a different directory name and press RETURN if you want to keep two sets of overflow files. This scenario doesn't occur too often, thank goodness!

 Tip: A better bet if you're not sure is to press F1 Cancel to return to the DOS prompt. You could then rename the overflow files. Load WordPerfect again and retrieve the overflow files individually to see if you lost any work. Thus, the overflow files can help you recover lost work. Accidental destruction of a file may never happen to you, but it's comforting to know that there are ways to recover work when you're in dire straits.

Dear Reader, there's a lot to learn, and everyone makes mistakes! But I hope that the examples in these first two chapters showed you ways to redeem yourself and save a lot of frustration and work, too.

3

Moving, Copying, and Joining

In this chapter you'll learn the following new commands . . .

Function Key Command

CTRL-F4 Move	(1) Move, copy, or delete text, (2) append a block to another file

Numeric Keypad Commands

ALT-F4 Block, CTRL-HOME,CTRL-HOME or **F12 Block,CTRL-HOME,CTRL-HOME**	Rehighlight the last block
CTRL-HOME,CTRL-HOME	Cursor to the last "major motion"
CTRL-HOME,ALT-F4 Block or **CTRL-HOME,F12 Block**	Cursor to the beginning of the last marked block or the currently marked block

. . . and you'll discover another use for these commands:

F10 Save	Save a block to a new file
SHIFT-F10 Retrieve	Retrieve text from the move buffer

WordPerfect has powerful and versatile commands to move text from one spot in a document to another. A companion to the move facility is the copy command, another topic of this chapter. You'll also learn how to copy text from one document to another document in a different file. These operations are all part and parcel of the word processor's trade.

DO WARM-UP

Conservation of Energy

Dear Reader, by now you should know the steps for doing basic operations like retrieving and saving a document or moving the cursor, so I won't go through them every time. They would make the book larger than it is, and my editor is already complaining that the book is too big. I'll just use a special symbol to tell you what to do before you continue an example, like this:

✔Retrieve the document NEWS.

That means, of course, press **SHIFT-F10 Retrieve**, type **news** , and press **RETURN**. Do it now!

A Fake Editing Session

In the examples that follow, you'll make changes to your original newsletter document. Then you'll *abandon* these editing decisions and keep the document as it was when you started. So, don't save the document at any time.

Moving Text

Before you learn how to move, here's a short summary of the steps you'll take. The Move command actually lets you do one of four operations: (1) physically move text from one spot in a document to another, (2) copy text within a document, (3) delete text, and (4) append, that is, copy text from one document to another. Here are the basic steps:

1. You first *select* the text. If it's a sentence, paragraph, or page, Word-Perfect can select them directly. Otherwise, use a block.

2. Next, you *choose* the operation you want: move, copy, delete, or append.

3. Finally, for move or copy operations you position the cursor at the location where you want the text to go, then press RETURN to *retrieve* the text. You can also complete a move or copy later. To append text, you supply a file name. If the file exists, WordPerfect appends the text to the end of the file. If the file doesn't exist, WordPerfect creates the new file.

The rest of the chapter illustrates these basic steps.

Moving a Paragraph

Writers are never satisfied! You decide that you don't like the flow of your newsletter, so you want to switch the last two paragraphs. WordPerfect has a very powerful and easy move feature. You simply cut text from its current position and paste it somewhere else, almost as if you had a giant electrical scissors and glue in your computer.

WordPerfect has built-in commands to move a sentence, a paragraph, and a page. That is, WordPerfect will automatically move any of these entities for you. All you have to do is make sure the cursor is somewhere in the sentence, paragraph, or page you want to move before you start.

✔Position the cursor at the left margin on the first line of the paragraph that begins *The Board of Directors*. Make sure the cursor is in front of the tab. Then:

Press   **CTRL-F4 Move**

WordPerfect presents the move menu:

Move: 1 Sentence; 2 Paragraph; 3 Page; 4 Retrieve: 0

Type   **2 or p [Paragraph]**

WordPerfect highlights the entire paragraph, then it presents another menu:

1 Move; 2 Copy; 3 Delete; 4 Append: 0

Type   **1 or m [Move]**

The paragraph has disappeared! Don't worry: It's not lost. WordPerfect keeps it in a separate *buffer* while you position the cursor to the move location. Recall that a buffer is a holding zone for text. At the bottom of the screen, WordPerfect tells you to:

Move cursor; press Enter to retrieve.

That is, WordPerfect is waiting for you to position the cursor where you want to move the text. You should complete the move now:

Press   **ESC,UP ARROW**

to position the cursor at the left margin of the paragraph that begins *Among the new arrivals*. If the cursor isn't there, position it there before you continue.

Now, retrieve the paragraph:

Press   **RETURN**

There's your paragraph again, in its new location. A nice touch is that WordPerfect also moved the two hard returns at the end of the paragraph to keep the correct spacing between paragraphs after the move.

Deleting with the Move Key

Although I won't step you through an example, you can use the CTRL-F4 Move command to highlight a sentence, paragraph, page, or block. Then delete the text with the **3** [Delete] choice.

Caution: The deleted text is stored in the undelete buffer (Chapter 2) and knocks out the first deletion in the buffer.

When you move or copy text, however, the text goes into the move buffer. The move buffer is separate from the undelete buffer, so it's technically possible to have four different sections of text or blocks in buffers and to restore or retrieve each one as many times as you wish.

Completing the Move Later

The **4** [Retrieve] choice on the CTRL-F4 Move key lets you retrieve the last moved text, too. Suppose you just want to cut the text, but you *don't* want to move it right now. Press **F1 Cancel** to remove WordPerfect's message from the status line. Later, but before you try to move anything else, position the cursor where you want to move the text. Then press **CTRL-F4 Move** and type **4** or **r** [Retrieve]. WordPerfect prompts:

```
Retrieve: 1 Block; 2 Tabular Column; 3 Rectangle: 0
```

Type **1** or **b** [Block] to retrieve the cut text. You can repeat the operation to copy the same text any number of times. Later you'll learn about block moves. **Tip:** Once you've moved or copied the text with the CTRL-F4 Move key, you can quickly retrieve the text from the move buffer by pressing **SHIFT-10 Retrieve** then **RETURN**.

Moving a Sentence

Take a look at what happens when you move a sentence. The cursor should be at the left margin.

Press   **CTRL-F4 Move**

Type   **1** or **s** [Sentence]

WordPerfect highlights the sentence, *including* the two spaces that separate it from the next sentence, but it doesn't include the tab stop at the beginning of the paragraph. Neat! You decide not to move this sentence, so:

Press   **RETURN** or **F1 Cancel**

How does WordPerfect "know" what's a sentence or a paragraph? Think about how sentences and paragraphs are formed and try to understand what WordPerfect "looks for" when you instruct it to cut a sentence or a paragraph.
 Hint: What begins and ends a sentence, and what begins and ends a paragraph?
 Tip: If you're moving the cursor across several pages before you can move something, use the Go To command, CTRL-HOME, to position the cursor on the correct page after you cut the text.

Another Way to Move Text: Undelete It

Suppose you don't want to move just one sentence, an entire paragraph, or a complete page. What if you want to move *two* sentences, or *part* of a paragraph, or only *half* a page? Can you do it? Of course, and you already know how: Just delimit what you want to move as a block, *delete* the block, move the cursor to the new location, and then *undelete* the block. Make sure you do this as soon as you can, because WordPerfect only "remembers" the last three deletions.

 When you use the *block method* to move text, you must take care to delimit all the text you want, including any necessary tabs, hard returns, and other codes. WordPerfect won't do it for you. Now block out and move the last two paragraphs together with the section heading. This block should thus include the center codes, the tabs at the beginning, and the hard returns at the ends of the paragraphs.

 ✔Position the cursor on the centered line, *Corporate News.*

 Wait! Exactly where's the cursor? Is it under the *C* of *Corporate?* If so, you're not ready yet. The cursor has to be at the left margin, in front of any codes, if you want to move the line and the center codes. Just to make sure, take a look at the codes:

Press   **ALT-F3 Reveal Codes** or **F11 Reveal Codes**

Aha! The cursor is directly past the begin center code. You want to include it in the block, so:

Press   **LEFT ARROW**

to move the cursor under the [Cntr] code.

Press   **ALT-F3 Reveal Codes** or **F11 Reveal Codes**

to turn the codes off.

The cursor is now at the left margin.

Press   **ALT-F4 Block** or **F12 Block**

Press   **HOME,HOME,DOWN ARROW**

Note that the cursor is two lines below the last paragraph. Although WordPerfect doesn't highlight the two hard returns, they're still part of the block.

Press   **DEL** or **BACKSPACE**

Type   y

to delete the block.

    ✔Position the cursor at the left margin on the first line of the paragraph that begins *The Board of Directors.* Then:

Press   **F1 Cancel**

Type   1 or r [Restore]

to restore and, hence, move the block here.

Yet Another Way to Move Text: Move a Block

One final way to move text is to use a block and then the CTRL-F4 Move key. This brings up a new and important issue, so pay close attention! Suppose you want to move the first two sentences in the paragraph (when you do, of course, the text won't make any sense, but just pretend it will).

    ✔Position the cursor under the *T* of the word *The* that begins the paragraph. You don't want to include the tab code in the block. Then:

Press   **ALT-F4 Block** or **F12 Block**

Type   . twice

(That's two periods.)

Wait! You haven't extended the block to include the two spaces after the second sentence:

Press   **RIGHT ARROW** twice

Now comes the point I'm trying to make:

Press   **CTRL-F4 Move**

What's this? WordPerfect presents another menu, the block move menu:

Move: 1 Block; 2 Tabular Column; 3 Rectangle: 0

Note: You'll find that often a menu changes when you bring up the menu and block is on. That's because some operations work only with blocks and some only with normal text. Tabular columns and rectangles are more advanced topics that I'll cover in other chapters.

Type   **1 or b [Block]**

Type   **1 or m [Move]**

Press   **DOWN ARROW**

Press   **END**

to position the cursor at the end of the paragraph.

Stop again! Are there two spaces after the sentence? If not, press the **SPACEBAR** twice before you move the block here. Then:

Press   **RETURN**

to retrieve the block.

Moving Text with Codes

Will writers ever be satisfied? (Probably not.) You decide to put the block back where it was originally, but this time you'll block it from the bottom up.

✔Position the cursor at the left margin of the paragraph that begins *Among the new arrivals.* Then:

Press   **ALT-F4 Block** or **F12 Block**

Press   **ESC,UP ARROW** twice or **UP ARROW** sixteen times

to position the cursor under the *C* of *Corporate.*

You still aren't there yet, because the cursor isn't at the left margin. How do you get past the begin center code with the block on? That's right!

Press   **HOME,HOME,HOME,LEFT ARROW**

to move past the codes.

Now you're ready to begin.

Press   **DEL or BACKSPACE**

Type   y

Press   **HOME,HOME,DOWN ARROW**

Press   **F1 Cancel**

Type   **1 or r [Restore]**

The moral of this example was: Don't forget the codes! To be doubly sure that you've included the codes in a block operation, use HOME, HOME,HOME,LEFT ARROW to position the cursor in front of the codes when you're in doubt.

Tip: You can also reveal the codes while a block is on to check them, too.

Well, there are the basic ways to move text. Because you now want to *abandon* the edit and return the document to the way it was before you started, do this:

Press   **F7 Exit**

Type   n twice

to clear the screen.

Copying Text

When you move text you are actually cutting it from its current location and physically pasting it at another location. If you decide that you don't like it there, you can move it back or elsewhere. When you *copy* text, you're following the same basic pattern, so you still begin by delimiting the text. But you then leave the original in its place and put a copy—or several copies—somewhere else in the document or in another file altogether.

A Real Helper

The Copy command can save you a lot of frustration and boredom—not to mention work—when you need to type repetitious text. But you have to be careful: Make sure that the text you want to copy has no typographical or grammatical mistakes *before* you copy it. Otherwise, you'll have to correct the same mistakes many times later! Take a look at the following form:

Record Loan Form

```
Catalogue No._____Date_____
Label I.D._____
Borrower_____
Street Address_____
City_____
```

Suppose you want to repeat this form as many times as you can on the page. Why type each repetition? Just type it once, and then let Copy do the rest of the work.

✔Center and type the title, **Record Loan Form**. Then press **RETURN** three times for spacing. Type **Catalogue No.** and stop.

Can you think of an easy way to do the underlines? Right! Use the ESC key. You want the date to begin at column 5.5, and the cursor is now at column 2.3. So $55 - 23 = 32$.

Press   **ESC**

Type   **32**

Type   _

(That's an underline, **SHIFT-HYPHEN**.)

There's your line. Type the word **Date** . The cursor is now at column 59. Use the ESC key to repeat the next underline 15 times. Then:

Press   **RETURN**

to end the line.

✔Create the other lines the same way, using these numbers with the ESC key for each underline:

Label I.D.	54
Borrower	56
Street Address	50
City	60

When you're finished, for spacing:

Press   **RETURN** three times

Eventually you'll learn how to use the spelling checker to catch typos (Chapter 12). Here, just "eyeball" it to make sure that there are no mistakes. Okay, when you've finished typing, the cursor should be on line 2.66″. Now, copy the text. What command would you use first?

Why not copy the text as a page? Try it, you'll like it!

Press   **CTRL-F4 Move**

Type   **3** or **a** [P<u>a</u>ge]

Type   **2** or **c** [<u>C</u>opy]

Because you're not moving the text, WordPerfect just makes a copy of it in the move buffer. The Move cursor; press Enter to retrieve message is at the bottom of the screen again. Now, the cursor is exactly where you want the new copy to go, so:

Press   **RETURN**

to copy the text here.

For the other copies, you first move the cursor and then retrieve the text as a block:

Press   **HOME,HOME,DOWN ARROW**

Press   **CTRL-F4 Move**

Type   **4** or **r** [<u>R</u>etrieve]

Type   **1** or **b** [<u>B</u>lock]

to insert the third copy.

✔Repeat these three steps two more times to copy the text. In all you should have five copies. When you're finished, save the document as FORM.1, then clear the screen.

Another Way to Copy: Use a Block

You can also block out the text, press **CTRL-F4 Move**, type **1** or **b** [<u>B</u>lock], then type **2** or **c** [<u>C</u>opy]. However, when the text is a sentence, paragraph, or page, it's easier just to use the regular move.

How Do YOU Spell Relief?

Now look at a slightly more complicated example of how to use the Copy command. The following excerpt is taken from a list of interrogatories from one party in a lawsuit to another.

INTERROGATORY NO. 1

According to your knowledge or belief, did Consolidated Toupee, on the day the purported events took place, August 15, 1988, knowingly, and with malice of forethought, refuse to respond to Plaintiff's questions regarding his new hairpiece?

INTERROGATORY NO. 2

According to your knowledge or belief, did Consolidated Toupee, on the day the purported events took place, August 15, 1988, knowingly, and with malice of forethought, refuse to send Plaintiff a hairpiece that did fit properly?

INTERROGATORY NO. 3

According to your knowledge or belief, did Consolidated Toupee, on the day the purported events took place, August 15, 1988, knowingly, and with malice of forethought, refuse to credit Plaintiff's account for the unwanted hairpiece?

Each interrogatory is the same up to a certain point. This could, and usually does, go on for pages. If you were typing this deposition, how would you do it with the Copy command? (There's a far easier way, but this is just for practice. The easier way is discussed in Chapter 7.)

What I would do is:

1. Type the first heading and question once (make sure the spacing and typing are correct!) up to the words *refuse to*, including the space.
2. Block out this much and then copy the block. Press F1 Cancel to turn copy off.
3. Type the rest of the question.
4. Space down with the RETURN key.
5. Retrieve the block, change the interrogatory number to 2, and finish the second question, and so on.

6. Save the document as DEPO.1.

I'll let you do this one yourself . . . have fun!

Copying Text Between Documents

As long as you're investigating the move and copy features, you should learn a little about how to copy text from one document to another. There are several ways to do this; I'll introduce only the easiest ways here. Basically, how you copy text depends on what document is open, to wit:

- You can *save* a block from the document on the screen to a new file on the disk.
- You can *append* a sentence, paragraph, page, or block from the document on the screen to the end of an existing file on the disk. If the file doesn't exist, WordPerfect creates it.
- You can *retrieve* or *join* another document into the one currently on the screen.
- You can retrieve *two* documents, either in two different *windows* or on two full screens, then move or copy text between them (Chapter 11).
- You can *copy* an entire file on the disk to a new file (Chapter 9).

Now for the steps you'd take to accomplish the first three options.

Saving a Block to a New File

When you want to save a block to a new file, do this:

1. Block the text as normal.
2. Press **F10 Save**, to which WordPerfect responds:

   Block name:

3. Type a *new* file name and press **RETURN**. If the file already exists, WordPerfect asks you to confirm the overwrite.

Appending Text to Another File

When you want to append a sentence, paragraph, page, or block to the end of an existing file, do this:

1. Press **CTRL-F4 Move** and type **1** or **s** [S̲entence], **2** or **p** [P̲aragraph], or **3** or **a** [P̲age].
   or
   Block the text as normal, press **CTRL-F4 Move**, then type **1** or **b** [B̲lock].

2. Type **4** or **a** [A̲ppend]. WordPerfect prompts:

   Append to:

3. Type the file name and press **RETURN**. If the file doesn't exist, WordPerfect creates the file and copies the text to it.

Note: You can append text to a *locked* document (Chapter 9) only if you know the password.

Joining Documents

To join one document into another, follow these steps:

1. Clear the screen and retrieve the first document.
2. Position the cursor where you want to join the next document. It doesn't matter whether insert mode or typeover mode is on, but you'll probably want to have the cursor at the left margin.
3. Press **SHIFT-F10 Retrieve**.
4. Type the file name and press **RETURN**.
5. Check the spacing between the documents to make sure it's correct, then save the new document.

All these copying operations let you set up reusable documents that word processors call *boilerplates* (Chapter 14). Even this early in your WordPerfect apprenticeship, though, you can see how copying can save you a lot of work!

Cursor Movement with Blocks

WordPerfect considers any block operation, such as moving or copying a block, a *major motion*. You can quickly go to the location of the last major motion operation by pressing CTRL-HOME,CTRL-HOME. If you have a large document, this command can get you *back* to where you were in a snap. You can also use CTRL-HOME,CTRL-HOME to move the cursor to the last major deletion location when you want to "undelete." Search and replace (Chapter 8) are also major motion operations.

The command CTRL-HOME,ALT-F4 Block or CTRL-HOME,F12 Block positions the cursor at the beginning of the last marked block.

Tip: If you turn the block on *first* and *then* press CTRL-HOME,ALT-F4 Block or CTRL-HOME,F12 Block, WordPerfect returns to the beginning of the block but the block is still on. Use this feature when you extend the block too far and you want to start over.

Finally, you can *rehighlight* the same block to perform another operation. Just press **ALT-F4 Block**, then **CTRL-HOME,CTRL-HOME** (yes, CTRL-HOME twice) to rehighlight. Alternately, press F12 Block, CTRL-HOME, CTRL-HOME.

Dear Reader, such are the essential move and copy operations that you'll want to learn. The next chapter takes you in another direction. It introduces special printing effects and the very important concept of fonts.

4

Fonts for Special Effects: Bold, Underline, Italics, and More

In this chapter you'll learn the following new commands . . .

Function Key Commands

F6 Bold	Turn boldface on/off
F8 Underline	Turn underlining on/off
CTRL-F8 Font	Change fonts

. . . and you'll learn some new codes:

[BOLD] and [bold]	Begin and end boldface
[DBL UND] and [dbl und]	Begin and end double underline
[Font]	Base font change
[ITALC] and [italc]	Begin and end italics
[OUTLN] and [outln]	Begin and end outline printing
[SHADW] and [shadw]	Begin and end shadow printing
[SM CAP] and [sm cap]	Begin and end small caps
[SUBSCPT] and [subscpt]	Begin and end subscript
[SUPRSCPT] and [suprscpt]	Begin and end superscript
[UND] and [und]	Begin and end underlining

Until Version 5.0 arrived, WordPerfect was firmly ensconced in the world of the office typewriter. For instance, recall from the the discussion of units of measure (Chapter 1) that previous versions of WordPerfect used a standard pica-size measurement: ten characters per horizontal inch and six lines per vertical inch. All that has changed. Now WordPerfect wants you to understand the rudiments of *desktop publishing*, an entirely different world from that of the typewriter indeed.

As a prelude to the general discussion of printing (Chapter 5), this chapter introduces the most common special printing effects. Even as simple a thing as boldface print can now take you into the world of desktop publishing, also called *personal publishing*. That's because WordPerfect is more "printer oriented" than ever and formats a document according to the printer you're currently using.

That was the bad news; now for the good news. You don't have to learn very much about desktop publishing to work with WordPerfect. This chapter gets you started on the right foot. When you become a "power user," you can explore other aspects of desktop publishing in later chapters. Dear Reader, please bear with me for a few pages, because you have some essential reading to do! This may all seem like advanced stuff, but you'll quickly get the hang of it.

DO WARM-UP

Blame It on the Laser Printer

What made desktop publishing an interesting and potentially revolutionary idea in the first place was the appearance of the desktop size laser printer. Provided you have a couple of grand to buy a laser printer, and the cost is dropping substantially, you can create near typeset quality documents for a fraction of the cost of typesetting.

There's the key word: *typesetting*. The laser printer evolved from the world of typesetting, not from the world of the typewriter. With typesetting came a whole new set of terms, but the only ones you need to know now appear in the next two sections.

Typestyles, Fonts, and Families

A dot matrix or daisy wheel printer prints in a particular typestyle that may either be built into the character set of the printer or reside on a daisy wheel or thimble. A *typestyle* is, as its name implies, one particular style of type such as Times Roman or Courier. This book is printed in a typestyle called English Times. You'll also see the word *typeface* to mean typestyle.

A *font* is one particular version of a typestyle in one particular size. So, Courier 10 is one font and Courier 12 is another, because the two are different sizes of the same typeface. Some dot matrix printers have a couple of different fonts, while daisy wheel printers let you change fonts by inserting a different print wheel. Laser printers, however, offer you many different fonts simultaneously.

The distinction between typestyles and fonts becomes significant when you print special effects. Conventional printers handle many effects by a purely mechanical printing action. For example, to print text in boldface, the printer normally overprints each letter two or three times, sometimes even moving the printhead slightly to make a filled in look. However, there is only a limited number of special effects that you can coax out of a conventional printer.

A laser printer, like a typesetting machine, however, usually prints a special effect by switching to a *different font*. For example, boldface print is an emboldened version of a particular typestyle in a particular size. The same procedure applies for italics.

This means that a laser printer needs several different versions of the same typestyle in the same size. Each version is a different font. For example, a laser printer that contains the Times Roman typestyle might have *four or five* Times Roman fonts: one for regular text, one for boldface, one for italics, one for bold italics, and one for super/subscripts. What's more, if you want to use a larger or smaller version of the same typestyle, you need other fonts.

A *family*, or *font family*, then, is a collection of all fonts available in a particular typestyle on a particular laser printer. For instance, the Times Roman family may include regular, bold, and italic fonts in a variety of sizes.

Points, Picas, Pitch, and Proportionals

Well, that wasn't too difficult to understand, but now the confusion begins in earnest. Typesetters normally refer to font sizes in terms of *points* or *picas*. There are 72 points in an inch, 12 points in a pica, and thus 6 picas per inch. One of WordPerfect's new units of measure is the printer's point, although the default unit of measure is the inch.

On laser printers, font size is usually given in points and is generally just a little bigger than the height of a font's tallest character. So think of font size as a vertical measurement. (To save your sanity, you'll bypass the metric system altogether!)

Pitch refers to the number of printed characters per horizontal inch. The larger the font, the fewer characters will fit in an inch. Traditional typewriter pica type prints ten characters per horizontal inch, while typewriter elite prints twelve.

On typewriters and most printers, every character takes up the same amount of space on a printed line. For instance, in the default pitch (10), a character occupies one-tenth of an inch. This is *fixed-width* printing. However, some characters are actually narrower than others. Consider the *i* compared to the *W* and you'll understand what I mean. You'll also then understand why "rivers" of white space appear on pages that have been printed with fixed-width fonts and justified right margins.

The reason that books look much better than computer printouts is in part because typesetting equipment can take into consideration the actual width of each character individually. This is known as *proportional spacing*. To print in proportional spacing, WordPerfect maintains a *table of spacing values* and continually refers to this table when it sets up a line. It totals all the characters' widths on each line and figures out the extra spacing *between* words according to the result. This certainly takes more computational ability than with nonproportional fonts.

Okay, what does all this font business mean to you if you *don't* own a laser printer? Not very much, so relax! For you the word *font* should just be a synonym for "special effect." All you have to remember is that whenever you want to print in a special effect other than the regular typestyle, you're working with fonts. That is, for every special effect you'll tell WordPerfect to change to a different font.

The Base Font

 Now you come to the gist of the matter. When you select a printer, WordPerfect also chooses the most common font that works with your printer. This is the *base font*, or *initial font*, and as you'd expect it's the starting point (base) for all font selection. WordPerfect always prints a special effect with the base font as its guide. That is, when you choose boldface print, WordPerfect switches to the boldface version of the base font.

For example, suppose you select the Diablo 630 daisy wheel printer. WordPerfect then "assumes" that the base font is Multipurpose 10, which is a fixed-width font that prints ten characters per horizontal inch. You can also choose one or two other fonts as the base font if you have the correct print wheel installed in your printer (Chapter 5). Another printer might use a 12-point, proportionally spaced base font. WordPerfect also stores the name of the base font along with the printer's file name (the .PRS "resource file") in the document prefix.

This brings up several important notions:

- You'll have to add new font change codes to documents from previous WordPerfect versions, because the old codes won't work anymore. See File Format Changes in the Prelude.

- You should be aware of what the base font is for the printer you're using. Most of the time, of course, you'll work with just one typestyle if you don't have a laser printer. That typestyle becomes your base font. As a matter of fact, even if you *do* own a laser printer, you won't get too heavily involved with multiple fonts until the latter part of this book.

- Your printer may not be able to print all the special fonts that Word-Perfect supports. To see what special effects work with a base font, print the PRINTER.TST document that WordPerfect Corporation supplies. Wait! You don't know how to print yet! Just learn the special effects now, then print later.

- Whenever you change to another font from the base font to print a special effect, you have to tell WordPerfect when you want to switch *back* to the base font. See Begin and End Codes, next.

- Although WordPerfect selects a base font when you set up your printer, you can choose another as the initial base font. Depending on your printer, there may be several base fonts from which you can choose.

- All size and appearance font changes refer to the base font. For example, if the base font is Times Roman 12 point and you select the large font, WordPerfect looks for a larger version of Times Roman. If it doesn't find one, it retains the base font. If you include italics codes and there's an italicized version of the base font, WordPerfect uses it. Otherwise, it retains the base font.

- When you select a different printer, WordPerfect normally reformats the text to take into account the new base font. For example, if you're using an Epson printer with a 12-point proportionally spaced font and switch to the Diablo 630 with its fixed-width font, then WordPerfect readjusts the lines for the new base font. Recall from the Prelude that WordPerfect calls this *intelligent printing*.

- If you select another printer for a document, WordPerfect uses a base font that most closely approximates the original printer's base font. WordPerfect also finds the closest matching fonts for all other size, appearance, color, and base font changes in the document. This aspect of intelligent printing is known as *automatic font changes,* or *AFC's.*

- Finally, WordPerfect displays special effects on the screen in a variety of ways that depend on your monitor. Boldface usually appears as highlighting, and underlining either appears as itself or a shading. If you have a color monitor, you'll probably see different colors. Some monitors can actually show the effects, for instance, italics. See also Changing the Screen Display of Fonts later in this chapter.

Begin and End Codes

All special printing effect font changes appear as codes that you insert into a document. The difference between these codes and others, such as hard returns or tabs, is that most of the time you need *two* codes: one to turn the special printing on and another to turn it off. I call them *begin* codes and *end* codes, but old-time computerists refer to them as *toggles*. WordPerfect Corporation calls them *paired* codes.

A printer, like a computer, is a dumb machine that will do everything you tell it to do and will *continue to do so* until you tell it to stop. If you instruct it to begin underlining but forget to tell it to stop underlining, then the rest of your text will be duly underlined. Figure 4-1 illustrates toggle switches that begin and end underlining.

Fortunately, WordPerfect indicates on the screen the text that will print in a different font. For instance, it can show underlining either as underlining or in a different shading or color. So if you look up and see the entire file being underlined before your very eyes, this indicates that you forgot to turn off the underlining code. It's a simple procedure to right this minor wrong at any time. WordPerfect also inserts both begin and end codes for you.

You can insert special effects into a document in two ways:

1. While you're typing the text, turn the effect on (select a different font) just before you type the text. When you get to the point where you want to stop the special effect, return to the base font.

2. Around existing text. With only a couple exceptions, this requires that you set up the text as a block. See Adding Special Effects to Existing Text later in the chapter.

Are you thoroughly confused, or perhaps bored, by all this? Don't be, because you're now ready to learn about the most common special effects. It's really quite easy!

Boldface Print As You Type

Most printers, laser and otherwise, can print underlining and boldface. Before you learn about the jazzier special effects, concentrate on the two you'll probably use most often. As usual, I'll step you through the new aspects of the example, but then you're on your own. Take a look at this sample memo,

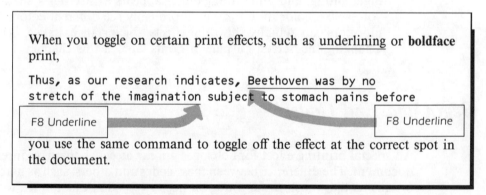

Figure 4-1   Printer Toggle Switches

but don't type it yet. Notice that the centered title is in boldface and that some words are underlined.

Confidential Memo

To: Jaime Pescado, Director of Marketing

From: Randolph D. Sturgeon, Head Buyer

Re: Some Thoughts

I am <u>sick and tired</u> of being a big fish in a little pond! When are you going to realize my true potential by getting me out of this rathole and into a job with more bite? As you know, I have repeatedly broached the subject of the company's marketing plans with you. Here are some more ideas to illustrate my great potential.

It seems that the Felt Platypus chain is suffering from what I call the <u>ho-hum syndrome</u>. Diners are bored by our menus and would rather eat at the golden arches. I suggest the following two ad campaigns to get the FP back into the swing of things.

First, the broadside: Dine with a Platypus Tonight. How's that for a catchy title? Then the more subtle approach: Is There A Platypus In Your Future? Both would feature, of course, Pete the Platypus, the company mascot.

You owe it to yourself and to the organization to get me involved with marketing, where I <u>really</u> belong.

Overlook Mr. Sturgeon's rather forceful style and just get the work done. Make sure the screen is clear. Start by centering the first line:

Press   **SHIFT-F6 Center**

Insert the begin bold instruction like this:

Press   **F6 Bold**

Notice that the Pos *number* on the status line has changed to whatever is your monitor's way of displaying boldface print. The position number will remain in this display until you turn boldface off. The Pos number always reflects the font at the cursor location of a document. Although the codes aren't revealed right now, trust me that WordPerfect has inserted both a begin and end bold code.

Tip: You can change the colors that WordPerfect uses to display different fonts on the screen (Appendix A).

✔Type the title, then stop! Always turn off a special printing effect as soon as you're finished with it:

Press   **F6 Bold**

The Pos number returns to its normal appearance, and WordPerfect has positioned the cursor past the end bold code. In a moment you'll take a look at the codes.

Press   **RETURN** three times

for spacing.

✔Continue typing the memo. For instance, type To: and press **TAB** twice. Then type Jaime Pescado, and so on. When you get to the word *sick*, stop!

Underlines As You Type

To begin underlining this word:

Press   **F8 Underline**

Notice that the Pos *number* on the status line has changed to whatever is your monitor's way of displaying underlining. The position number will remain in this display until you turn underlining off. See also How Word-Perfect Underlines Spaces and Tabs in Chapter 6.

Type   sick and tired

Press   **F8 Underline**

to turn underlining off.

✔Continue typing the memo, making sure to turn underlining on for the phrase *ho-hum syndrome*. Notice that you turn underlining off *before* you type the period in this example. Remember the underlines around the word *really* in the last paragraph. When you're finished typing the memo, save it as MEMO.1 and leave it on the screen.

The Bold and Underline Codes

Now it's time to take a look at how WordPerfect sets up the boldface and underline codes:

Press   **HOME,HOME,UP ARROW**

Press   **ALT-F3 Reveal Codes** or **F11 Reveal Codes**

The begin bold code is [BOLD], and the end code is [bold]. The begin underline code is [UND], and the end code is [und]. As with the center codes, the begin code contains uppercase letters, and the end code is in lowercase.

Adding Special Effects to Existing Text

Remember that the only way you can add boldface or underlining to existing text is with the block approach. Mr. Sturgeon is waxing strong, so he decides to underline the words *great potential* in the first paragraph.

✔Position the cursor under the *g* of *great* in the first paragraph.

Press   **ALT-F4 Block** or **F12 Block**

Type   l

(that's a lowercase *L*) to extend the block.

Press   **F8 Underline**

to underline the block.

Although you won't do this, how would you extend the underlining in a phrase? For instance, Mr. Sturgeon tells you to underline the phrase *to illustrate my great potential*, which already contains underlining. You could first delete the codes and start over, as the next section discusses, but a faster method is just to block the entire phrase and press F8 Underline. When you do, WordPerfect adjusts the codes. Neat!

Removing Special Effects

Mr. Sturgeon feels that perhaps he's being just a *little* too forceful, so he wants you to delete the underlining codes surrounding *sick and tired*. To remove a special effect, you simply have to delete *one* of the codes. It could be the begin code or the end code—whichever is closer! WordPerfect will then delete the matching code in the set for you. It can do this trick because it distinguishes between begin and end codes. If you delete a begin code, WordPerfect finds the next end code. If you delete an end code, WordPerfect finds the previous begin code.

✔Position the cursor under the *s* of *sick and tired*.

Stop! Do you *really* know where the begin underlining code is? No! It's best to be sure:

Press   **ALT-F3 Reveal Codes** or **F11 Reveal Codes**

The cursor is probably under the begin underline code. If it isn't, position it there now. With the codes still on:

Press   **DEL**

Question: If the cursor were positioned directly after the code, what key would you use? *Answer:* Right! The BACKSPACE key. You can also search and replace font codes (Chapter 8).

Press   **ALT-F3 Reveal Codes** or **F11 Reveal Codes**

to turn the codes off.

✔Save the document again, but leave it on the screen.

Again, you won't stop to do this now, but guess what happens when you attempt to delete a boldface or underline code when the codes aren't revealed. Right! Because it's so easy to position the cursor on a hidden code, when you press DEL to delete a character or BACKSPACE to rub out the previous character, WordPerfect asks you to confirm what you're doing:

```
Delete [BOLD] (Y/N)? No
```

or

```
Delete [UND] (Y/N)? No
```

You'd type y to delete, of course.

The CTRL-F8 Font Key

So there are quick keys for boldface print and underlining, F6 Bold and F8 Underline, respectively. To get other special effects, you work with the font key, CTRL-F8 Font. (This was the Print Format command in previous versions.) Before you experiment with the special effects on this key, take a look at how WordPerfect organizes font changes:

Press   **CTRL-F8 Font**

WordPerfect presents the font menu:

```
1 Size; 2 Appearance; 3 Normal; 4 Base Font; 5 Print Color: 0
```

WordPerfect organizes font changes according to the following topics:

■ *Size* deals with fonts that are smaller or larger than the base font or are on a different position on the line. Guess what that means? Right! Subscripts and superscripts. Here's what the size menu looks like:

1 Suprscpt; 2 Subscpt; 3 Fine; 4 Small; 5 Large; 6 Vry Large; 7 Ext Large: 0

You'll investigate superscripts and subscripts in this chapter and sizes in future chapters.

■ *Appearance* handles most of the other printing effects that you'll use, such as italics and double underlines. The appearance menu looks like this:

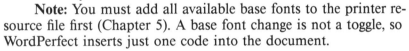
1 Bold 2 Undrln 3 Dbl Und 4 Italc 5 Outln 6 Shadw 7 Sm Cap 8 Redln 9 Stkout: 0

Wait a minute! Boldface and underline are here, too! You'll understand why when you look at all options on this menu except **8** [Redln] and **9** [Stkout], because the redline and strikeout features have their own discussion (Chapter 24).

■ *Normal* means returning to the normal, or base, font when you're finished using any other special effect. There's another way to accomplish the same thing.

■ *Base Font* lets you select another available font in your printer as the base font. When you select this option, WordPerfect shows the fonts from which you can choose.
    Note: You must add all available base fonts to the printer resource file first (Chapter 5). A base font change is not a toggle, so WordPerfect inserts just one code into the document.

■ *Print Color* is for selecting different color printing if your printer can do this (Chapter 15).

How to Use the CTRL-F8 Font Key

Whenever you select a different font with the CTRL-F8 Font key, WordPerfect inserts both begin and end codes. When you try your hand at italics, you'll see the codes in action. That means, in essence, the following:

■ When you select one or more fonts *before* you type the text, you push the end codes along as you type. When you're ready to turn the fonts off and return to the base font, you can press **CTRL-F8 Font** and type **3** or n [Normal] *or* just press **RIGHT ARROW** to move the cursor past the end codes. That way, you avoid having to go through the CTRL-F8 Font menu again.

Note: The **3** [N̲ormal] choice doesn't add a new code. It just positions the cursor past the end font change codes for the fonts you're using.

- When you change a block to a different font, WordPerfect encloses the block with begin and end codes, just as it did when you added underlining to a block in a previous example.

- The only exceptions to this rule are for changing the base font and print colors. Again, I'll defer discussion of colors for the moment.

Italics As You Type

I'll step you through two more examples, then discuss the other special effects on the appearance menu. Suppose you want to insert italicized text into your memo.

Note: If your printer doesn't do italics, WordPerfect will probably print underlines instead. That's yet another aspect of intelligent printing.

✔Position the cursor at the end of the document and make sure there is a blank line between the last paragraph and the new one you'll type now. Reveal the codes to see what happens when you turn on italics:

Press   **ALT-F3 Reveal Codes** or **F11 Reveal Codes**

Press   **CTRL-F8 Font**

Type   **2** or **a** [A̲ppearance]

Type   **4** or **i** [I̲talc]

Notice that WordPerfect has inserted [ITALC] and [italc] codes and that the cursor is under the end code. You'll push the end code along as you type the new paragraph:

`It's very important that I speak about this matter to you as soon as possible.`

The italicized text appears in a different color or shading, or in italics on some monitors! Notice the Pos number, too. By the way, if typeover mode were on you'd *still* push the end code along. WordPerfect won't ever let you type over a code. Now, return to the base font and continue:

Press   **RIGHT ARROW**

to move past the end italics code.

Press   **SPACEBAR** twice

for spacing.

    Type the rest of the text: `I'll call your office later.`

Press   **ALT-F3 Reveal Codes** or **F11 Reveal Codes**

to turn the codes off.

    ✔Save the document again and leave it on the screen.

Italics Around Existing Text

Suppose pushy Mr. Sturgeon has pulled out all the stops. He now wants you to insert italic codes around his two marketing ideas. Here's an example of how to block text and add a special effect from the CTRL-F8 Font key.

    ✔Position the cursor under the *D* of *Dine* in the third to last paragraph.

Press   **ALT-F4 Block** or **F12 Block**

Type   .

(that's a period) to extend the block.

    Wait! Do you want to italicize the period? Some people do; some don't. It's up to you.

Press   **CTRL-F8 Font**

This time you see the font attribute menu, a condensed version of the font menu:

`Attribute: 1 Size; 2 Appearance: 0`

Recall from Chapter 3 that WordPerfect often presents a different menu when block is on.

Type   **2** or **a** [Appearance]

Type   **4** or **i** [Italc]

    There you are!

    ✔Repeat the steps for inserting italic font codes around the other marketing idea that begins with *Is* and ends with a question mark. Then save the document again and clear the screen.

The Rest of the Font Appearance Choices

When you need them, there are several other special printing effects on the appearance menu.

Note: Keep in mind that some printers can't print all these effects. Here's a brief summary of how they look and their codes:

- Choice **3** [Dbl Und] prints double lines under text. See also How WordPerfect Underlines Spaces and Tabs in Chapter 6. The codes are [DBL UND] and [dbl und].

- Choice **5** [Outln] reverses the printing so that the letters appear white on a black background, if your printer can do this! The codes are [OUTLN] and [outln].

- Choice **6** [Shadw] stands for *shadow print*, where the print head moves over to print a dark shadow behind each character. Shadow differs from boldface in that boldface prints a dark character, whereas shadow prints a distinct shadow behind the character. The codes are [SHADW] and [shadw].

- The final choice, **7** [Sm Cap], prints lowercase small capitals instead of lowercase. Initial caps and versions of the word *I* (*I'm*, *I'd*, and so on) still print in regular caps. The codes are [SM CAP] and [sm cap].

Superscripts and Subscripts

The next topic involves two popular choices on the size menu: superscripts and subscripts. I'll discuss the other sizes in later chapters.

Note: Version 4.2 had a separate key, SHIFT-F1 Super/Subscript, for these print effects. The SHIFT-F1 key means something totally different in WordPerfect 5.0 (Appendix A).

When you do superscripts and subscripts on a typewriter, you have to stop and shift the platen up or down a notch or two manually before you can type. After you type the superscript or subscript, you shift the platen *back* to the regular line. This is exactly what WordPerfect tells the printer to do when you insert codes for superscripts and subscripts.

Note: Some printers don't support superscripts and subscripts. Generally, WordPerfect prints superscripts and subscripts one-third of a line above or below the regular text line. Your printer may only be able to print in half line or full line increments, so it might be a good idea to use one-and-a-half or double spacing when you're doing text with superscripts and subscripts (Chapter 6). Depending on the base font, WordPerfect may even use a smaller font for superscripts and subscripts! That's why they're on the size menu.

By the way, it makes no sense to use superscripts for *footnote references*, because WordPerfect has an impressive automatic footnoting feature that takes care of numbering and printing footnote references for you (Chapter 22).

You don't have to do this example, but just think about the steps you'd perform:

```
With all due respects to Comrade Khrushev, he obviously doesn't
understand the meaning of e = mc² or even H₂0.
```

That's right! When you get to the first *2*, press **CTRL-F8 Font**, type **1** or **s** [Size], then type **1** or **p** [Suprscpt]. Type the **2**, then press **RIGHT ARROW** to move past the end code and continue the sentence.

Type **2** or **b** [Subscrpt] for the subscripted second *2*, then press **RIGHT ARROW** once to finish the sentence. The codes are what you'd expect: [SUPRSCPT] and [suprscpt] for superscript, and [SUBSCPT] and [subscpt] for subscript.

The Normal and Base Font Choices

It's definitely easier to press RIGHT ARROW to move past the end code when you're finished with a special effect. If you decide to use the **3** [Normal] choice to return to the base font, you should know that there's no special code for this. WordPerfect just positions the cursor past whatever end codes are already there.

The **4** [Base Font] choice is different. It lets you *switch* to an entirely different base font altogether. When you switch base fonts, WordPerfect uses the new font as the base font. Any special effect codes that appear in the document past this location will work with the new base font. Because you may want to use the new base font throughout the rest of the document, this change inserts only one code. WordPerfect Corporation refers to this type of code as an *open* code. You can't insert a base font change when block is on.

Depending on your printer, you may see only one base font. Figure 4-2, for example, shows what you might see if you were using the Hewlett-Packard LaserJet II printer. At the bottom of the screen is this menu:

```
1 Select; N Name Search: 1
```

You can select a different base font in two ways:

1. Use the **ARROW** keys to move the highlight to the font. Alternately, type **n** [Name Search], then type the first letter of the font name to position the highlight on the first font that starts with that letter. Then press **RETURN**. WordPerfect takes you back to the document.

2. Use the **ARROW** keys or name search to move the highlight to the font and type **1** or **s** [Select]. WordPerfect takes you back to the document.

```
Base Font

* Courier 10 pitch (PC-8)
  Courier 10 pitch (Roman-8)
  Courier Bold 10 pitch (PC-8)
  Courier Bold 10 pitch (Roman-8)
  Line Printer 08.5pt 16.66 pitch (PC-8)
  Line Printer 08.5pt 16.66 pitch (Roman-8)
  Tms Rmn 12pt (AC)
  Tms Rmn 14pt Bold (AC)
  Tms Rmn 18pt Bold (AC)
```

```
1 Select; N Name search: 1
```

Figure 4-2   Base Fonts on a Laser Printer

WordPerfect inserts a [Font] code with the name of the new base font listed after the colon. For example, [Font:Courier 12pt 10 pitch (PC-8)]. In other chapters you'll learn how to work with different base fonts. If you haven't set up a printer yet, you'll see this message:

ERROR: Printer not selected

Follow the steps under Adding a Printer Resource File in Chapter 5 to select your printer first.

A Few More Important Points

Dear Reader, you're almost through with this chapter. There are just a couple other points (no pun intended!) about special effects, and then you'll learn about printing.

Changing the Screen Display of Fonts

You can change how WordPerfect displays special fonts on the screen. That's an advanced topic that appears with all the various setup options in Appendix

A. If special effects don't appear in a different color or highlighting on your screen, you may want to take a look at the discussion of the screen attributes in Appendix A. (In previous versions this was on the CTRL-F3 Screen key.)

Why Word Processors Go Gray

Sometimes what seems the simplest thing in the world turns out to be a hassle. Take this example. You want to underline the first word in the following sentence:

```
"What did you say to your mother?"
```

So you press F8 Underline and type "**What**, followed by the end code. The result?

```
"What did you say to your mother?"
```

You didn't place the underline code at the right spot! You should have *first* typed the beginning quotation marks, *then* pressed the F8 Underline key. These are the little things that try word processors' souls. But if you know how to handle them, they're a piece of cake. Still, it's a relief that they don't crop up too often.

Combining Special Effects

You can combine all special effect fonts, but you may have to add them one at a time to the same block.

 Tip: After you've blocked the text and inserted a special effect once, the cursor should be at the end of the block. Press **ALT-F4 Block**, then press **CTRL-HOME,ALT-F4 Block** to extend the block back to its original beginning. Then choose the next font. If you've turned on several fonts, then the fastest way to turn them all off in one fell swoop is to use the **3 [Normal]** choice from the font menu.

How Font Changes Affect Line Height

Line height refers to the amount of space from the base, or bottom, of one line to the base of the next. Normally when you choose an appearance font that works with the base font, line height doesn't change. However, it you choose a different *size* font, then WordPerfect will adjust the line height to accommodate the new size. You can also control the line height setting yourself (Chapter 17).

Beware the WordPerfect Blob!

When you work with a lot of fonts or other special printing features like graphics elements (Chapter 34), the size of your document may grow substantially. To overcome this "blob" effect and put your document on a diet, save the document, clear the screen, retrieve the document, and save it again. See Freeing Up Disk Space in Chapter 9 for more information.

The Printer Test Documents

WordPerfect Corporation supplies a variety of printer test documents with WordPerfect. They all end in the extension .TST. You can print these documents to see how your printer handles various fonts.

Dear Reader, you're already starting to get into the real nitty-gritty of word processing with WordPerfect. Now would be an excellent time to review what you've learned before you continue.

5

Printing Essentials

In this chapter you'll learn the following new commands:

Function Key Commands

SHIFT-F3 Switch   Switch the foreground and
background colors in the print
view

SHIFT-F7 Print   Control most printing operations

Typewriter Keyboard (DOS) Command

SHIFT-PRT SC   Print a screen dump

You've created a couple of documents and learned how to work with special printing fonts. So far, you haven't been concerned with printing your documents, because you wanted to get your thoughts down and even fine-tune them a bit first. This chapter finally gets you involved with the hard copy stage of word processing. You'll learn the basics of printing and printers. If you haven't set up WordPerfect to work with your printer, this is the place to look! You can study this chapter independently of all others, by the way.

DO WARM-UP

Ways to Print a Document

You can print a document in two different ways: (1) from the screen or (2) from the disk. If you print from the screen, you can choose to print the current page, the entire document, or a marked block. If you print from the disk, you can print specific pages or page ranges as well as the entire document. (A third way to print is to have WordPerfect pretend to be a typewriter, in which case you just print as you type from the keyboard. See WordPerfect, the Typewriter in Chapter 34.)

When you print a document from the screen, you're printing from *memory*, because that's where a copy of the document is located. Your printout reflects all editing changes you've made to the document during the current session, even if you haven't saved the edited document yet. The printout also depends on the printer you're currently using, because WordPerfect formats each document according to the printer specifications. There's that intelligent printing again!

You should eventually get accustomed to editing from the screen, because it's faster. But you might find at first that you're more comfortable when you can see a hard copy version of your document in front of you. That's natural! In fact, it took me a long time to get used to editing from the screen only. Don't worry if the document's formatting isn't totally correct yet. You can always polish that later.

When you print from the disk, you're using the *last* previously saved file. If you're working on the document and save it at least once, the printout includes those saved changes when you print from the disk. However, there are some very important concepts to learn before you can print . . .

The Document and Your Printers

Every time you create a new document, WordPerfect sets up the document's format according to the printer that's currently selected. WordPerfect gets its printer information from a *printer definition* or *printer resource* file that ends in the extension .PRS. You can, of course, change any specific formats that you want to within the document, as many other chapters will discuss. You know already how to change the appearance of a document with the addition of font codes.

When you save the document, WordPerfect saves ("attaches") the name of the printer resource file with the document in a special *document prefix* that you don't see. However, the original printer whose name is in the document prefix may not be the currently selected printer.

Here's what all this means to you:

1. If you use just one printer, you're more or less on easy street and can skip to the next section.

2. If you have more than one printer, you can switch printers as often as you wish. See Selecting a Different Printer later in the chapter. You can select only one printer at any one time.

3. No matter what printer is currently selected (the "default printer"), when you retrieve a document, WordPerfect selects the original printer whose name is in the document prefix. When you save the document, WordPerfect selects the default printer again. If WordPerfect can't find the printer resource file for the original printer, WordPerfect uses the default printer and tells you that it is reformatting the document for that printer.

    Note: If the initial fonts of the two printers are different, Word-Perfect may *not* reformat the document on the screen. That's because WordPerfect saves the original printer's initial font for the document in the document prefix. However, WordPerfect will still pick a font on the new printer that matches or approximates the original font. To change the original font instruction in a document, see the discussion of the format: document menu in Appendix A.

4. To save a *new* printer resource file with a document, retrieve the document, select the new printer, then save the document again.

Here are the points to know about how WordPerfect formats before it prints a document:

1. Complete formatting normally occurs only to the printed version of the document. Some formats, such as top and bottom margins, don't appear on the screen.

2. The formatting depends on the printer resources, including the initial font you've assigned to the printer, together with the default formats.

3. WordPerfect still honors any format codes that you've inserted in the document. That is, if you added underlining or italics codes, Word-Perfect uses those codes, too. WordPerfect never deletes any codes that you insert.

Before you get to some real printing, learn the reason for this lengthy introduction.

Fast Save and How It Affects Printing

The *fast save* feature is supposed to reduce the time WordPerfect needs to save a document. If you turn fast save on—the default is off—from the Setup menu (Appendix A), WordPerfect does *not* save general formatting with the document. WordPerfect just saves the name of the printer resource file. The notion of fast save brings up several related issues. At the moment the two most important issues are what happens when (1) WordPerfect can't find the printer resource file or (2) you attempt to print a document from the disk.
    I just mentioned that if WordPerfect can't find the printer resource file, it tells you:

```
Document formatted to default printer
```

That is, WordPerfect uses the currently selected printer. Thankfully, WordPerfect then takes it upon itself to format the document according to the new printer. At least you can continue working!

The second issue is more crucial to the topic at hand. Bad English aside, WordPerfect won't let you print a document that's been "fast saved" and will tell you this:

```
ERROR: Document was Fast Saved -- Must be retrieved to print
```

So, you normally can't print a "fast saved" document from its disk file unless you do one of three things:

1. Retrieve the document and print it from the screen. This is by far the fastest way to print in WordPerfect.

2. Press **HOME,HOME,DOWN ARROW** to move the cursor to the end of the document *just before* you save the document. When you move the cursor to the end of the document, this is a signal to WordPerfect to format the entire document. You can then save the document and print it from the disk. Make sure that you select the correct printer before you save the document!

3. Turn the fast save feature off. That way, WordPerfect will format the document whenever you save it (Appendix A). Remember that fast save is off by default.

For the time being, assume that you'll print from the screen—the easier approach—most of the time.

Printing from the Screen

You control virtually all printing from one command and one menu. Before you investigate general printing, you should retrieve a document.

✔Retrieve the NEWS document now. Turn on your printer and make sure it has paper (I won't mention this obvious step again.) Then:

Press   **SHIFT-F7 Print**

WordPerfect presents the print menu, shown in Figure 5-1. Dear Reader, I'll cover most of the choices in due time and in order of importance. Some printing topics are advanced, so you won't learn about them in this chapter. WordPerfect has *so many* features!

Note: To leave this menu without doing anything, press **F1 Cancel**, **RETURN**, the **SPACEBAR**, or any key on the numeric keypad, or type **0**.

When you print from the screen, you can print the full document, just one page, or a marked block.

```
Print

        1 - Full Document
        2 - Page
        3 - Document on Disk
        4 - Control Printer
        5 - Type Through
        6 - View Document
        7 - Initialize Printer

Options

        S - Select Printer          Standard Printer
        B - Binding                 0"
        N - Number of Copies        1
        G - Graphics Quality        Medium
        T - Text Quality            High




Selection: 0
```

Figure 5-1   The Print Menu

Note: WordPerfect prints the page where the cursor is currently located. If you want to print another page, go to that page before you start printing. If you want to print the full document, it doesn't matter where the cursor is in the document.

Type   **2** or **p** [Page]

to print the current page or

Type   **1** or **f** [Full Document]

to print the entire document.

After a brief pause, WordPerfect prints the first page or entire document, provided your printer has continuous form paper. If you have to insert individual sheets of paper, WordPerfect beeps at you. That means it's waiting for you to tell it when "all systems are go." See Telling the Printer to Go later in the chapter.

Tip: Now that you know how to print, why not try printing the PRINTER.TST document to see the special effects that your printer can handle?

Printing a Block

To print a portion of a document that doesn't break down evenly into specific pages, block out the text *first* and then press **SHIFT-F7 Print**. You don't have to do the steps now. WordPerfect then prompts:

```
Print block? (Y/N) No
```

Make sure you prepare your printer and paper before you type y to continue. WordPerfect prints the block using the document's format settings.

Controlling the Print Job

Every time you tell WordPerfect to print a document, it sets up a print job in the *print queue* or *job list* in the order that you issue the printing command. The print queue is a lineup of documents waiting to print, like a check-out line in the supermarket but not nearly as frustrating. You can queue up several print jobs at once, and WordPerfect prints each job in its turn. You handle all aspects of the print queue, including any problems that occur during printing, from the print: control printer menu.

Tip: If the printer isn't printing or something seems to be wrong or WordPerfect beeps at you, first check the print: control printer menu for a message that WordPerfect might be giving you.

I'll list the steps that you perform to see the print: control printer menu once, right now:

Press   **SHIFT-F7 Print**

Type   **4** or **c** [Control Printer]

Figure 5-2 shows what the print: control printer menu looks like when there are no print jobs in the queue.

Note: To leave this menu without changing anything, press **F1 Cancel**, **RETURN**, the **SPACEBAR**, or any key on the numeric keypad, or type **0**.

Telling the Printer to Go

If WordPerfect is waiting for you to insert a sheet of paper before it can begin printing, take a look at the Current Job information at the top of the print: control printer menu. Does it say something like this?

```
Job Status: Waiting for a "Go"
Message:    Insert 8.5"x11" Standard Form in Manual Feed--Press "G" to continue
```

```
Print: Control Printer

Current Job

Job Number: None                        Page Number:  None
Status:     No print jobs               Current Copy: None
Message:    None
Paper:      None
Location:   None
Action:     None



Job List


Job   Document            Destination       Print Options




Additional Jobs Not Shown: 0




1 Cancel Job(s); 2 Rush Job; 3 Display Jobs;  4 Go (start printer); 5 Stop: 0
```

Figure 5-2   The Print: Control Printer Menu

The form name may be different. If you get this message, then you have to tell WordPerfect when to start printing the first page. Notice that WordPerfect tells you the *type of form* you're using. Here, it's a standard page that's 8½ by 11 inches. Your form type may differ. Soon you'll learn how to change forms if you use different paper sizes.

Type   **4** or **g** [G̲o]

to print the first page.

Press   **RETURN**

to exit the print: control printer menu.

If you're printing a long document on paper that you have to insert by page, WordPerfect will beep at the end of each page and present a message that's similar to this one:

```
Job Status: Waiting for a "Go"
Message:    Printing stopped--Press "G" to continue
```

When you're ready, type **4** or **g** [G̲o] to continue.

Caution: Make sure that the printer has finished printing the *previous* page and that you've inserted another piece of paper before you issue a go. Often WordPerfect will beep to signal a new page several seconds before the printer has completed printing.

Background and Foreground

If you were printing a multiple-page document, WordPerfect would beep at you at the end of every page to remind you to insert the next sheet of paper and issue a go. (A short aside: It seems like a lot of steps just to get the printer to print, but you can make your life easier by setting up the go in a *macro*. A macro is a shortcut. See Chapter 7.)

WordPerfect thus prints in the background to let you continue editing. That is, after you start printing another page, you can leave the print: control printer and print menus and return to the document. Printing is the background task, because you're editing in the foreground. If you stay in the print: control printer menu, printing is the foreground task. Depending on your printer, printing in the foreground may be slightly faster than printing in the background.

Displaying the Entire Print Queue

At the bottom of the screen on the print: control printer menu is a listing of the current print jobs. WordPerfect can show only three print jobs on the print: control printer menu, but the message Additional jobs not shown always tells you how many more there are. To see all print jobs at once, type **3** or **d** [Display Jobs]. WordPerfect clears the screen and displays the entire job list, an example of which is in Figure 5-3. When you're finished looking at the list, press any key to return to the print: control printer menu.

Rushing a Print Job

You can rearrange the print jobs in the queue with the **2** [Rush Job] option. This command reorders the jobs in the queue so the one you select becomes first in line, thus *prioritizing* the job. When you type **2** or **r**, WordPerfect prompts:

Rush which job?

WordPerfect supplies the *last* job number, but you can type whatever number you want to rush and press RETURN. Notice that WordPerfect reorders the job list at the bottom of the screen with the rushed job at the top of

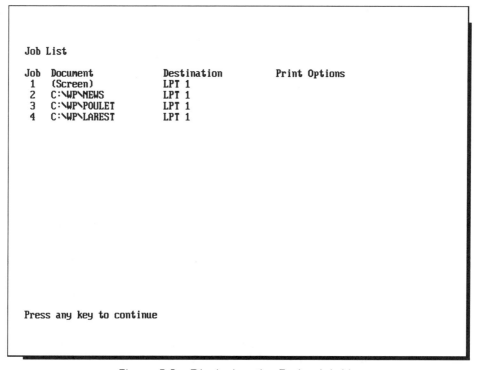

```
Job List

Job  Document           Destination       Print Options
 1   (Screen)           LPT 1
 2   C:\WP\NEWS         LPT 1
 3   C:\WP\POULET       LPT 1
 4   C:\WP\LAREST       LPT 1













Press any key to continue
```

Figure 5-3 Displaying the Entire Job List

the list. The word RUSH appears next to a rushed job, too. Of course, you can't rush a print job if it's the only one in the queue. WordPerfect would admonish:

```
Job is already printing
```

If you rush a print job while another is still printing, WordPerfect stops printing the first job temporarily. It then prints the rush job. When that is finished, WordPerfect continues printing the previous job at the top of the interrupted page. Neat!

Stopping and Canceling

If for some reason you have to stop the printing temporarily, type **5** or **s** [Stop] after you call up the print: control printer menu. WordPerfect waits for you to issue a go to resume printing where you left off.

To *cancel* a print job, type **1** or **c** [Cancel Job(s)] from the print: control printer menu. WordPerfect prompts:

```
Cancel which job? (*=All Jobs)
```

WordPerfect assumes that you want to cancel the current job, so it supplies that number. You can type another job number and press RETURN. In either case, WordPerfect then cancels that job only. If you type a job number that doesn't exit, WordPerfect presents this message:

```
Job is not in queue
```

You can cancel all jobs in the queue by typing an asterisk (*). In that case, WordPerfect asks you to confirm your decision:

```
Cancel all print jobs? (Y/N) No
```

Type **y** or **n** as you wish.

Note: Printers work decidedly more slowly than computers. The computer sends the text to be printed very quickly. Some printers hold this text in a buffer until they can catch up. When you stop or cancel a print job, it may take a while for the printer to empty the buffer. A few additional lines may print (on a laser printer, it may be an entire page or several pages). This is completely normal.

If you attempt to exit WordPerfect and there are still some jobs in the print queue, WordPerfect again asks if you want to cancel the print jobs. This is WordPerfect's reminder that you haven't finished all the printing left in the queue. You can't exit WordPerfect until you either finish printing or cancel the remaining print jobs.

Printing Problems?

When it begins printing, WordPerfect first checks to see if the printer is on and ready to work. If not, you'll hear a beep. Go into the print: control printer menu and check the Current Job status. Does it say something like this?

```
Job Status:  Trying to print
Message:     Printer not accepting characters
```

Turn on your printer and type **4** or **g** [Go]. If that doesn't work, check the connection and then the settings.

Note: You may see other printing-related messages. If you're still having problems, consult the section on error messages in the WordPerfect documentation.

However, if WordPerfect doesn't present an error message but your printer doesn't print, or if your *printer* displays an error message (laser printers) or a warning light, write down the error message or determine from the printer's manual what's causing the problem. Then call WordPerfect Corporation's Customer Support and explain the problem.

If the margins of the printed page are off center, you have two choices: Either change the margin settings (but you don't know how to do that yet!) or change the paper position in the printer. It's best to establish a paper position in the printer that works well for you and then *stick with it*. For the time being, use whatever paper position makes the text print with a 1-inch left margin. If the top margin isn't 1 inch, then check the *top-of-form* setting on your printer and adjust it accordingly.

The last problem is more a matter of aesthetics. When WordPerfect justifies each line, it adds enough spaces or even microspaces between words on the line to print each line the same length. On printers that use *fixed-width* characters, there may be a visual effect known as "rivers" of white space that appear to flow down the page. One way to correct this problem is to tighten up the lines by hyphenating some words (Chapter 20). An even better way is to use a *proportionally spaced* font (Chapter 35). You can also change the way WordPerfect adds spaces to justified text. See the discussion of the word spacing justification limits in Chapter 34.

Printing from the Disk

The major advantage to printing from disk is that you can specify which pages of a document you want to print. The major disadvantage is, as I've mentioned, that fast save business. Remember that fast save must be off (the default) if you want to print the document from disk later. See Appendix A to learn how to turn the fast save feature on and off.

Suppose, for the sake of example, that you're working on one document and you want to print another document at the same time. Suppose further that you've already saved the format with the second document or that the fast save feature is off. After you press **SHIFT-F7 Print**, do this:

Type   **3** or **d** [Document on Disk]

WordPerfect prompts:

`Document name:`

Type the document's file name and press **RETURN**. WordPerfect then asks you to specify which pages to print and assumes you want to print all pages:

`Page(s): (ALL)`

Press   **RETURN**

to print all pages.

To print certain pages only, see the next section.

Here's another potential problem. You attempt to print a document that you created or edited with one printer and you're now using another printer. You'll see this message:

`Document not formatted for current printer. Continue (Y/N)? No`

Type **y** or **n**. If you don't want to use the current printer, select the printer that works with the document.

Note: Whenever you print from disk, remember that you use the *most recently saved* version of the file. If you're working on the document, save it first before you print it.

Printing Specific Pages

When you print a document on the disk, you can print selected pages or page *ranges* that need not be continuous. Type individual page numbers separated by commas (for example, **1,4,7**) and ranges by hyphens (**10-25**). Press **RE-TURN** to start printing.

Caution: Don't use *spaces* between ranges. For instance, typing the range **10 -25** can get you into a lot of trouble. You'll see why in Chapter 17. For the time being, just use the examples in Table 5-1 as guides when you want to print selected pages.

Tip: WordPerfect doesn't handle too many ranges at a time, so you may have to queue up several print jobs.

Viewing the Printout Before You Print

As you know, WordPerfect doesn't show justified right margins or some fonts on the screen. There are other special features, such as footnotes, headers, and footers, that don't readily appear until you print a document. To avoid wasting paper, especially with long documents, you may want to *view* or *preview* the printing before you actually do it, just to make sure everything's satisfactory. You'll see all correct margins, line spacing, and page breaks.

The print view has been greatly expanded in WordPerfect 5.0 and includes the following features:

- You can view all pages in the document individually or two facing pages together.

- You can scroll through the print view with some of the cursor movement commands.

- You can view an entire page "greeked" (I'll explain what that means in a moment) or *zoom in* to 100% or 200% of the actual printed page size.

Table 5-1   Printing Selected Pages

Example	What It Means
3	Print page 3 only
25-27	Print pages 25 through 27
2,4,7-10	Print pages 2, 4, and 7 through 10
6-	Print starting at page 6 to the end of the document
-12	Print starting at the beginning of the document up to and including page 12
2,5,8-	Print pages 2, 5, and the rest of the document starting at page 8
-9,20	Print starting at the beginning of the document up to and including page 9, and then print page 20

■ WordPerfect shows a typeface that's similar to the one in your printer. For example, on daisy wheel printers you'll see something that resembles the standard Courier typeface. Laser printer owners will see a different typeface if they're using a proportionally spaced font.

Note: What you *can't* do, however, is switch back and forth between the actual document and the print view. There is no longer a "Doc 3" as in WordPerfect 4.2.

The NEWS document should still be on the screen. Unfortunately, this document contains only two pages, so you won't get the full effect of viewing two facing pages. Just pretend that the document is longer or clear the screen and retrieve a long document if you have one now.

You can start the print view from any page in the document, and WordPerfect will show you that page first. To start the print view:

Press   **SHIFT-F7 Print**

Type   **6 or v** [**V**iew Document]

WordPerfect first displays the outline of a piece of paper and the current page. You can see the actual page makeup, but you can't read the individual letters. That's what *greeked* means. The term greeked is also from the world of desktop publishing. At the bottom of the screen is this menu:

```
1 100%   2 200%   3 Full Page   4 Facing Pages: 3
```

The print view is using the **3** [Full Page] option at the moment. There are no mnemonics in this menu. The first two choices are the zoom options. WordPerfect shows the document and page number on the right side of the status line.

✔Take a look at choices 1 and 2 to familiarize yourself with the zoom options. As you view a document, especially a long document, you can use the cursor movement commands listed in Table 5-2 to move across pages or on the current page. When you're finished looking at the zoom options, do this:

Type   **4** [Facing Pages]

Depending on the current document page, you'll see two facing pages. However, because page 1 doesn't face with another page, you won't see facing pages if the cursor is in page 1. Because the NEWS document only contains two pages, you won't see facing page 3 either! That's why I suggested that you use a longer document. In any case, the facing pages choice can only show the pages in greeked form.

To leave the print view, press **F1 Cancel**, **RETURN**, or the **SPACEBAR**. WordPerfect returns to the print menu but retains the last size choice (100%,

Table 5-2 Cursor Movement in the Print View

Command	Action	
DOWN ARROW	Scrolls the view down a line	
UP ARROW	Scrolls the view up a line	Works with choices 1 and 2 only
HOME,DOWN ARROW or GRAY +	Scrolls to the bottom of the current page	
HOME,UP ARROW or GRAY −	Scrolls to the top of the current page	
PG DN	Displays the next page	
PG UP	Displays the previous page	
HOME,HOME, DOWN ARROW	Displays the last page	
HOME,HOME,UP ARROW	Displays the first page	
CTRL-HOME	Goes to a page number you specify	

Full Page, and so on) that you used. The next time you view the printout WordPerfect starts with that size.

Note: How many different print effects, such as font changes or italics, you can see in the print view depends on the kind of graphics card you have. On some screens WordPerfect can display different fonts as they'll appear in the actual printout. On other monitors you'll see a different shading, highlighting, or color for special effects. You can press SHIFT-F3 Switch to switch the foreground and background colors of the print view. Use a setup option to select a black on white display on a color monitor (Appendix A).

The Print Options

The five options in the lower part of the print menu control a variety of printing features. I'll discuss the Binding, Number of Copies, and Text Quality options here; I'll cover Graphics Quality in Chapter 34. Because the Select Printer option is so important, it's in a separate section later in the chapter.

Tip: Always set the print options *before* you start a print job. WordPerfect "remembers" each setting until you exit the program or change the setting. You can assign default print options from Setup menu (Appendix A).

Printing on Paper with Holes

Use the Binding setting when you have to print on both sides of paper that is punched with binder holes. Adjusting the binding width prevents the printer from printing over the holes. The binding width temporarily moves the text over on the page: Text moves right on odd numbered pages and left on even numbered pages. Of course, if you want to print two sides directly on your sheet fed paper, you have to insert the page twice to get a printout on both sides.

Note: Any binding setting takes precedence over the document's left margin when you print the document.

To change the Binding option, type **b** [Binding], type a new number, and press **RETURN**. WordPerfect normally measures binding in inches, so a binding setting of 1 equals 1 inch. You can also set increments in half or quarter inches, for instance, .5 or 1.25.

Tip: If you plan to print on single sided paper with binder holes, just change the left margin of your text, if necessary (Chapter 6). Make sure you change binding back to 0 when you no longer need this option.

Printing Multiple Copies

Use option **N** [Number of Copies] to print multiple copies of the next job and all other jobs that you queue up. For example, if you want to print two copies of each page, do this:

Type   n [Number of Copies]

Type   **2**

Press   **RETURN**

Note: If you want to print only one copy of the *next* job, make sure you change the number of copies back to 1 before you queue up the job.

Text Quality

Some printers, most notably the dot matrix variety, can print in various *modes:* draft, medium, or high. Draft mode is the fastest, but the printout is not of the same quality as medium or high mode. Often, however, you'll want just a fast printout and you won't be concerned about print quality.

Note: WordPerfect sets up the Text Quality selection according to your printer. Some printers don't use some of the modes listed. When in doubt, select high quality. You can set a different default text quality, too.

To change the text quality, type **t** [Text Quality], and you'll see this menu:

```
Text Quality: 1 Do Not Print; 2 Draft; 3 Medium; 4 High: 4
```

Choose the mode you want. Choice **1** [Do Not Print] is for printers that can't print text and graphics in one pass (Chapter 34). You can print the text on a page first, then turn text printing off and reinsert the page to print the graphics. To be able to print text again after you use this option, you must choose one of the other options.

Selecting and Editing Printer Resource Files

WordPerfect keeps information about each printer you use in a printer resource file. This file ends with the extension .PRS, as in STANDARD.PRS for the standard printer. Although you can easily work with the standard printer, eventually you'll want to tell the program about your own printers.

Note: Printer definitions from previous WordPerfect versions won't work in Version 5.0. You must set up your printers again.

Actually, the term *printer resource* is perhaps a bit misleading. When you tell WordPerfect about your printer or printers, you also tell WordPerfect about other things, too, most notably the type of *forms* you're planning to use. What's more, you can tell WordPerfect *how* a form goes into the printer, *where* it's located, and its *type*. For the moment, however, just get started!

When you select, add, or change printer resources, WordPerfect extracts the information from the master printer file and creates a separate .PRS file for each printer if one doesn't exist already. It also updates the file that contains all your settings, WP{WP}.SET (Appendix A). You select or change a printer resource from the same location:

Press   **SHIFT-F7 Print**

Type   **s** [Select Printer]

The print: select printer screen appears. At the top is a list of the printers you've already added. An asterisk notes the currently selected printer. On the status line is this menu:

```
1 Select; 2 Additional Printers; 3 Edit; 4 Copy; 5 Delete; 6 Help; 7 Update: 1
```

I'll cover all these options in their turn. Just make sure you see this menu before you follow the steps outlined in the next few sections.

Selecting a Different Printer

Once you've added printer resources, discussed next, you can easily switch to a different printer. Use the **UP ARROW** or **DOWN ARROW** key to high-light the printer on the list. Then:

Type **1 or s** [Select]

or

Press **RETURN**

to select that printer.

An asterisk appears next to the printer you've selected. Then:

Press **F7 Exit**

to return to the print menu.

WordPerfect now lists the new printer on the Select Printer line, and you can continue your work.

Note: The new printer remains in effect even when you exit WordPerfect, and WordPerfect may reformat any document on the screen to accommodate the new printer.

Adding a Printer Resource File

You can't select a different printer or edit the printer resource until you've added the printer to the list. You can add as many printers as disk space will allow for the printer resource files. This is a slightly complicated procedure, so pay close attention! From the print: select printer screen, do this:

Type **2 or a** [Additional Printers]

WordPerfect keeps all printer information in large composite files that end with .ALL, for example, WPRINTA.ALL and WPRINTB.ALL. When you add a printer resource, WordPerfect takes the information for that printer from the composite file and sets up a separate printer resource file. That way, you don't have to store all printer information on the disk.

The composite printer files should already be in the WordPerfect direc-tory of your hard disk. If they aren't where WordPerfect expects or if you're using floppy disks, WordPerfect won't be able to find the files and will tell you this:

```
Selct Printer: Additional Printers
```

```
Printer files not found
```

```
    Use the "Other Disk" option to specify a directory for the printer
    files.  Continue to use this option until you find the disk with the
    printer you want.
```

At the bottom of the screen is this menu:

```
1 Select; 2 Other Disk; 3 Help; 4 List Printer Files; N Name Search: 1
```

Floppy disk users: Insert the printer disk in a drive. Then:

Type   **2 or o** [Other Disk]

WordPerfect prompts:

```
Directory for printer files: A:\
```

Your drive letter may be different. Suppose you've inserted the disk with
the printer information in the B drive. Do this:

Type   **b:**

Press   **RETURN**

Hard disk users: If the printer file is in another directory, type **2 or o**
[Other Disk] and supply the directory path.

Tip: You can also press **PG DN** to see this message:

```
Directory for printer files: C:\WP\
```

Type a new directory path and press **RETURN**. In all cases, WordPerfect
then takes you back to the select printer: additional printers menu and lists
the printer resources. You see the same menu at the bottom of the screen:

```
1 Select; 2 Other Disk; 3 Help; 4 List Printer Files; N Name Search: 1
```

Use the **DOWN ARROW** key to highlight the printer you want to add, or type n [Name Search] and the first letter of the printer.

Tip: If your printer isn't on the list, try to find one that's similar. Once the highlight is on the printer you want:

Type   **1** or **s** [Select]

to select the printer.

WordPerfect tells you the printer resource's file name (most of which change with the seasons, it seems). For instance, if you select the Hewlett-Packard LaserJet II, you see:

```
Printer file name: HPLASEII.PRS
```

Press   **RETURN** or **F7 Exit**

Floppy disk users: WordPerfect will then tell you to insert the "WordPerfect 2" disk back in the drive if you removed the disk. Press any key to continue.

(An aside: You can type **4** or **l** [List Printer Files] to refresh your memory of what printers you've already added. Then continue as above. If you select a printer that's already on your printer list, WordPerfect asks you to confirm that you want to overwrite the previous printer resource file.)

WordPerfect may tell you that it's updating the printer's fonts. It may also present some information about the printer you've selected. Use the standard cursor movement commands to look at the information. Press SHIFT-F3 Switch to see any information about sheet feeders, and the same key to return to the main help screen. When you're finished:

Press   **F7 Exit**

The select printer: edit menu appears (Figure 5-4). To the right are the default settings that WordPerfect "assumes" for this printer. To the left are the change settings options. I know that all this looks terribly confusing, especially if you're just starting out. Here's a consolation: You'll work with the same options when you change (edit) a printer resource file, so eventually you'll get the hang of it. (I know, I know! That's little consolation!)

Note: Always press **F7 Exit** to save any information. If you press any other key, you'll get unexpected results.

Tip: Accept the default settings and see if your printer works okay. The only settings you may have to change initially are those for the port, sheet feeder, and location of the standard form. I'll discuss all the options below or mention the chapter where I'll cover them if they're advanced options.

The Printer's Name. The **1** [Name] option lets you change the descriptive printer name that appears on the printer list. For example, you may want the

```
Select Printer: Edit

        Filename

  1 - Name

  2 - Port

  3 - Sheet Feeder

  4 - Forms

  5 - Cartridges and Fonts

  6 - Initial Font

  7 - Path for Downloadable
      Fonts and Printer
      Command Files




Selection: 0
```

Figure 5-4   The Select Printer: Edit Menu

name to be LaserJet with B Cartridge or Printer - No Sheet Feeder. Type
1 or n [Name], type the new name, and press **RETURN**. The name can be
about 37 characters long. You do not have to change the name if you don't
want to.

   Ports, Baud Rates, and More. Option **2** [Port] is important. It tells
WordPerfect where you've connected your printer to the computer. Word-
Perfect "assumes" that you're using the first parallel port, what DOS calls
LPT1. If you've connected the printer to a serial port (COM1, COM2, and
so on) or a different parallel port (LPT2, LPT3), you must change the setting.
Type **2** or **p** [Port] to bring up the port menu:

Port: 1 LPT 1; 2 LPT 2; 3 LPT 3; 4 COM 1; 5 COM 2; 6 COM 3; 7 COM 4; 8 Other: 0

Type the number of the correct printer port. Notice that there are no mnemonic letters in this menu except for "other." If you select a serial port (COM), WordPerfect then asks for other information germane to serial-type printers on the select printer: COM port menu (Figure 5-5). Here's where you can get out the printer manual and attempt to find the correct settings, or you can run to your local printer *guru* and yell!

Tip: Check the help information that WordPerfect supplies for the printer resources. It may list the correct settings that you need.

The **1** [Baud] choice brings up the baud menu with the available baud rates:

Baud: 1 110; 2 150; 3 300; 4 600; 5 1200; 6 2400; 7 4800; 8 9600: 0

Similarly, you'll see the parity menu when you select choice **2** [Parity]:

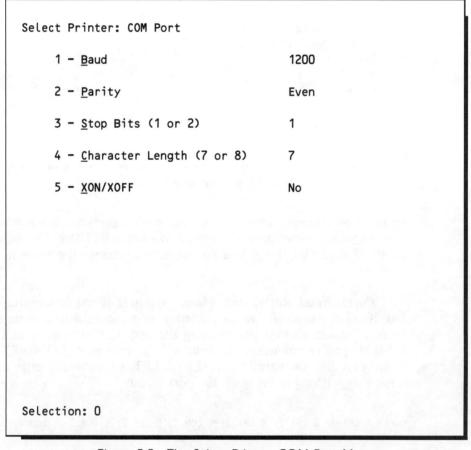

```
Select Printer: COM Port

    1 - Baud                        1200

    2 - Parity                      Even

    3 - Stop Bits (1 or 2)          1

    4 - Character Length (7 or 8)   7

    5 - XON/XOFF                    No











Selection: 0
```

Figure 5-5   *The Select Printer: COM Port Menu*

```
Parity: 1 None; 2 Odd; 3 Even: 0
```

Make sure you press **F7 Exit** to accept all changes to the COM port.

Sheet Feeders. Choice **3** [Sheet Feeder] tells WordPerfect if this printer works with a sheet feeder. Type **3** or **s** [Sheet Feeder] to call up the select printer: sheet feeder screen. WordPerfect lists only those sheet feeders that work with the printer you've selected. Use the **DOWN ARROW** key to highlight the sheet feeder, then type **1** or **s** [Select], or press **RETURN**. Type **2** or **n** [None] for no sheet feeder. Use the help and name search options as normal.

Tip: Use this option to select a sheet feeder that works for most of the documents you print. You can switch sheet feeders, for instance, to print the first letter on letterhead stationery from one feeder bin and subsequent letter pages on stationery that's in another bin. In that case, you'd select a different *form* (Chapter 13). You can also set up two printer resources with two different sheet feeders if necessary. If you don't normally use a sheet feeder, don't change this setting.

Caution: Laser printer owners should *not* set up a new sheet feeder if they're using the one that is built into the printer.

Forms and Type of Paper. The **4** [Forms] option is without a doubt the most confusing. It lets you set up or select different types of forms and tell WordPerfect everything it needs to know about those forms, but more than you *ever* care to know! To WordPerfect, a *form* is more than just paper of a certain size. A form also has a location and an orientation, among other things.

By default, WordPerfect uses an 8½ by 11 inch sheet of paper as the *standard form*. You insert this form vertically in the printer, what is known as *portrait orientation* (Chapter 13). But WordPerfect also "assumes" that the location of the form is a continuous roll of paper.

At its most basic level, the Forms option lets you indicate to WordPerfect the type of paper you have in the printer. For the time being, assume that you want to change the paper location: Type **4** or **f** [Forms]. WordPerfect displays the forms that it "knows" for your printer and this message and menu at the bottom of the screen:

```
If the requested form is not available, then printing stops and WordPerfect
waits for a form to be inserted in the ALL OTHERS location.  If the requested
form is larger than the ALL OTHERS form, the width is set to the maximum width.

1 Add; 2 Delete; 3 Edit: 3
```

Don't worry about the message. All will become clear in Chapter 13. Now, select the standard form if WordPerfect hasn't already selected it. Then type 3 or e [Edit] to see the select printer: forms menu, shown in Figure 5-6.

Note: You must tell WordPerfect the exact specifications of each form that you plan to use before you can work with the form. Otherwise, WordPerfect chooses the "ALL OTHERS" setting or whatever form is the closest match (Chapter 13).

On the Filename line is the name of the printer resource file you're working with. Below that is the form type. For each other option there's a setting that you can change.

Sheesh! Are you ever going to learn all these options? Of course! But for the sake of your sanity, I'll defer discussion of all options but one until Chapter 13. Right now, you need learn only how to tell WordPerfect what kind of paper you're using. That is, you can choose continuous form paper, a sheet feeder, or individual sheets that you insert manually. So, type 4 or l [Location] to bring up the location of forms menu:

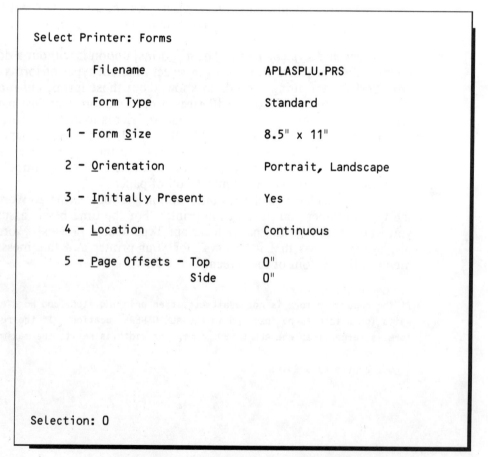

```
Select Printer: Forms

        Filename                APLASPLU.PRS

        Form Type               Standard

  1 - Form Size                 8.5" x 11"

  2 - Orientation               Portrait, Landscape

  3 - Initially Present         Yes

  4 - Location                  Continuous

  5 - Page Offsets - Top        0"
                    Side        0"




Selection: 0
```

Figure 5-6 The Select Printer: Forms Menu

```
Location: 1 Continuous; 2 Bin Number; 3 Manual: 0
```

Type **1** or **c** [Continuous] for paper on continuous rolls or **3** or **m** [Manual] for individual sheets. If you type **2** or **b** [Bin Number], WordPerfect requests the sheet feeder bin number. Type it and press **RETURN**. Then make sure you've told WordPerfect which sheet feeder is attached to your printer.

✔ If you changed the standard form from continuous to manual or sheet feeder, press **F7 Exit** twice to return to the select printer: edit menu. Or press **F1 Cancel** twice to return to the menu without changing the forms information.

Cartridges and Fonts. This choice is a little confusing, because "cartridges and fonts" can also mean print wheels if you have a daisy wheel printer. In fact, WordPerfect is "smart" enough to know your printer's *font resources.* Choice **5** [Cartridges and Fonts] thus lets you tell WordPerfect what cartridges, fonts, and print wheels your printer uses. WordPerfect then knows when to tell you to switch wheels if you select a font on a different wheel as the base font for a document.

Note: Laser printer owners must first tell WordPerfect what cartridges and soft fonts they're using before they can choose an initial font or make font changes within a document. I'll cover this procedure in greater detail in Chapter 35.

When you type **5** or **c** [Cartridges and Fonts], WordPerfect displays the select printer: cartridges and fonts screen. If you have a conventional printer, you'll see one or more selections under the Resource column. If you have a laser printer, you'll work with both the Cartridge Fonts and maybe the Soft Fonts resources (Chapter 35). Notice that WordPerfect tells you how much memory is available for soft fonts. At the bottom of the screen is this menu:

```
1 Select Fonts; 2 Change Quantity; N Name Search: 1
```

Change Quantity means to change the number of font cartridges you have. To tell WordPerfect about a cartridge or print wheel, highlight the Font Slot you want or the message Cartridge Fonts and type **1** or **f** [Select Fonts]. A screen of fonts appears. Move the highlight to the font you want to use. Then mark the font with either a plus sign (+) or an asterisk (*). Laser printer owners can mark cartridges with an asterisk only, because cartridges must be initially present when you turn on your printer.

Tip: If you mark the wrong font, press the asterisk key again to "unmark" it.

In general, use an asterisk to tell WordPerfect that the cartridge or font is *present when the print job begins.* If you have the option to use the plus sign to indicate that you can load the font during a print job, WordPerfect will beep when you print and ask you to change the print wheel for the font. If you're selecting laser printer font cartridges, you can select as many as the quantity shown on the select printer: cartridges and fonts screen.

When you're finished selecting cartridges and fonts, press **F7 Exit** twice to return to the select printer: edit menu. WordPerfect will tell you that it's updating the fonts for your printer.

If you have a conventional printer that does not work with multiple cartridges, fonts, or print wheels, you'll probably see this message:

```
This printer has no other fonts or cartridges
```

Initial Font. The next choice, **6** [Initial Font] is where you instruct WordPerfect what *base font* you want to use with your printer (Chapter 4). Laser printer owners: You'll see on the list both the printer's internal fonts (Chapter 35) and the fonts on the cartridges you've selected.

To select an initial font, type **6** or **i** [Initial Font] to see the select printer: initial font screen. The current base font has an asterisk next to it. Highlight the font you want, then type **1** or **s** [Select]. Use the **N** [Name Search] choice to find a font by name. Until you're comfortable with fonts, it's best to accept the default that WordPerfect supplies.

Directory Path for Fonts. Choice **7** [Path for Downloadable Fonts and Printer Command Files] is also for laser printer owners (Chapter 35).

Okay, after you've made *all* the choices you want, you're ready to finish the process of adding a printer. Do this:

Press   **F7 Exit** twice

to add the new printer and return to the print menu.

Editing (Changing) a Printer Resource File

To make any changes to all those settings that you just learned in the previous section, move the highlight to the printer you want to change.

Tip: You don't have to select the printer if you're just editing the resource file. Then type **3** or **e** [Edit] and find the settings you want to edit. When you're finished, press **F7 Exit** enough times to save the settings.

Copying a Printer Resource File

Sometimes you'll want to use the *same* printer resource file as the base for another. See Using the Same Printer with Different Paper later in this chapter. Instead of going through all the steps, just copy the information to a new printer. Highlight the printer you want to copy, then type **4** or **c** [Copy]. WordPerfect shows the printer information screen again. Press **F7 Exit** to continue.

Caution: If you don't supply a new name, you'll see two printers with the same name. Here's a good time to use another name, like `Printer with Envelope Feeder`, or whatever. After you change the name, change any settings and continue.

Deleting a Printer Resource File

Mercifully, deleting a printer from the active list is easy. Just *highlight, but don't select* the printer's name. Then type **5** or **d** [Delete]. WordPerfect asks you to confirm what you're doing:

```
Delete <Printer> (Y/N)? No
```

where `<Printer>` is the name you're attempting to delete. Just type **y** to delete or **n** to cancel.

Note: This operation just deletes the printer's *name* from the list. You must now also delete the .PRS file if you wish (Chapter 9). You can't delete the selected printer. WordPerfect gives you this message if you try:

```
Must select another printer before deleting this printer
```

WordPerfect is telling you that there must always be a selected printer.

The Help Option

When you type the last choice, **6** or **h** [Help], WordPerfect presents the same information on the selected printer that you saw when you first added the printer. If there is no additional information for a printer, you'll see briefly:

```
No help available
```

The Update Option

WordPerfect Corporation is continually changing and improving printer resource information in the composite printer files. The final choice, Update, gives you the option to update printer resources when you purchase a new set of composite files. This choice does *not* change the current font setup in your printer resource file, so you don't have to start from scratch. The Update option just adds any new capabilities from the composite printer file to your printer resource file.

Using the Same Printer with Different Paper

Suppose you want to use the same printer to print on either continuous form or manual feed paper, but at different times. Set up *two* printers on the list. That is, copy the printer and change the location of forms setting. The rest of the two resources will be the same.

 Tip: Give different names to the printers so that you know which is for continuous form paper and which for manual feed paper.

A Quick-and-Dirty Printout

As long as you're exploring printing, here's a DOS command that you can use within WordPerfect for a "quick-and-dirty" printout that requires just two keystrokes. First, make sure that the screen displays the text that you want to print. Then, after you have turned on your printer and prepared the paper:

Press   **SHIFT-PRT SC**

There are several disadvantages to using SHIFT-PRT SC. First, it gives you a printout of the *entire* screen, including the status line! Second, you would have to repeat the operation for additional screens of text. Finally, the command won't format the lines as they appear when you print the document with WordPerfect. I *told* you it was quick and dirty!

However, one nifty use of SHIFT-PRT SC is to print out specific WordPerfect help screens or menus that you want to refer to without stopping your work or fumbling through the manual. Keep these visual aides near your computer or in a notebook. By the way, if you press PRT SC by itself, it will insert an asterisk (*). The official computerese for what SHIFT-PRT SC does is the inelegant but descriptive term, *screen dump*—you're dumping the current contents of the screen to the printer.

Well, there you have the basics of printing in WordPerfect. See Chapters 34 and 35 for a discussion of other printing features. For the time being, however, you have all the information you need to print your WordPerfect documents. Now it's time to learn about formatting.

6

Introduction to Formatting

In this chapter you'll learn the following new commands . . .

Function Key Commands

CTRL-F3 Screen (1) Rewrite the screen, (2) display the tab ruler at the bottom of the screen

SHIFT-F5 Date/Outline (1) Insert the date as text, (2) insert the date as a code

SHIFT-F8 Format Change most formats

Numeric Keypad Command

HOME,HOME,HOME, UP ARROW Position the cursor at the beginning of the document in front of any codes

. . . and you'll learn some new codes:

[Center Pg] Center text between the top and bottom of the page

[Date] Date code

[Just Off] Right margin justification off

[Just On] Right margin justification on

[Ln Num:Off] Line numbering off

[Ln Num:On] Line numbering on

[Ln Spacing] Line spacing change

[L/R Mar] Left and right margin change

more . . .

[Tab Set]	Tab set change
[T/B Mar]	Top and bottom margin change
[Undrln]	Underlining of spaces or tabs off
[Undrln:Spaces]	Underlining of spaces on
[Undrl:Tabs]	Underlining of tabs on

You can use any word processing program like WordPerfect to do at least three basic operations: (1) writing and editing, that is, typing in text and making corrections and changes easily; (2) formatting documents to look the way you want them to; and (3) printing.

By far the most complicated aspect of word processing is formatting. You'll spend a great deal of time exploring WordPerfect's extensive formatting capabilities. When you used a typewriter, you had to consider formatting, too, but there were not nearly as many choices available to you as there are in WordPerfect.

Everyone has different format requirements, so the examples in this book illustrate some popular document types. You can use them as models from which to customize documents for your own needs. This chapter covers the format changes you'll do most frequently, as well as a few other WordPerfect features. You'll also learn how to reuse a document without having to retype it.

DO WARM-UP

Formats in a Nutshell

A *format* is a set of rules that governs the document's printed appearance. In Chapter 1 I listed the most important default formats, for instance, line length, justification, and page margins. You've also learned that WordPerfect may reformat a document according to the printer definition you've selected to ensure that the document prints correctly with the default formats. Now you'll learn how to insert formatting codes that change those defaults.

Although WordPerfect offers you almost unlimited freedom in determining formats, there are several general points to consider. They apply to all format changes:

■ Until you change the format settings, WordPerfect uses the default settings that come with the program.

- A format change tells WordPerfect to change one of the default formats or a previous format change.

- All format changes are represented by codes that you insert in the document and save with the document.

- Most formatting commands are in the format menu that appears when you press SHIFT-F8 Format. There are a few special keys, such as the indent commands (Chapter 10), for quick formatting. Version 4.2 used three different commands for line, print, and page formatting.

- A format change starts from its position in the document and affects *only* the text following the change. Like the base font change (Chapter 4), format changes insert open codes in the document.

- Format changes remain in effect until you change the format somewhere else or delete the format change code from the document.

- If you issue an incorrect format change, you should delete the incorrect code. Otherwise, you'll get some strange printouts! (See Revising a Format Change in this chapter.)

- You have to keep track of where the codes are when you enter or change text in the document. You should keep codes together whenever possible.

The Three Simple Rules

Before you begin, and with the foregoing points in mind, you should know these three easy rules regarding format changes:

1. Whenever possible, use the default formats. If they don't produce the correct format for the majority of the documents you produce, change the defaults after you've worked with WordPerfect a while (Appendix A).

2. If a format change is to govern the entire document—or most of it—insert the necessary format change codes at the *beginning* of your document in front of any text. Not only will this eliminate the possibility of missing text that you want to reformat, but it also lets you find the codes easily to check them or change them. What's more, if you format *before* you begin, then you don't have to worry about it again.

3. If you have to work with two or more format changes within a document—such as changing the line spacing from double to single for indented text, and then back to double—try whenever possible to insert the format change at the *left margin* for line or print format changes or at the *top of the page* for page format changes. There are only a couple format changes, such as a font change, that should be in the middle of the line.

In this chapter you'll learn how to make line and print format changes that govern an entire document, as well as a few page formatting instructions. You'll explore other page formats in Chapters 16 and 17. Chapter 11 covers how to change formats *within* a document. Of course, one great advantage of word processing is the capability to change formats at any time. Many people don't worry about the fine points of formatting until they get the document text correct, that is, when the document reaches its "final" stages.

The Format Key

Before you begin a real-life formatting example, take a look at the format menu. Throughout the rest of this chapter, you'll use this menu almost exclusively, so I'll show it just once. Version 4.2 users: Take note of this!

Press   **SHIFT-F8 Format**

Figure 6-1 shows what you see. Most common format changes are in the Line or Page sections, choices 1 and 2. Although the third section is called Document, you'll find that you still work with line and page formats when you change the format of an entire document. After all this hullabaloo, it's time to try your hand at changing formats.

Correspondence Quality: A Letter Format

You'll first do a simple business letter with nondefault formats. Specifically, you'll change the left and right margins and the tab settings, turn off right margin justification, and switch from single spacing to line-and-a-half spacing. Later you'll deal with the top and bottom margins.

Assume that your company has a standard letterhead that takes up about 2 inches at the top of the page. By default, WordPerfect sets the top margin of a printed document to 1 inch. This prints far too high up on the page, but WordPerfect has a nifty feature that eliminates the problem: You can *center* the page from top to bottom on the paper.

Changing the Left and Right Margins

First, you'll learn some line format changes. Because the left and right margin settings often affect other formatting considerations—such as tabs—it's a good idea to change these settings *first*.

Note: I assume that you've already pressed **SHIFT-F8 Format** and that the format menu is now on the screen.

```
Format

    1 - Line
                Hyphenation                Line Spacing
                Justification              Margins Left/Right
                Line Height                Tab Set
                Line Numbering             Widow/Orphan Protection

    2 - Page
                Center Page (top to bottom)   New Page Number
                Force Odd/Even Page           Page Number Position
                Headers and Footers           Paper Size/Type
                Margins Top/Bottom            Suppress

    3 - Document
                Display Pitch              Redline Method
                Initial Settings           Summary

    4 - Other
                Advance                    Overstrike
                Conditional End of Page    Printer Functions
                Decimal Characters         Underline Spaces/Tabs
                Language

Selection: 0
```

Figure 6-1   The Format Menu

Type   **1** or **l** [Line]

The format: line menu, shown in Figure 6-2, appears. Notice that the left and right margins are by default 1 inch. You now want to change them to 1½ inches.

Note: The left and right margins are the amount of blank space from the left and right edges of the page. After it subtracts these settings from the width of the page (usually 8½ inches) WordPerfect arrives at the length of the text line.

Type   **7** or **m** [Margins]

WordPerfect positions the cursor on the left margin setting.

Type   **1.5**

```
Format: Line

    1 - Hyphenation                        No

    2 - Hyphenation Zone - Left            10%
                          Right            4%

    3 - Justification                      Yes

    4 - Line Height                        Auto

    5 - Line Numbering                     No

    6 - Line Spacing                       1

    7 - Margins - Left                     1"
                 Right                     1"

    8 - Tab Set                            0", every 0.5"

    9 - Widow/Orphan Protection            No




Selection: 0
```

Figure 6-2   The Format: Line Menu

Press   **RETURN**

WordPerfect shows the new setting as 1.5" and positions the cursor on the right margin setting.

 Note: You must use decimals to indicate fractions, such as half inches. You can use other fraction settings, too (for example, 1.35). Throughout this book I use inches as the units of measure for format settings, but refer to Appendix A for information about the other possibilities.

✔Repeat the last two steps to set the right margin to 1.5" and return the cursor to the bottom of the screen. Stay in the format: line menu.

It makes no sense to set a right margin that's less than the left, and WordPerfect will tell you this if you attempt such a thing:

ERROR: Right margin overlaps left margin

Unfortunately, there's no way to change just one setting without going through both. Just press **RETURN** if you want to accept the current setting.

By the way, laser printers can't print near the four edges of the paper. To see how wide this *unprintable* region is, change the left and right margins to 0 (zero). WordPerfect will display the smallest available left and right margin setting. Similarly, change the top and bottom margins to 0 (page 124) to determine the top and bottom unprintable regions.

Clearing and Setting Tabs

By default, WordPerfect sets tab stops at every half inch (0.5), starting at position 0.0 and extending to position 8.5. Try clearing the tabs and setting a new tab at position 2.2:

Type   **8** or **t** [Tab Set]

The tab set area appears (Figure 6-3). It shows all the current tabs and the line divided into inches. Below are instructions for clearing and setting tabs. You'll set up standard tabs, what WordPerfect calls *left-justified* tabs, in this chapter. Chapter 10 discusses the other types of tabs.

Note: In the tab set area, the L markers indicate left-justified tabs, *not* the left margin. The cursor is at the new left margin, position 1.5.

First clear all the tabs because you want only two new tab stops in the document. Notice that you use the Delete EOL (end of line) command to clear tabs:

Press   **CTRL-END**

Caution: The CTRL-END command clears all tab stops to the right of the cursor position. If the cursor isn't at the left margin, press HOME,LEFT ARROW to move the cursor to the left end of the ruler line before you use CTRL-END to delete all tabs. In this example, the tab stops to the left of the left margin won't affect the document anyway, so you don't have to worry about them.

To set or delete *individual* left-justified tabs, you have two options:

1. Use the **ARROW** keys to position the cursor on the tab line at the correct column. Then type **l** or press **RETURN** or **TAB** to *set* a tab there, or press **DEL** or **BACKSPACE** to *delete* the tab.

```
L....L....L....L....L....L....L....L....L....L....L....L....L....L....L....L....L...
   ¦    ^    ¦    ^    ¦    ^    ¦    ^    ¦    ^    ¦    ^    ¦    ^    ¦    ^
0"       1"       2"       3"       4"       5"       6"       7"
Delete EOL (clear tabs); Enter number (set tab); Del (clear tab);
Left; Center; Right; Decimal; .= Dot leader; Press EXIT when done.
```

Figure 6-3   The Tab Set Area

2. Type the column position and press **RETURN** to move the cursor to that column quickly *and* at the same time set a left-justified tab at that column. Press **DEL** or **BACKSPACE** to *delete* the tab.

I like the second approach better, so to set a tab at column 2.2:

Type   **2.2**

Press   **RETURN**

to place an L marker at column 2.2.
You also need a tab stop for indenting the closing of the letter. Put it at column 4.5:

Type   **4.5**

Press   **RETURN**

You're now finished setting tabs, so:

Press   **F7 Exit**

A later section discusses how to set tabs at specific intervals. Notice that WordPerfect shows the first few tabs on the format: line menu. Don't worry! The new ones are there, too.

Changing Line Spacing

The next change alters line spacing. The default, as you know, is single spacing, but now you want line-and-a-half spacing:

Type   **6** or **s** [Line Spacing]

Type   **1.5**

Press   **RETURN**

You can also set spacing to just half a line (0.5) for mathematical equations (Chapter 15).
Be careful when you change the line spacing in existing documents, because you might get some unexpected results. For example, when you change a single spaced document to a double spaced one, WordPerfect substitutes *two* soft or hard returns for every one in the original document. You may have to delete some extra hard returns when the document is double spaced.

Tip: Use the Replace command to search for and replace hard returns (Chapter 8).

Turning Justification Off

A letter with justified right margins often turns the reader off, because it was obviously composed on a computer! To fool people into thinking that they're getting more individualized correspondence, use a "ragged" right margin, as on a typewriter:

Type   **3** or **j** [Justification]

Type   **n**

for no.

Tip: When justification is on, WordPerfect normally adds microspaces between words only to fill out the lines. If you don't like the results, you can adjust the *word spacing justification limits* to have WordPerfect put micro-spaces between characters (Chapter 34).

You're now finished with the line format changes that you want to make, so:

Press   **F7 Exit**

to return to the document.

Tip: Using F7 Exit bypasses the format menu and takes you back to the document. If you had pressed RETURN, you'd be back in the format menu and would have to press F7 Exit or RETURN again to leave that menu.

Checking the Codes

The status line now tells you that the left margin is at Pos 1.5". There are now four format codes in the document. Because you're just learning how to make format changes, it's a good idea to check the codes to make sure they're correct. Take a look at them now:

Press   **ALT-F3 Reveal Codes** or **F11 Reveal Codes**

The tab ruler shows the new left and right margins and tab stops. Below that are the codes:

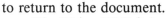

```
[L/R Mar:1.5",1.5"][Tab Set:L0",L0.5",L1",L2.2",L4.5"][Ln Spacing:1.5][Just Off]
```

WordPerfect breaks the line in the reveal codes area to show all codes on the screen, but that won't affect the document. Notice that the left and right margins settings are separated by a comma and that WordPerfect has included the extra tabs at positions 0, 0.5, and 1 in the tab set code.

Question: If you were turning right justification back on, what code would WordPerfect insert? *Answer:* Right! A [Just On] code.

If there are more than these four codes in the document, position the cursor under each extra code and press DEL to delete it. When you're finished, make sure the cursor is directly past the codes. Then:

Press   **ALT-F3 Reveal Codes** or **F11 Reveal Codes**

to hide the codes.

Whenever you set a different format for a document, the new format stays with the document when you save it to a file. If you work on a document today, save it, and then come back to it tomorrow, you *don't* have to reset the format.

Step-by-Step Through the Letter

Here's the entire letter to type. Just look at it for a moment, but don't type it yet.

```
Mr. J.Q. Suds

P.O. Box 507

Juneau, AK  99901



Dear Mr. Suds:



    Thank you for your recent inquiry concerning the

availability of Consolidated Toupee's newly-announced

product line, Five Easy Pieces.  We, too, feel that

this will be an exciting addition to our family.
```

Two returns here

Unfortunately, our production schedule for Five
Easy Pieces was disrupted by delays in the shipment of
materials, so at present the product is not yet in the
stores. We anticipate that it will be available
sometime in December.

I have taken the liberty of enclosing a brochure
that describes our other products and of putting your
name on our mailing list for future product
announcements.

Regards,

R. Jackson Frump
Director of Sales,
Western Region

✔Type the interior address lines, pressing **RETURN** to end each line. Notice that WordPerfect shows line-and-a-half spacing as double spacing on the screen. After the city and state line, press **RETURN** twice for spacing.

Because of the hardware limitations of your computer, WordPerfect can't show true line-and-a-half spacing on the screen, so it uses double spacing instead. But notice that WordPerfect shows the half lines on the status line as you type. I'm stepping you slowly through the first part of the letter to emphasize that, just as with the typewriter, you must end short lines with hard returns. By the way, I didn't forget the date—it's a special feature discussed later.

✔Type the salutation and press **RETURN** twice. Type in the rest of the letter as you see it here. Use one **TAB** for each paragraph. Let WordPerfect wrap the lines for you, but remember to press **RETURN** twice at the end of each paragraph. Press the **TAB** key twice for the closing section and **RETURN** four times for the signature space. Press **RETURN** twice to space down for the date.

(An aside: You may want to hyphenate some long words, but you won't learn about hyphenation until Chapter 20.)

Entering the Date

WordPerfect has a command that types the current date into a document, provided you supplied the correct date when you started your computer. But it does much more than that. You can use it to choose the format of the date from an astounding array of choices; it can enter the current time; and you can even have it update the current date and time whenever you edit or print the document. This latter feature becomes very useful if you reuse documents frequently, because you then won't have to change the date yourself.

WordPerfect distinguishes between the date purely as *text* and the date as a *code*. When you tell WordPerfect to enter the current date as text, it provides the text equivalent for today's date. This text won't change if you later go back into the document: It's essentially a one-shot deal.

When you tell WordPerfect to enter the date as a code, WordPerfect shows today's date in the format that you desire. However, WordPerfect will later update the date whenever you edit or print the document. Some people call this a *hot code*, because it can change.

Press   **SHIFT-F5 Date/Outline**

WordPerfect presents the date/outline menu:

1 Date Text; 2 Date Code; 3 Date Format; 4 Outline; 5 Para Num; 6 Define: 0

You'll learn about the outline and paragraph numbering features in other chapters. If you had used choice **1** [Date Text], WordPerfect would insert just text. Instead, insert the date as a code because you'll be using this letter on another day:

Type   **2 or c** [Date Code]

There's the date, but see how the code appears:

Press   **ALT-F3 Reveal Codes** or **F11 Reveal Codes**

You see this code: [Date:3 1, 4]. The numbers indicate the default date format. At this point, don't worry about the date format or how to enter the time—those topics are covered in Chapter 15. For the most part, you'll use the default format anyway. But the code stays in the document and will show the current date.

Press   **ALT-F3 Reveal Codes** or **F11 Reveal Codes**

to turn the codes off.

Centering the Text on the Printed Page

Assume that Consolidated Toupee has a standard letterhead that takes up about 2 inches at the top of the page. By default, WordPerfect sets the top margin of a printed document to 1 inch. The letter will print too high up on the page, but WordPerfect has a nifty feature that eliminates this problem. You can *center* the page from top to bottom on the paper.

Note: The center page feature works correctly *only* if the code is at the very top of the page in the document.

Now, you may think that you can press HOME,HOME,UP ARROW to return the cursor to the beginning of the document. You're wrong! That command only positions the cursor directly past the format codes, so you can type text without moving any codes at the beginning of the document. Here's what you can do instead:

Press   **HOME,HOME,HOME,UP ARROW**

to position the cursor at the real beginning of the document.

This command is a combination of HOME,HOME,UP ARROW and HOME,HOME,HOME,LEFT ARROW.

The center page feature is, as you would expect, a page format change.

Press   **SHIFT-F8 Format**

Type   **2** or **p** [Page]

The format: page menu, shown in Figure 6-4, appears.

Type   **1** or **c** [Center Page (top to bottom)]

WordPerfect changes No to Yes next to this option.

Press   **F7 Exit**

to return to the document.

```
Format: Page

    1 - Center Page (top to bottom)          No

    2 - Force Odd/Even Page

    3 - Headers

    4 - Footers

    5 - Margins - Top                        1"
                  Bottom                     1"

    6 - New Page Number                      1
          (example: 3 or iii)

    7 - Page Numbering                       No page numbering

    8 - Paper Size                           8.5" x 11"
              Type                           Standard

    9 - Suppress (this page only)


Selection: 0
```

Figure 6-4   The Format: Page Menu

You won't see any immediate change to the line numbering, but WordPerfect inserts this code into the document: [Center Pg]. If you print the document now, you'll see the document centered on the printed page. WordPerfect deducts the total line count of the document from the number of lines on the standard form, then divides this figure by 2 to determine the new top and bottom margins. If your letter runs long, or if the letterhead takes up a large amount of space, this feature probably won't work. You would have to change the top margin. The center page command only applies to the current page.

✔Save this document as SUDS.LTR before you continue. If you wish, print the letter now to see the results. (I won't mention printing again; just print whenever you want to.)

Now that you have a letter, what about an envelope? That'll wait until Chapter 13, which discusses forms and more advanced page formatting. (Actually, the best way to set up an envelope is to use a "fill-in document," the topic of Chapter 29.)

Revising a Format Change

If you find that you entered a format change incorrectly—for example, you selected the wrong margin settings—or if you want to remove a format change from the document, I *strongly* urge you to delete the original change code and enter a new one. You can get unpredictable results if you insert two codes that do the same thing, even if the new code occurs after the old one. If your printouts are not what you expected, always check the codes to see if a superfluous code appears somewhere.

As an example, you'll remove the line spacing change code and see what happens to the document.

✔Because you may not remember exactly where the code is, reveal the codes and position the cursor under the [Ln Spacing:1.5] code. Then press **DEL** to delete the code. Turn the codes off when you finish.

The letter now appears in single spacing, but it will still print centered on the page.

Tip: You can "undelete" an individually deleted code with the F1 Cancel key. However, make sure the codes are revealed so you can see the deletion that you want.

✔Save the document again but leave it on the screen.

Other Common Format Changes

Now that you've investigated line and page formatting, take a look at a few other format changes that you'll probably want to learn now. You'll learn how to set tabs at specific intervals, change the top and bottom margin of the page, set the underline style, and print line numbers in the left margin of the page.

Setting Tabs at Intervals

Besides setting individual tabs, you can set tabs at specific intervals. Although you don't have to do anything right now, just follow these steps when you need this feature.

1. Press **SHIFT-F8 Format**.
2. Type **1** or l [Line].
3. Type **8** or t [Tab Set].
4. Position the cursor at the left margin if it isn't there already, then press **CTRL-END** to delete all tab stops.
5. Type the *starting* column position, a comma, then the *interval amount*. Press **TAB** or **RETURN** to set the tabs. For example, to set tabs every 0.5 inch starting at column 1.0, you'd type **1,.5**.

6. Press **F7 Exit** to return to the document.

Note: If there's already a tab at the beginning column, WordPerfect uses its *type* (left-justified, right-justified, centered, or decimal) for the new tabs; otherwise, it "assumes" left-justified tabs. You'll learn about the other types of tabs in Chapter 10.

Changing the Top and Bottom Margins

You can change the top and bottom margins of the printed page, but remember that WordPerfect doesn't show these margins on the screen except when you view the printout. The default settings are 1-inch top and bottom margins. Follow these steps when you want to change the settings, but don't do the steps now:

1. Press **SHIFT-F8 Format**.
2. Type **2** or **p** [Page].
3. Type **5** or **m** [Margins].
4. Type the new top margin setting and press **RETURN**, or press **RETURN** alone to accept the current setting.
5. Type the new bottom margin setting and press **RETURN**, or press **RETURN** alone to accept the current setting.
6. Press **F7 Exit** to return to the document.

When you change the top or bottom margin, WordPerfect inserts this code: [T/B Mar] with the new settings. In earlier versions you had to change the top margin, page length, and number of text lines to arrive at a bottom margin.

Tip: Always check the other codes that are currently in the document before you insert page formatting codes. If, for example, you've inserted a center page code, make sure this code is first. In general, put all other page formatting codes at the beginning of the document, or at least at the top of the current page.

Underlining Spaces and Tabs

Normally WordPerfect underlines the spaces between words in a phrase, but it won't underline the tab stops. You can change the underlining style, and your changes affect both single and double underlines.

Note: Your monitor may not show the underlining of spaces, but underlining will still print correctly. This is your first introduction to the format: other menu, although you don't have to follow the steps below right now.

To change how WordPerfect underlines spaces and tabs:

1. Press **SHIFT-F8 Format**.

2. Type **4** or **o** [Other] to bring up the format: other menu (Figure 6-5).

3. Type **7** or **u** [Underline].

4. Type **n** or **y** to change each setting.

5. Press **F7 Exit** to return to the document.

Here are the codes associated with the underline style: [Undrln:] turns off the underlining of whatever is the previous on setting, spaces or tabs; [Undrln:Spaces] turns on the underlining of spaces; and [Undrln:Tabs] turns on the underlining of tabs.

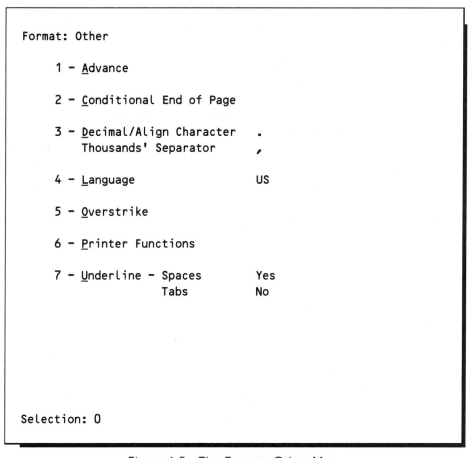

```
Format: Other

    1 - Advance

    2 - Conditional End of Page

    3 - Decimal/Align Character       .
        Thousands' Separator          ,

    4 - Language                      US

    5 - Overstrike

    6 - Printer Functions

    7 - Underline - Spaces            Yes
                    Tabs              No




Selection: 0
```

Figure 6-5   The Format: Other Menu

Printing Line Numbers

If you work in a law office, here's a nifty feature. WordPerfect can print line numbers in the left margin of the page. You can choose to print each line number, certain line numbers at a set interval, or numbers for lines containing text only (thus skipping blank lines). You can also change the position of the printed number in the left margin white space, start numbering with a number other than 1, or restart numbering at the top of each page. Follow these steps when you need this feature:

1. Press **SHIFT-F8 Format**.
2. Type `1` or `l` [Line].
3. Type `5` or `n` [Line Numbering].
4. Type `y` for yes. WordPerfect displays the format: line numbering menu (Figure 6-6).
5. Change any settings that you wish.
6. Press **F7 Exit** to return to the document.

When you turn line numbering on, WordPerfect inserts a `[Ln Num:On]` code in the document. Keep in mind that line numbering starts from the

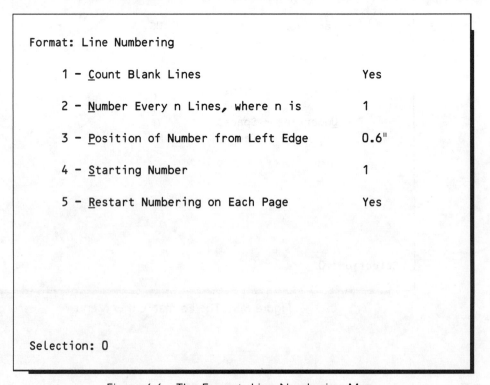

```
Format: Line Numbering

     1 - Count Blank Lines                        Yes

     2 - Number Every n Lines, where n is         1

     3 - Position of Number from Left Edge        0.6"

     4 - Starting Number                          1

     5 - Restart Numbering on Each Page           Yes







Selection: 0
```

Figure 6-6 The Format: Line Numbering Menu

position of the code, so it's a good idea to put this code at the beginning of the document. Although you won't see the numbers on the screen, you can view them with the print view feature.

To stop line numbering, position the cursor at the correct spot in the document and follow steps 1 through 3 above. Then type **n** and press **F7 Exit** to insert a [Ln Num:Off] code.

Brief Interlude: Why Retype?

Take a short break from format codes and do an exercise in reusing the SUDS.LTR document. Assume that you get another inquiry and that you can send the very same letter to a different person. Why retype the whole letter when you can print it again with just a few minor changes? Later, you'll see other, perhaps better, ways of setting up stock reply letters, but even at this early stage in your word processing apprenticeship you can use WordPerfect to your advantage. This example provides an opportunity for you to work with typeover mode.

You can change the letter, print it, and save it under a new name, if you wish. But it may make more sense just to change the letter and print it without saving it. You might not want to save all documents in files, because you'll clutter up precious disk space with files that you don't really need.

✔ If SUDS.LTR isn't still on the screen, retrieve it now.

WordPerfect automatically inserts today's date, and you just type the new material over the interior address and the salutation. *However*, always make sure of where the codes are when you change your text. When in doubt, reveal the codes.

✔ Position the cursor under the *M* of *Mr.* Is the cursor really where you want it? Reveal the codes to see. The cursor should be past all formatting codes before you continue. When you're ready:

Press   **INS**

to turn typeover mode on.

Type   **Ms. Terri Mahoney**

When you're in typeover mode you don't type over the hard return at the end of the line. That would cause real trouble! Why? Because it would make lines merge together. Don't press RETURN, because even in typeover mode, this will insert a hard return into the document. Instead:

Press   **END,RIGHT ARROW**

(A nifty trick to position the cursor at the beginning of the next line!)

Type   **1511 Ridge Road West**

Type over the city, state, zip line with:

Rochester, NY 14603

Are you finished? No, you must type over part of the salutation line so that it reads *Dear Ms. Mahoney:*. But you don't have to type over the *Dear,* do you? (Make sure that you type in the colon, though.) The letter is now ready to go.

Question: If you type over a long line with a short line, how to you get rid of the extra characters? *Answer:* Just press **CTRL-END** to delete to the end of the line (the fast way), or type over the extra characters with *spaces* by pressing the **SPACEBAR** (the slow way).

Whenever you're finished working in typeover mode, *always* get out of it. It can be very dangerous at times, especially if you *think* you are in insert mode and you accidentally press the INS key and replace some old text with the new text as you type.

Press   **INS**

to return to insert mode.

You can print the document if you wish, but *don't* save it as SUDS.LTR! By the way, typeover mode won't let you type over codes. If the cursor is under a code, WordPerfect acts as if it were in insert mode and will push the code ahead as you type. Be careful!

More Ways to Work with Formats

Okay, that was a very brief interlude. Now you'll learn just a few more tricks that you can use when you're dealing with format changes.

Rewriting the Screen

I've found that sometimes when you change a format, WordPerfect doesn't immediately show the effects of the change on the screen. This is especially true with advanced formatting, but you should be aware that you can *rewrite* the screen at any time to update the display.

Rewriting the screen brings up a related issue. Normally, WordPerfect automatically reformats entire paragraphs when you edit a line and then move the cursor out of the line or type past the right margin. You can set the defaults so that WordPerfect only reformats lines individually (Appendix A). In that case, you can still rewrite the screen at any time.

Although you don't have to follow these steps now, here's how to rewrite the screen:

1. Press **CTRL-F3 Screen** to see the screen menu:

   0 Rewrite; 1 Window; 1 Line Draw: 0

2. Type **0** or **r** [Rewrite], or simply press **RETURN** to rewrite the screen.

Here's another way to use the CTRL-F3 Screen key.

Showing the Margins and Tabs Settings on the Screen

If you like to see the left and right margin and tab settings on the screen as you work, you can display the tab ruler at the bottom of the screen. The tab ruler changes to show the current settings as you move the cursor through the document. That is, if the cursor moves past a left/right margin change or tab set code, the tab ruler reflects the new settings. To show the tab ruler:

1. Press **CTRL-F3 Screen** to bring up the screen menu.

2. Type **1** or **w** [Window], and WordPerfect prompts:

   # Lines in this Window: 24

   WordPerfect may show another number if you're using a monitor that can display more than 24 lines at a time. You need to reduce the number of lines by one so that WordPerfect will display the tab ruler. These steps work with any monitor.

3. Press **UP ARROW** to make the tab ruler appear. The window shrinks one line and WordPerfect prompts:

   # Lines in this Window: 23

4. Press **RETURN** to set the tab ruler.

To remove the tab ruler from the screen, repeat steps 1 and 2. Then press **DOWN ARROW** to extend the window one line down. Press **RETURN** to finish. The **1** [Window] choice also lets you split the screen into two windows when you want to display and edit two documents at the same time (Chapter 11).

Copying Format Codes

It's entirely possible to copy just codes, but you have to be *very* careful to block the codes and nothing else. Fortunately, you can reveal the codes after you turn a block on or before you begin a block. That way, you'll know exactly what's in the block.

✔Clear the screen and retrieve the document SUDS.LTR if it isn't on the screen now. Position the cursor at the beginning of the document, in front of all format codes.

Suppose you wanted to copy just the codes into a new file and use the new file as a *format document*. As its name implies, a format document contains just formatting instructions that you can call up whenever you start a document with the very same format. (In Chapter 11 you'll learn about format macros, which do the same thing.) To copy the codes, first reveal the codes to see what's what:

Press   **ALT-F3 Reveal Codes** or **F11 Reveal Codes**

If you've been following all the examples, there should be *four* codes that you want to block and copy: [Center Pg], [L/R Mar:1.5",1.5"], [Tab Set:L0",L0.5",L1",L2.2",L4.5"], and [Just Off]. There are three ways to copy these codes. Leave the codes on! Now:

Press   **ALT-F4 Block** or **F12 Block**

Press   **RIGHT ARROW** four times

to establish the limit of the block.

Press   **F10 Save**

As you saw in Chapter 3, WordPerfect requests a block name.

Type   `letter.fmt`

(The extension .FMT reminds you that this is a format document.)

Press   **RETURN**

Press   **ALT-F3 Reveal Codes** or **F11 Reveal Codes**

to turn the codes off.

To start a new letter at any time, clear the screen and retrieve the LETTER.FMT document as the format. Go ahead, try it! Then reveal the codes to see that they're there. (What you did was create a *boilerplate*, about which you'll learn more in Chapter 14.)

Caution: WordPerfect will "remember" the last file name when you save a new letter, so remember to supply a *new* name so that you don't overwrite the LETTER.FMT file.

Another way to block out the codes would be to reveal the codes, position the cursor directly *past* the codes (assuming they're all together), and then start the block. To delimit the entire block, press HOME,HOME, HOME,LEFT ARROW. Instead of saving the codes to another file, you can cut them or copy them as a block to other parts of the same document with the CTRL-F4 Move command.

Finally, nothing prevents you from blocking out text *and* codes, moving or copying the block as you wish, and then deleting the text to leave just the codes. It's up to you! Remember: Always block out exactly what you want to copy, including any codes, and make sure that the text is correct before you copy it. When in doubt, reveal the codes!

By the way, you can also copy text from one WordPerfect Corporation program to another through the WordPerfect Library. See the discussion of the Library's *Clipboard* feature in Appendix E.

This is not the last you'll hear about formatting! Many other chapters present examples of typical formatting situations, but the format changes in this chapter are the most common ones.

7

Macros Save Keystrokes!

In this chapter you'll learn the following new commands:

Function Key Commands

ALT-⟨letter⟩	Run a WordPerfect macro assigned to ⟨letter⟩
ALT-F10 Macro	Run a WordPerfect macro by file name
CTRL-F10 Macro Define	Turn WordPerfect macro definition on/off

Typewriter Keyboard Commands

HOME,INS	Force typeover mode on
HOME,HOME,INS	Force insert mode on
CTRL-V	Insert an editing command in a macro definition

Dear Reader, isn't word processing great? It relieves you of so much drudgery and gives you the time to be *creative,* or at least to take longer coffee breaks. Don't be chagrined if I tell you, however, that you're still *working too much!* This chapter shows you why and explains what to do about it. You'll learn about important keystroke and time savers known as macros. And guess what? Finally, you'll study a relatively short chapter!

DO WARM-UP

Macros Explained

Think about the steps you have to go through to print a document. First, you have to stop typing, find the SHIFT key and position your finger on it while you position another finger over the F7 key, press SHIFT-F7 Print, and then type a number choice, such as **2** or **p** [Page]. In other words, a modicum of fumbling and three keystrokes. If you have to insert individual sheets of paper into your printer, you must then press SHIFT-F7 Print *again*, type **4** or **c** [Control Printer], and then **4** or **g** to issue the go command—four *more* keystrokes. Sheesh!

WordPerfect's designers realized that there must be a better way. They added a very powerful macro capability to the program. Using macros is the number one keystroke saver in WordPerfect. Remember Alfieri's motto: Saving keystrokes means saving work. Users of the newer, extended keyboards will definitely appreciate WordPerfect macros. (In case you haven't realized it yet, the word *extended* refers to what your fingers feel like when you try to reach those faraway function keys!)

But I digress from the topic at hand. A *macro* is simply a collection of many keystrokes that you can issue with only a few keystrokes—usually two. For instance, you can have a macro to change the left and right margins, all with two keystrokes. A macro can contain text that you want to type into a document, commands, or a combination of both.

How does WordPerfect do it? It *stores* the macro instructions in a special file, with the extension .WPM. When you begin a macro, WordPerfect finds the file for that macro on the disk and issues the commands in the file.

Note: Version 4.2 users should refer to Macros from Previous WordPerfect Versions later in the chapter to learn what happened to the .MAC macros.

Once you've set up a macro, you can use it as many times as you wish. There are two ways to issue, or run, WordPerfect macros:

1. Hold down the **ALT** key and press one of the 26 alphabet keys on the keyboard (**A** through **Z**). You don't have to use uppercase, so ALT-a and ALT-A are identical.

2. Press the **ALT-F10 Macro** key and type a two- to eight-letter *macro name*, followed by a **RETURN**.

For example, you could have the macro ALTP issue printing commands (which is exactly what you'll do in a moment), or you could use the ALT-F10 Macro key with the macro named ST to have WordPerfect type out your street address. WordPerfect saves the former in a file called ALTP.WPM, and the latter in ST.WPM.

Tip: You can also assign macros to CTRL keys, such as CTRL-G. See the discussion of keyboard layout in Appendix A.

Everyone has different needs and uses some commands more than others, so besides saving you work, macros *customize* WordPerfect to suit your tastes and requirements. For example, I have a macro that prints my name, but that would be useless for you! Consult the documentation for information about the sample macros that come with WordPerfect.

Introductory Macro Tips

Devising a system for naming and storing macros is up to you, of course. I find that it's beneficial to save frequently issued *commands* in the ALT key macros and frequently used *text* in the ALT-F10 Macro key macros. Use *mnemonics* to jog your memory about what a macro does. For example, you can set up ALTP as a mnemonic for your print document macro. Using ALT key macros for command sequences is especially useful, because then your fingers don't have to stray too far off the keyboard.

With ALT-F10 Macro key macros, use *short, but suggestive* names. After all, the whole idea of a macro is to save keystrokes, so a macro called AD-DRESS, which types your address, requires more keystroking than a macro called AD that does the same thing. Limit macro names to two letters if possible. Whichever way you decide to go, be consistent. (Only *foolish* consistency is the "hobgoblin of little minds"; useful consistency is another thing.) You may even want to print out a crib sheet that describes each macro name and what it does, at least until they become second nature to you.

You can also append a description to the macro when you create or edit it. That way, you'll know exactly what the macro does when you later edit the macro.

And for heavens sake *save* all your macro files to a backup disk so that you have them in the case of an accident. By now, you should be making backups of *all* new files. If you don't know how to make backups, see Chapter 9.

Note: The number of macros that you can have is limited only by the amount of disk space available to you.

Macros from Previous WordPerfect Versions

The keystrokes for many commands and menus have changed in Version 5.0, so you'll have to set up new macros. What's more, the enhancements to the macro feature have required a change in the macro file format. The bottom line is that you can't use the old .MAC macros any more. So sorry! If you attempt to run a 4.2 macro, WordPerfect gives an error message. For instance, you want to use the ALTB macro, which was in a file called ALTB.MAC. So, you think you'll outsmart WordPerfect. You first rename the file to ALTB.WPM, because that's the way Version 5.0 expects to see the file name. WordPerfect still won't run the macro and tells you:

```
ERROR: Incompatible file format -- ALTB.WPM
```

Although you can now *edit* existing Version 5.0 macros, you can't edit macros from previous versions. The solution? Recreate your macros from scratch, or use the separate MACROCNV.EXE program to convert 4.2 text and command keystrokes that haven't changed in 5.0.

ALT Key Macros

The fastest macros are those you issue by holding down the ALT key as you press a letter, such as ALT-A. You'll first set up a standard print routine in a macro called ALTP. This macro prints an entire document from the screen.

✔Clear the screen now if it isn't clear already. You don't have to have a document open to create the first macro.

To create any macro, you *define* the keystrokes that you want to include in the macro:

Press   **CTRL-F10 Macro Define**

WordPerfect prompts:

```
Define macro:
```

It's waiting for the macro name. You don't have to use the SHIFT key to type the *p* or any other letters you define as macros.

Note: To cancel macro definition, press **F1 Cancel** before you get to the actual steps that you want to include in the macro.

Press   **ALT-P**

WordPerfect now prompts:

```
Description:
```

You can type a descriptive name for the macro or press RETURN to leave the description blank. In all examples, you'll add descriptions.

Type   **Print doc from screen**

Press   **RETURN**

You can edit the description line with any editing key before you press RETURN. Next, WordPerfect flashes this message on the status line and continues to flash it until you end the macro definition:

`Macro Def`

WordPerfect will now include in the macro *every* key you press until you press **CTRL-F10 Macro Define** again, so be careful. At this point, for instance, you can't cancel a macro with the F1 Cancel key (just press CTRL-F10 Macro Define to cancel). In a moment, I'll show you how to edit macros.

Press   **SHIFT-F7 Print**

Type   1 or f [Full Document]

Press   **CTRL-F10 Macro Define**

to finish the macro definition.

WordPerfect saves the macro in the file called ALTP.WPM. It also probably beeped at you because there isn't a document on the screen, but don't worry. You've created the macro correctly. Whenever you want to print an entire document from the screen, prepare your printer and paper, then press **ALT-P** (don't do it now, though).

If you have to issue a go command for individual sheets of paper, why not set it up in a macro, too? Call this one ALTG.

Press   **CTRL-F10 Macro Define**

Press   **ALT-G**

Type   Issue a go

Press   **RETURN**

for the description.

Press   **SHIFT-F7 Print**

Type   4 or c [Control Printer]

Type   4 or g [Go]

Press   **F7 Exit**

to return to the document.

Press   **CTRL-F10 Macro Define**

to finish the macro definition.

No more fumbling to print the next page . . . hurray!

Caution: Remember not to issue this macro until the printer has finished printing the previous page and you've inserted a new sheet of paper.

Owners of the newer keyboards will want to set up macros that prevent unnecessary finger stretching. One of my favorites, ALTC, is simple yet effective. It clears the screen without saving the current document:

Press	**CTRL-F10 Macro Define**
Press	**ALT-C**
Type	`Clear the screen`
Press	**RETURN**
Press	**F7 Exit**
Type	n twice
Press	**CTRL-F10 Macro Define**

Stay tuned: There are more useful ALT key macros later in this chapter.

ALT-F10 Macro Key Macros

Now you'll create a simple macro to type out your name and address whenever you need it. The macro includes the hard return at the end of each line. You'll issue this macro with the ALT-F10 Macro key. Give it any name you like, for instance, your initials.

Press	**CTRL-F10 Macro Define**
Type	`[your initials, or whatever you want for the macro name]`
Press	**RETURN**
Type	`My name`
Press	**RETURN**
Type	`[your first name]`
Press	**RETURN**
Type	`[your street address]`

Press   **RETURN**

Type   [your city, state, and zip code]

Press   **RETURN**

Press   **CTRL-F10 Macro Define**

Now, run the macro:

Press   **ALT-F10 Macro**

WordPerfect says:

Macro:

It's waiting for the macro name.

Type   [the macro name]

   Note: You don't have to type the .WPM extension. Just type the first part of the file name. For instance, I set up this macro as VA.WPM, so all I have to type is **va**.

Press   **RETURN**

   It's like magic! Your name and address appear. If you type the macro name incorrectly, use the BACKSPACE key to correct your mistake before you press RETURN. If *you* want to cancel the macro, press F1 Cancel before you finish issuing the Macro command.

   Tip: It's possible to set up ALT-F10 Macro key macros with *one-letter* names, such as N for "name and address." WordPerfect stores the macro as N.WPM and no longer considers these macros as temporary. To run a single-letter macro, press **ALT-F10**, type the letter, and press **RETURN**. You can thus have two macros associated with each key, for instance, ALTN.WPM and N.WPM. Press ALT-N to issue the former.
   By the way, if you try to issue an incorrect macro name or a macro that doesn't exist, WordPerfect tells you it can't find the macro file:

ERROR: File not found -- <file>.WPM

where <file> is the name you typed.

Editing a Macro

Say something went wrong and your macro doesn't work as you anticipated. There are three ways to go: (1) redefine the entire macro, (2) edit the macro with WordPerfect's *macro editor,* or (3) edit the macro with the Macro Editor in the WordPerfect Library. I'll discuss only the first two options here.

Tip: If the macro is short, it makes most sense just to redefine it.

For the time being, however, learn how to edit an existing macro. Suppose you want that ALTP macro to print the current page rather than the entire document.

Press   **CTRL-F10 Macro Define**

Press   **ALT-P**

WordPerfect tells you:

`ALTP.WPM is Already Defined.  1 Replace; 2 Edit: 0`

Type   **2 or e** [Edit]

WordPerfect presents the macro: edit screen, as shown in Figure 7-1. Notice the Description and Action sections. The Action box shows all the keystrokes in the macro. For each function key command in a macro, WordPerfect supplies a *command tag* in braces. The command tags are all self-explanatory, such as {Print} for SHIFT-F7 Print or {Format} for SHIFT-F8 Format. A list of all command tags is in Appendix D. WordPerfect stores macro command tags and other information for the macro editor in a file called WP.MRS. The WordPerfect Library's Macro Editor also uses this file to identify WordPerfect commands.

To add new function key commands to a macro, just press the command as you would normally. For example, to insert the {Screen} command tag, press CTRL-F3 Screen. The *exceptions,* discussed below, are for the ESC, F1 Cancel, and F7 Exit commands, as well as for all cursor movement, insertion, and deletion commands. That's because these commands function in their normal editing capacity when you edit macros, too. You must, therefore, tell WordPerfect when you want to insert them as commands in a macro definition.

A Simple Example

In this first example, all you want to do is to change the 1 or f for full document to a 2 or p for page, but you should also change the description. So:

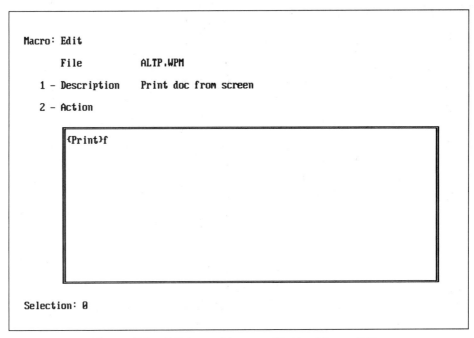

```
Macro: Edit

        File            ALTP.WPM

   1 - Description      Print doc from screen

   2 - Action

        ┌──────────────────────────────────────────────────┐
        │{Print}f                                          │
        │                                                  │
        │                                                  │
        │                                                  │
        │                                                  │
        │                                                  │
        │                                                  │
        │                                                  │
        └──────────────────────────────────────────────────┘

   Selection: 0
```

Figure 7-1   Editing a Macro with the Macro Editor

Type   **1** or **d** [Description]

WordPerfect positions the cursor at the beginning of the description. In the macro editor you can use the standard deletion and cursor movement commands, including the scrolling commands if the entire macro definition doesn't appear in the action box.

✔Use the **RIGHT ARROW** key to position the cursor under the *d* of *doc*. Delete this word, then type **page** instead. Make sure the spacing between words is correct. To exit the description line, press **F7 Exit** or **RETURN**. Now for the action:

Type   **2** or **a** [Action]

✔Press **RIGHT ARROW** to position the cursor under the **1** or **f**. Delete this character and type **2** or **p** instead. Press **F7 Exit** to leave the action box.

Caution: Don't press RETURN while the cursor is in the action box, because then you'll insert a hard return into the macro definition.

To save the edited macro:

Press   **F7 Exit** or **RETURN**

Inserting Editing Commands

The ESC or F1 Cancel keys will let you escape out of the macro or restore a deleted command tag or character. WordPerfect will ask you to confirm the cancelation if you've made any changes to the Action box:

```
Cancel changes? (Y/N) No
```

The F7 Exit key exits macro editing and saves the edit. The various cursor movement, insertion, and deletion keys let you edit the macro. That is, these editing commands function as normal.

To insert the commands as actual commands in a macro definition, you must use a different approach. What you do is simply press **CTRL-V** *immediately before* you issue the command.

The special command CTRL-V tells WordPerfect to treat the next command—and *only* the next command—as a command tag. You must repeat the CTRL-V for every ESC, F1 Cancel, F7 Exit, insertion, deletion, or cursor movement command that you want to include in the macro. (Actually, CTRL-V tells WordPerfect to accept the next command or character *literally*. Later you'll investigate other uses for this command.) To learn a couple important macro editing techniques, follow these examples:

✔Using the basic steps for redefining a macro, edit the ALTC macro that you created previously. The screen should look like Figure 7-2. Now, follow these steps:

Type   **2 or a** [Action]

Press   **DEL**

to delete the {Exit} tag.

Oops! You didn't want to delete that!

Press   **F1 Cancel**

to restore the tag and leave the action box.

Type   **2 or a** [Action]

Press   **DEL**

to delete the {Exit} tag again.

This time, learn how to insert an editing command into a macro definition:

Press   **CTRL-V**

```
Macro: Edit

        File          ALTC.WPM

   1 - Description    Clear the screen

   2 - Action

   ┌──────────────────────────────────────────────────────────┐
   │ {Exit}nn                                                   │
   │                                                            │
   │                                                            │
   │                                                            │
   │                                                            │
   │                                                            │
   │                                                            │
   └──────────────────────────────────────────────────────────┘

   Selection: 0
```

Figure 7-2   Editing Another Macro

Nothing seems to happen, but now do this:

Press   **F7 Exit**

to insert an {Exit} tag.
  The macro definition should look exactly as it did when you started.

Press   **F1 Cancel**

Type   y

to cancel macro editing.

  Tip: If you're editing a macro and you can't seem to insert a command correctly in the macro definition, press CTRL-V first. That should do the trick. You can also press CTRL-F10 Macro Define *while in the Action box* to toggle to command tag mode. WordPerfect tells you:

Press Macro Define to enable editing

  Now, *every* key you press (except CTRL-F10 Macro Define) inserts a command tag. Be careful! You have to toggle out of this mode with another press of CTRL-F10 Macro Define if you just want to move the cursor and edit the actions. I like the CTRL-V approach better!
  Chapter 32 continues the discussion of macro editing, but for the time being you now know the basics. As I mentioned, you could just use the **1** [Replace] option to replace a macro definition with new steps. That way, you avoid having to use the macro editor altogether. Be careful that you don't overwrite a macro you really want to keep.

Creating a Macro with the Macro Editor

As you know, when you define a new macro, you just issue all the commands and characters you want in the macro. The only way to bring up the macro editor is to edit an existing macro. However, suppose you *like* the macro editor and want to create your macros with it. That way, you can leisurely watch as you build a macro definition.

What you must do is first define a new macro that does *nothing* and then edit it. Here are the steps that you'd take (you don't have to follow them now):

1. Press **CTRL-F10 Macro Define** to begin the definition.
2. Supply the new macro name.
3. Press **RETURN** to bypass the description.
4. Press **CTRL-F10 Macro Define** again to end the definition.
5. Repeat steps 1 and 2.
6. Type **2** or **e** [Edit] to bring up the blank macro in the macro editor. Continue editing as normal.

Deleting a Macro

To delete a macro completely, simply delete the macro file from the disk. Recall that each macro file has the extension .WPM. I'll show you a fast way to do that in Chapter 9.

A RETURN Key Macro

You can also create a macro assigned to just the RETURN key. WordPerfect saves this macro to a file called WP{WP}.WPM, so the macro is no longer temporary as in previous versions. However, you can't edit this macro; you can only redefine it.

To assign a macro to the RETURN key, after you press **CTRL-F10 Macro Define**, press **RETURN**. WordPerfect bypasses the description altogether. After you define the macro, whenever you want to run it, press **ALT-F10 Macro**, and then press **RETURN**.

Where Are the Macro Files?

WordPerfect looks for and saves macro files in the drive or directory where the WordPerfect program resides. Even if you change directories (Chapter 9), WordPerfect still uses the program location for macros. If you wish, you can tell WordPerfect to find its macro files on another drive or in another directory. That's one of the setup options (Appendix A).

Tip: Use this feature if you want to isolate all macros in a special directory or if you want to set up different macros with the same names for different editing situations.

Forcing Insert or Typeover Mode On

When you press the INS key, you toggle from insert mode to typeover mode. So, using INS in a macro just reverses the *current* insert or typeover status. You may need to ensure that either insert or typeover mode is on regardless of the current setting. In that case, use **HOME,INS** to force typeover mode on, or **HOME,HOME,INS** to force insert mode on.

Tip: Make sure you force the correct insert or typeover mode back at the end of the macro.

Other Useful Macros

You're probably eager to set up your own macros now, but here are a few that I find useful. The first is a true line delete, ALTL. The second, which I've named ALTS, saves whatever document you're working on without clearing the screen, so you can continue editing. The third, ALTX for exit, it a variation of ALTC. It uses the F7 Exit command to save the current document and clear the screen.

Note: You must have a document on the screen for these macros to work properly, and the document must have been saved to disk at least once.

The next macro, ALTR, displays the tab ruler line; the macro ALTI inserts italics codes into a document; the last, ALTT, transposes the word at the cursor with the next word. It, too, requires a document on the screen.

✔Retrieve any document, such as NEWS or MEMO.1. Position the cursor on any line of text in any paragraph.

A Macro to Delete an Entire Line

The line delete macro, ALTL, deletes not only to the end of the line, but also the hard or soft return at the end. It's a substitute for the lack of a true line delete in WordPerfect, and it works with the cursor anywhere on the line. Here are the keystrokes for creating this macro:

Press	**CTRL-F10 Macro Define**
Press	**ALT-L**
Type	`Line delete`
Press	**RETURN**
Press	**HOME,HOME,LEFT ARROW**
Press	**CTRL-END**
Press	**DEL**
Press	**CTRL-F10 Macro Define**

Because you've deleted text that you really want to keep, you must now restore the deletion. Do this before you continue!

Press	**F1 Cancel**
Type	`1` or `r` [Restore]

Question: Why did I include the **HOME,HOME,LEFT ARROW** command? *Answer:* That command ensures that the cursor is at the left margin before the macro deletes the entire line. Notice, however, that the macro doesn't move the cursor in front of any codes on the line, because you may *not* want to delete the codes!

A Macro to Save the Current Document

Leave the document on the screen as you define the next macro, ALTS, to save a document quickly. However, make sure the document is complete before you start.

Press	**CTRL-F10 Macro Define**
Press	**ALT-S**
Type	`Save document/continue editing`
Press	**RETURN**

Press   **F10 Save**

Press   **RETURN**

Type   y

Press   **CTRL-F10 Macro Define**

The reason you need a document on the screen is that the macro then will request that you confirm the overwrite of the existing document.

A Macro to Save a Document and Clear the Screen

And now for the ALTX macro that saves the current document and clears the screen.

Press   **CTRL-F10 Macro Define**

Press   **ALT-X**

Type   `Save document/clear the screen`

Press   **RETURN**

Press   **F7 Exit**

Press   **RETURN** twice

Type   y

Press   **RETURN**

Press   **CTRL-F10 Macro Define**

Tip: You can also set up a macro that saves the document and exits WordPerfect altogether. Even though you don't officially end the macro— because you've exited WordPerfect—the macro would still work. The macro's steps are the same as ALTX, except the second to last line. Instead of pressing RETURN, type y.

A Macro to Display the Tab Ruler

You've probably figured out the ALTR macro, but here it is anyway. The macro will work with any monitor.

Press	**CTRL-F10 Macro Define**
Press	**ALT-R**
Type	`Display tab ruler`
Press	**RETURN**
Press	**CTRL-F3 Screen**
Type	`1 or w` [Window]
Press	**UP ARROW**
Press	**RETURN**
Press	**CTRL-F10 Macro Define**

If you wish, try your hand at a macro that removes the tab ruler from the screen.

A Macro to Insert Italic Codes

If you're like me, you'll want a lot of macros that avoid the seemingly endless levels of menus in WordPerfect. Here's one that lets you insert italics codes without "menu madness":

Press	**CTRL-F10 Macro Define**
Press	**ALT-I**
Type	`Italics`
Press	**RETURN**
Press	**CTRL-F8 Font**
Type	`2 or a` [Appearance]
Type	`4 or i` [Italc]
Press	**CTRL-F10 Macro Define**

Make sure you delete the italic codes now. By the way, this macro will work with text that you'll now type or with a marked block. Neat!

A Macro to Transpose Words

Now for the macro to transpose words, ALTT. This macro transposes the first word with the next. First, position the cursor on any word in any line. Then:

Press   **CTRL-F10 Macro Define**

Press   **ALT-T**

Type   Transpose

Press   **RETURN**

Press   **CTRL-BACKSPACE**

Press   **CTRL-RIGHT ARROW**

Press   **F1 Cancel**

Type   1 or r [Restore]

Press   **CTRL-F10 Macro Define**

I'll let you figure out for yourself just how this macro works! Throughout this book, I'll mention other useful macros as examples of this powerful WordPerfect feature. As further practice, why not create macros to block out a sentence, a paragraph, and a page? When you're feeling comfortable with basic macros, refer to Chapter 32 for a discussion of more advanced macro concepts. At this stage, however, you can still use simple macros to cut down on a lot of keystroking.

Repeating a Macro

What if you have to type the following address lines over and over? Boring!

Name_____Date_____

Why not have a macro do it for you? Instead of issuing the macro just once, you can repeat the macro as many times as you need. This example shows two good uses of the ESC key. First, when you define this macro, use the ESC key to draw the lines. Then use it to repeat the macro. Call the macro LI for lines.

Press   **CTRL-F10 Macro Define**

Type   li

Press   **RETURN**

Type   Name and date line

Press   **RETURN**

Type   Name

Press   **ESC**

Type   40

Type   _

(That's **SHIFT-HYPHEN.**)

Type   Date

Press   **ESC**

Type   15

Type   _

Press   **RETURN** twice

for spacing between lines.

Press   **CTRL-F10 Macro Define**

    ✔Clear the screen now.
    If you want, say, ten name and date lines, do this:

Press   **ESC**

Type   10

Press   **ALT-F10 Macro**

Type   li

Press   **RETURN**

You can also have a repeating macro that keeps calling itself or another macro (Chapter 32).

✔ Clear the screen again.

One Final Example

It turns out that you work for the Department of Biofeedback of the University of Northwestern California. It's bad enough having to work at all, but at least you can cut down the keystroking. Assume you're typing the following text (you don't have to if you don't want to):

```
Thank you for your recent letter of application for the
position available in the Department of Biofeedback of the
University of Northwestern California.  We have carefully
reviewed your credentials and have concluded that the Department
cannot utilize your services at the present time.

Although your background is definitely in line with the
Department's current hiring plans, we call your attention to the
job description originally published by the Department, which
clearly stated that the Ph.D. degree in-hand is a requirement for
the position.

We would like to keep your resume on file should another
position more in line with your present qualifications become
available in the Department of Biofeedback.
```

Why not set up three macros, one to type *Department,* one to type *Department of Biofeedback,* and one to type *University of Northwestern California?* How would you do them?

Hint: Add the space after each word or phrase, so you don't have to type that either. Note that this won't work in all cases, for instance, *Department's* in the second paragraph. But you can easily backspace, and it's much better than all that boring typing.

WordPerfect has many features that can save you time and work. The trick is to learn how to use these features for your own needs. Macros are perhaps your hardest working friends. Get to know them!

8

Searching and Replacing

In this chapter you'll learn the following new commands . . .

Function Key Commands

F2 ▶Search	Forward search
ALT-F2 Replace	Search and replace
SHIFT-F2 ◀Search	Backward search

Typewriter Keyboard and Numeric Keypad Command

CTRL-V,CTRL-X	Search for pattern matches in the middle or at the end of a string

. . . and you'll discover other uses for these commands:

CTRL-HOME,CTRL-HOME	Return the cursor to the last search location ("major motion")
DOWN ARROW	Indicate a forward search or replace
UP ARROW	Indicate a backward search or replace

Continuing in your exploration of important work and time savers, you'll learn how to search for words and even replace one word with another. Like macros, Search and Replace are helpful friends indeed. Professional word processors couldn't live without them. Neither should you!

DO WARM-UP

Finding Text with the Search Command

WordPerfect lets you find text *and* codes both forward and backward through the document with the **F2 ▶Search** and **SHIFT-F2 ◀Search** keys, respectively. The Search operation starts from the *cursor location* and proceeds in the direction you specify. Search works only in the document on the screen, but you'll eventually learn how to search through all the documents on the disk, too (Chapter 9).

Technically, the Search commands can find any *string* of text, codes, or what have you. As its name implies, a string is a series of characters and codes "strung together," that is, connected to each other. A word is a string, as is a code attached to a phrase, which in turn is a string of words and spaces. Although *you* see your documents neatly arranged in lines and pages on the screen, your computer (and, hence, WordPerfect) sees documents as one continual string of text and formatting codes.

Normally you'd use the Search command in long documents to find a specific reference when you don't remember the exact page on which the reference occurs. Because you haven't created any long documents, however, use a little imagination in the next examples.

🖙Clear the screen and retrieve the NEWS document.

Simple Searching

You want to check the number of times you use the word *Consolidated* in this document. Begin the search:

Press   **F2 ▶Search**

WordPerfect says:

```
-> Srch:
```

Type   **consolidated**

Stop! Don't press RETURN, because then you'd include an [HRt] code in the search. Type the search word in lowercase, because then WordPerfect will match the word, no matter what its case. Now that you've told WordPerfect what to look for, start the search:

Press   **F2 ▶Search**

WordPerfect stops at the first occurrence of the word. To continue the search:

Press   **F2 ▶Search**

WordPerfect "remembers" the last text you looked for during this session, so all you need do is:

Press   **F2 ▶Search**

 Tip: To avoid unnecessary retyping, you can *edit* the search string just as you can edit a file name. That is, use the ARROW keys to position the cursor and make your changes. Other keys that work here are CTRL-END, DEL, and BACKSPACE.

Continue searching for *consolidated*. Eventually WordPerfect won't find any more occurrences of the text and tells you:

```
* Not Found *
```

WordPerfect continues a search until it finds the word, until it reaches the end of the document, or until you press F1 Cancel to stop.

Other Case Matching

When you type the string you're looking for in lowercase letters, WordPerfect will look for all occurrences of the string, no matter what the case. In the previous example, WordPerfect would find *Consolidated*, *consolidated*, or *CONSOLIDATED*. You can also type the entire string in uppercase if you're looking for occurrences of the string in uppercase *only*. There's no way to look for just lowercase occurrences, though.

Searching Backward

Assume that you want to find the occurrences of the name *Glatzkopf*, but you want to search backward. To see how this feature works, press **HOME,HOME,DOWN ARROW** to position the cursor at the end of the document. Then:

Press   **SHIFT-F2 ◀Search**

WordPerfect still remembers the last search text and presents this message, but notice that the arrow is now reversed:

```
<- Srch: consolidated
```

You must edit or type over the last search word, if there is one.

Tip: You don't have to type the whole word if it's unique and only a few letters will do. As soon as you begin to type, WordPerfect removes the former search text from the message:

Type   glatz

Press   F2 ▶Search

Even though you're searching backward, you can still use the F2 ▶Search key to begin the search. You can also press SHIFT-F2 ◀Search, but that's one more keystroke. To repeat the backward search, however, you must still initiate the search with SHIFT-F2 ◀Search. Try it!

Tip: You can *reverse* a search once you've started it. Press **UP ARROW** to change a forward search to a backward search, or **DOWN ARROW** to change a backward search to a forward search.

Unexpected Results

Sometimes you'll look for text that you *know* is in the document somewhere, but WordPerfect won't be able to find it. That's probably because the cursor is presently *past* the text and you're searching forward, or vice versa. So, a good rule of thumb for working with the Search command is to go either to the beginning or the end of the document before you start searching. Another unexpected result is when you're searching for text that may be contained in other words. Here's an example. First, go to the beginning of the document with HOME,HOME,UP ARROW. Then:

Press   F2 ▶Search

Type   is

Press   F2 ▶Search

WordPerfect stops at *Issue*. If you continue the search, it stops at words such as *is* and *this*, too. How can you get around this aggravation? Enclose the word in *spaces* after you start the search. That is, instead of typing **is** alone, press the **SPACEBAR**, type **is**, and press the **SPACEBAR** again. WordPerfect then searches only for *is* as a whole word, which as a word has spaces separating it from other words.

As another example, if you want to find *her*, keep in mind that WordPerfect would stop at words such as t*her*e, too.

Note: When you enclose a whole word in spaces, WordPerfect won't find the word if it's followed by a punctuation mark. Be careful!

One other problem that people have when they use the Search command is not being accurate enough. If you type an incorrect word, how can you expect WordPerfect to know what you want? So always be careful about (1) knowing the present cursor position and (2) typing the search string exactly. As usual, you can cancel a search or replace operation with the F1 Cancel key.

Searching for Pattern Matches

You just learned that you don't have to type the whole word in if you're sure that only a few letters are unique enough for WordPerfect to find the word. Sometimes you might want to search for *word patterns*. For example, say you want to find words that begin with *t* and end with *p—tap, tip, top,* and so forth. Use the character matching feature, CTRL-V,CTRL-X. There are two ways to use this feature:

1. You can match *one* character within a string. For example, after you begin a search, type **t**. Then press **CTRL-V**. WordPerfect prompts:

   `Key:`

   Recall from Chapter 7 that the CTRL-V command tells WordPerfect to accept the next key literally. Here, you want the special pattern matching command, so press **CTRL-X**. WordPerfect displays an ^X in the search string. Finally, type **p**. This is what you see on the screen:

   `-> Srch: t^Xp`

   Continue the search as normal.

2. You can also match *all* characters at the *end* of the string. That is, use CTRL-V,CTRL-X as the last character in the search string. For example, `top^X` would match words like *tops, topiary,* and *topology.*

Note: The pattern match feature matches text only, not codes. Use one CTRL-V,CTRL-X for each character within a string, but don't use it as the first character in the search, because it then matches *all* words.

Searching for Codes

Now that you know about format changes and some special printing effects, you should be aware that you can search for their respective codes. This can be a great time saver when you're trying to locate codes that may not be where you thought you originally put them.

Tip: You might want to search for codes with the codes revealed.

✔Position the cursor at the beginning of the document. Then:

Press   **F2 ▶Search**

Press   **SHIFT-F6 Center**

WordPerfect supplies the name of the code: [Cntr]. If there are begin and end codes, you'll see the begin code. See also the next section.

Press   **F2 ▶Search**

to begin the search.

When there are two codes, as for centering, WordPerfect positions the cursor at the begin code, no matter whether you're searching forward or backward. If you repeat the search, WordPerfect goes to the *next* pair of codes.

What happens if you press **F2 ▶Search** and then press the **SHIFT-F8 Format** key? Try it! What happened? WordPerfect first prompts for the *general* format codes you're looking for:

1 Line; 2 Page; 3 Other: 0

You'd then type the general code, such as **1** or ι [Line]. WordPerfect then brings up the line formatting codes, some of which you don't know yet:

1 Hyphen; 2 HZone; 3 /; 4 Justification; 5 Line; 6 Margins; 7 Tab Set; 8 W/0: 0

Depending on the code you now choose, WordPerfect may present yet *another* menu. For example, if you type **5** or ι [Line], you will see this:

1 Line Height; 2 Line Numbering; 3 Line Spacing: 0

Menu madness again! If you often search for the same codes, set up the search in a macro. There are some commands that don't insert codes in a document, so it makes no sense to press these keys during a search. Try searching for the **F7 Exit** key to see what I mean.

Searching for Begin and End Font Codes

As you know, WordPerfect distinguishes between begin and end font codes. You can search for begin or end codes, too. This can be useful when you have to replace the codes separately with other font change codes. For example, you may need to replace underline codes with italics codes for your laser printer.

WordPerfect used to be able to replace begin and end codes with the normal Replace command (discussed next). Now, you'd have to set up a macro and use the ESC key to repeat the macro many times (use a ridiculously high repetition number). You can also create a macro that calls itself (Chapter 32). The macro searches for the underline codes and along the way blocks the text and puts the block in italics. It then deletes the underline codes.

The basic macro, UTOI.WPM, should contain these keystrokes after you've pressed CTR-F10 Define Macro and entered a description: (1) HOME,HOME,UP ARROW to position the cursor to the beginning of the document; (2) F2 ◆Search to start the search; F8 Underline to search for the next [UND] code; (3) F2 ◆Search to start the search; (4) ALT-F4 Block or F12 Block to begin the block; (5) F2 ◆Search to start another search and extend the block; (6) F8 Underline *twice* to search for the next begin and end [UND] [und] codes; (7) LEFT ARROW to position the cursor under the begin code on the edit line; (8) BACKSPACE to delete the begin code but leave the end code; (9) F2 ◆Search to continue the search and thus extend the block to the end underline code; (10) CTRL-F8 Font, 2 or a [Appearance] and 4 or i [Italc] to surround the block with italic codes; (11) LEFT ARROW to position the cursor under the ending [und] code; (12) BACKSPACE and y to delete the underline codes. Whew!

Notice in the macro that for each press of a font key, WordPerfect inserts a begin or end code. That is, press the key once to insert a begin code. Press the key again to insert an end code. To create a macro that repeats itself, you'd add as the last instructions: ALT-F9 Macro, utoi, and RETURN. This was just a taste of things to come!

Search in Block Mode

When a block is on, the Search command lets you extend the block to the next occurrence of the search string. This may be a convenient way to find the end of the block quickly. Make sure you turn on the block before you search in this fashion.

The Replace Command

A sibling to the search feature is the Replace command, ALT-F2 Replace. This command searches for text and replaces it with new text.

Forward Replace

There are many uses for the Replace command; here's one. It turns out that Jane R. Pomegranate is really Janice R. Pomegranate, so you want to replace the incorrect name with the correct one.

🖝Position the cursor at the beginning of the document. Then:

Press   **ALT-F2 Replace**

WordPerfect first asks:

w/Confirm? (Y/N) No

If you type **n** or merely press **RETURN**, WordPerfect won't stop and ask you to confirm the replace operation. When you type **y**, WordPerfect stops at each occurrence of the text and asks you for confirmation before replacing it. Better be on the safe side this first time:

Type   y

WordPerfect asks for the text to search for.

Type   jane

Caution: Don't press RETURN here unless you want to include a hard return code in the search string. A neat trick! WordPerfect *is* case-sensitive when it replaces text, so you can still type it in lowercase letters. When WordPerfect finds *Jane*, it automatically replaces it with *Janice* (using an initial cap).

Press   **F2 ▶Search**

to identify the search string.
WordPerfect then prompts:

Replace with:

Type   janice

Press   **F2 ▶Search**

to begin.
WordPerfect finds the first *Jane* and asks:

Confirm? (Y/N) No

Type   y

Backward Replace

WordPerfect "assumes" that you want to search and replace *forward* through a document, but you can replace backward, too. Here are the steps you'd take (you don't have to do them right now):

1. Press **ALT-F2 Replace** and determine the confirm option.

2. Just before you type the search string, press **UP ARROW** to replace backward. Notice that the search arrow on the status line has reversed its direction: <-Srch:.

3. Type the search string and continue the replace as normal.

If you decide you don't want to replace backward after you press UP ARROW, immediately press DOWN ARROW to reverse the replace again.

Block Replace

You can replace text or codes in a block, and you don't have to determine the direction even if the cursor is positioned at the end of the block. Just set up the block and make sure it's on before you start a replace.

Tip: If you know that what you're replacing is confined within a specific block of text in a long document, use the block replace feature to save time.

Positioning the Cursor Where You Left Off

If you're working on a long document, you may want to return to the spot where you began a search or replace. Recall that WordPerfect considers a block operation a major motion. A search or replace is also a major motion. You can quickly return to the starting location of a search or replace by pressing **CTRL-HOME,CTRL-HOME**. Try it!

✔Save the edited version of NEWS, if you wish. Then clear the screen.

Searching and Deleting Codes the Easy Way

Here's a useful application of the Replace command. You can have WordPerfect search for text or codes and delete them automatically. What you're doing is searching for something—be it codes or text—and replacing the search string with *nothing*.

✔Retrieve the MEMO.1 file now.

You want to delete all underline and boldface codes from this document. The cursor should be at the beginning of the document.

Press   **ALT-F2 Replace**

Type   n

or press **RETURN** so WordPerfect skips the confirmation.

Press   **F8 Underline**

Press   **F2 ▶Search**

Now, to delete the codes, when WordPerfect prompts you for the replacement string:

Press   **F2 ▶Search**

Well, I'll be darned! All the underline codes are gone. Try your hand at deleting the boldface codes but make sure you first go back to the beginning of the document. Then use the ALT-F2 Replace command to find some text and delete it, too.

    ✔When you're finished, clear the screen *without* saving the document, because you do want to keep the original codes.

Here's a macro that I've named UN that positions the cursor at the beginning of the document, finds all underlining codes and deletes them, and then returns the cursor to the beginning of the document:

Press   **CTRL-F10 Macro Define**

Type   un

Press   **RETURN**

Type   Delete underlines

Press   **RETURN**

Press   **HOME,HOME,UP ARROW**

Press   **ALT-F2 Replace**

Type   n

Press   **F8 Underline**

Press   **F2 ▶Search**

Press   **F2 ▶Search**

Press   **HOME,HOME,UP ARROW**

Press   **CTRL-F10 Macro Define**

To run this macro on a document, press **ALT-F10 Macro**, then type un and press **RETURN**.

Other Practical Applications

When I was writing this book, I didn't know exactly how I was going to arrange the chapters. So I typed two question marks (??) for the chapter references. When the chapter numbers became final, I went back and plugged them in where necessary by merely searching for the ??.

You can thus choose an unusual character from the keyboard and use it as a *place marker* in the document to help you locate text for reference. For example, I never use the @ sign for anything but as a place marker. But if you can't spare a special character, then make one up. Use a combination of letters that you couldn't possibly use for anything else, such as @!, or whatever. Make sure you search and delete the place markers when you're finished with them.

Here's another example. You are typing in a long mailing list that contains names and addresses of people who live for the most part in one or two cities. Suppose that you prefer not to set up a macro. You could instead use a special character and the correct spacing and then later have WordPerfect plug in the entire city names later.

For instance, you might use the % sign for *Rochester, NY* and the ^ for *Syracuse, NY.* You might also consider the two spaces that normally follow the state and precede the ZIP code, which would presumably change for many of the city listings. Two of your entries would then look something like this: %14604 and ^13222.

When you use the Replace command to do the dirty work, make sure that you do code in the two spaces. You would instruct WordPerfect to search for % and replace this with *Rochester, NY_* (the underscore means two spaces here). Similarly, you would have WordPerfect search for ^ and replace this with *Syracuse, NY_.*

Now for a literary diversion. Here is a very brief excerpt from your latest novel (again, you don't have to type this example if you don't want to).

CHAPTER ONE

```
    Flo sat dejectedly at her window, staring without seeing at
the view of Abilene below.  What did it all mean?  Where was she
going?  Who could she turn to?
    She saw the truck coming up the driveway.  "Abilene Cleaners
and Launderers," it proudly proclaimed on its side.  What did he
want with her now?
    She thought perhaps she could pretend that no one was home,
but George saw her dash from the window.  He certainly won't take
no for an answer, she thought.
    "Howdy, Flo, how's tricks?  I was in the neighborhood and
thought I might just stop by a minute."
    "That's mighty kind of you, George, but I don't have any
```

```
cleaning today."
     "Aw, Flo, you know that's not why I came over.  Gee whiz,
can't we ever just be alone together, just you and me?  I've been
thinking about you all week, Flo.  Abilene would be a desert
without you.  Oh, Flo, do you really have to leave?"
     "I think Abilene will get used to my leaving very well,
George.  And as far as it matters to you, well, we've hashed this
over too many times already.  Why can't you get it into your
thick skull ..."
```

You get the picture. Then, after hours, weeks, months, perhaps years of work, your first novel is finished. A prestigious publisher is beating down your door, and the movie rights will net you at least seven figures. You can bask in the glory for years to come and think of the spinoffs: t-shirts, cookies, chewing gum, maybe even a sit-com.

But then that publisher throws a wrench in the works: The leading lady's name should be changed from Flo to Samantha, and her erstwhile boy friend should be Joe instead of George. What is more, the story *has* to take place in Albuquerque instead of Abilene. Is it back to the typewriter, or perhaps to your analyst?

Neither! Just have WordPerfect search for all those nasty words and replace them with the new ones. You're happy, your family is happy, your publisher is happy, and your agent is happy. This is a silly example, but don't think it doesn't happen all the time!

Another practical application of the Replace command with confirm set to yes is as a pseudostyle checker. That is, see how often you have used a word and then change only certain occurrences of this word. Every lawyer in the country should read this section, because lawyers are by far one of the worst (but not the only) offenders when it comes to repetitiousness! Here is what I mean:

```
     Accordingly, we hope to have shown that the case before this
Court is utterly without merit and should be dismissed in its
entirety.  We accordingly ask that the following judgments be
made:
     1.    That Plaintiff Consolidated Toupee be released of all
           pecuniary obligations to Defendant J.Q. Suds.
     2.    That Defendant J.Q. Suds be charged for all Court and
           attorneys' fees in this case.
     3.    And, accordingly, any other judgment that the Court
           wishes to grant in favor of Plaintiff Consolidated
           Toupee.
```

Yes, this is also a silly example. But I think you get the point that sometimes we all use certain words too much. Replace some of the occurrences of the overworked word with another to vary your style.

Finally, say you're typing a long document that includes many occurrences of a name. Much to your chagrin, you discover that you have misspelled the name a zillion times. That's another job for the Replace command.

A Note on Place Markers

Although WordPerfect doesn't have a separate command to insert place markers, here's a neat trick. Use begin and end bold or underline codes as a marker. That is, at the spot where you want the place marker to go, press F6 Bold or F8 Underline *once*. Because there's no block, WordPerfect inserts the begin and end codes "back-to-back," as it were. The codes don't appear unless you reveal them. Then, to search for or replace your place marker, press F6 Bold or F8 Underline *twice* to insert the begin and end codes on the search edit line.

So there you have Search and Replace in a nutshell. There's more to these commands. When you learn about headers and footers, I'll introduce WordPerfect's *extended search* feature (Chapter 16).

Beyond the Basics

Document and File Management

In this chapter you'll learn the following new commands . . .

Function Key Commands

CTRL-F1 Shell	Go to DOS or to the WordPerfect Library
F5 List Files	(1) Display the file listing, (2) manage files, drives, and directories
ALT-F5 Mark Text	Mark or "unmark" all files in the file listing
CTRL-F5 Text In/Out	(1) Insert a document comment, (2) lock or unlock documents by adding or removing password protection

Typewriter Keyboard Commands

*	Mark or "unmark" individual files in the file listing
HOME, *	Mark or "unmark" all files in the file listing
CTRL-S	Scroll the document down on the look screen
SHIFT-TAB	Move the highlight to the previous marked file

. . . you'll discover new uses for these commands . . .

F2 ▶Search	Start a name search
SHIFT-F8 Format	Add or edit the document summary
DEL	Delete the highlighted file

more . . .

> **PG DN** and **PG UP**   Scroll quickly through the document on the look screen
>
> **TAB**   Move the highlight to the next marked file
>
> . . . and you'll learn this new code:
>
> [Comment]   Document comment

By now you've created several documents and saved them in files. The more you work with computers, the more you'll realize that files have a tendency to multiply like rabbits, so keeping track of your documents and files will become a high priority. That's what *file management*, or file maintenance, is all about. If you have a hard disk that you've divided into many directories, consider regular file management a must.

This chapter discusses the essential file maintenance operations you should master for your day-to-day activities. It's a long chapter, but you don't have to study it in one sitting.

> ### *DO WARM-UP*

File Management in a Nutshell

DOS is actually your computer's file manager. For example, DOS monitors whether file names are correct and keeps track of where files are located on the disk. When you retrieve or save a file, WordPerfect calls on DOS's assistance. Normally, to manage files you'd have to work at the DOS prompt and issue commands like DEL (delete), REN (rename), COPY, and so on.

Fortunately, WordPerfect has extensive file management features on the **F5 List Files** command that mimic DOS's and are easier to use. While DOS is notoriously taciturn (and sometimes downright *rude*), WordPerfect provides prompts and even warning messages when you're about to do something potentially dangerous, for instance, delete a file. In fact, for the most part you can manage your files quite nicely within WordPerfect.

With all its power, though, WordPerfect still can't perform certain DOS operations. Don't worry: There's a way to go out to DOS temporarily from WordPerfect. For example, if you find you need a new, formatted disk and there's none available, you can go to DOS and format one on the fly. See WordPerfect and DOS later in the chapter.

There are three important points to keep in mind about file management. First, name your files logically. Use file extensions to identify files that contain similar documents, such as .LET or .LTR for "letters" (SUDS.LTR). You can then filter out inapplicable files when you're looking for a specific document. When I was writing this book, for example, I kept each chapter in a file called CH.1, CH.2, etc. I could then do a variety of file management tasks with just these files and leave the others alone. See also Housekeeping later in the chapter.

Second, use the modular approach to keep the size of files small. Why? Because if you break your longer files into small modules, they're easier to work with. What's more, if something goes wrong to a large file, you run the risk of losing more of your efforts. In the case of a book, it's sheer madness to have the entire book in one file. I would suggest keeping file modules of no more than 20 or 25 pages or so. You can combine the chapters later, or use the *master document* feature (Chapter 25).

The third point is for hard disk users: Set up related files in different directories. Hard disks can store hundreds, if not thousands, of files. You wouldn't want all files in the same directory, would you? In fact, you've probably already divvied up your hard disk into directories, one for DOS commands, one for WordPerfect's program files (\WP50), one for the Library if you have it (\LIBRARY), and so on.

Identifying and Annotating Documents

Before you work with the F5 List Files key, learn how to identify documents or call your attention to specific sections of a document. Why? You may have several current versions of a document floating around, and there may be several people who're working on the same document. Later you'll learn how to search for documents by content or other criteria, too.

Adding a Document Summary

One way to reduce "file frustration" when you're trying to determine which file contains which document version is to use WordPerfect's *document summary* feature. WordPerfect keeps track of who created the document and on what date you added the summary, among other things. You did enter the date when you started today, didn't you? WordPerfect can only work with whatever you entered as today's date.

 ✔ Retrieve the NEWS document now.

The summary is part of the document format. You can add or change the summary from anywhere in the document. There is only one summary per document, and the summary does not print. (Version 4.2 users: It's on the CTRL-F5 Text In/Out key.)

Press   **SHIFT-F8 Format**

Type   **3** or **d** [<u>D</u>ocument]

WordPerfect presents the format: document menu (Figure 9-1). Your initial font may be different. See also Appendix A.

Type   **5** or **s** [<u>S</u>ummary]

WordPerfect presents the document summary screen, shown in Figure 9-2, and supplies the System File Name and its Date of Creation. If this were a new, unsaved file, WordPerfect would display (Not named yet) for the system file name. Genesis notwithstanding, the date of creation is misleading. It just means *today's* date, or so my experience tells me.

Before you add any descriptive information to the summary, notice that WordPerfect displays the first few text lines of the document in the Comments box as a reminder about the document's contents. (Actually, it inserts about 400 characters but attempts to end the comments at a word boundary or at the end of a sentence.)

```
Format: Document

    1 - Display Pitch - Automatic    Yes
                        Width         0.1"

    2 - Initial Codes

    3 - Initial Font                  Courier 12pt 10pitch (PC-8)

    4 - Redline Method                Printer Dependent

    5 - Summary





Selection: 0
```

Figure 9-1   The Format: Document Menu

```
Document Summary

        System Filename              C:\WP\NEWS

        Date of Creation             April 8, 1988

    1 - Descriptive Filename

    2 - Subject/Account

    3 - Author

    4 - Typist

    5 - Comments
   ┌────────────────────────────────────────────────────────────────┐
   │ "Permanent Wave" August Issue ;  The most important news of the month is │
   │ the company picnic. That's right!  Consolidated Toupee is giving us a     │
   │ real, honest to goodness picnic.  After all, don't we deserve it?  So come│
   │ one, come all to Founder's Park on August 21st and join in the fun. Bring │
   │ the kids, bring your friends, bring food and drink.                       │
   └────────────────────────────────────────────────────────────────┘


Selection: 0
```

Figure 9-2   The Initial Document Summary Screen for the NEWS
Document

I won't step you through a summary editing session. I'll merely explain
the five options and show an example of a completed summary. You don't
have to fill in all the choices, by the way. Choices 1 through 4 are limited to
40 characters, while the largest comment (choice 5) can contain 780 characters.
To set an entry, press **F7 Exit** or **RETURN** for choices 1 through 4, or **F7
Exit** for choice 5.

Tip: You can use any editing command in the various entries. To cancel
an operation, press F1 Cancel or ESC.

1. Type **1** or **d** [Descriptive File Name] to enter a name that expands on
   DOS's limitations of 11 characters. For example, you could describe
   this document as August Newsletter, Draft 1.
   Note: If you haven't named the document yet and you add a descriptive file name on this line, WordPerfect "intuits" that you might
   want to use the same or similar name when you save the document.
   For example, if you type A new document for the descriptive file name,
   WordPerfect thinks you want to save the file as ANEWDOC. You'll
   see the name on the status line when you exit the summary screen.
   When you save the document for the first time, you can supply a different name if you wish.

2. Type **2** or **s** [<u>S</u>ubject/Account] to add a different subject or account designation. Later when you work with the F5 List Files key, you'll see that you can search for a file on this information.

   Note: By default, WordPerfect uses *RE:* as the subject search string. If the string *RE:* appears in the first 400 characters of the document, WordPerfect automatically inserts this string in the summary. You can provide any other subject/account string now or change the default (Appendix A).

3. Type **3** or **a** [<u>A</u>uthor] to designate the author of the document, who may be different from the typist.

4. Type **4** or **t** [<u>T</u>ypist] to designate the person who typed the document, who may in turn be different from the author.

5. Type **5** or **c** [<u>C</u>omments] to position the cursor in the comments box. Use CTRL-END to delete the default comment lines and supply new comments if you wish. WordPerfect will wrap the lines within the box. Comments can be longer than the box area: WordPerfect will scroll the display as you type. You must press **F7 Exit** to save the new comments.

   Tip: To make the text stand out, you can add underlining or boldface to any entry in the document summary. If you made a mistake, type the letter choice and correct the mistake. Figure 9-3 shows a completed summary for the NEWS document. Go ahead: Add the same summary or a similar one.

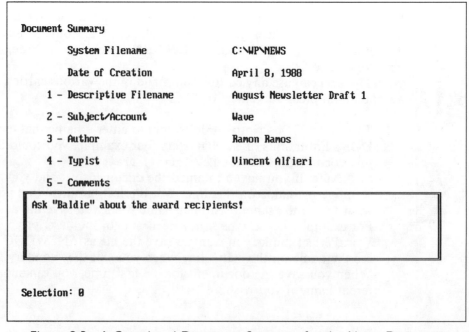

Figure 9-3   A Completed Document Summary for the News Document

174

To save the document summary:

Press   **F7 Exit** twice

Keep in mind that you must also save the document again to save the summary. You won't see the summary until you look at the file's contents from the file listing, discussed later. There is no summary code.

Tip: You can change the WordPerfect defaults so that WordPerfect always asks for a document summary when you save a *new* document for the first time (Appendix A).

Inserting Notes to Yourself

You can also insert nonprinting annotations in your document as reminders. This is the *document comment* feature. You must first position the cursor where you want the comment to appear before you enter the comment. You cannot, however, insert comments in text columns (Chapter 18) or math columns (Chapter 19).

✔Position the cursor at the left margin of the second paragraph. Then:

Press   **CTRL-F5 Text In/Out**

WordPerfect presents the text in/out menu:

1 DOS Text; 2 Password; 3 Save Generic; 4 Save WP 4.2; 5 Comment: 0

Type   **5** or **c** [Comment]

WordPerfect presents the comment menu:

Comment: 1 Create; 2 Edit; 3 Convert to Text: 0

Type   **1** or **c** [Create]

The document comment screen and a blank comment box appear.

Type   **Ask "Baldie" about the award recipient.**

As you type a long comment, WordPerfect will scroll the lines within the comment box if the comment is longer than the box. A comment can be up to 1024 characters long. Comments don't affect the true line count of the document, although the comment may appear to break up the text if you insert a comment in the middle of a line. (Editors will *love* this capability!)

Tip: Use boldface and underlining for emphasis.

Press   **F7 Exit**

to save the comment.

By default, WordPerfect displays comments on the screen as you work, but you can change the setup to hide the comments (Appendix A). However, even if you reveal the codes you won't see the text of a comment until you edit it. You'll only see the [Comment] code.

To edit a comment, position the cursor past the comment code, press **CTRL-F5 Text In/Out**, type **5** or **c** [Comment], then **2** or **e** [Edit]. Continue as normal. To search for a comment, start the search, then press **CTRL-F5 Text In/Out**.

Tip: You can move a comment by deleting its code and restoring the code somewhere else in the document.

You can also change a comment to document text or change text to a comment. This is the only way you can print a comment with the rest of the document. Here are the steps you'd take:

1. To change a comment to text, position the cursor past the comment's code, press **CTRL-F5 Text In/Out**, type **5** or **c** [Comment], then type **3** or **t** [Convert to Text]. Check the spacing and formatting of the text in relation to the text around it.

2. To change text to a comment, block out the text, but make sure you include all characters, including tabs and hard returns. Then press **CTRL-F5 Text In/Out**, and WordPerfect prompts:

```
Create a comment (Y/N)? No
```

Type **y** to create the comment.

The F5 List Files Key

As organized a you may be, eventually you'll have a lot of files on the disk, and occasionally you'll forget a file name. No problem! It's time to learn about the F5 List Files key and file management. Suppose you want to retrieve a document, but its file name has slipped your mind. With a blank screen, do this:

Press   **F5 List Files**

On the status line WordPerfect says:

```
Dir B:\*.*                          (Type = to change default Dir)
```

The actual drive or directory name may be different. The *.* means that WordPerfect is prepared to give you the directory of *all* files on the disk or in the current directory. This is a DOS wildcard about which you'll learn more later in the chapter. (The DOS equivalent of what WordPerfect is doing would be the command DIR *.*.) Here, accept WordPerfect's suggestion to display all files:

Press   **RETURN**

 Tip: You can also type a new disk designator, such as **a:**, or a new directory path, as in **\wp50\memos**, before you press RETURN to see the file listing for that disk or directory. However, you still remain on the default drive or in the default directory. See also Working with Drives or Directories if you want to switch to a different drive or directory.

The File Listing

There's the file listing. At the top, WordPerfect provides the date, time, directory name, the size of the document you're currently editing, and how much free disk space is available. The cursor has changed to a highlight that's on the current directory, shown as:

```
. <CURRENT>    <DIR>
```

The dot is another DOS convention for the current directory. You may also see the parent directory, shown as:

```
.. <PARENT>    <DIR>
```

If you're using a hard disk and you're in the \WP50 directory, the current directory is \WP50 and the parent directory is the root directory. DOS shows the root directory as \.

Notice that the files appear in alphabetical order, but from *left to right* and then from top to bottom. (To arrange the files in order of extension or date and time, you'll need the WordPerfect Library's File Manager.) At the bottom of the screen you see this menu:

```
1 Retrieve; 2 Delete; 3 Move/Rename; 4 Print; 5 Text In;
6 Look; 7 Other Directory; 8 Copy; 9 Word Search; N Name Search: 6
```

WordPerfect "assumes" you want to use the **6** [Look] choice to view the contents of a file. You'll do that later.

Note: To exit the file display and return to editing, type **0** or press **F7 Exit**, **F1 Cancel**, or the **SPACEBAR**. For the time being, stay in the file listing!

Highlighting and Retrieving a File

You probably don't have too many files yet, so it's easy to find the name you want. Just use the ARROW keys to move the highlight to the file. But if the drive or directory contains many file names, they may not all fit on the screen. A down-pointing arrow appears at the bottom of the divider line to indicate that there are more files below the screen. Use the cursor movement keys shown in Table 9-1 to see more screens. An up-pointing arrow on the divider line indicates that there are more files above the current screen.

At the bottom of the file listing you'll probably see strange file names like WP}WP{.BV1, or {WP}.BV1 in previous versions. Where did they come from? These are the temporary overflow files that WordPerfect uses to store the backup of a document or parts of a document that don't fit entirely into memory. As you learned in Chapter 2, when you exit WordPerfect, the program deletes these temporary files automatically.

✔Use the ARROW keys to move the highlight to MEMO.1

Type   **1** or **r** [Retrieve]

No more typing in file names! Just find the file and retrieve it from the file listing.

Note: If you're already working on a document and you attempt to retrieve another, WordPerfect's prompt reminds you that you'll be joining two documents:

```
Retrieve into current document? (Y/N) No
```

Table 9-1   Scrolling Keys for WordPerfect's File Listing

Key	Action
PG DN	Moves to the next screen
GRAY +	Moves to the bottom of the screen
HOME,DOWN ARROW	
PG UP	Moves to the previous screen
GRAY −	Moves to the top of the screen
HOME,UP ARROW	
HOME,HOME,UP ARROW	Moves to the beginning of the list
HOME,HOME,DOWN ARROW	Moves to the end of the list

Type   y

By the way, the **5** [Text In] choice is for DOS text files (Chapter 36).

Tip: You can also press **SHIFT-F10 Retrieve** *first*, and then press **F5 List Files** to view the file listing and choose a file to retrieve.

✔Clear the screen now. Then use the F5 List Files key to go back into the file listing.

Name Search: Selecting a File Quickly

You can also move the highlight to a specific file with the *name search* feature. Try it:

Type   n [Name Search]

Tip: You can also press **F2 ▶Search** to start a name search. The status line now says:

```
(Name Search; Enter or arrows to Exit)
```

Now, type the first letter or a few letters of the file name. For example:

Type   n

WordPerfect highlights the first file name that begins with the letter N. If there are other files that begin with N, you may have to type a second letter. For instance, if WordPerfect doesn't find NEWS, type an **e** to restrict the search further. If no file begins with the letter you type, WordPerfect positions the highlight on the file that begins with the next letter of the alphabet.

Note: You can search backwards and forwards, but you still press the F2 ▶Search key to start a name search.

Once you've found the file name you want, you must then leave the name search feature and *select* the file:

Press   **RETURN**

to select the highlighted file.

You can now do any operation you want on the file you've selected.

Using Wildcards to Restrict a File Listing

When there are a lot of files, you can restrict the file listing to only those you need. As you poker players know, a *wildcard* can substitute for any other card. DOS has wildcards, too. Use the **?** and * wildcards as *templates* to match file names. The first wildcard matches any one character, and the second matches all characters.

For example, the template MEMO.* restricts the listing to only those files with the name MEMO, no matter what the extension (MEMO.1, MEMO.XXX, and so on, but not MEMONEW). The DOS equivalent to what WordPerfect is doing would be DIR MEMO.*. The other DOS wildcard, ?, matches individual characters in file names, so the template M?M*, for instance, finds MEMO, MEMONEW, or MOMS.TOO. See your DOS manual for more information about wildcards.

There are two ways to restrict the file listing with DOS wildcards:

1. From the edit screen, press **F5 List Files**, then type the template and press **RETURN**.

2. From the file listing itself, highlight the <CURRENT> directory at the top of the screen and type **6** or **l** [Look], or press **RETURN**. Then type the template and press **RETURN**.

Once you've restricted the file listing, other file operations work on the restricted file list.

Tips: You can quickly restore all names to the list. Highlight the <CURRENT> directory and press **RETURN** twice to see all files again. From the editing screen, press **F5 List Files** *twice* to use the same file name template.

Mark: Selecting Specific Files

Say you want to work with selected files, but you can't restrict them by extension or name because the names are dissimilar. You can *mark* files. Position the highlight on each file name and press the asterisk key (*), SHIFT-8. To remove the mark next to file name, press the asterisk key again. On some computers you can press PRT SC to mark a file.

Tip: You can quickly mark all files in the current listing with the ALT-F5 Mark Text key or HOME,*. Press this key a second time to "unmark" all marked files. Or press * to unmark individual files. Keep marking only the files you need. A quick way to mark *most* files is to press **ALT-F5 Mark Text** or **HOME,*** to mark all files. Then "unmark" the files and directories you don't need, including any that may not be visible on the current screen. (An aside: This was not an official introduction to the ALT-F5 Mark Text command. That's in Chapter 23.)

Once you've marked files, you can move the highlight quickly to other marked files. Press **TAB** to move to the next marked file or **SHIFT-TAB** to move to the previous marked file. You can now perform a word search, copy, delete, or print command, all discussed later in the chapter. For instance, if you mark several files and then type **2** or **d** [Delete], WordPerfect asks:

```
Delete Marked Files? (Y/N) No
```

You would type **y** to continue the deletion. Similar messages appear when you attempt to copy or print marked files. If you type **n**, WordPerfect then performs the copy, delete, or print operation on the highlighted file only.

Look: Is This the Right Document?

If you just want to see the contents of a document without retrieving the document, use the **6** [Look] choice. As a matter of fact, it's the default because WordPerfect "assumes" that you'll use this choice most often. The idea of Look is just to let you view a document—including it's summary—quickly.

↙Make sure all files appear in the file listing. Move the highlight to the NEWS file. Then:

Press   **RETURN**

or

Type   **6** or ∟ [Look]

WordPerfect first shows the document summary if there is one and indicates that you can use the cursor keys to view more text. You must press one of the downward moving keys to view the text.

Press   **DOWN ARROW** or **PG DN**

The summary disappears, and you can now move the cursor both down and up through the document. You can't edit the document on the look screen.

Tip: Once the text appears, you can *hold down* the PG DN or PG UP key to scroll the document quickly down or up, then release the key to stop the scrolling. If you don't like to hold the keys down, press **CTRL-S** to start scrolling down, then any key to stop. You can also use the other cursor movement commands, such as HOME,HOME,DOWN ARROW to go to the end of the document.

Press   **F7 Exit** or **F1 Cancel** or **ESC**

to return to the file listing.

(An aside: There is a TYPE command in DOS that displays a file's contents, but it won't work with WordPerfect files.)

Word Search: Where Is That Document?

Sometimes you'll forget in exactly which file the document you need is located. Use the **9** [Word Search] choice from the file listing to have WordPerfect restrict the listing to only those files that contain the word or words you specify. Word search actually does much more than its name implies. You can search by date and summary information or restrict the search to only the first page of documents. Word search works on the current drive or in the current directory. Unless you instruct it otherwise, WordPerfect searches all files. If there are a lot of files, you might as well go get a cup of coffee.

Tip: Before you begin a word search, restrict the file listing with wildcards if you can. You can also mark selected files for a search.

Type   **9** or **w** [Word Search]

WordPerfect presents the word search menu:

```
Search: 1 Doc Summary; 2 First Page; 3 Entire Doc; 4 Conditions: 0
```

Most of the time you'll probably use choices **2** [First Page] or **3** [Entire Doc] to search documents.

Tip: Searching just the first page of documents is faster than searching the entire document. After you select choice 1, 2, or 3, you'll see this prompt:

```
Word pattern:
```

Type the word or word pattern and press **RETURN**. See the next section, Word Search Patterns, for more information.

Note: Once you've set up a search in this menu and you want to perform another search, you must blank out the previous search conditions from the **4** [Conditions] choice, as outlined next.

If you type **4** or **c** [Conditions], the word search menu appears (Figure 9-4). The number of files that you have will be different. If you've already performed a search, WordPerfect shows the word pattern on the correct line. Here's what the various options mean (press **RETURN** to complete an option, **F1 Cancel** to cancel):

1. Type **1** or **p** [Perform Search] only *after* you've selected any other options that you want to use. WordPerfect lists the number of files that you've restricted or marked, or the total number of files.

2. Type **2** or **u** [Undo Last Search] to return to the previous search conditions.

3. Type **3** or **r** [Reset Search Conditions] to start over or blank out any previous conditions that you've set.

4. Type **4** or **d** [File Date] to search only those files that were last created or edited on a certain date or within a range of dates. WordPerfect changes No to Yes. Press **RETURN** to move the cursor to the From line. Type the beginning date and press **RETURN**. The cursor moves to the To line. Type the ending date and press **RETURN**.

```
Word Search

   1 - Perform Search on              All 107 File(s)

   2 - Undo Last Search

   3 - Reset Search Conditions

   4 - File Date                       No
       From (MM/DD/YY):                (ALL)
       To   (MM/DD/YY):                (ALL)

               Word Pattern(s)

   5 - First Page
   6 - Entire Doc
   7 - Document Summary
       Creation Date (e.g. Nov)
       Descriptive Name
       Subject/Account
       Author
       Typist
       Comments

Selection: 1
```

Figure 9-4   The Word Search Menu

Tips: To search on just one date, enter the date on the first line, and press **RETURN** alone to see (ALL) on the second, or enter the date on both lines. You don't have to use leading zeros (6/6/88 is the same as 06/06/88), and you can leave part of the date blank. For example, 6// uses dates in June of the current year, while //90 uses dates in 1990. Another example is 6// for the beginning date and 8// for the ending date to restrict the search to June through August.

5. The next two choices are the same as their counterparts on the first word search menu. Type **5** or **f** [First Page] or **6** or **e** [Entire Document] to search for a word or word patterns either in the first page of documents or in the entire documents you've selected.

6. Type **7** or **s** [Document Summary] to supply search information for the various summary categories. Again, you don't have to enter conditions on all lines. Use the ARROW keys to move between lines. Here's where you would search for the Subject/Account string.

After you select the search conditions, type **1** or **p** [<u>P</u>erform Search] to see WordPerfect's message:

```
Searching File
```

and the file count at the bottom of the screen. You can cancel a word search by pressing F1 Cancel at any time.

If WordPerfect finds files that contain the stated conditions, WordPerfect marks those files on the file listing. You can then look at the files individually.

Tip: Once WordPerfect marks files, you can quickly unmark them all with ALT-F5 Mark Text or HOME,* to start a new word search.

Word Search Patterns

Normally, you type just the word you're looking for in response to Word-Perfect's prompt. You don't have to type the entire word if only the first few letters are enough to restrict the word search. You also don't have to use uppercase. For example, if you were searching for Mr. Pescado's name, you could type just **pesc** on the reasonable assurance that those four letters are unique enough for the search. Try to restrict the search string to less than 30 characters.

You can use the **?** wildcard to find files that match a word pattern where one letter in the word may be different. For example, you want to find all files containing the pattern *t?p*. WordPerfect may find files containing *top*, *tip*, *tap*, and so on.

Similarly, use the ***** wildcard to match one or more characters. For instance, you want to find files that contain any word beginning with *top*, so you type **top***. WordPerfect would match this template with words such as *top*, *topology*, or *Topper*.

What if you want to find all files that include *Pescado* as well as *Sturgeon*? Instead of typing just **pesc**, type **pesc;stur**. The semicolon is an *operator* that tells WordPerfect to search for files that contain both words. Assume you want to find all files containing *either* word. Use the comma operator. Type **pesc,stur**. The comma instructs WordPerfect to find files that contain one or the other word, or both words.

Tip: You can also use the ***** wildcard to search for files that contain both words. For example, if you type **eat*restaurant** as the word search, WordPerfect looks for files that have the word *eat* followed somewhere by the word *restaurant*.

If you want to find files that contain *Pescado* or *Sturgeon* and also *marketing*, use this pattern: **pesc,stur marketing**. Make sure a space separates the last two terms. The semicolon, comma, and space are known as *logical* operators, because they restrict the selection to certain choices. Be careful with the "and" operator (;). WordPerfect finds only those files that fill *both* conditions. Table 9-2 lists the operators that you can use in the word search.

Finally, you can search for a *phrase*, but you must enter the phrase in double quotes. That's because normally the space is an operator. For example, you want to search for the phrase *President Glatzkopf*, so you type `"President Glatz"`. If you need to search for a question mark, asterisk, comma, or semicolon as text, enclose the entire phrase in quotes, too. For example, to find the phrase *Dear John,* (with the comma) enter it as `"Dear John,"`.

Copying Files and Making a Quick Backup

Don't *ever* forget to *back up your work* regularly. That way, you shouldn't have a problem with full disks. "An ounce of prevention" now is certainly worth a pound of headaches later. If you only work on a few documents each day, the easiest way to back up your work is to follow this pattern. After saving your document in its file, select the file from the directory and type **8** or **c** [Copy]. WordPerfect prompts:

`Copy this file to:`

Supply a drive name with colon or a complete path name for a directory. Then press **RETURN**.

Tip: If you're copying a file to another drive or directory and you want to retain the same file name, just supply the drive name (for example, B:), or the directory path (\WP\MEMOS). You don't have to repeat the file name.

This operation mimics the DOS COPY command. If you copy a file to another file on the same drive or directory with the same name, WordPerfect requests that you confirm your decision to replace the original file with the updated version (you'll see the actual file name instead of <file> below):

Table 9-2   Word Search Operators in WordPerfect

Operator	Meaning
?	Matches one letter
*	Matches one or more letters, or one first word followed somewhere by second word
,	Either first or second
;	Both first and second
(space)	Combination of , and ;
"	Enclose a phrase

```
Replace <file> (Y/N)? No
```

This is the easiest way to do backups of individual files from within WordPerfect.

 Tip: To copy all macro files to a backup disk, restrict the file listing with the template *.WPM and mark all files before you copy.

One other message may crop up if you didn't have enough coffee today and you're still half asleep. Suppose you're making a backup copy from drive C to a floppy disk in drive B, but you forgot to put a disk in drive B or to close the door. WordPerfect gives you a stern warning:

```
Drive door may be open - Drive not ready reading drive B
1 Retry 2 Cancel and return to document 1
```

Insert a disk or close the door, then type **1** [Retry]. Choice **2** [Cancel and return to document] doesn't return to the document here. It just returns to the file listing.

A Reminder About Disk Space

Use the F5 List Files key regularly to check the amount of available disk space at the top of the file listing. If you're working on a large document, check its size *before* you retrieve it and make sure you have enough space to save a changed version. Otherwise, WordPerfect will honor you with this message:

```
ERROR: Disk Full--Strike any key to continue
```

In this case you can insert another disk that has enough room and save the document there, or delete some unnecessary files (discussed next). What if you don't have a formatted disk ready? See WordPerfect and DOS later in the chapter for a way out of this dilemma.

Deleting, Moving, and Renaming Files

You can choose a file name from the directory listing and either delete the file or give it another name with the **2** [Delete] and **3** [Move/Rename] choices, respectively. These operations mimic the DOS DEL (or ERASE) and REN (or RENAME) commands, although DOS has no special command just to move a file (you'd have to copy the file to another drive or directory, then delete the original). WordPerfect *can* move a file!

To delete a file, highlight it and type **2** or **d** [Delete].

 Tip: You can also highlight a file and press **DEL**. Be careful when you delete files, however: You can't *undelete* a file within WordPerfect once you've deleted it. (There *is* a way to undelete files using another program. See Chapter 36.) In fact, WordPerfect always asks you to type **y** to confirm what you're doing:

```
Delete <file> (Y/N)? No
```

To delete a *macro*, position the highlight on its file name (with the .WPM extension) and type **2** or **d** [<u>D</u>elete]. Then type **y** to confirm.

To rename a file, highlight it and type **3** or **m** [<u>M</u>ove/Rename]. Word-Perfect prompts:

```
New name:
```

Type the new name and press **RETURN**. If the name already exits, WordPerfect tells you:

```
ERROR: Can't rename file
```

Choose another name! By the way, when you rename a file, you aren't altering the file's contents. To move a file, give it *the same name* on a different drive or in a different directory.

Working with Drives or Directories

This section outlines ways to work with drives or directories from the file listing.

Directory Paths. Hard disk users: A word about DOS *paths* is in order here. Figure 9-5 shows a typical directory structure. DOS views each directory as a path that starts at the root directory and works its way down through the disk. Think of the directory structure as an inverted tree with the root at the top and branches below it.

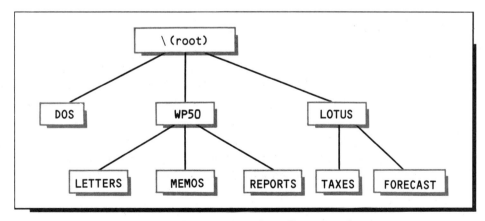

Figure 9-5   A Typical Hard Disk Directory Structure

The directory structure in Figure 9-5 contains three directories—DOS, WP50, and LOTUS—that branch from the root directory, \. The WP50 directory contains *sub*directories LETTERS, MEMOS, and REPORTS, while LOTUS contains subdirectories TAXES and FORECAST. WP50 and LOTUS are the *parent* directories for their respective subdirectories, which in turn are the *children*. The root directory is the *grandparent* of them all.

DOS looks for directories starting at the *current* directory and working downward through the directory path. That is, if you're in the WP50 directory and you want to switch to the MEMOS directory, you identify the directory simply as MEMOS. However, if you want to switch to another directory that's at the same or higher level, or in a child directory of another directory, you must designate its path starting at the root directory.

For example, you're in the WP50 directory and you want to switch to the TAXES directory that's a child of the LOTUS directory. You would identify the directory as \LOTUS\TAXES. The first backslash designates the root directory.

Changing the Drive or Directory. If you keep your work on separate disks or in separate directories, you can change drives or directories at any time. Then you can do a file listing or any other file management command. All documents that you save will be stored on the new drive or in the new directory during the current work session. Here's how to change directories. Press **F5 List Files**, then type an equals sign: =. WordPerfect prompts:

```
New Directory =
```

Type the drive name *with* the colon (for example, **a:**), or the path name of the directory (for example, **memos** or **\lotus\taxes**). Then press **RETURN**. You can also use the **7** [Other Directory] choice in the file listing menu to accomplish the same thing. When you switch to a different directory, this procedure mimics the DOS command CHDIR or CD.

This procedure actually changes the currently active drive or directory. Previously you learned how to view a different drive or directory without changing the default.

Note: If you're in one directory and you retrieve a document from another, WordPerfect always saves the document to its original location unless you specify otherwise. For example, you retrieve the document \WP50\ MEMOS\FILE.1 in the \WP50\MEMOS directory, but you're currently in the \WP50 directory. WordPerfect will still save the document back to \WP50\MEMOS.

Creating or Removing Directories. If you type a directory name that doesn't exist, WordPerfect asks you if you want to *create* this new directory. For example, you typed **a** instead of **a:** to designate the A drive. WordPerfect prompts:

```
Create a (Y/N)? No
```

If you typed the wrong directory name, type **n** to start again. If you *do* want to create the new directory, of course, type **y**. The new directory becomes a "child" of the current directory. This feature mimics the DOS command to make a directory, MKDIR or MD. To delete a directory, you must first delete all the files in that directory. Otherwise, WordPerfect will honor you with this error message:

```
ERROR: Directory not empty
```

Caution: Do you *really* want to delete these files? Maybe you should copy them to a floppy disk first in case you actually want to keep them. Once you've deleted all the files in the directory, highlight the directory name in the file listing and type **2** or **d** [Delete]. WordPerfect asks you to confirm your decision (here, the directory is \WP50\MEMOS):

```
Delete C:\WP\MEMOS (Y/N)? No
```

Type **y** to delete, or **n** to retain the directory. This procedure mimics the DOS remove directory command, RMDIR or RD.

Viewing Other Directory Listings. Sometimes you *still* can't find a file, but you don't want to continue changing directories until you locate the file. You can view the contents of other directories after pressing **F5 List Files** and **RETURN** by positioning the highlight on a directory and typing **6** [Look] or pressing **RETURN**. Then either restrict the listing to certain files or just press **RETURN** for a listing of all files in the new directory. Other directories have <DIR> following their name on the file listing, too.

Printing a File or the File Listing

As you probably noted, the **4** [Print] choice in the file listing lets you print a document quickly.

Yes, it will let you print only certain pages or page ranges, as outlined in Chapter 5. To print several files in succession, mark them and then type **4** or **p** [Print]. Remember that you can't print files that have been fast saved.

You can also print the file listing to keep it for reference. First, select the files whose names you wish to print by restricting the file listing as previously outlined, then prepare your printer and paper. With the highlight on the <CURRENT> directory at the top of the listing, or any file name that isn't a directory, press **SHIFT-F7 Print**.

If you highlight a different directory from <CURRENT>, WordPerfect prints the files names in that directory. Once you've started the printing, you can control the print job like any other in the print queue. You must, however, exit the file listing if you want to go into the print: control printer menu.

Locking Documents for Security Reasons

You might not want other computer users around you to be able to change or view certain documents. If you're working on a *local area network (LAN)*, read this! WordPerfect can *lock* a document, that is, it can lock out others from viewing the document. To lock a document, you attach a password to it when you save the document. Then the *only* way you—or anyone else—can retrieve the document is by entering the correct password. When it locks a document, WordPerfect "scrambles" its contents. You can retrieve the document, look at the contents of the document, perform word searches, copy, or print the document from the file listing only if you supply the correct password.

Note: When you copy a locked document, the copied document takes the same password. You can rename a locked document, but that doesn't remove the password.

Caution: If you forget the password for a document, there is *no way* you can retrieve it ever again! I strongly urge you to think carefully about how you'll set up locked documents. Make sure you pick a password that you can remember, but don't write the password where others will see it.

✔Return to the edit screen and retrieve any document.

To save and lock this document:

Press   **CTRL-F5 Text In/Out**

Type   **2** or **p** [P̲assword]

WordPerfect presents the password menu:

Password: 1 A̲dd; 2 R̲emove: 0

Type   **1** or **a** [A̲dd]

WordPerfect prompts:

Enter Password:

Type a password and press **RETURN**. You won't see the password as you type it. The longest possible password is 76 characters. The password doesn't appear on the screen. To make sure that you've entered the right password, WordPerfect asks you to enter the password a second time:

```
Re-Enter Password:
```

Type it again. If you goof and don't type the same password, WordPerfect says:

```
ERROR: Incorrect password
```

You have another chance to try again. Now, when you save the document again and only when you save it, WordPerfect locks it. To *change* the password, repeat the steps.

Later, when you retrieve the document, WordPerfect will request the password. If you don't supply the right one for <file>, you see this message:

```
ERROR: File is locked -- <file>
```

✔Leave the NEWS document on the screen.

You *unlock* a document by removing the password, but the document must be on the screen. So, you have to give WordPerfect the password to retrieve the document. Try unlocking the same document:

Press   **CTRL-F5 Text In/Out**

Type   **2 or p [P̲assword]**

Type   **2 or r [R̲emove]**

And there you are!

Note: Make sure you save the document to remove the password. If you just clear the screen, the document is still locked.

WordPerfect and DOS

Sometimes you might need to access a DOS command, but you don't want to leave WordPerfect or disrupt your work. For example, you may find that a disk is full and you have to format another disk quickly before you can save the current document, or you may want to change the date or time. WordPerfect lets you go out to DOS temporarily. Here's how:

Press   **CTRL-F1 Shell**

WordPerfect says:

```
1 Go to DOS: 0
```

Type   1 or **g** [Go to DOS]

If you're running WordPerfect within the WordPerfect Library, you'll see this menu instead:

```
1 Go to Shell; 2 Retrieve Clipboard: 0
```

You must first type **1** or **g** [Go to Shell], and then go to DOS from the Library. When you go to DOS from WordPerfect, you'll see the DOS prompt and this message:

```
Enter 'EXIT' to return to WordPerfect
```

You could then insert the DOS disk in the A drive and format a new floppy disk. Or, better yet, you could have the FORMAT.COM program on the WordPerfect disk so that you don't have to switch disks. Then all you need do to format a disk in the B drive is to type **a:format b:** and press **RETURN**. When you're finished with DOS, type **exit** and press **RETURN** to go back to WordPerfect.

How much you can do in DOS depends on how much memory your computer has. It's possible to go to DOS and run an entirely different program with WordPerfect still in memory. However, always make sure that you go back into WordPerfect and exit WordPerfect properly to close all documents before you quit for the day.

Caution: Never try to load a *memory-resident program*, such as a desktop utility or keyboard enhancer, from within WordPerfect. You'll probably lock your computer and lose any new work that you haven't saved. Always load memory-resident programs *before* you enter WordPerfect. Also, don't use the DOS DELETE command (you can easily delete files from the file listing) or the DOS CHKDSK command with the /F switch when you go to DOS from within WordPerfect. Use *only* the standard CHKDSK command, as outlined in the next section.

How Much Memory Do You Have?

The DOS command CHKDSK gives you the amount of available memory in bytes. Use the CTRL-F1 Shell key to go to DOS, then type **chkdsk** and press **RETURN**. If CHKDSK.COM is on the A drive and you're checking the default B drive, the command would be **a:chkdsk**.

Caution: Never use the /F switch with CHKDSK from within Word-
Perfect. See your DOS manual for details about this switch.

Housekeeping

Dear Reader, you probably have one of them in your house, too. It's that
closet into which you throw things that you don't want to deal with at the
moment. I call mine "Siberia." You should see all the junk in there! Every
few months or so, of course, things come to such a pass that I can't find
anything in Siberia, so I have to clean it out, one of my least favorite tasks.

When you work with computers, you run the risk of creating "mini-
Siberias" on all your disks. Documents and files seem to multiply like rabbits,
and disk space is at a premium. If you don't check your directory often, you'll
tend to overlook superfluous files, unless you include in your work routine
a very important operation known, aptly enough, as *housekeeping.*

Housekeeping means cleaning up your act and, as with cleaning closets,
you need not do it (thank goodness) on a daily basis. But do set up a housekeeping schedule for your work disks and stick to this schedule. If you have
a hard disk system, housekeeping on a frequent basis is absolutely essential.
But even with floppy disk based computers, you will find that you are wasting
disk space if you don't clean house every so often.

Here are some additional Alfieri tips for organizing files and housekeeping:

1. Separate files by subject or type. For instance, create a disk or directory for letters and one for memos.

2. Label disks properly so you know what's in them. The introduction
   shows you how to add a volume label to a disk, but you should also
   use tags on the outside of the disk itself or on the disk jacket. Give
   directories descriptive names, like LETTERS and MEMOS.

3. Differentiate between documents that are *active*, that is, on-going, and
   those that are *inactive*, finished and no longer needed on a daily basis.
   You'll want to keep inactive documents and perhaps reuse them later,
   but they don't have to clutter up your day-to-day work disks.

4. Spread out active documents over many disks to allow enough space
   for multiple editions. Once you're finished with a document, you can
   then free up this space by *archiving* inactive files together.

5. For day-to-day word processing activity, using short file names is a
   work-saver. But rename your files with longer and more descriptive
   names later when the files become inactive.

6. Make liberal use of document summaries and comments. Enough
   said!

"Trashed" Files

With any luck, this scenario may never happen to you, but several of my readers have written to me about it. You save a document, and everything seems okay. Later when you retrieve the document you see "garbage" characters. What's worse, WordPerfect won't let you edit the document, and your keyboard may lock up so that you have to turn off your computer and start again. You have a *trashed* file!

This unnerving situation is generally not WordPerfect's fault. It's probably a bad sector, a section on the disk, that's the culprit. My recommendation? Salvage all the files you can by copying them to a freshly formatted, new disk. Then throw the problem disk away! (There are utility programs that check the disk for bad sectors to warn you in advance if problems may occur.) If the situation reoccurs with alarming frequency, maybe you need to clean your disk drive heads or have the drive's alignment checked.

There may be another cause of this problem: You're using different versions of DOS or WordPerfect on different machines. Check all product versions and standardize everything!

Freeing Up Disk Space

When you save a document, DOS may not store its entire file in the same place on the disk! DOS records the new parts where it can and then keeps track of where all the separate parts of a file are. This may seem strange to you, but it is a good way to use the disk space *dynamically*. Think of the alternative. DOS would have to rearrange *all* the files on the disk each time you saved another file. This would take a great deal of time, because DOS would have to read each file into memory and write it back to the disk.

Even the dynamic storage method can waste some disk space, so once in a while it's a good idea to copy the file to a new disk or a new file name. By copying the file, you are also compressing its disparate parts. If you have a large file that has gone through many heavy editing sessions, it would be a good idea to do this periodically.

WordPerfect documents may also grow inordinately large at times. This increase in document size happens because WordPerfect maintains font and graphics information in the hidden document prefix but doesn't automatically discard this information when you edit your document. That is, the prefix comprises various *packets* of information. When you edit a document, WordPerfect creates another packet and marks the previous packet as unused. So, the prefix grows like a blob! WordPerfect doesn't free unused packets until you retrieve the document the next time. To reduce the size of the prefix and hence of your document: save the document, clear the screen, retrieve the document, and save it again.

Dear Reader, I can't emphasize enough the importance of file management. Learn the techniques that I've outlined in this chapter and apply them to your files regularly. You'll be glad you did.

10

Tabs as Tools

In this chapter you'll learn the following new commands . . .

Function Key Commands

F4 ◗Indent Indent the left side of the line or paragraph to the next tab stop

SHIFT-F4 ◗Indent◖ Indent both sides of the line or paragraph to the next tab stops

CTRL-F6 Tab Align Cursor to the next tab stop and align figures at the alignment character (usually the decimal point)

. . . you'll discover new uses of these commands . . .

SHIFT-F5 Date/Outline Turn outline mode on/off

SHIFT-F8 Format (1) Clear and set centered, decimal, and right-justified tabs with or without leaders, (2) change the decimal/align character and thousands' separator

TAB Move to the next outline level

SHIFT-TAB (1) Left margin release, (2) move to the previous outline level

. . . and you'll learn some new codes:

`[Align]` and `[C/A/Flrt]` Begin and end tab align

`[Decml/Algn Char]` Decimal/align character or thousands' separator change

more . . .

> [→Indent]   Left indent
>
> [→Indent←]   Both sides indent
>
> [←Mar Rel]   Left margin release
>
> [Par Num:Auto]   Outline number

With apologies to Shakespeare and Gertrude Stein, a tab is a tab is a tab—at least on a typewriter. On a word processor, the TAB key can do many more things than just move over to the next tab stop. In fact, coupled with certain features like quick indent keys and automatic outline numbering, tabs become powerful word processing tools. This chapter continues the discussion of tabs from Chapter 6.

> ### DO WARM-UP

Using Decimal Tabs

Take a look at the following example sales report that you'll create in a moment.

United Bakeries of Santa Clara County

Welcome to the Friendly Pies

Sales Report - 1987

January	$97,325.01
February	97,559.15
March	98,001.77
April	100,021.22
May	93,559.77
June	66,990.20
July	9,582.35
August	9,901.50
September	12,101.75
October	95,602.32

November	96,888.50
December	105,159.99

Notice that the sales figures are different lengths and that each figure is aligned under the previous one around the decimal point. This is standard *statistical typing* practice.

WordPerfect has a special command to help you enter the figures without having to fuss about getting the alignment correct. It's called *tab align*, but you'll hear other word processors refer to it as *decimal tab*. When you type the figures, WordPerfect sees to it that everything moves to the left until you type the alignment character, which is by default the decimal point. (You'll see how to change the alignment character, too.) Then the characters move to the right. You can use the tab align feature only at a tab stop.

The Tab Align command is CTRL-F6 Tab Align. Each time you press this command, you advance the cursor to the next tab stop and tell WordPerfect to align the text that you'll next type around the alignment character. You can also accomplish the same results by setting up *decimal tab* stops from the tab setup area. That way, you merely press TAB to move to a decimal tab stop. This first example uses the tab align key.

Because it's always a good practice to determine the format settings for a document before you begin, do so now.

✔Use the SHIFT-F8 Format key to go into the tab set area.

You don't want all the tab stops, because they would get in your way when you use the TAB key for the report.

✔Clear all tabs with CTRL-END, then set left-justified tabs at columns 2.5 and 5.5 only. Press **F7 Exit** twice to return to the document. Center and type the three titles (don't forget to underline the second line), and press **RETURN** twice between titles.

Now, to enter the first sales figure, do this:

Press   **TAB**

Type   January

Stop! Here's where you use the tab align instead of the regular tab.

Press   **CTRL-F6 Tab Align**

The cursor jumps to the next tab stop, and WordPerfect tells you:

Align char = .

The message disappears as soon as you type the alignment character, but watch as WordPerfect moves the characters to the left until you type that decimal point.

Type   **$97,325.01**

Press   **RETURN**

to end the line.

    ✔Continue typing each line by first pressing the **TAB** key once, entering the month, then using **CTRL-F6 Tab Align** to move to the sales figure column. If you make a mistake and press TAB instead of CTRL-F6 Tab Align, use the BACKSPACE key to delete the tab and start again.

    If you wish, reveal the codes to see how WordPerfect sets up a tab align instruction. It surrounds the part of the figure that is to the left of the alignment character with a begin [Align] and an end [C/A/Flrt] code. You saw the latter when you learned about centering in Chapter 2.

    ✔When you're finished, save the document as SALES.87.

    Keep one important point in the back of your mind when you do aligned columns of figures: To perform totals or other arithmetic operations on the figures, set them up instead as *math columns* (Chapter 19).

What Happens When You Change the Tab Settings

If you decide to change the tab stops after you've entered text, WordPerfect automatically adjusts the text around the new settings. You decide to do just that. Remember to delete the previous format change code and insert another.

    ✔Position the cursor at the beginning of the document, reveal the codes, and delete the [Tab Set] code.

    Whoa! The text is a mess now, because there are *no* tab stops in the document. Don't worry!

    ✔Use the SHIFT-F8 Format key to set new left-justified tabs at columns 2.0 and 5.0. Press **F7 Exit** twice to return to the document.

    There's the text, all prettied up! With the codes off, if you attempt to delete an align code, WordPerfect asks you to confirm what you're doing.

    ✔You may wish to change some of the figures to see what happens. Go ahead, try it! When you're finished, clear the screen.

The Other Types of Tabs

You have a choice of regular (left-justified), right-justified, center, and decimal tabs. The next few sections present examples that use some of these tabs. Here's how to set these tabs. Make sure the cursor is at the left margin.

    ✔Use the SHIFT-F8 Format key to go into the tab set area. Then clear all tabs before you follow these steps.

Type   **3**

Press   **RETURN**

to set a left-justified tab at column 3.0.

Type   **d**

The tab changes to a decimal tab.

Type   **c**

The tab changes to a center tab.

Type   **r**

Now the tab changes to a right-justified tab.

Type   **5**

Press   **RETURN**

WordPerfect by default sets left-justified tabs, this time at column 5.0. Again, you could change this to a different tab by typing the appropriate letter. Another way to go is to position the cursor at the desired column and then type L, R, C, or D as necessary.

Press   **CTRL-END**

Notice that this clears all tabs from the cursor position only.

Type   **4.5**

Press   **RETURN**

Type   **d**

A decimal tab stop appears at column 4.5. To set multiple decimal tabs from column 4.5, first set a left-justified tab. Then change it to a decimal tab. Finally, set up the multiple columns:

Type   **4.5,1.0**

Press   **RETURN**

Now you have decimal tabs every tenth column starting at column 4.5. The same procedure applies for setting multiple center and right-justified tabs.
   ✔Press **F1 Cancel** or **ESC** enough times to return to the blank screen without saving the new tab stops.

If you want to practice an example with right-justified, center, and decimal tabs, try this one. I won't step you through it, but I'll just mention how I did it. I first typed the titles, then set a right-justified tab at column 2.5, a center tab at column 4.5, and a decimal tab at column 6.5. Save this document as PIES.1, and have fun!

United Bakers of Santa Clara County

Welcome to the Friendly Pies

Seasonal Availability and Price

Apple	All Year	$2.25
Cherry	May-September	2.30
Blueberry	June-July	2.55
Peach	June-October	2.45
Pecan	All Year	3.00
Pumpkin	All Year	2.00
Rhubarb	July-August	2.25
Strawberry	May-September	2.75

Changing the Decimal/Align Character and Thousands' Separator

You can have only *one* decimal/align character active at one time. If you're entering population figures, for instance, you might want the comma to be the alignment character. A related issue is the *thousands' separator*. In some European countries, for instance, the comma is the decimal character, and the space separates thousands.

To change the decimal/align character and thousands' separator, follow these steps (you don't have to do them now):

1. Press **SHIFT-F8 Format**, type **4** or **o** [Other], then type **3** or **d** [Decimal Character].

2. Type the decimal/align character or press **RETURN** alone to accept the period. Repeat the steps for the thousands' separator.

3. Press **F7 Exit**.

WordPerfect inserts a [Decml/Algn Char] code in the document that shows the new characters.

Tip: If you have to type several columns, each with its own different alignment character, you can switch back and forth between alignment characters as often as you wish. Set up a macro to do this. For instance, say you have to type aligned columns of figures, some arranged under commas and some, under decimal points. Use one macro to switch the alignment character from the default decimal point to a comma and one to switch it back.

Tabs with Leaders

This next example shows how to set up tab stops with dot leaders. Leaders are characters that precede something, in this case a tab stop. Take a look at the example before you try it.

```
           United Bakeries of Santa Clara County

              Welcome to the Friendly Pies

              Seasonal Availability


            Apple . . . . . . . . . All Year
          Apricot . . . . . . . . . April-October
     Banana Cream . . . . . . . . . All Year
     Black Bottom . . . . . . . . . All Year
           Cherry . . . . . . . . . May-September
        Blueberry . . . . . . . . . June-July
    Concord Grape . . . . . . . . . August-October
         Key Lime . . . . . . . . . All Year
   Lemon Meringue . . . . . . . . . All Year
            Peach . . . . . . . . . June-October
            Pecan . . . . . . . . . All Year
          Pumpkin . . . . . . . . . All Year
          Rhubarb . . . . . . . . . July-August
       Strawberry . . . . . . . . . May-September
```

✔To set up the formatting, go into the tab set area and clear all tabs. Set a left-justified tab at column 3.0. Then:

Type   r

Type   .

(That's a period.)

The R is now shaded to indicate that dot leaders will appear preceding this right-justified tab stop at column 3.0. Wait! That's not what you want. The dot leaders should precede the *second* tab stop. To delete the dot leader:

Type   .

The tab stop reverts to a right-justified tab without dot leaders.

Type   **5.1**

Press   **RETURN**

Type   .

That's where you want the dot leaders!

Press   **F7 Exit** twice

Type the titles as before. To do the first pie, press **TAB** once and type the name. It appears right-justified as you type. Then press **TAB** to move to the next tab stop and have WordPerfect insert the dot leaders. Enter the second column information and continue.

✔When you're finished, save this document as PIES.2. Then clear the screen.

Centering Lines Over Tab Stops

Recall from Chapter 2 that the cursor should be at the left margin before you attempt to center a line. That's because if you tab over and *then* press SHIFT-F6 Center, WordPerfect will center the line you type over the last tab stop.

Note: Center tabs act in the same way as if you were using the Center command over a tab stop. It's up to you.

Indenting Text

Moving right along, turn your attention now to indented text. Even though WordPerfect supplies special commands for indenting, the **F4 ▶Indent** and **SHIFT-F4 ▶Indent◀** keys, the indentations are determined by the tab stops.

The indenting commands indent a line or paragraph of text one tab stop from the left margin or from *both* margins. As you type, the lines still wrap, but they don't wrap back to the left margin. Instead, they wrap back to the *temporary indentation*, the tab stop. If you indent from both margins, the lines wrap at the temporary right margin indentation, too.

The indentation stays in effect until you press the RETURN key to end the paragraph. You *don't* have to press the TAB key to begin each indented line, but you can have regular tabs in the indented text, too.

Left Side and Both Sides Indents

Here is an example of how to indent. You'll type the following report:

At the monthly Executive Committee meeting, held as usual on the second Wednesday of the month, the Committee's presiding officer, Professor Lawrence Papadoupoulos, presented the following prepared statement, which read in part:

For quite some time now, the Executive Committee has been wrestling with the problem of student attendance, or, rather, lack of attendance. Of course, students have always skipped classes, but this practice seems to be on the increase lately. We are making every effort to ascertain the reason for this distressing development, and we shall keep you apprised of our findings.

A general discussion of this statement followed. It was apparent after some debate that no consensus was to be reached, because Ms. Maude Keeper, representing the Student Body at large, was unwilling to accept the opinions of the rest of the Committee. She cited as her defense the following extract from the student paper, The Daily Noise:

It has recently been brought to our attention that certain members of a certain department (are you listening, Professor P.?) have been absent from classes on a more than regular basis. One professor, students assert, has not shown up for class or consultation in over three weeks ...

The Committee decided to postpone a final decision of this matter until a later date.

✔Type the *first* paragraph as usual; use the default format to save time. Press **RETURN** twice when you're finished. When you're ready to do the indented paragraph:

Press   **F4 ▸Indent**

The cursor jumps to the next tab stop. Type the indented portion as you would any other paragraph. WordPerfect indents each line one tab stop from the left margin. The *only* time you should press RETURN is at the end of the paragraph.

Press   **RETURN** twice

for spacing.

You should now have two hard return codes at the end of the document. Type the third paragraph and press **RETURN** twice when you're finished. The fourth paragraph is tricky. It is indented one tab stop from *both* margins, and it includes a *regular* tab.

Press   **SHIFT-F4 ▶Indent◀**

That's the command to indent one tab stop from both margins.

Press   **TAB** once

That's the regular tab. Now, type the paragraph, press **RETURN** twice to space down, and finish the example. Press **RETURN** twice when you're finished.

✔Save the document as MINUTES but leave it on the screen.

When you press RETURN to end an indented paragraph, WordPerfect cancels whatever indent command you are using. Because an indentation is a *temporary* formatting situation in the document itself, it is not set up from the SHIFT-F8 Format menu. However, there are codes for the indentation instructions, and these codes remain in the document. For the F4 ▶Indent key, the code is [→ Indent]; for the SHIFT-F4 ▶Indent◀ key, it's [→ Indent ←].

If you edit the portion of text that is temporarily indented, WordPerfect still indents properly when it adjusts the lines. If you wish to delete the indentation, delete the code at the beginning of the paragraph. The text adjusts back to the normal margins. You can always insert an indent instruction later, too. To change the column location of an indentation, change the tab settings.

Using More Than One Indentation

You can indent as many tab stops as you like, one tab stop for each indent command. You'll add more text to the MINUTES document to see what I mean.

✔Make sure there are two hard returns at the end of the document. Type the first short paragraph in the following example. Press **RETURN** twice for spacing.

Other business discussed at this meeting included the following:

1. The Dean's Office has decided not to proceed with its intention to purchase 50 microcomputers until a better pricing policy can be arranged with the vendor.

2. The University is considering a wage freeze on all academic appointments, effective immediately. The Committee is considering what action to take in response to this proposal.

3. There is growing concern that the new offices will not be available by the date promised. The Committee has been advised that Smudge & Smudge, Solicitors to the University, are negotiating with the building contractor about this matter.

Do the list of items with *two* indentations:

Press   **F4 ▶Indent**

Type   **1.**

Press   **F4 ▶Indent**

✔Type the entry for number 1. Press **RETURN** twice to space down. Repeat these steps for the other two entries. WordPerfect honors both indentation commands, but it always indents text to the rightmost command only. When you're finished, save the edited version of MINUTES and clear the screen.

With this example in mind, you now know how to do an *outline* using the temporary indentation feature. But don't do outlines this way! WordPerfect has a much better way, as you'll see in a moment. First, I'll round out the discussion of indented text with a little gastronomic diversion.

Hanging Indents

By now you're probably tired of dry academic texts, so I'd like to change the mode a bit. Here's a little gift for you: a real recipe that works. This easy recipe was handed down to me from my mother, Alda Alfieri, who lives in East Rochester, New York. She in turn got it from friends, so I guess it's been passed around a lot. Now it's yours!

SOUR CREAM COFFEE CAKE

Grease and flour a bundt pan; preheat oven to 350 degrees. Cream
    together 1/2 cup butter and 1 cup sugar until the mixture is
    light and fluffy. Add 2 eggs and beat well.

In a large bowl, sift together 2 cups all-purpose flour, 1
    teaspoon baking soda, and 1 teaspoon baking powder. In
    another bowl, add 1 teaspoon vanilla to 1 cup sour cream.

Add one-half of the dry ingredients to the creamed mixture, then
    add one-half of the sour cream mixture. Continue in this
    fashion, ending with a final addition of dry ingredients.

Place half the batter in the prepared pan. Put in half the
    filling (see below); repeat. Top with the remaining
    filling. Bake for 50 minutes.

Filling: Mix together 1/2 cup tightly packed light brown sugar, 1
    tablespoon flour, 2 teaspoons cinnamon, 1/2 teaspoon nutmeg,
    and 1/2 cup chopped walnuts.

Take a look at the text before you begin. The first line of each paragraph is standard, but the other lines are indented. This is called a *hanging indent*.

✔Center and type the title as you see it, with the CAPS LOCK key on, then space down three lines. Turn the CAPS LOCK key off. To do each hanging indent:

Press   **F4 ▸Indent**

Press   **SHIFT-TAB**

The key combination SHIFT-TAB is the Left Margin Release command. It moves the cursor back to the previous tab stop. As on the typewriter, use the margin release to go past the default left margin setting temporarily. Note, however, that you can't go left of column 0 on the screen nor is there a release command for the right margin. (You would have to change the right margin to go past it.) Here, the margin release disables the indentation of the first line only. The margin release code that you inserted in this document is [◂Mar Rel].

✔Type the first paragraph and watch the results. Space down and repeat the steps above for each successive paragraph. When you're finished, save this document as COFFEECK, and then clear the screen.

You can also do a hanging indent with the SHIFT-F4 ▸Indent◂ key. However, first make sure that the right indent is set for the correct tab stop.

Simple Outlining

If you have to type outlines often, you're going to love WordPerfect's automatic outlining feature. That's right! You don't have to worry about numbering the outline, because WordPerfect does that for you. Just be careful about how many tab stops you use.

Outlining is the second of several *modes* that you'll use in WordPerfect. The first was typeover mode (Chapter 1). Other modes are for text columns (Chapter 18) and math (Chapter 19). You must tell WordPerfect when it should number outlines. That is, you turn outline mode on.

As an example of a simple outline, you're about to write an article about some of your favorite restaurants in Los Angeles, so you decide to collect your thoughts in an outline first. (The article itself is in the next chapter.) Here's the entire outline. Notice that it has two outline *levels* (there are eight possible levels).

```
L.A. Restaurants

I.    El Colmao
      A.    Cuban
      B.    Picadillo, ropa vieja
II.   Palermo
      A.    Italian
      B.    Check address
      C.    Pizza, veal parmigiana
III.  House of Chan Dara
      A.    Thai
      B.    Meat/vegetable combinations
      C.    Great ambiance
IV.   Maya
      A.    Japanese
      B.    "Country" style
      C.    Teriyaki, tempura, sukiyaki
V.    Talpa
      A.    Mexican
      B.    Good food, lousy parking
VI.   La Fuente
      A.    Mexican, too
      B.    Close to downtown
      C.    Sonoran food
VII.  Tommy's
      A.    Hamburgers
      B.    24 hours
VIII.Hampton's
      A.    More hamburgers
      B.    Great desserts
```

```
IX.  Gorky's
     A.   Russian
     B.   Artists' hangout
X.   Vickman's
     A.   Bakery
     B.   Strange hours
     C.   Bran muffins
XI.  Clifton's Cafeteria
     A.   "Soup Easy"
     B.   515 West 7th Street
XII. Hunan
     A.   L.A.'s Chinatown
     B.   Eggplant!
XIII.     Seafood Bay
     A.   Fresh fish, low prices
     B.   Mention Onyx Cafe
```

✔Type the title, which isn't part of the outline, and press **RETURN** *once* for spacing. You'll see why you don't press RETURN twice in a moment. Now follow the steps to add the first outline section.

The outline feature is on the SHIFT-F5 Date/Outline key. Version 4.2 users: It's on the ALT-F5 Mark Text key.

Press   **SHIFT-F5 Date/Outline**

Type   **4** or **o** [<u>O</u>utline]

At the bottom of the screen, WordPerfect tells you that outline mode is on. But you don't see any numbers yet!

Press   **RETURN**

to start the numbering.

Because you must press RETURN to add a first level number, you now have the correct spacing between it and the title. As with almost every format setting, WordPerfect "assumes" a default setting. In the case of outlines, it provides a Roman numeral I. for the first level, but there are many other outline styles (Chapter 21). Continue by indenting the text for the level one entry:

Press   **F4 ▶Indent**

If you go too far, press **BACKSPACE** to delete the extra indent code or codes.

Caution: Don't use the TAB key alone to indent, because that's a signal to WordPerfect that you want a different outline level. If you don't want the text to indent, press the SPACEBAR and *then* the TAB key to insert a normal tab.

Type   El Colmao

Press   **RETURN**

Wait! WordPerfect inserted a Roman II., because it thinks you want another entry at the first level. Don't worry! Here's how to do the second level entries:

Press   **TAB**

to change the II. to an A.

If you go too far, you can press **BACKSPACE** to delete the tab, or press **SHIFT-TAB**. The latter command moves back to the previous outline level.

Press   **F4 ◗Indent**

Type   Cuban

Press   **RETURN**

The trick is that for every press of the TAB key WordPerfect moves the outline to the next level and renumbers the outline accordingly. You can have up to *eight* levels of outlines, more than enough for most pedants and other organized types. You must use the F4 ◗Indent key to indent when outline mode is on.

✔Finish the rest of the outline, but after you type the last entry about the Onyx Cafe, *don't* press RETURN. Leave the cursor at the end of the line.

If you did press RETURN at the end of the last line, WordPerfect adds another outline number. To delete the superfluous number, press **BACK-SPACE**. Now, turn outlining off and return to normal insert mode:

Press   **SHIFT-F5 Date/Outline**

Type   **4** or **o** [Outline]

to turn outline mode off.

Always turn outlining off so that you don't get any superfluous outline numbers when you want regular text. Note that you can't use the F1 Cancel key to cancel outlining: You must specifically turn it off from the SHIFT-F5 Date/Outline key. Later, if you want to continue outlining, position the cursor where you want outlining to start before you turn outline mode on again.

If you look at the code that WordPerfect supplies for each outline number, you'll see this: [Par Num:Auto]. WordPerfect considers outlining an automatic paragraph numbering instruction, because the two features are related (Chapter 21). If you attempt to delete one of these codes in normal insert mode, WordPerfect asks you to confirm what you're doing.

✔Save the document as ARTICLE.OUT but leave it on the screen. (It might be a good idea to use the file extension .OUT for all outlines you create so you can identify them easily.)

Did you notice that there's one thing not particularly pleasing about this outline? Look at section VIII. How would you fix this? That's right! Go to the beginning of the document and change the tabs. Remove the tab stop at column 1.5 and put one at column 1.6 instead. Then insert a left indent in front of the word *Hampton's*. I'll let you do this example on your own.

To align the section numbers around the decimal point, what would you do? Right! Use the standard Tab Align command. Later you'll learn that when you delete, add, or move outline sections WordPerfect automatically renumbers the outline (Chapter 21).

Dear Reader, tabs are useful tools indeed. But at the moment aren't you hungry? Go ahead: bake that coffee cake. *Bon appétit!*

11

A Double Dose of
Documents

In this chapter you'll discover new uses of these commands:

F1 Cancel	Move or copy text to the other window or screen
CTRL-F3 Screen	(1) Split the screen into two windows, (2) restore the screen to one window
CTRL-F4 Move	Move or copy text to the other window or screen
SHIFT-F3 Switch	Cursor to the other window or screen

Dear Reader, nimble up your fingers, because there's a lot of typing in this chapter! So far, you've been working with short documents, but now you'll turn to a longer text. Besides typing in a more substantial example, you'll work with two documents at the same time. You'll also learn how to change formats within a document. All this is the meat and potatoes of word processing.

DO WARM-UP

Working with Two Documents

You can have two documents open at one time in WordPerfect. You can either split the screen into two *windows* to view both documents simultaneously or switch between two separate screens, each showing a different document or different parts of the same one. However, you can *work* in only one window or screen at any time.

A typical example of working with two documents is when you're writing something—a letter, an article, the chapter of a book—and you're referring to notes or an outline. Instead of turning from your computer whenever you want to check your notes, set them up as the second document. In this example, you'll use the outline from the last chapter to guide you as you write your article on restaurants in Los Angeles.

Dear Reader, if you *didn't* type the outline in the last chapter, don't fret! You can still follow along here; just don't retrieve a document into the second window. However, *do* type the long document in this chapter, because you'll use it a lot throughout the rest of the book.

On most monitors, the screen shows 24 lines of text in Doc 1. Some monitors can display 43 or more lines. You can split the screen into two windows of equal or unequal size. Depending on your work style, you can have the outline in the top window and the article in the bottom, or vice versa. Here, you'll write the article in the top window, using the outline in a smaller window at the bottom.

Splitting the Screen into Two Windows

When you retrieve a document, WordPerfect uses Doc 1. Because you want the new article in Doc 1 and the outline in Doc 2, you must first split the screen into two windows.

Press   **CTRL-F3 Screen**

Type   **1** or **w** [<u>W</u>indow]

WordPerfect displays:

```
# Lines in this Window: 24
```

Your number may be different. To split the screen equally, you would type **12**, or whatever is the number that represents half the lines on your monitor. When you use two windows, WordPerfect requires three screen lines for the two status lines and the tab ruler. Here, however, you want more screen space for the article, so you decide to give the second window only 8 lines. Because you're still in the first window, you give it $24 - 8 = 16$ lines. If your monitor can display more lines, use other figures, such as 33 lines for the top window and 10 for the bottom.

Type   **16**

or whatever number of lines you want for the top window.

Press **RETURN**

You can also press the **UP ARROW** and **DOWN ARROW** keys to size the window visually, instead of typing a number. Then press **RETURN** to set the window. The cursor is still in Doc 1 in the top window. Note that WordPerfect uses the tab ruler to divide the two screens and that the tab settings (the little triangles) are pointing *up* as a reminder that the cursor is in the upper window, the active window at the moment.

Whenever you want to *switch* to the other window and to make it the active one, do this:

Press **SHIFT-F3 Switch**

The cursor is now in the bottom window, Doc 2, and the tab settings on the tab ruler point *down* to remind you where you are. Once you're in the correct window, you can retrieve a document.

✔Retrieve the document ARTICLE.OUT now.

Now you're ready to begin, or are you? No! You must switch back to Doc 1.

Press **SHIFT-F3 Switch**

WordPerfect keeps track of the different cursor positions in the two windows when you switch. One last note: You can view the printout of only one document, the one in the active window.

Some Real Work

You're now ready to type the article, which is one of the longest examples in this book. Take your time and make sure you include the correct center and underline codes. Assuming that you're following the outline, whenever you get to the point when you need to see more of the outline, switch to Doc 2 and use a scrolling command (such as the ESC key) to bring more of the outline into view. Then, switch back to Doc 1 and continue "writing."

Dear Reader, little did you know what a *bargain* you received when you bought this book. Not only is it a tour through WordPerfect, but it also gives you my own personal guide to some of the nicest (and cheapest) "little" restaurants in Los Angeles!*

The entire article is in the default format for the standard printer. Type it exactly as you see it, correcting your mistakes as you go. Note that there are no extra blank lines between paragraphs this time.

---

*Readers of the Version 4.2 edition will notice a new addition and a few other alterations to this long example. Los Angeles is constantly changing, so make sure you call ahead before you visit any of these restaurants.

The Little Restaurants of Los Angeles

San Francisco, eat your heart out! Los Angeles has some of the <u>best</u> restaurants in the state, with more appearing all the time. I'm not talking big and fancy here. For the most part, these are smaller places, generally ethnic, but the food is great and the prices are right.

Certainly at the top of my list is <u>El Colmao</u>, purveyors of excellent Cuban food. If you don't like rice and beans, then skip this place, because rice and beans are the staple of the menu. But you'll be missing several treats, such as the <u>picadillo</u> (ground beef cooked in a sauce), or the <u>ropa vieja</u> (literally, "old clothes"--shredded beef simmered in tomato sauce), or <u>boliche</u> (Cuban-style pot roast). The atmosphere is bouncy and unpretentious, and the portions are enormous. El Colmao is at 2328 West Pico Boulevard (closed Tuesdays).

Then there's <u>Palermo</u>, my choice for good Italian fare at very good prices. Palermo has had a loyal following for many years, so you'll probably have to wait for a table. The thin-crust pizzas are highly recommended, as is the <u>veal parmigiana</u>. Palermo has recently moved into bigger quarters at 1858 North Vermont Avenue and is now open every day.

Los Angeles has more Thai restaurants than you can shake a bamboo at, but the one I always find myself returning to is the <u>House of Chan Dara</u>. Here's another spot where you'll wait in line, and for good reason. The food is inexpensive and beautifully prepared. Try any of the meat and vegetable combinations, as well as the ubiquitous Thai iced tea or iced coffee. The ambience is definitely part of the fun at the Hollywood location (1511 Cahuenga Boulevard), while the Larchmont Village branch (310 N. Larchmont Boulevard) is more subdued.

Ah, <u>Maya</u>! No, this is not another taco joint, but rather the best Japanese restaurant in Los Angeles. No snooty sushi here, just well-prepared and delicious "country-style" food: <u>teriyaki</u>, <u>tempura</u>, <u>sukiyaki</u>. Small, intimate, reasonable -- maybe even the find of the century. I could never leave L.A. because I'd miss Maya (874 Virgil Avenue, closed Mondays).

"Good food, lousy parking" is what the sign says at the <u>Talpa</u>. That's exactly right, but don't let the lack of parking deter you. The Talpa has authentic Mexican food, a lively atmosphere, and rock-bottom prices. Any of the combination platters are good, as well as the <u>albondigas</u> soup. The Talpa is open every day except certain holidays, and you'll find it at 11751 West Pico Boulevard.

If you're on the east side, here's an equally good Mexican Restaurant near downtown. It's called <u>La Fuente</u>, and at it you'll enjoy excellent food from Mexico's state of Sonora. What you won't experience is a fancy decor, but who cares? La Fuente is at 5530 Monte Vista Street in Highland Park, and it's open every day.

Angelenos (yes, that's what they're called) love hamburgers, and people develop very strong loyalties to their favorite hamburger haven. Perhaps the place with the strongest following is <u>Tommy's</u>, open 24 hours a day to satisfy that urge. All Tommy's hamburgers come with tomato, pickle, mustard, onion, and chili sauce, but you can have it your way, too. It must be good, because no one minds the absence of french fries. Although there are several Tommy's locations throughout the city, the <u>only</u> one to go to is at 2575 Beverly Boulevard.

If, however, you want to have your cake and your burger, too, you should consider <u>Hampton's</u>, a pleasant place to experiment with a variety of different hamburger combinations, as well as salads and other, more "formal," entrees. Hampton's also has wonderful desserts. They're at 1342 North Highland Avenue in Hollywood, and at 4301 Riverside Drive in Burbank.

Los Angeles, not to be outdone by New York's Soho, has its own thriving artist colony that has taken over many of the warehouses downtown and turned them into studios and living quarters. Most of the artists appear regularly at <u>Gorky's</u>, and their influence shows in the decor. The food is, of all things, Russian—and good, too. The service is cafeteria style. Open for breakfast, lunch, and dinner. Park your car in the lot across the street, and don't get <u>too</u> freaked out by the neighborhood: 536 East 8th Street.

If you're a night person like me and you get the munchies at 4 o'clock in the morning, head over to one of Gorky's neighbors, <u>Vickman's Restaurant and Bakery</u>. Many people consider Vickman's an L.A. institution. It caters to the produce mart workers and keeps their hours: 3 a.m. to 3 p.m.! All baking is done on the premises, and they have one of the cheapest and best breakfasts in town. I do <u>love</u> their bran muffins! (1228 East 8th Street, closed Sundays.)

Another L.A. tradition is called <u>Clifton's Cafeteria</u>, and it, too, is downtown. Clifton's has been around L.A. longer than most of us, and it still prepares home-made food at very reasonable prices. The dark-panelled interior may remind ex-New Yorkers of Schrafft's, but skip the crowd upstairs and go down to the "Soup Easy." There you'll find several different kinds of home-made soups (they change daily), salads, and desserts. The corn bread is out of this world. Clifton's is at 515 West 7th Street (open until 3 p.m., but closed on weekends).

Everyone loves Chinese food, right? Did you know that Los Angeles has quite a flourishing Chinatown? My favorite eating

place there is the <u>Hunan Restaurant,</u> at 980 North Broadway. The
cuisine is on the hot and spicy side, as you might expect. Try
the eggplant! If you're going on to the Music Center for a
concert or play, make reservations and come early: this is
another place with a continual line.

Fish fanatics will not believe the prices at <u>Seafood Bay</u> in
Silver Lake, 3916 West Sunset Boulevard. How can this restaurant
serve such a variety of fresh fish and charge so little? Mind
you, I'm not complaining at all. All entrees come with your
choice of fresh mushrooms, rice pilaf, potatoes, or other
selections. Highly recommended! When you're finished, have a
cappuccino at the <u>Onyx Cafe</u> a few blocks up the street.

✔Save the document as LAREST but leave it in the top window.

As you can imagine, the major rule of thumb for working with two
screens is to know in which window the cursor is currently located. Also, if
you're working with two documents and you attempt to exit WordPerfect
without saving one or the other—or both of them—WordPerfect warns you
accordingly.

Before you go on, take a look at the document. Some of the lines will
"space out" too much when you print the article, because you didn't attempt
to hyphenate some longer words. That's a topic of Chapter 20.

Closing or Resizing Windows

Now that you're through with the outline, you'll clear it from the screen so
you can restore the entire screen for your article.

Press   **SHIFT-F3 Switch**

to move the cursor to the bottom window.

✔Use the **F7 Exit** key to clear the outline from the screen without saving
it.

Note: If you close a window that is showing an open document,
WordPerfect still keeps the document in Doc 2, and you can switch to it (see
Using Two Separate Screens). WordPerfect will remind you to save *both* doc-
uments before you attempt to exit the program.

To close the bottom window, first switch to the top window:

Press   **SHIFT-F3 Switch**

Now, give the top window the full screen:

Press   **CTRL-F3 Screen**

Type   1 or w [Window]

Type   24

or whatever is the maximum number of lines your monitor can display.

Press   **RETURN**

You can also use the **DOWN ARROW** key to expand the window until it takes up the entire screen. Follow the same steps if you want to *resize* the windows. Just supply a different line number for the window size or move the tab ruler with the arrow keys.

Using Two Separate Screens

Say you're working on a document and you have a sudden brainstorm, or just a simple inspiration. Better write it down before you forget it! But you don't want to bother splitting the screen. Just use Doc 2 as it's normally set up, which I call the "WordPerfect Flip-Flop."

Press   **SHIFT-F3 Switch**

There's another blank screen, and the status line tells you that this is Doc 2 . You can then get your thoughts down, save them to a new file, and switch back to what you were doing before the Muse blew in your ear.

Press   **SHIFT-F3 Switch**

to return to Doc 1.
In Chapter 32, you'll learn an interesting use of two document screens together with an advanced macro feature to help you enter postal state codes.

 Tip: You can change the screen defaults to have different *colors* for the two documents. That way, it's always clear to you which document you're editing (Appendix A).

Two Versions of the Same Document

Suppose you're working on a long document and you have to keep track of or check a reference somewhere else in the same document. You can split the screen and have two copies of the document in use. But be careful which document you save! You might save the wrong document and abolish any editing changes you've made to the right one. In this case, it's a good idea to avoid switching between the two documents if at all possible and to stay in the one you're editing.

Moving or Copying Text Between Two Documents

There's nothing to prevent you from using any move or copy operation to transfer text from one document to the other. For instance, if you want to move text, just use the standard block move technique, switch to the other document, and retrieve the block. You can also use the undelete feature to cut text from one document and paste it in the other.

It turns out that you'll put part of the original article in *another* article with a similar theme. After all, if J.S. Bach could repeat melodies and themes, you can, too! Of course, if you copy text, make sure it's correct first. Then follow these steps:

Press   **HOME,HOME,UP ARROW**

to position the cursor at the top of the document.

Press   **ALT-F4 Block**

Press   **DOWN ARROW** eight times

to block the title and the first paragraph.

Press   **CTRL-F4 Move**

Type   **1** or **b** [Block]

Type   **2** or **c** [Copy]

Press   **SHIFT-F3 Switch**

Press   **RETURN**

to copy the block into Doc 2.

Suppose you want to change this article to one that discusses the little restaurants of Eureka:

Press   **ALT-F2 Replace**

Type   **n**

Type   **Los Angeles**

Press   **F2 ▶Search**

Type   **Eureka**

Press   **F2 ▶Search**

Notice that WordPerfect recentered the title when it replaced *Los Angeles* with *Eureka*. Use the **F7 Exit** key to clear the screen and then switch back to Doc 1. When you do, WordPerfect asks:

```
Exit Doc 2? (Y/N) No
```

Type   y

to exit Doc 2.

Using Different Formats in a Document

This section shows you how to create a document that contains two different formats. Of course, the basic concepts apply if you have more than two formats, but just keep things simple for the time being.

The Primary Format

Always determine what the *primary* format for the document should be—that is, the format for the bulk of the document. The first example comprises part of the chapter of a book. Most of the chapter is double spaced, but it uses the default 6½ inch line and right margin justification. However, certain quotations are single spaced and indent from both margins. Because you want to switch back and forth between these two formats frequently, you'll set up two macros to do this for you.

✔ Make sure you've saved LAREST. Clear both screens, return to Doc 1, then use the SHIFT-F8 Format key to set line spacing to double for the new document's primary format.

Type the first paragraph as you see it. When you get to the end of the paragraph, press **RETURN** twice for spacing. Now that the document is in double spacing, when you press **RETURN** twice you will get *four* blank lines between the paragraph and the next section.

```
In 1812, Beethoven moved from the west side of Vienna to the

east side, but apparently the move was not without frustration.

Although little extant material remains to help scholars unravel

the personal experiences of this time, the sources that are
```

```
available point to a feeling of loneliness and unhappiness on

Beethoven's part, or, to use a modern phrase, a "downer."  In a

letter to his brother on April 26 of that year, Beethoven writes:
```

The Secondary Format

The other format is the *secondary* format. It will be for indented, single spaced quotations. Of course, you can have as many different secondary formats as you need.

Recall from Chapter 6 one of the rules of thumb for working with format changes: Put format change codes at the *left margin*, so that they are easy to find when you reveal the codes. Inserting codes in the middle of lines can cause real problems, because some of your text may not print in the correct format. The only important format changes that you should use within a line are font changes.

Before you start typing the next paragraph, set up a macro to change to the secondary format. Call it IN for "indented section." I'll step you through this one:

Press	**CTRL-F10 Macro Define**
Type	in
Press	**RETURN**
Type	Indented section
Press	**RETURN**
Press	**SHIFT-F8 Format**
Type	1 or l [Line]
Type	6 or s [Line Spacing]
Type	1
Press	**RETURN**
Press	**F7 Exit**
Press	**SHIFT-F4 ▶Indent◀**
Press	**CTRL-F10 Macro Define**

There's your macro. Because you actually performed the steps to create the macro, you've already changed the format for the first indented section.
✔Type the first indented section now.

```
Ach!  You should only know how miserable I am here in
this hole, trapped between the Scylla of a distempered
and continually inebriated landlady and the Charybdis
of a neighbor who leads a life in reverse.  When all
other human beings are trying to sleep, he is awake and
pounding away at his heels (yes, he is a shoemaker).
During the day his snoring can be heard for miles.  Why
did I ever move?
```

Watch the Spacing When You Change Formats

How many times did you press RETURN at the end of the paragraph? You probably pressed it twice, but that's not correct! The first paragraph is separated from the indented section by *four* blank lines, because of the double spacing. However, at the moment the format is for single spacing, so you need two more blank lines.

Keep in mind that the RETURN key advances the printer down the number of blank lines that are *currently* set for the line spacing. The first paragraph was in double spacing, so when you pressed RETURN twice at the end of it, you added a "double-double," that is, four blank lines. But then you changed the format to single spacing, so each time you press RETURN, you only add one blank line to the document.

You do want your printout to be as aesthetically pleasing as possible, don't you? The moral of this example is to watch the spacing *between* paragraphs or sections of text when you switch line spacing settings. So, make sure you now have four blank lines at the end of the document.

Returning to the Primary Format

Now, set up a macro to change back to the primary format. However, recall that when you pressed RETURN you automatically turned off the indent feature. So, all you need do is change the line spacing back to double. Call this macro RE for "return."
✔Create the macro RE that changes line spacing to double.

Tip: You could also include in the macro the *tab* that begins the next paragraph if you wish.

Of course, this is a simple example of how to use two formats, but just think of all the keystrokes you've saved with macros. You'd have used many more keystrokes if you had to change the margin settings for the secondary format. Time to type the next paragraph. Remember to press RETURN twice at the end for correct spacing.

Is this perhaps the beginnings of the "Hammerklavier" sonata that would appear soon? The nocturnal working of a shoemaker, whose hammering undoubtedly kept Beethoven up many a night? One can only imagine the incessant pounding and the insomniac artist, growling and cursing to himself in the next room. And the unfortunate landlady: where would she appear in the great master's works? Perhaps the next part of the same letter provides us with a clue:

Finishing the Example

Now for another indented section, but this time you'll use your IN macro:

Press   **ALT-F10 Macro**

Type   in

Press   **RETURN**

You're ready to go: Type the indented section below, remembering to press **RETURN** four times for spacing at the end. Then use the RE macro to change back to the primary format before you type the last paragraph:

And Frau Kram is a bothersome thing who won't leave me
alone for a moment! She has taken it into her pickled
brain that I am the cat's meow. She even brings me
little gifts, worthless trinkets and such. Too bad she
can't cook: the midday meal is a disaster. I find
myself sneaking off to the local pub when I can, yet
another unexpected and unwanted expense.

Researchers have searched far and wide for a "Frau Kram" figure in Beethoven's works. They have looked for a drunken female and have found none. Remember the sweetness of Leonore in

<u>Fidelio</u>. And yet the answer has been staring them in the face

all this time. For isn't one of the admittedly lesser-known

works of this period the secular cantata, "Ach! Es Schmerzt Mir

der Magen" ("Oh, My Stomach Hurts!")? Certainly if Frau Kram is

anywhere in Beethoven's music, it would be in this piece.

✔When you're finished, save the document as CHAPTER.2.

It's a good idea to establish a *consistent* way of spacing between paragraphs or indented sections. Later, if you add to or delete sections of the document, the spacing will still be correct. But for the moment take a look at the page break display between pages 1 and 2. What's "wrong" with it?

WordPerfect breaks the pages depending on the length of the form (the page) and the number of blank lines in the top margin and bottom margins. Page 2 will print with an extra blank line at the top, because of the spacing between paragraphs. Don't worry about this yet. But keep in mind that, when the document gets to its "final" stage, you should make a quick run through your document and check the page endings (Chapter 17).

✔You may wish to use the F5 List Files key to delete the two macro files, IN.WPM and RE.WPM, unless, of course, you plan to use them for *real* work!

(An aside: Another way to switch formats, but one that doesn't require macros, is to use WordPerfect's powerful *style* feature. Because that's a more advanced topic, however, you'll have to wait until Chapter 26.)

Dear Reader, working with two documents in WordPerfect couldn't be easier. Now that you've typed a long article, it's time to check your typing and maybe even improve your writing style.

Grammarian's Delight: Speller and Thesaurus

In this chapter you'll learn the following new commands:

Function Key Commands

ALT-F1 Thesaurus   Find synonyms or antonyms for a word

CTRL-F2 Spell   Check the spelling of a word, page, document, or block

Even if you're not a grammarian, you'll like WordPerfect's speller and thesaurus. These features check your documents for misspellings and typographical errors or help you find just the right word. Assuming that you typed the LAREST document in Chapter 11, you're ready to begin.

DO WARM-UP

How the Spelling Checker Operates

When you prepare short documents, you can easily see your mistakes on the screen. But that's unrealistic! When you work with longer documents like LAREST, you won't be able to see everything at once. Even if you scroll through the document, your eye can easily overlook misspellings. WordPerfect has a built-in spelling program that checks your documents for possible mistakes. Note the word *possible*. Like everything else in this world, computers are not perfect, and spelling checkers aren't either.

WordPerfect has a dictionary of many common—and not so common—English words. When you ask the program to check the spelling in a document, it matches each word in the document against the words in its dictionary. If it finds an *exact match*, it considers the word correct. (It will disregard upper- and lowercase, by the way.) If not, it stops and shows you the word in context and even suggests possible corrections.

There are two limitations to all spelling checkers like WordPerfect's. First, they can't possibly have all words in their dictionaries. Sometimes, a word *is* correct, but the program can't find it so it flags it as an "error." *You*, as the captain of your fate, must make the final decision about the correctness of a word. The second limitation is that WordPerfect can't read a word for its meaning in the document. For example, if you typed *from* instead of *form*, WordPerfect won't help you, because both these words are correctly spelled.

If you're confused by *there* for *their* or *they're*, or *its* for *it's*, WordPerfect can't help you with your grammar, either, but it can suggest possible sound-alike words to jog your memory. What's more, WordPerfect's speller can check if you mistakenly typed a word twice (a "double word") or if you typed a digit in a word (such as *thi9s*).

When I first started using the spelling checker, it stopped at *Alfieri*. Of course, *I* know that it's a perfectly good word, but the program didn't. It would be a hassle if WordPerfect stopped every time it came to your name, so you can customize the dictionary by adding your own words to it. WordPerfect also automatically reformats your document while the spelling check is in operation if spelling corrections change some lines.

The speller uses a *main* dictionary file, WP{WP}US.LEX, and a *supplemental* dictionary file, WP{WP}US.SUP. The US stands for American English. I refer to both files collectively as the dictionary. Hard disk users: The dictionary files are normally in the WordPerfect directory, but you can put them elsewhere (Appendix A). The first time you add any words to the dictionary during a spelling check, WordPerfect creates the supplemental file. Version 4.2 users know these files as LEX.WP and {WP}LEX.SUP, respectively.

Note: Owners of Version 4.2 must convert their supplemental and specialized dictionaries to 5.0 format with the Speller utility (Chapter 36).

Checking a Document

Now it's time to begin. WordPerfect lets you spell-check an individual word, just one page, or an entire document. You can also check just part of a document as a block. The steps for checking a word, a page, or a document are essentially the same. In this example you'll check an entire document.

✔Retrieve the LAREST document.

Stop! If you have a dual floppy system, remove your work disk from the B drive and insert the Spell disk. If you have a hard disk, the dictionary should already be in the WordPerfect directory.

Press   **CTRL-F2 Spell**

If you forgot to insert the Spell disk, WordPerfect tells you:

`WP{WP}US.LEX not found: 1 Enter Path; 2 Skip Language; 3 Exit Spell: 3`

Insert the Spell disk if you have to, then type **1** or **p** [Enter Path] to continue. WordPerfect requests the dictionary path:

`Temporary dictionary path:`

Type the drive letter and colon or the complete path name, then press **RETURN**. Use the **2** [Skip Language] choice is if you've inserted a code to change languages (Chapter 36) and WordPerfect can't find the dictionary for that language.

If WordPerfect can find the dictionary, you'll then see the spell menu:

`Check: 1 Word; 2 Page; 3 Document; 4 New Sup. Dictionary; 5 Look Up; 6 Count: 0`

Although you won't stop to check a word or a page right now, keep this in mind. You must position the cursor under the particular word (or under the space directly past the word) or anywhere on the page you wish to check before you start the speller.

Type   **3** or **d** [Document]

WordPerfect begins to check the entire LAREST document. You can cancel at any time by pressing **F1 Cancel**. If you do cancel, WordPerfect presents a word count of the words checked so far and tells you to press any key to continue editing.

Caution: The corrections you've made before you canceled or at the end of a spelling check remain in the document, but they aren't permanent corrections until you save the document again.

Unless you made a typing mistake before the word *Colmao*, that's the first unknown word, so WordPerfect stops there. Figure 12-1 shows how your screen should look. The highlight on the word *Colmao* identifies the word WordPerfect can't find in its dictionary.

The Spell Options

WordPerfect first attempts to find a correct spelling for the word that it doesn't know and lists one or more suggested alternates. For this word WordPerfect

```
        San Francisco, eat your heart out!  Los Angeles has some of
    the best restaurants in the state, with more appearing all the
    time.  I'm not talking big and fancy here.  For the most part,
    these are smaller places, generally ethnic, but the food is great
    and the prices are right.
        Certainly at the top of my list is El Colmao, purveyors of
    excellent Cuban food.  If you don't like rice and beans, then skip
    this place, because rice and beans are the staple of the menu.  But
    you'll be missing several treats, such as the picadillo (ground
    beef cooked in a sauce), or the ropa vieja (literally, "old
    clothes" -- shredded beef simmered in tomato sauce), or boliche

    ==========================================================================

    A. calm




    Not Found: 1 Skip Once; 2 Skip; 3 Add; 4 Edit; 5 Look Up; 6 Ignore Numbers: 0
```

Figure 12-1   Using the Spelling Checker

finds only one alternate, calm, which isn't correct. At the bottom of the screen
is this message:

Not Found: 1 Skip Once; 2 Skip; 3 Add; 4 Edit; 5 Look Up; 6 Ignore Numbers: 0

There are no mnemonics because you could type the letter next to the
alternate to correct the spelling with that alternate, and there may be many
alternates (A., B., and so on). Here's what the options on this menu mean.
In a moment you'll continue the example.

1. Type **1** [Skip Once] to skip the word once if it's correctly spelled.
   WordPerfect will stop at the word again elsewhere in the document.
   Don't use this option unless you want to check *every* occurrence of an
   unknown word.

2. Type **2** [Skip] to skip the word throughout the rest of the document, if
   the word is correctly spelled. This is by far the best way to bypass
   words that the speller doesn't know and that you don't want to add to
   the supplemental dictionary.

3. Type **3** [Add] to add the word to the supplemental dictionary. Make
   sure the word is correctly spelled! WordPerfect won't stop at the word
   with the same spelling again. Use this option to customize the dictionary with your name, and so on.

Caution: There is a limit to the number of words you can add to the supplemental dictionary. I suggest adding only those words that you *know* you use a great deal or putting them in the main dictionary eventually to free up the supplemental dictionary (Chapter 36).

4. Type **4** [Edit] to enter a correction directly into the text if Word-Perfect doesn't suggest alternate spellings or if the alternates aren't the correct word.

Tip: You can also press **LEFT ARROW** or **RIGHT ARROW** to begin editing. After you've typed the correction, press **F7 Exit** or **RETURN** to return to the speller.

5. Type **5** [Look Up] to find the correct spelling of any word or a word pattern. See Looking up Words and Sounding Out a Word later in the chapter. If you choose a correction, the speller replaces the original word with your choice.

6. Type **6** [Ignore Numbers] so that WordPerfect doesn't stop when it finds a word, like *8th,* that contains numerals.

7. Type **0** or press **RETURN** to have WordPerfect show more alternates if all the alternates don't fit on one screen. If you then find the correct word, type the letter next to it.

Once you've determined how to deal with the highlighted word, WordPerfect finds the next unknown word. Continue with the example. Because *Colmao* is correct:

Type   **2** [Skip]

I originally misspelled the word *purveyors* in this document, so WordPerfect dutifully stopped and suggested the correct spelling, together with the plural! WordPerfect also honors the *case* of the misspelled word and substitutes the correct word in the same case. When you skip a word, WordPerfect keeps it in a special buffer until you finish spelling the document, at which points WordPerfect clears the buffer.

Because I haven't a clue about how many mistakes you made, continue checking the document on your own. The next word that WordPerfect thinks is misspelled is probably *picadillo.* Type **2** [Skip] and continue to check all words. Make any corrections. (Apparently WordPerfect knows *tempura* and *sukiyaki,* but not *sushi* and *teriyaki.* Maybe the WordPerfect folks in Utah have never eaten those delicious dishes—too bad!)

Another Menu You Might See

There's a variation of the previous menu that may appear at times. If it finds a double occurrence of a word, WordPerfect stops and tells you:

```
Double Word: 1 2 Skip; 3 Delete 2nd; 4 Edit; 5 Disable Double Word Checking
```

Normally, you'd type **3** [Delete 2nd] to remove the double word. When the spelling check is completely finished, WordPerfect tells you:

```
Word count: 1050     Press any key to continue
```

Press   [any key]

to leave the spelling checker.

✔Floppy disk owners: Remove the Spell disk and insert your work disk. Everyone: Save the document after you've made any corrections but leave the document on the screen.

Looking Up Words

A very useful feature of the spelling checker is its ability to look up the spelling of a word based on a template with the standard **?** or * wildcards. Suppose you more or less know how to spell *occurrence*, but is it *occurence* instead? Start the speller and type **5** or ι [Look Up]. WordPerfect prompts:

```
Word or word pattern:
```

Type a word pattern template and press **RETURN**. For instance, in this example you could type occur* or occur?ence. To return where you left off, press **F1 Cancel** or **ESC**. When WordPerfect stops at an unknown word during a spelling check, the **5** [Look Up] choice serves the same function.

Sounding Out a Word

WordPerfect uses a special formula for suggesting alternate words that sound like the unknown word. But sometimes the alternates aren't what you want either. Use the **5** [Look Up] choice to instruct WordPerfect to continue "sounding out" the word and suggesting alternates. Keep in mind, though, that this takes a little time, especially if you have a floppy disk system. Version 4.2 users: There used to be a Phonetic option, but that's now part of Look Up.

Use this choice to help you with *homonyms*, words that sound the same but are spelled differently and have different meanings, such as *there* and *their*. If seeing the words doesn't help, try working with the thesaurus, explained later, to check the part of speech (noun, adjective, adverb) of a word. For example, *there* is a pronoun or an adverb, but *their* is an adjective.

Spelling a Block

What if you've already checked a long document and you don't want to go through the entire spelling procedure if you've added just a few new paragraphs or pages? Use your old friend, block, instead. Block out whatever text you want to check, then start the speller. Continue as normal, then press any key when WordPerfect is finished checking the block.

Getting a Word Count

Use the speller to give you a count of the words in your document or in just part of the document. For the entire document, press **CTRL-F2 Spell**, and type **6** or **c** [Count]. This choice bypasses the spelling check. Press any key to return to the document after you ascertain just how wordy you really are!

To count part of a document, block out the part you want to count and then begin the spelling check. This time, you have no choice but to check the entire block before you can get a word count. (If you press **F1 Cancel** when WordPerfect stops at a misspelling, you'll get a count of only those words in the block up to that point.) Sometimes you'll luck out: If WordPerfect doesn't find any misspellings in the block, it ends the check with a word count anyway.

Question: What's another way to count a block? *Answer:* Save it to another file and then count that file. (You may wish to retrieve this file in Doc 2.) That way, you don't have to go through the spelling check just to get a word count.

Dealing with Dictionaries

I think you'll find that the main dictionary, WP{WP}US.LEX, contains a large percentage of the words you use normally. It also includes many words specific to the professions. However, it's possible that your work requires the use of jargon, foreign, or other industry-specific words. You may have to set up your own *specialized dictionary* for these words or use one of the foreign language dictionaries. That's what choice **4** [New Sup. Dictionary] is for.

For instance, if you write mostly about food and about computers, you could have two different specialized dictionaries. You might also find that you'll want to delete words from a dictionary or add new words. Say that one of your bosses leaves the company, so you want to remove her name from the dictionary.

WordPerfect's separate Speller utility—it's in a file called SPELL.EXE—helps you do all these things and more (Chapter 36). At this point, however, you now know how to work with the spelling checker on a day-to-day basis.

Using the Thesaurus

Another writer's aide is WordPerfect's built-in thesaurus. At any time, you can ask WordPerfect to give you a synonym for the word at the cursor location. You can also use the thesaurus to help you find what the French call *le mot juste,* the "correctly chosen word according to its use in the sentence," and to offer some assistance if you have problems with homonyms. WordPerfect even offers *antonyms,* opposites, of many words. The thesaurus is in a file called WP{WP}US.THS (in previous versions the file was TH.WP.)

The cursor should first be anywhere under the word you want to check, or under the space immediately following the word.

✔Position the cursor on the word *loyal* in the third paragraph of LAREST. Stop! If you have a dual floppy system, remove your work disk from the B drive and insert the Thesaurus disk. If you have a hard disk, the thesaurus should already be in the WordPerfect directory.

To find synonyms for *loyal:*

Press   **ALT-F1 Thesaurus**

WordPerfect highlights the word *loyal* and moves the text containing this word up to the top of the screen. As Figure 12-2 shows, the rest of the screen is taken up by the thesaurus. WordPerfect notes that *loyal* is an adjective by displaying (a) and offers two groups of synonyms depending on its two basic meanings. It also presents some antonyms (ant) for the word.

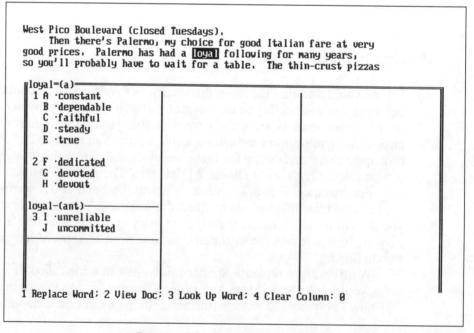

Figure 12-2   Using the Thesaurus

There may be several groups of words, depending on the different meanings of the word you're checking. Each group is marked with a number, and each replacement word is marked with a letter. If there are more synonyms and antonyms than can fit on the screen, use the standard scrolling commands (HOME,DOWN ARROW, PG DN, and so on) to move the cursor through the list. You can also press CTRL-HOME and type the number of a group that you want the cursor to select.

At the bottom of the screen is this menu:

```
1 Replace Word; 2 View Doc; 3 Look Up Word; 4 Clear Column: 0
```

Type   1 [Replace Word]

This choice lets you replace the original word with one of the synonyms or antonyms. WordPerfect prompts:

```
Press letter for word
```

Type   c

the letter next to *faithful*.

WordPerfect replaces *loyal* with *faithful*, exits the thesaurus, and adjusts the text. The cursor is now on the space directly after *faithful*. You can still check the previous word.

Press   **ALT-F1 Thesaurus**

This time you'll learn about the other options.

Type   2 [View Doc]

This choice temporarily suspends the thesaurus so you can look at the text. Use the standard cursor movement keys to move around. Sometimes you'll want to check a synonym against the text, but you won't be able to see the text you need. Use this choice, then press **F7 Exit** to return to the thesaurus, as WordPerfect notes. WordPerfect again highlights the word *faithful*.

Use the **3** [Look Up Word] choice to check one of the other words. WordPerfect asks for the word. Type the word or the letter next to the word. However, it's faster just to type the letter without having to type **3** [Look Up Word] first.

Type   a

the letter next to *allegiant*.

WordPerfect says:

Word not found

WordPerfect is telling you that this word is not a headword. A *headword* is a word that has references in the thesaurus. The words marked with little dots are all headwords.

Type   c

for *dedicated*.

WordPerfect shows you synonyms and antonyms for *dedicated*. The letter choices are now in the second column.

Type   a

for *committed*.

More words! Use the **LEFT ARROW** or **RIGHT ARROW** keys to move between columns and thus make another column active. When you're finished looking at all these words, move the cursor to the third column. Then:

Type   4 [Clear Column]

to remove the listings in column 3.

Tip: You can also press **DEL** or **BACKSPACE** to clear a column.

Type   4 [Clear Column]

You're back to only one column of synonyms and antonyms.

Press   **RETURN** or **F1 Cancel**

to leave the thesaurus.

Tip: You can check any word, even if it's not in a document. First, position the cursor on a blank line, *then* press **ALT-F1 Thesaurus**. Word-Perfect says:

Word:

Type the word and press **RETURN**. If it can't find synonyms for that word, WordPerfect displays a blank thesaurus screen. Type **3** [Look up word] to try another word or press **F1 Cancel**.

✔Press **RETURN** or **F1 Cancel** to leave the thesaurus. Floppy disk owners: Remove the Thesaurus disk and insert your work disk. Everyone: Save the document now.

If you want more practice with the speller and thesaurus, why not retrieve any other documents you've created and try your newly found skills on them? What words did you misspell or change?

13

The Forms Fandango

In this chapter you'll learn the following new command . . .

Typewriter Keyboard and Numeric Keypad Command
CTRL-RETURN   Insert a hard page break into the document

. . . you'll discover new uses for these commands . . .
SHIFT-F7 Print   Create or edit forms for your printer
SHIFT-F8 Format   Change the paper size or type (form change)

. . . and you'll learn some new codes:

[HPg]	Hard page break
[Paper Sz/Typ]	Paper size or type (form) change
[SMALL] and [small]	Begin and end small font
[SPg]	Soft page break

Until now you've used the standard *form*, an 8½ by 11 inch page, for your documents. This chapter teaches you how to change forms so that you can work with other paper sizes and types. Recall from Chapter 5 that I deferred a lengthy discussion of how to set up forms for your printer. Well, the time has come for you to take the deep plunge into the world of forms, because so much formatting depends on them. Dear Reader, study this chapter carefully!

DO WARM-UP

Forms in a Nutshell

Another feature of WordPerfect's intelligent printing is that you can set up different forms for each of your printers. Before you actually try your hand at creating and using forms, here are the general points to learn about them:

1. Every form has certain specifications, the most important being *paper size* and *paper type*, that you must determine.

2. Form information is attached to the printer resources, because one printer may work with forms in a different fashion from another printer. Depending on the printer, WordPerfect may provide a few default forms automatically. You can add others, even different size forms for the same form type. There is always at least the standard form available to you.

3. For every form you want to use, you must define the form for the printer *before* you can access the form. You either add a new form or edit an existing form.

    Tip: After you add a form, see if WordPerfect's default settings for the form work for your needs before you make any changes.

4. Once you've defined the forms you need, you can insert a code to change forms at the beginning of or within a document. For instance, a later exercise will show you how to insert an envelope form change within a document.

    Caution: A form change is a *page formatting* instruction, so always make sure you insert the form change code at the top of the page.

5. When you change the paper size and type, WordPerfect tries to find a form for the printer that corresponds to the settings you selected. If no form is available, WordPerfect uses the "ALL OTHERS" definition. If you didn't set up an "ALL OTHERS" definition, WordPerfect uses the form that's the closest match. See Forms Confusion later in the chapter.

6. If the printer can't use the form you select, you'll see this message in the print: control printer menu:

    `ERROR: Printer doesn't support selected form`

    Try another form, or the "ALL OTHERS" choice.

7. You must still adjust the page formatting for the form change from within a document after you've selected a form. For example, you may want to set the margins to zero (0) to have WordPerfect display the unprintable regions on a form for a laser printer (page 115).

8. The standard form's dimensions may be different in other countries. WordPerfect uses the current language setting (Chapter 36) to assign the standard form for the country represented by the language.

Tip: Use a *format document*, described later in the chapter, to reuse form changes with their corresponding page formatting changes.

Seems complicated, no? I must reassure you that it isn't complicated at all, once you get the hang of it. The importance of forms is that, when you switch printers, WordPerfect can still print documents on the forms, provided you've set up the forms. That is, you don't have to insert any format change codes for the same form on different printers.

Adding a Form to the Printer Resource File

Most of the time, you'll work with the standard form, an 8½ by 11 inch page that you insert vertically in the printer. This section shows you how to create or edit other forms.

The standard printer resource doesn't have an envelope form by default, so you'll set one up and in the process learn all you need to know about forms. Because I'm a nice person, I'll step you through the entire process.

Tip: Substitute your printer for the standard printer if you want to set up an envelope form for it. WordPerfect may already have provided one for you, but you may want to edit the settings.

Press   **SHIFT-F7 Print**

Type   **s** [Select Printer]

Highlight the Standard Printer if it's not selected. Then:

Type   **3** or **e** [Edit]

to bring up the select printer: edit menu.

Type   **4** or **f** [Forms]

to display the select printer: forms menu.

Form Types. Only the standard form should be on the screen, so you'll add a new form for envelopes.

Type   **1** or **a** [Add]

to bring up the select printer: form type menu (Figure 13-1).

Before you go on, understand that the form types are more descriptive than anything else, and their names are meant to indicate their functions. *Bond,* for instance, might be that special paper you use once in a while or a

```
Select Printer: Form Type

        1 - Standard

        2 - Bond

        3 - Letterhead

        4 - Labels

        5 - Envelope

        6 - Transparency

        7 - Cardstock

        8 - [ALL OTHERS]

        9 - Other




Selection: 1
```

Figure 13-1   The Select Printer: Form Type Menu

higher quality paper for final printouts. It doesn't necessarily have to be bond paper at all! *Letterhead* could be the first page of your stationery with its preprinted name and address. You might want to use *Cardstock* for printing on index cards.

You'll want to select the envelope form next, but before you do, read on. In addition to using some or all of the seven named form types, you can add many others with your own names or use a "catch-all" category. Here are the steps, but don't follow them now:

1. To create a totally new form, type **9** or **o** [Other]. WordPerfect prompts:

   `Other form type:`

   Type a name as you want it to appear in the forms list, then press **RETURN**. You can create as many new form types as you need, as long as you have enough disk space to save the printer resource files.

2. To set up any other forms that you may need in a generic category, type **8** or **a** [ALL OTHERS].

Here, of course, you'll do this:

Type   **5** or **e** [Envelope]

to choose the envelope form and bring up the select printer: forms menu.
WordPerfect provides default settings for the form on the select printer: forms menu. Again, I'll explain the options as you work with them.

Form Size. You have complete control over the actual size of the form, but WordPerfect can help. It provides a number of popular sizes, so you don't have to fidget with a ruler.

Type   **1** or **s** [Form Size]

Wow! The select printer: form size menu appears. See Figure 13-2. The *inserted edge* means the top left corner of the form. Select one of the sizes that WordPerfect provides or create your own size. You'll accept the envelope size, which is for legal envelopes by the way:

Type   **5** or **e** [Envelope]

to select the legal envelope size and leave this menu.
To enter a size that isn't listed, type **o** [Other]. WordPerfect then prompts:

```
Width: 0"      Length:
```

Type the width and press **RETURN**. Then type the length and press **RETURN**.

Note: If you selected ALL OTHERS as the paper type, the Form Size changes to Maximum Width. Enter the widest possible size for all forms that will use this type. WordPerfect uses this definition when it can't find the paper size and type that you specify as a format change in the document.

Paper Orientation. The next option, *orientation*, brings up another topic from the world of desktop publishing (Chapter 4). Laser printer paper enters the printer from a paper tray and can enter only one way. You can't shift the paper around to print, say, horizontally on the page. Normally, you print across the width of the paper. This is *portrait orientation*, so named because most portrait paintings are vertical. When you want to print across the length of the page, that's called *landscape orientation*, because landscape paintings are generally horizontal.

```
Select Printer: Form Size
                              Inserted
                              Edge

    1 - Standard             8.5"    x    11"

    2 - Standard Wide        11"     x    8.5"

    3 - Legal               8.5"     x    14"

    4 - Legal Wide          14"      x    8.5"

    5 - Envelope            9.5"     x    4"

    6 - Half Sheet          5.5"     x    8.5"

    7 - US Government        8"       x    11"

    8 - A4                  210mm    x    297mm

    9 - A4 Wide             297mm    x    210mm

    0 - Other

Selection: 1
```

Figure 13-2   The Select Printer: Form Size Menu

This won't mean much to you if you don't own a laser printer. In fact, you can leave the orientation at portrait or change it to landscape for the envelope form. To see what happens when you select this option:

Type   **2 or o [Orientation]**

WordPerfect presents the orientation menu:

```
Orientation: 1 Portrait; 2 Landscape; 3 Both: 0
```

Choice **3** [Both] tells WordPerfect that the form can go into the printer in either landscape or portrait mode.

  ✔ If you do have a laser printer, you *must* set landscape orientation for an envelope, so do that now. If you don't have a laser printer, just press **F1 Cancel** to leave this menu.

Initially Present. Suppose you normally use continuous form paper, so your envelopes aren't anywhere near the printer most of the time. The *initially present* option tells WordPerfect that the form is already in the printer. You'll change it:

Type   **3** or **i** [Initially Present]

Type   **n**

for no.

When you use a form that's not initially present, WordPerfect reminds you to issue a go before you print the page.

Location. You already know how this option lets you determine the type of paper you're using (Chapter 5). If you have to insert envelopes manually, change this option to choice **3** [Manual]. Well I'll be a monkey's uncle! When you select manual, WordPerfect also changes the initially present option to no if you didn't do it yourself!

Make sure you've selected the correct bin number if your printer uses sheet feeders.

Note: If your printer has two or more sheet feeder bins, the only way you can switch from the default sheet feeder to another bin within a document is to set up different forms for each bin first. Then insert a form change code in the document to select the form in a different bin. See also Changing Paper Trays later in the chapter.

Page Offsets. This choice refers to the positioning of the form in the printer. Change the offset settings—top and left—only if you insert the form in the printer at a different position from that of the standard paper. That way, WordPerfect can keep track of where to start printing on the form. The settings work in conjunction with the normal top margin and left margin settings. You can enter a negative page offset, too.

Tip: Don't change the page offsets until you've printed the form once with the standard position. Then make any adjustments.

Okay, you've determined all the settings for your envelope form. To save the form definition:

Press   **F7 Exit**

to see your added form on the list.

Press   **F7 Exit** enough times

to return to the document screen.

Editing or Deleting a Form

To edit a form, follow the steps to edit the printer and bring up the list of forms. Highlight the form and type **3** or **e** [Edit]. Continue as above.

To delete a form, highlight the form name and type **2** or **d** [Delete]. WordPerfect prompts:

```
Delete form? (Y/N) No
```

Type **y** to delete or **n** to cancel. The form no longer exists!

Caution: Make sure you check any documents that used this form and delete any form change codes that refer to the form.

Keeping Track of Forms

The select printer: forms screen always shows the forms you've defined for a particular printer, as well as each form's characteristics.

Tip: Call up this screen, prepare your printer, then do a screen dump of the screen (SHIFT-PRT SC) to make an instant *crib sheet* of the form list.

Envelope Exercises

Now that you have your envelope form, it's time to put it to use. This section discusses how to set up an envelope in two different ways: with a letter or as a separate document. In the process you'll learn some important new commands that govern page formatting.

Letter and Envelope Together

Assume that you want to attach an envelope to a letter document for each letter that you write. This approach has obvious advantages. You can block out the interior address and copy it for the envelope, and you can print both letter and envelope from one document, provided that your printer lets you insert the paper first and the envelope later.

The disadvantages to this approach are that you still have to change some of the formats in the document and you can't use this example if your printer works with tractor feed paper. But it's still useful, because it illustrates what to look out for when you use two different forms in a document and what happens if you're not on your toes.

✔Clear the screen and retrieve the SUDS.LTR document now. Position the cursor at the end of the document. If there isn't a hard return after the date, insert one now.

Because you're going to print the envelope separately from the letter, the two have to be on different pages in the document. However, the letter doesn't take up an entire page, so WordPerfect hasn't supplied a page 2 yet. This brings me to a new command that you have to learn first . . .

The Hard Page Code

If you reveal the codes at a regular page break, that is, a line of hyphens, you'll see the *soft page* code: [SPg]. WordPerfect inserts this code at the end of each page, except on the last page and on those pages that you break yourself. Whenever you want to force a page break before WordPerfect expects it, you must insert a *hard page* code in the document. Here's how:

Press   **CTRL-RETURN**

WordPerfect breaks the page here and positions the cursor at the top of page 2. To distinguish between WordPerfect's own page breaks and your hard page codes, WordPerfect shows hard page breaks as a line of equal signs. You can thus identify hard page breaks easily when you scroll through a document. The code for a hard page looks like this: [HPg]. Figure 13-3 illustrates the Hard Page command.

Tip: Get into the good habit of always inserting hard page codes at the left margin. That way, you don't inadvertently break a page in the middle of a text line.

Changing the Paper Size and Type (Form Change)

Now you'll learn how to insert a form change in the document. As I mentioned at the beginning of the chapter, a form change is a dual instruction: a paper size and a paper type change. The cursor should be at the top of the page, exactly where you should insert the form change.

Press   **SHIFT-F8 Format**

Type   **2 or p** [Page]

Type   **8 or s** [Paper Size]

The format: paper size menu appears. Select a size that matches one of your forms, in this case:

Type   **5 or e** [Envelope]

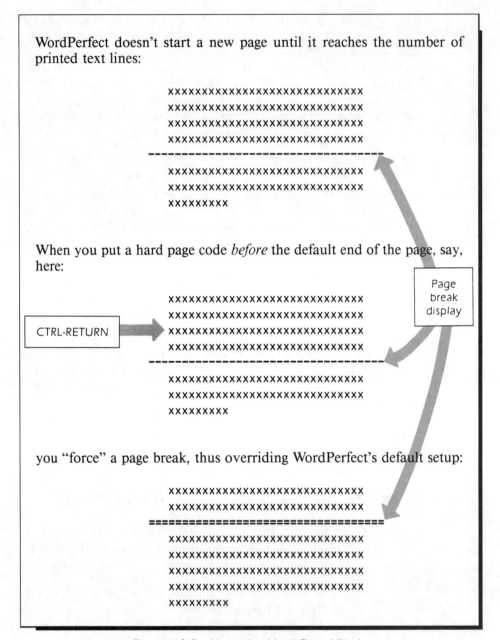

WordPerfect doesn't start a new page until it reaches the number of printed text lines:

```
xxxxxxxxxxxxxxxxxxxxxxxxxxxxxx
xxxxxxxxxxxxxxxxxxxxxxxxxxxxxx
xxxxxxxxxxxxxxxxxxxxxxxxxxxxxx
xxxxxxxxxxxxxxxxxxxxxxxxxxxxxx
------------------------------------
xxxxxxxxxxxxxxxxxxxxxxxxxxxxxx
xxxxxxxxxxxxxxxxxxxxxxxxxxxxxx
xxxxxxxxx
```

When you put a hard page code *before* the default end of the page, say, here:

Page break display

```
xxxxxxxxxxxxxxxxxxxxxxxxxxxxxxxx
xxxxxxxxxxxxxxxxxxxxxxxxxxxxxxxx
xxxxxxxxxxxxxxxxxxxxxxxxxxxxxxxx
xxxxxxxxxxxxxxxxxxxxxxxxxxxxxxxx
------------------------------------
xxxxxxxxxxxxxxxxxxxxxxxxxxxxxx
xxxxxxxxxxxxxxxxxxxxxxxxxxxxxx
xxxxxxxxx
```

CTRL-RETURN

you "force" a page break, thus overriding WordPerfect's default setup:

```
xxxxxxxxxxxxxxxxxxxxxxxxxxxxxxxx
xxxxxxxxxxxxxxxxxxxxxxxxxxxxxxxx
====================================
xxxxxxxxxxxxxxxxxxxxxxxxxxxxxx
xxxxxxxxxxxxxxxxxxxxxxxxxxxxxx
xxxxxxxxxxxxxxxxxxxxxxxxxxxxxx
xxxxxxxxxxxxxxxxxxxxxxxxxxxxxx
xxxxxxxxx
```

Figure 13-3   How the Hard Page Works

The format: paper type menu appears. Why do you have to choose envelope again when you've just selected the envelope paper size? Actually, this menu lets you select a different *type* of form for the size you specified. Many paper types may use the same paper size, or vice versa. Because your envelope form uses the envelope size, do this:

Type   **5** or **e** [Envelope]

to return to the format: page menu.

WordPerfect shows the new paper size and type on the format: page menu.

Press   **F7 Exit** or **RETURN**

to return to the document.

You've just inserted a [Paper Sz/Typ] code that lists the paper size and type.

Forms Confusion

If the paper size and type don't match an existing form, WordPerfect won't be able to find the form in the printer resources. WordPerfect then displays an asterisk next to the setting or settings it doesn't "know." You'll see the asterisk in the paper size/type code and on the format: page menu. Below that is this message:

```
(*requested form is unavailable)
```

WordPerfect will look for an "ALL OTHERS" definition and use it if there is one. If you didn't set up a definition for all other forms, WordPerfect selects the form that's the closest match to the paper size and type change.

I recommend that you always have a specific form definition for each form you plan to use. That is, if the form doesn't exist, you have two options: (1) delete the paper size/type code and insert one for a correct form or (2) create the form for your printer now or any time before you print. Once you've created the form that uses the paper size and type that you specified in the form change, WordPerfect removes the offending asterisk and shows the correct paper size and type in the code.

Format Changes for the Envelope

Even though you've inserted the correct form change, you still might want to change the actual page formatting for the form. For instance, you'll probably want the interior address lines to print higher up on the envelope page. Assuming that you use the same top of form setting for the envelope as for regular paper, you'll change the top margin. One inch is too much of a blank space at the top of an envelope! You may also need to set the left margin over a bit.

Note: These settings depend on how and where you insert the envelope into your printer. This is just an example.

🖊Change the top margin to something like 0.3 or 0.5 inch but leave the bottom margin alone. Then change the left margin to 0.5 but leave the right margin as it is. Type your return address lines, just as you would on an envelope. Then use the **RETURN** key to space down about ten blank lines.

What now? Well, you want the recipient's name and address to print in the center of the envelope. You *could* just tab over, but there's a better way.

🖊Change the left margin to 4.5 and the right margin to, say, 0.5.

The new right margin setting ensures that WordPerfect won't wrap any long address lines. Darn! You forgot the recipient's name and address. No problem! Just go back to the beginning of the document, block out the interior address, return to the end of the document (where you left off), and copy the block here. Be careful! You *don't* want to copy the format change codes at the beginning of the document!

🖊Press **HOME,HOME,UP ARROW** to go to the beginning of the document but past the codes. The cursor should be under the *M* of *Mr.* Block and copy the interior address lines. Press **HOME,HOME,DOWN ARROW** to position the cursor at the end of the envelope page, then retrieve the copied block. When you're finished, save the document but leave it on the screen.

You may want to try your hand at printing both pages if your printer accepts individual sheets. Use scrap paper if you don't want to spoil a good envelope! You may have to make some adjustments to the envelope's page formatting for your printer setup. When it encounters a form change during printing, WordPerfect beeps at you. Go into the print: control printer menu to see this message:

```
Message:    Insert form--Press "G" to continue
```

When you're ready to print the form, type **4** or **g** [<u>G</u>o].

A Separate Envelope Document

As you can well imagine, you wouldn't want to go through these formatting steps every time you print an envelope! Why not set up the envelope—form change, page formatting, interior address, and all—in a separate document? It will then be your own envelope boilerplate that you can use whenever you need it. In this example you'll learn how to change the paper size, too. (Chapter 29 shows you another way to address envelopes.)

You have a sudden brainstorm: You'll *copy* the envelope setup from the SUDS.LTR document to the new envelope file. (You're learning fast, Dear Reader!) But be careful to copy only the text and codes that you need. The cursor should be at the end of the document.

🖊Position the cursor at the top of page 2. Turn the codes on to make sure. Block out the paper size/type change code, the margin change codes, your return address, the blank lines below your address, *and* the left and right margin change code. Do not include the recipient's name and address in the block. Then:

Press   **F10 Save**

Type   env

Press   **RETURN**

to save the block to a file called ENV.

Whenever you want to print an envelope, retrieve the ENV document. Alternately, set up a new page in a letter document and copy the envelope document there. In either case, just press **HOME,HOME,DOWN ARROW** to move the cursor to the bottom of the envelope page, then insert the address.

Caution: Print the envelope from the screen, but *don't* save it, because you don't want to add a name and address in this "generic" envelope.

✔Clear the screen now.

Getting Along With Long Lines

In this section you'll create documents with long text lines, and you'll work with smaller fonts. You'll also use a couple of new forms. There's a lot of good word processing practice here!

Using a Legal Form: A Trust Account

In the law firm where I worked, wills and trust accounts were printed on paper that was 14 inches long and in an elite typestyle appropriately termed "prestige legal elite." This example shows you how to change both the form and the font. Again, it's only an example. The type of fonts you have available depend on the printer you've selected.

Your first order of business is to set up a legal form specifically for wills and trusts. Do *not* use the standard printer; instead, set up the form for your printer.

✔Follow the steps to add a new form to your printer resources. When you get to the select printer: form type menu, type **9** or **o** [Other]. For the other form type, use **Will**. For the form size, use **3** [Legal] (8½ by 14 inches). Change the other settings as necessary. Press **F7 Exit** enough times to save the form and return to the blank edit screen.

Selecting Other Forms

When you want to use a form that you've created, follow these steps:

Press   **SHIFT-F8 Format**

Type   **2** or **p** [<u>P</u>age]

Type   **8** or **s** [Paper <u>S</u>ize]

Type   **3** or **l** [<u>L</u>egal]

Type   **8** or **o** [<u>O</u>ther]

The defined form types screen appears. Highlight the Will form and type **1** or **s** [<u>S</u>elect]. If you don't see the form on the list, type **2** or **o** [<u>O</u>ther], then select it. Use the name search feature if your list of forms is a long one!

Press   **F7 Exit**

to return to the document.

Using a Smaller Font

A traditional elite typeface prints 12 characters per horizontal inch. That means that there will be more characters per line than with a traditional pica typeface. Well, as you know WordPerfect wants you to think in terms of fonts now. Still, when you select a smaller font, the line length remains at the default 6½ inches unless you change it. WordPerfect's intelligent printing takes care to adjust the number of characters per line for you automatically.

Because the entire example will print in a smaller font, insert a font change code at the beginning of the document. However, the actual lines of the example may be different from what I show here, depending on the printer and font you've selected. Look at the fonts that are available to you first:

✔Use the SHIFT-F7 Print command to select the printer and then edit the printer resources. Do *not* use the standard printer in this exercise, because there is only one font available for it. When the select printer: edit menu appears, type **6** or **i** [<u>I</u>nitial Font] to see the fonts that WordPerfect "knows" for your printer. Make a note of the point sizes. Then exit back to the edit screen.

You can change to a smaller font two different ways.

1. Use the special *small* font. Press **CTRL-F8 Font**, type **1** or **s** [<u>S</u>ize], then type **4** or **s** [<u>S</u>mall]. WordPerfect takes upon itself to find a smaller version of the base font that's in the font list. This action inserts begin and end [SMALL] and [small] codes in the document, and the cursor is between the codes.

    Note: If no smaller font is available, WordPerfect disregards the font change, although the codes stay in the document. Later chapters introduce the other font sizes.

2. Change the *base font*. Press **CTRL-F8 Font**, type **4** or **f** [Base **F**ont], then select the font from the list. Highlight the font you want, then type **1** or **s** [**S**elect] or press **F7 Exit**. This action inserts only an open [Font] code, because WordPerfect assumes you want to stay in the base font. The code lists the font's name.

When you change the font's size to a small font, WordPerfect displays the new font in a different color. I like the second approach better, because then the entire document doesn't appear in a different color on the screen. So, I changed the base font before I typed the example. In my case, the new base font is Courier 12, which prints 12 characters per inch.

✔Change the base font to a smaller font now.

As you type the example, WordPerfect adjusts the lines to accommodate as many characters as possible with the smaller font. If you're using a proportionally spaced font, you may see that some lines appear longer than others on the screen. That's because WordPerfect can fit more characters on those lines. Of course, if you don't like the default left and right margins, you can change them, too.

There's one more change to make before you begin.

✔Change the line spacing to double now.

Go for It

Type the entire trust agreement, shown next. Center the title, and press **RE-TURN** twice after the title and before each subheading. Use one **RETURN** between each subheading and the paragraph following it. Note also that each paragraph starts with *two* tabs rather than one. This was not meant to throw you off, but merely to illustrate a typical legal format. And watch the spacing between sections!

The signature lines are eight tab stops over, but here I *have* thrown you a curve. The two signature lines are single spaced, so what do you have to do? Right! Change back to single spacing. And do you remember an easy way to do the underline at the end? Right again! Use the **ESC** key with the repeat value of 30.

When you type a long line, the screen scrolls to the left when the cursor gets near the end of each line so that you can see the rightmost characters. When WordPerfect starts a new line, it brings the left side of the line back into view.

REVISED TRUST AGREEMENT

I, GRACE T. GOODBODY, do hereby make known my intention to revise

and amend the original Trust Agreement (the "Trust Agreement"), dated April 26,

1947, which established the "Grace T. Goodbody Memorial Trust Account" (the

"Trust"), to include the following stipulations:

Designation of Beneficiary

Whereas the recent actions and lifestyles of the original Beneficiary

to the Trust, my erstwhile friend, Franklyn K. Rake, are now personally

reprehensible to me, I have decided after painful deliberation to change the

Beneficiary to the Trust. The new Beneficiary shall be my nephew, Stanley D.

Sycophant, who presently resides in Los Alamitos, California.

I should also like it known that, as of this date, I shall not be

responsible for any debts incurred by the original Beneficiary, or by his agent

assigns, or representatives.

Adjustment in Attorneys' Fees

In recognition of the long and devoted service of my attorneys,

Smudge & Smudge, and of the great increase in legal and administrative costs,

I give my consent to an adjustment of the original attorneys' fees. The new fees

shall total no less than fifty percent (50%) of the proceeds from my Estate,

before taxes.

<u>Other Requests</u>

       I ask that, as soon as possible upon the dissolution of my Estate,

the bundle of papers and other memorabilia contained in the large, wooden chest

which is presently located under the mattress of the last bed to the right of

the third guest bedroom in the South Wing, be destroyed, most particularly those

letters addressed to a personage named "Poopsie." I further request that my

Executor, WOLFGANG AMADEUS SMUDGE, not show these letters to anyone.

       EXECUTED this fifth day of December, 1989, in Claremont, California.

                        ————————————————————

                        Grace T. Goodbody

On your screen the title line may not appear centered over the text, but when you view the printout or print the document, everything will be okay. By the way, when you view a document that uses a different form, WordPerfect shows the new form's length, too.

    ✔Save the document now as GOODBODY.ELT but keep it on the screen. The file extension .ELT reminds you that this document is in an elite typestyle.

    You may want to refer to Chapter 2 to reacquaint yourself with the various horizontal scrolling commands and try them out on this document. When I typed this example, the very last line appeared on page 2. In word processing parlance that's an *orphan* line (Chapter 17). You could use a hard page code to break page 1 earlier, perhaps at the beginning of the last paragraph, but for the time being leave it alone. You also haven't added a *witness* section to the end of the trust agreement. That'll come in Chapter 14.

    ✔Save the document and clear the screen.

Printing on Horizontal Paper

If you do a lot of statistical tables, you might run into the situation where you would want to print on paper positioned horizontally in the printer. Later, you'll learn how to total columns of figures (Chapter 19). In this example you'll work on yet another form.

When you print on a horizontal page, the width of the page is 11 inches, and the length is 8½ inches. WordPerfect's intelligent printing automatically adjusts the line length when you change the form. You don't have to insert left or right margin changes unless you want to.

✔Set up a standard form that uses the **2 [Standard Landscape]** paper size. Make sure that the form's orientation is landscape. Then on a clear screen insert a form change code that uses this form size and type.

Notice that you can have several forms that are called *standard form*, each with a different paper size. In this example, you'll use tab stops for the various columns, so the next order of business is to set up the tabs.

✔Clear all tabs and set left-justified tab stops at columns 3.5, 6.0, and 8.0 only.

You have done enough typing work in this chapter already, so this example is refreshingly brief!

✔Type each name and then use the **TAB** key to move the cursor before you type the other entries on the line. Press **RETURN** to end each line. Add other names if you wish.

```
Grace T. Goodbody        22 West Street      Calumet City, IL    (607) 552-0981
Cyrus P. Anybody         101 Main Street     San Leandro, CA     (415) 339-2044
Gwendolyn D. Somebody    Route 5             South Dallas, TX    (712) 201-7747
```

✔Save this document as NAMES.

Changing Paper Trays

One of a form's characteristics is its *location* in the printer. When you want to select a different sheet feeder bin for a document, you must insert a form change code at the top of that page in the document. Be sure to define the form first. There is no longer a separate bin change code.

Alternating Between Different Types of Paper

If your printer has a dual bin sheet feeder, and if you find that you alternate between two different types of paper in your documents, set up the two forms for the different paper. For example, say your document contains straight text and statistical typing, where the figures are on a separate horizontal page. Set up the regular form in one bin and the horizontal form in the other. Then, on the first line of those pages in the document using the horizontal paper, make the necessary form change.

Forms don't present any great problems, but they do call for a bit of forethought on your part. That is, you must define a form before you can use it and keep track of the forms you've defined. Often there are other format changes that come into play, such as font selection or tab stops. As your knowledge of word processing increases, all these fine points will become the tools of your word processing trade.

14

A Boilerplate and Block Party

In this chapter you'll learn the following new command . . .

Function Key Command

ALT-F6 Flush Right   Align text to the right margin

. . . you'll discover new uses of these commands . . .

SHIFT-F3 Switch   (1) Change a block from uppercase to lowercase, (2) change a block from lowercase to uppercase

CTRL-F4 Move   Move, copy, or delete tabular columns

. . . and you'll learn some new codes:

`[Flsh Rt]` and `[C/A/Flrt]`   Begin and end flush right alignment

I've already mentioned the term *boilerplate* a couple of times, and by now you've realized that the block technique is an important WordPerfect feature. Now you'll take a closer look at what boilerplates are and how to use them. In the process you'll learn more about the many ways to work with blocks. Dear Reader, you did enough work with forms, so this is a short chapter!

DO WARM-UP

Boilerplates Explained

Years ago, syndicated newspapers would make one set of typeset copy on printer's *plates* for an article and then send these plates around to their syndications for publication. Because of the way it was done, this process became known as boilerplating. Word processors now employ the term *boilerplate* for any text that you use over and over.

Remember that word processing means you never have to retype. You'll find boilerplates one of the most useful word processing tools. For example, if you don't have your own printed stationery, why not set up a standard letterhead, with your name and address and all necessary format codes, in a boilerplate?

Technically, you should have each boilerplate in a different file with an easily recognizable name. You can set up a boilerplate document from scratch, of course, and then save the document to a new file. Again, make sure the typing and formatting are correct, because you'll be copying the boilerplate many times later.

Creating a Boilerplate

Recall from Chapter 13 that you created a separate envelope document (ENV) by saving part of a letter and envelope document (SUDS.LTR) to a new file. You first blocked the codes and text, then pressed F10 Save to save the block to a file. Why retype if you don't have to? In this example you'll create a boilerplate from scratch.

You'll set up a "generic" witness boilerplate that you can add to other documents as necessary. Use the default form and format but note the two tabs at the beginning of each paragraph. Follow the alignment of the text above the underlines when you type them. Later when you add this boilerplate to the revised trust agreement that uses a different font, WordPerfect will reformat the boilerplate in the new font of the main document.

Question: What other interesting things are in this document? (See the next two sections for the answer.)

        We, the witnesses to this agreement, attest that the
above signature is the correct signature of the signee.
        Each of us is now more than eighteen (18) years of age
and a competent witness and resides at the address set forth after
his or her name.
        We are acquainted with the above signee. At this time
we attest that he/she is over the age of eighteen (18) years, and
to the best of our knowledge he/she is of sound mind and is not
acting under duress, menace, fraud, misrepresentation, or undue
influence.

```
        We declare under penalty of perjury according to the laws
of the State of California that the foregoing is true and correct,
and that this declaration is executed on the _____ day of
_____, 198_, at _____, California.
```

✔Press **RETURN** twice at the end of the last paragraph for spacing.

Flush Right Alignment

Here's a partial answer to the question about the interesting features of the example. Because this boilerplate will eventually end up in a document with a different format, there's a way to get the signature lines lined up at whatever will be the right margin: Use the Flush Right command. You'll type the following example:

```
                residing at  _____
                             _____
                             _____
```

Here's how:

Press   **ALT-F6 Flush Right**

The cursor jumps to the right margin. To create the first underline:

Press   **ESC**

Type   **35**

Type   **_**

(That's SHIFT-HYPHEN.)

Press   **RETURN**

The first signature line is added flush at the right margin. WordPerfect inserts begin and end flush right codes, [Flsh Rt] and [C/A/Flrt], respectively, on each line. Later you'll see how to flush right an entire block.

✔To continue, press **ALT-F6 Flush Right**, type residing at and a space, and then create the same underline as just outlined. Press **RETURN** and add the third underline as you did the first and second. Press **RETURN** twice for spacing.

For a second set of signature lines, copy the first set as a block:

✔Press **UP ARROW** enough times to position the cursor on the first signature line. The cursor should be at the beginning of the line in *front* of the flush right codes on that line. Continue the block copy as normal.

You should have two sets of signature lines now. Make sure the document has no typing errors or misspellings when you're finished.

✔Save the document as WITNESS. Then clear the screen and retrieve the document GOODBODY.ELT. Position the cursor at the end of the document.

Using the Boilerplate

An important point rears its head now: Always check the spacing between sections before you add a boilerplate. When you originally typed the GOOD-BODY.ELT document, you probably changed to single spacing to do the signature line for Ms. Goodbody at the end of the document. Make sure that there are *four* blank lines between her name and the witness section before you continue. Now, because you want the witness section to be double spaced:

✔Change the line spacing back to double now. Then retrieve the WITNESS document. Note how the signature lines for the witnesses are aligned flush to the current right margin.

There's another thing to do, which brings up the other interesting thing about this example. Because of the "generic" nature of the witness boilerplate, you must search for the string *he/she* and replace it with *she*. Please do that now. (Some law firms have *two* generic boilerplates, one for men and one for women. The combined approach here works just as well, provided you remember to delete the inappropriate pronouns after you insert the boilerplate!)

✔Save the GOODBODY.ELT document now, then clear the screen.

Joining Documents Redux: A Summary

Now that you know about boilerplates, consider the methods available to you when you want to *join* documents. Depending on where in the first document you want to insert a second document, you could:

- Retrieve the second document, mark it as a block, and use the CTRL-F4 Move key to append the second document to the end of the first.

- Retrieve the first document, position the cursor, then use SHIFT-F10 Retrieve to insert the second document into the first.

- Retrieve each document in its own window and use the cut, copy, or delete block commands to insert the second into the first.

Document Assembly, Format Libraries, and Styles

Working with standard boilerplates and the techniques from this chapter, you can quickly and easily *assemble* a variety of documents. For example, most law firms use certain contract paragraphs over and over (such as a *force majeure* clause). Once you set up your boilerplates, just use them whenever you need them. Don't retype! When you learn about WordPerfect's merge features, you'll discover another, more complicated and powerful, form of document assembly (Chapter 30).

If you need a variety of different document formats, both primary and secondary, why not set up a macro for each? Then you'll have an entire *format library* that's ready whenever you are to save unnecessary work. You may want to keep a little list of the macro names at your computer to remind you what each macro does. Most word processing centers also use format libraries to maintain the consistency of the output among many different operators. You can even set up a *menu* to get a specific format, as an example in Chapter 31 will show you.

Another way to set up a format library is to have all the different formats that you use for a particular document in a separate *style document*. You could, for instance, include an underline style, margins, tabs, and a hyphenation setting (Chapter 20). Whenever you begin a new document, first retrieve the style document and its styles to set the formats for the new document. Style documents are an advanced feature (Chapter 26).

Caution: When you retrieve a format document, WordPerfect may "remember" its name as the last document. After you've entered some text and decide to save the new document, you press **F10 Save**. WordPerfect shows the *format* document's name on the edit line. Make sure you type a new file name! Otherwise, you'll overwrite the format document, which you don't want to change, with the new document on the screen.

Of course, it's a good idea to set up the WordPerfect format defaults for the document type that you use the most. If the standard defaults aren't exactly what you need, you can customize the program (Appendix A).

Blocks and Commands

Often a command changes when block is on. In Chapter 3, for example, you saw that the CTRL-F4 Move command presents the block move menu. Appendix C lists the normal results of all commands and their block equivalents. Not all WordPerfect commands work with blocks. If you press a nonapplicable command when a block is on, either nothing happens or WordPerfect beeps at you.

Other Block Operations

There are many other block operations, most of which you'll learn in chapters that relate to their functions. For example, you can add redlining and strikeout to blocks (Chapter 24) or use a block as an index, table of contents, list, or table of authorities entry (Chapter 23). Here are a few more block features.

Flush Right and Centered Blocks

Just as you can center or flush right text as you type it in, you can center and flush right blocks of existing text. The most practical use for this feature is in titles or other text that you want to stand out in a document. (You might be using boldface or a fancy font, too.)

To flush right or center a block, merely establish the block. When you block a paragraph, make sure you include the entire short line at the end of a paragraph. Then press either **ALT-F6 Flush Right** or **SHIFT-F6 Center**. WordPerfect asks you to confirm your decision. WordPerfect then inserts the correct begin and end code on each line of the block.

Caution: I've found that the only way to restore the block would be to use the Replace command to find all the codes and delete them. However, this doesn't restore the block completely as it was before you flushed it to the right margin.

Changing Case

When a block is on and you press **SHIFT-F3 Switch**, you can *switch* the text in the block from lowercase to uppercase, or vice versa. You'll see the case menu:

1 Uppercase; 2 Lowercase: 0

If you type **1** or **u** [Uppercase], WordPerfect converts the entire block to uppercase. If you then change the block to lowercase, WordPerfect is smart enough to switch text to *mixed* case, with the first letter of each sentence in uppercase, *only* if you've included the ending punctuation of the previous sentence in the block. That's the signal to WordPerfect to convert the case of the sentence correctly. Otherwise, you'd have to add the correct uppercase letters where necessary. WordPerfect also leaves all variations of the word *I* (*I'm, I'll*, and so on) in uppercase, no matter where they appear in a block.

A Word About Large Blocks

Although you can make blocks as large as you like, WordPerfect may slow down considerably when it has to move or copy a large block. That's because WordPerfect writes the entire block to a temporary file on the disk first. If this speed degradation annoys you, divide a large block into several smaller blocks and work with the smaller blocks individually.

Working With Tabular Columns

Later in this book, you'll learn what WordPerfect means by *text columns* and *math columns*. Suffice it to say that these are special formatting situations, and—as confusing as this may be to you—they have nothing to do with the topic of this final section. The *tabular column* feature under consideration here refers to moving or copying columns of text or numbers that have been set up around tab stops or with the Indent commands.

Sometimes you might find it necessary to move or copy just one tabular column as a block. To give you an idea how to do this, and the factors to think about, you'll work with one of your earlier examples.

✔Clear the screen and retrieve the document SALES.87.

Say you want to switch the two columns in this document by moving the first to be after the second. You can't block out just one column with the standard Block command, because WordPerfect would include the entire line in each block. This is a job for tabular column move.

The first trick to tabular column move is to position the cursor at the beginning of the column, not at the beginning of the line, before you block the column. The second trick is to highlight only as much of the column as you need. The third trick is not to worry what the block looks like, as long as you use the special tabular column commands.

✔Position the cursor directly under the *J* of *January*. Then:

Press   **ALT-F4 Block** or **F12 Block**

Press   **DOWN ARROW** eleven times

The cursor is now under the *D* of *December*, but you're not finished yet.

Press   **RIGHT ARROW** eight times

The cursor should be directly under the *r*. At this point, WordPerfect highlights part of the second column in the block, but don't worry. Figure 14-1 shows how your screen looks.

Caution: Don't extend the block any farther than this. Now you're ready to use the tabular column command:

Press   **CTRL-F4 Move**

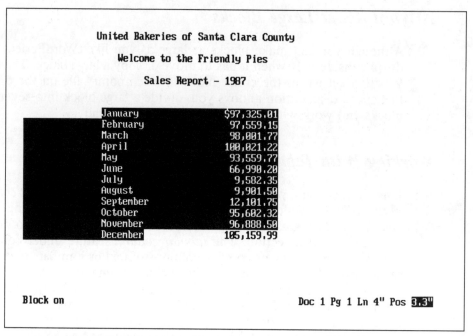

United Bakeries of Santa Clara County

Welcome to the Friendly Pies

Sales Report - 1987

January	$97,325.01
February	97,559.15
March	98,001.77
April	100,021.22
May	93,559.77
June	66,990.20
July	9,582.35
August	9,901.50
September	12,101.75
October	95,602.32
November	96,888.50
December	105,159.99

Block on   Doc 1 Pg 1 Ln 4" Pos 3.3"

Figure 14-1   Blocking a Tabular Column

Type   **2** or **c** [Tabular **C**olumn]

WordPerfect now shows only the first column highlighted. (If part of the second column is highlighted, that means you've delimited too much of the column, and you'll have to start again.) Figure 14-2 shows how the block looks before you move it.

You're ready to move the block:

Type   **1** or **m** [**M**ove]

WordPerfect cuts the first column and is waiting for you to position the cursor at the move location:

Press   **UP ARROW** eleven times

Press   **END**

to position the cursor at the end of the first line of figures.

Press   **RETURN**

to retrieve the column.

Oops! WordPerfect moved the column correctly, but the columns now look too spaced out. Why? Well, the tab settings really haven't changed, but

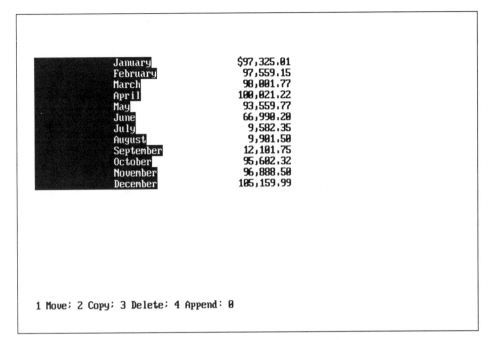

January	$97,325.01
February	97,559.15
March	98,001.77
April	100,021.22
May	93,559.77
June	66,990.20
July	9,582.35
August	9,901.50
September	12,101.75
October	95,602.32
November	96,888.50
December	105,159.99

1 Move; 2 Copy; 3 Delete; 4 Append: 0

Figure 14-2   Moving a Tabular Column

remember that the figures are aligned around the decimal points, while the months are flush left at regular tabs. The point here is that, even though you can move or copy columns easily, you may have to change the tab stops to pretty up the results. (If you wish, find the [Tab Set] code, delete it, and change the tabs to, say, columns 3.2 and 4.8. That should make things look better.)

✔Clear the document from the screen now.

When you study boxes and equations, you'll learn about how to cut and copy a rectangular block (Chapter 15).

Dear Reader, like Alice at the Mad Hatter's tea party, you may feel a bit overwhelmed right now. As your word processing experience grows, though, you'll appreciate all that WordPerfect has to offer.

The Nitty-Gritty

Chapter

15

A Potpourri of
Special Effects

In this chapter you'll learn this new command . . .

Typewriter Keyboard Command

CTRL-2   (1) Compose a character, (2) insert a
WordPerfect character set character

. . . you'll discover new uses of these commands . . .

ALT-⟨*number*⟩   Enter an extended character whose
code is ⟨*number*⟩

CTRL-V   Insert a WordPerfect character set
character

CTRL-F3 Screen   (1) Draw lines and boxes, (2) fill the
screen with spaces

CTRL-F4 Move   Move, copy, or delete rectangular
blocks

SHIFT-F5 Date/Outline   Change the date and time format

SHIFT-F8 Format   (1) Overstrike one character with
others, (2) advance the line up, down,
left, right, to a line, or to a column

CTRL-F8 Font   (1) Change font size, (2) change print
colors

. . . and you'll learn some new codes:

[AdvDn]   Advance down

[AdvLft]   Advance left

[AdvRgt]   Advance right

more . . .

[AdvToCol]	Advance to a column
[AdvToLn]	Advance to a line
[AdvUp]	Advance up
[Color]	Print color change
[EXT LARGE] and [ext large]	Begin and end extra large font
[FINE] and [fine]	Begin and end fine font
[LARGE] and [large]	Begin and end large font
[Ovrstk]	Overstrike
[VRY LARGE] and [vry large]	Begin and end very large font

It's now time to take a look at some other special formatting and printing effects that you can do with WordPerfect, and there are quite a few! This chapter has a mixed bag of features, but you can study the examples a little at a time or just explore the features when you need them. Other printing effects are in Chapters 34 and 35.

You'll learn how to select different font sizes and colors; compose a special character; print one or more characters over another; gain access to your computer's extended characters set; advance to another line or column; and draw lines and boxes. If you type complex scientific or mathematical equations, WordPerfect has the means to help you. This chapter also discusses the many ways to print the date and time in your documents.

DO WARM-UP

Using Different Font Sizes

You've already worked with the *small* font size when you were setting up a trust account document (Chapter 13). Although size changes depend on the fonts available for your particular printer, and although they're most useful if you have a laser printer and many fonts, you might as well learn about the different sizes now. After all, they're special effects, too! You'll see examples of how to use these sizes in Chapter 35.

Recall the rule of thumb about font changes: If there's a different font size available for the *base font*, WordPerfect will use it. If not, WordPerfect retains the base font. Always know what fonts you can select, that is, what base font the printer is using and what other sizes of the base font are available.

In any case, the sizes are all on the CTRL-F8 Font key. Here are the begin and end codes that represent the font sizes: [FINE] and [fine], [SMALL] and [small], [LARGE] and [large], [VRY LARGE] and [vry large], and [EXT LARGE] and [ext large].

Printing in Colors

The last option from the CTRL-F8 Font key lets you print in different colors, provided your printer has this capability. To change print colors, follow these steps:

1. Position the cursor where you want to insert the change in the document.
2. Press **CTRL-F8 Font**.
3. Type **5** or **c** [Print Color].
    The print color screen appears. If you remember your elementary physics, then you'll know that all colors are composed of various percentages of red, green, and blue. WordPerfect shows the percentages for each color you choose. If you *don't* remember any physics, no matter.
4. Type the number or letter of the color you want. If you type **o** [Other], WordPerfect lets you determine the "mix" of red, green, and blue to create your own color!
5. Press **F7 Exit** to return to the document.

WordPerfect inserts a [Color] code here that lists the color you've chosen. There is just one code, not a pair of begin and end codes, so remember to switch back to the default color (probably black) later.

Inserting Special Characters

WordPerfect has three different ways to help you insert into a document those special characters that aren't on the standard American keyboard, such as the British pound sign, foreign language letters with accents, or graphics characters. You can (1) use the compose key, (2) work with the overstrike command, or (3) enter an extended character with the ALT key. Which method you use depends on what you want.

There are many characters lurking in the background of your computer. They are part of the *extended character set*. The American Standards Committee for Information Interchange (ASCII) originally standardized a number of codes for printable characters. This was the ASCII code chart. IBM added more codes and thus "extended" this basic set to bring the total to 256 characters. People now refer to the entire extended character set as the *ASCII codes*.

Note: You aren't restricted to just 256 characters, as the section called The WordPerfect Character Set describes. Some printers, however, can't print all extended characters.

I don't want to go any further into the history of computer keyboards or codes. All you have to know is that the extended character set supplies many legal, foreign language, scientific, and graphics characters. For some bizarre reason, it even includes *two* versions of the Happy Face! The WordPerfect documentation includes a chart of the code numbers. You can also use CTRL-V to compose characters.

The Compose Key

The compose key, CTRL-2, lets you insert a number of common extended characters quickly without having to know their code numbers. You can compose *digraphs*, two characters joined together (for instance, the pound sign—£), or *diacriticals*, one character struck over with an accent mark (like the French or Spanish *c* with a cedilla—ç). Consult the WordPerfect documentation for all the characters that are available and what normal characters you type.

Note: Not all extended characters are available from this key.

For example, to create the British pound sign, you enter these characters: a hyphen (-) and an uppercase L. You can type them in either order but make sure you use the correct case. So:

Press   **CTRL-2**

Now, release both keys. Nothing happens!

Type   **-L or L-**

There's the pound sign. How about the ç?

Press   **CTRL-2**

Type   **,c or c,**

There is no special WordPerfect code for the ASCII extended characters. Please note, however, that some printers can't access these characters.

The Overstrike Command

In WordPerfect, the BACKSPACE key has nothing to do with moving the print head while a document is printing. You can, however, insert a special directive to the printer to position the print head back a column and print something else over the previous character. That's basically what the Compose feature does. WordPerfect also has an Overstrike command, not to be confused with the Strikeover command for soon-to-be-deleted text (Chapter 24). Please note that some printers can't backspace, so you might not get the correct results in the next example.

Probably the most common use of the Overstrike command is for accent marks or special symbols, just like the Compose key. However, the Overstrike command lets you strike over a character with more than one character, or one character and a font change. So the Compose key is fast and easy, but the Overstrike command is more powerful.

Although you could use the Compose key in the next example, you'll work with the Overstrike command instead. You want to type the word *vis-à-vis*, which includes a grave accent that prints over the *a*. (Don't confuse the grave accent with the single quote. The grave accent is on the same key as the tilde, ˜.) You must include *all* characters in the overstrike.

Type   **vis-**

The Overstrike command has moved to the Format key. In previous versions you'd press SHIFT-F1 Super/Subscript, but that key has disappeared in WordPerfect 5.0.

Press   **SHIFT-F8 Format**

Type   **4** or **o** [<u>O</u>ther]

Type   **5** or **o** [<u>O</u>verstrike]

Type   **1** or **c** [<u>C</u>reate]

WordPerfect submits for your approval an [Ovrstk] code on the status line. Type the "struck" and "overstriking" characters:

Type   **a`**

to insert the *a* and the grave accent mark.

Press   **RETURN**

to complete the overstrike.

Press   **F7 Exit**

to return to the document.

Type   **-vis**

The entire word looks like this on the screen: vis-`-vis. Take a look at the codes. There's the [Ovrstk] code and the characters.

Tip: You can include font changes and other characters in the overstrike. Make sure, however, that the begin and end font codes surround the other overstriking characters. Also, keep in mind that for every one overstrike that you create, the characters following the [Ovrstk] code all print in the same position.

To edit an overstrike code, position the cursor directly past the code, go into the format: other menu, select overstrike, then type **2** or **e** [Edit].

✔Clear the screen after this and all other examples before you try the next example. I won't repeat this message!

Accessing the Extended Character Set

All well and good, but you can create only a limited number of characters with the standard keyboard keys and the Compose feature or Overstrike command. For all other extended characters you can access the extended character set directly.

The codes for extended characters are between 1 and 31 and between 128 and 255. Please note, however, that some printers can't print these special characters. What's more, you may have to add a font change code in your document before you can print them. Many dot matrix printers can generally print the extended character set with no extra fuss. Laser printer owners may have to choose a different *internal font* to print some extended characters (Chapter 35).

There used to be two ways to insert extended characters into a document: (1) issue them directly from the keyboard or (2) use a special menu from the CTRL-F3 Screen command to assign them to CTRL or ALT keys. The latter approach is no longer in WordPerfect, but you can set up CTRL and ALT keys with the keyboard layout feature (Appendix A). You can also create macros that insert extended characters.

To enter any extended character, hold down the ALT key and type the character's code number on the *numeric keypad only.* Don't use the regular number keys on the top line of the keyboard. For instance, ALT-227 gives the lowercase Greek p (π) that represents *pi*. There is no code attached to an extended character.

Note: If you're using a memory resident program with WordPerfect, you might have to press both the ALT and the SHIFT keys together to insert the extended characters.

Try these two examples, then clear the screen when you're finished. You'll use the following extended characters:

20 = the paragraph symbol (¶)

21 = the section symbol (§)

148 = the umlauted o (ö)

225 = the German double s (ß)

For the umlauted o and double s, you have a choice. Either enter the code number that's shown or use the Compose key. To compose the umlauted o, press **CTRL-2**, then type "o or o"; to compose the double s, press **CTRL-2**, then type **ss**.

```
The Court refers Plaintiffs to Mr. Smudge's deposition at ¶49,
§§512-513.
```

```
Neulich sagte mir Beethoven:   "Ach, die Kram wird mir endlose
Schwierigkeiten machen!  Wissen Sie, daß sie noch mal die Miete
erhöhen will?"
```

The WordPerfect Character Set

WordPerfect Corporation provides even more characters than the standard extended character set. There are several different WordPerfect character sets. Consult the documentation for charts of these characters. You may also have a file called CHARACTR.DOC that contains the WordPerfect character sets. To enter a WordPerfect character set character, use the Compose key:

1. Press **CTRL-2** or **CTRL-V** and then release both keys.

2. Type the character set's number, a comma, then the code number of the character itself. For example, type **1,27** to insert the lowercase *a* with an acute accent—á.

3. Press **RETURN** to finish.

Tip: One especially useful character set contains the common typesetting symbols that aren't in the ASCII set. It's WordPerfect character set 4. If your monitor can't display a character, WordPerfect puts in a little box. But the printed character will be correct if it's in the printer's character set.

The Advance Command

The Advance command moves the printer in several directions, usually from the *current* cursor position. You can move down, up, left, or right any distance you choose. The amount of the advance is relative to the present cursor position. That is, you might want to advance up one-half inch. You can also advance up or down to a specific line or left or right to a column position, but this is tricky. You must use an offset measurement in inches from the *top edge* of the page when you're advancing to a line, or from the *left edge* of the paper when you're advancing to a column. Thus, a line advance of 2.5 is 2½ inches from the top edge of the page.

Tip: You can give WordPerfect an "absolute" line number: Just type a **v** after the number. For instance, **33v** advances to line 33. In the code, WordPerfect still shows the amount of the advance in inches.

Note: Some printers can't advance at all. This feature has been expanded in WordPerfect 5.0, and it's now on the format key. In previous versions it was on the SHIFT-F1 Super/Subscript key. When you use this feature, remember to return to the correct line when you want to turn the advance off. That is, if you advance up, make sure you advance back down later. If you advance right a certain distance, remember to advance left later. In this example, you'll use the Advance command to imitate superscripts and subscripts. Take a look at the entire line first:

```
I forgot how to do ⁽ˢᵘᵖᵉʳ⁾scripts and ₍sub₎scripts with WordPerfect!
```

It turns out on my laser printer that the advance is about ¹⁄₁₀ inch. Type the normal text. When you get to the word *super*, do this:

Press   **SHIFT-F8 Format**

Type   **4** or **o** [Other]

Type   **1** or **a** [Advance]

WordPerfect presents the advance menu:

```
Advance: 1 Up; 2 Down; 3 Line; 4 Left; 5 Right; 6 Column: 0
```

Type   **1** or **u** [Up]

WordPerfect prompts:

```
Adv. up 0"
```

Type   **.1**

(Don't forget the decimal point.)

Press   **F7 Exit** twice

to return to the document.

Type   **super**

WordPerfect doesn't show you how the text will print. If you reveal the codes, however, you'll see [AdvUp] and the distance you specified. The Ln indicator on the status line tells you the new line number for the advanced section. You now have to advance back down, and you have two options: (1) advance down the same distance or (2) advance to the original line number. You did note the line number, didn't you?

✔Advance down the same distance (.1), then continue typing the example. When you get to *sub*, advance down first and then back up at the appropriate spot. Finish the example and print it to see the results.

The remaining advance codes are self-explanatory: [AdvDn], [AdvLft], [AdvRgt], [AdvToLn], and [AdvToCol]. With the advance feature in effect, WordPerfect does *not* create a blank space on the screen, but the Ln and Pos numbers on the status line show the correct lines as you cursor through the document. The page endings change automatically, too.

Tip: One nifty application for the advance to line feature comes immediately to mind, though. Remember the ENV document you created in Chapter 13? Instead of having all those extra blank lines between your return address and the recipient's name and address, why not just use the advance to line? Go ahead, try it if you like!

Drawing Lines and Boxes

WordPerfect's Line Draw command draws lines or boxes in a number of styles. You can even draw boxes around existing text. This feature is tricky in that it works in typeover mode, so you have to be careful when you're drawing lines or boxes around or near existing text and codes.

A Box Example

The line draw feature uses certain graphics characters from the extended character set.

Note: Your printer may not be able to print these extended characters. On my daisy wheel printer, WordPerfect substituted the box characters with others that the printer could handle. You'll first draw a box and then insert text into the box. Make sure the screen is clear. Then:

Press   **CTRL-F3 Screen**

Type   **2** or **l** [Line Draw]

WordPerfect presents the line draw menu:

1 |; 2 ||; 3 *; 4 <u>C</u>hange; 5 <u>E</u>rase; 6 <u>M</u>ove: 1

Caution: While the line draw menu is on the screen, when you move the cursor you insert lines into the document. You can draw a single or double line or a line of asterisks from this menu. Later you'll learn how to set other drawing characters.

Type   1 [|]

You can use the ARROW keys to draw the top of the box across to the right margin, but remember the faster way:

Press   **ESC**

Type   **65**

Press   **RIGHT ARROW**

It takes a few seconds for WordPerfect to draw the line. In the latest version of WordPerfect you can use HOME with an ARROW key to draw a line quickly to the edges of the screen or margins. Little boxes represent the corners, but when you change directions for the side of the box WordPerfect inserts the corners of the box for you:

Press   **ESC**

Type   **10**

Press   **DOWN ARROW**

Press   **ESC**

Type   **65**

Press   **LEFT ARROW**

Press   **UP ARROW** ten times

Just to keep you alert, I changed the pattern here. If you go too far, type **5** [Erase], move back with an ARROW key to erase the extra sections of a line, and then type **1** to continue drawing the line.

Press   **F7 Exit**

to return to the document.

You can also type **0** or press the **F1 Cancel** key when you're finished. WordPerfect returns to the document and turns typeover mode off. There's your completed box. The cursor should be where you started.

Erasing Part of the Box

It turns out that you want the sides of the box to extend only *nine* lines down, so you have to erase part of the box. Nothing to it!

Press   **DOWN ARROW**

Press   **CTRL-END**

Press   **DEL**

to delete one line.

Press   **HOME,HOME,DOWN ARROW**

Press   **RETURN**

to add a hard return at the end of the box.

✔Save the document as BOX.9 but leave it on the screen. You could use it as a boilerplate when you want to insert a box in other documents.

Inserting Text into a Box

Time to put something in the box.

Caution: Remember that, because WordPerfect is normally in insert mode, the text would push the right side over and ruin the symmetry of your box. What do you do?

Press   **INS**

to turn on typeover mode.

✔Position the cursor at the left margin of the middle of the box.

Press   **RIGHT ARROW** sixteen times *or* **ESC RIGHT ARROW** twice

Press   **CAPS LOCK**

Type   `SPECIAL!  FOR A LIMITED TIME ONLY!!`

Caution: If you make a mistake, *don't* use the BACKSPACE key, because that will bring back the right side of the box, too. Use the LEFT ARROW key to move the cursor back, and then type the correction. When you're finished:

Press   **CAPS LOCK**

Press   **INS**

   ✔Save the new document as SPECIAL.BOX if you wish.

Moving Around and Erasing in the Box

Use the **6** [Move] choice from the line draw menu to move around in a box without disturbing the box setup, and the **5** [Erase] choice to erase parts of the box or text. Try this:

   ✔Type **6** [Move], position the cursor on the *S* of *SPECIAL*. Then type **5** [Erase] and, with the **RIGHT ARROW**, erase the entire heading. Press **F1 Cancel** when you're finished.

You can also bypass the line draw routine at times with typeover mode: Position the cursor with the ARROW keys and erase sections by typing over them with spaces.

   ✔Clear the screen when you're finished.

Drawing Boxes or Lines in Existing Documents

When you want to *insert* lines or boxes in existing documents, make sure you have enough blank lines. Remember that WordPerfect switches to typeover mode with the line draw feature, so a line or box may replace a blank line. Try these next examples to experiment with a variety of commands.

   ✔Retrieve the document NEWS now.

Press   **DOWN ARROW** twice

Press   **RETURN**

to add an extra blank line.

Press   **UP ARROW**

Press   **SHIFT-F6 Center**

to center the line.

Press   **CTRL-F3 Screen**

Type	**2** or **ι** [L̲ine Draw]
Type	**2** [‖]
Press	**ESC**
Type	**25**
Press	**RIGHT ARROW**
Press	**F7 Exit**

You just learned how to center a double line on the screen.

✔ *Keep* the original NEWS file intact and save this version as NEWS.LN, if you wish. Then clear the screen and retrieve the document LAREST.

Press	**RETURN**

to add an extra blank line.

Press	**DOWN ARROW**
Press	**RETURN**

to add another blank line.

Press	**HOME,UP ARROW**
Press	**CTRL-F3 Screen**
Type	**2** or **ι** [L̲ine Draw]
Type	**6** [Move]
Press	**RIGHT ARROW** ten times
Type	**2** [‖]
Press	**ESC**
Type	**43**
Press	**RIGHT ARROW**
Press	**DOWN ARROW** twice
Press	**ESC**

Type   **45**

That's right!

Press   **LEFT ARROW**

Oops! You went too far.

Type   **5** [Erase]

Press   **RIGHT ARROW** twice

Type   **2** [‖]

Press   **UP ARROW** twice

Press   **F7 Exit**

✔ *Keep* the original LAREST file and save this version as LAREST.BOX, if you wish. Then clear the screen.

You just learned how to put a box around existing text, as well as how to erase lines. Always make sure that you don't inadvertently type over existing text when you add lines or boxes to documents. See Moving Rectangular Blocks later in the chapter for information on how to move or copy a box.

Changing Line Draw Characters

The extended character set has a limited number of other graphics characters that you can use to draw boxes and lines to give your documents more pizzazz. Take a look at them:

Press   **CTRL-F3 Screen**

Type   **2** or ∟ [Line Draw]

Type   **4** [Change]

WordPerfect presents eight *more* graphics characters for line or box drawing. You can mix and match characters by selecting a number, drawing your line, typing **4** [Change] again, selecting another number, and continuing. If *that* isn't enough, you can supply other characters, but you must know the character's ASCII code. For example, you want a line of solid Happy Faces across the screen. That's ASCII code 02 (the other Happy Face character is 01). Type **9** [Other], to which WordPerfect responds:

`Solid Character:`

Hold down the **ALT** key as you type **02** *from the numeric keypad.* WordPerfect displays your new choice as **3** on the line draw menu. (Follow the same steps to bring the asterisk back.)

Press   **F1 Cancel**

when you're finished to leave the line draw feature.

✔Clear the screen before you continue.

Entering Complicated Equations

Multiline equations require a little thought and planning on your part, as well as several extra formatting steps. Here's a sample equation with many superscripts and subscripts, but please don't ask me what it does! You'll type this example in a moment.

$$x^2 \frac{d^2 y}{dx^2} + x \frac{dy}{dx} + (x^2 - a^2)y = 0$$

Follow these general steps when you're typing a complicated equation in WordPerfect:

1. Determine the total number of *half* lines in the equation, including the superscript or subscript lines, too. The example here has six half lines. Then determine the *middle* line of the equation (the fourth line in this example), which will be your starting point when you type in the equation.

2. Position the cursor at the location in the document where you want the equation to appear. You may wish to add blank lines for spacing from the preceding text.

3. Set the line spacing to .5 (one half line) and turn right margin justification off. Make sure that these format changes are on a *separate line* from the lines you use for the equation.

4. Fill the required number of half lines in the document with spaces using the **6** [Move] choice from the line draw menu.

5. On the line directly after the equation area, change the format back to the original settings.

6. Turn typeover mode on.

7. Position the cursor at the correct line and type the equation. Start with the middle line and work up and down as necessary. Use the UP ARROW and DOWN ARROW keys to position the cursor. Do *not* use the BACKSPACE key to correct mistakes. Rather, just type over the mistakes with corrections. Type from the left margin, unless you know exactly how far over you have to move the cursor to center the equation on the page. Later, you can move the entire formula over as a rectangular block.

8. When you're finished, turn typeover mode off.

9. Save your work!

10. Position the cursor past the format change codes to begin normal operation. Whew!

Now, do the example equation, step by step (slowly I turned . . . Niagara Falls!—oops, wrong movie). Just use a clear screen and pretend you're in the middle of another document with the default format.

✔Change line spacing to 0.5 inch and turn justification off. Press **RETURN** to add a hard return. Then, fill the six half lines needed in the equation with spaces:

Press   **CTRL-F3 Screen**

Type   **2** or **l** [Line Draw]

Type   **6** [Move]

To be on the safe side, insert spaces on the entire 65-character line. How do you do this quickly?

Press   **ESC**

Type   **65**

Press   **RIGHT ARROW**

The cursor should be at the end of the line. Now, quickly fill the other five lines down, with one for good measure:

Press   **ESC**

Type   **6**

Press   **DOWN ARROW**

Press   **F7 Exit**

to leave the line draw menu.

Make sure that the cursor is past the filled area before you change the document format back to its original setting:

Press   **RETURN**

✔Set the line spacing back to single and turn justification on. When you've done that, position the cursor at the left margin of line 1.5" to begin typing the equation.

Press   **INS**

to use typeover mode.

Type   **x**

Press   **UP ARROW** once

Type   **2**

Notice that you aren't adding a superscript font here.

Press   **SPACEBAR**

Press   **SHIFT-HYPHEN** eight times for the underline

✔Using this section of the equation as your guide, finish the entire equation. Then press the **INS** key to return to insert mode. Notice that the equation appears single spaced on the screen because your monitor can't normally show half line spacing, but the spacing should print correctly. Save your work as EQUATION but leave the document on the screen.

Moving Rectangular Blocks

Say you now want to center the finished equation on the screen, because it's too far to the left. You can block it out and move the block. In WordPerfect special equations and box drawings are block *rectangles*. You only block out the equation itself, not the entire line or lines containing the block. To delimit a block rectangle, tell WordPerfect the *upper left* and *lower right* corners of the block.

Use the following example as a pattern for moving or copying boxes or other rectangular blocks. Make sure you first position the cursor at the beginning of the block, which may or may not include formatting codes. In this example, however, you don't want to move the codes. Reveal the codes if you're not sure.

✔Position the cursor at the left margin of the line beneath the format codes. Do *not* include the format change codes in the block. Then:

Press   **ALT-F4 Block** or **F12 Block**

Press   **DOWN ARROW**

enough times to block out the entire equation *except* the last line with the two dx's. Leave the cursor on the line with the two dx's.

You aren't finished yet! Notice that the block contains all characters on each line, including the hard returns. You now have to position the cursor at the lower right corner of the rectangle to tell WordPerfect the limits of the block.

Press   **RIGHT ARROW**

enough times to move past the entire equation (Pos 5.6 or thereabouts).

Press   **CTRL-F4 Move**

Type   **3** or **r** [Rectangle]

Now WordPerfect highlights only the rectangular block, as Figure 15-1 shows.

Type   **1** or **m** [Move]

✔Position the cursor on line 1.5". Then:

Press   **SPACE BAR** ten times

Press   **RETURN**

to retrieve the block.

And there you are!

✔Save your edited document, then clear the screen.

Date and Time Formats

You've already learned how to insert the current date in a document, either as text or as a code that WordPerfect updates whenever you later work with

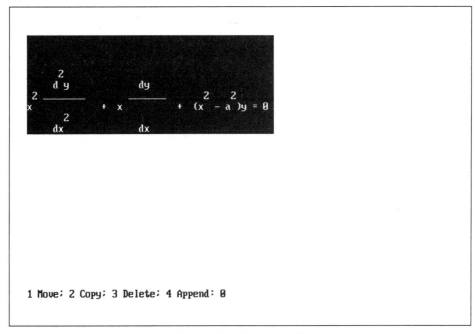

Figure 15-1   Highlighting a Rectangle

the document (Chapter 6). WordPerfect considers the current *time* to be part of the date feature, too. Now look at some ways to show the date and time.

Press   **SHIFT-F5 Date/Outline**

to bring up the date/outline menu.

Type   **3** or **f** [Date Format]

The date format menu shown in Figure 15-2 appears. The numbers here are functions that represent a specific format. They *don't* mean the current date or time. Use the numbers and explanations as guides to how you want the date and/or time to appear. Note that the default date is set up as 3 **1,** 4, that is, the month spelled out and followed by a space, then the day of the week followed by a comma and a space, and finally the year in four digits. You can include any other text in the formula that you want, but the longest format is 29 characters.

WordPerfect gives you a few examples as guides. Here's how to set the time in a 12-hour format, which is slightly different than the example on the screen:

Type   **8:9 0**

```
Date Format


       Character    Meaning
          1         Day of the Month
          2         Month (number)
          3         Month (word)
          4         Year (all four digits)
          5         Year (last two digits)
          6         Day of the Week (word)
          7         Hour (24-hour clock)
          8         Hour (12-hour clock)
          9         Minute
          0         am / pm
          %         Used before a number, will:
                       Pad numbers less than 10 with a leading zero
                       Output only 3 letters for the month or day
                          of the week



       Examples:  3 1, 4       = December 25, 1984
                  %6 %3 1, 4   = Tue Dec 25, 1984
                  %2/%1/5 (6)  = 01/01/85 (Tuesday)
                  8:90         = 10:55am



Date format: 3 1, 4
```

Figure 15-2   The Date Format Menu

Notice that you must type the colon and the space if you want to separate the time from the am/pm.

Press   **RETURN**

to return to the date/outline menu.

Now you can enter the new format either as text or as a formula:

Type   1 or t [Date Text]

I prefer *a.m.* and *p.m.* with periods, but you can't have everything.

Note: There is no code for a date format change, but the new format will appear in a [Date] code. Remove any previous [Date] codes to make sure WordPerfect uses the new date format. Now try a more complicated example—one that shows the date and time in a continental style:

Press   **SHIFT-F5 Date/Outline**

Type   **3** or **f** [Date Format]

Type   **6, 1 3 4 7:9**

Note the spaces!

Press   **RETURN**

Type   **1** or **t** [Date Text]

If it's 3/26/89 at 1:16 p.m., this is what you see on the screen:

Sunday, 26 March 1989 13:16

Tip: If you didn't set the correct date before you started WordPerfect, use the CTRL-F1 Shell command to go to DOS (Chapter 9), then the DOS DATE command to change the date.

Here are two macros to try. The first is called D1. It enters the correct date and time as text in the form MM/DD/YY HH:MM am/pm. The percent sign (%) in the function enters leading zeros for numbers less than 10. You can use this macro to keep a log of when you worked on a document.

Tip: When you insert a percent sign in front of a month or day code, WordPerfect shows only the first three characters. For example, the code %6, %3 1 displays Mon, Mar 21.

Press   **CTRL-F10 Macro Define**

Type   d1

Press   **RETURN**

Type   Date format #1

Press   **RETURN**

Press   **SHIFT-F5 Date/Outline**

Type   **3** or **f** [Format]

Type   **%2/%1/5 8:9 0**

Press   **RETURN**

Type   **1** or **t** [Date Text]

Press   **CTRL-F10 Macro Define**

The second macro, called D2, prints the date as a code with the name of the day of the week. Because WordPerfect remembers the *last* date and time format that you set, this macro also resets the date format to the default:

Press   **CTRL-F10 Macro Define**

Type   **d2**

Press   **RETURN**

Type   **Date format #2**

Press   **RETURN**

Press   **SHIFT-F5 Date/Outline**

Type   **3** or **f** [Date Format]

Type   **6, 3 1, 4**

Press   **RETURN**

Type   **2** or **c** [Date Code]

Press   **SHIFT-F5 Date/Outline**

Type   **3** or **f** [Date Format]

Type   **3 1, 4**

Press   **RETURN**

Press   **RETURN**

Press   **CTRL-F10 Macro Define**

Use the **ALT-F10 Macro** key to run these two macros. Be careful that you know what format you're using.

Tip: You can include other text in the date or time format. For example, you set up a date format like this:

Today's date is: 3 1, 4.

Type two spaces at the end of the format

Today is the 26th day of April, 1989, so every time you enter a date in the document you get this result: Today's date is: April 26, 1989. The date format even includes the period and two spaces at the end of the sentence!

Dear Reader, I bet you thought WordPerfect was *only* a word processing program! You may not use all these special features all the time, but eventually you'll want to learn how to take advantage of all the power at your fingertips.

Chapter

16

Headers, Footers, and Page Numbering

In this chapter you'll learn the following new commands . . .

Numeric Keypad and Function Key Commands

HOME,F2 ▸Search	Extended forward search
HOME,ALT-F2 Replace	Extended replace
HOME,SHIFT-F2 ◂Search	Extended backward search

. . . you'll discover new uses of this command . . .

SHIFT-F8 Format	(1) Determine page numbering settings, (2) set up headers, (3) set up footers, (4) suppress a page format setting for the current page only

. . . and you'll learn some new codes:

^B	Page number in a header or footer
[Footer A]	Footer A change
[Footer B]	Footer B change
[Force]	Force odd or even page numbering
[Header A]	Header A change
[Header B]	Header B change
[Pg Num]	New starting page number or numbering style

more . . .

[Pg Numbering]	Page number position change (start page numbering or change the page number location)
[Suppress]	Suppress page format on the current page

Work, work, work, it's enough to make you sick! Dear Reader, take heart. Although no word processing program can do everything for you, WordPerfect can save you a great deal of tedium. For instance, it can print incremented page numbers or any other "running" text at the top or bottom of each page. These *headers* and *footers*, as they are called in the word processing trade, are the subject of this chapter.

DO WARM-UP

Some Introductory Notes

Headers and footers are part of the *page format* of a document. The only real difference between a header and a footer is where it appears on the page. The setup for both is essentially the same. You decide about headers and footers once, usually at the beginning of the document, and WordPerfect takes care to print them on each page. You can also have *alternating* headers and footers, that is, different setups for odd numbered and even numbered pages.

Version 4.2 users: Recall that there is no longer the ALT-F8 Page Format command. Use the SHIFT-F8 Format key for most page formats.

In deference to the podiatrists of this world, I should mention that footers have only a casual relationship to *footnotes* (Chapter 22), and both in turn have only a semantic relationship to *feet*. WordPerfect has definite opinions about the first two commodities but takes little interest in the third. By the way, a footer prints below everything else on the page, including footnotes.

WordPerfect prints headers in what would normally be the top text lines of the page, *not* in the top margin space, and footers in the bottom text lines. It then adjusts the number of text lines on the page to account for the number of header and footer lines. WordPerfect also automatically puts 0.16 inch of blank space (about one line) between the header and footer and the body of the text. That includes a "plain vanilla" page number or fancier headers and footers.

So, you may have to adjust the top and bottom margin settings of the document's page when you use headers or footers. There are ways to change the blank space, known as the header and footer margins, between headers or footers and normal text, too.

You can have WordPerfect print headers or footers—or both—on all pages, or on selected pages. As a convenience, WordPerfect provides special commands for page numbering alone, or you can create your own customized format with text and page numbering. You can even insert a graphics element in a header or footer (Chapter 34).

WordPerfect keeps header and footer information in separate areas. You don't see headers or footers until you print the document or view the printout. You can reveal the header and footer codes, but WordPerfect may not show the entire header or footer text. Like all "open" code format changes, any page numbering, header, or footer instruction applies to the rest of the document forward from the location of the instruction. Whenever possible, then, it's a good idea to establish the header or footer format at the beginning of the document.

Except for the page number, if any, a header or footer text doesn't change. WordPerfect just prints the same header or footer on each page and continues to do so unless you tell it otherwise. If you want to turn off a header or footer or change it at a specific point in the document, you must give WordPerfect the correct instructions at the correct location. It's easy to change a header or footer in the middle of a document.

Recall the basic rules of format changes that you learned in Chapter 6. Most page formatting changes should be at the very top of the page, in front of any text (including blank lines). Otherwise, you'll get unexpected results! If, for example, a header code isn't at the top of the page, WordPerfect won't print the header until the *next* page. With footers, the instruction can be anywhere before the bottom of the page, but it's still a good idea to insert footer instructions at the top of the page, too. That way, you can locate the codes easily.

Note: If you change the base font and you want page numbering, headers, or footers to print in the new base font, the font change code must be *in front of* the other page format codes. If the font change code is after the page format codes, WordPerfect prints page numbering, headers, or footers in the original base font. See also What Happens When You Change the Document's Format later in the chapter.

Setting Up Page Numbers

WordPerfect does *not* number the pages for you by default, unless you change the defaults (Appendix A). Once you do instruct WordPerfect to print page numbers, you don't have to worry about them. WordPerfect increments the page number for each page and prints the number either at the top or bottom of the page. Numbers can be Arabic or Roman numerals.

Nevertheless, you should be aware of the *two* ways to set up page numbering in WordPerfect. If all you need is a simple, unembellished number, use WordPerfect's *predefined page numbering feature.* (WordPerfect inserts a blank space of 0.16 inch—about one line—between the page number and the normal text.) If the page number is to be part of a header or footer with other text, you must set up the header or footer to include a special page numbering command.

So, the rule of thumb about page numbering is: Use either (1) the predefined setup or (2) a header or footer. (Needless to say, you wouldn't want page numbers in both a header and a footer.) Indeed, you might get some strange results, such as *two* page numbers on a page, if you're not careful!

Predefined Page Numbering

First you'll learn how to use the predefined page numbering feature. Predefined page numbering is the simplest form of header or footer, one with no text except the page number. WordPerfect uses the top two text lines of the document for a page number at the top of the page, or the bottom two lines if the page number is at the bottom of the page. WordPerfect will also then set up new page breaks. To save time, you'll work with a document from previous chapters.

✔Retrieve the document LAREST now.

Press   **SHIFT-F8 Format**

Type   **2** or **p** [Page]

To set up predefined page numbering, tell WordPerfect the page number position:

Type   **7** or **p** [Page Numbering]

The format: page numbering menu appears (Figure 16-1). WordPerfect shows a visual representation of the page numbering menu. You have an impressive array of choices: page numbers at the left, center, or right of the page, either at the top or the bottom of the page, or alternating left and right at the top or the bottom of the page. Try a "plain vanilla" page number at the bottom of the page:

Type   **6**

to position page numbers in the bottom center of every page.

Press   **F7 Exit**

to return to the document.

If you reveal the codes now, you'll see: [Pg Numbering:Bottom Center]. If you change your mind about where a page number should go, it's best to

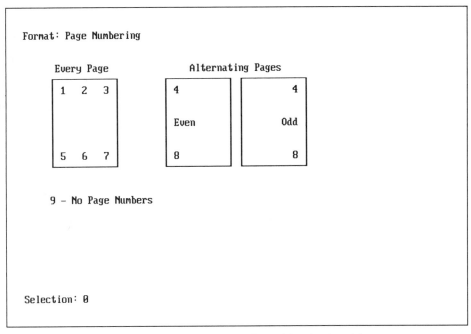

Figure 16-1   The Format: Page Numbering Menu

delete the previous code and insert a new one, following the steps I just outlined. You can also choose choice **9** [<u>N</u>o Page Numbers] from the format: page numbering menu to turn page numbers off later in the document.

    ✔Print the first page or view the printout to see the results. Save the document now but give it the name LAREST.PAG, because you'll use the original LAREST document elsewhere. Then clear the screen.

How Other Formats Affect the Page Number

You don't have to determine what WordPerfect should consider the left corner, center, or right corner of the page when you change the left and right margins settings or select a different font. WordPerfect automatically adjusts the page number position to the new left, center, or right position. Remember, however, to put the font change in front of the page format codes. If you want an unadorned page number somewhere else, set it up as a header or footer, as outlined later in the chapter.

Skipping or Repositioning Page One

If you don't want a page number to print on the first page, but you *do* want numbers for all subsequent pages, you can still set up page numbering at the beginning of the document. You then instruct WordPerfect to *suppress*, that is, skip, the page numbering for the current page, page 1. The Suppress command does not alter the actual page number; it only suppresses the printing of the number on the current page. Here's how to use this command (you don't have to follow these steps right now):

1. Press **SHIFT-F8 Format**.
2. Type **2** or **p** [Page].
3. Type **9** or **u** [Suppress (this page only)].
    Whoa! WordPerfect presents more choices in the format: suppress (this page only) menu, shown in Figure 16-2. You'll learn about the others later, in my discussion of headers and footers. What you want here is:
4. Type **4** or **p** [Suppress Page Numbering].
5. Type **y** for yes if necessary.
6. Press **F7 Exit** enough times to return to the document.

WordPerfect inserts a [Suppress] code into the document. The code lists the specific page format that you want to suppress.

Tip: The Suppress command is especially helpful when you're typing multipage letters but you don't want page numbering on the letterhead page.

If, for example, you don't want a page number on page 10 of a document, go to that page and insert the suppress code. It's a good idea to do this when the document is in its *final* stages; otherwise, you may move the code to a different page if you insert or delete text. Chapter 17 discusses at greater length how to take full control of the page.

You may have noticed choice **3** [Print Page Number at Bottom Center] in the format: suppress menu. Often the first page of a document has pagination at the bottom center of the page, while subsequent pages print with page numbering elsewhere. Those folks at WordPerfect Corporation think of (almost) everything!

Changing or Skipping a New Page Number

Suppose your document is actually the continuation of a longer document that you've broken down into separate, easy-to-work-with module files. The chapters of a book come immediately to mind, don't they? Using the steps below, you can also change the *numbering style* from Arabic, the default, to lowercase Roman numerals. Here's how to tell WordPerfect to start with a new number or numbering style:

```
Format: Suppress (this page only)

     1 - Suppress All Page Numbering, Headers and Footers

     2 - Suppress Headers and Footers

     3 - Print Page Number at Bottom Center   No

     4 - Suppress Page Numbering              No

     5 - Suppress Header A                    No

     6 - Suppress Header B                    No

     7 - Suppress Footer A                    No

     8 - Suppress Footer B                    No




Selection: 0
```

Figure 16-2   The Format: Suppress (this page only) Menu

1. Press **SHIFT-F8 Format**.
2. Type **2** or **p** [Page].
3. Type **6** or **n** [New Page Number].
4. Type the new number either as an Arabic numeral or as a lowercase Roman numeral.

   Tip: To change the numbering style but not the page number, type the same number in the new style. For instance, if the cursor is at the top of page 1 but you want lowercase Roman numerals, type **i**.
5. Press **F7 Exit** enough times to return to the document.

WordPerfect inserts a [Pg Num] code with the new starting number and numbering style.

Tip: You can also use this feature within a document to *skip* a page number. For instance, say you're inserting an illustration of teriyaki and tempura between pages 1 and 2 of the LAREST document, so page 2 of the document should be numbered 3 instead. You'd go to the top of page 2 and insert a page number change there (don't do it now, though).

Caution: When you add any page format code in the middle of a document, say, on page 2, the text lines and page breaks may change if you add text before this spot later. There's a way to keep the codes at the top of the page; this is discussed in Chapter 17.

Forcing an Odd or Even Page

Another way to change the page number is to *force* an odd or even number for a particular page. For example, your document may contain a lengthy report and you want to ensure that sections within the report start printing on odd numbered pages.

This feature works no matter what the other page numbering instructions are. That is, if the page is currently numbered 22 in sequence but you insert a force odd page number instruction, WordPerfect renumbers the page to the next odd number, 23. Here's how to force an odd or even page:

1. Press **SHIFT-F8 Format**.
2. Type **2** or **p** [Page].
3. Type **2** or **o** [Force Odd/Even Page]. WordPerfect prompts:

   1 Odd; 2 Even: 0
4. Type **1** or **o** [Odd] or **2** or **e** [Even].
5. Press **F7 Exit** enough times to return to the document.

WordPerfect inserts a [Force] code here with odd or even as you chose. The status line shows the forced page number.

Alternating Page Numbers

Do you recall choices **4** and **8** on the format: page number position menu? They let you print *alternating* page numbers, that is, to the left on even numbered pages and to the right on odd numbered pages. Many books have this type of pagination. You can also have alternating headers and footers, the subject of a later section.

A Note on Printing Specific Pages

You've already learned how to print selected pages of a document (Chapter 5). Be cautious when your document contains a variety of page numbering, whether in a footer or a header, to give WordPerfect the correct page numbers *according to the document's pagination.* See the end of the next chapter for more information about printing page ranges when you have complicated page numbering setups.

Customized Page Numbering

There are many possibilities available with just the predefined page numbering feature, but you can experiment with them yourself. Now imagine you want a more elaborate page number, say, one enclosed in hyphens, like this: − 3 −. Here's where you must forego the predefined setup and use a footer (or, for the top of the page, a header).

Headers and Footers

Headers and footers can contain other text besides page numbering. In the first example, you'll include hyphens around the page numbers. When you set up customized numbering in a header or footer, you decide how the page number is to appear and its column position.

First, however, bear in mind that if you set up page numbering in a header or footer, you *must* turn off any predefined page numbering feature. The best way to do this is to delete all page numbering codes (remember that by default there is no page numbering) or use the **9** [No Page Numbers] choice from the format: page number position menu.

✔Clear the screen and retrieve the CHAPTER.2 document.

Your First Footer

This footer example sets up the page numbers centered on the line and enclosed in hyphens and shows you how to increase the number of blank lines between the regular text and the footer. It also illustrates a potential problem with centering.

Press	**SHIFT-F8 Format**
Type	**2** or **p** [Page]
Type	**4** or **f** [Footers]

WordPerfect asks which of two footers you want to set up:

1 Footer A; 2 Footer B: 0

You can have two different headers and two different footers—labeled A and B—in each document. They can print on every page, odd numbered pages, or even numbered pages, as you'll now decide.

Type   **1** or **a** [Footer A]

WordPerfect asks for information about Footer A:

```
1 Discontinue; 2 Every Page; 3 Odd Pages; 4 Even Pages; 5 Edit: 0
```

Type   **2** or **p** [Every Page]

WordPerfect presents the footer setup area.

Tip: You can reveal the codes in the footer or header setup area if you wish. To add an extra blank line between the footer and the text in addition to the space WordPerfect normally adds:

Press   **RETURN**

Now, center the page number:

Press   **SHIFT-F6 Center**

Type   **-**

(That's a hyphen.)

Press   **SPACEBAR**

for a space.

Here's where you must instruct WordPerfect about the incremented page number. You insert a special code:

Press   **CTRL-B**

WordPerfect shows this code as ^B on the screen. Remember that the caret means the CTRL key. The code represents page numbering in a header or footer.

Note: Although the manual may say that you can also use CTRL-N, don't do it! As you'll see later, CTRL-N has a different meaning in merge operations. You can insert a ^B code anywhere in a document, but it makes most sense to use it only in a header or footer. Finish the setup:

Press   **SPACEBAR**

Type   **-**

(Again, a hyphen.) Your screen will look like Figure 16-3.

Stop! Don't press RETURN at the end of the line, because then you'd have an extra blank line in the footer. You're finished now.

Press   **F7 Exit** twice

to return to the document.

Once you set up a footer or header, WordPerfect indicates that the footer or header exists on the format: page menu. You'll see FA (Footer A), FB (Footer B), HA (Header A), or HB (Header B) and the occurrence that you've chosen for each.

Turn on the codes now, and you'll see the footer code followed by the occurrence instruction and the actual text of the footer. The code in this example is [Footer A]. Still, there's something wrong here: The ending center code, [C/A/Flrt], is missing, but the footer should still print correctly centered. Try it!

If, however, WordPerfect does *not* center the text correctly, do this. Edit Footer A, as outlined under Editing a Header or Footer, and add a **RETURN** to the second line of the footer. This should insert the ending [C/A/Flrt] code (reveal the codes to make sure). Then use the **BACKSPACE** key to delete the hard return code, so that you don't have an extra blank line in the footer. Press **F7 Exit** twice when you're finished and try printing the page again.

Here's something else to try. Go to the top of page 2 and try changing the second page to page number 3 and the numbering style to lowercase

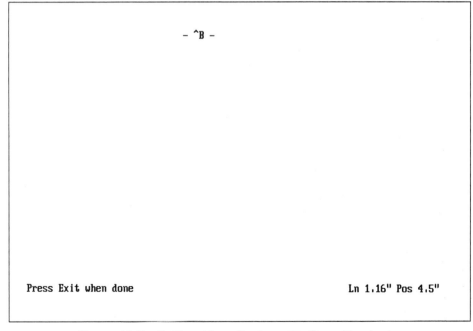

Figure 16-3   Setting Up a Footer with Page Numbering

Roman numerals. Print the page. You can "mix-and-match" page formatting features. Delete these codes on page 2 when you're done.

✔When you're finished, position the cursor at the beginning of the document.

Note: You can use special printing effect fonts, such as boldface or italics in headers and footers. The suppress, new page number or numbering style, and force odd/even page features work with any page numbering in a header or footer, too. Remember to put a font change code in front of any header or footer instruction.

Your First Header

Creating a header is essentially the same as creating a footer. That is, there's a special setup area in which you'll type the text you want.

Press   **SHIFT-F8 Format**

Type   **2** or **p** [<u>P</u>age]

Type   **3** or **h** [<u>H</u>eaders]

Type   **1** or **a** [Header <u>A</u>]

Type   **2** or **p** [Every <u>P</u>age]

You'll put some text at the left margin:

Type   `"Inside Beethoven" - Chapter 2`

Press   **ALT-F6 Flush Right**

to flush the next text to the right margin.

Now you want the date as a code so that it will be updated each time you print the document:

Press   **SHIFT-F5 Date/Outline**

Type   **2** or **c** [Date <u>C</u>ode]

Don't press RETURN at the end of the line, because that would add an extra blank line between the header and the document text. Your screen looks like Figure 16-4.

Press   **F7 Exit** twice

to return to the document.

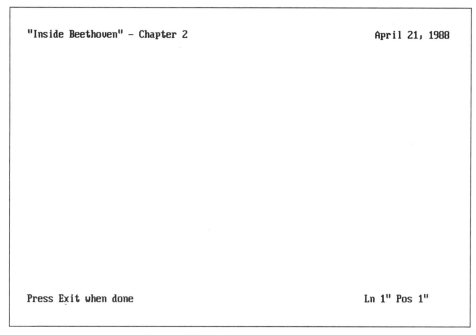

Figure 16-4   Setting Up a Header

Now, take a look at the codes in the document. WordPerfect shows only part of the [Header A] code with an ellipsis (...) to indicate that there's more. WordPerfect can display only a certain number of characters in the header or footer codes.

✔Print the first page if you wish.

Editing a Header or Footer

So how do you check the contents of the entire footer or header or change the setup? Go back into it, using the special edit choice. The cursor can be anywhere in the document. To edit a header or footer, follow these steps (you don't have to do them now):

1. Press **SHIFT-F8 Format**.

2. Type **2** or **p** [P̲age].

3. Type **3** or **h** [H̲eaders] or **4** or **f** [F̲ooters].

4. Select which header or footer you want to edit, A or B.

5. Type **5** or **e** [E̲dit].

6. Edit the header or footer, then press **F7 Exit** twice to return to the document.

Tip: You can use any cursor movement or editing command in the header and footer setup areas. If you wish, try this example.

✔Follow the steps to edit the Footer A setup area, then follow the instructions below.

You want to add some more text to the footer, but you don't want to move the page number from the center of the page, so what do you do? Right!

Press   **INS**

to turn typeover mode on.

Press   **DOWN ARROW**

Press   **HOME,HOME,HOME,LEFT ARROW**

to position the cursor at the beginning of the line in front of the center code.

Type   `Draft #1`

Press   **INS**

Press   **F7 Exit** twice

to return to the document.

✔Print this page or view the printout to see the results. Then save the edited CHAPTER.2 document.

The Header or Footer Margin

The blank lines between headers and footers and the normal document text are known as the *header and footer margins*, respectively. You may want to include extra hard returns in a header or footer for a larger margin. That is, to increase the header margin, insert blank lines *below* the header text. To increase the footer margin, insert blank lines *above* the footer text. (Think about it!)

Copying Document Text into a Header or Footer

You can also move or copy text from the document into a header or footer setup. (The same techniques work for footnotes, too; see Chapter 22.) That is, work with the CTRL-F4 Move key or the F1 Cancel key. Go into the header or footer area that you want, then retrieve or restore the text. It's that simple!

What Happens When You Change the Document's Format

By default, WordPerfect uses the current left and right margin settings in headers and footers. If you later change these margins in the document, you don't have to edit the header or footer setups. You can also determine different margin, tab, line spacing, and hyphenation settings (Chapter 20) for headers and footers. To do that, just edit the header or footer and press SHIFT-F8 Format to insert the desired format change codes within the header or footer only.

Tip: To make headers or footers stand out from the rest of the document, set up different margins. For example, use left and right margins of 0.5 inch in headers or footers and the default 1.0 inch for normal document text.

Note: WordPerfect retains single spacing for headers and footers even if you change the line spacing of the entire document. Usually, you'd want to keep header or footer text in single spacing, but there's no law against using a different setting.

Suppressing a Header or Footer

You can use the Suppress command, described earlier in the chapter, to suppress the printing of any header or footer on the current page. Make sure you know what you want to suppress! For example, if you want to print Footer A but suppress Header A, you would type **5** or **h** [Suppress <u>H</u>eader A], then **y** in the format: suppress menu. Version 4.2 users: You can no longer type several suppress instructions separated by a plus sign. You must type each one individually.

Multiple Line Headers and Footers

Headers or footers can take up more than one line. Use hard returns to end the separate lines. Make sure that you adjust the document's top and bottom margins to accommodate the added lines, if necessary.

Alternating Headers and Footers

To print different headers and footers on odd or even pages, set up each separately, A for odd pages and B for even, or vice versa. Here's how:

1. Press **SHIFT-F8 Format**.
2. Type **2** or **p** [<u>P</u>age].
3. Type **3** or **h** [<u>H</u>eaders] or **4** or **f** [<u>F</u>ooters].
4. Type either **a** or **b** to set up odd numbered pages.

5. Type **3** or **o** [Odd Pages].

6. Type the header or footer text and press **F7 Exit** once.

7. Repeat steps 3 and 4, but this time choose the other header or footer (A or B), the one you didn't use in step 4. This will be for even numbered pages.

8. Type **4** or **v** [Even Pages].

9. Type the header or footer text and press **F7 Exit** twice to return to the document.

WordPerfect shows in the codes which setup is for odd and which for even numbered pages.

Changing the Starting Page Number in a Header or Footer

If you have page numbering in a header or footer, you can still change the starting number of the page, or the numbering style (Arabic or lowercase Roman numerals), with choice **6** [New Page Number] from the format: page menu, just as you learned with the predefined numbering. WordPerfect uses the new page number and numbering style whenever it sees the ^B code in a header or footer.

Removing a Header or Footer

You can, of course, delete a header or footer code if you want to start with a clean slate. But if you want to stop printing a header or footer somewhere in the *middle* of a document, first position the cursor on the correct page. Select the header or footer that you want to remove, then type **1** or **d** [Discontinue].

Tip: Once you discontinue a header or footer, here's how to reinstate it. Copy the original code to the page where you want to restart it. That is, delete the original code, immediately restore it, go to the restarting page, and restore the code again. Neat!

You can search for a header, footer, or page numbering code as any other. But you better know what code you need! First start the search command, press **SHIFT-F8 Page Format**, then type **2** or **p** [Page]. Here's what you see:

```
1 Cntr 2 Force 3 Hdr 4 Ftr 5 T/B Mar 6 New PgNum 7 PgNum Pos 8 Sz/Typ 9 Sup: 0
```

You've learned all these codes. Can you figure them out? Now learn how to search for text *within* a header or footer . . .

The Extended Search Feature

Because WordPerfect stores the information for headers, footers, footnotes, and endnotes (Chapter 22) in a separate area from the document text, you can't use the regular search commands to find header or footer text. Use the *extended search* instead. This feature searches these separate areas as well as the normal text. To use extended search, merely press the **HOME** key *before* you start any search or replace operation: **HOME,F2 ▶Search**, **HOME,SHIFT-F2 ◀Search**, or **HOME,ALT-F2 Replace**. (The extended search does not work with text in the document summary or comments.)

There are two "tricks" to working with the extended search feature. First, because header or footer codes are usually at the beginning of the document, make sure the cursor is positioned in front of the codes before you attempt a forward extended search. Press HOME,HOME,HOME,UP ARROW to be sure. Second, you must implicitly start *each* extended search with the HOME key after WordPerfect stops in a header, footer, or footnote area when it finds the search string.

✔Clear the screen and retrieve the CHAPTER.2 document again if it's not on the screen.

You want to find all occurrences of the word *Beethoven* in the entire document, including the headers and footers. But where is the cursor when you retrieved the document? Better be on the safe side: Reveal the codes. If the cursor is past the header and footer codes, press **HOME,HOME, HOME,LEFT ARROW** before you continue. Then:

Press   **HOME,F2 ▶Search**

WordPerfect prompts:

-> Extended srch:

Type   **beethoven**

Press   **F2 ▶Search**

There's the header area. Press **F7 Exit** after you've viewed the header, or continue the extended search.

Caution: If you just pressed F2 ▶Search now, you'd start a regular search in the document only. Assuming you'd want to search some footnotes or endnotes for the word *Beethoven*, you must again press **HOME,F2 ▶Search** to continue the extended search throughout the document.

Tip: Once you start an extended search or replace, you can press UP ARROW or DOWN ARROW to reverse the direction. You can also use the extended search to find the ^B page numbering code.

Specifying Total Page Numbers

I've stuck this new section here to avoid disrupting the page breaks and *really* giving my editor a fit until we can prepare a totally revised version of this book. Suppose you want to print page numbers like so: Page 1 of 31. You can do it, but you don't know how yet!

To have WordPerfect compute the actual total page numbers of a changing document, first insert a *cross-reference* "target" code at the end of the document. Then create your header or footer and tie a "reference code" to the target as a page number. You'll find the instructions for inserting cross-references in Chapter 23.

For example, a cross-reference target code called *totalpages* that you insert at the end of the document looks like this when you reveal the codes: `[Target(TOTALPAGES)]`. You can then set up a footer with a reference to this target like this: `Page ^B of [Ref(TOTALPAGES)Pg :?]`. The ? indicates that WordPerfect will calculate the total pages when you tell it to *generate* the cross-references, another topic of Chapter 23.

I have emphasized the tricky parts of setting up page numbering, headers, and footers so that you're well prepared when you do your own. Most of the time, you'll have standard header and footer formats—say, predefined page numbering throughout a document or a header on all but the first page. When you do need a more complicated setup, WordPerfect is at your disposal.

Taking Control
of the Page

In this chapter you'll discover new uses of these commands . . .

SHIFT-F7 Print   Print page ranges in documents with complicated pagination

SHIFT-F8 Format   (1) Turn widow/orphan control on/off, (2) insert a conditional end of page instruction, (3) protect a block, (4) change the number of lines per vertical inch (line height or leading)

. . . and you'll learn some new codes:

[Block Pro:Off]	Block protection off
[Block Pro:On]	Block protection on
[Cndl EOP]	Conditional end of page
[Ln Height]	Line height or leading change
[W/O Off]	Widow/orphan protection off
[W/O On]	Widow/orphan protection on

Dear Reader, there are two unfortunate entities that will crop up every so often in your documents and cause some sad looking printouts: a widow line stranded all by itself at the bottom of a page and an orphan line at the top of the page. Widows and orphans are among the bugbears of editors and finicky word processors, but they need not occur. WordPerfect can help you deal with widows and orphans.

There are other times when you'd want to adjust the page breaks, for instance, when you don't want WordPerfect to break a page in the middle of a table. What I'm really talking about here is advanced page formatting and how you, in tandem with WordPerfect, can control the look of the page.

> **DO WARM-UP**

Draft Versus Final Copy

Before you begin, however, here's a practice that professional word processors commonly follow, one that can save you time and frustration. They differentiate between the *draft* stages of a document and its *final* form.

A document generally goes through any number of drafts until it reaches that stage of *semi*perfection (nothing's perfect in this imperfect world, after all—sorry, WordPerfect!) when it's ready to be sent out into the world. All the many versions of a document comprise the *document history*. You should only know how many drafts I did of this book before I was able to pass it on to the publisher! By the way, WordPerfect can help you keep track of different document versions (Chapter 24).

In general, during the draft stage you type text and make editing changes, while during the final stage you're more concerned with formatting. That is, you want your final document to look its best. In the law firm where I worked, the lawyers insisted that draft versions of documents be in double spacing, sometimes even in triple spacing, to give them enough room to pencil in corrections and changes. Later, we changed the spacing back to single where necessary. We used cheap paper for drafts and the expensive stuff only for final printouts. (Dear Reader, lawyers use a lot of paper!)

Getting your final document version to be of the highest quality takes a bit of time and extra effort, but it's worth it. If you did the extra "prettying up" steps each time you printed a document draft, you'd be wasting time, because you may have to move the codes around for each version. Many word processing operators choose not to delve too deeply into elaborate page formatting until the document reaches the final stage.

A Reminder

You've already learned how to center a page from top to bottom, how to change the top and bottom margins (Chapter 6), ways to work with forms (Chapter 13), and how to set up pagination, headers, and footers (Chapter 16). These features are all part of page formatting, too.

The Good, the Bad, and the Ugly

A *widow* is the beginning line of a paragraph stranded at the bottom of a page; an *orphan* is the ending line of a paragraph left by itself at the top of a page. Because they are both short lines, widows and orphans look terrible if they're not "related" to at least one other line in the paragraph (hence the colorful terminology). The normal way to correct the widow or orphan situation is to make sure that these short lines print with either the next line (for a widow), or the previous line (for an orphan) in the paragraph. That means changing the page endings, as Figure 17-1 illustrates.

There is good news and bad news about WordPerfect's handling of widows and orphans. The good news is that there is built-in *widow and orphan control*, or—to follow WordPerfect's nomenclature, *widow/orphan protection*. If you tell it to, the program will try not to end a page with a widow or begin a page with an orphan. It "protects" the widow or orphan.

Now for the bad news: WordPerfect is just not "smart" enough to catch *all* widow and orphan situations, as a simple little example in this chapter will show you. Ultimately, the final arbiter of all this should be *you*. You don't want any ugly pages, do you?

Version 4.2 users: WordPerfect now considers widow and orphan protection a line format.

When I set up page numbering for the LAREST document and saved the new document as LAREST.PAG (Chapter 16), WordPerfect broke the pages differently. Where the page breaks occur depend on the printer and font, so your example may be different. In any case, take a look at this typical page break:

```
experience is a fancy decor, but who cares?  La Fuente is at 5530
Monte Vista Street in Highland Park, and it's open every day.
    Angelenos (yes, that's what they're called) love hamburgers,
-----------------------------------------------------------------
and people develop very strong loyalties to their favorite
hamburger haven.  Perhaps the place with the strongest following is
```

There's a lonely widow at the bottom of the page. Here's how to set up widow and orphan protection to avoid this problem:

1. Position the cursor at the location in your document where you want widow and orphan protection to begin. Generally, this will be at the beginning of the document or at the top of a page.

2. Press **SHIFT-F8 Format**.

3. Type **1** or **l** [L̲ine].

4. Type **9** or **w** [W̲idow/Orphan Protection].

5. Type **y** for yes.

6. Press **F7 Exit** to return to the document.

A [W/O On] code is now in the document. If you were turning widow and orphan protection off, you'd repeat the steps but type **n** for no. The code would be [W/O Off] ... natch! Here's how the page break appears with widow and orphan protection on:

Before widow/orphan protection: WordPerfect breaks pages using the default page format

| Widow line at bottom of page | Orphan line at top of page |

xxxxxxxxxxxxxxxxxxxxxxxxxxxxxx   xxxxxxxxxxxxxxxxxxxxxxxxxxxxxx
xxxxxxx   xxxxxxxxxxxxxxxxxxxxxxxxxxxxxx
    xxxxxxxxxxxxxxxxxxxxxxxx   xxxxxxxxxxxxxxxxxxxxxxxxxxxxxx
----
xxxxxxxxxxxxxxxxxxxxxxxxxxxxxx   xxxxxxxxx
xxxxxxxxxxxxxxxxxxxxxxxxxxxxxx   xxxxxxxxxxxxxxxxxxxxxxxx
xxxxxxxxxxxxxxxxxxxxxxxxxxxxxx   xxxxxxxxxxxxxxxxxxxxxxxxxxxxxx

Page break display

After widow/orphan protection: WordPerfect breaks pages early to keep widows and orphans "related" to rest of paragraph

Widow starts at top of next page   Orphan connected to previous line

xxxxxxxxxxxxxxxxxxxxxxxxxxxxxx   xxxxxxxxxxxxxxxxxxxxxxxxxxxxxx
xxxxxxx   xxxxxxxxxxxxxxxxxxxxxxxxxxxxxx
----
    xxxxxxxxxxxxxxxxxxxxxxxx   xxxxxxxxxxxxxxxxxxxxxxxxxxxxxx
xxxxxxxxxxxxxxxxxxxxxxxxxxxxxx   xxxxxxxxx
xxxxxxxxxxxxxxxxxxxxxxxxxxxxxx   xxxxxxxxxxxxxxxxxxxxxxxx
xxxxxxxxxxxxxxxxxxxxxxxxxxxxxx   xxxxxxxxxxxxxxxxxxxxxxxxxxxxxx

Figure 17-1 Before and After Widow and Orphan Control

```
experience is a fancy decor, but who cares?  La Fuente is at 5530
Monte Vista Street in Highland Park, and it's open every day.
-------------------------------------------------------------------
        Angelenos (yes, that's what they're called) love hamburgers,
and people develop very strong loyalties to their favorite
```

WordPerfect breaks the page one line sooner than normal, and the widow is now related to its paragraph at the top of the next page.

A Problem Situation

I strongly urge you to use widow and orphan protection, because it takes care of most situations—but not all. Take a look at this example page break:

```
Other Requests

        I ask that, as soon as possible upon the dissolution of my Estate,

-------------------------------------------------------------------------------
the bundle of papers and other memorabilia contained in the large, wooden chest

which is presently located under the mattress of the last bed to the right of
```

Now you have both a widow line and a subheading problem. Technically, a title or heading should always be connected to at least the first *two* lines of the paragraph that follows it. So, you dutifully turn widow and orphan protection on at the beginning of the document. The result? WordPerfect didn't catch the problem, because it has limited intelligence in determining what is a widow or orphan and what is not. Apparently, the *Other Requests* line threw WordPerfect off.

How do you handle this problem? Well, you could go through the document and insert hard page codes manually during the final stages. Or you could use something else . . .

The Conditional End of Page Command

When you have text lines that are separated by blank lines but should still be kept together—as with a subheading and the first two lines of the paragraph following it—use the Conditional End of Page command. This feature tells WordPerfect not to break a page if there are fewer than a certain number of lines left on the page. That's the "conditional" part.

You must insert conditional end of page codes on the line directly above *all* sections that you don't want WordPerfect to split between pages. Therefore, this is one page formatting change that doesn't necessarily appear at the top of the page. It's always attached to the text you want to keep together.

Version 4.2 users: It's been moved, too! Here's how to use this command:

1. Position the cursor on the line *above* the first text line that you want to keep together. Don't fret if the line above has text on it, but do make sure the cursor is at the left margin.
2. Press **SHIFT-F8 Format**.
3. Type **4** or **o** [Other].
4. Type **2** or **c** [Conditional End of Page]. WordPerfect prompts:

   `Number of Lines to Keep Together:`
5. Type the exact number of *single-spaced* lines to include in the condition. Include in the count any blank lines if the document is double or triple spaced *and* the line above the text.
6. Press **F7 Exit** twice to return to the document. (You may have to rewrite the screen, too, to see the new page break.)

WordPerfect inserts a `[Cndl EOP]` code in the document with the number of lines you stipulated. As you can see, this type of formatting is something you'd want to do only in the final stage of the document history, after you've made all editing changes. You *can* set up a macro to insert a Conditional End of Page command in front of every subheading when you're typing the document, too, if you wish.

Protecting a Block

Sometimes you'll have a large section of text, such as a table or chart, that you wouldn't want split between pages. Furthermore, you might not wish to count the number of lines and use the conditional end of page feature. Instead, make the text a block and then *protect* the block.

✔Clear the screen and retrieve the document SALES.87, or just follow along.

Assume that this sales chart is somewhere in the middle of a document. You want to make sure that WordPerfect doesn't break the page in the middle of the chart. First, make sure the cursor is at the beginning of the document in front of all codes. Then:

Press   **ALT-F4 Block** or **F12 Block**

Press   **HOME,HOME,DOWN ARROW**

to delimit the block.

Press   **SHIFT-F8 Format**

This key has changed. In previous versions you'd press ALT-F8 Page Format. WordPerfect asks:

```
Protect block? (Y/N) No
```

Type   y

WordPerfect surrounds the block with [Block Pro:On] and [Block Pro:Off] codes. You don't have to worry about this block any more! You may have figured out that the block protect feature is also a substitute for any situation in which you would use the conditional end of page. For instance, with subheadings, just block out the subheading and two lines of the following paragraph and protect the block.

✔Save the document and clear the screen.

Note: If you're protecting a regular paragraph of text, include in the block the first character in the paragraph (probably a tab code) and the entire paragraph *except* the hard return code at the end of the paragraph.

Breaking a Page Yourself

Sometimes it's easier to give the document—in its final stage—a quick run-through to check for page endings. Then adjust the endings yourself. Merely scroll through the document by page and insert Hard Page commands, CTRL-RETURN, wherever you want a page to break before WordPerfect expects. As an example, take a look at part of the trust account you created in Chapter 13:

```
letters addressed to a personage named "Poopsie."  I further request that my

Executor, WOLFGANG AMADEUS SMUDGE, not show these letters to anyone.



                EXECUTED this fifth day of December, 1989, in Claremont, California.




                                  _____
-------------------------------------------------------------------------------
                                  Grace T. Goodbody
```

```
        We, the witnesses to this agreement, attest that the above signature

is the correct signature of the signee.
```

That won't do at all! The line with Ms. Goodbody's name is not connected to its section, but where would you place the page break? If you put it one line up, the document still looks ugly because then just the signature and name lines are at the top of the page. I would put it at the left margin of the line that starts *EXECUTED*, so the result would be this:

```
letters addressed to a personage named "Poopsie."  I further request that my

Executor, WOLFGANG AMADEUS SMUDGE, not show these letters to anyone.




================================================================================
        EXECUTED this fifth day of December, 1989, in Claremont, California.




                              _____

                              Grace T. Goodbody




        We, the witnesses to this agreement, attest that the above signature

is the correct signature of the signee.
```

Recall that WordPerfect shows your hard page breaks with equals signs. You can search for and delete a hard page code like any other.

Keeping Codes at the Top of the Page

I mentioned in Chapter 16 that you can make sure header, footer, and page numbering instructions stay at the top of the page, even when you change the text. Just insert a hard page code directly in front of the other code.

Recall that WordPerfect always obeys a Hard Page command. If you add lines to the document in front of a hard page code, you may push the code into the middle of the page. It's best to wait until the final stage of a document and *then* insert any hard page codes that you might need.

Leaving Room for Illustrations

Whenever you want to leave a blank space for illustration or other paste-up work in your documents, you can do that, too. How you do it depends on where the illustration is to appear. Assume that you want a separate illustration page, but you still want to print the page with whatever headers or footers you've already set up. Position the cursor at the top of the page following the illustration and add a hard page code there. Note that WordPerfect shows the blank, numbered page.

What if you want to leave space at the *bottom* of a page for an illustration? Merely break the page early with a hard page code at the desired location.

Finally, what if the illustration is in the *middle* of the page, surrounded on either side by text? Then you must tell WordPerfect to leave a certain number of lines blank. For that you use the advance to line feature (Chapter 15). When you print the page you'll get the illustration space.

Tip: Use the paragraph numbering feature to number sequential figures and illustrations for you throughout the document (Chapter 21). If you're working with *graphics* elements, then WordPerfect can help you even more (Chapter 34).

Squeezing More Lines on a Page

There is one last point to make about formatting, and it involves a setting known as *line height*. Line height used to refer to the number of printed lines per vertical inch. Now it means the amount of space that a line occupies. WordPerfect measures line height from the base of one line, the *baseline*, to the base of the next line. WordPerfect automatically adjusts the line height when you switch to a larger or smaller font! If you use fixed-width characters, line height is normally six lines per vertical inch.

In the world of typesetting and laser printers, line height is called *leading*. The word, by the way, rhymes with "bedding." You might want to change the amount of leading to make type look less dense on the printed page. Conversely, you might want to squeeze more lines on a page, another time when you'll determine the line height yourself.

Follow these steps when you wish to change line height (or leading) to a fixed amount that you determine:

1. Position the cursor at the correct spot in the document.
   Note: To ensure that header and footer text prints with the new line height, make sure the cursor is in front of any codes.

2. Press **SHIFT-F8 Format**.

3. Type **1** or **l** [Line].

4. Type **4** or **h** [Line Height]. WordPerfect prompts:

   1 Auto; 2 Fixed: 0

5. Type **2** or **f** [Fixed]. WordPerfect shows the default setting for your printer.

6. Supply a new setting, that is, a smaller setting for more lines per inch and a larger setting for fewer lines per inch. Press **RETURN** after you've typed the new setting.

    Caution: Depending on the font size, too small a line height setting will force the lines to print over each other! Be especially careful if the document is single spaced.

7. Press **F7 Exit** to return to the document.

WordPerfect inserts a [Ln Height] code with your new setting and adjusts the page breaks to accommodate the change.

Note: Make sure you turn line height back to automatic when you want WordPerfect to adjust the line height for you. When you tell WordPerfect to return to automatic line height, the code is [Ln Height:Auto].

Printing Specific Pages Revisited

When you learned the essentials of printing (Chapter 5), I mentioned that you'd get into trouble if you didn't accurately specify page ranges. Now that you know about page numbering and controlling the page, you should take another look at how to print specific pages or page ranges in WordPerfect.

When you first learned about printing specific pages, there was no explicit page numbering in your documents. WordPerfect still finds page numbers according to the normal page breaks. It's also possible that you'll have several different sections in a document, each with a different page numbering. WordPerfect then keeps track of page numbering according to your instructions—the codes—in the document.

For example, you may have different sections with different Arabic page numbering. Or you may have table of contents pages numbered with lowercase Roman numerals, regular text with Arabic numbers, and an index or appendix with other Arabic numbering, for example, I-1. (You'll learn how to create tables of contents and indexes in Chapter 23.) This second example thus has three distinct sections.

You can instruct WordPerfect to print certain pages from different document sections, but you must include specific references to the sections in your print ranges.

Caution: The other issue that can hang you up if you're not careful is whether the document you want to print has been fast saved or not. Recall that you print specific pages or page ranges from a document on the disk, and that you must not have fast saved this document prior to printing.

If you have several sections all in one numbering style, such as Arabic numbers, the procedure is relatively straightforward. For example, a document that contains four chapters of a book, with each chapter numbering starting at 1, would have four sections: 1, 2, 3, and 4.

After you press SHIFT-F7 Print, type **3** or **d** [Document on Disk] and select a file to print, indicate sections by number. Divide the section number from the page ranges with a colon (:), and pages with a comma (,). Do *not* uses spaces except when you want to indicate ranges within a section, such as 1-5 7-11, because WordPerfect may interpret a number as a section rather than a page.

Caution: Make sure you type the correct pages according to their numbering in the section. That is, if section 2 has pages 1 through 10, it makes no sense to try printing page 15. WordPerfect doesn't let you enter too many ranges at a time, so you may have to queue up several print jobs. The easiest way to print specific pages and sections is to do the sections individually.

For example, to print Arabic pages 1, 3, and 5–7 of section 1, page 4 of section 2, and all of section 4, you would start three different print jobs with the following page ranges:

```
1:1,3,5-7
2:4
4:1-
```

If you had typed just **4:** for the last section, WordPerfect would have printed only page 1 of that section. You could print the second and third ranges in one print job: (2:4,4:1-).

Things get a little confusing, however, when you're using sections with both Roman and Arabic numbers. If you have a Roman section and an Arabic section (sort of like medieval Spain!), as in the second example, WordPerfect considers them two types of section 1. Here's what I mean.

Assume you want to print pages ii and iii of the table of contents section (Roman section 1), pages 2, 5–7 and 10 of the text section (Arabic section 1), and all the index (Arabic section 2). Here are the page ranges you'd enter:

```
ii-iii
1:2,5-7,10
2:1-
```

In this example, you could print the first and third ranges together: ii-iii,2:1-.

While it's printing, WordPerfect displays the current section and page number on the print: control printer menu. You'll also see the page numbers change as WordPerfect scans the document looking for sections and numbering. Depending on your printer, WordPerfect may ask you to issue a Go command when it finishes one section and before it goes to the next. That means that you type **4** or **g** [Go] from the print: control printer menu to move through the sections, and then another **4** or **g** each time you have to insert a new page in the printer.

Of course, if you follow my advice about keeping the parts of a large document (such as chapters of a book) in individual, modular files and changing the numbering in each document, you'll avoid having to specify different *sections* altogether.

As far as widows and orphans are concerned, WordPerfect has a lot of "eleemosynary" spirit! Still, ultimate control rests with you. Professional word processors know that the proof of the pudding is in the printout. So they take the extra bit of time to get their pages exactly the way they want them. How do you want *your* documents to look?

Working with Multiple Text Columns

In this chapter you'll learn the following new commands . . .

Function Key Command

ALT-F7 Math/Columns (1) Define text columns, (2) turn column mode on/off

Numeric Keypad Commands

CTRL-HOME,HOME, LEFT ARROW Cursor to the leftmost column

CTRL-HOME,HOME, RIGHT ARROW Cursor to the rightmost column

CTRL-HOME,LEFT ARROW Cursor to the next column to the left

CTRL-HOME,RIGHT ARROW Cursor to the next column to the right

. . . you'll discover new uses of these commands . . .

CTRL-HOME,DOWN ARROW Cursor to the bottom of the current column

CTRL-HOME,UP ARROW Cursor to the top of the current column

CTRL-RETURN Cursor to the next parallel column

END Cursor to the right side of the line in the current column

more . . .

> **HOME,LEFT ARROW**   Cursor to the left side of the line
> in the current column
>
> ... and you'll learn some new codes:
>
> [Col Def]   Text column definition
>
> [Col Off]   Text column mode off
>
> [Col On]   Text column mode on

One of the many features that separates WordPerfect from most other word processing programs is its extensive *column formatting* capabilities. If you prepare a great deal of columnar text, you'll appreciate this feature. You can create up to 24 *newspaper style* columns where the text "flows" or "snakes" from one column to the next on the page, or *parallel* columns that line up alongside each other.

Normally the biggest problem you'd face with multiple text columns is learning how to align them on the page so that they print properly within the margins. Most word processing programs can set up columns, but few actually *adjust* the positions of the columns automatically. Not only does WordPerfect do precisely that, but it also allows you to move or copy columns or to change them as you wish. If you have to make revisions to the material within a column, you won't upset the formats of the other columns on the page.

This chapter discusses text columns only. In Chapter 19 you'll learn how to perform mathematical operations on columns of figures.

> ***DO WARM-UP***

Before You Begin

Formatting columnar text is easy in WordPerfect, but there are *two* special rules to follow:

1. You must *define* the columns, that is, tell WordPerfect how to format them. You determine whether columns are evenly spaced from each other, how far apart they'll be, how many columns you want, and the left and right margins of each column. The column definition is stored in a special formatting code that you insert into the document.

2. Because it can't read, WordPerfect has to know exactly where the column formatting begins and ends, so you must tell it by turning the column feature *on* and *off* at the correct locations in the document. The on and off of columns is similar to the on and off of outline mode (Chapter 10).

When you're working with that section of the document that contains columns, you can move the cursor, insert and delete text, delete columns, move columns, or copy columns as you wish. WordPerfect readjusts the columns accordingly.

 Note: WordPerfect won't let you create footnotes in text columns. Set up endnotes instead (Chapter 22). Comments are also not allowed!

Newspaper Style Columns

The first example shows you how to format a document with two columns, as in a newspaper or newsletter. Text "snakes" from one column to the next. That is, any changes in the text changes the column formatting. This is also the longest typing example in the book, so you're getting some good practice here.

As usual, always decide on the main document formatting at the beginning of the document. For this example, use the default margins, spacing, and right margin justification. However, you might find *after* you set up the columns that you may not have the correct tab stops. You can change the tabs later, but for this example I'm supplying the tab stops that work.

✔You can't set tabs from within a column, only in the main document. So, go into the tab set area and clear all tabs. Then set left-justified tabs at columns 1.3 and 5.1 only.

Next, put in a title for the article. Because this title should be centered over *both* columns, do not include it within the columns themselves.

✔Center and type this title: *Texan's Chili Conquers All.* Press **RETURN** three times for spacing.

The next step is to define the columns that you want and insert the definition code into the document. This procedure is only slightly different from previous versions. When you define columns, you must instruct WordPerfect about the following:

1. The type of columns you want, that is, whether they're to be evenly spaced within the document's left and right margins (newspaper style) or not (parallel).

2. How many columns you want.

3. How much blank space you want to separate the columns, that is, the distance between them.

4. Whether you want regular or protected parallel columns, discussed later.

5. Any margin adjustments. You can determine the column margins yourself, or have WordPerfect do it (I like that!), in which case it then automatically figures out the column margins within the document's margins.

   Tip: WordPerfect "assumes" you want columns of equal width that use the default line length. To have newspaper columns of une-qual widths, type the new margin settings to override WordPerfect's suggestions. To have columns that extend past the margins or use a smaller line length, change the left margin setting of the first column and the right margin setting of the last column.

If you plan to switch between column mode and regular text and the column definition is the same throughout the document, you only need one definition. Make sure, however, that the column definition appears before the first columns but after any line format changes.

   Time to begin:

Press   **ALT-F7 Math/Columns**

WordPerfect presents the math/columns menu:

`1 Math On; 2 Math Def; 3 Column On/Off; 4 Column Def: 0`

Type   **4** or **d** [Column **D**ef]

The text column definition screen shown in Figure 18-1 appears. Your margin settings may be different. WordPerfect defaults to two newspaper col-umns that are a half inch apart, so you don't have to do *anything!* You'll even accept WordPerfect's margin suggestions, so:

Press   **F7 Exit**

to return to the math/columns menu.

   What could be easier? Not much. Another example will show you how to change the column definition. However, after you define your columns, you must still turn column mode on:

Type   **3** or **c** [**C**olumn On/Off]

WordPerfect inserts a `[Col Def]` code and a `[Col On]` code into the doc-ument. The column definition code shows the number of columns and their margins. Column mode is now on. Note that WordPerfect shows the current column number on the status line: Col 1. You'll soon see Col 2, too.

```
Text Column Definition

    1 - Type                              Newspaper

    2 - Number of Columns                 2

    3 - Distance Between Columns

    4 - Margins

    Column    Left     Right     Column    Left      Right
      1:      1"       4"          13:
      2:      4.5"     7.5"        14:
      3:                           15:
      4:                           16:
      5:                           17:
      6:                           18:
      7:                           19:
      8:                           20:
      9:                           21:
     10:                           22:
     11:                           23:
     12:                           24:

Selection: 0
```

Figure 18-1   The Text Column Definition Menu

The next step is to get the typing done. Alas, WordPerfect can't help you there! If you've moved the cursor, make sure it's directly past the [Col On] code before you begin. The entire article is shown here. Type it, using one tab to begin each paragraph and making your corrections as you go along. I've indicated where the columns end—don't type my little reminders!

When it reaches the bottom of the first column, WordPerfect starts the second column at the top of the same page, and so on.

Note: The lines and pages may break differently depending on the printer you're using.

327

Texan's Chili Conquers All

POULET, Texas. When he was a boy, Stanley Beburp dreamed of becoming the King of Chili. "Other boys wanted to be firemen and policemen. Not me! I wanted to be the world's expert on chili, the Reigning Monarch of the Red Hot."

Now it looks as if Beburp's dreams have come true. Not only did his "Buckaroo Chili" take first prize in the All-Texas Chili Round-Up, but it did so for the tenth consecutive year, a record that no one has ever come close to beating.

What's more, a large international food conglomerate has approached Beburp with an offer to mass produce and distribute his prize-winning chili as part of a new line of frozen food products emphasizing "regional American cuisine."

"It's like what I always knew would happen," he exclaimed. "Someday people everywhere would appreciate me for my true worth, would recognize the grandeur and majesty of good chili."

Beburp, or Stan, as he is most often known to virtually everyone in these parts, dipped a huge ladle into a steaming cauldron of—what else?—Buckaroo Chili, and offered it to the unsuspecting writer. Not being one to refuse a kind gesture, I took up the challenge. Thank what appeared to me to be a diabolical scheme to destroy my entire insides. "People who aren't used to chili, and especially to my chili, find it at first a bit hard to swallow. Get it? Hard to swallow. Hah!"

I smiled meekly, all the while trying to ascertain exactly where I was and what in heaven's name I was doing with the uncontrollable, burning sensation that writhed down my throat and ended in the pit of my stomach. The beer helped a little, but only a little, and only if I continued to down it like water. I was also thinking wistfully of quiche lorraine and other more, well, civilized food.

"Are you from New York?" he asked, as I politely refused another brimming ladleful. "I've found New Yorkers the most difficult to please. They never seem to enjoy my chili. I think their taste buds must have been destroyed in early childhood. Probably has something to do with the subways, I think."

(Little did Stan realize that the hottest of Hunan food, so much praised by residents of the Big Apple and elsewhere, couldn't come even close to the pinnacle of picantness that was and is Buckaroo Chili. As one who has always considered himself a relentless pursuer of the

goodness there was a pint of cold beer also readily available!

"It's hot, isn't it?" Stan asked, offering to help wipe the tears away from my eyes as I nearly swooned in

Bottom of first column: Go to the top of the second column.

head was reeling, and my stomach was giving me notice that I would pay long and hard for my sins.

Meanwhile, Stan was blithely and rather rapidly rattling on about his childhood. All I could catch were snips and snatches here and there:

"Poor family ... never had enough to eat, it seemed ... father disappeared when he was 10 ... mother had to work and not the best of cooks anyway ... can't blame her ... neighbor's wife made chili for them every week ... it became an obsession, a craving that he couldn't satisfy ... he would spend hours over the pot ... she gave him the task of stirring the chili ... that was the real secret: in the stirring ..."

Soon the minor revolution that had begun in my stomach was turning into an event of major proportions, an uproar that swelled and took with it my sense of decorum and all my Eastern-bred reliance on the balance between the Inner and Outer Man. At the moment, the Inner Man was a devil who had

ultimate "hot trip," I felt that, at long last, I had met my match.)

Things were getting a bit befuddled and confused as I tried to listen to Stan recount his life story. My

Bottom of second column: Continue with the first column of page 2 below.

buzzing in the hot, midday sun: "Who knows, maybe I can sell the t-shirt concession soon, too!"

```
totally subverted the Outer
Man to his wishes.  I excused
myself and stumbled towards
the restroom.
    Later, I would look
around and see what appeared
to be thousands of fiends
calmly spooning down huge
bowls of perdition, drinking
beer and soda, and all the
while laughing and having a
jolly good time.  I wondered
whether I had finally gone
through the looking glass and
were not, in fact, viewing the
world through the distortion
of some insidious fever.
    Somewhere, far off in the
distance now, a voice was
```

Bottom of the first column:
Go to the top
of the second column

When you're finished:

Press   **ALT-F7 Math/Columns**

Type   **3** or **c** [Column On/Off]

WordPerfect inserts a [Col Off] code here.

Tip: Get into the habit of turning column mode off at the point where the columns end. Because the second column is shorter than the first, WordPerfect starts a new page when you turn columns off. Later you'll see how to even out column lengths.

Once you've defined the column setup, you can turn column mode on and off many times throughout a document. For example, suppose you now inserted text that was in regular paragraphs. Later, you could switch back to the same column setup. All you need do is turn column mode back on. You *don't* have to define the columns again, as long as the formatting is the same.

✔Save this document as POULET, but leave it on the screen. Print the document or view the printout to see the results, if you wish.

Tips: You may have noticed that, because the columns are narrow, some lines will print more "spaced out" than others. Soon you'll learn how to hyphenate words to close up lines (Chapter 20). If you wanted page numbering, set that as part of the main document's formatting before the column definition code. Widow/orphan protection also works within columns. In this example, you added a title that you centered over both columns. You can also center title lines above individual columns. Make sure the cursor is within a column. Then use the RETURN key to add some blank lines before you insert a title.

Cursor Movement in Columns

The normal cursor movement keys work as you might expect within each column. Just think of the column as a full page. For example, position the cursor at the beginning of the document, and then use the **DOWN ARROW** key to move into the first column. Then:

Press **END**

The cursor moves to the last character of the column.

Press **HOME,LEFT ARROW**

The cursor is now at the left edge of the column, the left margin.

Press **CTRL-HOME,DOWN ARROW**

The cursor is at the bottom of the "page," that is, the first column.

Press **CTRL-HOME,UP ARROW**

The cursor is at the top of the first column, not at the top of the page. You can move between columns quickly, too:

Press **CTRL-HOME,RIGHT ARROW**

The cursor is in the next column, at the same line relative to the previous column line.

Press **CTRL-HOME,DOWN ARROW**

The cursor is now at the bottom of the second column.

Press **CTRL-HOME,UP ARROW**

Now, it's at the top of the second column.

Press **CTRL-HOME,LEFT ARROW**

Finally, you've moved the cursor to the previous column. If you were working with *more* than two columns, use the commands **CTRL-HOME,HOME,LEFT ARROW** to move the cursor to the first (leftmost) column and **CTRL-HOME,HOME,RIGHT ARROW** to move the cursor to the last (rightmost) column.

Press   **PG DN**

The cursor is at the top of the first column on page 2. Get the picture? Table 18-1 lists the cursor movement commands you've just learned. By the way, the delete keys work within a column, too. That is, CTRL-END deletes to the end of the line in the current column, and CTRL-PG DN deletes to the bottom of the column.

Editing a Column

If you add to or delete text in a column, WordPerfect adjusts all other columns accordingly. First, go where you want the new text to be. Position the cursor on the first line of the paragraph that begins *Later, I would look*. It's on page 2. Then add a blank line:

Press   **RETURN**

Press   **UP ARROW**

Watch what happens when you add this paragraph to the article:

Table 18-1 Cursor Movement in Text Columns

Press	To move to the . . .
HOME,LEFT ARROW	Left side of the current column
END	
HOME,RIGHT ARROW	Right side of the current column
HOME,UP ARROW	Top of the screen in the current column
HOME,DOWN ARROW	Bottom of the screen in the current column
CTRL-HOME,LEFT ARROW	Next column to the left
CTRL-HOME,RIGHT ARROW	Next column to the right
CTRL-HOME,HOME,LEFT ARROW	Leftmost column
CTRL-HOME,HOME,RIGHT ARROW	Rightmost column
CTRL-HOME,UP ARROW	Top of the current column
CTRL-HOME,DOWN ARROW	Bottom of the current column

There was still what
seemed to me to be an enormous
pile of Buckaroo Chili left on
my plate. I knew that there
was no getting out of the
inevitable without some form
of drastic action. Stan had
turned his back for a moment
to address a friend, so I knew
that here was my golden
opportunity for salvation.
The plate "slipped" from my
hands. A close call!

✔Type the new paragraph, but don't add an extra hard return at the end. How do the two columns look now? Then save your edited version of POULET, but leave it on the screen.

Moving or Copying Text within Columns

You can block out text within a column and move it somewhere else. However, if you're moving a paragraph that's split *between* two columns, as is the additional paragraph you just typed, with the standard block operation you'd have to block out the two parts and move or copy them *separately*. WordPerfect has a better idea. Say you want to move the new paragraph somewhere else.

✔Position the cursor at the left margin of the first line of paragraph that begins *Later, I would look* on page 2. Then:

Press   **CTRL-F4 Move**

Type   **2** or **p** [<u>P</u>aragraph]

Type   **1** or **m** [<u>M</u>ove]

✔Position the cursor at the very end of column 2 on page 2. If you didn't add a RETURN at the end of the last paragraph, press **RETURN** now. The cursor should be on the line below the end of the second column.

Press   **RETURN**

to retrieve the paragraph.

      Caution: Don't use the tabular column feature on the block move menu to move text within columns. That's for moving or copying columns of text or numbers that you've set up around tab stops or indents (Chapter 14). You can, of course, use the block technique to move or copy text that is entirely *within* a column, including all the text in an entire column. In that case, be careful that you *don't* move any column definition or column on/off codes.

Evening Out Column Lengths

WordPerfect assumes that the columns should extend down the entire page to fill in the total number of text lines for the page. On page 2 of the POULET document, the second column is shorter than the first. What if you wanted to even out the length of the two columns on this page? Although you shouldn't stop now and do it as an example, you could count the number of total lines in a full column and the number of lines presently in column 2. Then, by simple arithmetic, figure how many lines from column 1 should be put in column 2.

For example, if column 2 contains 11 text lines and column 1 54 text lines, then there are 54 + 11 = 65 total column text lines on the page. So, there should be 65 / 2 = 33 text lines in column 1 and 32 in column 2. Position the cursor on the 34th text line in column 1 and press CTRL-RETURN to add a hard page break there. WordPerfect adjusts the second column, and you now have even columns on the page.

Turning Off the Column Display

WordPerfect has to do a great deal of on-screen formatting when you're working with newspaper style columns, so it slows down a bit. It slows down a lot if you have many columns on the page. If this is an annoyance, you can turn off the on-screen display of columns side by side. The cursor can be anywhere in the document.

Version 4.2 users: This feature has moved. Because it's now part of the setup options, refer to Appendix A for information.

When you turn off the side-by-side columns display, WordPerfect shows only one column per screen "page," and screen rewriting is much faster. Use the PG UP and PG DN keys to see the other column on a second "page." The columns will still print correctly. Just turn the display back on when you do want to see columns side by side on the screen.

Note: If text *within* columns appears to overlap on the screen display, refer to Appendix A to learn how to change the display pitch.

Changing the Column Definition

Because it's a format code, you can change a column definition. You have two options: (1) delete the previous column definition code and start with a new one or (2) position the cursor directly past the [Col Def] code but in front of the [Col On] code, press **ALT-F7 Math/Columns**, and type **4** or **d** [Column Def] to see the previous definition. Then make any changes to this definition. I prefer the first method, because then you aren't confused by all the extra codes! When you change an existing code WordPerfect inserts a new code next to the original.

✔If you wish, change the two column layout to a three column one (make sure you save the document in two column format first). First, position the cursor at the beginning of the document. Press **DOWN ARROW** three times to get to the column setup. Then, reveal the codes and delete the [Col Def] code but leave the cursor where it is and don't delete the [Col On] code. Press **ALT-F7 Math/Columns**, then type **4** or **d** [Column Def]. Then follow these steps:

Type   **2** or **n** [Number of Columns]

Type   **3**

Press   **F7 Exit** twice

WordPerfect doesn't show the new columns yet. Just rewrite the screen, and there they are! Neat, huh?

✔If you wish, save this document as POULET.2, but don't change the original POULET document. You'll use that in another chapter. Then clear the screen.

Drawing Lines Between Columns

Although you can't use the normal line draw feature (Chapter 15) to draw a vertical or horizontal line between text columns, you *can* accomplish this trick with a graphics element. See Chapter 34.

Parallel Columns

Parallel columns are columns of text that line up horizontally, usually to the first line. The formatting for each column is separate from the others, and you can change this formatting as you wish. Needless to say, text doesn't flow from one parallel column to the next.

As an example of parallel columns, I've chosen a little test document that probably reveals my age. The test consists of a question section, in one column, and a series of multiple choice answers in the other column. The test column is wider than the answer column. Again, to save time you'll use the standard defaults. Don't bother with a title this time, but get right into setting up the column definition.

Press   **ALT-F7 Math/Columns**

Type   **4** or **d** [Column Def]

This time, you must supply some answers:

Type   1 or t [Type]

WordPerfect presents the column type menu:

```
Column Type: 1 Newspaper; 2 Parallel; 3 Parallel with Block Protect: 0
```

Use choice **1** [Newspaper] if you've already set up parallel columns before this spot in the document and you now want newspaper columns. WordPerfect always "remembers" the last column type you've chosen. WordPerfect lets you have parallel columns that span page breaks or parallel columns enclosed in block protect codes (Chapter 17). The former was a request of script writers. You'll choose the latter to make sure that WordPerfect doesn't split a question and answer section over page breaks:

Type   3 or b [Parallel with Block Protect]

Normally, you'd have to determine the left and right margins for each column when you're setting up columns that are not evenly spaced. I've done the thinking for you in this example.

Type   4 or m [Margins]

Type   1.0

Press   **RETURN**

Type   4.5

Press   **RETURN**

These are the margin settings for the larger first column.

Type   5.5

Press   **RETURN**

Type   7.5

Press   **RETURN**

These are the margin settings for the smaller column.
Note: You can't overlap column margins. For example, if you typed **4.5** for the left margin of the second column, that conflicts with the right margin of the first column. WordPerfect would give you this error message:

```
ERROR: Text columns can't overlap
```

Try again! If you've typed the margins correctly, it's time to turn column mode on:

Press   **F7 Exit**

to return to the math/columns menu.

Type   **3** or **c** [<u>C</u>olumn On/Off]

Look at the codes now. WordPerfect sets up the column definition and column on codes, but it also inserts a [Block Pro:On] code. That's because you've told it to protect each group of parallel columns. Now, type the first question, shown below, but don't type the answer part yet!

```
What was the name of Clarabelle's        ____ Annabelle
sister on the "Howdy Doody Show"?        ____ Bozette
                                         ____ Clarabella
                                         ____ None of the
                                               above
```

It's always a good idea to work your way across the columns. After you type the first column, here's how to get to the top of the other column:

Press   **CTRL-RETURN**

Now, type the answer lines, ending *each* with a hard return. The underlines are four across. When you're finished with the first set of parallel columns, you can begin another set. With the cursor directly after the word *above:*

Press   **CTRL-RETURN**

The cursor moves down to begin another set of parallel columns. Type the second question and its answers. Remember to press **CTRL-RETURN** to move from the first column to the second:

```
Which famous personality did Lucy        ____ Harpo Marx
not imitate or pretend to be on          ____ Superman
either of the "Lucy" shows?              ____ J. Edgar Hoover
                                         ____ Ethel Merman
```

There's your little test. Now, turn column mode off:

Press   **ALT-F7 Math/Columns**

Type   **3** or **c** [Column On/Off]

Note that WordPerfect moves the cursor to the next line when you turn column mode off. If you reveal the codes, you'll see both a [Block Pro:Off] and a [Col Off] code.

 Tip: Suppose you have four parallel columns across a page but you don't know the entry for each column yet. You must still press CTRL-RETURN to move into the column, then CTRL-RETURN to move to the next column. Later you can fill in the missing information. Use the cursor movement keys discussed in a previous section to move between parallel columns.

✔Save the document as TEST.1.

Moving, Copying, and Deleting Text Columns

When you move, copy, or delete entire columns, make sure that you block out the column definition and on/off codes at the beginning and end of the column setup along with the column text. For parallel columns, include the block protection codes, too. Then perform the move, copy, or delete operation on the block. Do *not* use the tabular column choice from the block move menu!

Tired of text? How about trying columns of figures and boning up on your arithmetic at the same time?

Chapter

19

Fun with Figures

In this chapter you'll discover new uses of this command . . .

ALT-F7 Math/Columns   Define, set up, and calculate math columns

. . . you'll investigate these math *operators* . . .

+	Addition
—	(1) Subtraction *or* (2) negative number
*	Multiplication
/	Division
+/	Average a numeric column
=/	Average a total column
( )	Negative number

. . . and you'll learn some new codes:

!	Math formula to be calculated or recalculated
??!	Incorrect calculation formula
+	Subtotal of a column of numbers directly above the code
*	Grand total of all totals above the code
=	Total all subtotals above the code
[Math Def]	Math column definition change
[Math Off]	Math mode off

more . . .

[Math On]	Math mode on
N	Subtract number but don't display a minus sign
t	Extra subtotal entry
T	Extra total entry

In Chapter 18, I mentioned that columns of figures are decidedly different from columns of text. That's because most of the time figures involve arithmetic, and that brings up WordPerfect's built-in math features—the subject of this chapter. The examples are all easy, but when you're a pro you can develop much more complicated math applications.

DO WARM-UP

Preliminary Notes

As usual, you should learn some points about how to work with figures and WordPerfect's math operations. The math feature requires you to follow these precepts:

- You turn the math feature on, like the text column feature, where you need it and then off when you're finished with it.
- You have to set up columns of figures to work with the math operation if you want to get any results. That means you have to turn math on *before* you start.
- You must define the types of math columns you need, just as you define text columns. There are four types of math columns in WordPerfect:

  1. *Numeric* columns (the default when you turn math on) contain numbers to total or subtotal.

  2. *Text* columns display descriptive labels (when math is on, you have to tell WordPerfect when you want it not to try to calculate column entries—hence, text columns).

  3. *Total* columns are separate columns that total whatever column is to the left of the total column.

4. *Calculated*, or *formula*, columns contain special formulas for a variety of situations, including totaling figures *horizontally* across a page. (Actually, total and calculated columns are special types of numeric columns, because they still give numeric results. You can have figures in text columns, too, but WordPerfect won't calculate them.)

■ You *must* set up columns of figures around tab stops. When math is on, WordPerfect uses the decimal tab align character automatically when you press the TAB key. Most of the time you'd use the decimal point when you type columns of figures anyway. But do keep in mind that *all* columns that you want to perform math operations on must be with figures at tab stops. As you'll see, you can perform math operations either down a column or across the page, provided that the figures are at tab stops.

Note: WordPerfect is essentially a word processing program with a lot of "perks," but its basic purpose is to work with words, not figures. If you plan to do a lot of "number crunching" (for instance, financial analysis or complicated accounting), WordPerfect may not be your best bet. What you need is a *spreadsheet* program that is devoted to handling heavy-duty numbers. WordPerfect Corporation can sell you PlanPerfect for this purpose, or you may want to investigate any number of other programs such as Lotus 1-2-3.

Back to the task at hand. As usual, a bit of planning helps before you start. Determine how you want to arrange your math columns *before you begin*.

Tip: WordPerfect's math features work best when you set up calculations down columns, although you can perform calculations across columns, too. You'll do both!

A Sales Report

You want to create a sales report for the United Bakeries of Santa Clara County and in the process discover some of WordPerfect's math features. Here's what the initial report will look like when it's finished (it will look a little different on the screen for reasons you'll learn later):

Product	January	February	March	April
Apple Pie	5,344.25	5,487.65	6,001.50	4,123.00
Bear Claw	2,567.80	2,010.36	1,998.66	1,989.05
Chocolate Eclair	3,558.22	(500.01)	2,775.12	950.00
Linzertorte	1,783.15	776.75	765.43	865.02
Strawberry Shortcake	981.00	865.40	1,115.50	4,111.15

Truffled Delight	3,299.25	3,005.22	4,004.04	3,050.25
	———	———	———	———
TOTAL	17,533.67	11,645.37	16,660.25	15,088.47

Because you'll add two more columns to the report later, use paper positioned horizontally in the printer. That means you'll switch to a different form.

✔If you didn't create the standard form with horizontal wide paper in Chapter 13, do so now (see Printing on Horizontal paper in that chapter). Everyone: At the top of a blank screen insert a paper size and type change to select the standard form with horizontal wide (landscape) paper.

Because WordPerfect uses 1-inch left and right margins, you'll change them so that the long horizontal lines will fit correctly.

✔Change the left and right margins to 0.5 inch now.

Now, *before* you get to the math part, determine the correct math column locations.

Caution: If numbers in one column extend into the next column, the calculations will not be correct. Make sure each column has enough space!

You must use the TAB key to move into each math column, so the next step is to change the tab settings. Always set your tabs *before* you turn math mode on. For this example, you'll have left-justified tabs beginning at column 3.5 and spaced 1.3 inches apart. Do you remember how to set tabs at intervals? Okay, I'll give you a break. Here's how:

Press	**SHIFT-F8 Format**
Type	1 or l [Line]
Type	8 or t [Tab Set]
Press	**CTRL-END**

to clear all tabs from the left margin.

Type	**3.5,1.3**

to set tabs at intervals of 1.3 inches, starting at column 3.5.

Press	**F7 Exit** twice

to return to the document.

Caution: When you're doing columns of text or figures, make sure that the *rightmost* column is wide enough to hold the figures. That is, don't make it too close to the right margin, because the column width then might not be able to fit figures of a certain length. For example, if the column width is 0.5 inch, you might not be able to fit a number such as 12,345.

Don't worry about the titles yet; they're above the math section, so you'll add them later. You must now define the math columns. Make sure that the cursor is positioned past the page and line format change codes. Note that the example *appears* to contain five columns. The leftmost "column" is strictly for text, while the other columns contain figures. *However*, because the leftmost column is *not* set at a tab stop—it's at the left margin—WordPerfect doesn't even consider it a math column.

Press   **ALT-F7 Math/Columns**

The ALT-F7 key is labeled Math/Columns to remind you that you use this key for both text columns and columns of figures.

Type   **2** or **e** [Math D̲ef]

Figure 19-1 shows the math definition screen that appears. This is a lot less complicated than it looks! The columns themselves are identified by letters, A being the leftmost column. The column type is shown as a number, 0 through 3. WordPerfect assumes by default that you're using numeric type columns, 2.

If the result of a math calculation is negative, you can choose whether to show the number enclosed in parentheses or preceded by a minus sign. WordPerfect assumes parentheses by default. The Number of Digits to the Right (0-4) line means the number of decimal places in the number, which will be to the right of the tab stop. The default decimal place setting is 2, exactly what you need! You'll learn about calculation formulas later.

The cursor is positioned under the type for column A, which is actually the *second* column in the sales report and the *first* tab stop. Why? Because the column with the product names is *not at a tab stop*. Get it?

As it turns out, you don't have to change anything! Just keep in mind that you won't include the first column of this example in the math column lettering scheme.

Press   **F7 Exit**

to return to the math/columns menu.

Type   **1** or **m** [M̲ath On]

The message, Math, appears on the status line as long as math mode is on, and WordPerfect inserts a [Math On] code into the document. If you had changed the default math definition, you would also see a [Math Def] code.

```
Math Definition          Use arrow keys to position cursor

Columns                  A B C D E F G H I J K L M N O P Q R S T U V W X

Type                     2 2 2 2 2 2 2 2 2 2 2 2 2 2 2 2 2 2 2 2 2 2 2 2

Negative Numbers         ( ( ( ( ( ( ( ( ( ( ( ( ( ( ( ( ( ( ( ( ( ( ( (

Number of Digits to      2 2 2 2 2 2 2 2 2 2 2 2 2 2 2 2 2 2 2 2 2 2 2 2
  the Right (0-4)

Calculation     1
  Formulas      2
                3
                4

Type of Column:
     0 = Calculation    1 = Text     2 = Numeric    3 = Total

Negative Numbers
     ( = Parentheses (50.00)         - = Minus Sign  -50.00




Press Exit when done
```

Figure 19-1   The Math Definition Screen

You're finally ready to type the products and their sales figures. I'll step you through part of the example, but then you're on your own.

Type   **Apple Pie**

At this point, should you use the CTRL-F6 Tab Align key? You *could*, but because this is a numeric column, and because math mode is on, WordPerfect assumes the tab align anyway when you press TAB alone. Why press two keys when you need to press only one?

Press   **TAB**

 Notice that the status line says Align Char = . Math to remind you that the default alignment character is a period. You can also change the decimal/ align character or thousands' separator (Chapter 10).

Type   **5,344.25**

Press   **TAB**

Continue typing the figures, remembering to press **TAB** to move the cursor into each column first. Press **RETURN** at the end of each line. Apparently there was a problem with chocolate eclairs in February, and instead of sales, the bakery showed a loss. You can type negative figures either with a minus sign, **-500.01**, or enclosed in parentheses, **(500.01)**, as here.

   ✔Type all six products and their sales figures. The cursor is on the next line when you're finished. Press **RETURN** again for spacing. For the underlines, use the **SPACEBAR** to move the cursor to the correct spot first. Working with the same technique, type the underlines below the figures. Because each underline is 8 characters long, use the **ESC** key to create the underlines quickly. Make sure you press **RETURN** twice at the end of the line and type the word **TOTAL** at column 1″. Leave the cursor directly after the word *TOTAL* on the last line, because you'll add to the line in a moment.

Setting Up Column Totals

To have WordPerfect automatically total down a column by adding all the positive numbers and subtracting the negative ones, you insert an *operator*. An operator tells WordPerfect what math operation to perform. Operators don't print with the document. There are three operators for doing totals: a plus sign (+) creates a subtotal, an equals sign (=) creates a total of subtotals, and an asterisk (*) generates a total from other totals. Confusing? Not really, as you'll see.

   Caution: You must use the TAB key to move the cursor into the column before you type the operator you want.

Press   **TAB**

Type   +

The plus sign operator tells WordPerfect to subtotal the column of figures above the +. Why a subtotal? Because you're going to add other figures to this report later. The WordPerfect documentation suggests that you allow space for the two decimal places when WordPerfect inserts the subtotals or totals in a column. It instructs you to press the SPACEBAR twice before going on to the next column. Actually, you *don't* have to do this, so why waste time?

   ✔Continue pressing the **TAB** key and entering the + operators for each column. At the end of the line, press **RETURN** to space down. Here's what the figures now look like on the screen:

Apple Pie	5,344.25	5,487.65	6,001.50	4,123.00
Bear Claw	2,567.80	2,010.36	1,998.66	1,989.05
Chocolate Eclair	3,558.22	(500.01)	2,775.12	950.00
Linzertorte	1,783.15	776.75	765.43	865.02
Strawberry Shortcake	981.00	865.40	1,115.50	4,111.15
Truffled Delight	3,299.25	3,005.22	4,004.04	3,050.25
	———	———	———	———
TOTAL	+	+	+	+

Well, so where are the subtotals? WordPerfect doesn't insert them until you specifically instruct it to *calculate* them.

Press   **ALT-F7 Math/Columns**

Because math is now on, the math/columns menu has changed slightly.

Type   **2** or **a** [Calculate]

There they are! Don't worry about the + operators in the totals line—they don't print with the document.

✔Save the document as SALES.HOR but leave it on the screen. The file extension reminds you about the paper setup.

A Useful Trick

When you do statistical typing, you may want to use the numeric keypad for data entry. Because it's set up in WordPerfect for cursor movement, normally you'd have to press the NUM LOCK key for numbers, and then press it again to move the cursor. What a drag! There's a way to get around this problem: Whenever you need to type a number, press the SHIFT key and the number key. The keypad remains a cursor movement pad, but you can still enter numbers quickly!

Prettying Things Up

Now add the titles above the columns, but be careful. You may *think* that you can just tab over and center each title over the figures with the SHIFT-F6 Center command, but that won't work as you'd expect. WordPerfect would center the titles over the tab stops, and they won't look very good. There are two ways to make the titles visually appealing: (1) set up center tab stops, but that takes time, or (2) "eyeball" the titles, a much faster approach.

✔Position the cursor at the beginning of the document. Then, make sure the cursor is positioned past all the format change codes, but in front of the [Math On] code. Use the **RETURN** key to insert two blank lines and then the **UP ARROW** key to position the cursor on line 1". Then use the **SPACE-BAR** to position the cursor before you type the titles. Refer to the original example as your guide. Save the document again and print it if you wish. Leave it on the screen.

Changing Figures and Recalculating

You glance at the columns of figures on the screen and notice that something seems to be wrong with Truffled Delight! Isn't the March figure a bit too high? Sure enough, you've made a mistake. No problem. Just go back into the specific column and correct it.

✔Position the cursor under the first *4* of *4,004.04*. As soon as you go into the math area, the status line tells you so. Then:

Press   **DEL**

Type   **3**

Once again, WordPerfect doesn't recalculate until you tell it:

Press   **ALT-F7 Math/Columns**

Type   **2** or **a** [C<u>a</u>lculate]

✔Save the document again.

Calculated Columns

You can change the math definition at any time, but first make sure that the cursor is positioned directly *past* the original [Math Def] code, if there is one, and directly *in front of* the [Math On] code. This is one time where you wouldn't want to delete the previous code, because then you'd delete any specific math definition. If you leave the code and press **ALT-F7 Math/Columns** to redefine the setup, all you'd have to do is make the new changes.

In this example, you'll set up two more columns of figures. One will show a standard commission rate, while the other contains a total of each row (horizontal line) of the table. Both are calculated columns.

A calculated column contains *only* a formula that refers to other columns. You can have at most four different calculated formulas, one per column. Here, the fifth math column computes a commission of 10% of the total of the line. The sixth math column adds the lines together to get a total of sales less commissions. After prettying the document up a bit, you'll see this on the screen (sorry about the smaller type!):

Product	January	February	March	April	Commissions	Net Total
Apple Pie	5,344.25	5,487.65	6,001.50	4,123.00	2,095.64!	18,860.76!
Bear Claw	2,567.80	2,010.36	1,998.66	1,989.05	856.59!	7,709.28!
Chocolate Eclair	3,558.22	(500.01)	2,775.12	950.00	678.33!	6,105.00!
Linzertorte	1,783.15	776.75	765.43	865.02	419.04!	3,771.31!
Strawberry Shortcake	981.00	865.40	1,115.50	4,111.15	707.31!	6,365.74!
Truffled Delight	3,299.25	3,005.22	3,004.04	3,050.25	1,235.88!	11,122.88!
	‾‾‾‾‾‾	‾‾‾‾‾‾	‾‾‾‾‾‾	‾‾‾‾‾‾	‾‾‾‾‾‾	‾‾‾‾‾‾
TOTAL	17,533.67+	11,645.37+	15,660.25+	15,088.47+	5,992.79+	53,934.97+
Other Income						t30,222.76
GRAND TOTAL						84,157.73=

I'll step you through the new math features. You can add the new titles later.

✔First, change the math definition by positioning the cursor at the beginning of the document and then directly in front of the [Math On] code. Then:

Press   **ALT-F7 Math/Columns**

Type   **2 or e** [Math D<u>e</u>f]

There's the default math definition setup. For the fifth column, labeled E, you must indicate that it's a calculated column.

Press   **RIGHT ARROW** four times

Type   **0** [Calculation]

WordPerfect displays the column label in the Calculation Formulas list. Use the standard microcomputer operators shown here to set up the calculation formula:

+   addition
−   subtraction
*   multiplication
/   division

You must include the column letter in the formula for each column that you need. You don't have to type letters in uppercase. So, to enter the formula to compute a 10% commission of the total of the other four columns:

Type   **.10*(a+b+c+d)**

Note the use of parentheses to *group* the four columns together. If you had typed **.10*a+b+c+d**, WordPerfect would have taken 10% of column A *only*. That's because it calculates formulas from left to right. Using parentheses *changes* the order of calculation to add the columns first and then multiply the result by 10%. (Computer gurus call this changing the *order of precedence*, but you don't have to know that!) WordPerfect always calculates the figures within the parentheses first. Be careful when you set up formulas that you have the correct groups. That is, use parentheses where necessary.

Press   **RETURN**

You must press **RETURN** so that the cursor moves back into the Type line before you can continue. For the next calculation (column F):

Type   **0** [Calculation]

Type   **a+b+c+d-e**

Press   **RETURN**

Here, parentheses aren't necessary, because WordPerfect adds the first four columns and *then* subtracts column E in the correct order. At this point, stop and consider both formulas more carefully. If Column E represents a sales commission that has to be deducted from columns A, B, C, and D, why didn't I set up the formula as a negative number, like this?

-(.10*(a+b+c+d))

The answer? Because you can only have *one* set of parentheses in a formula. WordPerfect would have presented the following message:

ERROR: Illegal character(s)

Fortunately, in this document, I could get around the restriction by using subtraction in the other formula. Still, it's a good idea to plan calculated columns wisely.

Press   **F7 Exit**

A [Math On] code is already in the document, so:

Press   **RETURN**

To get WordPerfect to use these two new calculated columns, you must move the cursor into them. Position the cursor at the end of the Apple Pie line:

Press   **END**

Move into the next column:

Press   **TAB**

WordPerfect inserts a ! into the column. In math mode, this means that the column is a calculated column.

Press   **TAB**

Another ! appears for the second calculated column.

Press   **DOWN ARROW**

Don't press RETURN, because you already have the correct line endings. Continue adding two tabs at the end of each line. Don't worry about the underlines yet. When you're finished,

Press   **ALT-F7 Math/Columns**

Type   **2** or **a** [Ca̲lculate]

If you put a ! operator in the wrong column, or if something is incorrect in your formula, you may see this when you calculate the column: ??!.
    ✔Now that you have the calculated figures, use them as a guide for inserting the titles and underlines (the second-to-last column needs nine underlines, and the last column, ten underlines). After doing those steps, try to set up totals for the two new columns on the *TOTALS* line. Position the cursor at the end of that line and press **TAB**. What happened?
    WordPerfect inserted the ! operator, but that's not what you want. You want a + to add the column *down*. You can bypass the ! by *deleting* it:

Press   **BACKSPACE**

Type   +

Press   **TAB**

✔Repeat the steps to delete the ! operator and add a + operator instead. Then recalculate the entire document.

Extra Subtotals and Totals

To finish the sales report as shown, add an extra figure to the result in the endmost column. You can have as many *extra* totals or subtotals as you want, but you must indicate them with special operators.

✔Use the **RETURN** key to position the cursor two lines below the *TOTALS* line. With the space bar, move the cursor over to add the title **Other Income**. After typing the title, do this:

Press   **TAB** five times

WordPerfect reminds you that the fifth numeric column is a calculated column. However, you don't want to perform any calculation, so delete the ! operator:

Press   **BACKSPACE**

Press   **TAB**

Press   **BACKSPACE**

to delete the ! operator in the last column.

Enter the following figure exactly as you see it:

Type   **t30,222.76**

The lowercase t tells WordPerfect to add this figure as an extra subtotal. Use an uppercase т for an extra total. These special total operators ensure that the figures aren't considered part of a column of other figures during calculation.

Press   **RETURN** twice

✔Space over, type the last label, **GRAND TOTAL**, tab over to the rightmost column, removing the ! operators in the last two columns on the way.

For the final total, you'd use either the = operator (total), or the * operator (grand total), depending on what type of totals you already have in the column above this spot. If there are subtotals, use =. If there are only totals in the column, use *. So, which one do you type here? Right! Because there are subtotals (+) above:

Type   =

✔Now, recalculate the entire document.

Get into the habit of turning math off when you're finished:

Press   **ALT-F7 Math/Columns**

Type   1 or m [<u>M</u>ath Off]

✔Save the document now. If you print it, make sure to use paper positioned horizontally in the printer. When you're finished, clear the screen.

Dear Reader, you'd be in a pretty pickle indeed if you tried to cut or copy one of these math columns with the tabular column feature (Chapter 14)! It won't work, especially if you attempt to move or copy just the figures. In fact, you'll "lock" your computer! If you try to copy the column *and* its title, the results will be fascinating but, alas, garbage. That's why a stitch in time really does save nine: *Plan ahead* before you set up math columns!

Total Columns and Other Things

The next example hits many birds with one stone. First, it uses the other two types of math columns: text columns and total columns. Second, it works with a different alignment character and illustrates what happens when you're not careful. Third, it includes negative figures and dollar signs in totals. Here's the *completed* document on the screen:

```
                         Expense Report

          January                    $1,245
          February                    2,090
          March                       1,167
          April                       1,988
          May                         2,450
          June                        3,222
          July                        2,404
          August                      2,010
          September                   1,873
          October                     2,399
          November                    1,700
          December                    4,500

          Subtotal                 $27,048+
```

```
Mortgage                      10,678
Travel                         4,332
Other Expenses                 5,699

Subtotal                              $20,709+

Total Expenses                        N$47,757=

Income                                T65,987

Total Before Taxes                    $18,230*
```

✔First, set the tab stops. Clear all tabs and set left-justified tabs at columns 2.5, 5.0, and 6.0. Then, change the decimal/align character to a comma (,). Leave the thousands' separator as it is. Do you remember how to do this change?

Hint: It's on the format: other menu. When you've done that, center and type the title. Press **RETURN** three times for spacing. Then press **ALT-F7 Math/Columns** to get into the math definition menu. Change column A to a text column by typing **1**. Move over to column C and change it to a total column by typing **3**. Then:

Press   **F7 Exit**

Type   1 or m [<u>M</u>ath On]

For the first line,

Press   **TAB**

Type   January

Press   **TAB**

Type $1,245

Press   **RETURN**

✔Continue adding the text and numbers in the example. Notice that the other figures don't include dollar signs—a standard accounting convention. Press **RETURN** twice after the December line for spacing. Tab once and type Subtotal, then stop. To add up figures as a subtotal, press the **TAB** key twice to move into the third column, a total column. A total column totals the figures in the column *to the immediate left*. Then:

Type   **$+**

Here you've added a dollar sign to make the total stand out. Calculate the subtotal by pressing **ALT-F7 Math/Columns** and typing **2** or **a** [Ca̲lculate]. Oops! What happened? WordPerfect shows the subtotal as **$27,05**+. Why? Because you forgot to change the Number of Digits to the Right selection in the math definition menu! Remember that *to the right* means to the right of the tab stop, that is, whatever alignment character you're using. Here, you need three spaces to the right of the comma in all figures.

✔Go back to the top of the document, position the cursor direction past the [Math Def] code, and go back into the math definition menu. Then:

Press   **DOWN ARROW** twice

Press   **RIGHT ARROW**

Type   **3** three times

to change the number of places to three for columns B, C, and D.

Press   **F7 Exit**

Press   **RETURN**

because math is already on.

✔Move into the math area and recalculate the document. There's your correct total. (Notice that WordPerfect rounded up the incorrect total.) Press **RETURN** a couple of times for spacing, then add the next three lines (**Other Expenses**, and so on) and their figures. Remember to press **TAB** first to go into each column. Type **Subtotal** and the + operator with a dollar sign in front of it in the third column.

Now, press **RETURN** twice to space down, press **TAB** once, and type **Total Expenses**. Press **TAB** twice to get into the third column. You'll use the = operator to add the subtotals in the column to the left, but with a twist. Because you want to subtract this amount from your total income, make it a negative number and include the dollar sign. How?

Type   **N$=**

The **N** operator subtracts the total figure, but a minus sign doesn't appear in the printout.

✔Recalculate the document to see the result. Then press **RETURN** twice for spacing. Tab over, type the title (**Income**), and then press **TAB** twice to get into the third column. Then:

Type   **T65,987**

Again, press **RETURN** twice, tab over and type `Total Before Taxes`, press **TAB** twice, and enter the final operator. This time, you have only totals above you, so:

Type   `$*`

✔Recalculate the document. Then save the document as MYMONEY and clear the screen.

Taking an Average

The next and last example is a refreshingly short one. It shows you how to compute an average of figures across columns. WordPerfect has special operators for doing an average, which is just the sum of the columns divided by the number of columns. Here's the example:

```
Beethoven            22   34   59   60   21   39.20!
Mozart               19   12    9   86   35   32.20!
Sibelius             39    2   36   44   18   27.80!
Vaughan Williams     62   91   13   10    7   36.60!
```

✔First, clear all tabs and set left-justified tabs every 0.5 column, starting at column 3.5. That is, type **3.5,.5**. Return to the document and go into the math definition menu. Then:

Press   **RIGHT ARROW** five times

to move the cursor to Column F.

Type   **0** [Calculation]

Type   `+/`

Press   **RETURN** twice

This special operator computes an average of numeric columns. To compute the average of total columns, type `=/`.

Note: When you use a special formula, you can't include another formula in the same column.

Press   **F7 Exit**

Type   **1** or **m** [Math On]

✔Type the composer's name, then use the **TAB** key to enter each column of figures. Don't forget to tab over into the sixth column so that WordPerfect inserts the ! operator. When you're finished, calculate the document. Save it if you wish.

Caution: The math feature may not be "smart" enough to work with numbers in different decimal formats. Be consistent in how you enter numbers for WordPerfect to calculate. That is, if you use a decimal point in some numbers, use it in all. For example, certain figures appear like this: 24.3, 22.1, and so on. Follow the same pattern even if you don't actually need a decimal point; for example, 24 would be 24.0.

Finding Math Operators

Guess what? Just as you can search for any other code in WordPerfect, you can search for math operators, too. Say that you put in total operators (=), but you really wanted subtotal operators instead (+). You can replace one with the other. After you start the Replace command, press **ALT-F7 Math/ Columns**. This is what you see:

```
Math: 1 Def 2 On 3 Off 4 + 5 = 6 * 7 t 8 T 9 ! A N   Column: B Def C On D Off: 0
```

Now for the tricky part. After you type the code number for the operator you want to search for (say, **5**), press the **F2 ▶Search** key as usual to select the replacement. However, don't *type* in the new operator. Instead, press **ALT-F7 Math/Columns** *again* and enter the new code number (**4**). Then press **F2 ▶Search** to begin the replacement. Note that you can search for text column codes, too.

WordPerfect is an excellent word processor, but it's also a pretty good mathematician. Now it's time to explore the world of the bibliophile and meet a host of new and useful features.

Dedicated to Bibliophiles

20

Hyphenation and Hard Spaces

In this chapter you'll learn the following new commands . . .

Typewriter Keyboard and Numeric Keypad Commands

CTRL-HYPHEN	Insert a soft hyphen manually
HOME,HYPHEN	Insert a dash or minus sign (hard hyphen)
HOME,RETURN	Insert an invisible soft return
HOME,SPACEBAR	Insert a hard space
HOME,/	Insert a do not hyphen code manually

. . . you'll discover new uses of these commands . . .

ESC	Insert a soft hyphen at the hyphenation prompt
F1 Cancel	Tell WordPerfect not to hyphenate a word at the hyphenation prompt
F7 Exit	Temporarily suspend hyphenation
SHIFT-F8 Format	(1) Turn hyphenation on/off, (2) change the hyphenation zone (HZone)

. . . and you'll learn some new codes:

[ ]	Hard space
[-]	Regular hyphen
-	Soft (discretionary) hyphen
-	Hard hyphen
/	Don't hyphenate this word

more . . .

[DSRt]	Deletable Soft Return
[Hyph On]	Hyphenation on
[Hyph Off]	Hyphenation off
[HZone]	Hyphenation zone change
[ISRt]	Invisible soft return

Dear Reader, WordPerfect has a host of editorial niceties that take it well into the realm of the serious bibliophile. The next few chapters explore these features in depth. Even if you aren't a true bibliophile, a lover of books, you'll appreciate all the ways WordPerfect can help you create the best looking documents possible. Two features that you shouldn't overlook are the focus of this chapter. Both are related to line endings and how you can overcome the limitations of wordwrap.

> ***DO WARM-UP***

A Big Hype for Hyphenation

Think for a moment about what is was like in the dark ages of the typewriter. Whenever you reached the end of a line, the bell would ring to remind you that the end of the line was near. Sometimes you also had to think about whether or not to hyphenate a long word.

When you work with WordPerfect you never have to worry about breaking the lines, because WordPerfect does that for you. All you have to do is put in a hard return at the end of each paragraph or other short line. You don't have to stop and look up to see where to break a line or fiddle with hyphenating words. So when *do* you hyphenate words? Glad you asked. In a moment you'll know. But first, here is a little discussion about hyphenation and its relationship to wordwrap.

How WordPerfect Breaks the Lines

How does WordPerfect "know" where to break each line when you type text into a document? It's not magic—after all, a computer cannot read. But it *can* distinguish letters and numbers from spaces because everything you type in from the keyboard has a code number associated with it. (Remember the ASCII codes from Chapter 15?) That's why the spaces are so important. They have their own code number, and every time you press the SPACEBAR you enter the code for a space in the document.

Whenever you type in a new word, you also separate it from the next word with a space. WordPerfect normally breaks lines *only* at the spaces and won't ever extend the line past the right margin setting. That is why it doesn't split up a word at the end of a line. If the word is too long to fit in the present line, WordPerfect brings it down in its entirety to begin a new line.

A computer can only follow its instructions to the letter and will *never* break them on its own initiative. Computers are very much different from human beings in this respect, because a computer doesn't know that "rules were made to be broken." A computer will never even *bend* the rules. By the way, WordPerfect does not eliminate the spaces between words at the end of the line. If you edit the line later and move the words around, the spaces are still there, provided that you didn't delete them yourself.

To justify right margins, WordPerfect fills some lines with extra spaces. You have probably seen documents with such "spaced-out" lines, and I bet you knew that these documents were done with a computer. I've already mentioned that, with a fixed-width font, justified lines can also cause rivers of white space to ripple down a printed page.

Using a good word processor like WordPerfect, you can avoid either situation if you hyphenate longer words to close up the extra spaces. When you take the trouble (and it really isn't much trouble at all) to hyphenate a word, you put part of it on one line and part on the next. The printout looks much better and definitely more professional.

Two Kinds of Hyphens

For hyphenating regular text, WordPerfect distinguishes between *two* kinds of hyphens, just as it uses two types of carriage returns. These hyphens both look exactly the same in the printout, but they are decidedly different in the context of the document.

The first kind of hyphen is the normal one that you type whenever a word contains a hyphen. Think of it as a *necessary* hyphen—often this is called a *regular* hyphen. Such words as *twenty-five* or *fixed-width* contain regular hyphens. You instinctively typed hyphens like these with the HY-PHEN key in previous examples. That is exactly how you should treat hy-phenated words: as you always have. WordPerfect shows the hyphen as [-] in the codes. It normally breaks words at regular hyphens when it can.

WordPerfect inserts the other kind of hyphen with your help when you go back to check if any words could *possibly* be hyphenated at the ends of lines to fill up these lines. You need not do this at the time you enter the text. Do it later when you've finished the typing and editing stage—the draft—and want a professional looking printout for the final version of your document.

This second type of hyphen is called a *soft hyphen*. It represents a con-ditional hyphen that only appears at a syllable break if the word is at the end of the line and if the word won't fit entirely on one line. That's the condition. Some word processors like to think of soft hyphens as *discretionary*, that is, they appear only at the discretion of the line breaks.

There's also a third kind of hyphen, a *hard* hyphen, that you'll want to use in dashes and minus signs. See the separate section later in the chapter.

By default, the hyphenation feature is off in WordPerfect. When you want to check which words could possibly be split at line endings, you must turn hyphenation on and instruct WordPerfect to find the possible hyphenation spots. WordPerfect distinguishes between *manual* and *auto* hyphenation. In previous versions, manual hyphenation was called aided hyphenation. When manual hyphenation is on, WordPerfect stops and requests your decision when it finds a likely candidate for hyphenation. You decide if and where to hyphenate the word.

When auto hyphenation is on, WordPerfect attempts to hyphenate words according to a set of rules for syllable breaks and a hyphenation dictionary. The rules are in the file WP{WP}US.HYC, and the dictionary is in the file WP{WP}US.HYL. In auto mode, if WordPerfect can't figure out a hyphenation spot, it temporarily switches into manual mode. You then must choose a syllable break or instruct WordPerfect not to hyphenate the word at all. You can turn hyphenation on or off anywhere and as many times as you wish in a document.

At this point you may be remonstrating that these extra steps mean extra time. That's true, of course, but the time you save *not* having to consider hyphenation during typing and editing is more than compensated by the little bit of time it takes to hyphenate later.

During the hyphenation process, WordPerfect considers a paragraph a distinct entity, because it ends with a hard return. WordPerfect thus hyphenates to maintain the flow of the entire paragraph. That is why it is so important not to press RETURN when you're typing normal paragraphs until you get to the very end of the paragraph. WordPerfect would "hang up" at any misplaced hard return codes. It does, however, readjust all the soft return codes and puts in new ones for the newly adjusted lines.

Manual Hyphenation

I am not a big fan of automatic hyphenation in *any* word processing program, for a reason I'll explain later. So, your first example will concentrate on manual hyphenation. Because it involves the line endings, hyphenation is on the format: line menu.

✔Retrieve the LAREST document. Make sure the cursor is at the beginning of the document. Then:

Press   **SHIFT-F8 Format**

Type   **1 or ʟ [Line]**

Type   1 or y [Hyphenation]

WordPerfect prompts:

1 Off; 2 Manual; 3 Auto: 0

Type   2 or m [Manual]

Press   **F7 Exit**

to return to the document.

WordPerfect has inserted a [Hyph On] code here. When you turn hyphenation off, you'll see a [Hyph Off] code instead.

Tip: To *bypass* hyphenating certain sections of a document, enclose those sections with off and on hyphenation codes.

What's this? WordPerfect beeps and presents the first word that could be hyphenated.

Note: You may see a "file not found" message if the current drive or directory is not the same as the WordPerfect directory where the hyphenation files are located. You can tell WordPerfect to use a different directory (Appendix A). Version 4.2 users must move the cursor down through the document first (using PG DN or even HOME,HOME,DOWN ARROW). Depending on the font and printer you're using, your hyphenation spots will be different. On my screen WordPerfect first stops at *picadillo* and prompts:

```
Position hyphen; Press ESC picadil-lo
```

Here's the reason why I don't like auto hyphenation: aesthetics or a lack of same. WordPerfect has no aesthetic sense. Suppose that there *is* a correct syllable break between the two *l*'s. How does the word look? I think a more aesthetically pleasing break is elsewhere:

```
pica-dillo
```

Of course, your aesthetic sense is undoubtedly different from mine. Still, I like to control hyphenation—and hence the look of all my documents—myself. For example, if there are already too many hyphenated words in a paragraph, I'll choose not to hyphenate just to make the lines look as pleasing as possible.

Tip: There's another way to control hyphenation. Use the separate Hyphen program to create an *exception dictionary*, in the file WP{WP}US.HYC (Chapter 36). You must purchase this program separately for a nominal charge.

Your Decision, Please

In any case, here's how to hyphenate words. Just follow these basic patterns:

1. To accept the syllable break that WordPerfect suggests, press **ESC**.
   Note: In manual hyphenation this may or may not be a correct syllable break.
2. To choose another syllable break, press **LEFT ARROW** or **RIGHT ARROW** to move the hyphen to the letter after which the break is to occur (see my example above). If you attempt to select a syllable break that would make the word too long to fit on the line, Word-Perfect won't let you. Press **LEFT ARROW** to select another spot.
3. To tell WordPerfect *not* to hyphenate the word at all, press **F1 Cancel**. WordPerfect inserts a "do not hyphenate" code in front of this word and brings the entire word down to start the next line.

Here are the hyphenation codes that you may insert: (1) a hyphen without brackets (-) is a soft hyphen; (2) a slash (/) at the beginning of a word indicates that you told WordPerfect not to hyphenate this word.

After you decide the hyphenation, WordPerfect tries to find other words. In fact, it will stop at all possible hyphenation spots on the current screen. To continue for the rest of the document, press any downward cursor command, such as PG DN or HOME,HOME,DOWN ARROW.

Tip: The latter command lets you check the entire document in one fell swoop. See also Suspending Hyphenation Temporarily.

As I mentioned, your hyphenation spots may be different. Table 20-1 lists the other words that WordPerfect selected and how I chose to deal with them.

✔When you're finished, save the edited document as LAREST.HY. Print it or view the printout to see the results, then clear the screen.

Table 20-1   Examples of Proper Hyphenation

Word	Hyphenated Word
literally	(did not hyphenate)
beautifully	beauti-fully
experiment	experi-ment
neighborhood	neighbor-hood
reasonable	reason-able

Suspending Hyphenation Temporarily

When you scroll through a document and hyphenation is on, WordPerfect will stop at each long word. You can temporarily suspend hyphenation, for example, when you're checking the spelling or trying to move to the end of the document with HOME,HOME,DOWN ARROW. When WordPerfect stops at the first long word, press **F7 Exit** to suspend hyphenation.

A Very Useful Purchase

If you're as much of a nitpicker about hyphenation but as bad at hyphenating as I am, how do you quickly find the correct hyphenation spot for a word? Get one of those paperback *speller/divider* books and keep it next to your computer at all times. Buying one of these books is a good investment!

Auto Hyphenation

If you had selected auto hyphenation instead of manual hyphenation on LAR-EST, WordPerfect would hyphenate the words according to its rules. (If you wish, retrieve the original LAREST document and try auto hyphenation.) WordPerfect can't figure out a hyphenation spot for *picadillo*, so it stops and asks for your guidance. But look at how WordPerfect hyphenated *literally: litera-lly*. That's ugly and incorrect! I think you get the picture. Dear Reader, bone up on your sense of aesthetics, please!

If you wanted to, you could turn auto hyphenation on before you type a document. WordPerfect would hyphenate in the background as you go along. The only disadvantage to this is that WordPerfect may occasionally stop and ask you to decide on a hyphenation spot for words that it couldn't figure out itself. This can be distracting when you're just trying to get your thoughts down. My advice is to turn on hyphenation only when you need it.

Hyphenating Text Columns

Text columns have shorter lines and, hence, more possibilities for that horribly spaced-out effect. I urge you to hyphenate text columns—either manually or with the auto hyphenation feature—if you want a high quality printout.

Hyphenating Part of a Document

To hyphenate just part of a document, position the cursor at the beginning of the section you want to check and turn hyphenation on. Use the DOWN ARROW to move slowly through that section and, if you're using manual hyphenation, make your decisions. When you've reached the end of the section, turn hyphenation off.

Hyphenating a Word with a Regular Hyphen

Some words that already have required hyphens in them are rather long. Think, for example, of *hard-to-find* or *down-to-earth*. At times, WordPerfect might stop at such a word and ask you if you want to hyphenate it. Every book on style will tell you the same thing: It is not considered proper form to hyphenate a word with a regular hyphen anywhere other than at the hyphen itself. So when WordPerfect stops at a word with a regular hyphen, use the F1 Cancel key.

(An aside: If WordPerfect stops at *proper nouns* such as *Vermont*, good form again dictates that you shouldn't hyphenate these words. Of course, that decision is ultimately yours.)

Ghosts

The great thing about soft hyphens is that they only appear at the end of a line. If you edit the document and move the words around, the soft hyphen won't print if the word ends up in the middle of a line, but the hyphen will still be in the word! That's why some people call them *ghosts:* They're there, but they don't appear all the time. You *don't* have to remove soft hyphens if you rearrange the lines. That would be a hassle indeed. The soft hyphens will stay in the word and will reappear if the word can again be split at the end of a line. They're "friendly ghosts." To insert a do not hyphenate code manually, press **HOME,/** at the beginning of a word.

Manually Inserting a Soft Hyphen

Occasionally you may want to insert a soft hyphen yourself without going through the entire hyphenation rigmarole. First position the cursor under a correct syllable break, then press **CTRL-HYPHEN**. You won't see the soft hyphen unless you reveal the codes, but it will be there. And it will stay in the word and work at the end of a line.

Dashes and Minus Signs

Use a double hyphen for a dash (--), but you don't want WordPerfect to break the line at the second hyphen. Similarly, you'd want a minus sign (-) in mathematical expressions to stay with its figure.

Note: If math mode is on (Chapter 19), WordPerfect automatically considers a hyphen to be a minus sign in math columns. To insert dashes and minus signs, use what WordPerfect calls a *hard hyphen*, the command for which is **HOME,HYPHEN**. For a dash, then, press HOME,HYPHEN, then type a regular hyphen. The hard hyphen code is an unhighlighted -.

The Invisible Soft Return

This strange beast isn't a hyphen, but it can be useful to help you adjust the lines. If a word is longer than the line length, WordPerfect inserts an invisible soft return to break the word over two lines. The code is [ISRt]. You can use the invisible soft return in composite words that contain a slash, for example, *backup/restore*. If there's an invisible soft return directly after the slash and WordPerfect can fit the *backup/* part on the line, it will break the composite word correctly without inserting a superfluous hyphen. To insert an invisible soft return, position the cursor at the correct spot and press **HOME,RETURN**. See also the end of the chapter.

The Hyphenation Zone

How does WordPerfect determine where to stop and request hyphenation? It has two zone settings at the end of the line. These settings comprise the *hyphenation zone,* or *H-Zone.* The default hyphenation zone is 10% to the left and 4% to the right of the right margin. This means that if a word falls within the last 10% of the line and extends at least 4% into the right margin, WordPerfect stops and requests your hyphenation decision. WordPerfect just wraps words shorter than the left zone down to the next line.

You can adjust the hyphenation zone to your needs. This might be necessary when you're printing right-justified text columns to get a "tighter" line. To do so, follow these steps:

1. Press **SHIFT-F8 Format**.
2. Type **1** or **l** [**L**ine].
3. Type **2** or **z** [Hyphenation **Z**one].
4. Supply the new percentage settings. That is, if you want a tighter looking line, enter a smaller left zone setting.

Caution: Unless you really know what you're doing, I recommend that you always accept WordPerfect's default for the right zone.
5. Press **F7 Exit** enough times to return to the document.

When you change the hyphenation zone, WordPerfect inserts a [HZone] code with the new settings in the document. You should then cursor through

367

the document and check for other hyphenation spots. WordPerfect gives you a great deal of power to determine how your documents will look, but *you* have to decide how to use this power.

Finding and Deleting Hyphen Codes

I repeat: You do *not* have to remove soft hyphens, but you can delete a soft hyphen code if you wish. For example, if you find that you have incorrectly hyphenated a word, locate the soft hyphen code. Delete it as you would any other with the BACKSPACE or DEL key. If hyphenation is on, WordPerfect will still ask you if you want to hyphenate the word. Press F1 Cancel to bypass hyphenation. Better yet, turn off hyphenation before you delete any soft hyphens.

You can use the Search command to search for a soft or hard hyphen. After you start the search, press CTRL-HYPHEN or HOME,HYPHEN as the search character. To search for the other hyphenation codes, start the search, press SHIFT-F8 Line Format, then type 1 or l [Line]. You'll see this crowded menu:

```
1 Hyphen; 2 HZone; 3 /; 4 Justification; 5 Line; 6 Margins; 7 Tab Set; 8 W/O: 0
```

In sum, type regular hyphens when you type in normally hyphenated words. They always appear, no matter where the word appears in the document. Soft hyphens appear only at the ends of the line and are inserted during the hyphenation process. You are getting farther and farther away from typing now!

By the way, you can now turn off hyphenation for a document: Just delete the [Hyph On] code. The soft hyphens and other hyphenation codes stay in the document.

The Hard Space

Now for a question: When is a space not a space? When it's a *hard space!* Using hard spaces is another way to overcome the limitations of wordwrap. Look at the following example, but *don't* type it. What's wrong with it?

We hereby acknowledge receipt of your letter postmarked June 15, 1989. Our records indicate that an order was placed for 200 Disposable Dipsy Diapers on May 16, 1989, by someone named Sylvia Q. Roper of your company. Therefore, our invoice postmarked May 19, 1989, is correct. We at Dapper Dandy Diaper Delivery feel that there is no cause to contest that invoice. If, however, you

```
wish to contact our attorneys, send all correspondence to Smudge
& Smudge, Solicitors, at 15 Barristers Court, San Francisco, CA
91405. Thank you.
```

In this example, WordPerfect breaks the lines to fit them within the margins, regardless of what the words mean. Any editor, lawyer, supervisor, or even a client would have a conniption because certain phrases are split over two lines. It just does not look good when a first name (*Sylvia*) is separated from a middle initial (*Q.*), or when the month is not together with the day (*June 15*).

WordPerfect has a way to avoid this problem, but you have to know how to use it. Instead of a regular space, you enter a *hard space* code at those spots where you do not want two words (or any two terms) to be split at the end of a line—ever. Whenever you reach a spot where you want to ensure that two words do not get separated, use the hard space *instead* of a regular space. The space will still "print" as a space. (Oh, yes, as far as the printer is concerned, there is such a thing as a "printable" character called the space. It's an instruction to move over one character position.)

WordPerfect never breaks a line at the hard space. If both words don't fit on a line, WordPerfect brings them down to start the next line. Like all codes, the hard space *stays* in the document and still works if the lines get moved around later. Now try the example with hard spaces in certain spots. Start typing, but when you get to the word *June* on the first line, stop. The cursor should now be directly after *June*. Do this:

Press   **HOME,SPACEBAR**

WordPerfect apparently just entered a space on the screen, but it's really a hard space. Type the date (**15**), but *do not type an extra space*. When you do type *15*, WordPerfect finds that it cannot fit all of the phrase *June 15* on one line, so it begins another.

Continue typing but make sure that you insert hard spaces instead of regular spaces between *Sylvia* and *Q.*, between *May* and *16* and *May* and *19*, and between the first *Smudge* and the ampersand. (There are three other spots which could use a hard space. Can you figure out where?) Now, compare the two examples: the original one and yours.

The other spots are between *15* and *Barristers*, between *San* and *Francisco*, and between *CA* and the zip code (use two hard spaces here). Now that you have used hard spaces, WordPerfect forms the lines differently, and some of the phrases are in the middle of the line. Here are examples of the most important places to use a hard space (shown by an underline):

- Between a title and a name—Dr._Einstein, Miss_Lizzie Borden
- Between a first name and middle initial—John_F. Kennedy
- Between a last name and such designations as *Jr.* or *III*—Salvatore Tetrazzini,_Ph.D.

- Between a street number and street name—507_Sycamore Street
- Between a month and day—April_26, 1947
- Between the words of a multiword name—Santa_Fe
- Between a state and zip code—CA__90065
- Between an ampersand and the word preceding it—Harry_& David

Other places where you would perhaps wish to consider using hard spaces might be:

- Between the parts of mathematical formulas—a^2_ +_b^3_ = _c
- Between section numbers or letters and the first word of the text—(a)_when it is necessary . . .
- Between such words as *section* or *page* and the number following these words—Section_II or Chapter_6 or pp._254
- Any time and for any reason that you do not want two words to be separated

Can you think of situations in your own work where the hard space might come in handy? What does the hard space code look like? Reveal the codes and take a peek. It's [ ]. You can delete the hard space code like any other. It takes a while to get into the habit of using the hard space feature, because it's probably totally new to you. But it can really improve the look of your work.

✔Save the document as HARDSP.EX, if you wish, and then clear the screen.

The Deletable Soft Return

I'm sticking this here to avoid changing the page breaks, but it should go after my discussion of the invisible soft return. If a "word" or line of characters stretches from the left to the right margin and WordPerfect can't determine a proper hyphenation spot, it inserts a *deletable soft return* code—[DSRt]—at the right margin to split the line. This may happen, for example, when you're formatting multiple text columns that are quite narrow or when you've typed a line of hyphens.

The name indicates the code's function. The deletable soft return is there only as a reminder to you to fix the syllable break later. That is, insert a soft hyphen or invisible soft return in a word that contains a deletable soft return code to set a syllable break. WordPerfect then automatically deletes the [DSRt] code from the word. By the way, *you* can't insert a deletable soft return code at all—only WordPerfect can do it!

Hyphenation and hard spaces are, to continue the alliteration, handy helpers indeed! Dear Reader, use them to improve the quality of your work.

21

Advanced Outlining and Paragraph Numbering

In this chapter you'll discover other uses of this command . . .

SHIFT-F5 Date/Outline   (1) Begin or end paragraph numbering, (2) change the outline or paragraph numbering style

. . . and you'll learn a new code:

`[Par Num Def]`   Outline or paragraph numbering style change

Anyone who writes for a living needs all the help possible, and WordPerfect is definitely there to help. For instance, WordPerfect lets you organize your thoughts in an outline. You've already learned how to create a simple outline (Chapter 10). This short chapter shows you other ways to work with WordPerfect's outline feature and its close relation, paragraph numbering.

DO WARM-UP

A Good Tip

If you plan to use outlines and paragraph numbering a great deal, then it behooves you to set up the various techniques that you'll learn—for example, deleting, moving, or changing outline levels—in macros. That way, you avoid many unnecessary keystrokes.

Manipulating an Outline

To refresh your memory, I'll step you through how to create a new outline that you'll then use in some of the examples. Here's what you're to type; it's only the beginning of a long outline:

I.   Objective: This course will study the rise and fall of the
     city-state, from its beginnings in Mesopotamia to the end of
     the Middle Ages.

     A.   Mesopotamia: How the city developed from the
          administrative machinery that became the normal political
          structure of the region.

          1.   History: Where did the actual political forms come
               from, and how did the people change them to suit
               their particular needs?

No matter what you want to do to an outline, the first rule of thumb is to make sure outline mode is on. Version 4.2 users: Remember that this feature has moved from the ALT-F5 key to SHIFT-F5.

Press   **SHIFT-F5 Date/Outline**

Type   **4** or **o** [Outline]

Press   **RETURN**

to add the first section number.
    Unfortunately, WordPerfect also adds a blank line, but you can delete that later if you wish.

Press   **F4 ▶Indent**

✔Type the first paragraph and press **RETURN** twice when you're finished. Type the second and third paragraphs but make sure you've moved the cursor to the correct level. That is, press **TAB** to select the level, then press **F4 ▶Indent** before you type the paragraph. After you press RETURN at the end of the third paragraph, press **BACKSPACE** once to delete the extra outline number. When you're finished, save the document as COURSE.OUT and leave it on the screen.

Inserting and Deleting Outline Sections

You can insert or delete outline sections, and WordPerfect will renumber the outline for you. Now add a new section. Outline mode should still be on.

✔Position the cursor on the blank line between the first and second sections. Why here? Because you have to press RETURN to insert a new outline number, so WordPerfect also inserts another hard return code for spacing.

Press   **RETURN**

to add a new section II.

Press   **F4 ▶Indent**

Type   `Pre-History`

Press   **RETURN**

WordPerfect adds a new number III., but you don't want that:

Press   **BACKSPACE**

Now the spacing between outline sections is correct. Take care when you insert new outline sections, because in outline mode when you press RETURN WordPerfect automatically adds a new number.

Tip: Turn outlining off before you use RETURN to add a lot of blank lines to an outline.

✔Now delete the section you just added. Move the cursor to the left margin of new section II. Make sure the cursor is under the [Par Num:Auto] code, because you want to delete that, too. Then:

Press   **ALT-F4 Block** or **F12 Block**

Press   **DOWN ARROW** twice

to delimit the block.

Press   **DEL** or **BACKSPACE**

Type   `y`

to delete the block.

Promoting or Demoting an Outline Section

You can promote or demote an outline section by moving it left or right, respectively. This changes the numbering according to how many tab stops you move the section, provided that outlining is on. To promote a section, delete the tab or tabs to move the section left. To demote a section, insert a tab or tabs to move the section right.

✔Position the cursor under the A of the second section.

Press   **BACKSPACE**

You've just deleted the tab, and the promoted section moves back one tab stop. If the numbering didn't change, it will as soon as you move the cursor or rewrite the screen. Notice that when you promote an outline section, those parts of the outline that are dependent on that section don't move with it. You now have to adjust section 1.

✔Position the cursor under the 1. Then:

Press   **SHIFT-TAB**

Press   **DOWN ARROW** or **UP ARROW**

to renumber the outline.

I used SHIFT-TAB just to show you that it works, too. Here's what the outline looks like now:

```
I.   Objective: This course will study the rise and fall of the
     city-state, from its beginnings in Mesopotamia to the end of
     the Middle Ages.

II.  Mesopotamia: How the city developed from the administrative
     machinery that became the normal political structure of the
     region.

     A.   History: Where did the actual political forms come from,
          and how did the people change them to suit their
          particular needs?
```

✔Next, demote the second section and see what happens. Position the cursor under the first *I* of section II. Then:

Press   **TAB**

Press   **DOWN ARROW**

The two demoted sections are renumbered as A. and B. The idea here is that if you promote or demote outline sections, other sections at different levels won't move over. You have to move each one yourself.

✔Save the document as COURSE.OUT, if you wish. Then clear the screen.

Moving an Outline Section

There are products on the market that advertise themselves as *thought processors*. This misleading term has nothing to do with zapping your brainwaves. It refers to programs that help you organize your ideas. Although it's not as powerful as these programs, WordPerfect's outlining feature can serve as a rudimentary brainstorming tool. That is, you can rearrange an outline to make your thoughts more organized. In this example, you'll move a section.

✔Retrieve the ARTICLE.OUT document.

Pretend that you haven't yet written the article for this outline. You decide to move the first restaurant so that it's second on the list.

✔Position the cursor under the I. Then:

Press   **ALT-F4 Block** or **F12 Block**

Press   **DOWN ARROW** three times

The cursor is now at the left margin of the next section, exactly where you want it. That is, you want to include the hard return at the end of the previous line to keep proper spacing, but you don't want the next paragraph numbering code. Reveal the codes if you're not sure. Then:

Press   **CTRL-F4 Move**

Type   **1** or **b** [Block]

Type   **1** or **m** [Move]

Press   **DOWN ARROW** four times

Press   **RETURN**

to retrieve the block.

The point of this lesson is that you have to move the hard returns, but not the paragraph numbering for the next section.

Changing the Outline Style

You can change the numbering style or starting number for an outline, but make sure to position the cursor *in front of* the entire outline first. That is, the code to change the outline style should appear before the outline itself. Outlining doesn't have to be on when you want to change the numbering style.

✔Position the cursor at the beginning of the document. Then:

Press   **SHIFT-F5 Date/Outline**

Type   **6** or **d** [Define]

The paragraph number definition menu appears (Figure 21-1). To change the starting number, type **1** or **s** [Starting Paragraph Number] and supply the new number. Choices 2 through 5 are predefined styles, including a bulleted style. You can also create your own custom style. For the moment, try an easy example:

Type   **5** or **b** [Bullets]

```
Paragraph Number Definition

    1 - Starting Paragraph Number          1
        (in legal style)


                                        Levels
                           1    2    3    4    5    6    7    8
    2 - Paragraph          1.   a.   i.   (1)  (a)  (i)  1)   a)
    3 - Outline            I.   A.   1.   a.   (1)  (a)  i)   a)
    4 - Legal (1.1.1)      1    .1   .1   .1   .1   .1   .1   .1
    5 - Bullets            •    o    –    ■    *    +    ·    x
    6 - User-defined

    Current Definition     I.   A.   1.   a.   (1)  (a)  i)   a)

        Number Style            Punctuation
        1 - Digits              #    – No punctuation
        A - Upper case letters  #.   – Trailing period
        a - Lower case letters  #)   – Trailing parenthesis
        I - Upper case roman    (#)  – Enclosing parentheses
        i - Lower case roman    .#   – All levels separated by period
        Other character - Bullet     (e.g. 2.1.3.4)


Selection: 0
```

Figure 21-1   The Paragraph Number Definition Menu

WordPerfect shows the new current definition.

Press   **F7 Exit** twice

to return to the document.

Nothing happened! That's because you should now rewrite the screen or move the cursor through the document to update the outline:

Press   **HOME,HOME,DOWN ARROW**

to renumber the outline.

There is now this code in the document: [Par Num Def]. If you switch numbering styles again, it's best to delete the previous code first and enter a new one.

✔Save the updated ARTICLE.OUT document and clear the screen.

Numbering Paragraphs

Moving right along, take a look at paragraph numbering in general. Recall that the outline feature is just one special aspect of paragraph numbering. That's why the code for an outline section is a paragraph numbering code.

One difference between outline numbering and paragraph numbering is that you might want to add paragraph numbering sometime after you've typed your text. Usually you'll outline as you go along. For instance, if you didn't want numbers for all paragraphs, you'd have to turn outline on and off repeatedly—too much trouble. So, use paragraph numbering only when you need it, either as you type or later.

The other difference is that you can force a different paragraph number *at the same level* if the one that WordPerfect supplies isn't correct. Like outlining, paragraph numbering works around tab stops or indented sections. There are at most eight numbering levels. The left margin is the first level, provided there is a tab stop there (which is the case for the default format), and each tab stop or indent is another level.

✔Retrieve the document MINUTES.

Automatic Numbering

You'll number the paragraphs in this short document. The cursor is exactly where you need it, at the left margin of the first paragraph. Always position the cursor correctly before you number a paragraph.

Press   **SHIFT-F5 Date/Outline**

Type   **5** or **p** [Para Num]

WordPerfect prompts:

`Paragraph Level (Press Enter for Automatic):`

Press   **RETURN**

WordPerfect inserts a Roman I. as the number but doesn't push the text ahead. If you reveal the codes, this is what you see: `[Par Num:Auto]`.

✔Position the cursor at the beginning text of the next paragraph. Repeat the above steps to insert the paragraph number, which turns out to be an uppercase A. for the second level. However, note the *spacing* in the text. What should you do?

Press   **TAB**

The point here is that sometimes, depending on the original text, you might have to add tabs or spaces between the paragraph number—which by default includes a period—and the body of the text.

✔Move the cursor down to the second regular paragraph and repeat the steps for adding section number II. Then *skip* the second indented section and do the same for the last paragraph to insert number III. When you're finished, move the cursor to the beginning of the second indented section directly under the *I* of *It*. Enter the paragraph number.

Manual Numbering

Well, that's not what you wanted! WordPerfect thought that this was the third level and put in a 1. for the paragraph number. That's because it counted the tab and indents and computed that this was level three. You could do one of two things: (1) move the cursor back to the second level at the indent or (2) force the correct number. First, delete the code:

Press   **BACKSPACE**

to delete the code.

Now, force the correct number by doing this:

Press   **SHIFT-F5 Date/Outline**

Type   5 or p [Para Num]

Type   2

to enter your own paragraph number level.

Press   **RETURN**

There's now an **A.** in the text, and the code is [Par Num:2]. Enter a tab to pretty up the paragraph. Keep in mind that you can reset the paragraph numbering at any point in the document, just as you can reset outline numbering.

Changing the Paragraph Numbering Style

You decide that you don't like the default paragraph numbering style or the other preset styles, so you'll create your own. Whenever you change numbering styles, make sure you position the cursor before the *first* paragraph number code in the document. As with all other formatting changes, it's best to put this change at the beginning of the document so you can locate it quickly.

✔Position the cursor at the beginning of the document and go into the paragraph numbering definition menu. Then:

Type   **6** or **u** [User-defined]

When you set up a custom style, you should define the style for *each* level or accept WordPerfect's default.

Tip: Start with a preset style that approximates the style you want, then change only the levels you need. Here, you just want to change levels 1 and 2, because that's all you're using in this document. Level one is set for **I.**, which the guide at the bottom of the screen tells you is for uppercase Roman letters. You want to change the numbering style for the first level to an Arabic number followed by a period.

Type   **1.**

(don't forget the period) for numbers (digits) followed by a period.

Press   **TAB**

to move to the next level.

If you want to move back to the previous level's definition, press SHIFT-TAB. For the second level you want lowercase Roman letters.

Type   **a.**

for lowercase letters followed by a period.

You don't have to change any other level, so:

Press   **F7 Exit** enough times

to return to the document.

You now have to rewrite the screen. Use HOME,HOME,DOWN AR-ROW or the Rewrite command on the CTRL-F3 Screen key.

✔Save the document as MINUTES.2 if you wish.

Numbering Figures

Despite its name, paragraph numbering doesn't have to be at the beginning of a paragraph. You could, for instance, use the paragraph numbering feature to number consecutive figures *within* a paragraph. That way, if you later delete a figure, WordPerfect will renumber the remaining figures for you.

There are two tricks. To use the first trick, set the paragraph numbering style to paragraph or legal numbering, depending on whether you want WordPerfect to insert a period after the number. The second trick is to force the *same* numbering level—level one—for each number. Figure 21-2 shows a sample sentence that contains three paragraph numbering codes, each at level one. The screen codes reveal the definition and numbering codes.

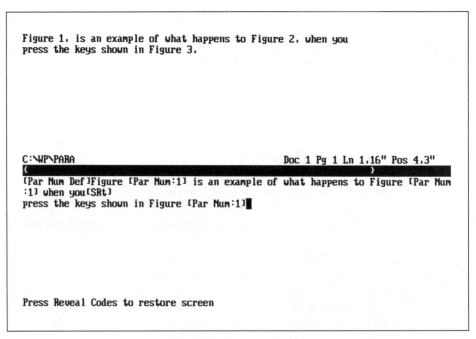

Figure 21-2   Numbering Figures

Tip: If you plan to insert graphics elements in your document, WordPerfect can also number the captions below the graphics (Chapter 34).

A Numbered List

You can also use paragraph numbering to create a list of sequential numbers, even if there aren't any paragraphs! Here's a macro that does just that. I'll call it NU for numbers. The macro also adds a tab after each number.

Press   **CTRL-F10 Macro Define**

Type   nu

Press   **RETURN**

Type   List of numbers

Press   **RETURN**

Press   **SHIFT-F5 Date/Outline**

Type   **5** or **p** [Para Num]

Press   **RETURN**

for automatic numbering.

Press   **TAB**

Press   **RETURN**

to add a hard return.

Press   **CTRL-F10 Macro Define**

Once you've defined this macro, use the ESC key to repeat it as many times as you want numbers in the list. For example, press **ESC**, type **20**, then press **ALT-F10 Macro** and enter the macro name to create 20 numbers. Then, go back to the top of the document and change the paragraph numbering style so that level one is just digits. Voilà: A list of numbers!

So much for outlines and paragraph numbers. There are many more writers' tools waiting for you in WordPerfect—for instance, footnotes and endnotes.

Chapter

22

Footnotes and Endnotes

In this chapter you'll learn the following new command . . .

Function Key Command

CTRL-F7 Footnote (1) Create or edit a footnote or endnote,
(2) change the footnote or endnote style,
(3) change the location of endnotes

. . . and you'll learn some new codes:

[Endnote]	Endnote
[Endnote Placement]	Endnote location change
[End Opt]	Endnote style (options) change
[Footnote]	Footnote
[Ftn Opt]	Footnote style (options) change
[New End Num]	Endnote number change
[New Ftn Num]	Footnote number change
[Note Num]	Footnote or endnote number in the note text

Dear Reader, WordPerfect has many features, but my editor claims her heart condition is threatening to be serious if I don't get this book finished! So, this chapter moves right along and covers two items that are the stock-in-trade of serious writers: footnotes and endnotes.

DO WARM-UP

Some Preliminaries

Trying to type footnotes was, as Joan Rivers would say, *the worst*. Not only did you have to keep track of the amount of space left at the bottom of the page, but you also had to know in advance just how many lines each footnote required and then mesh the two together. More than likely, you allocated too much space so there was an ugly blank space at the bottom of the page, or you didn't leave enough room and couldn't fit the entire footnote on the page. That meant retyping the page.

Enter WordPerfect and its *automatic footnoting* feature. Not only does WordPerfect put a footnote correctly at the bottom of the page—complete with footnote number—and adjust the page endings, but it also keeps track of the numbering should you add or delete any notes. Although there is a default format for footnotes, it's easy to set up your own. If you prefer endnotes, or a combination of footnotes and endnotes, you can have them, too. Usually endnotes print at the end of the document, but you can position them elsewhere. The procedures for creating footnotes and endnotes are similar.

The only major caveat to mention about footnotes is that you can't have them in text columns or math columns. WordPerfect will let you insert only endnotes in text columns. A note can be as long as 300 pages, although I doubt whether even the most serious scholar would need such capabilities. WordPerfect keeps footnote and endnote text in separate areas, similar to those for headers and footers (Chapter 16).

Footnotes

Practically the only thing you have to think about is where you want to place your footnote references. You'll use existing documents in the examples.

✔Retrieve the LAREST document. Press **END** to position the cursor at the end of the title line.

Inserting Footnotes

Stop! Make sure you're at the correct location for the footnote reference in the text before you insert the footnote instruction. Here, you want the reference to be centered along with the rest of the line. However, the cursor is now *past* the end center code (turn the codes on if you don't believe me). So:

Press   **LEFT ARROW**

By default, WordPerfect uses the standard superscripted number for the footnote reference. You *don't* have to enter the number yourself.

Press   **CTRL-F7 Footnote**

The note menu appears:

1 Footnote; 2 Endnote; 3 Endnote Placement: 0

Type   1 or f [Footnote]

WordPerfect displays the footnote menu:

Footnote: 1 Create; 2 Edit; 3 New Number; 4 Options: 0

Type   1 or c [Create]

WordPerfect presents the footnote edit area, indents the footnote five spaces, and supplies the next available footnote number.

Caution: To ensure that WordPerfect keep track of footnote numbers, never *type* a footnote number yourself. It's a special code. Remember that the screen can't show superscript numbers as they'll print. Now, all you do is enter the footnote text, which is shown here along with its number (1). Notice that you can use different fonts in notes, too. By the way, this is a purely fictitious book.

    1From <u>Avocados to Zany: A Guide to Eating Funky in Los Angeles,</u> by Vincent Alfieri, Ph.D. New York: Aubergine Press, 1988. Reprinted by permission of the author.

Caution: Don't add any extra hard returns after the footnote. WordPerfect separates several notes on one page with a blank line between each, so you don't have to worry about that. Within the footnote area, the cursor keys move as if the footnote were a page. For instance, HOME,HOME,DOWN ARROW takes the cursor to the end of the note, and so on. When you're finished:

Press   **F7 Exit**

to save the note.

Reveal the codes to see what you did. WordPerfect inserted *two* codes: [Footnote:1;] and [Note Num]. The first code tells WordPerfect what kind of note it is and its number, and the second is the numbering instruction within the note. As with headers and footers, WordPerfect shows only the first part of the note in the code, but it's all there. Ready for another?

✔Position the cursor at the end of the paragraph on the Talpa restaurant. The cursor should be directly past the period. Then:

Press   **CTRL-F7 Footnote**

Type   1 or f [Footnote]

Type   1 or c [Create]

Type the note, but not the number 2:

```
        2It's on the north side of the street, in the middle of the
block.  So if you're coming from Santa Monica, you have to make a
U-turn on Pico Boulevard to park on the same side.  Don't try to
cross the street during rush hour!
```

WordPerfect will warn you if you attempt to delete the footnote number. Should you inadvertently delete it, position the cursor at the beginning of the note and press **CTRL-F7 Footnote** to reinstate it. WordPerfect also adds the five spaces to indent the note. When you're finished:

Press   **F7 Exit**

to save the note.

If you're using the standard printer, the note won't fit on page 1 so WordPerfect broke the pages differently. The reference and note are now on page 2.

Tip: You can use any move or copy technique to move text from the document into a footnote area. That is, work with the CTRL-F4 Move key or the F1 Cancel key. Then go into the footnote area that you want and retrieve or restore the text.

✔Save the document as LAREST.NOT. View the printout of the first two pages to see the results. Then position the cursor at the beginning of the document.

Notice that WordPerfect supplied a dividing line between the text and notes. You can change the style of this line if you wish.

Editing a Footnote

Pretend that you want to edit footnote 2 but you don't remember where the reference in the text is located. Should you search for it? No! All you need do is supply the number to edit. Here's how.

Press   **CTRL-F7 Footnote**

Type   **1** or **f** [Footnote]

Type   **2** or **e** [Edit]

WordPerfect asks:

Footnote number?

and supplies the closest footnote number, which is not what you want here.

WordPerfect lists the note number according to the current cursor location. If the cursor is in the middle of a document, WordPerfect searches backward for the previous number. If the cursor is at the beginning of the document or WordPerfect doesn't find a note number ahead of the cursor position, WordPerfect searches forward.

Type   **2**

Press   **RETURN**

Press   **HOME,HOME,DOWN ARROW**

to position the cursor at the end of the note.

If you haven't done so already, type two spaces, and then add the following sentence to the end of the note:

L.A.'s finest are very happy to issue jay-walking tickets to unsuspecting visitors of our lovely city.

Press   **F7 Exit**

If you've changed the footnote numbering style (discussed later), supply the appropriate letter or number when you want to edit a note. For example, if you plan to edit note A, supply A as the note "number."

If you're using the standard printer, what's wrong with the document? When WordPerfect moved the reference for note 2 to the top of the second page, it created an orphan line (Chapter 17). If you wish, you can turn widow/orphan protection on at the beginning of the document to clear this up.

Document Formatting and Footnotes

WordPerfect uses the current left and right margins as the margins for footnotes, but it *does not* adjust the notes if you later change these settings. That's because some margin changes are for indentations, but you still may want the notes to print in the original margins.

Tip: One easy way to change the margins in all footnotes is to use the extended search feature (Chapter 16), but make sure you look for some string that you know *isn't* in any of the notes. That way, WordPerfect goes through all the notes and reformats them, but it doesn't stop the search until it reaches the end of the document. Tricky, huh? After you position the cursor at the beginning of the document, press HOME,F2 ▶Search. Supply an unusual string, such as @#@, and continue the search. You can also run a spelling check to reformat footnotes after you've changed the margin settings.

Normally notes are single spaced, but you can adjust the line spacing within a note if you want this setting to be different. See Customizing Footnote Styles. In a note you can also spell-check or hyphenate text separately from the document or use different fonts.

Finding, Deleting, and Inserting Footnotes

You can search for footnote text with the Extended Search command. If you forget a note number, you can use either Search command to find footnote codes. It's best to reveal the codes before you look for footnotes in this way, so that you can identify the note by its text quickly. After you press F2 ▶Search or SHIFT-F2 ◀Search, press CTRL-F7 Footnote, then type **1** or **f** [Footnote]. WordPerfect presents this menu:

```
1 Note; 2 Number Code; 3 New Number; 4 Options: 0
```

You'll learn about new footnote numbers and options soon. Make your selection, then continue the search. However, it may take some time if you're at the beginning of the document and you want to get to footnote 10, because WordPerfect stops at each note along the way. You'd have to repeat the search, or better yet, use a repeating macro (Chapter 32).

If you start a footnote at the wrong spot, just press F7 Exit and delete the note codes. Although you won't actually delete a footnote now, the procedure is simple. Position the cursor directly under the reference number in the text and press DEL (alternately, position the cursor directly past the number and press BACKSPACE). WordPerfect asks you to confirm your decision:

```
Delete Footnote? (Y/N) No
```

and supplies the footnote number. If you type **y**, WordPerfect deletes the footnote text, the two codes, and the reference number. It then renumbers the remaining footnotes past this location.

To insert a footnote, just choose the correct location and follow the steps listed for setting up a new note. Again, WordPerfect renumbers all the notes that are affected by the change.

✔Save the document but leave it on the screen.

Moving or Copying a Footnote

You can position a footnote reference somewhere else by moving it—that is, moving the footnote codes—but be careful. Now move footnote 2.

✔Position the cursor on the number 2 in the text. Then:

Press   **ALT-F4 Block** or **F12 Block**

Press   **RIGHT ARROW**

to extend the block past the code.

Press   **CTRL-F4 Move**

Type   **1** or **b** [<u>B</u>lock]

Type   **1** or **m** [<u>M</u>ove]

✔Position the cursor directly after the period of the sentence that ends *deter you* in the same paragraph. Then:

Press   **RETURN**

to retrieve the block.

The second note will appear at the bottom of the first page, because there's enough room for both notes. The above steps apply to copying a note, too. For instance, if you use lots of *op. cit.* notes, block the first such note out and copy the note wherever you need it. Set up a macro to do this. Yes, WordPerfect renumbers the notes accordingly. What if you use *op. cit.* and *ibid.* notes? Set up the text in separate documents, then use a macro to insert a new footnote, retrieve the document, and exit the note.

✔Save the document again.

Splitting a Note Between Pages

WordPerfect will split a long note between two pages if it can fit part of the note on one page. By default, it keeps at least 0.5 inch of footnote text on the page. You can change this default and even have WordPerfect indicate a continued note. See Customizing Footnote Styles.

Setting a Different Note Number

To start or continue footnote numbering at a number that isn't the next in order, follow these steps (you don't have to do them now):

1. Press **CTRL-F7 Footnote**.

2. Type **1** or **f** [Footnote].

3. Type **3** or **n** [New Number]. WordPerfect prompts:

   `Footnote number?`

4. Type the new number and press **F7 Exit**.

WordPerfect inserts a `[New Ftn Num]` code in the document with the new number and renumbers the footnotes past the code.

Tip: If you plan to use a *master document* (Chapter 26) and you want to restart note numbering with 1 for each chapter, insert numbering change codes at the beginnings of the chapters.

Customizing Footnote Styles

In the law firm where I worked, we used a different footnote setup, an example of which follows.

<u>1/</u>   Because of the Court's refusal to hear this case, Plaintiff
         Smudge and Smudge have decided to settle privately with
         Defendant.

Notice that the number in the footnote is not superscripted and the text lines are indented. The reference number in the text will look like this:

... so it appears from the proceedings$^{1/}$ that Mr. Smudge has
agreed ...

To customize your footnote numbering like this one, you have to change both the footnote reference number format and the footnote text format. As with all formatting changes, it's always a good idea to put the change at the beginning of the document. Make sure it's at least in front of the first footnote code. (Why not set up a format macro or a format document?)

✔Position the cursor at the beginning of the document. Then:

Press   **CTRL-F7 Footnote**

Type   **1** or **f** [Footnote]

Type   **4** or **o** [Options]

Heavens! The footnote options menu in Figure 22-1 appears. You certainly have a variety of choices. Actually, you don't have to change most of them, just the ones you want. The options are slightly different in previous versions. Here's what they mean:

1. Choice **1** [Spacing Within Footnotes] lets you set a different line spacing for notes or adjust the amount of blank space between two or more notes on a page.

   Tip: You can also adjust the spacing within a particular note with the SHIFT-F8 Format key. Suppose you set double spacing for notes here, but within a note you want single spacing for a quotation. You can do it!

2. Choice **2** [Amount of Note to Keep Together] lets you determine how much of a note must fit on a page. By default, WordPerfect will keep at least 0.5 inch of note text on the page.

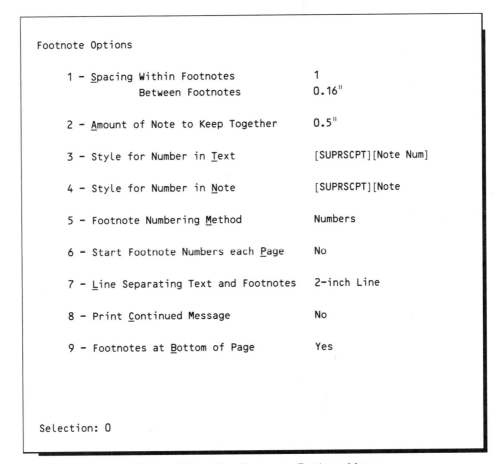

```
Footnote Options

    1 - Spacing Within Footnotes          1
              Between Footnotes           0.16"

    2 - Amount of Note to Keep Together    0.5"

    3 - Style for Number in Text          [SUPRSCPT][Note Num]

    4 - Style for Number in Note          [SUPRSCPT][Note

    5 - Footnote Numbering Method         Numbers

    6 - Start Footnote Numbers each Page   No

    7 - Line Separating Text and Footnotes  2-inch Line

    8 - Print Continued Message            No

    9 - Footnotes at Bottom of Page        Yes




Selection: 0
```

Figure 22-1   The Footnote Options Menu

3. Choices **3** [Style for Number in Text] and **4** [Style for Number in Note] are where you change the reference number and note styles. See the example later in the section.

4. When you select choice **5** [Footnote Numbering Method], Word-Perfect presents this menu:

   `1 Numbers; 2 Letters; 3 Characters: 0`

   Numbers and letters are self-explanatory. The third option, characters, lets you pick a character such as an asterisk. WordPerfect prints the first note on the page with one asterisk, the second with two, and so on. You may want to make sure that you restart note numbering on each page (the next option) so that you don't have *too* many characters!

5. Choice **6** [Start Footnote Numbers Each Page] restarts the numbering at the top of each page. By default this setting is off.

6. Use choice **7** [Line Separating Text and Footnotes] to change the divider line from this menu:

   `1 No Line; 2 2-inch Line; 3 Margin to Margin: 0`

7. Choice **8** [Print Continued Message] will print the message *(continued. . .)* at the end of a partial note that doesn't fit entirely on one page.

8. Finally, choice **9** [Footnotes at Bottom of Page] is so useful that it's the default. Where necessary, WordPerfect will add blank lines to push a note to the bottom of the page.

When you change the options, WordPerfect inserts a `[Ftn Opt]` code in the document. Here's how you would set up the two styles shown at the beginning of the section. Make sure WordPerfect is displaying the footnote options menu. Then:

Type   **3** or **t** [String for Number in Text]

WordPerfect prompts:

`Replace with:[SUPRSCPT][Note Num][suprscpt]`

Now, you can just move along the line and edit it:

Press   **RIGHT ARROW**

to position the cursor under the `[Note Num]` code.

Press   **F8 Underline**

to insert a begin [UND] code.

Press   **RIGHT ARROW**

Press   **F8 Underline**

to insert an end [und] code.

Type   /

The new string is now this:

```
[SUPRSCPT][UND][Note Num][und]/[suprscpt]
```

Press   **RETURN**

to finish.

WordPerfect can't show the entire string on the line, but it's there. Notice that you must repeat the font change to add the end code. For each font selection, WordPerfect alternates between begin and end codes. Now do the footnote text style change:

Type   **4** or **n** [Style for Number in Note]

Notice that there are five spaces, instead of a tab, for the beginning of each note. That's because WordPerfect wants to indent the note five spaces, regardless of what the document's tab settings are. This example prints footnotes at the left margin.

Press   **CTRL-END**

to delete the line and start with a clean slate.

Press   **F8 Underline**

to add a begin [UND] code.
Now you must insert a note number code, like so:

Press   **CTRL-F7 Footnote**

Type   **1** or **f** [Footnote]

Type   **2** or **c** [Number Code]

Press   **F8 Underline**

to add an end [und] code.

Type   /

Press   **RETURN**

to finish.

You can't have an indent code in the footnote text, so you'll have to add it to each note if you're using this new style. Also, whenever you start a new footnote with this format, just press F4 ▶Indent to indent the text of the note.

Press   **F7 Exit**

to return to the document.

✔If you wish, print the document to see how the notes look now. Then clear the screen, but *don't* save the document.

Examples of Endnotes

Creating endnotes is essentially the same as preparing footnotes. Just type **2** or **e** [Endnote] after you press CTRL-F7 Footnote, then select the choice you want. WordPerfect takes care to position all endnotes at the end of the document when you print the document. Try experimenting with endnotes a little.

✔Retrieve the document CHAPTER.2 now.

This Beethoven scholar is going to pepper his manuscript with numerous endnote references so that his tenure review committee will be suitably impressed. (He probably won't get tenure anyway, but there's no harm in trying.) You'll use the standard endnote defaults to save time.

✔Position the cursor directly past the period at the end of the first sentence. Then:

Press   **CTRL-F7 Footnote**

Type   **2** or **e** [Endnote]

Type   **1** or **c** [Create]

Notice that the default format for endnotes is slightly different than for footnotes. Type the note as you see it below, but press **TAB** first to indent the first line of the note.

1.   Indeed, what in Beethoven's life was <u>without</u> frustration?
It is one of the ironies of history that such a gifted composer,
whose works have inspired millions, should lead such a troubled
and difficult life.

Caution: Don't add a return at the end of the note. WordPerfect will take care of the spacing between notes for you. When you've typed the endnote:

Press   **F7 Exit**

The code for endnotes is [Endnote] followed by the endnote number, [Note Num] code, and part of the endnote text.

✔For the second endnote, position the cursor directly after the question mark at the end of the last sentence in the first indented text. Repeat the above steps to add this endnote:

2.   Kirsten Grimstad, "Beethoven's 'Kram' Letters: An Exercise
in Frustration," <u>Journal of the American Beethoven Society</u>, 6:1,
pp. 35-92.

When you've typed the endnote:

Press   **F7 Exit**

✔Save the document as CHAPTER.2N and view the printout to see the results. Then clear the screen.

If there are footnotes and endnotes in a document, WordPerfect keeps track of them separately but uses Arabic numbering for both. You can change the numbering style for the notes if you wish.

Editing Endnotes

Follow the patterns you've learned with footnotes, but type **2** or **e** [Endnote] to edit an endnote, to change the starting endnote number, or to create a new endnote style. If you change the starting number, you'll insert a [New End Num] code. If you decide to change the endnote style, you'll see the endnote options menu (Figure 22-2). Follow the steps listed previously in the footnotes section to change these options. WordPerfect then inserts an [End Opt] code into the document.

```
Endnote Options

        1 - Spacing Within Endnotes          1
                Between Endnotes             0.16"

        2 - Amount of Endnote to Keep Together  0.5"

        3 - Style for Numbers in Text       [SUPRSCPT][Note Num][

        4 - Style for Numbers in Note       [Note Num].

        5 - Endnote Numbering Method        Numbers




Selection: 0
```

Figure 22-2   The Endnote Options Menu

Changing Endnote Placement

WordPerfect normally prints endnotes on the last page of the document directly below any regular text. If you want to separate the text from the endnotes, insert a few blank lines at the end of the document. If you want WordPerfect to print endnotes on a separate page at the end of the document, insert a hard page break there.

However, suppose your document has several sections and you'd like WordPerfect to print endnotes at the end of each. To change the *endnote placement* location, follow these steps (you don't have to do them now):

1. Position the cursor at the spot where you want WordPerfect to print the endnotes.

   Tip: You may want to add blank lines about this spot to separate the endnotes from the text. However, don't try to insert endnote placement codes in text or math columns.

396

2. Press **CTRL-F7 Footnote**.

3. Type **3** or **p** [Endnote Placement]. WordPerfect prompts:

```
Restart endnote numbering? (Y/N) Yes
```

That is, WordPerfect will restart the numbering for any endnotes past this spot. Type **y**.

WordPerfect inserts the following message in what looks like a comment box:

```
Endnote Placement
It is not known how much space endnotes will occupy here.
Generate to determine.
```

That is, WordPerfect doesn't really count the endnote lines until it prints the endnotes. So, it can't determine how much space it needs for the endnotes. By *generate* WordPerfect means to create all tables, lists, and indexes, but you can use the same generate feature to have WordPerfect figure out how much space it needs for the endnotes (Chapter 23). You could also print the document or view the printout. There's now an [Endnote Placement] code here, and a [New End Num] code if you told WordPerfect to renumber the remaining endnotes. What's more, WordPerfect inserts a hard page code just to be on the safe side.

Tip: After you view the printout, you can adjust the spacing between the endnotes yourself. Then delete the hard page code if you wish but make sure you don't delete the endnote placement code.

Formatting Endnotes in Columns

Several readers have asked me if WordPerfect can format endnote text as newspaper style columns. Normally, no, but you can "fool" the program if you use a combination of endnote and paragraph numbering (Chapter 21). Here's how.

1. Go to the end of the document and set the formatting for the paragraph numbering and columns. Because the default paragraph numbering style for level one is Roman numerals, change the style to "mimic" endnotes: 1., 2., and so on. (You may want to set all this up on a new page. Use CTRL-RETURN to force a page break.)

2. For every endnote reference in the document text, create a new endnote, but *leave it blank*. That is, delete the [Note Num] code within the endnote area. Press F7 Exit to save each blank note. That way, WordPerfect will continue to number the endnotes, but it won't print them!

3. For each note text, go to the end of the document, insert an automatic paragraph numbering instruction, then type the text.

4. If you delete an endnote reference, make sure you delete the corresponding text. WordPerfect will then renumber the endnotes and paragraph numbers for you.

What if you've already set up endnotes? Simple! Edit each one, block the text *and* number code, then delete the block. Save the blank endnote with F7 Exit, position the cursor at the end of the document, and restore the deletion. Because the endnote numbering doesn't work outside an endnote, WordPerfect won't restore it. WordPerfect just restores the endnote text. (You can create a macro to automate these steps for you.)

Footnotes and endnotes have come a long way! Far from being "the worst" and a typist's nightmare, they're now a piece of cake in WordPerfect.

23

Generating Tables, Lists, Indexes, and Cross-References

In this chapter you'll learn the following new command . . .

Function Key Command

ALT-F5 Mark Text	(1) Mark table of contents entries, (2) mark list entries, (3) mark index entries, (4) mark table of authorities entries, (5) mark cross-references, (6) generate tables, lists, indexes, and cross-references

. . . and you'll learn some new codes:

[Def Mark:Index]	Location of index definition
[Def Mark:List]	Location of list definition
[Def Mark:ToA]	Location of table of authorities section definition
[Def Mark:ToC]	Location of table of contents definition
[End Def]	End of table, list, or index after generation
[Index]	Index entry
[Mark:ToC] and [End Mark:ToC]	Begin and end table of contents entry
[Mark:List] and [End Mark:List]	Begin and end list entry
[Ref]	Automatic reference (cross-reference) location
[Target]	Target reference location
[ToA]	Table of authorities long or short form entry

One of the world's most boring and tedious editorial jobs is creating a table of contents, list of figures or illustrations, index, or cross-references. You have to locate all the passages, jot down the page numbers, then consolidate them somewhere else. Thank goodness WordPerfect has ways to help you in this most thankless task. If you're a "legal bibliophile" or work for one, Word-Perfect can create tables of authorities, too. Dear Reader, this is a long chapter, but you can study it in sections. Do the sections in order, though.

> **DO WARM-UP**

Generalities

The procedure for creating tables, lists, indexes (or is it indices?), and cross-references is basically the same. What's more, all operations are on one key, **ALT-F5 Mark Text**. Here are the steps in brief (I'll cover them more thoroughly later).

1. *Locate* each reference in your document. That is, position the cursor at the reference. Most of the time you'll block the reference, too.

2. *Mark* each reference as a table of contents, list, or index entry or as a cross-reference. WordPerfect calls cross-references *automatic references*, by the way, and requires you to "tie" the cross-reference to another spot in the document. For tables of authorities you supply a full form and a short form, as I'll describe later.

3. When you're finished, tell WordPerfect where you want it to put the tables, lists, and index in the document and *define* the appearance of each. Usually tables go at the beginning of a document and the index at the end. Cross-references occur in the text, so you don't have to define them.

4. Finally, have WordPerfect *generate* the tables, lists, index, and cross-references. WordPerfect creates the table of contents, as many as nine different lists, the table of authorities if you're using it, an index, and the cross-references. You don't have to use all the features, just the ones you need.

5. Save the document often during the marking process and definitely after you generate everything!

Note: WordPerfect normally generates tables, lists, indexes, and cross-references for the document on the screen only. However, you can also combine many documents into a *master document* and generate tables and so on for the entire show. This chapter discusses the one-document approach, but refer to Chapter 25 for information about master documents.

For tables and lists, your job is more or less straightforward. You'll probably use existing and easily recognizable headings and subheadings in your document as sections in the table of contents. Tables of authorities require a bit more planning, but a caveat is definitely in order about doing an index. WordPerfect can only *help* you; its power is necessarily limited in this area. Why? Because even the most experienced bibliophile—and every editor—knows that generating an index is an art in itself. It's one thing to mark entries, but quite another to be organized enough to get them right the first time.

Tables of Contents and Lists

The procedure for setting up a table of contents is essentially the same as for a list, so you'll do an example using both. For tables of authorities, see the separate discussion later in the chapter.

✔Retrieve the document GOODBODY.ELT or any document that contains headings that you can set up as table of contents entries.

Marking Table of Contents Entries

When you mark table of contents entries, you (1) block out the text that's to appear in the table of contents and (2) tell WordPerfect the entry's *level* in the table's structure. Generally, any chapter title is level 1, with subtitles being levels 2, 3, and so on.

Caution: Make sure you include only the text you want in the block. That is, don't block any superfluous spaces or blank lines. For example, the title of this document will constitute the first level, but you don't want to include the spaces in front of it in the listing. So:

Press   **CTRL-RIGHT ARROW**

to position the cursor under the *R* of *REVISED*.

Press   **ALT-F4 Block** or **F12 Block**

Press   **END**

to block the text.

Press   **ALT-F5 Mark Text**

WordPerfect presents the block mark menu:

```
Mark for: 1 ToC; 2 List; 3 Index; 4 ToA: 0
```

Type   1 or c [ToC]

WordPerfect asks:

```
ToC Level:
```

Type   1

WordPerfect has just surrounded this block with two codes. The first, [Mark:ToC], is the begin code, and the second, [End Mark:ToC], is the end code. The code includes the table of contents level, too. Note that, fortunately, WordPerfect didn't include the center codes in the block. Each subheading of this document will be part of table level 2.

✔Position the cursor at the left margin of the line that contains the heading, *Designation of Beneficiary*. Stop! Do you want the underlining in the block? Probably not, so reveal the codes and position the cursor under the *D*. Then:

Press   **ALT-F4 Block** or **F12 Block**

Type   y

to extend the block.

Press   **ALT-F5 Mark Text**

Type   1 or c [ToC]

Type   2

for level 2.

✔In the same fashion, mark the other two subheadings for table of contents level 2. Don't include any underline codes in the blocks! Then save the document, but leave it on the screen.

Marking List Entries

When you mark a list entry, you (1) block the text and (2) indicate the *list number*. You can have nine different lists, and WordPerfect will generate each one separately. Now, change the document a bit to include a title for the witness section. You'll then block the title and mark it as part of list #1.

✔Position the cursor at the left margin of the first sentence in the witness section (*We, the witnesses* and so on).

Press   **RETURN** twice

for spacing.

Press   **UP ARROW** twice

✔Center, underline, and type this title: `Testimony of Witnesses`. Block it out (without the underline codes), then:

Press   **ALT-F5 Mark Text**

Type   **2** or **l** [<u>L</u>ist]

WordPerfect asks:

`List Number:`

Type   **1**

WordPerfect encloses list entries in `[Mark:List]` and `[End Mark:List]` codes that include the list number.

Tip: A "list" can be any collection of information, such as a table of figures, illustrations, or graphs. In fact, WordPerfect can use lists 6 through 9 for tracking graphics elements (Chapter 34).

✔Save the document again and leave it on the screen.

Generating a Table of Contents and Lists

When you're ready to generate the table of contents, you must complete the following steps (they hold true for generating lists and indexes, too):

1. Add any descriptive titles or other text to identify the table, list, or index. This is just text in the document itself.

   Tip: You may also want to add a hard page code so that the table, lists, and index print on separate pages.

2. Tell WordPerfect where the table, list, or index should go. That is, you insert a "define mark" code at the correct spot in the document.

3. Decide on the definition style, that is, define how the table, list, or index will look.

4. Generate.

5. Save your work!

Fortunately, you accomplish steps 2 and 3 at the same time. In this example, however, there are other pitfalls along the way. Be alert!

Press   **HOME,HOME,UP ARROW**

It makes sense that the table of contents should be at the beginning of the document, and you'll probably want it on a separate page.

Caution: If you have format change codes in this document, you want them to stay at the very beginning of the document.

✔Reveal the codes and press **RIGHT ARROW** as many times as necessary to get past any formatting codes. The cursor should be under the [Cntr] code in this example. Now you're ready to add a page break here.

Press   **CTRL-RETURN**

to insert a hard page code.

Press   **UP ARROW**

✔Center, bold, and type this title: `Table of Contents`. Don't forget to move the cursor past the end boldface code! Then press **RETURN** twice for spacing (remember that this document is double spaced).

Now for the table of contents definition mark and style definition, which must be *exactly* where you want the entries to go.

Tip: Always enter this information at the left margin. WordPerfect inserts a code that marks the beginning location of the table and the style you've chosen. Later when you generate the table, the cursor can be anywhere in the document and WordPerfect will still insert the table entries at the code location.

Press   **ALT-F5 Mark Text**

Because block is not on, WordPerfect presents the mark text menu:

`1 Auto Ref; 2 Subdoc; 3 Index; 4 ToA Short Form; 5 Define; 6 Generate: 0`

Type   **5** or **d** [Define]

The mark text: define menu appears (Figure 23-1).

Type   **1** or **c** [Define Table of Contents]

The table of contents definition menu appears (Figure 23-2). You tell WordPerfect how many levels there are in the table, the way you want page numbers to appear, and, optionally, how you want the last level to appear. That is, if you answer yes to choice **2** [Display Last Level in Wrapped Format],

```
Mark Text: Define

    1 - Define Table of Contents

    2 - Define List

    3 - Define Index

    4 - Define Table of Authorities

    5 - Edit Table of Authorities Full Form


















Selection: 0
```

Figure 23-1   The Mark Text: Define Menu

WordPerfect shows the entries for the lowest level of the table as one unit. It separates each entry with a semicolon instead of placing each entry on a separate line. WordPerfect wraps the lines according to the margin settings.

   Tip: Always indicate the number of levels first:

Type   1 or n [Number of Levels]

Type   2

for two levels.

Type   3 or p [Page Number Position]

   Now that you've entered the number of levels, WordPerfect shows the default page numbering for each level (Flush right with leader). At the bottom of the screen you see this:

```
Table of Contents Definition

    1 - Number of Levels                    1

    2 - Display Last Level in               No
           Wrapped Format

    3 - Page Number Position - Level 1      Flush right with leader
                               Level 2
                               Level 3
                               Level 4
                               Level 5




Selection: 0
```

Figure 23-2   The Table of Contents Definition Menu

1 None; 2 Pg # Follows; 3 (Pg #) Follows; 4 Flush Rt; 5 Flush Rt with Leader

The choices are self-explanatory. Note that choice **2** and **3** are the same except for parentheses surrounding the page number. You'll accept the default for both levels, so:

Press   **F7 Exit** twice

to return to the document.

WordPerfect has inserted this code into the document: [Def Mark:ToC] with the number of levels. Now it's time to insert the definition for list #1.

Caution: You must have a separate definition mark for each list. Here, you *could* set up the list on a separate page, but instead do this:

✔Press **RETURN** twice for spacing. Center and type this title: List of Figures. Press **RETURN** twice for spacing. Then:

Press   **ALT-F5 Mark Text**

Type   **5** or **d** [<u>D</u>efine]

Type   **2** or ι [Define <u>L</u>ist]

WordPerfect prompts:

```
List Number (1-9):
```

Type   **1**

The list 1 definition menu, shown in Figure 23-3, appears. Similar menus would represent other lists. This is just like the page numbering menu in the table of contents definition menu.

```
List 1 Definition

    1 - No Page Numbers

    2 - Page Numbers Follow Entries

    3 - (Page Numbers) Follow Entries

    4 - Flush Right Page Numbers

    5 - Flush Right Page Numbers with Leaders




Selection: 0
```

Figure 23-3   The List 1 Definition Menu

Type   **5** or **l** [Flush Right Page Numbers with <u>L</u>eaders]

There's now a [Def Mark:List] code for list #1 in the document.
✔Before you continue, save the document.

Tip: Make sure your page breaks are correct before you begin generating the table and lists. When you're ready:

Press   **ALT-F5 Mark Text**

Type   **6** or **g** [<u>G</u>enerate]

The mark text: generate menu appears (Figure 23-4). I'll cover the first four choices in later chapters.

Type   **5** or **g** [<u>G</u>enerate Tables, Indexes, Automatic References, etc.]

```
Mark Text: Generate

    1 - Remove Redline Markings and Strikeout Text from Document

    2 - Compare Screen and Disk Documents and Add Redline and Strikeout

    3 - Expand Master Document

    4 - Condense Master Document

    5 - Generate Tables, Indexes, Automatic References, etc.
```

```
Selection: 0
```

Figure 23-4   The Mark Text: Generate Menu

WordPerfect warns:

```
Existing tables, lists, and indexes will be replaced.  Continue? (Y/N): Yes
```

Normally, you'd want to update the tables, so WordPerfect will delete any previous ones. Because there *are* no previous ones:

Type   **y**

WordPerfect begins the generation and tells you:

```
Generation in progress.
```

Soon you'll see the completed table and list. The only thing that WordPerfect *doesn't* do for you is number the pages. Traditionally, the page numbers on contents pages are Roman numerals. You've already learned how to set them up yourself (Chapter 16), but remember to switch to Arabic numerals and back to page number 1 for the main document page numbering. In this example, make sure the page numbering code for the table of contents page is in front of the definition codes and at the top of the page. See Chapter 17 for information on how to print specific pages with Roman numerals.

After generation is complete, WordPerfect inserts an `[End Def]` code to mark the end of each table, list, and index. You can search for this code as any other.

Caution: Don't insert any text between the begin and end definition codes. WordPerfect deletes all text between the codes when you generate the tables, lists, and indexes the next time.

✔Save the document, then clear the screen.

An Aside: Generating Endnotes

If you've set up an endnote placement code in the middle of a document (Chapter 22), you can generate the endnotes as I just outlined, even if you don't have any tables, lists, or indexes. Here *generate* means to set up enough space for the endnotes at the placement code. This is not a mandatory step: WordPerfect will still print the endnotes correctly. It's just an option to let you see exactly how much space the endnotes require.

Regenerating a Table

Say you're like me and you mistakenly included some underline codes in one of the blocks. So, you want to correct your mistake and generate another table. First, find the block that's incorrect. Because there may be many table of contents marks in the document, use the Search command. After you begin the search, press **ALT-F5 Mark Text** to see this menu:

1 ToC/List; 2 EndMark; 3 Index; 4 ToA; 5 Defs and Refs; 6 Subdocs: 0

If you type **1** or **c** or **l** [ToC/List], WordPerfect shows a [Mark] code as the search string. Continue searching until you find the code you need. Then delete the code and insert a new one. When you delete the begin or end code, WordPerfect deletes the other for you. After you make your corrections, re-generate the table. You don't have to define the table again, because the definition code is still in the document.

Note: If you add another level to the table of contents, however, you must delete the original definition code and redefine the table to include the new level.

Indexing a Document

A few preliminary words of advice about creating an index are in order. First, try to determine the specific index topics you want *before* you begin. Do you want separate entries for *Apple Pie* and *Pie, Apple?* If you do, you must put in a code for each. You may wish to make a list of these topics, split the screen into two windows, and have the topics visible in the other window for quick reference. WordPerfect can't help you decide on your index topics, but a good style book—such as the *The Chicago Manual of Style*—can.

Second, even though it takes more time, try to find the entries for each topic separately and mark them, one topic at a time. That way, you can concentrate on one topic without being distracted by others, and you won't miss a reference location. What's more, you can then set up a macro to set up the index code for the topic any number of times throughout the document. Use the Search command to help you find the correct spots in the document, or a repeating macro (Chapter 32).

Third, and most important, *be consistent.* If you mark one section of text as an entry called *Pies*, make sure you mark all other applicable text in the same fashion. For instance, if you marked a section with the entry *Apple Pies*, then WordPerfect will generate a separate entry in the index for this entry. It might be better if you used a heading and a subheading in the index. The heading, of course, would be *Pies*, while each subheading would be a type of pie: *apple, cherry*, and so on.

Be consistent in your use of case, too. If you type **pies** in some places and **Pies** in other places, WordPerfect considers these separate entries for the index. Again, an ounce of prevention is worth a pound of headaches later. Decide if your index entries will be in mixed case (*Pies*) or lowercase (*pies*) throughout. One way to get around this hassle is to use a *concordance file.* A concordance file contains an alphabetical listing of the important words in the document. WordPerfect can generate index entries for the concordance list (see the separate section Using a Concordance File).

And for heaven's sake, make sure your page breaks are correct before you begin generating the index. Obviously, WordPerfect can only refer to the page numbering according to the current page setup. It can't read your mind! Use hard page codes to set the correct pages if necessary. If you edit the document and the page breaks change, you'll have to regenerate the index.

Finally, there's no getting around the harsh reality that *after* WordPerfect generates an index for you, you'll still have to do a bit of housekeeping to clean it up. Even the best planned index may not turn out exactly as you intended. For instance, you might decide to consolidate a few entries or add some cross-references. But it's a relatively easy matter once you *have* the finished index to make any last-minute changes to it.

Caution: Make last-minute changes only to the final index. Remember that WordPerfect deletes everything between the definition mark codes if you regenerate an index.

✔Retrieve the LAREST.NOT document or any document that you want to index. I'm using LAREST.NOT because it contains footnotes.

Marking Index Entries

There are two ways to mark an index entry: (1) mark the current word at the cursor location or (2) mark a block. WordPerfect assumes that the word or block will become the index entry, called the *heading*, but you can override that decision and type your own heading. You can then determine if the entry needs an optional *subheading*. When it generates the index, WordPerfect consolidates all subheadings under the same heading. You'll first mark all restaurant names for index entries.

✔Position the cursor under the *E* of *El Colmao* in the second paragraph. Because this name contains two words, you must block it out to include the entire name in the entry.

Press   **ALT-F4 Block** or **F12 Block**

Type   **,**

(That's a comma.)

Press   **LEFT ARROW**

because you don't want the comma in the block.

Press   **ALT-F5 Mark Text**

Type   **3** or **i** [Index]

WordPerfect says:

Index heading: El Colmao

Press　　　**RETURN**

to accept this.

WordPerfect then asks for the Subheading . You don't want one, so:

Press　　　**RETURN**

for no subheading.

There is now an [Index] code followed by the exact index entry here. Note that WordPerfect doesn't include the underlining in the code. The next restaurant, Palermo, is one word.

✔Position the cursor anywhere under the word *Palermo*.

Press　　　**ALT-F5 Mark Text**

Type　　　**3** or **i** [Index]

Press　　　**RETURN** twice

WordPerfect inserts the index code at the cursor location, which may be in the middle of the word. That's okay, although it looks a little funny when you reveal the codes.

✔Go through the entire document and mark *each* restaurant name as an index heading. When you're finished, save the document as LAREST.NDX before you continue. Then return the cursor to the beginning of the document.

Note: When you mark index entries, WordPerfect assumes the entire word at the cursor. Say the word is at the beginning of a quote, like this: *"Palermo . . ."*. WordPerfect would mark the quote, too. The same applies if the word contains an apostrophe: *Palermo's*. To get around the problem, block out only that part of the word that you need before you press ALT-F5 Mark Text.

Now you want to index each type of cuisine. This time you'll use one general heading, *food*, and then a subheading for each type.

✔Position the cursor under the word *Cuban* in the second paragraph. Because you'll be supplying your own heading, don't bother to block out the text.

Press　　　**ALT-F5 Mark Text**

Type　　　**3** or **i** [Index]

Don't accept the heading Cuban. Instead, just start typing a new heading (WordPerfect will delete the original heading):

Type　　　**food**

Press   **RETURN**

You're using lowercase for entries. When you override the suggested heading, WordPerfect uses it as the subheading instead. You can override that, too, if you wish, but here you want to accept it.

Press   **RETURN**

to accept Cuban as the subheading.

The code for this entry is [Index:food;Cuban]. Note the case of the text.

✔Position the cursor under the word *Italian* in the third paragraph and repeat the steps to make the heading *food* and the subheading *Italian*. Mark the words *Thai*, *Japanese*, and *Mexican* in the next four paragraphs in a similar fashion, substituting the correct "ethnicity."

The next restaurant presents a conceptual problem. Tommy's is a hamburger joint, so how will you refer to it? Here's where you have to use your own philosophy of index creation. There's no definitive rule. I chose to use *two* entries, one for *food, American* and one for *hamburgers*. But where to put them? How about at the word *hamburgers* in the first line, which you'll use as an entry anyway? Position the cursor at this word.

Press   **ALT-F5 Mark Text**

Type   **5** [Index]

What's this? WordPerfect assumes that index headings should be capitalized! Say you don't want them capitalized. You must then enter the heading yourself.

Type   hamburgers

Press   **RETURN**

WordPerfect then inserts the subheading, in lowercase. You don't want it, so:

Press   **F1 Cancel**

to delete the subheading.

You can also press CTRL-END to delete the subheading, then RETURN to continue.

✔Now, mark the same spot with the heading *food* and the subheading *American*. You'll have to override both suggestions on WordPerfect's part for this one. Repeat these steps to add *food, American* and *hamburgers* as entries for Hampton's, the next restaurant. For Gorky's, use *food* and *Russian*.

Vickman's is another exception. I chose again *food, American* for one entry and *bakeries* for the other. Use just *food, American* for Clifton's Cafeteria, but I also put an entry for *soups* at the phrase *Soup Easy*. Continue with *food* and *Chinese* for the next paragraph, and *food, seafood* for the next. Finally, make an entry for *cappuccino*, lowercase, on the last line.

✔Save the LAREST.NDX document again and leave it on the screen.

With a little luck, you can also insert an index entry in a footnote. Try this if you're brave!

Press	**CTRL-F7 Footnote**
Type	**1** or **f** [F̲ootnote]
Type	**2** or **e** [E̲dit]
Type	**1**
Press	**RETURN**

✔Position the cursor under the *A* of *Alfieri.*

Press	**ALT-F5 Mark Text**
Type	**3** or **i** [I̲ndex]
Press	**END**

to move the cursor to the end of the heading.

Type	**, Vincent**
Press	**RETURN**
Press	**CTRL-END**

to delete the subheading.

Press	**RETURN**
Press	**F7 Exit**

✔Save the document, then position the cursor at the end of the document.

Generating the Index

The index belongs on its own page.

Caution: Make sure the location of your index definition code is past all index entry codes in the document. That means, put the index at the end of the document where it rightly belongs.

Press   **CTRL-RETURN**

to add a hard page break.

✔Center, bold, and type the title, **Index**. Make sure you turn boldface off. Press **RETURN** three times for spacing. Now, insert the definition mark and determine the index style:

Press   **ALT-F5 Mark Text**

Type   **5** or **d** [Define]

Type   **3** or **i** [Define Index]

WordPerfect first requests:

Concordance Filename (Enter=none):

Press   **RETURN**

because you're not using a concordance file. (That's covered later in the chapter.)

The index definition menu appears. It's exactly like the list definition menu you saw earlier. Use the standard index style here:

Type   **2** or **p** [Page Numbers Follow Entries]

WordPerfect inserts a [Def Mark:Index] code in the document. Now, generate the index:

Press   **ALT-F5 Mark Text**

Type   **6** or **g** [Generate]

Type   **5** or **g** [Generate Tables, Indexes, Automatic References, etc.]

Type   **y**

When WordPerfect is finished, you should see an index similar to the one in Figure 23-5. Not bad, no? Now, reveal the codes to see exactly how WordPerfect sets up each index entry. It turns out that the program uses indents and the margin release command.

✔Save the document, then clear the screen.

Index

```
Alfieri, Vincent  1
bakeries  2
cappuccino  3
Clifton's Cafeteria  2
El Colmao  1
food
      American  2
      Chinese  2
      Cuban  1
      Italian  1
      Japanese  1
      Mexican  1, 2
      Russian  2
      seafood  3
      Thai  1
Gorky's  2
hamburgers  2
Hampton's  2
House of Chan Dara  1
Hunan Restaurant  3
La Fuente  2
Maya  1
Onyx Cafe  3
Palermo  1
Seafood Bay  3
Talpa  1
Tommy's  2
Vickman's Restaurant and Bakery  2
```

Figure 23-5   A Completed Index for the LAREST Document

Caution: If you have a document with endnotes and an index, Word-Perfect will put the notes after the index when you print the document. To get around this, insert an endnote placement code on the last page of the document or somewhere before the index definition code.

Using a Concordance File

You can include a concordance file during index generation. This is a separate WordPerfect document that contains a list of index references. Instead of having to put an index code for all occurrences of, say, *food* in your document, you can include this word in the concordance file and set up the index reference once. WordPerfect matches the concordance file entries with the document and generates index entries whenever it finds one of the words from the concordance in the document.

By definition, a concordance is in alphabetical order. You can type the list in any order and then sort the concordance file with WordPerfect's sorting feature (Chapter 33).

Caution: Make sure that each entry in the concordance file, including the *last*, is on a separate line that ends with a hard return. Include both subheadings and headings as necessary. For example, the following file called LAREST.CON contains these entries (I've already sorted them for you):

```
American
Chinese
Cuban
Italian
Japanese
Mexican
Russian
seafood
Thai
```

After setting up the list and sorting it, you'd make *food* the heading and each of the different cuisines a subheading. Position the cursor on *American*, press **ALT-F5 Mark Text**, and type **3** or **i** [Index]. Type **food** as the heading, then use **American** as the subheading. Repeat the procedure for each word on the list, but substitute the correct type of cuisine.

In this example, it makes no sense to have each word, such as *American*, a separate entry, but at times you may want to set up individual words or phrases as headings with no subheadings. For example, if you included the names of the restaurants in the concordance, you'd set up index entries for them. When it's time to generate the index, supply the file name of the concordance file when WordPerfect asks:

```
Concordance Filename (Enter=none):
```

Notice that I used the extension .CON for my concordance file (LAREST.CON). This isn't necessary, but it is an easy way to distinguish file types.

Doing a Table of Authorities

Guess what? You legal types can generate a *table of authorities* that combines elements of both a table of contents and an index. The "table" part shows court cases, laws, and statutes arranged according to *sections*. The "index" part lists the page numbers of all occurrences of a particular case, law, or statute. The authority appears once with its full title, and below that are the page references for individual citations.

 Question: If you're not a legal type but you want to create a bibliography, how can you do so with a table of authorities? Think!

Sections in the Table of Authorities

You must do a little planning to determine how you want to arrange the table of authorities. That is, you first decide what you'll name the section headings. For example, you have sections titled *Supreme Court Cases, State Appellate Court Cases*, and *Other Statutes*, in that order. You give each section a number: Supreme Court Cases can be number 1; State Appellate Court Cases, 2; and Other Statutes, 3. The maximum number of sections is 16. Make sure you remember your section numbers when you mark the authorities.

The Long and the Short of It

To mark the authorities in the document, you find the *first* occurrence of the authority and mark it as the long or *full form*, that is, the complete name of the case, law, or statute. For example, suppose one case is called *Smudge & Smudge v. The State of California*, 24 Cal.App.9 (1987). That's the long form. You also give the authority a *short form* to identify all subsequent occurrences of it in the document without having to retype the long form. The short form must be unique and refer to one full form. The short form here is *Smudge*.

For the full form, use whatever special printing effects you need. For instance, court cases are usually underlined, so include the underline codes in the full form. Thus, after finding the first occurrence of the example, you block it out, including the underline codes in the block. Then press **ALT-F5 Mark Text** and type **4** or **a** [To**A**]. WordPerfect prompts:

```
ToA Section Number (Press Enter for Short Form only):
```

This example falls under state appellate court cases, so you would type **2** and press **RETURN** to add this case to the second section. WordPerfect shows the block in the table of authorities editing area. You can edit it to make sure it appears as you want it. For example:

Smudge & Smudge v. The State of California,
      24 Cal.App.9 (1987)

Here the full form is on two lines and the second line is indented, which makes the listing appear nicely uncluttered in the table. When you're finished editing the full form, press **F7 Exit**. WordPerfect prompts:

Short Form:

and supplies the long form.

Use the standard cursor and editing keys to modify the line, or in this instance type **Smudge** and press **RETURN**. You'll insert a [ToA:2;Smudge;[Full Form]] code, and it includes the first part of the full form text.

Then, find all subsequent occurrences of the authority and mark them with the short form.

Tip: Use the extended search (Chapter 16) to search through notes. If the short form (for example, *Smudge*) appears by itself in the document, you don't have to block the authority. Just press **ALT-F5 Mark Text** and type **4** or **a** [ToA Short Form]. Type the exact short form name and press **RETURN**. A [ToA:;Smudge;] code represents the short form in this example.

If the authority appears with section numbers, block it out entirely and press **ALT-F5 Mark Text**. Type **4** or **a** [ToA] and press **RETURN** alone for the short form. Enter the short form name and press **RETURN**. WordPerfect matches each short form occurrence with the full form, but it also includes any different citations when it generates the table.

Generating the Table of Authorities

After you mark all authorities, you then define the style, decide where the table should go, and set up the page accordingly. Generally tables of authorities precede the actual text, so put in a hard page break and whatever page numbering you want.

Then define each section in the table. Type the section heading and press RETURN as many times as you want for spacing. Press **ALT-F5 Mark Text**, type **5** or **d** [Define], then type **4** or **a** [Define Table of Authorities]. WordPerfect prompts:

Section Number (1-16):

Type the section number and press **RETURN**. The definition for table of authorities 1 menu, shown in Figure 23-6, appears (you'd see similar menus for other sections). You now decide how the listings are to appear. I suggest using yes for all three entries. (You can also set new table of authorities

```
Definition for Table of Authorities 1

      1 - Dot Leaders                          Yes

      2 - Underlining Allowed                  No

      3 - Blank Line Between Authorities       Yes

















Selection: 0
```

Figure 23-6   The Definition for Table of Authorities 1 Menu

defaults, as Appendix A will show.) Press **RETURN** when you're finished
with the first section, add any spacing between sections, and continue defining
the others. WordPerfect inserts a [Def Mark:ToA] code for each section.

Finally you're ready to generate the table as you would any other. Or
are you? Apparently WordPerfect prefers that you add a correct beginning
page number for the actual text of the document, which normally follows the
table of authorities. So go to the top of the first page of text and set the page
number as you want it. If you don't add a page number to the beginning of
the actual text, WordPerfect gives you this message after it generates the table:

WARNING New page num not found between ToA def and first mark (Press any key)

But it still generates the table for you. To edit any full form name later,
position the cursor directly past the code. Then press **ALT-F5 Mark Text**,
type **5** or **d** [Define], and type **5** or **e** [Edit Table of Authorities Full Form].

Press **F7 Exit** when you're finished and supply the correct section number for the authority. Whew!

Creating Automatic Cross-References

The last topic concerns automatic cross-references. A cross-reference is a referral to some other spot in the document. Because the page breaks may change as you edit, you'd find it hard to keep track of cross-references if WordPerfect weren't there to help you. Cross-references can refer to other document text, footnotes, endnotes, page numbers, paragraph or outline numbers, or even graphics boxes (Chapter 34)!

The Ties That Bind

WordPerfect can't read, so you have to supply special codes to tell it about your cross-references. There are at least two codes: (1) a code at the *original* location of the reference in the text and (2) a code at the *target reference location*, that is, the spot to which you're referring. You tie the two together with an *ID name* that identifies the target. The ID name must be unique for the target so that WordPerfect can make the match later when you generate the references.

A cross-reference can refer to another location either ahead of or after the location of the reference. It can even refer to other elements of a master document (Chapter 25). You can also set up several cross-references that refer to the same target. That is, you just refer to the same target ID. Still, there must be at least one match between the two codes, reference and target. Because my editor's condition gets worse and worse the longer I take to write this book, I can only show you a few examples of how to work with cross-references!

The easiest way to mark cross-references is to mark both the reference and target at the same time. However, sometimes you'll know the location of one but you won't know the other yet. Not to worry: You can mark references and targets separately.

Caution: Make sure that *eventually* you mark both, though, before you attempt to generate the references. Otherwise, WordPerfect just ignores the cross-reference altogether, as you'll see in due time.

✔Retrieve the document LAREST.NDX again, or any other document into which you plan to insert cross-references.

Marking Both the Reference and the Target

Suppose you plan to include full-page illustrations of various types of food with this document, and you'll refer to them in the text. The illustrations will be at the end of the document. First, create a new blank page for the first illustration:

Press **HOME,HOME,DOWN ARROW**

to position the cursor at the end of the document, directly past the index.

Press **CTRL-RETURN**

to insert a hard page code.

 ✔Position the cursor at the end of the second paragraph about the El Colmao restaurant. If you didn't add two extra spaces, do so now (there's your end of paragraph trick again!).

 The first part of the cross-reference is just text within the document:

Type   **See Illustration, Page**

Press **SPACEBAR**

for spacing.

 Tip: Always make sure that the cross-reference is correctly spaced from the rest of the text. Here's where you insert a reference code. The code will refer to a page number that may change, so let WordPerfect keep track of the numbering for you:

Press **ALT-F5 Mark Text**

Type   **1** or **r** [Auto **R**ef]

 The mark text: automatic reference menu appears (Figure 23-7).

Type   **3** or **b** [Mark **B**oth Reference and Target]

 The tie reference to: menu appears, as in Figure 23-8. Notice Word-Perfect's message about how to select the target.

Type   **1** or **p** [**P**age Number]

WordPerfect returns to the document and prompts:

`Press Enter to select page.`

 That doesn't mean to press RETURN *yet!* First, go to the page to which you'll tie the reference.

Press **HOME,HOME,DOWN ARROW**

```
Mark Text: Automatic Reference

     1 - Mark Reference

     2 - Mark Target

     3 - Mark Both Reference and Target

















Selection: 0
```

Figure 23-7 The Mark Text: Automatic Reference Menu

You can use any cursor movement command, but you can't edit while WordPerfect is waiting for a target location. Make sure the cursor is directly past the target; here, you've moved to the top of the page directly past the soft page code.

Press   **RETURN**

to select this page.
WordPerfect now prompts for the target's ID name:

Target Name:

Type   **cuban food**

Press   **RETURN**

```
Tie Reference to:

     1 - Page Number

     2 - Paragraph/Outline Number

     3 - Footnote Number

     4 - Endnote Number

     5 - Graphics Box Number

After selecting a reference type, go to the location of the item you want to
reference in your document and press Enter to mark it as the "target".




Selection: 0
```

Figure 23-8   The Tie Reference To: Menu

WordPerfect doesn't distinguish the case of the target ID, so use lower-case to save time. You've now successfully tied the reference and target together, and you've given the target a unique ID name. WordPerfect returns to the location of the reference and supplies the correct page number.

Stop! You haven't finished the sentence yet! Always make sure about the rest of the text surrounding the reference.

Type

(That's a period to end the sentence.)

If you now reveal the codes, you'll see a [Ref] code at the reference location. The code includes the target's ID name and current page number. If you look at the end of the document, you'll see a corresponding [Target] reference code, again with the ID name.

Marking Several References to One Target

The next example shows you how to refer to the same target more than once in a document.

✔Go to the end of the document and insert another hard page code to create a new, blank page. This will be for an illustration of Mexican food. Then position the cursor directly under the period that ends the sentence *as well as the albondigas soup* in the sixth paragraph.

This time, because you've already referred to the illustrations in general, your message will be shorter:

Press   **SPACEBAR**

for spacing.

Type   **(Page**

(Note the open parenthesis.)

Press   **SPACEBAR**

for spacing.

Press   **ALT-F5 Mark Text**

Type   **1** or **r** [Auto <u>R</u>ef]

Type   **3** or **b** [Mark <u>B</u>oth Reference and Target]

Type   **1** or **p** [<u>P</u>age Number]

Press   **HOME,HOME,DOWN ARROW**

Press   **RETURN**

to set the page number.

Type   **mexican food**

for the target ID name.

Press   **RETURN**

Type   **)**

to complete the reference.

✔Now, repeat the steps to add a **(Page)** reference after *Sonora* in the next paragraph, but be careful! The target already exists, so do you have to mark it again? As it turns out, yes! After you type the text beginning—*(Page*—as in the previous example, press **ALT-F5 Mark Text**. Then type **1** or **r** [Auto Ref] and follow along:

Type   **3** or **b** [Mark Both Reference and Target]

Type   **1** or **p** [Page Number]

Press   **HOME,HOME,DOWN ARROW**

to position the cursor at the end of the document.

Press   **RETURN**

to set this page as the target.

WordPerfect understands that you want to use the same target ID, so it returns to the document and inserts the new [Ref] code. You now have two references to the same target.

Type   **)**

to complete the reference.

Tip: When you move the cursor, WordPerfect may split the page number from the word *Page* at the end of the line. Do you know how to overcome this problem? Right! Use a hard space instead of a regular space (Chapter 20). I'll let you do that on your own some time if you wish.

✔Save the document but leave it on the screen.

Marking Reference and Target Separately

This next example shows you how to mark the reference and target locations at different times. It also uses a footnote as the target reference instead of a page number. You'll first refer to the footnote; then you'll create it and the target separately.

✔Position the cursor at the end of the next paragraph about Tommy's restaurant. Insert two spaces to separate the last sentence from the new one you'll type. Then:

Type   **(Please see footnote**

Press   **SPACEBAR**

for spacing.

Press   **ALT-F5 Mark Text**

Type   **1** or **r** [Auto <u>R</u>ef]

Type   **1** or **r** [Mark <u>R</u>eference]

Type   **3** or **f** [Footnote <u>N</u>umber]

Type   `noteit`

Press   **RETURN**

for the target name.

    WordPerfect doesn't know where the target is yet, so it displays a ? at the reference location. This is its reminder that you haven't yet completed the reference. If you generate the references now, WordPerfect would still just show a question mark.

Type   `.)`

to complete the sentence.

    On the screen the text looks like this: `(Please see footnote ?.)` Suppose it's now later and you're ready to insert the target. That means adding the footnote, too.

    ✔Position the cursor at the end of the next paragraph on the Hampton's restaurants. This time, you want to attach the footnote reference to the sentence, so make sure the cursor is directly past the period. Then:

Press   **CTRL-F7 Footnote**

Type   **1** or **f** [<u>F</u>ootnote]

Type   **1** or **c** [<u>C</u>reate]

    Now, you could type the text of the note, but for the sake of example insert the target reference first. The order doesn't really matter, but you must insert the target within the note area.

Press   **ALT-F5 Mark Text**

Type   **1** or **r** [Auto <u>R</u>ef]

Type   **2** or **t** [Mark <u>T</u>arget]

    WordPerfect remembers the last target ID name, which just so happens to be the one you want. If, however, you were working on this document later, you'd have to type the *exact* ID name as you originally supplied in the reference code. Be careful!

Press   **RETURN**

to accept the target name.

Pretend you've now typed the text of the note and you're finished:

Press   **F7 Exit**

to save the new note.

Marking One Reference to Many Target Locations

Suppose the target occurs in several parts of the document and you want to refer to all occurrences of it. You need only mark the reference spot once, then mark each separate target location with the same target ID. That's how you get a result like this one: See also Mexican food, pages 2, 7, 10, 11. When it generates the references, WordPerfect separates each target page with a comma and space.

Generating the References

Wait! The ? hasn't disappeared! You must now generate the automatic references to update everything. There is no definition step, however:

Press   **ALT-F5 Mark Text**

Type   **6** or **g** [<u>G</u>enerate]

Type   **5** or **g** [<u>G</u>enerate Tables, Indexes, Automatic References, etc.]

Type   **y**

If you now look at the references, you'll see that WordPerfect has correctly updated them.

✔Save the document again, then clear the screen.

Wow! WordPerfect's power just goes on and on. The next chapter will show you how to use the ALT-F5 Mark Text key to keep track of the changes you make to a document. Carry on!

24

Redline, Strikeout, and Document Comparison

In this chapter you'll discover other uses of these commands . . .

ALT-F5 Mark Text (1) Remove redline and strikeout codes and struck text, (2) compare the screen and disk versions of a document and mark the differences

SHIFT-F8 Format Change the redline method

CTRL-F8 Font (1) Mark redline text, (2) mark strikeout text

. . . and you'll learn some new codes:

[REDLN] and [redln] Begin and end redlining

[STKOUT] and [stkout] Begin and end strikeout

In my discussion of a typical document history, I mentioned that a document may go through any number of drafts before it reaches its final version (Chapter 17). Often several people must review and correct a document draft. WordPerfect has *redline* and *strikeout* features to help you keep track of additions to and deletions from a document. WordPerfect can even *compare* two documents and mark the differences for you.

> ### DO WARM-UP

Preliminaries

Redlining is the process of marking text for possible addition to a document, while *strikeout* means marking text for possible deletion. WordPerfect now thinks of redline and strikeout as fonts, and so they've moved to the CTRL-F8 Font key. That means there must be begin and end font codes. Users of previous WordPerfect versions know that redline and strikeout were originally on the ALT-F5 Mark Text key. Well, that key still comes into play, as you'll see later.

The reason WordPerfect regards these two features as fonts is because redlined and struck sections print differently depending on your printer. You can change the printing defaults for redlining (discussed later) or strikeout (with the PTR utility, Chapter 36), but right now just understand the basics. To wit: either redline text prints in a different shading or font, or a special character prints in the left or right margin of every line that contains redlining. On my laser printer, for instance, a shading prints behind redlined text. Struck text is normally overprinted with a solid line or a line of hyphens. By the way, the print view may display the redlined text with the color red!

Once your boss or whoever else is in charge has approved the redlined and struck text, you can have WordPerfect remove the codes quickly. In fact, WordPerfect does more: It removes all redline and strikeout codes, leaves the redlined text, but deletes the struck text automatically!

Redlining

As in other chapters, you'll work with previous documents so you don't have to type your fingers to the bone. Actually, you can just follow along if you don't want to key in the examples, or use a different document.

✔Retrieve the LAREST document.

Because redline is a font, you have two ways to enter redline codes: (1) as you type new text or (2) around a block of existing text. When you redline new text, first insert the codes. Then type the text and press RIGHT ARROW once to move past the end code. Alternately, you could press CTRL-F8 Font, then type **3** or **n** [Normal] to return to the base font. When you redline a block, you set up the block and then select the font change.

Suppose your editor, like mine, doesn't like everything you write (just kidding!). She's going to make a suggested addition.

✔Position the cursor at the end of the first paragraph. Insert two spaces after the sentence if you haven't done so already. Then:

Press   **CTRL-F8 Font**

Type   **2** or **a** [Appearance]

Type   **8** or **r** [Redln]

The Pos number changes to the screen style or color that indicates redlining.

✔Type this sentence: **For example, a dinner for two normally costs less than $20, quite a bargain these days.**

WordPerfect inserts begin [REDLN] and end [redln] codes. Remember to move the cursor past the end code when you're finished:

Press   **RIGHT ARROW or DOWN ARROW**

Although you won't stop to redline a block, the procedure is the same as for all other font changes. That is, set up the block, then choose the font change from the CTRL-F8 Font key.

✔Save the document as LAREST.2 and leave it on the screen.

Strikeout

Now your editor is going to tear your fine prose apart (just kidding again!). Once in Guadalajara she contracted Montezuma's Revenge, so she *hates* Mexican food. She's decided to get rid of those sections that deal with Mexican food and to warn you accordingly. She'll strike out the text.

✔Position the cursor at the left margin of the sixth paragraph about the Talpa restaurant.

Most of the time, strikeout text is already in the document, so you'll use a block. Remember to include everything you want to strike (for instance, tabs) in the block.

Press   **ALT-F4 Block or F12 Block**

Press   **RETURN twice**

to extend the block to two paragraphs.

Press   **CTRL-F8 Font**

Type   **2** or **a** [A̲ppearance]

Type   **9** or **s** [S̲tkout]

WordPerfect displays strikeout as a different shading or color. There are now begin [STKOUT] and end [stkout] codes in the document.

Please don't confuse Strikeout with the Overstrike command. That command backspaces the printer to print one or more characters over another (Chapter 15). What's more, keep in mind that even though the text prints struck over with lines or hyphens to indicate that it will probably be deleted, you still haven't *officially* deleted it from the document yet. You'll do that in a moment.

✔Save the LAREST.2 document again. Print the page now to see the results but leave the document on the screen.

Did you see this message when you tried to print the page?

```
Document needs to be generated. Continue? (Y/N) No
```

That just means that WordPerfect has sensed the presence of redline and strikeout codes and "assumes" you want to remove the codes first. That's the "generate" part. You can safely type **y** to continue, and the printout shows the redlining and strikeout.

Tip: Often strikeout and redline text appear close together. For example, an editor may strike out a sentence and then suggest a replacement. Put the suggested addition right past the struck version so that you or others working on the project can quickly see the document's editorial history. What if you don't like the default redline or strikeout screen fonts? You can change the defaults (Appendix A).

Changing the Redline Method

If you don't like the way WordPerfect printed the redline, you can change what WordPerfect calls the *redline method*. Here's how (you don't have to follow these steps right now):

1. Press **SHIFT-F8 Format**.

2. Type **3** or **d** [Document].

3. Type **4** or **r** [Redline Method]. WordPerfect presents the redline method menu:

   ```
   Redline Method: 1 Printer Dependent; 2 Left; 3 Alternating: 1
   ```

   Depending on your printer, the default may be printer dependent or redlining as a box or vertical bar in the blank left margin space. Choice **3** [Alternating] prints the redline character in the left margin space on even numbered pages and in the right margin space on odd numbered pages.

4. Type your choice. If you select left or alternating, WordPerfect asks for the redline character and shows a little box:

   ```
   Redline character: ■
   ```

5. This does *not* represent any specific character, so be sure to supply your choice. Type the character and press **RETURN**. (The vertical bar is SHIFT-\, by the way.)

6. Press **F7 Exit** to return to the document.

The redline method change governs the *current* document only. See Appendix A for information about the other settings on the format: document menu.

Removing Strikeout and Redline Codes

Now assume that your editor has decided that the text she marked for deletion with the Strikeout command should be permanently removed from the document, while the redline text should be accepted as an addition to the document. WordPerfect gives you an easy way to remove the struck out text itself *and* the strikeout and redline codes, all in one fell swoop.

However, take care before you use this feature: WordPerfect doesn't stop and ask you to confirm the removal of each individual set of strikeout or redline codes. It just deletes them all quickly, deletes the struck text, and positions the cursor at the end of the document when the remove operation is finished.

Tip: Make a copy of your document just for safe measure.

The cursor can be anywhere in the document when you begin the remove operation:

Press   **ALT-F5 Mark Text**

Type   **6 or g** [Generate]

Type   **1 or r** [Remove Redline Markings and Strikeout Text from Document]

WordPerfect asks:

```
Delete redline markings and strikeout text? (Y/N) No
```

Type   **y**

There *is* one escape valve. You can use the F1 Cancel key to "undelete" the blocks that were struck out with the remove choice. The strikeout codes will be restored along with text, too. Remember that WordPerfect only "remembers" the last three deletions, so if there were many strikeout sections, you couldn't restore them all. In addition, make sure that the cursor is at the correct spot in the document before you restore a struck block. You can't undelete the removed codes.

If you don't want to remove *all* strikeout and redline codes, or if you don't want to delete strikeout text but you do want to delete the codes, you can't use the automatic remove feature. Instead, as with other begin and end codes, just delete either one of the two codes. If you have several sections of strikeout or redline text in a long document, use the ALT-F2 Replace command to find and delete the codes quickly.

That is, after you press ALT-F2 Replace, press the CTRL-F8 Font key as the code to be replaced. Because there are many font changes, you'll have to select the code carefully. When you delete strikeout codes in this fashion, you must also manually delete any text to be struck out of the document.

✔Clear the screen but don't save the document.

Comparing Two Documents

Okay, it's one thing to have someone enter redlined text and codes and strikeout codes manually. It's quite another thing to have WordPerfect do the entire operation for you! This is the *document comparison* feature. Word-Perfect compares whatever document is on the screen with another document on the disk. It then inserts *into the screen document only* redline text and codes and strikeout codes where there are differences between the screen and disk versions.

Tip: You can compare the document on the screen with the *same* document on the disk. That is, if you've made changes to the screen document and you want to see what those changes were, you can. However, keep in mind that WordPerfect uses whatever is the last saved version of the document on the disk.

There is one good rule to follow *before* you compare documents: Make sure you have a backup copy of the screen document with another file name in case you want to restore the document to its original form. That is, you may inadvertently save the document on the screen with the added redline and strikeout codes. If there's a backup copy, you have an escape valve.

Although you won't follow a specific example, here are the steps for comparing two documents:

1. Retrieve one of the documents you want to compare.

2. Press **ALT-F5 Mark Text**.

3. Type **6** or **g** [Generate].

4. Type **2** or **c** [Compare Screen and Disk Documents and Add Redline and Strikeout]. WordPerfect prompts:

   Other Document:

   and supplies the last document name.

5. Type the document's file name, including any drive or path designator, or edit the file name on the edit line. Then press **RETURN**. WordPerfect displays a counter as it compares the two documents.

After it compares the documents, WordPerfect inserts redline codes around text that doesn't appear in the disk version. It inserts strikeout codes and a copy of any text that's in the disk version but not on the original screen document. If WordPerfect detects that a section has moved, it inserts this line ahead of the text:

THE FOLLOWING TEXT WAS MOVED

and this line after the text:

THE PRECEDING TEXT WAS MOVED

WordPerfect encloses both messages in strikeout codes. You can then save the new screen document if you wish, have WordPerfect remove the codes and struck text, or clear the screen without saving the document.

Dear Reader, with WordPerfect's help, your editorial skills are increasing rapidly. Now turn your attention to a truly "masterful" feature.

Mastering Master Documents

In this chapter you'll discover other uses of this command . . .

ALT-F5 Mark Text   (1) Set up a master document, (2) expand a master document, (3) condense a master document

. . . and you'll learn some new codes:

[Subdoc]   Location of a subdocument in a condensed master document

[Subdoc End]   End of a subdocument in an expanded master document

[Subdoc Start]   Start of a subdocument in an expanded master document

This chapter rounds out the discussion of the editorial niceties that are available to you on the ALT-F5 Mark Text key. You'll recall that normally WordPerfect can generate tables, lists, indexes, and cross-references only for the document on the screen (Chapter 23). That may be unrealistic if you write books, as I do, and you maintain each chapter as a separate document file. With the *master document* feature, you can generate composite tables and so on for an entire writing project.

DO WARM-UP

Master Documents Explained

As its name implies, a master document is a *controlling* document. It's a regular WordPerfect document that contains a list of all documents in a project, in their correct order. WordPerfect refers to each document within a master document as a *subdocument*, or *subdoc*. The chapters of a book are a prime example of subdocs that are part of an entire master document project. In a sense, you can think of the master document as the structure of your entire project. That is, it lists the subdocs in the order in which they'll print in the project.

You may be thinking that master documents take up a lot of disk space. After all, if they include all the subdocs, they'd be very large. Well, you'd be right and wrong! Most of the time a master document is a *condensed* version of the entire project. It just lists the names of the subdocs and as such is quite tiny. When you want to work with a master document—for instance, to generate tables, lists, indexes, and cross-references—you must *expand* the master document. It's only then that the master document grows to its real size.

When it expands a master document, WordPerfect substitutes the text of each subdoc at the location of the subdoc's file name in the master document. If you make editing changes to a subdoc in the expanded master document, you have the option of saving the changes to the original subdoc file. All numbering of paragraphs, outlines, graphics items (Chapter 34), footnotes, endnotes, and pages are consistent throughout the entire master document. Once you've generated everything you want, you can condense the master document back to its normal size. One of the beauties of master documents is that you can work with all your subdocs individually. Never one to pass up a chance to harp, I'll just remind you again that the modular approach to file management is essential. Deal with your documents as modular units, then use a master document later for the entire project.

It's also sensible to edit subdocs as separate entities, because you'll need a lot of memory for an expanded master document. What's more, WordPerfect may slow up when it works with large documents.

Tip: You can print the condensed master document and get a fast overview of the project's structure. If you want to print the entire project, you must first expand the master document.

A master document can contain text and even formatting codes. For instance, it probably will contain the composite tables and index. If you don't include any special line and page formats in the subdocs but rather include them at the beginning of the master document, the master document's formatting will govern all subdocs when you've expanded the master document.

Caution: If there *are* formatting changes in any subdocs, WordPerfect honors them in the subdoc text when it expands the master document. It always honors the last format changes it sees.

So the basic rule of thumb you should learn when you work with master documents is: Try to consolidate all formatting requirements in the master document. You don't *have* to follow this rule, but it will make your work a lot easier.

Creating a Master Document

I'm going to ask you to pretend that you're writing a book like this one (heaven help you!) and you're keeping each chapter in a different file. WP.I, for instance, contains the Introduction, Prelude, and all other "front matter," as my editor calls it. The chapters are in files like WP.1, WP.2, and so on. Suppose you want to create a master document for the entire book. Here are the basic steps (I'll give you some more tips later):

1. Clear the screen.
2. Enter any format changes for the entire project and other text that pertains to the project. A later figure will show what I mean.
3. Press **ALT-F5 Mark Text**.
4. Type **2** or **s** [Subdoc]. WordPerfect prompts:

   Subdoc Filename:

5. Type the file name, including any drive or path designator, and press **RETURN**. WordPerfect inserts a [Subdoc] code with the file name, and the subdoc's file name appears in a box on the screen.
6. Continue inserting all subdocs in the master document.
7. When you're finished, save the master document.

Caution: If you keep a master document on one drive or in one directory, and subdocs in another, make sure you tell WordPerfect where everything is!

Formatting and Editing Tips

You can edit the master document as any other to insert text or codes. Figure 25-1, for example, shows the first page of my master document, WPBOOK, for this entire book project. What do you see?

Well, first of all you see a *title page* for the book. Below that you see a hard page code so that the title page prints separately from the first subdoc, WP.I. Notice also that hard page codes appear after each subdoc. Thus, every chapter starts on a new page when I print the master document!

The idea here, of course, is that you can include other text that's germane to the project in the master document. Or you can have the text in the subdocs. For example, I keep the chapter titles in the subdocs, where they belong!

What about page formatting and pagination? Take a look at the codes that appear at the very top of the master document. I've listed them in a column, but they run together on the screen:

```
            "The Best Book of: WordPerfect"

                Second, Revised Edition

                By Vincent Alfieri, Ph.D.

         Copyright (c) 1987, 1988 by Vincent Alfieri, Ph.D.

                All Rights Reserved
=================================================================

 ┌─────────────────────────────────────────────────────────────┐
 │ Subdoc: WP.I                                                  │
 └─────────────────────────────────────────────────────────────┘

=================================================================

 ┌─────────────────────────────────────────────────────────────┐
 │ Subdoc: WP.1                                                  │
 └─────────────────────────────────────────────────────────────┘

=================================================================

 C:\WP\WPBOOK                          Doc 1 Pg 1 Ln 1" Pos 1"
```

Figure 25-1   A Typical Master Document

```
[Force:Odd]
[Footer A:1;"Best Book of: WordPerfect" [-] Page ^B]
[Suppress:Pg BC,FA]
```

Just for good measure, I inserted a Force Page command to make sure that this page prints on an odd page. I inserted the same command before every subdoc in the master document, too, so that each chapter starts on an odd page. Then I set up the footer for the entire project but suppressed the printing of the footer on the title page (FA in the suppress code). The BC in the suppress code means to print the page number on this first page at the bottom center.

As it turns out, I'll have to alter my pagination when I insert a table of contents and lists for the master document. But you get the idea about how creative you can be!

Note: The page formatting only governs the subdocs after you've expanded the master document. If you want to restart footnote or endnote numbering with 1 for each chapter, insert numbering change codes either at the beginnings of the chapters or directly ahead of each subdoc location in the master document.

Expanding the Master Document

Once you've created the master document to your liking, you can expand it to print the entire project or finish any cross-references between subdocs (discussed later in the chapter). Make sure you've included all the subdocs you need, although you can always add them later.

Note: Version 4.2 users: Retrieve and save documents from previous versions at least once in WordPerfect 5.0 before you use the documents as subdocs in a master document. To expand the master document:

1. Clear the screen and retrieve the master document.

2. Press **ALT-F5 Mark Text**.

3. Type **6** or **g** [<u>G</u>enerate].

4. Type **3** or **e** [<u>E</u>xpand Master Document].

WordPerfect tells you:

```
Expanding master document
```

If WordPerfect can't locate a subdoc, it informs you in no uncertain terms:

```
Subdoc not found:
```

Press F1 Cancel, correct your mistake, and try again. WordPerfect will expand the master document up to the point it can't find a subdoc.

Once it's expanded the master document, WordPerfect displays other codes that indicate the beginning and end of each subdoc. The codes are [Subdoc Start] and [Subdoc End], and they include the subdoc's file name. You'll see boxes as reminders to you about the subdoc divisions. You can search for these codes throughout a document to locate a particular subdoc.

Cross-References in the Master Document

You'll recall that sometimes you won't know the exact target or reference location for every cross-reference. If your cross-references "cross over" from one subdoc to other subdocs in a master document, make sure you complete the cross-references when you expand the master document. Otherwise, WordPerfect won't be able to display the correct reference location.

Caution: Save the subdocs individually if you've edited them in the expanded master document. That way, the next time you expand the master document, WordPerfect can find the cross-references.

Generating Tables, Lists, Indexes, and Cross-References

To generate tables and so on in the master document requires a multistep approach:

1. Mark each table, list, index, and cross-reference entry in each subdoc as you learned in Chapter 23.

   Tip: Don't forget (as I did the first time) to include chapter titles as table of contents level one entries!

2. Save each subdoc.

3. Expand the master document. Make sure that cross-references between subdocs are complete! If you don't have any cross-references between subdocs, you don't have to expand the master document (discussed below).

4. Define the tables, lists, and indexes and their location in the master document.

   Tip: Include the correct hard page codes and pagination, too, or set them up after you generate.

5. Generate the tables and so on from the expanded master document.

6. Condense the master document. The tables and so on stay in the master document. Later, to print the whole kit and caboodle, expand the master document first.

7. Save the condensed master document.

Tip: Make sure you have all pagination setups correct in the master document and all page breaks the way you want them *before* you generate. That way, any table, list, or index generation will use the right page numbers.

As it turns out, you *can* generate tables and so on from a condensed master document. After it is finished, WordPerfect asks:

```
Update Subdocs? (Y/N) Yes
```

This message means you can save the subdocs again if you think any changes have been made during generation. If you have cross-references between subdocs, type **y**; otherwise, type **n**. WordPerfect generates the tables, lists, index, and cross-references, then returns to the condensed master document.

Editing an Expanded Master Document

You can make any changes you like to the text of an expanded master document, including the tables, lists, and index. However, it makes more sense to condense the master document and edit its text then, because the document will be smaller and hence easier to manage. Edit your subdocs individually and your master document in its condensed form to save time.

Condensing the Master Document

To condense a master document, follow these simple steps:

1. Press **ALT-F5 Mark Text**.
2. Type **6** or **g** [<u>G</u>enerate].
3. Type **4** or **o** [C<u>o</u>ndense Master Document]. WordPerfect prompts:

   ```
   Save Subdocs (Y/N)? Yes
   ```

4. If you've made any editing changes to the subdoc text in the expanded master document, type **y**; otherwise, type **n**.

   WordPerfect says:

```
Condensing master document
```

If you told WordPerfect to save the subdocs, the first time it comes to subdoc text in the master document, it stops and prompts:

```
Replace <file>? 1 Yes; 2 No; 3 Replace All Remaining: : 0
```

where <file> is the first subdoc file name. You can selectively replace subdocs, or just type **3** or **r** [<u>R</u>eplace All Remaining] to have WordPerfect replace all of them. Soon you'll see just master document text and the subdoc boxes again.

Nesting Documents

You aren't limited to one master document and its subdocs. A master document can contain another master document as its subdoc! Similarly, a subdoc can contain other subdocs. This process is called *nesting*. However, until

443

you're quite familiar with the whole master document approach, I recommend that you not nest documents at all. Simple is best here.

Whew! That was some journey through the world of the bibliophile! Actually, this section of the book isn't complete yet. For good measure I've tacked on a discussion of one last feature that can help you create polished documents: style sheets.

A Matter of Styles

In this chapter you'll learn the following new command . . .

Function Key Command

ALT-F8 Style (1) Create, edit, and use styles, (2) update the style library

. . . and you'll learn some new codes:

[Open Style] Turn an open style on

[Style Off] Turn a paired style off

[Style On] Turn a paired style on

You've already learned how to create format documents that contain formatting codes and text, then use these documents as boilerplates when you want to format a new document. You can also maintain an entire library of format documents and insert them whenever you need a different format (Chapter 14). Well, WordPerfect has another and more powerful way to control formats: its style feature. Learning how to use styles will take you some time, but it's time well spent.

DO WARM-UP

Styles in a Nutshell

A *style* is just a particular format that may contain formatting codes and even text. For example, the chapter headings of this book are in one style, the subheadings are in another style, and the body of the text in yet another style. Styles often include font characteristics and placement on the page. That is, the chapter heads are in a large, bold font and are centered on the page, and the subheads print in a smaller font and are in the left margin "gutter." The book's text is in yet another font, proportionally spaced by the way, and uses a certain line length.

You can create as many different styles as you wish for a particular project. Using the example of this book again, you could set up a "chapter head" style, a "subhead" style, and a "body text" style, each with different formatting characteristics. You collect all the styles in a separate *style document*. The **ALT-F8 Style** key controls most aspects of style management. Version 4.2 users: This key has changed.

Once you establish the styles you need, you *attach* the style document to your regular document. Then you attach styles from the style document to specific parts of the document you're editing. WordPerfect refers to this operation as turning a style *on* and *off*. For example, you'd attach the chapter head style to each chapter opening by turning the style on and then typing the text. Because you don't want this style for all text in the chapter, you turn the style off at the correct spot. You can also attach a style to a block of existing text, just as you make font changes. WordPerfect saves the style document with the regular document.

So far you're probably thinking that format documents work the same way as style documents. You'd be right *and* wrong. Yes, you insert styles very much as you insert format documents. However, you can't turn a format document "on" or "off": You just use another format document to change the format again. The other major difference between format documents and styles is that, when you change the style or style document that's associated with a document, WordPerfect reformats the document that uses those styles automatically!

You can also have different style documents that contain styles with the same name. When you switch style documents, WordPerfect reformats any document that uses the style. For example, suppose you create a style document called DRAFT with three styles: chapter head, subhead, and text. These styles use boldface for the chapter style, underlined text for subheads, and a standard Courier-type font for text. Figure 26-1 shows part of a sample printed page of the document.

Later when the document is in its final form, you attach another style document called FINAL. It contains three styles with the *same* names as DRAFT, but their characteristics are different. The chapter head style is in a larger font, subheads are in a smaller, bold font, and text is proportionally spaced. When you attach this new style document to the original document,

26

A Matter of Styles

You've already learned how to create format documents that contain
formatting codes and text, then use these documents as boilerplates
when you want to format a new document. You can also maintain an
entire library of format documents and insert them whenever you
need a different format (Chapter 14). Well, WordPerfect has another
and more powerful way to control formats: its style feature.
Learning how to use styles will take you some time, but it's time
well spent.

Styles in a Nutshell

A style is just a particular format that may contain formatting
codes and even text. For example, the chapter headings of this book
are in one style, the subheadings are in another style, and the
body of the text in yet another style. Styles often include font
characteristics and placement on the page. That is, the chapter
heads are in a large, bold font and are centered on the page, while
the subheads print in a smaller font and are flush to the left
margin. The book's text is in yet another font, proportionally-
spaced by the way, and uses a certain line length.

You can create as many different styles as you wish for a
particular project. Using the example of this book again, you could
set up a "chapter head" style, a "subhead" style, and a "body text"
style, each with different formatting characteristics. You collect
all the styles in a separate style document. The ALT-F8 Style key
controls most aspects of style management. Version 4.2 users: This
key has changed.

Figure 26-1   A Document Printed with Draft Styles

WordPerfect reformats the text associated with each style. Figure 26-2 shows
how the same page would print.

Tips

It's easiest to set up styles *first* and then attach them to a new document as
you type. If you attach a style to an existing document, you have more thinking
to do. Why? Well, consider a chapter head style. It contains an instruction
to center the text, put it in a boldface font, then add three blank lines for
spacing. Suppose you attach this style to a chapter head that's already centered
and three blank lines above the text. WordPerfect would add *more* center
codes and blank lines! So, one basic tip is this: When you work with styles,
put all the formatting code in the styles, *not* in the document itself.

Planning is the essence of my second tip. Think about the styles you
want and plan how you'll use them before you actually work with styles.

26

A Matter of Styles

You've already learned how to create format documents that contain formatting codes and text, then use these documents as boilerplates when you want to format a new document. You can also maintain an entire library of format documents and insert them whenever you need a different format (Chapter 14). Well, WordPerfect has another and more powerful way to control formats: its style feature. Learning how to use styles will take you some time, but it's time well spent.

Styles in a Nutshell

A style is just a particular format that may contain formatting codes and even text. For example, the chapter headings of this book are in one style, the subheadings are in another style, and the body of the text in yet another style. Styles often include font characteristics and placement on the page. That is, the chapter heads are in a large, bold font and are centered on the page, while the subheads print in a smaller font and are flush to the left margin. The book's text is in yet another font, proportionally-spaced by the way, and uses a certain line length.

You can create as many different styles as you wish for a particular project. Using the example of this book again, you could set up a "chapter head" style, a "subhead" style, and a "body text" style, each with different formatting characteristics. You collect all the styles in a separate style document. The ALT-F8 Style key controls most aspects of style management. Version 4.2 users: This key has changed.

Figure 26-2   The Same Document Printed with Final Styles

Think about what formatting can be part of each style. *Plan ahead!* As Ben Franklin said, "An ounce of prevention is worth a pound of cure."

My third and last tip is the most important: Don't rush into styles willy-nilly. Take your time.

How to Work with Styles

There are several steps to working with styles. I'll list them as generalities here, then go on to explain them in an example:

1. Determine the styles you need and create them. You can edit styles, too, if you have to change them later.

2. Save the styles in a style document. This is just a WordPerfect document that contains only the styles and their characteristics.

3. Retrieve the document to which you want to attach the styles, then attach the style document.

4. Attach styles to specific parts of the regular document.

5. Save the results.

Once you create a style document, you can attach it to other documents.

Characteristics of a Style

When you create a style, you give it certain characteristics:

1. The style's *name* is a short tag by which you identify the style in the document. A style name can contain at most 11 characters.

2. The style's *type* can be one of two varieties: (1) paired or (2) open.

     Think of a *paired* style as a set of begin and end codes. Unlike normal begin and end font changes, however, paired styles automatically revert to the original formatting when you turn the paired style off. Because the comment code separates the "begin" and "end" formatting sections within a paired style, you can't insert a normal comment code within a style definition.

     An *open* style is a style that you can't turn off. You turn it on once, and it affects the document from that point forward.

     Tip: Use open styles only at the beginning of a document, for example, for page formatting.

3. The style *description* is a longer title that identifies more clearly what the style does.

4. The formatting *codes* and text that apply to the style, such as line spacing, margin, or font changes.

5. How you want the *enter*, the RETURN, key to work in a style. You can have the enter key act as normal to insert hard returns, or it can turn a style on or off. You'll see how in a moment.

Well, I think you've had enough preliminaries! Get a good grip on yourself, Dear Reader, and forge ahead.

Creating Styles

The example you'll use is the beginning of another chapter from your book on Beethoven. Your first order of business is to create the styles that you need. There will be four styles: (1) an open document style that controls page formatting, (2) a paired style for the chapter headings, (3) a paired style from the body text, and (4) a paired indent style for quotes. On a clear screen, do this:

Press   **ALT-F8 Style**

WordPerfect presents the styles screen that will soon list the styles you create. At the moment the screen is blank except for this menu at the bottom:

1 On; 2 Off; 3 Create; 4 Edit; 5 Delete; 6 Save; 7 Retrieve; 8 Update: 4

An Open Style

The first style, Doc, will be an open style:

Type   **3** or **c** [Create]

WordPerfect presents the styles: edit menu (Figure 26-3).

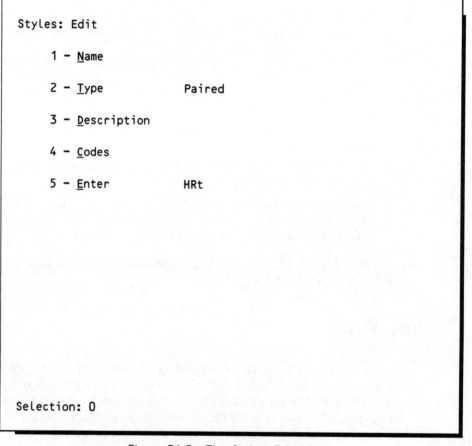

```
Styles: Edit

    1 - Name

    2 - Type          Paired

    3 - Description

    4 - Codes

    5 - Enter         HRt
```

```
Selection: 0
```

Figure 26-3   The Styles: Edit Menu

Type	**1** or **n** [<u>N</u>ame]

Type	**Doc**

Press	**RETURN**

for the style's name tag.

Type	**2** or **t** [<u>T</u>ype]

WordPerfect prompts:

Type: 1 <u>P</u>aired; 2 <u>O</u>pen: 0

Type	**2** or **o** [<u>O</u>pen]

Because you've chosen an open style, WordPerfect won't let you change the enter key. The enter key has significance only in paired styles.

Type	**3** or **d** [<u>D</u>escription]

Type	**Document Format**

Press	**RETURN**

for the description of what the style does.

Type	**4** or **c** [<u>C</u>odes]

WordPerfect presents a split screen to reveal the codes you'll now enter into the style. This style will only have two codes, one to print a footer and one to turn widow and orphan protect on. (Bear with me! Later you'll change the style and add more codes.)

✔Use the SHIFT-F8 Format key to turn widow and orphan control on. Then go into the edit area for Footer A. Make sure you tell WordPerfect that the footer is to print on all pages. Then set up the footer like this:

Type	**"Inside Beethoven" - Chapter 3**

Press	**ALT-F6 Flush Right**

Press	**SHIFT-F5 Date/Outline**

Type	**2** or **c** [Date <u>C</u>ode]

Press	**RETURN**

for a hard return.

Type   **`Draft Number 1`**

Press   **F7 Exit** twice

to save the footer and return to the codes screen.
You're now finished setting up this style, so:

Press   **F7 Exit**

to return to the styles screen.

WordPerfect lists your new style name, type, and description. Of course, styles can be—and often are—much more complex. They can contain lengthy sections of text and many different codes.

Paired Styles

The other three styles will be the default, paired. Follow these steps to create the Chapter style that will also make special use of the RETURN key.

✔Create a new style. For the name, type **Chap**; for the description, type **Chapter Openings**. Leave the style's type as paired. Then:

Type   **4** or **c** [Codes]

What's this? WordPerfect presents a comment box with this message:

`Place Style On Codes above, and Style Off Codes below.`

That means WordPerfect wants to know what the various on and off formatting codes will be when you turn the style on and off. The cursor is above the comment box. This style will center and bold the chapter openings, so:

Press   **SHIFT-F6 Center**

Press   **F6 Bold**

to enter the on codes.

Now, move below the comment box to enter the off codes:

Press   **RIGHT ARROW**

Press   **F6 Bold**

to insert the end bold code.

Press   **RETURN**

to insert the end center code and a hard return.

Press   **F7 Exit**

to return to the styles: edit menu.

    Finally, you want the RETURN key to turn this style off, then on, because you'll use it for more than one line in the chapter openings. Later, you'll see more clearly what I mean. For the moment, trust me:

Type   **5** or **e** [Enter]

WordPerfect prompts:

`Enter: 1 Hrt; 2 Off; 3 Off/On: 0`

Type   **3** or **o** [Off/On]

Press   **F7 Exit**

to return to the style screen.

    The next style will be for the body text.

    ✔Create a new style. For the name, type **Text**; for the description, type **Body Text**. Leave the style's type as paired and the enter choice as the default hard return. The format will be double spaced, with the default left and right margins. Go into the codes screen and use the SHIFT-F8 Format key to change the line spacing to double *above* the comment box. Don't enter any off codes below the comment box, though. Press **F7 Exit** enough times to return to the styles screen.

    The final style, Indent, will be for single spaced, indented quotes. This time you'll change the RETURN key so that it turns off the style.

    ✔Create a new style. For the name, type **Indent**; for the description, type **Indented Quotes**. Leave the style's type as paired. Go into the codes screen and use the SHIFT-F8 command to change the line spacing to single above the comment box. Then:

Press   **SHIFT-F4 ▸Indent◂**

to indent from both margins.

Press   **RIGHT ARROW**

to move below the comment box.

Press   **RETURN**

to end the indent.

Press   **F7 Exit**

to return to the styles: edit menu.
Finally, this style will use the RETURN key to turn off the style automatically:

Type   **5** or **e** [Enter]

Type   **2** or **f** [Off]

Press   **F7 Exit**

to return to the styles screen.

Creating Styles from Existing Codes

Although you won't stop to do it, I mentioned that you can attach a style to existing text. Just block the text, press **ALT-F8 Style**, and select the style. Similarly, you can create a *paired* style from codes and text that are already in a document. Block the codes and text, then press **ALT-F8 Style** and type **3** or **c** [Create].

 Caution: WordPerfect only inserts begin font change codes into a paired style that you create in this fashion. Make sure you insert end codes past the comment code in the new style with specific paragraphs of text.

Saving Styles in a Style Document

Okay, you've created the styles, but you haven't really saved them to disk yet. Make sure you save the styles; otherwise, when you exit WordPerfect you'll lose them and have to start over. You are now ready to save the four styles in a style document.

 Caution: Never save style documents with the F10 Save key. Always work with styles from the ALT-F8 Style key:

Type   **6** or **s** [Save]

Type   **draft.sty**

Press   **RETURN**

Tip: Because styles documents are special, give them a unique and easy-to-identify extension. I use .STY for all style documents. By the way, WordPerfect maintains style documents on the default drive or in the default directory, but you can use another. See The Style Library later in the chapter.

✔ Press **F1 Cancel** to leave the styles screen, then use the **F7 Exit** key to clear the screen.

But the screen is already clear! However, when you clear the screen, WordPerfect also clears the styles. I'm asking you to do this so that you understand the next section.

Attaching a Style Document

You're now almost ready to begin typing the new chapter, but first you want to attach the style document to this new document. WordPerfect uses the word *retrieve*, but you must still work with the ALT-F8 Style key.

Caution: Never retrieve a style document with the normal SHIFT-F10 Retrieve command, or from the file listing.

Press	**ALT-F8 Style**
Type	**7** or **r** [Retrieve]
Type	**draft.sty**
Press	**RETURN**
Press	**F7 Exit**

to return to the document.

Note: If you attach one style document, then attach another, WordPerfect *appends* the styles from the second style document to the styles already on the styles screen. If there are style names that match, WordPerfect asks if you want to replace the original styles:

```
Style(s) already exist. Replace? (Y/N) No
```

Type **y** to update the styles, or **n** to append only those styles with dissimilar names. The moral: Be careful when you work with styles!

Attaching Individual Styles

Now you're ready to attach the styles to your new document. You'll attach the first style, Doc, at the beginning:

Press   **ALT-F8 Style**

With the ARROW keys, highlight the Doc style. Then:

Type   1 or o [<u>O</u>n]

WordPerfect attaches the style and returns to the document. If you reveal the codes, you'll see an [Open Style] code with the style's name. Now you want to attach the paired Chap style:

✔Go into the styles screen, highlight the Chap style, and type 1 or o [<u>O</u>n].

Because this style contains a center code, WordPerfect moves the cursor to the middle of the line. Type the first line of the chapter head:

Press   **CAPS LOCK**

Type   `CHAPTER 3`

Press   **RETURN** twice

for spacing.

What happened? Because you set up the RETURN key to turn the style off and then on again, the style is now on! Don't worry:

Type   `Tales of the Vienna Woes`

then stop.

WordPerfect inserts [Style On] and [Style Off] codes around the text. These codes represent paired styles, and they show the style name and other format codes that are part of the style's characteristics. If you press RETURN, WordPerfect will continue to turn the style off and on. Here's how to turn the style off totally:

Press   **ALT-F8 Style**

Type   2 or f [O<u>f</u>f]

Now you can type the body text but first attach the correct style:

✔Press **RETURN** twice for spacing. Then go into the styles screen, highlight and turn on the Text style. Type the following paragraph but *leave* the cursor at the end of the paragraph:

The period from 1812 to 1815 is one of bad feelings and even worse living conditions for Beethoven. Although he had been in Vienna for some time and was familiar with the city, he continually refers to himself as an outsider. In one letter to his family in Bonn, Beethoven complains:

You now want to attach the Indent style, but where's the cursor? Reveal the codes to see what I mean. Aha! The cursor is ahead of the [Style Off] code, so you first have to move *past* the code. This is just like turning off font changes:

Press   **RIGHT ARROW**

to move past the code.

You could also go into the styles menu and type **2** of **f** [O_ff] to move past the end code of a paired style.

Press   **RETURN** enough times

for four blank lines, but watch the Ln number to make sure!

✔Go into the styles screen, highlight and turn on the Indent style. Then type this paragraph, but leave the cursor at the end of the paragraph:

Ach! Vienna is overwhelming me to no end! The crowds are exasperating, and I can't relate to the inhabitants with their boorish accent. The glittering shops near the Opera entice and repel me at the same time. I can hear them whispering as I walk by: "There goes Beethoven, that poor excuse of a composer who can't afford our finery." The food is too heavy and has wreaked havoc on my intestines. Rents are unbelievable. In short, I'm an outsider looking in, and I don't like what I see.

✔When you're finished, press **RETURN** enough times for spacing. Because you've defined the RETURN key to turn the style off, you don't have to move past the off code. Now, turn on the Text style, and type the next paragraph:

As if these feelings weren't bad enough, Beethoven was suffering from a problem that would plague him all his life. Two days before the date of the same letter, Beethoven's banker had pronounced the bad news that the young composer had spent his last groschen. In a word, Beethoven was broke. He continues:

✔Finally, move the cursor past the style off code, use the RETURN key to space down, turn on the Indent style, and type the last paragraph:

If you can, please send me a care package with all those goodies that Mutti makes so well. And, by the way, I could use a little spare cash if there's any lying around. Over and above everything else, Vienna is frightfully expensive.

✔Save the document as CHAPTER.3, but leave it on the screen. Print it or view the printout if you wish.

Changing Styles

Whew! That was a lot of extra work, but now you'll understand the power of styles. This section shows you how to *edit* a style document to create a new one, and in the process change the formatting for the chapter.

Suppose that you now want to print your chapter in a more polished manner, with proportionally spaced fonts. You'll set up a style document for final printouts, and you'll even use the original styles as the basis. That way, you save a lot of keystrokes, and when you attach the edited styles WordPerfect updates the document. It can do this because the style names are the same.

✔Go into the styles screen and highlight the Text style. Then:

Type   4 or e [Edit]

Type   4 or c [Codes]

✔Insert a base font change code that uses any proportionally spaced font on your printer, such as Times Roman 12 point. Make sure the code is past the line format changes but in front of the comment code. Then press **F7 Exit** enough times to return to the document screen.

Well I'll be darned! WordPerfect reformats the body text with the new font. But why didn't WordPerfect reformat the chapter heads or indented sections? Think! Well, the Chap style uses the base font, and the Text style is paired, so it's always off when you use the Indent style. You now have to edit the Chap and Indent styles:

✔Go into the style screen, highlight the Chap style, edit its codes to insert the same base font change as in the Text style. Make sure it's past the format codes but in front of the comment code. Do the same for the Indent style. Then return to the document.

And there you are! WordPerfect reformats everything correctly. Well, almost everything. If you print the document now, you'll notice that the footer prints in the default base font. That's because you didn't enter a base font change in the Doc style. Do it now if you wish.

Some astute reader may have noticed that you can insert a font change in just the Doc style, because it's an open style and will govern the rest of the document. That's correct. I took you down the straight-and-narrow path to emphasize that you may want different font changes in different sections.

Question: I've made one mistake—where is it? *Answer:* You should change the footer text in the Doc style, because you no longer want it to print *Draft Number 1*. If you wish, change the footer to print *Final Version*, or something similar.

You're almost finished:

✔Save the CHAPTER.3 document again. Then go into the styles screen and save the newly edited styles to a new style document called FINAL.STY.

You now have two style documents, DRAFT.STY and FINAL.STY, that use the same style names but give different results. You can attach them as you wish to other documents, perhaps the other chapters in your Beethoven book. (Remember to update the footer text to show the new chapter number!)

Deleting a Style

You can highlight a style name and type **5** or **d** [Delete]. WordPerfect prompts:

```
Delete Style (Y/N)? No
```

However, this action doesn't delete the style codes in the document. Be careful when you delete styles!

Tip: WordPerfect won't let you create a new style with the same name as an existing style. Either delete the original style, or edit it.

The Style Library

If you want a set of default styles that WordPerfect automatically attaches to *every* document, use the style library. However, keep in mind that you may not always want to attach the styles in the style library to all documents. What's more, the styles don't affect a document until you attach them manually to sections of the document.

Caution: Consider this a very advanced option! My suggestion is: Until you're comfortable with styles, create separate style documents and attach them only when you need them. You can always set up your own default formats that WordPerfect will use anyway.

You must first tell WordPerfect the name and location of the style library as one of the setup options (see Location of Files in Appendix A). I suggest LIBRARY.STY or MASTER.STY for the name. Then, whenever you retrieve and save a document, WordPerfect attaches the styles in the style library.

If you use the style library but you want to attach different styles, you must delete all style library styles individually to get rid of them. To update the style library, go into the style screen and type **8** or **u** [Update]. Then save the new style library document.

Dear Reader, I've only been able to scratch the surface of styles. They are perhaps the most powerful formatting tool available in WordPerfect, but it'll take you a while to get your styles the way you want them. Before you do, continue your exploration of WordPerfect and in the process discover an entirely different world.

Merge Features

Chapter

27

Form Letter Mailings, Part 1

In this chapter you'll learn the following new commands . . .

Function Key Commands

F9 Merge R	Insert an end of field merge code
SHIFT-F9 Merge Codes	Display and select merge codes
CTRL-F9 Merge/Sort	Begin a merge

. . . and you'll learn some *merge* codes:

^E End of record marker in the secondary document

^F Field number indicator in the primary document

^N Go to the next record in the secondary document

^P Use the enclosed primary document (two codes required)

^R End of field marker in the secondary document

^T "Type" (print) the merged document and clear memory

The next few chapters explore WordPerfect's extensive *merge* capabilities. You're on a different tack from standard word processing now. In fact, I suggest you take your time studying the examples and "merge with caution," just as you would on the freeway. The secret to successful merge operations is to be patient, precise, and careful. There are a variety of new codes involved with merge tasks, so you may not get the results you want if you're not on your toes.

Still, the merge feature can be one of your most hard working friends and well worth the effort to learn. You have a head start, because you can use the examples as the patterns to follow for your own needs.

Caution: Version 4.2 users must retrieve and save all their merge documents at least once in WordPerfect 5.0 before they begin a merge. Merge codes are now on the SHIFT-F9 Merge Codes key, and ALT-F9 has other functions.

> **DO WARM-UP**

Merge in a Nutshell

By far the most frequent use of the merge is for form letter mailings. If you've ever had to type the *same* form letter 100 times, you know what boring and back breaking work it can be. Never again! By setting up the form letter as a WordPerfect merge document, you need type the letter only once. The program then plugs in a different name and address from a separate document for each letter.

The term *merge* thus refers to the process of combining information from one or more documents into another. In the case of form letters, a merge involves putting name and address information at the appropriate locations in the letter itself. You can also merge a document with information that you type at the keyboard to create fill-in documents, such as a stock reply letter (Chapter 29).

What's more, you can merge boilerplate documents to make composite documents, such as contracts—a process WordPerfect calls *document assembly* (Chapter 30). When you merge documents, you don't change the originals; WordPerfect creates a new document during the merge. Normally, the merged document is in memory and appears on the screen for you to edit or view before you print. You can also save the merged document and print it later.

If a computer can't read, how can it know where to put text from one document, or from the keyboard, into another? It can only follow your explicit instructions that you insert in the document as a series of *merge codes*. For example, your form letter is like any other letter except that it also contains merge codes that instruct the program to merge in the name and address information. WordPerfect still prints each letter individually, and the correspondent never knows the letter was a merge!

The Primary Document

There is always one document that controls the merge. WordPerfect calls this the *primary* document. For a form letter mailing, the letter document is the primary document. The names and addresses are in what WordPerfect calls the *secondary* document. Both documents contain different merge codes. I prefer to think of the primary document as a *shell*, because it serves as the framework into which WordPerfect inserts information from the secondary document or from the keyboard.

The Secondary Document

For a form mailing, there's a different set of names and addresses in the secondary document for each printed letter. These changing names and addresses are *variables*. WordPerfect refers to variables as *fields*. A merge code delimits each field so that WordPerfect knows where one field ends and another begins. WordPerfect can't understand what *information* is in the fields. It only looks for the codes.

The combined fields for each separate listing in the secondary document form a *record*. Every record must contain the *same* number of fields, and the type of information in each field must be in the same *order* in each record. That is, if the first field contains a person's first name, then all first fields in all records must contain first names or else be blank. A different merge code tells WordPerfect where one record ends and another begins.

The secondary document is actually a simple *data base*. It can contain many fields, but you don't have to use all the fields all the time. You can select which fields you want for a particular merge task.

 Tip: If you have the WordPerfect Library, you can use its Notebook to help you maintain mailing lists as WordPerfect secondary merge documents.

Merging the Two Documents

Wherever field information from the secondary document is to appear in the primary document, you insert a special merge code that identifies the field number. This number corresponds to the field's *position* in each record. The numbering is from the top to the bottom of the record, so the first field becomes F1, the second field becomes F2, and so on. During the merge itself, WordPerfect inserts the field information into the letter by matching the reference number in the primary document with the correct field location in the secondary document. Figure 27-1 shows how this works.

Primary Document

contains merge codes telling
WordPerfect where to put variable
field information from secondary
document

```
^F1^ ^F2^ ^F3^
^F4^
^F5^, ^F6^  ^F7^

Dear ^F1^ ^F3^:

   Thank you for your interest
in being a part of the "A-Team
Good Guys Club."  We are sending
you ...
```

Secondary Document

contains the variable field
information, each field marked by
an ^R code and each record by
an ^E code

```
Mr.^R
John^R
Public^R
22 Main Street^R
Anytown^R
MA^R
02100^R
^E
===================
Ms.^R
Jane^R
Doe^R
507 West Ave.^R
East Nowhere^R
NY^R
14445^R
^E
```

One record

MERGE

Creates one letter for each set of names and addresses
in the secondary document

```
Mr. John Public
22 Main Street
Anytown, MA  02100

Dear Mr. Public:

   Thank you for your ...
```

```
Ms. Jane Doe
507 West Ave.
East Nowhere, NY  14445

Dear Ms. Doe:

   Thank you for your ...
```

Figure 27-1   How Merge Works

Note: The caret symbol (^) in merge codes represents the CTRL key. It's not the symbol, SHIFT-6, on the keyboard.

WordPerfect can now also identify a field in the secondary document by a descriptive *name*. I'll stick to the traditional approach in this chapter and discuss the new approach in Chapter 28.

After it finishes one letter, WordPerfect goes on to fill up another letter with information from the next record in the secondary document and continues to do so until there are no more records in the secondary document. With a minimum of effort, you can then reuse both the primary document for another form mailing with a different secondary document or the secondary document with any number of other primary documents. In the case of a form mailing, for instance, you would certainly want envelopes or mailing labels for the letters, and possibly a mailing list of recipients, which you could easily print with the *same secondary document* (Chapter 28).

Do keep in mind, though, that a merge application is *not* an editing application. You must first use WordPerfect as you would normally to create and revise the documents that you will eventually merge.

The Two Types of Merge

All well and good, you might say, am I ready to try a merge? Not quite. You have to learn about the *two* different types of merge operations in WordPerfect: the *simple merge* and the *regular merge*. Actually, the WordPerfect people didn't give a name to the not-so-simple merge, but I'll refer to it as "regular," because the simple merge is a special case.

Why two merges? Well, the folks who designed WordPerfect realized that the most popular use of merge operations is for form letter mailings. So, they set up the simple merge to handle form letters without too much work on your part. For instance, the simple merge automatically starts a new page for each new record in the secondary document, because you'd want each letter on a different page when you print the form mailing.

Sometimes, however, this is not what you'd want. Say you're setting up a mailing list of letter recipients, so you don't want each name and address on a different page—a waste of paper indeed. Instead, you'd want as many names and addresses on a page as possible. Here's where the regular merge comes in.

Merging and Printing

Once you've created the merged form letter document with a simple merge, you can either save the merged document to print it later, or you can print it directly from the screen. Normally, you wouldn't want to save the document, because it would just take up disk space.

Tip: Do check the merge document on the screen to make sure the merge was successful *before* you print it!

However, the merged form letter document may be too large to fit totally in memory. For example, say you're doing a mailing of 200 letters. Depending on how much memory you have in your computer, WordPerfect might not be able to create a merged document with 200 pages on the screen during a simple merge. You'd have to use a regular merge to merge directly to the printer. In that case, WordPerfect merges and prints one letter at a time, then clears memory and continues.

So, the rule of thumb for deciding which of the two types of WordPerfect merge operations you need is: For form letter mailings of a small number of names and addresses, use a simple merge. For almost everything else, use a regular merge. Don't fret! Often, all you have to do to change a simple merge setup to a regular merge setup is add a couple extra codes. You'll do a simple merge first to learn that things aren't all *that* complicated after all.

The Variable Information: A Secondary Document

In their documentation, the makers of WordPerfect instruct you to create the secondary document *first* to set up the information that each field is to contain. Depending on your style, you can also create a form mailing the other way around, with the primary document first. In either case, because you'll want to refer to *both* documents as you work to make sure you get the correct fields in the correct spot, this is a perfect time to use two *windows*. You'll do that when you create the letter document.

When you set up a secondary document, think about the type of information that is to go into each different field. The example secondary document contains customer records with eight fields, each one holding a different variable: the customer's title, first name, last name, street address, city, state, zip code, and last order date.

It's also a good idea to keep information that you might want to sort in *separate* fields. For example, if you decide later to sort this secondary document numerically by zip code to take advantage of bulk mailing rates, your task will be easier if the zip code is in its own field (Chapter 33).

There are several other important points to note about the secondary document:

1. The order of the fields in each record must be the same, and there must be the same number of fields in each record. If the ordering is inconsistent, WordPerfect would not be able to make a correct match between where it should insert the variables in the form letter itself and the actual data for each variable. Remember that WordPerfect is not reading the *information* in the field but is merely noting the field's location relative to the other fields in the record.

2. Each field must end with a special merge code (^R) and a hard return to tell WordPerfect where one field ends and another begins. That's because a field could contain more than one line of text.

3. The entire record must end with another merge code (^E) and a hard page to tell WordPerfect when to go to the next record for a new letter.

   Caution: Do *not* use extra blank lines between records, because this will confuse WordPerfect to no end. Version 4.2 users: Many people knew the trick about the hard page code to separate records visually in the secondary document. Now when you insert an ^E code, WordPerfect inserts a hard page instead of a hard return.

4. Don't insert any extraneous page or line formatting codes into a secondary file. It's technically an unformatted document. The only code you may have to insert is to change line spacing to single if the default is something else. Merge secondary documents should be in single spacing. You can use such printing effects as underlining or boldface for field information. For example, if a field contained a magazine title, that could be underlined.

A real example will make things clearer to you. Take a look at the first record that you'll type, but *don't* type it yet:

```
January 18, 1986^R
Ms.^R
Sue Ann^R
Montgomery-Simpson^R
3350 N.W. Fifth Street^R
Atlanta^R
GA^R
33030^R
^E
```

It's pretty obvious what each field contains, but notice the date information in the first field. This doesn't have to be the first field, but there's a method to my madness, as you'll soon see. Notice that each field ends with an ^R code and that the entire record ends with an ^E code. Now enter this information into the secondary document like so:

Type   **January 18, 1986**

Don't move the cursor! With the cursor positioned directly past the date, and *without* adding any extra spaces:

Press   **F9 Merge R**

This inserts an ^R code and a hard return at the end of the line and positions the cursor on the next line. The ^R code tells WordPerfect where a field ends.

Caution: Do not add any extra spaces between the end of a field line and the ^R code.

✔Continue typing the other lines, ending each with an ^R code, as shown.

When you get to the blank line below the fields, you must enter the ^E code from the SHIFT-F9 Merge Codes key:

Press **SHIFT-F9 Merge Codes**

WordPerfect presents quite an inexplicable list:

^C; ^D; ^E; ^F; ^G; ^N; ^O; ^P; ^Q; ^S; ^T; ^U; ^V:

Don't worry! You'll learn about all these codes in due time. The one you want right now is the code for end of record. I won't bother to put underlines beneath the mnemonics, because everything is a mnemonic here! (You don't have to type the caret symbol.)

Type **e**

This inserts an ^E code and a hard page and positions the cursor on the next line. The ^E code tells WordPerfect that that's the end of the first record. Remember not to add any blank lines between one record and the next. I'll let you do the next two yourself (you'll see a hard page break between them):

```
September 3, 1985^R
Mr. and Mrs.^R
Stanislaus^R
Mustard^R
22 Cherry Lane, Apartment 3B^R
Richmond^R
VA^R
22407^R
^E
April 26, 1986^R
Dr.^R
Vincent^R
Alfieri^R
Route 7^R
East Podunk^R
WY^R
75409^R
^E
```

✔Enter at least three or four more records for different people. Use your friends' names or invent new ones. Make sure that you separate each record from the next with an ^E code.

Caution: Insert an ^E code at the end of the *last* record in the secondary document, too. Otherwise, the last record won't print correctly. However, don't add any extra blank lines to the end of the document.

Note: You can press CTRL-R or CTRL-E from the keyboard to enter the merge codes, but then you'd also have to press RETURN for the hard return and CTRL-RETURN for the hard page. Heaven help you if line spacing is anything but single! Unless you have your wits about you, I don't recommend this approach. Use the SHIFT-F9 Merge Codes key.

In this example, there's a one-line street address for each record. Later I'll show you how to set up a secondary document that contains two or more lines *within* a field, and I'll show you what points to consider in the process (Chapter 28). For the time being, concentrate on an easy example!

Tip: Because each record is on a separate page, use PG UP and PG DN to move through the records quickly.

When you're finished entering records, *check your typing* to make sure that all entries are correct. Use the standard cursor movement and editing commands to make any changes, but take care not to delete any ^R and ^E codes inadvertently. If you do accidentally delete a merge code, put it back in at the correct spot. If you decide to delete an entire record, block it out and then *do* delete all text and merge codes that pertain to that record only.

✔Save this document as PATRONS but leave it on the screen.

Prelude of Things to Come

Before you go on to the primary document, consider this. It's obvious to you what each field contains, but it may not be so obvious to someone else who has to work with this secondary document! In previous versions of Word-Perfect you could add a nonprinting comment box to the top of the secondary merge document to list what each field number contains. Unfortunately, comments seem to throw off WordPerfect 5.0. Instead, you could use descriptive field names for the fields in the secondary document. It's slightly tricky, so I'll defer discussion until Chapter 28.

The Letter: A Primary Document

Continuing with the same reasoning, think about this. You might create a secondary document and then forget exactly what fields contain what information. So, why not use two windows as you create the primary document? In the lower window will be the secondary document so you can view the ordering of the fields as you compose the letter. You'll need more room for the letter, so make its screen window larger:

✔Use the CTRL-F3 Screen key to split the screen into two windows. Give the top window 14 lines. Retrieve the secondary document in the second window, then position the cursor in the top window.

Now for the letter itself. Just because the form letter is a special merge document, it's still a letter. That means that you should first consider the necessary formatting requirements of the letter. So . . .

✔Using the SHIFT-F8 Format key, change the right margin to 1.5 inches. Keep the left margin at 1 inch. Then turn justification off. Clear all tabs from the left margin and set two left-justified tabs at columns 1.5 and 4.0 only. Keep the other defaults as they are.

The entire letter is shown here. Take a look at it for a moment before you begin. Notice the field names, ^F1^, ^F2^, and so on. In a moment I'll step you through how to set them up.

                                        501 West Indiana Highway
                                        Calumet City, IL 61102
                                        March 18, 1988

^F2^ ^F3^ ^F4^
^F5^
^F6^, ^F7^ ^F8^

Dear ^F2^ ^F4^:

    Consolidated Toupee has a special offer for its good customers, and we think that it's so special that we've taken this opportunity to tell you about it personally.

    For a limited time, and only while supplies last, you can purchase any of our new line of men's or ladies' hairpieces at <u>25% off</u>! That's right: 25% off the already low price for Consolidated quality.

    Act now and avoid the disappointment of missing out on this special offer. Our phone lines are ready to take your order 24 hours a day. Just call <u>1-900-222-1111</u>. Sorry, no COD orders for this sale.

    We are sure, ^F2^ ^F4^, that you won't want to pass up this sale. And we note that your last order with us was on ^F1^. Isn't it time for another great Consolidated hairpiece?

```
Yours sincerely,



Stanley R. Cluck
Marketing Manager
```

✔Begin by typing the interior address. Use two tabs to indent each of these lines. For the date, use the **SHIFT-F5 Date/Outline** key to insert the date as a *code* so that the current date always appears when you merge and print this letter. Don't type the date you see. Press **RETURN** four times for spacing, then *stop*. Here's where you'll put the variable names and addresses for the interior address.

Entering Fields into a Primary Document

Because WordPerfect normally locates the fields in the secondary document by their position number, glance at the secondary document to remind yourself which field goes where. You notice in Doc 2 that the order date information is in field 1, but that is *not* the one you want first. The reason I set up the secondary file in this fashion is to point out that you don't have to use the fields in the order they appear in the secondary document. But you *do* have to use the correct field number.

The cursor should be at the left margin. To enter the title field in the interior address:

Press   **SHIFT-F9 Merge Codes**

Type   f

WordPerfect prompts:

Field:

Type   2

Press   **RETURN**

You've inserted the field reference like this: ^F2^. The field number is enclosed on both sides by carets (^). These carets are part of the merge code. Now for something tricky. You must still enter the correct spacing and punctuation *between* fields, because that's part of the letter setup. So . . .

Press   **SPACEBAR**

Time to add the next two fields for first and last names:

Press   **SHIFT-F9 Merge Codes**

Type	**f**
Type	**3**
Press	**RETURN**
Press	**SPACEBAR**
Press	**SHIFT-F9 Merge Codes**
Type	**f**
Type	**4**
Press	**RETURN** twice

once to enter the field number and once to end the line.

✔Continue typing and entering the fields as shown in the letter. Be careful about the punctuation for the city, state, and zip line. Also, did you put in a space after the word *Dear?* Notice that you're using two fields, numbers 2 and 4, *again* in the salutation line. You can use a field *as many times as you wish* in the primary document, provided that you always use the correct field number. Don't forget the colon at the end of the salutation line.

In the fourth paragraph, you're using fields 2 and 4 *once again*, and—finally!—you get around to putting in field 1. Because the fourth paragraph contains fields *within* the text of the paragraph, when you merge the documents WordPerfect will take care to adjust the line endings to the margins, no matter how long the field information is. You can search for merge codes, too (Chapter 31).

A Stitch in Time . . .

Because this letter will be going out to scores, maybe hundreds, of people, check that it is *absolutely correct* before you start the merge. Just think of the frustration if you discovered later that, say, 200 letters all contained misspellings! So take a moment to check the letter now. The easiest way to proofread this document is visually. But if your form mailing were longer, you should do a formal spelling check. And if you're as much of a nitpicker as I am, you might want to consider hyphenating words, too. Finally, you may also want to center the letter on the page. Do you remember how and where to do that?

✔When you're finished, save this document as MAILING.1. Then clear *both* screens and close the second window.

Deleting a Field from a Primary Document

Although you won't stop to do this, assume you don't want that last paragraph in the letter. Do you have to delete all field 1's in the secondary document? No! You can have as many fields in the secondary document as you wish, but you don't have to use them all in a primary document. Just make sure that you do use the correct field numbers.

Completing a Simple Merge

Now that you have your primary and secondary documents all set up, it's time to merge the two to create the form letter mailing. Because the secondary document only contains a few records, you can try a simple merge. During the merge, WordPerfect is not available for other tasks, such as editing another document.

Caution: Always make sure that the screen is clear and that there are no documents open when you begin a merge. Otherwise, WordPerfect would join the merged document to whatever is on the screen at the time. To start the simple merge:

Press   **CTRL-F9 Merge/Sort**

　　　　WordPerfect says:

1 Merge; 2 Sort; 3 Sort Order: 0

Type   1 or m [Merge]

　　　　WordPerfect requests the Primary file:

Type   mailing.1

Press   **RETURN**

　　　　WordPerfect requests the Secondary file:

Type   patrons

Press   **RETURN**

　　　　The merge begins, and WordPerfect tells you so with:

* Merging *

When it's finished, WordPerfect positions the cursor at the end of the newly created merged document. Take a look at the results by going to the beginning of the document and scrolling through it.

Canceling a Simple Merge

If for any reason you wish to cancel a simple merge, just use the **F1 Cancel** key. You'd then have to clear the screen to remove however much of the merged document was created before you canceled. To restart the merge, repeat the steps for beginning the merge.

Printing the Merged Document

After you finish a simple merge, you can save the merged document in a new file and print it later, or print it right away without saving it.

✔If you wish, print the merged document, or merely a page or two of it. Then clear the screen before you continue.

Merging Directly to the Printer

During a simple merge, WordPerfect makes certain assumptions about the newly created merge document and acts accordingly. It assumes that there should be a different page for each record. As I mentioned, that works fine for form mailings, but you won't always want page breaks after each record. WordPerfect also assumes that you want to create one merge page for *each* record in the secondary document, so it continues to read the records and merge them to form the merged document. Finally, WordPerfect assumes that you're using the same primary document for each record in the secondary document.

Remember that whenever the merged document is too large to fit in memory, you can't use a simple merge. You must instead set up a regular merge to the printer directly. However, when you merge to the printer, WordPerfect does not create a new page for each record, nor automatically merge all records in the secondary document, nor assume that you're using the primary document throughout the merge. *You* have to insert several more codes into your primary letter document to direct the entire show.

Pretend, then, that the form letter mailing is much larger than it really is, so you're planning to merge directly to the printer.

✔Retrieve the MAILING.1 document now. Then position the cursor at the end of the document. The cursor should be directly after the words *Marketing Manager.*

The new merge codes that change this simple merge setup to a regular merge have to be at the end of the primary document.

Press   **SHIFT-F9 Merge Codes**

Type   **t**

You've inserted a ^T code into the document. When you merge the document, this code instructs WordPerfect to *type out* the text so far, that is, print the first merged letter. The ^T code also then clears the first merged letter from memory once WordPerfect has printed the letter.

Press   **SHIFT-F9 Merge Codes**

Type   **n**

The ^N merge code tells WordPerfect to go to the *next* record in the secondary document and continue the merge.

Press   **SHIFT-F9 Merge Codes**

Type   **p**

Press   **SHIFT-F9 Merge Codes**

Type   **p**

The *two* ^P merge codes instruct WordPerfect to use the same *primary* document for the continuation of the merge. In other words, WordPerfect starts the merge cycle again with the next record (^N), but it *still* has to "know" what primary document to use. There must be a begin and end ^P code enclosing the file name. But because you'll use the very same primary document, you don't have to enter its name here. WordPerfect uses the same primary document that you indicate when you begin the merge.

As the manual mentions, the combination of ^N^P^P codes forces WordPerfect to start a new page—that is, a new letter—for the next record in the secondary document. With these codes in place, WordPerfect then can merge the entire form mailing to the printer. The end of the line should now look *exactly* like this:

```
Marketing Manager^T^N^P^P
```

Note: The ^T code only works correctly if it's *in front of* the other codes.
✔Save the MAILING.1 document and then clear the screen. Time for the merge. Prepare your printer and align the paper, then:

Press	**CTRL-F9 Merge/Sort**
Type	**1** or **m** [<u>M</u>erge]
Type	`mailing.1`
Press	**RETURN**
Type	`patrons`
Press	**RETURN**

When it finishes merging the first record information with the letter document, WordPerfect prints the merged document and continues to do so for all records in the secondary document. If you have to insert individual sheets of paper into your printer, you must enter a go from the print: control printer menu. Do you remember that in Chapter 7 you created a macro called **ALTG** to issue the go command? Can you use this macro during a merge? No!

WordPerfect doesn't allow you to issue macros while a merge is in progress, but you can set up instructions for WordPerfect to issue a macro *after* the entire merge ends (Chapter 29). Here, however, your macro is useless, because you'd want to use it after the merge creates each letter. So sorry.

Merging Selected Records

Assume that you print out your form mailing only to discover that the information from one or two records in the secondary document is incorrect. With a simple merge, you could just correct the merged document itself before you print. Make sure you correct the secondary document, too, for the next time.

If you've merged to the printer, do you have to go through the entire rigmarole again? No! Merely make your corrections to the records in the secondary document, block these records out, and save the block to another file. If the records are not contiguous in the secondary document, use the block append approach. Then merely merge the primary document with this new secondary document to the printer.

Use the same technique to select only certain records that don't fit into a sorting pattern. If you *can* sort out the records you need, this makes life easier. For example, if you have city information in a separate field, you might want to print letters only to people who live in a particular city (Chapter 33).

This chapter has been rather long, and you're probably ready for a break. In the next chapter, you'll learn how to prepare the envelopes, mailing labels, and a mailing list for your form mailing.

Chapter

28

Form Letter Mailings, Part 2

In this chapter you'll discover new uses of this command . . .

ALT-F7 Math/Columns   Generate multiple mailing labels

. . . and you'll learn some new *merge* codes:

- **?** Suppress the printing of a blank line in the merge document
- **^N** Identify fields by name in the secondary document
- **^Q** Stop the merge at this record in the secondary document

Well, now you have your form mailing ready to go. Or is it? Doesn't it need envelopes for the letters, or at least mailing labels? And you might want to print a mailing list to remind you to whom this mailing was sent. You already have the names and addresses ready to go, so it's just a matter of creating a couple of new primary documents for the envelopes, labels, or list. A primary merge document need not be just a letter; it can be *any* kind of document that accepts information from a secondary document during a merge.

> **DO WARM-UP**

Problems with Varying Field Lines and Blank Fields

Before you get to the new primary documents, however, there's something else to learn. The examples in the previous chapter used a secondary document that contained one line per field. This may not always be a realistic approach, because some addresses in a secondary document may require several lines or none at all. When you have varying numbers of lines, WordPerfect has a way to accommodate them. To illustrate what I mean, you'll add a couple of "problem children" to the PATRONS secondary document.

✔Retrieve PATRONS and position the cursor at the end of the document.

Type the following record, but notice that field 5 contains two address lines and that the ^R merge code occurs only after the second line. That's because you *want* the hard return at the end of the first line to be part of the field information. Make sure you end the record with an ^E code.

```
December 15, 1985^R
Mrs.^R
Ottilia^R
Hammer^R
55 Broadway
Suite 555^R
Brooklyn^R
NY^R
10101^R
^E
```

The point here is that, no matter how many lines a field contains, only the *last* line of the field should end in an ^R code. Remember that you must always have the same number of fields in each record of the secondary document. Now, enter the following new record below the previous one:

```
May 8, 1986^R
Prof.^R
Hugo^R
First^R
^R
New Brunswick^R
NJ^R
07004^R
^E
```

This record contains a *blank* street address, so you don't add anything to the field. However, you must still end the blank field with an ^R code. You now have two very different records in this secondary document, one with a two line address and one with no address line at all. Both addresses are still entirely in field 5.

✔Save the edited PATRONS document. Then clear the screen and retrieve MAILING.1.

As it turns out, just because an address field contains two lines won't bother WordPerfect, as long as there is only one ^R code at the end of the field, not at the end of each line. But the blank field would be a problem that you can easily rectify.

To merge this primary document with your new secondary document successfully, insert a special instruction in those fields that *may* contain blank lines. This instruction, a question mark code, tells WordPerfect not to create a blank line for empty fields.

✔Position the cursor on the line that contains the ^F5^ code. Move the cursor underneath the *second* caret, then:

Type   ?

Make sure there aren't any spaces in the code. The result should be this and only this:

^F5?^

The rest of the document doesn't change. However, because this is a simple merge, make sure that you don't have any regular merge codes such as ^T or ^N at the end of the document. If there *are* ^T, ^N, or ^P codes in the document, delete them before you continue the example.

✔Save the edited MAILING.1 document. Then clear the screen and merge MAILING.1 with PATRONS to see the results.

Tip: When you're adding fields to a new primary document, press SHIFT-F9 Merge Codes and type the field number and ? directly after it before you press RETURN.

Envelopes for the Form Letter

For envelopes, set up a different primary merge document that includes only the fields from the secondary document that you need. However, recall from your little "forms fandango" (Chapter 13) that WordPerfect wants you to create a special envelope form for your printer.

✔If you haven't set up an envelope form that uses the standard envelope form size, do so now. Laser printer owners: Make sure the envelope form's orientation is landscape. Then clear the screen and insert a paper size and type change that selects the envelope form.

Tip: You may also have to change the left margin so that WordPerfect prints the return address further to the left on the envelope and the top margin so that there is less space at the top of the envelope. So:

✔Change the left, top, and bottom margins to 0.25 inch.

(Another way to go would be to change the envelope form's page offsets for the left and top settings.) Regrettably, Consolidated Toupee has run out of printed envelopes, so you'll type their return address at the top left of the envelope document, as shown:

```
CONSOLIDATED TOUPEE, INC.
501 West Indiana Highway
Calumet City, IL  61102
```

Now, you have two choices: (1) press RETURN ten or twelve times for spacing or (2) use the Advance to Line command. I chose the former:

✔Press **RETURN** about ten times.

Now, instead of using tabs, why not just change the margins for the name and address lines? You want to change both margins so that WordPerfect doesn't inadvertently wrap long address lines at the right margin.

✔Change left margin to 4.5 inches and the right margin to 0.25 inch here. Then insert the following merge codes for the name and address lines (they'll appear further right on the screen), but make sure the spacing and punctuation are correct:

```
^F2^ ^F3^ ^F4^
^F5?^
^F6^, ^F7^  ^F8^
```

You certainly don't need the order date field in the secondary document, so just don't use it. What happens to the field? Nothing! It is not part of this merge, so WordPerfect will use only the fields listed in the envelope document and bypass any others. Of course, they are all still in the secondary document for other occasions.

Caution: After you change the left and right margins for the name and address lines, WordPerfect would use these margins for the return address lines on subsequent envelope pages. Fortunately, you have margin change codes for the return address lines, but keep in mind that WordPerfect always honors the last format change.

This primary document is set up for a simple merge. If you were merging to the printer, you'd include the ^T, ^N, and two ^P merge codes on the last line of the address, as outlined in Chapter 27. Notice also that the second line contains the ? code.

✔Save this document as MAILING.ENV and clear the screen. Then merge MAILING.ENV with the PATRONS secondary document. If you wish, print one or two pages of this document on scrap paper—don't waste envelopes! Or just view the printout. Clear the screen when you're finished.

Mailing Labels

You may have a preference for *mailing labels* instead of envelopes, because labels are cheaper and printing them takes less time. Sure, you can use your secondary document again! The format for mailing labels depends on whether you have rolls of labels or pages of labels that are two or three across.

Single Rolled Labels

One problem that many people have with mailing labels is a conceptual one, not a technical one. Labels are really a series of small forms, one strung after the other on a continuous roll, just like continuous form printer paper. So, half the battle is merely one of getting the form right. Here's a basic format for single rolled labels that are 5 inches wide and 3 inches long. Because this form is slightly tricky, follow **along with** me.

✔Select your printer **and edit** it to bring up the select printer: forms screen. Type **1** or **a** [Add] to **create a new** form. Then:

Type	**9** or **o** [Other]
Type	**Rolled Labels**

for the form type.

Press	**RETURN**
Type	**1** or **s** [Form Size]
Type	**0** or **o** [Other]
Type	**5**
Press	**RETURN**

for the width.

Type	**3**
Press	**RETURN**

for the length.

TO TYPE MAILING LABELS:

FORMAT: 1.   Take off R/L Margins
          2.   Take off T/B Marging

FORMAT: Paper Size

          Select (#2) - Paper Size/Type

          Then #8 (Menu will come up -
          hit Other. Then it will ask
          for width/height.

          Then paper type will come
          up -- hit #4 (Labels)

✔If you have your printer set up to accept manual paper, remember to change the location to continuous form. Everyone: Press **F7 Exit** enough times to return to the edit screen.

Now you need to insert the form change and fix the top and bottom margins.

✔With the SHIFT-F8 Format key, go into the format: page menu and type **8** or **s** [Paper Size]. Then:

Type   **0** or **o** [Other]

Type   **5**

Press   **RETURN**

for the width.

Type   **3**

Press   **RETURN**

for the height.

Type   **8** or **o** [Other]

for the paper type.

Type   **2** or **o** [Other]

Type   `Rolled Labels`

Press   **RETURN**

enough times to return to the document.

✔Now, change the top and bottom margins to 0.25 inch. Then enter the *same* merge codes in the same lines as you did for envelopes. Save the document as MAILING.RL, clear the screen, and merge this new document with PATRONS.

You still might have to change the left and right margins or the form's offset, too; again it depends on where you position the mailing labels to print in the printer. Trial print the label file on scrap paper to determine the necessary adjustments to your document. Or merely position the labels in the printer to use the default left margin setting.

Two- and Three-Across Mailing Labels on Sheets

Here's where things get a bit more tricky, so pay close attention. To print two- or three-across (or four, or five, and so on) labels on 8½ by 11 inch sheets, you must use a *parallel column format* and a couple of other tricks. Here are the basic steps and what you have to consider. You'll do two-across labels, but the procedure is the same for any multiple label setup.

✔First, create a new form for the printer. This time, you can use the predefined Labels form, but make sure you change the location setting if necessary. Retain the paper size as 8½ by 11 inches. Then, insert a paper size and type change in the new document that selects this form.

The next step is to use a ruler to figure out the left, right, top, and bottom margins and the number of spaces between the columns. Then adjust the settings but make sure you also adjust the line length so that any long address lines don't wrap around. Just for the sake of example, accept the default top and bottom margins. You can change them later. Now, assume that the left margin of the first label column is 0.5 inch, and the right margin of the entire page is at position 0.25 inch. The number of spaces between columns is 20. These settings depend, of course, on the labels you're using.

✔Change the left margin to 0.5 inch and the right margin to 0.25 inch now.

The next step is to define the parallel columns.

Caution: Don't use newspaper columns, because they won't give you the correct results.

Press	**ALT-F7 Math/Columns**
Type	**4** or **d** [Column D̲ef]
Type	**1** or **t** [T̲ype]
Type	**2** or **p** [P̲arallel]
Type	**3** or **d** [D̲istance Between Columns]
Type	**2.0**
Press	**RETURN**

You'll accept WordPerfect's suggestions for the column margins. Later, after you do a dry-run printing, you can adjust the margins if they're not correct.

Press	**F7 Exit**

to leave the column definition.

Type	**3** or **c** [C̲olumn On/Off]

✔Enter the same merge codes as for the previous envelope or rolled label example.

You also have to do a little trick: You must include enough blank lines to space one row of labels from the next. Again, only measurement and trial-and-error can help you here. You'll assume in this example that there are four blank lines between rows of labels.

Press   **RETURN** four times

Next you'll block the codes so you can copy them easily into the second column, but be careful!

Press   **ALT-F4 Block** or **F12 Block**

Press   **UP ARROW** six times

The reason I didn't instruct you to press HOME,HOME,UP ARROW is that you *don't* want to include the formatting codes in the block. If you reveal the codes right now, you'll notice that the block just includes the merge codes and blank lines. Now, you'll copy the codes and blank lines to the second column:

Press   **CTRL-F4 Move**

Type   **1** or **b** [<u>B</u>lock]

Type   **2** or **c** [<u>C</u>opy]

to make a copy of the block.

Press   **HOME,HOME,DOWN ARROW**

to position the cursor at the end of the first column.

Press   **CTRL-RETURN**

to move the cursor into the second parallel column.

Press   **RETURN**

to copy the block here.

Wait! There's one important other trick. Because you want WordPerfect to go to the next record in the secondary merge document and print this record in the second column, you must include an ^N merge code at the top of the second column. The cursor should be exactly where you want the code now—under the first caret (^) of ^F2^—so:

Press   **SHIFT-F9 Merge Codes**

Type   n

The screen should now look exactly like Figure 28-1. You're now ready to test the results.

✔Save the new file as MAILING.L2 to remind you that this is for two-across labels. Clear the screen and merge MAILING.L2 with PATRONS.

There they are! You can save the merged document or print it.

 Tip: Laser printer owners might want to print on plain paper and then photocopy the results onto the real label pages. That way, they avoid the risk of the labels coming unglued in the printer.

The only other consideration is to check the page format so that WordPerfect breaks each page at the correct spot. If necessary, change the top and bottom margins but make sure you put these changes at the top of the merged document. Better yet, put them at the top of the original primary document! Laser printer owners: See also the discussion of *unprintable regions* on page 115.

Use the same approach for any multiple label setup on individual sheets. Remember to include the ^N merge code at the top of each column *except* the first. For multiple labels on continuous rolls, you'd combine the two approaches. That is, follow these basic steps: (1) determine the form for the label as an entire page, (2) set up the correct left and right margins, (3) figure out the parallel column definition and turn column mode on, (4) enter the merge codes in each column, including the ^N code in all columns except the first, (5) save the results, and (6) merge and print. Good luck!

✔Clear the screen before you continue.

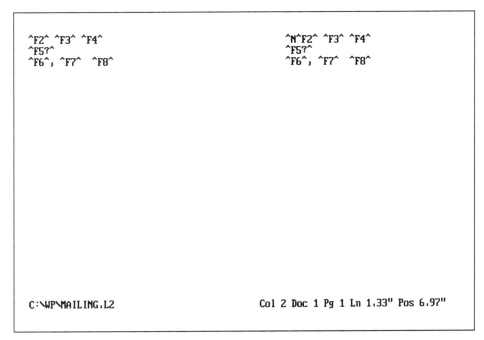

Figure 28-1   A Two-Across Mailing Labels Setup

Creating a Mailing List

If you want a mailing list, why not use the secondary document *again* with yet another primary document? This one, however, is slightly different for several reasons. First, you'll use the standard form, but you'll want to print as many names and addresses on each page as possible. So you have to forego the simple merge procedure. Second, you'll list the variable names in a slightly different order, with the last name first. Third, you'll add a header to the document. Finally, you'll use the block protect feature to ensure that WordPerfect doesn't split a name and address between two pages. Ready?

✔Enter the field numbers as you see them in this example, using the **SHIFT-F9 Merge Codes** key. Don't forget the commas and the proper spaces between the fields! Press **RETURN** three times after the third line for spacing. Then enter the extra merge codes shown at the end of the document.

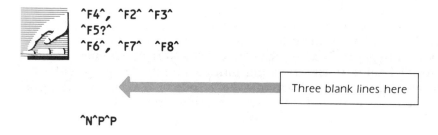

^F4^, ^F2^ ^F3^
^F5?^
^F6^, ^F7^ ^F8^

Three blank lines here

^N^P^P

You added the extra blank lines so that when WordPerfect plugs in a new record into the primary document, this record is nicely spaced down from the previous one. The extra codes ^N^P^P instruct WordPerfect to repeat the form as many times as it can on the page and continue until it's merged all records from the secondary document.

Another Trick

WordPerfect might possibly split a record at the bottom of a page, depending on how many lines are to be printed on each page. How could you make sure that WordPerfect keeps the record intact? Right! Use the Block Protect command. If WordPerfect finds that a record can't fit at the bottom of the page, it will start a new page. Here's how to do it:

Press   **HOME,HOME,UP ARROW**

Press   **ALT-F4 Block** or **F12 Block**

Now, you have to be careful about how much of the block to protect. Do *not* attempt to include the last line with the merge codes in the block, because that will "hang" your computer. So, do this:

Press   **DOWN ARROW** four times

The cursor should be on the fifth line. That's as much of the block as you want to protect.

Press   **SHIFT-F8 Format**

Type   y

to protect the block.

How about a header line for this mailing list? The header will print on each page to identify this list.

Caution: If you type a title in the body of the primary document, that title would appear before *each* record on the mailing list. That's not what you want! Use a header setup instead:

✔ Position the cursor at the top of the document. Then go into the setup area for Header A. Make sure you instruct WordPerfect to print this header on every page. Then center and type the header text: `Mailing List - Super Promotion`. Press **RETURN** a couple times to increase the header margin. Finally, press **F7 Exit** enough times to return to the document.

Finally, if this were a long list, you might want to have page numbers print. I'll let you do that setup yourself!

✔ Save the completed document as MAILING.LST. Then clear the screen and try merging the new document with the PATRONS secondary document. When you're finished, clear the screen again. The records in the secondary document aren't sorted in any order (Chapter 33).

Unfortunately, when you use the merge code combination ^N^P^P as here, you can't merge directly to the printer. If you inserted a ^T code in front of the ^N code in the primary document, WordPerfect would force a page break after each record in the secondary document. Most of the time, you should have enough memory to create the mailing list. However, if your form mailing is a really large one, you might have to break it up into sections. See Dealing with Large Secondary Documents later in the chapter.

Using Field Names Instead of Numbers

I've stressed the traditional WordPerfect approach to teach you how to identify fields by their position number. You can also set up field names in the secondary document, then list these names after the ^F codes in the primary document. But the procedure is slightly tricky, so pay close attention.

To use field names, you create a *dummy record* at the beginning of the secondary merge document. This record must be in front of all real records. It tells WordPerfect the names of the fields and their order. Here are the steps:

1. Insert an ^N merge code and a hard return.
2. Insert begin and end bold codes around *each* field name.
3. Type each field name *exactly* as you want to use it in the exact order that the fields appear in the secondary document. Each field name must be on a separate line that ends in a hard return. You can use spaces in field names.
4. End the entire list with an ^R code and a hard return. The resulting "field" contains the names of all real fields, but it's still just field 1.
5. Insert enough ^N^R codes and hard returns for the other fields.
6. Insert an ^E code below it all to end the dummy record.

Now that you're totally confused, take a look at the beginning of the edited PATRONS secondary document. Here's a sample setup for the fields in this document:

```
^N
order date
title
first
last
street
city
state
zip
^R
^N^R
^N^R
^N^R
^N^R
^N^R
^N^R
^N^R
^E
==============================================================================
January 18, 1986^R
Ms.^R
Sue Ann^R
Montgomery-Simpson^R
3350 N.W. Fifth Street^R
(and so on)
```

Notice that to save typing I've entered the field names in lowercase. The first field of the dummy record contains the field names, each one enclosed in bold codes, listed in the correct order. Because there are eight fields in each record, there must be *seven* more ^N^R codes below this first field.

Now, instead of using numbers in the primary document, you can insert the field names. That is, press **SHIFT-F9 Merge Codes**, type f, then type the field name and press **RETURN**. Take a look at the first part of the edited MAILING.1 primary document to see how I inserted the field names.

```
                        501 West Indiana Highway
                        Calumet City, IL  61102
                        March 18, 1988




^Ftitle^ ^Ffirst^ ^Flast^
^Fstreet?^
^Fcity^, ^Fstate^  ^Fzip^

Dear ^Ftitle^ ^Flast^:

    Consolidated Toupee has a special offer for its good
customers, and we think that it's so special that we've
taken this opportunity to tell you about it personally.
(and so on)
```

Notice also the ? code after the street field. Essentially, this setup with field names is the same one that the WordPerfect Library uses when you work with the Notebook utility.

Merge Codes in Headers and Footers

Suppose you have a two page form letter and you want to print the recipient's name in a header on the second page. Unfortunately, WordPerfect won't let you enter merge codes into header or footer setups, so you have to trick the program. Instead of inserting a regular header or footer code with the SHIFT-F8 Format command, type the header or footer as actual *text* in the primary document.

It's important that you first type the regular text of the letter document. Make sure everything is correct. Then *add* the header or footer text. For a header, you would position the cursor at the top of the second page. Change the top margin if necessary. (You could instead put the top margin change code on page 1 and suppress the change for that page only.)

Then press RETURN enough times to separate the "fake" header lines from the actual body of the text. Return the cursor to the top of the page past any codes. Type the fake header, including the merge codes you need. Using the original PATRONS secondary document, you might have this header at the top of page 2 in the primary document:

```
^F2^ ^F3^ ^F4^
Page 2
```

Notice that you must supply the correct page number as text, because if you used the normal ^B code WordPerfect would increment the page numbering for each letter page of the merged document. That's not what you want here!

Question: You could use the ^B code if you did one other thing—what is it? *Answer:* Insert a new page number code at the beginning of the primary document to restart numbering with page 1.

When you merge the primary document with the secondary document, here's what the fake header would look like for the first record:

```
Ms. Sue Ann Montgomery-Simpson
Page 2
```

A fake footer is more difficult than a fake header, because you may have to supply enough blank lines to fill up the page to the position at the bottom of the page where you want the footer to go. You may also have to change the bottom margin.

More Possibilities

Dear Reader, are you still with me? You haven't yet exhausted the possibilities of merge operations using the *very same* documents! Here are two other examples. You can reuse the original MAILING.1 letter with another set of variables. Just make sure that the fields match. Or use the same secondary document with an entirely different letter.

Tip: Copy the field setup for the interior address from MAILING.1 for the next letter to save time.

The Stop Merge Code

Later you'll learn how to *sort* a secondary merge document— say, by zip code— or to *select* only certain records, before you create a form letter merge. For the sake of example assume you want to merge all the records in a secondary document only up to a particular record. Instead of copying the records to another secondary document altogether, you could insert a stop merge code, ^Q, in the document.

Caution: I have found that you must insert this code directly in front of the ^E code for the last record you want to merge, so that the line looks like this: ^Q^E. If you insert the ^Q after the ^E or on its own separate line, the merge doesn't work properly. The stop merge code can be used in either primary or secondary documents. Make sure you delete the ^Q code after the merge operation if you want the next merge to include all records in the secondary document.

Dealing with Large Secondary Documents

It may behoove you to split up your secondary documents if they contain a great many records and if you need to create large form letter mailings. For example, you might have a secondary document called ATOL for the first half of the alphabet and one called MTOZ for the second half. So, if you're trying to create a large mailing that might not fit into memory, first merge the primary document with the ATOL secondary document. Save the newly created merged document. Then merge the primary document with the MTOZ secondary document.

Okay, that's all you need to know about form letter mailings. Merge has many more tricks up its sleeve, as you'll discover next.

Chapter

29

Fill-In Documents

In this chapter you'll discover new uses of these commands . . .

F9 Merge R Continue a merge from the keyboard

SHIFT-F9 Merge Codes Cancel a merge from the keyboard

. . . and you'll learn some new *merge* codes:

^C Wait for input from the keyboard

^D Print the current date in the merged document

^G Run the named macro after the merge is complete (two codes required)

^O Display the enclosed prompt (two codes required)

^V Insert the enclosed merge code into the merged document (two codes required)

Now that you know the basics of merge, you're ready to explore other powerful applications. Merge is not for form letters alone! For instance, it would be a colossal pain to have to do a form mailing for, say, just one or two letters. And it would be a waste of time to create a new document every time you wanted to print a standard envelope.

This chapter shows you how to create *stock* documents with fill-in variable locations. You can then reuse these stock documents as many times as you want. You set up the document only once. After that, it's a piece of cake to supply the correct information during the merge and print the document. WordPerfect even reminds about you what information goes where! What's more, you can expand your merge setup to include a *data entry* form for many other interesting possibilities.

> **DO WARM-UP**

Fill-In Documents Explained

In a stock reply document, such as a letter, there is a certain amount of variable information that will change for each new letter, although *most* of the letter remains the same. You could, if you wish, type the letter as normal, and then type over the old information with the new information. You have done this already, but that's kid's stuff! In a complicated or lengthy document you risk missing something.

WordPerfect has a much better way to avoid this potential problem and others. It lets you put special merge codes in a document wherever there is to be variable information. Unlike a form letter mailing that receives its information from a secondary document, however, these stock reply documents prompt you to supply the information from the *keyboard* at the time of the merge.

What are the other benefits of the fill-in document approach? First, you don't have to set up a secondary document for information you may not need. Second, you can have WordPerfect prompt you for the information that is to go into each code location. Finally, you avoid the hassle of matching fields between primary and secondary documents. Remember, however, to supply the correct spacing and punctuation around the variable information in the fill-in document.

A Stock Reply Letter

A stock reply letter is correspondence that you may send out once a day, once a week, or even less frequently. Wherever variable information is to appear in the letter, you set up two merge codes, one to prompt you for the information with a screen message and the other as a place marker for the information that you supply from the keyboard. Here's the example stock reply letter you'll create:

Busy Bee Bake-Off Contest
1776 North Highland Avenue
Hollywood, CA 90028
^D

^OEnter full name:^O^C
^OEnter street address:^O^C
^OEnter city, state, zip:^O^C

Dear ^OEnter salutation:^O^C:

   Thank you very much for your recipe for ^OEnter
recipe:^O^C, which you intend to enter in the Seventh Annual
Busy Bee Bake-Off Contest. This year's bake-off will be
held at Golden Gate Park in San Francisco on December 5,
1989.

   We have registered your entry in the ^OEnter
division:^O^C division. Please remember that the deadline
for all further entries is November 30, 1989.

   We certainly hope that your entry wins you first prize.
Good luck!

                    Sincerely,

                    Simone Fourchette
                    Director

   Notice that parts of the document contain some merge codes that you
haven't seen yet. I'll explain them in a minute.
   ✔First, put in a center page code at the beginning of the document
(remember, it has to be the first code). Then change the left margin to 1.5
inches but leave the right margin at 1 inch. Turn justification off. Use six tabs
to enter the address lines for the Busy Bee Bake-Off Contest. (You could also
delete all tabs and set new ones at columns 2.0 and 4.5 only so that you
wouldn't have to press the TAB key too often!)
   The fourth line contains a ^D code. This code instructs WordPerfect to
insert today's date during the merge. It's like the normal date code. To enter
this code:

Press   **SHIFT-F9 Merge Codes**

Type   **d**

Press **RETURN** four times for spacing, then *stop*. The ^O merge codes display messages on the screen. You must enclose each message with a begin and end ^O. The ^C code tells WordPerfect to suspend a merge and wait for input from the keyboard. Once you type the information, WordPerfect inserts it at the location of the ^C code.

It's a good idea to use both the ^O and ^C codes together, because you may not be able to ascertain from the context of the document exactly what information goes where. So, always supply a message that makes sense to you! To enter the first line of merge codes in the example:

Press   **SHIFT-F9 Merge Codes**

Type   **o**

Now for your message:

Type   `Enter full name:`

You must supply an ending ^O code to tell WordPerfect where the message ends:

Press   **SHIFT-F9 Merge Codes**

Type   **o**

Now for the code to accept input from the keyboard:

Press   **SHIFT-F9 Merge Codes**

Type   **c**

Press   **RETURN**

to go to the next line.

✔Using the example as your guide, continue adding the other codes and prompt messages for the interior address and the salutation lines. Use the correct number of hard returns for spacing. Notice that the ending colon on the salutation line is not part of the merge code setup.

Begin typing the first paragraph. Make sure of the spacing before you enter the message and fill-in merge codes. Even though the lines break to accommodate the current margins, WordPerfect will later adjust the lines to the correct information that you supply from the keyboard. Do the second paragraph in the same fashion. Then finish the letter and check your typing for any possible mistakes.

✔Save the document as REPLY.1, then clear the screen.

Note: A merge won't work correctly if there are font changes or other formatting codes *within* begin and end merge codes such as ^O or ^P. Don't do it!

Merging from the Keyboard

Whenever Ms. Fourchette needs to send this letter, she does this:

Press	**CTRL-F9 Merge/Sort**
Type	1 or m [Merge]
Type	reply.1
Press	**RETURN**

Because there's no secondary document:

Press	**RETURN**

WordPerfect shows the letter and displays your first message at the bottom of the screen. Note that the name line is now blank. Type in a correct full name, such as this:

Type	**Ms. Rose Terranova**
Press	**F9 Merge R**

Use the **F9 Merge R** command to continue the merge after you've entered information from the keyboard. Now for a tricky one: a street address that contains *two* lines:

Type	1543 Burnside Avenue
Press	**RETURN**
Type	Apartment B
Press	**F9 Merge R**

Finish the letter:

Type	Queens Village, NY 11453
Press	**F9 Merge R**
Type	Ms. Terranova
Press	**F9 Merge R**

Type	**Neapolitan Enchiladas**
Press	**F9 Merge R**
Type	**Light Lunches**
Press	**F9 Merge R**

And there's your letter that you can now save or just print from the screen.

✔Clear the screen when you're finished.

(An aside: There's a variation on the fill-in document theme in Chapter 31. There you'll learn about a "pseudo" fill-in document that handles correspondence to a limited number of regular clients but doesn't require you to set up a secondary merge document.)

Canceling a Keyboard Merge

The F1 Cancel key won't cancel the merge for a fill-in document. Press **SHIFT-F9 Merge Codes** and type **e** to cancel this type of merge. Then clear the screen.

Tip: You can insert an ^E code in a primary merge document to stop a keyboard merge.

Doing Several Fill-Ins at Once: Use a Macro

It turns out that Ms. Fourchette has to send out several stock reply letters today. So, she decides to set up a macro to start the merge operation and then repeat the merge a number of times. She'll insert a special merge code in the primary document to start the macro again after one letter is done. She'll call this macro RE for "reply."

✔Clear the screen and retrieve the REPLY.1 document. Then position the cursor at the end of the document. The cursor should be directly after the word *Director*. Press **RETURN** once to space down.

First, to start the macro from a primary merge document, enter the following codes and information into the primary document:

Press	**SHIFT-F9 Merge Codes**
Type	**g**

Two ^G codes delimit a macro name. WordPerfect begins the macro only *after* the entire merge is completed, although you can insert this macro instruction anywhere in the merge document.

Type	re

Press	**SHIFT-F9 Merge Codes**

Type	g

You don't have to provide the macro file extension, but make sure you add the ending ^G code so that the line looks like this: ^Gre^G. WordPerfect assumes the file extension .WPM for macros.

There's one other point to consider. As it stands right now, each new stock reply letter won't start at the top of a new page. Because there's technically no secondary document, the combination ^N^P^P doesn't work in repetitious fill-in documents. So, just insert a Hard Page command directly after the last ^G code:

Press	**CTRL-RETURN**

✔Save the document as REPLY.2, then clear the screen.

The procedure for setting up a macro to call a merge is slightly different than for other macros.

Press	**CTRL-F10 Macro Define**

Type	re

Press	**RETURN**

Type	Reply Macro

Press	**RETURN**

Press	**CTRL-F9 Merge/Sort**

Type	1 or m [Merge]

Type	reply.2

Press	**RETURN**

Press	**RETURN**

A macro definition automatically ends when a merge begins, but you must now cancel the merge itself:

Press	**SHIFT-F9 Merge Codes**

Type	e

✔Clear the screen now.

To do several fill-in reply letters at once, start the macro as usual:

Press   **ALT-F10 Macro**

Type   re

Press   **RETURN**

Keep entering fill-in information for each letter. When you get to the last letter and after you finish it, press SHIFT-F9 Merge Codes to end the macro. You would have to clear the last, incomplete letter from the screen. Then print the letters as normal. In Chapter 30, you'll *customize* this stock reply document for a variety of different recipients, using the document assembly operations of WordPerfect's merge feature.

In a similar fashion, you could start a macro to define two- or three-across columns after you merge a label document with a secondary name-and-address document.

The Best Way to Address Envelopes

You've already seen several envelope setups, but by far the best way to prepare individual envelopes is with the merge from the keyboard feature. That's because you'll often have to dash out a fast envelope but you won't want to keep the name and address information. Here's a standard envelope set up as a fill-in document with the simple name E:

```
<Your Name>
<Your Street Address>
<Your City, State, Zip Code>
```

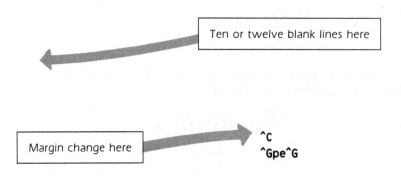

Ten or twelve blank lines here

Margin change here

```
^C
^Gpe^G
```

✔Retrieve the MAILING.ENV document from Chapter 28. Replace the return address with your name and return address. Then delete the original merge codes and insert the merge codes and macro name that appear in this example. Save the document as E but leave it on the screen.

I didn't even bother to add a screen message for the fill-in item, because it's obvious that you just supply the standard information for each line when you merge the envelope with information from the keyboard. Press RETURN to end each name and address line. This setup handles *any* envelope, because you don't press F9 Merge R until you've entered all address lines. That is, you press F9 Merge R at the end of the last envelope line only.

The best way to use this envelope is with two macros, one called SE for "start envelope" to begin the keyboard merge, and one called PE for "print envelope" to print the envelope. The PE macro starts as soon as you've filled in the envelope information.

The SE macro is essentially like the RE macro you created in the previous example, but I've added a twist. What is it?

Caution: You must first create the E document before you can define the SE macro.

Press	**CTRL-F10 Macro Define**
Type	se
Press	**RETURN**
Type	Start Envelope
Press	**RETURN**
Press	**F7 Exit**
Type	n twice
Press	**CTRL-F9 Merge/Sort**
Type	1 or m [<u>M</u>erge]
Type	e
Press	**RETURN** twice

You must now cancel the merge and clear the unfinished envelope. The answer to my little question is that this macro first clears the screen before it starts the keyboard merge—just in case you forget to clear the screen yourself!

Now for the second macro, PE:

Press	**CTRL-F10 Macro Define**

Type	**pe**
Press	**RETURN**
Type	**Print Envelope**
Press	**RETURN**
Press	**SHIFT-F7 Print**
Type	**2 or p [P̲age]**
Press	**CTRL-F10 Macro Define**

Whenever you want to fill in and print an envelope, prepare your printer and envelope form, press **ALT-F10 Macro**, type **se**, and press **RETURN**. Supply the name and address lines, ending each with a hard return except the last. To finish the keyboard merge, press **F9 Merge R** after the last envelope line. WordPerfect then starts the PE macro to print the envelope.

Filling In Preprinted Forms

If you have to fill in an occasional form, there's a way to make WordPerfect pretend it's a typewriter (Chapter 34). However, if you have to fill in certain forms all the time, set them up as fill-in documents. The most difficult part about setting up forms is getting WordPerfect to print the fill-in information at the correct spot on the form. The documentation's suggestion to use a *grid* and the Advance command (Chapter 15) is a good one. You can also get a special ruler in computer supply stores that lets you measure the lines and column positions. These rulers usually come with measurements for 6 and 8 lines per vertical inch.

Creating Data Entry Forms

The fill-in stock reply letter that you composed in the first example has a distinct disadvantage. You'd have to enter the same information each time you want to print that information elsewhere in the letter. For instance, say you want to include the name of the recipe in the first sentence of the last paragraph so that the sentence reads: *We certainly hope that (recipe) wins you first prize.* Normally, you'd have to set up two fill-in locations and type the recipe name twice from the keyboard.

Well, there's a way to *reuse* information that you've entered from the keyboard. It requires a more complicated merge setup, but it has so many useful applications that you should learn about it now. Once you master this technique, you can create any number of data entry forms.

A data entry form is a fill-in document that requests the information you need and then sets the information up in a secondary merge document, complete with ^R and ^E merge codes! This new secondary document contains only one record. Then, using macros, you'll merge this secondary document into the stock reply letter as if it were part of a larger form letter mailing. Take a close look at this data entry form:

```
^OTitle? ^O^C^V^R^V
^OFirst Name? ^O^C^V^R^V
^OStreet Address? ^O^C^V^R^V
^OCity? ^O^C^V^R^V
^OState? ^O^C^V^R^V
^OZip Code? ^O^C^V^R^V
^ORecipe Submitted? ^O^C^V^R^V
^ODivision? ^O^C^V^R^V
^V^E
===============================================================================
^V
```

Each line displays a prompt on the screen and then waits for your input from the keyboard. The spaces after each prompt and before the end ^O code are cosmetic. But what are the ^V codes? They enable you to insert other WordPerfect merge codes into the resulting merged document without losing the codes during the merge. So the pairs of ^V codes at the end of each line, except the last line, insert the correct ^R codes into the document. The last pair of ^V codes inserts the requisite ^E code to mark the end of the record.

✔Go ahead, type this form. Make sure to press **SHIFT-F9 Merge Codes** to enter each code and that there are begin and end ^O and ^V codes as shown. WordPerfect will insert the hard page break when you enter the ^E code. Save this document as REPLY.FRM, then clear the screen.

Merging a Data Entry Form with Another Document

You must now change the stock reply letter for the Busy Bee Bake-Off Contest. It has to be a standard primary document for a simple merge with the secondary document soon to be created by the fill-in document, REPLY.FRM.

✔Retrieve the document REPLY.1 now.

Why not just make the changes to this document so that you don't have to retype the whole thing?

505

✔Delete *all* ^o and ^c codes and messages and then insert the ^F codes, as shown here. Note that because you've split the fields into distinct entities, you can reuse the fields as often as you like throughout the letter. Make sure of correct spacing between the codes and check your typing when you're finished.

```
                        Busy Bee Bake-Off Contest
                        1776 North Highland Avenue
                        Hollywood, CA  90028
                        ^D


^F1^ ^F2^ ^F3^
^F4?^
^F5^, ^F6^  ^F7^

Dear ^F1^ ^F3^:

     Thank you very much for your recipe for ^F8^, which you
intend to enter in the Seventh Annual Busy Bee Bake-Off
Contest.  This year's bake-off will be held at Golden Gate
Park in San Francisco on December 5, 1989.

     We have registered your entry in the ^F9^ division.
Please remember that the deadline for all further entries is
November 30, 1989.

     We certainly hope that ^F8^ wins you first prize.  Good
luck!
                        Sincerely,




                        Simone Fourchette
                        Director
```

✔Save this new document as REPLY.3, then clear the screen.

Here's where things get a little tricky, so pay *close* attention. First, you have to set up a "dummy" file so that the file exists when you save the document that you create after you merge the ENTRY.FRM document with information from the keyboard.

Type   **dummy info**

Actually, you can type anything you want, because it'll soon be replaced by the real information.

Press	**F10 Save**
Type	`reply.dat`
Press	**RETURN**

Leave the dummy text on the screen. Next, you create a macro that starts as soon as you've filled in the data entry form. This macro saves the entire form as a block to the REPLY.DAT file and clears the screen. Call this macro SF for "save form."

Caution: Make sure that the cursor is at the very end of the dummy information line, because you'll use the block technique to save the document within the macro.

Press	**CTRL-F10 Macro Define**
Type	`sf`
Press	**RETURN**
Type	`Save Form`
Press	**RETURN**
Press	**ALT-F4 Block or F12 Block**
Press	**HOME,HOME,HOME,UP ARROW**
Press	**F10 Save**
Type	`reply.dat`
Press	**RETURN**
Type	`y`
Press	**F1 Cancel**
Press	**F7 Exit**
Type	`n twice`
Press	**CTRL-F9 Merge/Sort**
Type	`1 or m [Merge]`
Type	`reply.3`

Press	**RETURN**
Type	reply.dat
Press	**RETURN**

✔Clear the screen of the incomplete merged document now.

What the SF macro does is first block out and save the filled-in entry form as the document REPLY.DAT. Because you'll repeat this procedure a lot, you needed the "dummy file" on the disk so that WordPerfect asks you to confirm the replacement. The macro then cancels the block, clears the screen, and starts the merge of the REPLY.3 letter with the newly entered data that's now in the REPLY.DAT document.

Next you must change the REPLY.FRM document so that WordPerfect begins the SF macro as soon as you've filled in the form.

✔Clear the screen and retrieve the REPLY.FRM document. Position the cursor at the end of the document, which should be directly past the last ^V code. Then:

Press	**SHIFT-F9 Merge Codes**
Type	g
Type	sf
Press	**SHIFT-F9 Merge Codes**
Type	g

✔Save the edited document now, then clear the screen.

Time to test your new data entry setup. First, begin the normal merge to enter the information from the keyboard:

Press	**CTRL-F9 Merge/Sort**
Type	1 or m [Merge]
Type	reply.frm
Press	**RETURN** twice

Enter the information as you see it below next to each prompt that appears on the screen. Remember to press **F9 Merge R** to continue the merge after you type each entry.

```
Title? Dr.
First Name? Vladimir
Last Name? Blini
Street Address? 25006 Santa Rosa Dr.
City? Bakersfield
State? CA
Zip Code? 93010
Recipe Submitted? Flaming Borscht
Division? Special Soups
```

After you complete the form, WordPerfect starts the SF macro. The macro saves the form to the REPLY.DAT file, clears the screen, and merges the REPLY.3 letter with the new REPLY.DAT secondary document. (Dear Reader, I don't know what "flaming borscht" is either!)

Of course, you could get *really* fancy and have WordPerfect then print the new letter. Just insert the correct ^G codes and the print macro name in the REPLY.3 document. You then have a complete data entry system for fill-in documents.

✔Clear the screen now.

A Stock Contract

In Chapter 30, you'll learn how to assemble documents, such as contracts, from separate boilerplates using the merge feature. Here's another example of a stock contract. This one is for two parties to an agreement. Because their respective names appear frequently in the contract, why not set up a merge that (1) requests the names and (2) plugs in the names throughout the entire contract?

This time, do the contract first. To save space and prevent my editor from having her threatened heart attack, I'll make this a short example, but I'm sure you get the idea. It could go on for pages!

```
                    A G R E E M E N T

    BE IT KNOWN THAT the party of the first part, ^F1^, and the
party of the second part, ^F2^, in consideration of the mutual
interests outlined below, have duly signed their names to this
Agreement, dated this ^F3^ day of ^F4^, 19^F5^.

    WHEREAS, ^F1^, being presently a tenant of ^F2^, agrees to
be retained in the employ of ^F2^ as Apartment Manager for the
property listed below.
```

```
     WHEREAS, ^F2^ agrees to provide ^F1^ a remuneration for
services rendered as Apartment Manager.  Such remuneration shall
include, but not be limited to, rent for a one-bedroom apartment
at the said property and a monthly stipend not to exceed $^F6^
per month.
```

✔Use the standard defaults but make sure to insert the correct field numbers as you see them. Check your typing, too! Save the document as AGREE.1, then clear the screen.

Create a data entry form like the following one. (WordPerfect will insert a hard page break when you enter the ^E code.) Of course, there could be any number of other fields depending on how you arrange the contract. However, make sure that the order of the field information that you enter into the entry form—and in turn into the secondary merge document—matches the field numbers in the AGREE.1 primary document.

This entry form document calls the macro DO that does the same thing as the SF macro from the previous example. It saves the entry form to a secondary document and then runs the merge operation to merge the secondary document with the AGREE.1 primary document.

```
^OWho is the party of the first part?: ^O^C^V^R^V
^OWho is the party of the second part?: ^O^C^V^R^V
^OThe day (e.g., 1st, 2nd)?: ^O^C^V^R^V
^OThe month spelled out?: ^O^C^V^R^V
^OAnd the last two digits of the year?: ^O^C^V^R^V
^OWhat is the monthly stipend?: ^O^C^V^R^V
^V^E
```

```
================================================================================
^V^Gdo^G
```

✔Save this document as AGREE.FRM. Follow the procedure outlined above for the REPLY documents to create the dummy file (call it AGREE.DAT) and the DO macro to run the second merge. When you're finished, clear the screen. Merge the entry form with information from the keyboard, after which let WordPerfect take over and merge this information with the contract document.

With fill-in documents you get the best of both worlds. That is, you don't have to *re*type and you don't have to *over*type existing documents. Just supply the information from the keyboard and let WordPerfect's merge take care of the rest!

30

Document Assembly

In this chapter you'll learn some new *merge* codes:

^S   Use the enclosed secondary document (two codes required)

^U   Rewrite the screen

Dear Reader, this book is already a big one, so I can only briefly touch on some ways you can use WordPerfect's *document assembly* merge feature. As you saw in the last chapter when you set up data entry forms, you'll have to do some advance planning and experimenting to get your merges the way you want them. This holds true for document assembly merges, too.

DO WARM-UP

What Document Assembly Means

Do you remember the discussion of boilerplates in Chapter 14? Normally when you work with boilerplates you have to retrieve a boilerplate document manually into another document. Document assembly merge takes the boilerplate idea one step further. WordPerfect automatically handles the creation of a merge document from any number of boilerplates.

For instance, you can create personalized reply letters by combining a series of boilerplate paragraphs—the first example in this chapter. Similarly, you can create stock contracts or other agreements. You can even *chain* files together to print them in one fell swoop.

Often in a document assembly project, you set up a primary document that "controls the show" but may not contain any text. It merely includes the merge codes that assemble the final document. Because this document contains only merge instructions, I'll refer to it as a *command document*. Don't confuse this type of document with the master documents that govern large writing projects with tables, lists, indexes, footnotes, endnotes, and cross-references (Chapter 25).

Suppose Ms. Fourchette sends a number of different stock reply letters to applicants of the Busy Bee Bake-Off Contest. One letter notifies contestants of acceptances, as you've seen, but another indicates a rejection. Yet another advises the contestant that his or her application is incomplete. Ms. Four-chette *could* set up several different letters, but for the sake of example you'll have her take the document assembly approach instead.

Using document assembly techniques, you'd break down a stock reply document into separate *modules*. For instance, the beginning part of each letter is essentially the same: the overall format of the letter, interior address, recipient's name and address, and salutation. Then, depending on the required reply, you'd have WordPerfect insert the correct paragraphs that make up the letter. Finally, you'd add a stock ending that would be the same for all letters.

In fact, if you consistently think in terms of the *modular approach* when you design a document assembly project, you'll be able to create a very flexible setup. Break down your boilerplate modules into the smallest useful unit—such as a paragraph—if you plan to include this boilerplate in many different documents. Figure 30-1 illustrates document assembly techniques.

 Note: Keep in mind that the memory limitations of your computer may affect a merge if it's a long one. That is, you must have enough system memory to hold the entire document in memory. If you don't have enough memory, use the ^T merge code to merge the assembled document directly to the printer. Or break down the project into smaller units and test them separately by first merging them to the screen. When you've ascertained that all is well, combine the modules to create the final project.

The other important consideration is formatting, especially the *spacing* between boilerplate sections. Make sure that each boilerplate contains the correct number of blank lines that will separate it from the next part of the document. You can do this several different ways. Whatever method you adopt, be consistent! This will save you a lot of time later, because you won't have to think about the formatting when you merge the documents.

"Customizing" Stock Reply Documents

Use the original REPLY.1 letter as the basis for your first document assembly project. Recall that this letter contains merge fill-in locations. You'll break

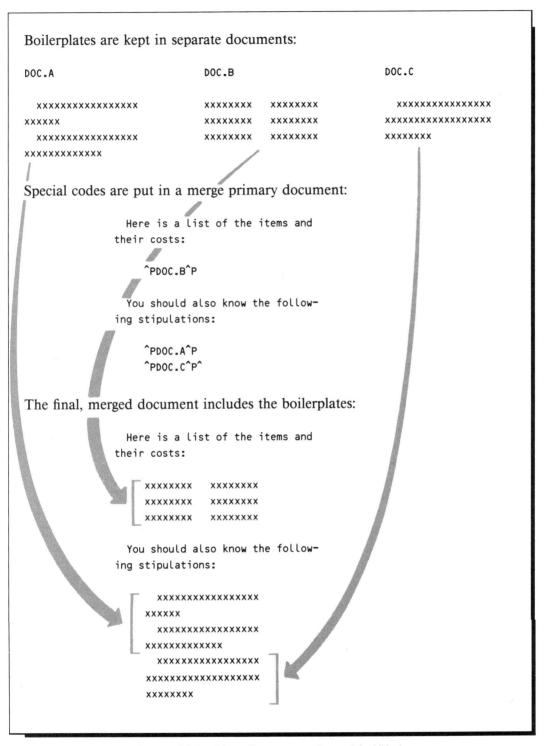

Boilerplates are kept in separate documents:

```
DOC.A                    DOC.B                    DOC.C

  xxxxxxxxxxxxxxxx       xxxxxxxx   xxxxxxxx        xxxxxxxxxxxxxxxx
xxxxxx                   xxxxxxxx   xxxxxxxx        xxxxxxxxxxxxxxxxx
  xxxxxxxxxxxxxxxx       xxxxxxxx   xxxxxxxx        xxxxxxxx
xxxxxxxxxxxxxx
```

Special codes are put in a merge primary document:

```
        Here is a list of the items and
      their costs:

          ^PDOC.B^P

      You should also know the follow-
      ing stipulations:

          ^PDOC.A^P
          ^PDOC.C^P^
```

The final, merged document includes the boilerplates:

```
        Here is a list of the items and
      their costs:

          xxxxxxxx   xxxxxxxx
          xxxxxxxx   xxxxxxxx
          xxxxxxxx   xxxxxxxx

      You should also know the follow-
      ing stipulations:

          xxxxxxxxxxxxxxxxx
        xxxxxx
          xxxxxxxxxxxxxxxx
        xxxxxxxxxxxxx
          xxxxxxxxxxxxxxxx
        xxxxxxxxxxxxxxxxxx
        xxxxxxx
```

Figure 30-1   How Document Assembly Works

the letter down into boilerplate sections, create several new boilerplates, and then do one or two document assembly merges to see the results.

✔Retrieve the REPLY.1 document.

Because you don't want to retype if you don't have to, you'll block out each paragraph and save each block to another file. At this point, however, think a bit about how you plan to use the modules, what names you'll give the files, and the spacing between modules. You decide to name the beginning of the stock letter, which includes the general first paragraph, as BEGIN.LTR. Here's how to block it out. First, press **DOWN ARROW** until you get to the left margin of the second paragraph (*We have registered . . .*). Then:

Press   **ALT-F4 Block** or **F12 Block**

Press   **HOME,HOME,HOME,UP ARROW**

Note that you've included the correct spacing between the opening section and whatever paragraph will come next when you assemble the document later. You've also blocked in the formatting codes for the letter in the opening section.

Press   **F10 Save**

Type   `begin.ltr`

Press   **RETURN**

To avoid confusion as you create the other boilerplates, delete the block:

Press   **ALT-F4 Block** or **F12 Block**

Press   **CTRL-HOME,CTRL-HOME,ALT-F4 Block**

to rehighlight the last block.

Press   **DEL** or **BACKSPACE**

Type   `y`

to delete the block.

✔Now, change the second paragraph by adding the extra sentences shown here. As you can see, you're rearranging the contents of the letter somewhat.

> We have registered your entry in the ^OEnter division:^O^C division. Please remember that the deadline for all further entries is November 30, 1989. We certainly hope that you win first prize. Good luck!

✔Move the cursor to the top of the document (WordPerfect reverts to the default margins, but don't worry). Then:

Press   **ALT-F4 Block** or **F12 Block**

Press   **DOWN ARROW** five times

Press   **F10 Save**

Type   yes.ltr

Press   **RETURN**

✔Delete the block now. For the "generic" closing of the letter, you'll change the last paragraph. Delete this paragraph and type the new paragraph shown below. Keep the closing section with Ms. Fourchette's name and title intact so that the entire closing reads:

> Thank you for your participation in the Busy Bee Bake-Off Contest.
>
>   Sincerely,
>
>
>
>   Simone Fourchette
>   Director

When you're finished:

Press	**F10 Save**
Type	`closing.ltr`
Press	**RETURN**

✔Clear the screen now. Time to set up the boilerplate paragraphs for the other reply letter possibilities. Type the following example.

```
    We note that your entry did not include the required
"Official Application Form."  Regrettably, we shall have to
disqualify you if you don't supply a completed form.  Please fill
out the attached blank form and return it to us as soon as
possible.
```

✔Press **RETURN** twice for spacing at the end. Make sure there are no typing mistakes. Then save the document as NEEDFORM.LTR and clear the screen.

Do the remaining examples in the same fashion. Press **RETURN** twice at the end of *each* for spacing. That's because you want the spacing in the boilerplates.

✔Type the next paragraph, press **RETURN** twice at the end, and save it as NOTCLEAR.LTR.

```
    Unfortunately, our Reviewing Committee cannot follow your
instructions, because they were not presented clearly enough.
Would you please submit your recipe in either a printed or
typewritten form?  By the way, each separate instruction should
begin on a new line.
```

✔Clear the screen and type this example. Press **RETURN** twice for spacing at the end. Save the example as BAD.LTR.

```
    Our Reviewing Committee has attempted on several occasions
to create this recipe, but has found the results consistently
inedible.  Perhaps you've left out some important ingredients?
Please check your original recipe and submit a corrected version
as soon as possible.
```

✔Clear the screen and type this example. Press **RETURN** twice for spacing at the end. (I used a hard space to keep *November* and *30* together.) Save the example as DISQUAL.LTR.

```
After painstaking review of your recipe by our Reviewing
Committee, we feel obliged to inform you that your entry does not
meet the qualifications for this contest.  Please feel free to
submit another entry before the cut-off date, which is
November 30, 1989.
```

You now have seven boilerplates that you can assemble to form a number of different stock reply documents. At this point, it's a good idea to make a list of your boilerplate file names and what they do. Here's the list:

BEGIN.LTR	standard letter opening
YES.LTR	acceptance of recipe
CLOSING.LTR	standard letter closing
NEEDFORM.LTR	no form
NOTCLEAR.LTR	recipe unclear
BAD.LTR	inedible recipe
DISQUAL.LTR	total rejection

Some bright souls out there in Readerland may already have realized that you can expand this setup to include a data entry form for the reply letters, too. Don't get *too* carried away yet!
✔Clear the screen now.

Command Documents

You'll now create a series of command documents to assemble the various letters. *Command documents* contain a list of the primary files that you'll merge, each one enclosed in ^P codes. Command documents direct the merge but don't necessarily have to contain any text other than the file names.
✔Using the **SHIFT-F9 Merge Codes** key, enter the following codes and type the file names for the first command document, shown here.

Caution: Make sure there are begin and end ^P codes around each file name.

`^Pbegin.ltr^P^Pyes.ltr^P^Pclosing.ltr^P`

Question: Why are the file names all on one line? *Answer:* Because you already have the correct number of blank lines in each boilerplate document. If you put the file names in the command document on separate lines, each line ending with a hard return, then there would be an extra blank line between the paragraphs when you assemble the boilerplates to create a reply letter. You *could* have set up the spacing in the command document, but then you'd have to remove the extra hard returns at the ends of each boilerplate paragraph. It's up to you.

✔Save this document as ACCEPT.LTR but leave it on the screen.

Create the other three command documents by just deleting the middle file name and inserting another. That way, you don't have to enter the merge codes or file extension again! Save the first command document as TRYAGAIN.LTR, the second as NOFORM.LTR, and the third as REJECT.LTR.

Note: These are *three* separate documents.

TRYAGAIN.LTR:

`^Pbegin.ltr^P^Pnotclear.ltr^P^Pclosing.ltr^P`

NOFORM.LTR:

`^Pbegin.ltr^P^Pneedform.ltr^P^Pclosing.ltr^P`

REJECT.LTR:

`^Pbegin.ltr^P^Pbad.ltr^P^Pclosing.ltr^P`

You're finally ready to try out the new document assembly setup.

Caution: Make sure that all documents are on the same disk or in the same directory and that you've made that disk or directory the default. Do a rejection letter but clear the screen first. Then:

Press   **CTRL-F9 Merge/Sort**

Type   **1** or **m** [<u>M</u>erge]

Type   `reject.ltr`

Press   **RETURN** twice

because there is no secondary document.

WordPerfect first calls up the standard letter opening and asks you to supply the fill-in information. Notice that the other two document names are on the screen, too, because WordPerfect hasn't gotten to them yet. Supply the following information from the keyboard or make up your own. Remember to press **F9 Merge R** to enter the information for each line.

```
Enter full name: Rev. Malcolm W. Small
Enter street address: 66 Coventry Way
Enter city, state, zip: Lexington, KY  28504
Enter salutation: Rev. Small
Enter recipe: Catfish Quiche
```

After you fill in these entries, WordPerfect finishes the letter by inserting the other two boilerplates, and the letter is then ready to print. Now, try the other three letters to get more experience with document assembly merge.

✔Clear the screen when you're finished.

Some Useful Tips

Keep track of the boilerplate documents with a "crib sheet" of what each boilerplate contains. In fact, why not print the documents with the normal print command and keep them in a folder for quick reference? Of course, boilerplates aren't restricted to single paragraphs. You can have multipage documents as boilerplates. For example, you could set up a contract document merge project that includes many different contract parts.

Sometimes you'll find that after a merge some words could possibly be hyphenated to fill in the lines better. You could then turn hyphenation on in the merged document and quickly check for hyphenation spots. Or insert soft hyphens in those words that you think may cause you problems at the ends of line. Do you remember how to do this? Right! Use CTRL-HYPHEN.

I repeat the two absolutely important points about working with boilerplate text: (1) check your spelling carefully and (2) make sure that you include the correct spacing between sections so that you don't have to add or adjust it later.

The format for Ms. Fourchette's various letters is in the BEGIN.LTR boilerplate, because that always comes first. It's also possible to have the command document itself govern the formatting. Just include the desired format changes at the beginning of the command document. How you determine your formatting requirements depends on the types of document you're assembling and the way you intend to set up your boilerplates.

A More Elaborate Boilerplate Example

Say that you want to "automate" a document assembly system for documents that require a set number of boilerplate sections, but with a choice of several boilerplates for each section. For instance, pretend you have to create a stock contract with different boilerplate sections depending on the terms of the contract.

You can have WordPerfect insert the correct document file in a merge. Use the fill-in technique instead of creating separate command documents. For instance, Ms. Fourchette sends several different letters, but each letter requires the same opening and closing sections. She could have set up just one command file to request the *middle* paragraph for each letter. So, for her rejection letter she would simply supply the name of the correct boilerplate document—in this case BAD.LTR.

Take a look at the following example. It illustrates how to set up a fill-in document assembly, as well as a few other interesting points.

`^Pbegin.ltr^P^U^OWhat middle paragraph do you want? (notclear, needform, or bad):^P^C.ltr^P^O^Pclosing.ltr^P`

This command document is similar to the three you just created—TRYAGAIN.LTR, NOFORM.LTR, and REJECT.LTR—in that each includes the standing opening and closing sections. However, this command document *requests* the middle section of the letter from you when you merge the document. Note the screen prompt after the first ^O code: it asks for the boilerplate file and tells you which file name you can supply— NOTCLEAR, NEEDFORM, or BAD.

Whatever file name you type replaces the ^C code within the ^P codes! What's more, because you've set up each boilerplate to end with the extension .LTR, the merge document supplies the extension so that you don't have to type it: `^C.ltr`. Note the position of the ^C code; whatever you type is added to the .LTR extension to form the complete file name. If you wanted to supply a beginning name and have the user finish the name, then put the ^C code after the beginning letters. For example, if each file begins with the letters *ch.*, set up the code like this: `ch.^C`.

However, notice where the ending ^O code is located. For some reason, the ^O codes must enclose the entire section here in order for the merge to work properly. The ^U code is an added touch. It merely *rewrites* the screen to make things appear less cluttered.

✔Retrieve the TRYAGAIN.LTR document and delete the section `^Pnotclear.ltr^P`. Add the codes and text shown in the last example. Make sure you use the **SHIFT-F9 Merge Codes** key correctly to add all the begin and end codes. When you're finished, save the new document as CHOICE.LTR.

To run this new merge document, clear the screen. Then:

Press   **CTRL-F9 Merge/Sort**

Type   1 [Merge]

Type   `choice.ltr`

Press   **RETURN** twice

Supply name, address, and recipe information, remembering to press **F9 Merge R** to continue. When WordPerfect prompts you for a middle paragraph, type one of the choices listed (without the .LTR extension), and press **F9 Merge R**. There's your reply letter!

Of course, this is a very simple example, but it does show you how to have WordPerfect insert information into merge codes and how to set up some pretty complicated document assembly procedures. The most important considerations are that you must set up your boilerplate documents correctly and that the merged document contain the same number of boilerplate choices. That is, the middle section of each letter is at present one paragraph, and you only have an instruction to insert *one* merge document here.

Be consistent at all times. If you had two insert instructions, they might apply for all letters. It is better to change the boilerplates if necessary and to leave the basic command document as generic as possible. For instance, if it turns out that the NEEDFORM.LTR boilerplate actually is composed of two paragraphs, set both up in the same document so that you can still call up the boilerplate as one file.

If you can keep track of which boilerplates to use, it makes sense to use short document names so that you don't have to type long names continually. Again, keep a crib sheet or supply information in your prompts. For example, you've renamed the three boilerplate files so that NOTCLEAR.LTR is N.LTR, NEEDFORM.LTR is F.LTR, and BAD.LTR is B.LTR. Your prompt could then read: `Type n for notclear, f for needform, or b for bad:`.

As with all merge tasks, planning is everything when you set up document assembly procedures. Determine your needs and the setup that's best for you. Try to make command documents as generic as possible and boilerplates as modular as possible for the most flexibility in creating many different documents easily.

A Generic Setup Example

Say that you do many different form letter mailings and you work with many different secondary documents. You can set up a generic "request" command document that asks for the names of the merge documents and provides helpful prompts for inexperienced users. Take a look at this simple example:

```
^OWhat is the secondary (name and address) document? ^S^C^S^O
^OWhat is the primary (letter) document? ^P^C^P^O
```

Notice the ^s codes. These codes insert a secondary merge document at the location of the first code. Note also that there is a space between the prompt and the first ^s code, so that the file name that the user types does not run into the prompt on the screen. Finally, I have found that you must request the secondary document name *first* before the primary document name.

✔Type this example exactly as you see it. Make sure to use the **SHIFT-F9 Merge Codes** key to insert the codes correctly. Save the document as FORMLET. Then clear the screen.

A good way to use this generic command document is with a macro to start it. Call the macro FL for "form letters." Here's how to set up the macro:

Press **CTRL-F10 Macro Define**

Type   fl

Press **RETURN**

Type   Form Letter Request

Press **RETURN**

Press **CTRL-F9 Merge/Sort**

Type   1 or m [<u>M</u>erge]

Type   formlet

Press **RETURN** twice

At this point, the merge will begin and request the secondary document name. You first want to stop the macro definition, so:

Press **SHIFT-F9 Merge Codes**

to end the merge and the macro definition.

Now, whenever you want to start another form letter mailing, press **ALT-F10 Macro** and supply the FL macro name. WordPerfect first requests the secondary document and then the primary document. Remember to press **F9 Merge R** after each.

Chaining Documents Together

Use the document assembly approach when you want to link, or *chain*, several documents in succession. The chapters of a book come immediately to mind. Say you're writing a book with an introduction and five chapters, each in a separate document. If you want to print the entire book in one fell swoop, you can set up a command document to do this. You may even want to include page numbering instructions in the command document so that you don't have to determine page numbering for each separate chapter document.

Of course, you can also create a master document (Chapter 25). The advantage to a merge command document is that you don't have to expand the command document as you would have to expand the master document before you print the entire book. The disadvantage to the command document is that WordPerfect can't keep track of note and cross-reference numbering. Still, a command document can come in handy when you just want to print a draft of a large project quickly.

You'll probably also want each chapter to start at the top of a new page. So, include hard page codes in the command document after each file name. Finally, if the book is a large one, remember that WordPerfect might not be able to merge it completely into memory. So, include ^T codes to print each chapter and then clear memory.

Here, then, is a command document that chain-prints several chapter documents together. This is just an example to use as a model for your own needs. You haven't actually created the files in the following list. Put in the ^P codes and type each file name. Directly after the ending ^P code for each file, add a ^T code to send the output to the printer. Then press CTRL-RETURN for a hard page. Notice that WordPerfect shows the page breaks in the document.

```
^Pintro^P^T
===============================================================================
^Pchapter.1^P^T
===============================================================================
^Pchapter.2^P^T
===============================================================================
^Pchapter.3^P^T
===============================================================================
^Pchapter.4^P^T
===============================================================================
^Pchapter.5^P^T
```

✔Save the document if you wish, then clear the screen.

Now take another break before you continue. All this talk about recipes and bake-offs has made me hungry. I wonder what's in the refrigerator?

31

More Merge Examples

Dear Reader, I could go on and on showing you ever more complex and powerful merge examples, but then I'd have to pay my editor's medical bills. There's time and space for just a few more typical merge tasks. You'll learn how to create a "pseudo" fill-in document, how to do a double merge, how to set up merge reports in neatly aligned columns, how to combine merge and math features, and how to develop your own customized menus—among other things!

> **DO WARM-UP**

A "Pseudo" Fill-In Document

Fill-in merge documents (Chapter 29) are great when you just want to zip out a fast letter or envelope and you aren't concerned with saving the recipient's name and address. Suppose, however, that you correspond with a certain number of people on a regular basis, but you don't want to set up their names and addresses in a secondary merge document because that's too much trouble. Is there a happy medium between the two, between a fill-in document and a full-fledged form letter mailing? Yes! Use a part fill-in, part document assembly document!

Take a look at the opening section of the letter below. This is not an example to type, so just relax! Instead of an interior address and salutation lines there are some ^O, ^C, and ^P merge codes. Can you figure out what they do?

```
                                    4118 Loony Tunes Blvd.
                                    Los Angeles, CA  90027
                                    ^D



^OThis letter is going to (type correct the letter):
     Centre Theater Group - C
     Ms. Jones - J
     Madame La Farge - L
     Nancy's Husband - H
     Queen Elizabeth - Q
     Mr. Smith - S
^O^P^C^P


     Thanks again for writing and for your order.  You should be
receiving your shipment in a matter of days.  If you have any
questions, and so on ...
```

Time's up! The ^O codes enclose a descriptive message that prompts you to type a one-character file name. Even though the message is composed of several lines that end in hard returns, these returns don't mess up the final merge document. After you type the file name you want, the ^C code inserts the name between the two ^P codes, which in turn instruct WordPerfect to merge that file into the letter.

The name and address information for each person or group is in separate documents: C, J, L, H, Q, and S. Here's what S, Mr. Smith's document, looks like:

```
Mr. Ronald Smith
507 Camino Real
El Paso, TX  77901


Dear Mr. Smith:
```

No hard return here!

The client document contains both the interior address and the salutation line. The document ends directly after the colon, because you don't want an extra hard return to throw off the spacing. Naturally, after you type one document, you can copy it as a basis for the others.

The advantage to this approach is that you can alter the salutation information. The C document for Centre Theater Group looks like this:

```
Centre Theater Group
600 West Temple Street
Los Angeles, CA  90012


Ladies/Gentlemen:
```

When you merge the letter document, supply its name as the primary document but *do not* supply a secondary document—just press RETURN. The message lines pop up from the bottom of the screen, and directly below that is WordPerfect's prompt, `Primary file:`. When you type `s` and press **F9 Merge R** or **RETURN**, you have your letter (the date, of course, will be different than the one here):

```
                         4118 Loony Tunes Blvd.
                         Los Angeles, CA  90027
                         January 13, 1988




Mr. Ronald Smith
507 Camino Real
El Paso, TX  77901

Dear Mr. Smith:

    Thanks again for writing and for your order.  You should be
receiving your shipment in a matter of days.  If you have any
questions, and so on ...
```

Neat, huh? By the way, the inspiration for this example came from one of my readers in San Francisco, who had a need for this type of arrangement. Keep those letters coming, Dear Readers!

A Double Merge

Now for a slightly more complicated example, one that does *two* merge operations. You'll use the original PATRONS secondary document as part of a merge to create a simple report. Here's what the final merged report looks like. Yours will also contain the extra names that you added to the PATRONS document (Chapter 27).

```
                    Consolidated Toupee

                      Customer List

            Name / Residence / Last Order Date
```

```
Montgomery-Simpson, Ms. Sue Ann / Atlanta, GA / January 18, 1986
Mustard, Mr. and Mrs. Stanislaus / Richmond, VA / September 3, 1985
      Alfieri, Dr. Vincent / East Podunk, WY / April 26, 1986
```

In addition to the PATRONS document, three new documents occur in this setup: (1) a "header" document for the title lines, (2) a primary merge document to print the customer information, and (3) a controlling command document for the entire merge. This time, you won't use a normal header setup. Instead, the title lines will be in a separate boilerplate that will be merged into the resulting document. Try doing that one first, because it's the easiest.

✔Center and type *only* the three title lines in the example. Note that the second line is in boldface. At the end of the third line, press **RETURN** twice for spacing. Then save this new document as PATRONS.HDR and clear the screen.

Now for the document to govern the merge of the customer information from the PATRONS document. The only tricky part of this document is that the first line is centered, but WordPerfect won't center the merge codes as you enter them. So center the line *after* you create it. That is, enter the merge codes and other text, then press **RETURN** to end the line. Move the cursor back up into the line to center it. Here is the entire document:

```
              ^F4^, ^F2^ ^F3^ / ^F6^, ^F7^ / ^F1^

^N^P^P
```

Note the spaces and slashes between fields, as well as the ^N^P^P codes at the end of the document. These codes instruct WordPerfect to repeat the line for each record in the secondary document.

✔Save this document as PATRONS.RPT. Then clear the screen.

Keep in mind that if you added the title lines to this document, WordPerfect would print one set of lines for each record, which is not what you want. So, the "header" information is in a separate document that you'll merge only *once* later.

The command document contains merge codes to insert first the "header" document and then the merge document for the names and addresses. What's more, because it's the controlling document, you should put any page or line formatting changes in it, too. After a bit of experimentation, I decided that the left and right margins should be 0.5 inch. Change them now. Then type the following merge codes and text. Note the file names within the set of ^P codes.

```
^Ppatrons.hdr^P
^Ppatrons.rpt^P
```

Because the spacing between the title lines and the report itself is in the PATRONS.HDR document, you don't add any blank lines between the ^P codes in this document.

✔Save the document as PATRONS.CMD and clear the screen.

Now for the merge itself. Make sure the three files you just created are on the same drive or in the same directory, and that that's the default directory. Then:

Press   **CTRL-F9 Merge/Sort**

Type   1 or **m** [<u>M</u>erge]

Type   **patrons.cmd**

Press   **RETURN**

Even though there are actually *two* primary documents, PATRONS.RPT and PATRONS.CMD, and even though the secondary document is technically merged into PATRONS.RPT, you must still use PATRONS.CMD for the primary document.

Type   **patrons**

for the secondary document.

Press   **RETURN**

And there's your simple report!

Note: If WordPerfect tells you it can't find the files, go into the PATRONS.CMD document and add a drive designator to the file names. For instance, if the three files are on the B drive, type **b:patrons.hdr** as the first file name and **b:patrons.rpt** as the second file name.

✔Clear the screen now.

Columnar Text Reports from Merges

Now you can change the report so that the information is neatly arranged in parallel columns. This means that you'll add a column setup to the PATRONS.RPT document. You'll find that the biggest problem with doing merged columnar reports is to get the margins right. Only trial and error can help you in this respect.

To remind you how you initially arranged the fields, set up the original PATRONS.RPT document as Doc 2. You have to make some major changes to the document for a column setup.

✔Split the screen into two windows with the first window having 14 lines. Switch to Doc 2 and retrieve the PATRONS.RPT document into the bottom window. Then switch back to Doc 1.

To arrange the field information in columns, you must first define the columns:

Press   **ALT-F7 Math/Columns**

Type   **4** or **d** [Column **D**ef]

Type   **1** or **t** [**T**ype]

Type   **2** or **p** [**P**arallel]

for parallel columns.

Type   **2** or **n** [**N**umber of Columns]

Type   **3**

Press   **RETURN**

for the number of text columns.

Here are the left and right margins for the three parallel columns. You'd normally have to experiment to get the correct settings, so I'm saving you a little time! Type each number and press **RETURN**.

```
Left: 0.5    Right: 3.5
Left: 4.0    Right: 5.5
Left: 6.0    Right: 8.0
```

Press   **F7 Exit**

Type   **3** or **c** [**C**olumn On/Off]

✔With the **SHIFT-F9 Merge Codes** command, enter the first column's merge codes and the correct spacing and punctuation so that everything looks like this:

^F4^, ^F2^ ^F3^

To enter the merge codes for the second column, you must position the cursor in that column. Do you remember how?

Press   **CTRL-RETURN**

The merge codes for this column look like this:

^F6^, ^F7^

After entering these codes, spacing, and punctuation,

Press   **CTRL-RETURN**

Enter the last column's code: ^F1^.
Caution: On the same line you must now turn column mode *off.*

Press   **ALT-F7 Math/Columns**

Type   **3** or **c** [Column On/Off]

Now, enter the ^N^P^P merge codes on the next line, as in the original example, so that the entire document looks like this:

```
^F4^, ^F2^ ^F3^                    ^F6^, ^F7^              ^F1^
       ^N^P^P
```

✔Save the document in the top window as PATRONS.R2. Then clear both windows and restore the screen to its full size.
Next, you change the original PATRONS.CMD command document so that it merges in PATRONS.R2 instead of PATRONS.RPT.
✔Retrieve the PATRONS.CMD document and change the second line so that the file to be merged is PATRONS.R2. Save this new document as PATRONS.C2, then clear the screen.
Now for the merge itself:

Press   **CTRL-F9 Merge/Sort**

Type   **1** or **m** [Merge]

Type   **patrons.c2**

Press   **RETURN**

Type   **patrons**

Press   **RETURN**

Note that WordPerfect couldn't fit some names on one line, so it forced the names onto two lines in the first column. You can readjust the margins of the columns if you wish. You may also want to redo the original header document so that the headings are centered over each column. Try it!

🖝 Clear the screen before you continue.

Math Reports from Merges

Setting up a math report as part of a merge is similar to doing columnar text reports. Make sure you define the math columns first, turn math on, and then insert the merge codes in each column. Recall also that you must separate the information in math columns with tabs. You may have to experiment a bit to get the tab settings the way you want them.

The following example uses a secondary document containing student names and grade scores for a school on a trimester system. The secondary document contains four fields: the student's name and the three grades. Here is what a few records in this document look like (remember that WordPerfect supplies hard page breaks after the ^E codes, so don't type them!):

```
Albatross, Ferdinand J.^R
92.5^R
88.0^R
90.1^R
^E

================================================================================
Bouchard, Constance B.^R
85.4^R
82.3^R
89.3^R
^E

================================================================================
Bouchard, Robert A.^R
98.3^R
95.0^R
96.1^R
^E

================================================================================
```

🖝 To do this example, create a document called GRADES and add as many records as you like, using the example as your guide. Make sure to end each field with an ^R code and each record with an ^E code. Clear the screen after you save the document.

Caution: The math feature may not be "smart" enough to work with numbers in different *decimal* formats. Be consistent in how you enter numbers. That is, if you use a decimal point in some numbers, use it in all. For example, in the GRADES document if a grade is 90, enter it as 90.0.

The merged document will contain the student's name, the grades for each trimester, and a final grade average in separate columns.

✔To set up this primary math document, first clear all tabs and set new left-justified tabs at columns 4.0, 5.0, 6.0, and 7.0. Then:

Press   **ALT-F7 Math/Columns**

Type   **2** or **e** [Math D*e*f]

Press   **RIGHT ARROW** three times

for column D.

Type   **0** [Calculation]

Type   **+/**

to average the numbers in the three previous columns.

Press   **RETURN**

Press   **F7 Exit**

Type   **1** or **m** [*M*ath On]

The first column, a text column, is not part of the numbering for the math columns. This column will contain the student's name. For the first field, just use the **SHIFT-F9 Merge Codes** command to enter ^F1^ at the left margin. To add each other field, first press the **TAB** key to go to each new column before you add the field. Make sure you press **TAB** to bring up the ! calculation operator in the fourth math column.

Don't turn math off at the end of the line, because you want the merged document to have math on. Press **RETURN** to space down, and add the ^N^P^P codes. The resulting document looks like this on the screen:

```
^F1^                         ^F2^      ^F3^      ^F4^     !
^N^P^P
```

✔Save the document as GRADES.RPT and clear the screen. Now, merge the two documents, using GRADES.RPT as the primary document and GRADES as the secondary document. (You could, if you wish, create a header for the report and a command document at this point. See Chapter 33 for information on how to sort the secondary document alphabetically.)

After the merge, you must still calculate the results (this assumes math is on, as it should be now):

Press   **ALT-F7 Math/Columns**

Type   **2** or **a** [C<u>a</u>lculate]

✔ Save the merge document if you wish, then clear the screen.

Searching for Merge Codes

You can use the various search commands to find merge codes in your documents. After starting a search, press **SHIFT-F9 Merge Codes**. Then just type the code you want. If you're searching for the ^R codes, use **F9 Merge R** instead.

Tip: You can also enter the merge code directly from the keyboard. Just hold down the CTRL key and type the letter.

If you want to search for the ^F merge codes in a document, you don't have to include the ending caret symbol. For example, you're looking for all ^F2^ codes from the beginning of the document. Press **F2 ▶Search**, press **CTRL-F**, and type **2**. The search string would thus be ^F2. Press **F2 ▶Search** to start the search.

Merged Menus

You can use the fill-in merge feature together with the display of prompts to make customized menus that guide you and your fellow WordPerfect users through various tasks. For instance, you'll learn how to create a menu for new documents that calls up the correct *format document* (Chapter 14). You never have to worry about setting formats or finding the right format document again. Here's the entire menu document:

```
^O                            New Document Menu

              A - Article

              C - Chapter

              L - Personal Letter
```

```
M - Memo

R - Daily Activity Report

S - Stock Reply Letter

Your choice? - ^P^C.new^P^O
```

Notice where the ^0 codes are, and also notice that screen prompts can extend over several lines. WordPerfect just assumes that everything between the ^0 codes, except for the other merge codes, is a prompt. When you set up menus, keep in mind that WordPerfect brings the menu up from the *bottom* of the screen when you merge the menu document.

Note: A merge won't work correctly if there are font changes or other formatting codes *within* begin and end ^0 merge codes. Don't do it!

What's more, think about how you'll *center* the menu items on the screen. The example above looks off-center right now, but it will display correctly when you merge it.

Caution: Use the **SPACEBAR** to position the entries over on the screen. The TAB key won't work. Take into account the two spaces taken up by the ^0 code on the first line. The word *New* starts at Pos 4.2", and each entry below it starts at Pos 3.5". The last line starts at Pos 3.3".

Each letter represents a different format document with the file extension .NEW. For example, the format document for a new article is in the file A.NEW. The L.NEW and S.NEW format documents may contain inside addresses and other merge codes, depending on your particular needs. (You haven't created these documents yet. This is just an example.)

✔Work with the example as a guide to create a menu for the document formats that you use. Save the menu document as MENU.NEW. Then set up each document format in another file with a one letter name and the extension .NEW. When you're finished, clear the screen.

To use this menu effectively, set up a macro that calls up the menu. You'll assign it to ALTM:

Press	**CTRL-F10 Macro Define**
Press	**ALT-M**
Type	Call Menu
Press	**RETURN**
Press	**CTRL-F9 Merge/Sort**
Type	1 or m [Merge]
Type	menu.new

Press   **RETURN** twice

WordPerfect automatically ends a macro definition when the macro starts a merge, but you must still stop the merge:

Press   **SHIFT-F9 Merge Codes**

From now on, whenever you or your colleagues want to start a new document, just press **ALT-M** to bring up the menu, then select the letter corresponding to the document type. Press **F9 Merge R** to complete the selection. Of course, if you type an incorrect letter, or more than one letter, WordPerfect would tell you that it can't find that particular file. By using menus like this, you can eliminate errors and needless keystroking! To get out of the menu without making a selection, just press **SHIFT-F9 Merge Codes**.

A Menu for Macros

As a tie-in to the next chapter, here's another menu that calls up certain predefined macros. Each macro is assigned to an ALT key, such as the ALPP macro to print a document. Note how the menu explains the macro, so that you or your friends never have to remember which macro does what.

Caution: This menu works best on a clear screen. If you attempt to merge this menu into the middle of an existing document, you'll get unexpected results.

   ^O   Macro Menu

                 M – New Document Menu

                 P – Print a Document from Disk

                 R – Retrieve a Document

                 S – Spell Check a Document

                 W – Word Count

                 Your choice? – ^Galt^C.wpm^G^O

✔After you type this document, save it as MACRO.MEN.

You may want to create a macro that calls up this menu, as you did in the previous example. When you select a letter from the menu, WordPerfect performs the macro associated with this item. Note the use of the ^G codes to run the macro, the letters ALT, and the file extension .WPM. WordPerfect sets up ALT key macros in files that begin with the word ALT followed by the letter. For example, the macro ALTR would be in a file called ALTR.WPM, so you have to supply these extra letters in the menu setup.

Did you notice that this menu calls a macro, ALTM.WPM, that in turn calls another menu? Neat!

I think you realize that an ounce of planning is worth a pound of problems later. Plan the names of your macros so that you can set them up like this in menus. For example, perhaps you can have the second letter of each macro be an X. After you set up your menu, change the fill-in section within the ^G codes to something like this: ^G^Cx.wpm^G .

Dear Reader, so much for the fascinating world of merge. This last section on merges and macros leads me to the next topic: advanced macro techniques.

For Power Users

32

Advanced Macros

In this chapter you'll learn the following new command . . .

Numeric Keypad Command

CTRL-PG UP (1) Set up a pause for keyboard input, (2) display
menus as a macro runs, (3) assign a value to a
variable, (4) enter a comment, (5) access advanced
macro programming commands

. . . and you'll discover a new way to use this command:

F2 ▶Search Set up a repeating macro

No doubt, you've been setting up your own personalized macros all along,
in addition to the ones I've mentioned in this book. There's a lot more to
macros than what you learned in Chapter 7. This chapter continues where
that one left off. It shows you ways to get the most out of WordPerfect's macro
feature, and even takes you a short distance into the realm of macro programming. Dear Reader, parts of this chapter are not for the timid, so forewarned is forearmed!

DO WARM-UP

The Startup Macro

Recall that in the Prelude I introduced some of the various WordPerfect startup options. When you load WordPerfect, you can supply a macro name after the /M switch, and WordPerfect will run the macro first. For example, in the last chapter you created the macro ALTM to present a menu of new document formats. Now say you want this menu to appear as soon as you start working with WordPerfect. Just load the program with this line: WP/M-ALTM. Note the hyphen that separates the /M switch from the macro name. You don't have to add the .WPM file extension.

Another useful startup macro would be one that lists all files on the disk or directory, so that you can just choose the file you want to retrieve and edit. Yet another good startup macro would change the drive or directory to one that doesn't contain the WordPerfect program. Or perhaps you'd like a startup macro that displays the tab ruler line at the bottom of the screen? You can do it!

You can go one step further and have your AUTOEXEC.BAT file (Chapter 36) load WordPerfect with a startup macro that presents a menu on the screen. This menu could in turn call other menus set up in other macros. You've essentially created a *turnkey system*, one that works automatically when you "turn the key," that is, start your computer.

Question: What if you want WordPerfect to start *two or more* macros automatically? *Answer:* Although the /M switch lets you start only one macro, you could have the first macro start a second when it's finished. The second could start a third, and so on. See Chaining Macros Together.

The Macro Commands Key

In many of the examples you'll work with the Macro Commands key, **CTRL-PG UP**. This command has enhanced functions that aren't in previous WordPerfect versions. It also acts differently under different conditions. In fact, so much has changed that experienced WordPerfect users should study this chapter carefully.

WordPerfect has a powerful and complex macro programming language, but you can perform many operations without programming. The first part of this chapter discusses the "nonprogramming" approach and gives you ideas about different types of advanced macros. Later you'll take a deep breath and learn a little macro programming, too.

Ten Temporary "Macros"

The basic function of CTRL-PG UP is to give values to variables. A *variable* is merely a temporary storage location in the computer's memory, like a post office box. When you store a value in the variable "box," you *assign* that value to the variable. You can use the digits (1–9) and zero (0) on the *top* row of the typewriter keyboard only, not the numeric keypad. Later, to retrieve the value from the variable you hold down the ALT key and type the digit or zero.

Although variables are the pawns of programming, there's no reason why you can't use them as ten temporary "macros" to call up text (codes won't work). For example, suppose you're typing a long article about Beethoven's *Ninth Symphony* today. You can set up a temporary variable that types Ninth Symphony. To assign values to variables, follow these steps (you don't have to do them now):

1. Press **CTRL-PG UP**. WordPerfect prompts:

   Variable:

2. Type the digit or zero on the top row of the typewriter keyboard to which you want to assign a text value. WordPerfect then prompts:

   Value:

3. Type the value and press **RETURN**.

   To insert the value of a variable at the cursor location, press ALT-<digit>, where <digit> is the number or zero that contains the value. Because they're temporary, variables disappear when you exit WordPerfect.

Macros That Pause for Keyboard Input

Another common and useful function of CTRL-PG UP is to insert a *pause* instruction into a macro. The pause lets you enter information from the keyboard during a macro. When you press RETURN, the macro continues.

A Window Opener

In the first example you'll define a new macro called ALTW that splits the screen into two windows. The macro is "generic": It lets you determine different window sizes when you run the macro.

Caution: If you've already assigned a different macro to ALTW, use another letter or replace the existing macro.

✔Clear the screen, then start the macro definition:

Press   **CTRL-F10 Macro Define**

Press   **ALT-W**

or any other key you want to use if you've already assigned a macro to ALTW.

Type   Window Change

Press   **RETURN**

for the macro's description.

Press   **CTRL-F3 Screen**

Type   1 or w [Window]

Here's where you want to insert a pause instruction so that you can enter the window size during the macro:

Press   **CTRL-PG UP**

WordPerfect presents this menu:

1 Pause; 2 Display: 0

 Note: At times you'll see a different menu when you press CTRL-PG UP:

1 Pause; 2 Display; 3 Assign; 4 Comment: 0

The three other choices are actually programming commands about which I'll have more to say later.

Type   1 or p [Pause]

Nothing seems to happen, but you must now tell WordPerfect that the pause is over:

Press   **RETURN**

Continue with the macro:

Press   **RETURN**

to set the number of lines in the window (it will be for the entire screen, but don't worry).

Press   **CTRL-F10 Macro Define**

to end the definition.

Now, when you press ALT-W to run this macro, WordPerfect pauses to let you specify the number of lines in the window. Type the number. When you press RETURN, the macro continues. That is, it splits the screen.

A Document Joiner

Here's another simple macro that comes in handy. I call it ALTJ, and it joins one document into another. It starts the normal retrieve operation but lets you specify a file name during the pause. Here are the steps:

Press   **CTRL-F10 Macro Define**

Press   **ALT-J**

Type   Join

Press   **RETURN**

Press   **SHIFT-F10 Retrieve**

Press   **CTRL-PG UP**

Type   1 or p [Pause]

Press   **RETURN** twice

Press   **CTRL-F10 Macro Define**

To use this macro, position the cursor where you want to join another document into the current one. Then press ALT-J.

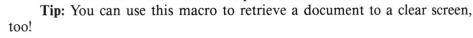

Tip: You can use this macro to retrieve a document to a clear screen, too!

A File Lister

Here's another example. This ALTF macro does a "file" listing, but it also stops so that you can either press RETURN to see all files or type a selection criterion.

Press	**CTRL-F10 Macro Define**
Press	**ALT-F**
Type	`File Listing`
Press	**RETURN**
Press	**F5 List Files**
Press	**CTRL-PG UP**
Type	`1` or `p` [P̲ause]
Press	**RETURN** twice
Press	**CTRL-F10 Macro Define**

Try this macro now. Press **ALT-F**. Then either press **RETURN** for all files or type a selection criterion, such as `*.ltr` to see all files with the extension .LTR.

A Macro That Inserts Format Documents

Finally, in Chapter 14 I mentioned a macro that inserts a format document from a format library when you begin work on a new document. To run this macro, you first have to have all your format documents in files with the same extension. For example, suppose each format document is in a file with the extension .FMT for "format." There may be files named LETTER.FMT, ARTICLE.FMT, REPORT1.FMT, and so on. This is your format library.

Once you've set up your format library, here's the macro, ALTI, to insert the format document of your choice. (You can use another letter, or a file name, for the macro name.)

✔Clear the screen before you define this macro.

Press	**CTRL-F10 Macro Define**
Press	**ALT-I**

or whatever is the letter you want.

Type	`Insert Format Doc`
Press	**RETURN**
Press	**SHIFT-F10 Retrieve**

Press   **CTRL-PG UP**

Type   1 or p [Pause]

Press   **RETURN**

to insert a pause.

Type   `.fmt`

Press   **RETURN**

At this point WordPerfect tells you that you've entered an invalid file name, but you can still complete the macro definition:

Press   **CTRL-F10 Macro Define**

Get rid of the error message:

Press   **F1 Cancel**

to cancel the retrieve operation.

This macro pauses to request a file name to retrieve, but it automatically supplies the file extension .FMT. All you do is type the name without extension and press RETURN to retrieve the file. For example, to retrieve the file called LETTER.FMT (if it existed!), you'd press ALT-I, type letter, and press RETURN.

Chaining Macros Together

The term *macro chaining* refers to three decidedly different ways to run one or more macros together:

1. You can have one macro call, or run, another in a direct chain. That is, when the first macro ends, it calls the second. The second could call a third, and so on.

2. You can, under certain circumstances, have a macro call itself. This is a *repeating* macro.

3. Finally, you can create a *conditional* macro. This is a macro that—at its most basic level—calls one of two other macros depending on whether a condition during the run of the original macro is true or false.

In previous versions of WordPerfect, repeating macros and conditional macros had to include a standard Search command as part of the macro definition. That's still the case in certain situations, and you can still chain or repeat macros without programming. But you'll need to learn programming to set up conditional macros.

A Simple Chain

When you want one macro to call another in a simple chain, you don't have to use the Search command. As an example of a simple chain, you'll define a macro called SP that saves a document, leaves it on the screen, and then prints the document. This macro calls the ALTP macro, which you've already defined, but you still want to keep ALTP separate to be able to use it alone.

Caution: There must be a document on the screen, and you must have saved the document once for this macro to work correctly.

✔Clear the screen and retrieve any document now.

Press	**CTRL-F10 Macro Define**
Type	sp
Type	Save and Print
Press	**RETURN**
Press	**F10 Save**
Press	**RETURN**
Type	y

Here's where you chain in the second macro.

Press	**ALT-P**
Press	**CTRL-F10 Macro Define**

to end the macro definition.

✔Try this macro out if you wish. Then clear the screen.

A Daisy Chain

Now be brave and create a macro called LOG that retrieves a document, pauses for you to enter a document name, and sets up a header with today's date as a log. It then calls the SP macro to save and print the edited document. This macro thus calls a macro that in turn calls another macro!

Press	**CTRL-F10 Macro Define**
Type	log
Press	**RETURN**
Type	Enter a Log
Press	**RETURN**
Press	**SHIFT-F10 Retrieve**
Press	**CTRL-PG UP**
Type	1 or p [Pause]
Press	**RETURN** twice
Press	**SHIFT-F8 Format**
Type	2 or p [Page]
Type	3 or h [Headers]
Type	1 or a [Header A]
Type	2 or p [Every Page]
Press	**SHIFT-F5 Date/Outline**
Type	2 or c [Date Code]
Press	F7 **Exit** twice
Press	**ALT-F10 Macro**
Type	sp
Press	**RETURN**
Press	**CTRL-F10 Macro Define**

✔Whew! Now, clear the screen of the header code, then run this macro on any document.

549

Repeating Macros

There are two nonprogramming ways to repeat a macro: (1) use the ESC key with a repetition value before you issue the macro or (2) set up a macro that calls itself continually. The ESC key is the more flexible method for two reasons. First, you can change the repetition value. Second, your macro doesn't have to include a Search command.

Tip: If you have to repeat a macro many times, but you don't know how many, use the ESC key with a *ridiculously high value*, such as 100.

A self-repeating macro may be more convenient in certain circumstances, but you must set up the repetition instruction within the macro definition. The macro must include a Search command as the first instruction. When you run such a macro, the macro repeats until WordPerfect can no longer find any occurrences of the search string.

As an example of a repeating macro, suppose you want to number the paragraphs in a document quickly. The document is single spaced, so there is one hard return code at the end of each paragraph. You can define a macro—PN here—to add a paragraph number, look for the next hard return code, and repeat itself until it reaches the end of the document.

Note: This macro works correctly only for the document format that I mentioned. Always make sure your macro fits the particular document format. You must also have a document in the correct format on the screen when you define this macro. This next example shows you some pitfalls to avoid when you define and use repeating macros.

✔Make sure the screen is clear before you retrieve the LAREST document.

This document contains a title line separated from the text by three hard returns. You must be very careful about what the document contains *before* you set up a repeating macro. For instance, if this document had a table of contents or an index, the macro wouldn't work as you desire. WordPerfect would blithely number all lines that end in hard returns as "paragraphs." Be careful! Fortunately, this document doesn't have any problem children except for the first few lines.

This example must first search for one hard return code, insert a paragraph numbering instruction, and then repeat itself. So, you put in the search instruction as the first part of the macro definition. To have WordPerfect enter a paragraph number in the first paragraph, do this:

Press   **DOWN ARROW** twice

The cursor is one line above the first paragraph. Now you're ready to define the macro.

Press   **CTRL-F10 Macro Define**

Type   **pn**

Press   **RETURN**

Type   `Paragraph Numbering`

Press   **RETURN**

Press   **F2 ▶Search**

Press   **RETURN**

Press   **F2 ▶Search**

Press   **SHIFT-F5 Date/Outline**

Type   **5** or **p** [Para Num]

Press   **RETURN**

for automatic numbering.

Now, to chain the macro to itself so that it repeats continuously, enter a begin macro instruction and supply the *same* macro name:

Press   **ALT-F10 Macro**

Type   `pn`

Press   **RETURN**

The macro definition is now finished, so:

Press   **CTRL-F10 Macro Define**

You've already numbered the first paragraph, and the cursor is directly past the number. You can use the repeating macro to number the other paragraphs:

Press   **ALT-F10 Macro**

Type   `pn`

Press   **RETURN**

WordPerfect goes through the document and numbers the paragraphs. If there's a hard return at the end of the document, WordPerfect supplies an extra paragraph number. Delete that. What you just did was create an *endless loop*. Of course, there is an end to the loop—the end of the document—but that's how to set up a repeating macro.

✔Clear the screen but don't save the document.

Here's another example. Suppose your document has many subheadings that you want to mark as level 2 entries in a table of contents. Each subheading is separated from the text above it by two hard returns, and each subheading is in boldface. Here are the steps that create a repeating macro called MT ("mark table"). The document is on the screen, and the cursor is at the beginning of the document (you don't have to follow these steps now if you don't want to).

Press	**CTRL-F10 Macro Define**
Type	mt
Press	**RETURN**
Type	Mark Table 2
Press	**RETURN**
Press	**F2 ▶Search**
Press	**RETURN,RETURN,F6 Bold**
Press	**F2 ▶Search**
Press	**ALT-F4 Block** or **F12 Block**
Press	**END**
Press	**ALT-F5 Mark Text**
Type	1 or c [ToC]
Type	2
Press	**ALT-F10 Macro**
Type	mt
Press	**RETURN**
Press	**CTRL-F10 Macro Define**

Note that this macro works correctly only for one line subheadings. Again, always be careful of the format requirements in your document when they affect the setup of a repeating macro.

This next macro, EN, shows every endnote text in a document to let you view the text. The macro searches for every endnote code, displays the note, and pauses so you can read the note. Press RETURN to go to the next note. (You could substitute footnote instructions for endnotes in the steps if you wish.)

✔Clear the screen and retrieve the document CHAPTER.2N that contains the endnotes you inserted in Chapter 22.

The EN macro has to search for each endnote code but be careful! The cursor must be *in front of* each endnote code so that WordPerfect will edit the current note and not the next.

✔Position the cursor at the beginning of the document. Then define the EN macro:

Press	**CTRL-F10 Macro Define**
Type	`en`
Press	**RETURN**
Type	`Display Endnotes`
Press	**RETURN**
Press	**F2 ▸Search**
Press	**CTRL-F7 Footnote**
Type	**2** or **e** [Endnote]
Type	**1** or **n** [Note]
Press	**F2 ▸Search**

View the note:

Press	**LEFT ARROW**
Press	**CTRL-F7 Footnote**
Type	**2** or **e** [Endnote]
Type	**2** or **e** [Edit]
Press	**RETURN**

for the current endnote.

Here's where you'll insert a pause to let you view the endnote:

Press   **CTRL-PG UP**

Type   **1** or **p** [**P**ause]

Press   **RETURN**

Leave the current note and continue:

Press   **F7 Exit**

Press   **ALT-F10 Macro**

Type   **en**

Press   **RETURN**

Press   **CTRL-F10 Macro Define**

✔Position the cursor at the beginning of the document before you run this macro. Press **ALT-F10 Macro**, type **en**, and press **RETURN**. Remember to press RETURN to view the next endnote. When you're finished, clear the screen.

Displaying Prompts and Messages

Although technically you can't put prompts or messages within a macro without programming, you could "fake it" with Doc 2. That is, suppose you want to show a message when the user calls a macro. Perhaps the message is a reminder about something, such as how to type in a file name to retrieve. Well, have the macro *switch* to Doc 2 with SHIFT-F3 Switch, retrieve the document that contains your message, pause for the user to read the message, and then close Doc 2 and switch back to Doc 1 when the user wants to continue.

Here's a nifty example. You can never remember those two-character postal state codes, nor do you have to. Einstein once said, "Never try to memorize what you can look up." So, here's a way to have WordPerfect do the memorizing.

First, with a clear screen, type the following document. Notice that the first paragraph is in boldface and that there are two spaces between states. There are hard returns at the ends of lines. (You could, of course, set this document up any way you want, maybe even with zip codes!)

Find the state code you want. Press RETURN to leave this
screen and return to your work.

Alabama AL Alaska AK Arizona AZ Arkansas AR
California CA Colorado CO Connecticut CT
Delaware DE District of Columbia DC Florida FL Georgia GA
Hawaii HI Idaho ID Illinois IL Indiana IN Iowa IA
Kansas KS Kentucky KY Louisiana LA
Maine ME Maryland MD Massachusetts MA Michigan MI
Minnesota MN Mississippi MS Missouri MO Montana MT
Nebraska NE Nevada NV New Hampshire NH New Jersey NJ
New Mexico NM New York NY North Carolina NC North Dakota ND
Ohio OH Oklahoma OK Oregon OR Pennsylvania PA Puerto Rico PR
Rhode Island RI South Carolina SC South Dakota SD
Tennessee TN Texas TX Utah UT
Vermont VT Virginia VA Virgin Islands VI
Washington WA West Virginia WV Wisconsin WI Wyoming WY

✔When you're finished, save the document as STATES and clear the
screen.

Use the following macro, SC for "state codes," whenever you're working
in Doc 1 and you need to look up a state code. Make sure there is no document
open in Doc 2. The macro switches to Doc 2, retrieves the STATES document,
then pauses. Presumably you'd read the helpful message at the top of the
screen. After you find the code you need, press RETURN. The macro then
clears Doc 2 and returns you to Doc 1. Here's how to define the SC macro:

Press   **CTRL-F10 Macro Define**

Type   sc

Press   **RETURN**

Type   Choose a State Code

Press   **RETURN**

Press   **SHIFT-F3 Switch**

Press   **SHIFT-F10 Retrieve**

Type   states

Press   **RETURN**

Press   **CTRL-PG UP**

Type	1 or p [Pause]
Press	**RETURN**
Press	**F7 Exit**
Type	n twice
Press	**SHIFT-F3 Switch**
Press	**CTRL-F10 Macro Define**

Can you figure out how this macro works? How would you change it to work with another document in Doc 2?

Making Macros Invisible

Normally, macros are *visible*. That is, they show all normal prompts and menus on the screen during the run of the macro. Usually this is acceptable because everything whizzes by anyway. But you may, at times, want to turn off the display and hence make the macro "invisible." For example, if there are some nervous Neds or Nellies in your office, you can at least make them feel more at ease. Just tell them to run the macro and wait for the results!

As an example, you'll define a macro, MA for "margins," that changes the left and right margins from the default 1 inch to 1.5 inches. It then changes the top and bottom margins to 0.75 inch. You'll include a no display instruction so that the macro doesn't show all those format menus. Later, you'll edit this macro, so bear with me, please!

Press	**CTRL-F10 Macro Define**
Type	ma
Press	**RETURN**
Type	Margin Changes
Press	**RETURN**

This time, you want to use the CTRL-PG UP key before anything else:

Press	**CTRL-PG UP**

Before you insert the second choice, enter a comment into the macro for good measure:

Type   4 or c [Comment]

WordPerfect prompts:

Comment:

Type   **This is just a test**

Press   **RETURN**

The comment is there just for your own use. Normally, you'd insert comments to remind you about what a macro does. Now for the display instruction:

Type   2 or d [Display]

WordPerfect prompts:

Display execution? ? (Y/N) Yes

Type   **n**

Continue with the macro definition:

Press   **SHIFT-F8 Format**

Type   1 or l [Line]

Type   7 or m [Margins]

Type   **1.5**

Press   **RETURN**

Type   **1.5**

Press   **RETURN** twice

Type   2 or p [Page]

Type   5 or m [Margins]

Type   **.75**

Press   **RETURN**

Type   **.75**

Press   **RETURN**

Press   **F7 Exit**

to return to the document.

Press   **CTRL-F10 Macro Define**

When you want to run this macro, press ALT-F10 Macro, type ma, and press RETURN. Well, it certainly ran quickly. What if you wanted it to run *more slowly?* That brings you to another world altogether.

Macro Programming

To have WordPerfect slow a macro down so that you can see what's happening, you'll have to learn a little about macro programming. Dear Reader, don't leave me yet! Although programming is an art unto itself, there's nothing difficult about it. You can appreciate the rudiments of programming and whet your appetite for more. You'll also get some more hands-on experience with the macro editor.

Note: To work with the macro editor, recall that you must have defined a macro at least once. The macro programming language is complex and powerful. I can only present a few examples of how to use it. My editor would hit the roof if I attempted to cover all the advanced programming commands. That would surely be the topic of a separate book!

Slowing Down a Macro

Your first programming lesson is easy. It shows you how to insert a *speed delay* in the macro to slow it down. In the process you'll remove the display off instruction in the MA macro:

Press   **CTRL-F10 Macro Define**

Type   **ma**

Press   **RETURN**

WordPerfect prompts:

MA.WPM is Already Defined. 1 Replace; 2 Edit: 0

Type   **2** or **e** [Edit]

There's the macro: edit screen. The commands in the Action box should resemble these:

```
{;}This is just a test~{DISPLAY OFF}{Format}lm1.5{Enter}1.5{Enter}
{Enter}2m.75{Enter}.75{Enter}{Exit}
```

Notice that a semicolon in braces—{;}—precedes the comment you inserted during the macro definition. This is a special programming command, all of which appear within braces. What's that little tilde (~) doing there? Users of spreadsheet programs like Lotus 1-2-3 (Chapter 36) will immediately fathom that the tilde represents the RETURN key.

Tip: In general, the tilde indicates use of the RETURN key as the *end* of a macro programming command, and the {Enter} code indicates the use of the RETURN key as an actual keystroke that the macro performs.

Following the comment is the {DISPLAY OFF} instruction you entered when you defined the macro, and the rest of the macro contains the formatting commands. You want to change the macro's actions so that there's a speed delay to slow down the entire macro:

Type   **2** or **a** [Action]

to enter the Action box.

Caution: The {DISPLAY OFF} command overrides any speed delays, so your first order of business is to delete this command:

✔With the RIGHT ARROW key, position the cursor directly under the first brace of {DISPLAY OFF}. Then press **DEL** to delete this command.

Here's where you want to insert a speed delay and at the same time enter the world of advanced macro programming:

Press   **CTRL-PG UP**

Whoa! A little box appears with a whole slew of inexplicable and advanced programming commands (Figure 32-1). On the status line, WordPerfect tells you that you can search for the programming command you want. Here, use the DOWN ARROW or PG DN keys to look at the commands:

Press   **DOWN ARROW** enough times

until the highlight is on the {SPEED} command.

If you go too far, press UP ARROW to go back. Make sure you've highlighted the correct command. Notice that WordPerfect tells you that you enter the speed in 100ths of a second, but also note the little tilde after this

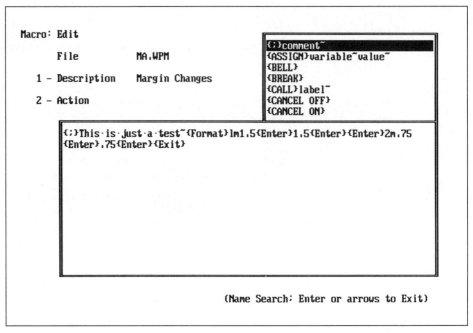

Figure 32-1   The Advanced Macro Programming Commands List

message. WordPerfect is telling you that you *must* enter the speed amount and follow it with a tilde. To select the speed command:

Press   **RETURN**

WordPerfect inserts a {SPEED} command into your macro. You're not finished yet—you must now enter the speed *and* a tilde to complete the command. Suppose you want the speed to be 0.5 second. Do this:

Type   **50**

Type   ~

By the way, you don't have to have the {DISPLAY ON} command in the macro for the {SPEED} command to work, but the speed command only affects the keys that come after it in the macro. That's why you inserted it before the other keys. The speed you choose is essentially a delay that occurs before each step in the rest of the macro. Figure 32-2 shows the edited macro.

A Short Aside

Before you finish the example, here are some other tips on how to use the Macro Commands key in the macro editor. To go back to the programming

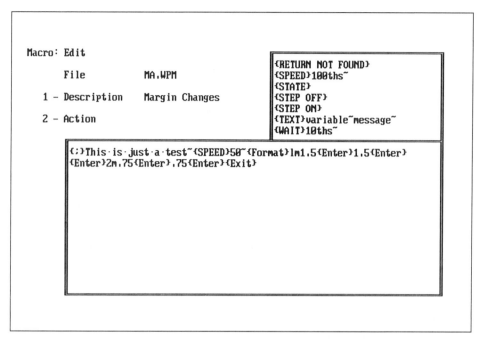

Figure 32-2   An Edited Macro with a Speed Delay

commands list from the Action box, press CTRL-PG UP. To leave the programming commands list without inserting a command into the Action box, press F1 Cancel or ESC. To use the name search feature, type the first letter of a command name to move the highlight to that command quickly. Press F1 Cancel to exit the name search if you don't want to select the command, or press an ARROW key to select another command near the first one.

You can also use the cursor movement keys to move the highlight quickly through the commands. That is, HOME,HOME,UP ARROW takes the highlight to the top of the list, while GRAY + moves down a screenful, and so on. Notice that you *must* enter a comment with the special {;} command in the list (it's the first one). Don't type the braces and semicolon yourself.

Keep in mind that the Macro Commands key, CTRL-PG UP, works with the advanced macro programming commands only. These commands are in uppercase. To insert regular WordPerfect commands such as {Format}, which are all in mixed case, use CTRL-V (Chapter 7).

Continue

You've now successfully edited the macro. Make sure the cursor is back in the Action box. Then:

Press   **F7 Exit** twice

to save the edited macro.

Now run the macro again:

Press   **ALT-F10 Macro**

Type   **ma**

Press   **RETURN**

Well, I'll be! WordPerfect slows the macro down quite a bit and shows you the macro's steps. Soon enough, your margin changes are in the document—again!

✔ Clear the screen before you continue.

Tip: To make the macro run at full speed again, edit the macro and delete the {SPEED} command, the speed amount, and the tilde from the Action box. You may have to experiment with the speed values that are most appropriate for you or your computer.

Inserting Delays

Just as you can slow down the macro speed to make the commands visible, so, too, can you insert *delays* into macros. Unlike the speed command, which slows down every step of the macro, the delay is a one shot deal. That is, after the delay the macro runs at its normal speed.

Delays are especially useful when you want to have a self-running demonstration with pauses between screenfuls of information. The following example flashes a message on the screen to remind the user what day it is:

Good Morning! Today is Friday, March 25, 1988

After a brief delay to give the user time to read the message, the macro then deletes the message to clear the screen. Because I wanted to center the message on the screen, I set it up in a separate document called TODAY.

✔ Clear the screen. Press **RETURN** ten times or so to position the cursor in the middle of the screen. Then press **SHIFT-F6 Center** to center the line. Type **Good Morning! Today is** and a space. Press **SHIFT-F5 Date/Outline**, type **3** or **f** [Date Format], and change the format to 6, 3 1, 4. Then insert the date as a code and return to the document. Press **RETURN** at the end of the line. Save the document as TODAY and clear the screen. (If I had wanted to be really fancy, I could have put the message in a pretty box, but you get the idea.)

You first have to create the macro to display this message, then you'll edit it to insert a delay. I call the macro TO for "today."

Press   **CTRL-F10 Macro Define**

Type   **to**

Press   **RETURN**

Type   **Greeting**

Press   **RETURN**

Press   **SHIFT-F10 Retrieve**

Type   **today**

Press   **RETURN**

Press   **F7 Exit**

Type   n twice

to clear the screen.

Press   **CTRL-F10 Macro Define**

Of course, if you run this macro now, the message will flash by too quickly!

✔Now, redefine the macro and enter the macro editor. Position the cursor in the Action box directly under the first brace of the {Exit} command. Here's where you want to insert a delay:

Press   **CTRL-PG UP**

to display the advanced programming commands.

It turns out that the command is {WAIT}, and it's at the bottom of the list, so:

Press   **HOME,HOME,DOWN ARROW**

Notice that WordPerfect tells you that a wait is in 10ths of a second, so a wait of 4 seconds is 40:

Press   **RETURN**

to insert a {WAIT} command into the Action box.

Type   **40**

Type   **~**

Press   **F7 Exit** twice

to return to the document.

✔With a clear screen, run the macro again to see the difference. You may want this or something similar to be your startup macro!

Tip: You can expand on this technique to display an "animation" of several screenfuls. Set up a document with different screens on each page. For every page in the document, have the macro wait a few seconds and then delete the page with CTRL-PG DN to bring up the next page, and so on. Another way to go would be to include a pause instruction that waits for the user to press a key before the macro displays the next screenful of information.

Conditional Macros

A *conditional macro* performs two different operations depending on whether a condition is true or false, or it selects one of several operations depending on a value. Here's where you'll just scratch a bit more on the tip of the macro programming iceberg, as it were. There are a variety of ways to set up conditional macros, the most common being: (1) use a *not found* condition, (2) use *if/then* conditions, or (3) set up a *multiple choice* situation. You'll learn how to do the first only.

Tip: The logic of programming often seems convoluted to mere mortals. You'll find that good old trial and error will probably be your guide until you get the hang of it—and even after you've mastered all the commands! Run your macros to test and debug them. (The original computer bug was actually an insect—a moth or something—that gummed up the works. Now the term *bug* means any unexpected problem in a program.)

In general, you must arrange the steps that WordPerfect has to perform in their correct order. A program is, in many respects, like a recipe. It contains all the necessary steps, clearly and unambiguously stated in their correct order.

The example not found condition also employs a variety of other interesting programming techniques. You'll edit an existing macro to learn them. The original EN macro just displayed the endnotes in a document, one by one. You'll now tell WordPerfect to perform another macro when it finds no more endnotes. This new macro, VIEW, views the printed endnotes at the end of the document. Here's how to define the VIEW macro (this is the easy part!):

Press   **CTRL-F10 Macro Define**

Type   `view`

Press   **RETURN**

Type   `View Endnotes`

Press   **RETURN**

Press   **HOME,HOME,DOWN ARROW**

to position the cursor at the end of the document.

Press   **SHIFT-F7 Print**

Type   **6** or **v** [Yiew Document]

Press   **CTRL-F10 Macro Define**

✔Press **F1 Cancel** enough times to return to the document. (You can, of course, use the VIEW macro to view the current page of any document.) Now, redefine the EN macro to enter the macro editor. The Action box should look something like this:

{Search}{Footnote}EN{Search}{Left}{Footnote}ee{Enter}{PAUSE}{Exit}
{Macro}en{Enter}

Type   **2** or **a** [Action]

In the original macro, when the search failed, the macro ended. You want to insert a not found instruction at the beginning of the macro so that when the search condition fails, the macro does something else.

Press   **CTRL-PG UP**

to display the advanced programming commands.
    Highlight the command {ON NOT FOUND}, then:

Press   **RETURN**

to insert this command.
    The "action" for the not found condition will be to continue the macro commands at another location. In programming parlance, this is a *branch* to another location in the macro itself. A branch skips over commands. To specify the branch location (no, this isn't a bank!), you give it a descriptive *label* with a name tag and tell WordPerfect to *go to* that label:

Press   **CTRL-PG UP**

to return to the commands.
    ✔Highlight the {GO} command and press **RETURN** to insert it.

Type   **end**

That will be the label's name. Now for something tricky: Both the {ON NOT FOUND} and {GO} commands require tildes to complete the command, so you have to enter *two* tildes!

Type   ~~

Okay, now you must tell WordPerfect where the label is and what to do at the label:

Press   **HOME,HOME,DOWN ARROW**

to go to the end of the Action box.
    ✔Find the {LABEL} command and insert it here. Then type **end** and a tilde (˜) to tell WordPerfect the label's name tag.
    By the way, you could have set up the label first and then the {GO} command. Because the not found action is to call another macro once, enter a macro instruction:

Press   **CTRL-V**

Press   **ALT-F10 Macro**

to enter a {Macro} command.

Type   view

Press   **CTRL-V**

Press   **RETURN**

to insert an {Enter} code.
    One final point: The original instructions {Macro}en{Return} now won't work. You must use the {NEST} command instead. In programming, the term *nesting* refers to one macro that's within another. When the first macro comes to a nest command, it runs the other macro. Here, you'll create a loop because the original macro continues to run itself!
    What's the difference between the normal {Macro} command and the {NEST} command? Apparently, when you use other advanced programming commands like {ON NOT FOUND}, you must tell WordPerfect to *repeat* a macro. The {NEST} command does that. Notice that this command takes a *macro file name* that must include the .WPM extension. So:
    ✔Delete the instructions {Macro}en{RETURN} and insert these commands instead: {NEST}en.wpm˜(Don't forget the tilde!) The entire edited macro Action box should look like this:

```
{ON NOT FOUND}{GO}end~~{Search}{Footnote}EN{Search}{Left}{Footnote}
ee{Enter}{PAUSE}{Exit}{NEST}en.wpm~{LABEL}end~{Macro}view{Enter}
```

Press   **F7 Exit** twice

to save the macro.

    ✔Retrieve the CHAPTER.2N document and try the new macro. Success!

    (An aside: WordPerfect Corporation supplies some sample macros that are attached to alternate keyboard setups, discussed in Appendix A. Many of these macros contain advanced programming techniques. One of the best ways to learn programming is to study the efforts of others before you. Take a look at the sample macros some time!)

    Dear Reader, that was just a brief exploration of WordPerfect's macro programming. Lest I fall victim to my editor's health problems, enough of this "macro madness." When you're *really* brave, try your hand at using variables, if/then conditions (the {IF}, {ELSE}, and {END IF} commands), multiple choice situations (the {CASE} command), macros that accept keyboard input (the {CHAR} and {TEXT} commands), and the built-in debugging capability ({STEP ON}). Good luck! Now you'll learn another powerful WordPerfect feature: sorting.

A Sorting Séance

In this chapter you'll discover new uses of this command . . .

CTRL-F9 Merge/Sort   (1) Start a sort, (2) determine the sort order

. . . and you'll learn some *sort* terms and operators:

+	Contains either
*	Contains both
=	Is equal to (numerically)
	Is the same as (alphabetically)
<>	Is not equal to (numerically)
	Is not the same as (alphabetically)
>	Is greater than (numerically)
	Comes after (alphabetically)
<	Is less than (numerically)
	Comes before (alphabetically)
>=	Is greater than or equal to (numerically)
	Comes after or is equal to (alphabetically)
<=	Is less than or equal to (numerically)
	Comes before or is equal to (alphabetically)
key\<n\>	Sorting key number (**\<n\>** equals **1**, **2**, and so on)
keyg	Global selection key

Although it's complicated, WordPerfect's sorting feature is versatile and powerful. If you study this chapter slowly and—as they say here in California—learn to *flow* with it, you'll quickly get the hang of sorting.

DO WARM-UP

Sorting Simplified

Now that you know a little about merge fields and records, you can apply the same terminology to WordPerfect's sorting feature. You'll frequently want to sort columns of text, so just visualize fields *across* the screen instead of down. Each line is a record. Later, you'll learn how to sort secondary merge documents, too.

When you sort columns, WordPerfect considers each column a field and refers to each field by its numerical position across the screen. Unless you tell it otherwise, WordPerfect assumes that the numbering is from left to right. Sort fields (columns) are separated by tabs or indent codes, but align characters are also considered tabs. What's more, *each* tab or indent code represents a column position.

In addition, bear in mind that any column of text at the left margin is also included in the numbering scheme if it's separated by the next column with a tab or indent. Later in this chapter you'll see why this is important to your sanity. Generally, when you sort paragraphs, the entire paragraph is the first sort field, because there aren't any columns.

Within each field are *words*. For instance, a field may contain a name such as *Ludwig van Beethoven*, which contains three words. As you know, words are separated from each other by spaces. During sorting, WordPerfect locates words by their numerical position *within* the field. *Ludwig* is in position number 1, if you're counting from left to right.

You have to tell WordPerfect which field and which word in the field you want to use as the base for the sort. This is the *key*. You can have several keys govern a sort. The first key takes precedence. If there's a tie—that is, if two key fields are exactly the same—the second key governs the sort, and the third, and so on. An obvious example of this is when you're sorting names and there are several Smiths or Joneses. In that case, WordPerfect would sort by first name, and then by middle initial if need be.

You can sort an entire document, or merely a block of text, either by paragraph or line. You can also sort secondary merge documents and even *sort out*—that is, select—certain records. WordPerfect calls this, understandably enough, "sort and select." If you have to create abstracts of documents, this feature could be a life-saver. You can sort, or sort and select, to the screen or to a file that you can later edit.

There's only one general rule to follow, and the manual states it clearly: *Save your document* before you sort it, just in case you don't like the results. I'll add another note of advice: *Watch the number of your tab settings*, because they affect column numbering. That's really all you need know at this point. As you work through the examples in this chapter, I'll introduce some more terms, but only a little at a time, so that you aren't overpowered by too many definitions all at once.

How Does WordPerfect Do It?

If WordPerfect can't read, how does it sort words? Quite simply, it determines the ASCII code number for the beginning letter in the field and then sorts the numbers in *numerical* order. When it's finished with the first letter, it goes on to sort according to the code number of the second letter in the word, and so on.

But there's more to it than that. In the ASCII scheme, all lowercase letters are numbered higher than uppercase letters, and many sorting programs would put any word that began with a lowercase letter after all capitalized words. Poor Ludwig van Beethoven! His last name would thus come after Wolfgang Amadeus Mozart's.

WordPerfect is smarter than that, as you'll see. It takes into account the case of the first letter and gives you a truly correct sort. How? It probably converts the first letter to uppercase internally, *then* sorts, and then returns the words to their proper case.

Sorting a Document by Paragraphs

When you sort an entire document by paragraph, you must follow three rules:

1. The paragraphs must be single spaced.
2. There must be at least one hard return code at the end of every paragraph.
3. No paragraph can be longer than a page.

It makes no sense to include titles or section headings when you sort paragraphs. You can, however, sort just a block of text that might contain several paragraphs.

Tip: Try to make the document format consistent before you sort it. That is, insert the same number of hard returns at the end of each paragraph. Normally, you'd do that anyway, wouldn't you?

Most of the time when you sort by paragraph, the issue of columns doesn't come up. There is only one "column": the paragraph. In the next example, however, you'll learn how to sort indented paragraphs.

The bibliophiles who basked in Part 4 will love the ability to sort bibliographies and notes. As a later section illustrates, you can even select paragraphs based on only a "global" criterion. Here's another type of document, more in line with my own interests (food!), for you to try. It uses the standard printer and defaults. Notice that one entry is capitalized.

```
tapas - in general, bite-size appetizers served during the daily
ritual in Spain preceding dinner, which happens much too late for
anyone's benefit

Cajun - also Creole; deriving from the style of cooking
indigenous to the original French settlers of Louisiana; a
multitude of gastronomic sins have been recently perpetrated
under the guise of "Cajun Cuisine"

quiche - a pastry shell filled with a combination of eggs, cream,
and either meats or vegetables, or both; also known as quiche
lorraine, from its district of origin; no longer in fashion

fajitas - strips of beef broiled and served sizzling hot with
side dishes of guacamole, salsa, and tortillas; now decidedly in
vogue

blue corn - a type of corn, found in New Mexico, used in the
making of tortillas and tamales; yes, it is really blue

home cooking - a ridiculous misnomer when applied to the eating
establishments that line the major interstate arteries of this
country; a trite and overworked phrase

pasteles - depending on the South American or Caribbean country,
a combination of meat, spices, and olives wrapped in a shell made
from ground roots or other pastry; the Puerto Rican version of
this, when prepared correctly, is excellent; when not, it's an
abomination of mush
```

✔After you type this document, save it as CUISINE. Here's how to sort it:

Press   **CTRL-F9 Merge/Sort**

The merge/sort menu appears. I'll just mention *en passant*, as it were, that WordPerfect determines the *sorting order* from the language you're currently using. If you've inserted a language code in the document (Chapter 36), the sort order may change to take into account any special characters in that language.

Type   **2** or **s** [Sort]

WordPerfect asks:

`Input file to sort: (Screen)`

You can use either a file on the disk or the current document on the screen.

Note: (Screen) here doesn't refer to just the current screen, but rather to the entire document in memory.

Press   **RETURN**

to accept the screen as the input file.

WordPerfect prompts:

`Output file for sort: (Screen)`

Again, you can direct the results of the sort to a disk file or to the screen.

Caution: *Never* direct the output to the same disk file as the input file!

Press   **RETURN**

to accept the screen as the output file.

WordPerfect splits the screen and shows part of the document at the top and the rather complicated sorting menu, shown in Figure 33-1. Notice that WordPerfect tells you by default that this is a Sort by Line, which is not what you want. You must first change the *type* of sort.

Type   **7** or **t** [Type]

The sorting type menu appears:

`Type: 1 Merge; 2 Line; 3 Paragraph: 0`

Type   **3** or **p** [Paragraph]

When you sort by paragraph, WordPerfect changes the first key definition to a 1 1 1. That means simply that:

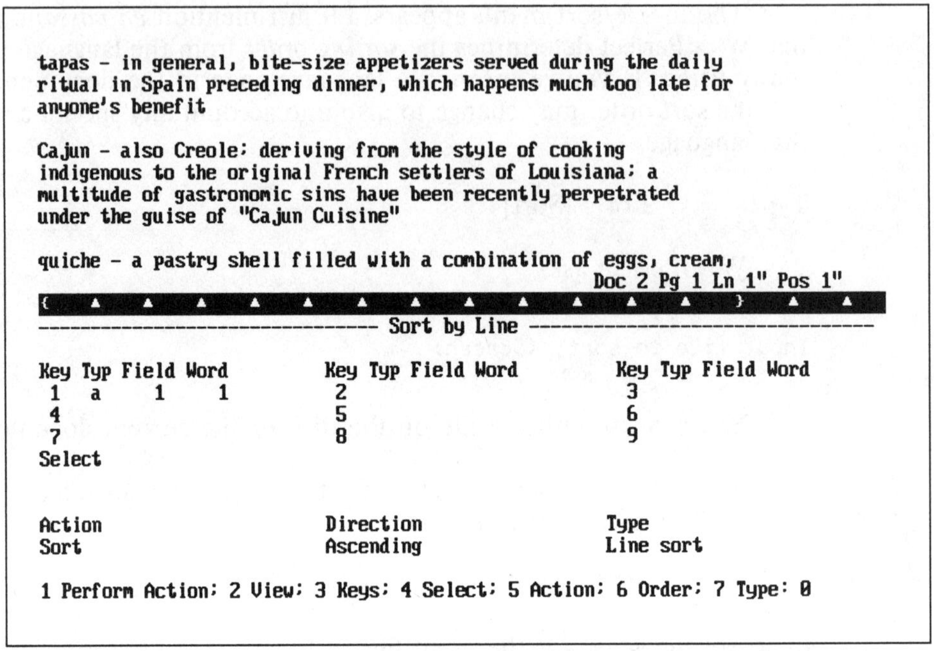

```
tapas - in general, bite-size appetizers served during the daily
ritual in Spain preceding dinner, which happens much too late for
anyone's benefit

Cajun - also Creole; deriving from the style of cooking
indigenous to the original French settlers of Louisiana; a
multitude of gastronomic sins have been recently perpetrated
under the guise of "Cajun Cuisine"

quiche - a pastry shell filled with a combination of eggs, cream,
                                        Doc 2 Pg 1 Ln 1" Pos 1"
{    ▲    ▲    ▲    ▲    ▲    ▲    ▲    ▲    ▲    ▲    ▲    }    ▲    ▲
---------------------------- Sort by Line ----------------------------

Key Typ Field Word    Key Typ Field Word    Key Typ Field Word
 1   a    1     1      2                      3
 4                     5                      6
 7                     8                      9
Select


Action                Direction             Type
Sort                  Ascending             Line sort

1 Perform Action; 2 View; 3 Keys; 4 Select; 5 Action; 6 Order; 7 Type: 0
```

Figure 33-1   The Sorting Menu

- The key is alphanumeric (a) because it contains letters, or numbers, of equal length.
- You want to sort according to the first line.
- You're using the first field, that is, the left margin in this case.
- You're using the first word in the field.

Most of the time this is the way you'll sort documents by paragraph. Once you've set up the characteristics of the sort, you *perform* it:

Type   **1** or **p** [Perform Action]

WordPerfect tells you it's sorting and gives a count. In a moment the sort is finished. Even though the ASCII coding scheme puts lowercase letters after uppercase ones, WordPerfect knows enough to sort the paragraphs correctly. Good show!

✔Save the document again, then clear the screen.

A More Complicated Example

This next example also sorts by paragraph, but with two twists. Each paragraph contains an indented section, but there are still soft returns at the ends of the lines and hard returns at the ends of paragraphs. In addition, you'll sort only part of the document that you'll set up as a block.

Those Golden Rules

Rule   Decide what's best for you, and then work at what
                you want to accomplish.

Rule   Always be on the alert for opportunities, even
                from the most unexpected sources.

Rule   Don't compromise on standards, that is, set your
                goals and stick to them.

Rule   Be yourself at all times. Don't try to be what
                other people expect or think you should be.

Just for the moment overlook how hokey this document is! Concentrate on sorting, please. You must be careful when you're setting up this document, because the default format has too many tab stops. It's best to clear all tabs and set new ones only where you need them. That way, you don't get confused about the numbering of the columns. Remember that WordPerfect counts each tab stop in the numbering of sort columns.

✔Clear all tabs and set a new left-justified tab at column 2.5. Center and type the title, then press **RETURN** three times for spacing. Type the rest of the example. Use one indent after the word *Rule* in each paragraph. Make sure that the last paragraph ends with two hard returns, just like the others. When you're finished, save this document as RULES.

Because you don't want to include the title in the sort, you must block out the paragraphs before you sort them.

✔Position the cursor at the left margin of the first paragraph. Then block the rest of the document.

Note: It's important that each paragraph end with the *same* number of hard returns for the sort to work correctly.

Now, start the sorting procedure as I instructed in the first example. Because you've defined a block, as soon as you press **CTRL-F9 Merge/Sort**, WordPerfect "knows" you can't do a merge. It automatically brings up the sorting menu. WordPerfect also "remembers" that the last sort was by paragraph, so you don't have to set the type. However, because this sort is to be on the second "column" in the paragraph, you must change the key definition.

Type   **3** or k [Keys]

WordPerfect positions the cursor in the first field definition. You can define up to nine fields. At the bottom of the screen WordPerfect tells you:

`Type: a = Alphanumeric; n = Numeric;  Use Arrows;  Press EXIT when done`

When you're defining keys, you should use the RIGHT ARROW or RETURN key to move through the definition. A key can contain numbers and letters (alphanumeric) or just numbers (numeric). By default, WordPerfect assumes alphanumeric.

Press   **RIGHT ARROW** twice

to accept the key as alphanumeric and the first line.

Type   **2**

to set field 2 as the sort field.

Everything else is okay, so press **F7 Exit** to leave the key menu and type **1** or **p** [Perform Action] to perform the sort. If the last paragraph had only one hard return at the end, WordPerfect would insert a superfluous hard return when it sorts the block, and you'd have to delete it for correct spacing between sections. Always make sure that each paragraph is set up exactly like the others before you begin sorting.

✔Save the document, then clear the screen.

Sorting by Line

When you sort columns of text by line, each line must end with a hard return and each column must be set up around a tab stop. You'll use this example to learn many different sorting techniques and some pitfalls to avoid.

✔First, set the left and right margins to 0.5 inch. Then clear all tabs and set new left-justified tabs at columns 3.5, 6.0, and 7.5. Type the example, but use tabs between columns. Make sure that each line, including the last line, ends with a hard return. When you're finished, save the document as the file RECORDS and leave it on the screen.

Wolfgang Amadeus Mozart	Eine kleine Nachtmusik	Beecham	M226
Jean Sibelius	Finlandia	Barbirolli	S102
Jean Sibelius	Kullervo	Berglund	S111
Bela Bartok	Bluebeard's Castle	Kertesz	B299
Ludwig van Beethoven	Symphony No. 3	Bernstein	B088
Ralph Vaughan Williams	A London Symphony	Barbirolli	V400
Igor Stravinsky	Rite of Spring	Stravinski	S765

Wolfgang Amadeus Mozart	Don Giovanni	Guillini	M333
Richard Wagner	Die Gotterdammerung	Solti	W543
Antonin Dvorak	New World Symphony	Szell	D332
Ludwig van Beethoven	Symphony No. 9	von Karajan	B071
Zoltan Kodaly	Hary Janos Suite	Dorati	B10
Ralph Vaughan Williams	Symphony No. 4	Bernstein	V387
Henry Purcell	Dido and Aeneas	Barbirolli	P227
Franz Josef Haydn	The Creation	Bernstein	H119
Ludwig van Beethoven	Late String Quartets	Julliard	B243
Wolfgang Amadeus Mozart	Symphonies 38 & 39	Klemperer	M102
Jean Sibelius	Symphony No. 2	Szell	S377
Giacomo Puccini	Tosca	Levine	P226
Giacomo Puccini	Madame Butterfly	Barbirolli	P302
Ludwig van Beethoven	Hammerklavier Sonata	Serkin	B070
Leos Janacek	Taras Bulba/Sinfonietta	Mackerras	J100
Ralph Vaughan Williams	A Sea Symphony	Previn	V291
Hector Berlioz	Romeo et Juliette	Davis	B99
Igor Stravinsky	Firebird/Petrushka	Bernstein	S202
Franz Josef Haydn	London Symphonies	Bernstein	H220

Sorting on One Key

Say you first want to sort this record inventory according to performers, the names in the third column. Start the sort, using the screen as both the input and output file. If you're continuing from the previous lesson, change the type to line sort: type **7** or **t** [Type], then **2** or **l** [Line]. Then:

Type   **3** or **k** [Keys]

Press   **RIGHT ARROW**

Type   **3**

to designate the third column as the sort field.

As WordPerfect tells you, press **F7 Exit** to leave the key menu, then type **1** or **p** [Perform Action] to perform the sort. You may have to press HOME,HOME,HOME,LEFT ARROW to see the left side of the sorted document on the screen.

Sorting on Two Keys

Well, that's okay, but say you now want to sort each composition alphabetically under the performer. You need a *second* key to order after the first key. Go back into the sort menu. Then:

Type   **3 or k [K̲eys]**

The first key is okay, so move into the second:

Press   **RIGHT ARROW** three times

WordPerfect puts in an a for alphanumeric in the second key.

Press   **RIGHT ARROW**

Type   **2**

for the second field.
 Exit the key menu and perform the sort. Much better!

Sorting by Left Words in a Field

This next example is a bit tricky. Pretend you now want to order the listings by composer's last name. Some names contain three words, some only two. Go into the sort menu. Then:

Type   **3 or k [K̲eys]**

Press   **RIGHT ARROW**

Type   **1**

Press   **RIGHT ARROW**

for the first field.
 Now, for the word within the field, you want WordPerfect to count from the *right* instead of from the left, as normal. So, use a negative number.

Type   **-1**

Leave the second key as it is so that WordPerfect sorts by composer and then by composition. Exit the key menu and perform the sort.

A Small Problem for Purists

Has anyone noticed what's wrong with Ralph Vaughan Williams? Technically, his last name is not Williams; it's Vaughan Williams. WordPerfect doesn't know that, so it sorted on the *W* instead of the *V*. If you're a purist, could you correct this situation? Yes! Remove the regular space and insert *hard space* codes—press HOME,SPACEBAR—between the *Vaughan* and the *Wil-*

liams for each listing, and then sort the document again. You've just fooled WordPerfect, because it only "knows" that sort words are separated by regular spaces. Now your sorted listing is complete and correct.

Viewing the Input File

Because the sort menu takes up a large portion of the screen, you may not be able to see the exact reference spot in your input document while you're setting up a sort. If you want to check your document temporarily, type **2** or v [Yiew], use the standard cursor keys to move around as normal, and press **F7 Exit** or **RETURN** to return to the sort menu when you're finished.

When Numbers Aren't Really Numbers

The rightmost column contains alphanumeric code numbers. You can sort the document by this number and see what happens. Go into the sort menu. Then:

Type   **3** or **k** [Keys]

Press   **DEL** three times

This erases all previous key definitions. WordPerfect won't erase key 1, because it needs at least one sort key. It reinstates key 1 to its default setting, **a 1 1**.

Press   **RIGHT ARROW**

Type   **4**

Exit the key menu and perform the sort. Is that exactly right? Not really. Number B10, for instance, should come before the others. The point here is that alphanumeric fields that contain numbers should be of *equal* length. A good way to get around this particular problem would be to change B10 to B010. Change B99 to B099, too. Then the sort will work.

Note: Because telephone numbers usually contain hyphens, you can't tell WordPerfect that they're strictly numeric. A numeric sort only works with true figures, which can contain decimal points, commas, and dollar signs, as another example will show you. So, when you're using telephone numbers or any other alphanumeric field with numbers, make sure each entry is of the same length.

Selecting Records

Now you're ready to learn how to sort out certain records based on selection criteria. That is, WordPerfect will filter the input file for only those records that meet the criteria you specify. You can then save the sorted and selected output to a new file if you wish. The original input file remains unchanged.

Using One Criterion

In the first example you'll choose all records that feature Bernstein as conductor, with the records sorted by composer. Go into the sort menu and set up the sorting keys:

Type   3 or k [Keys]

Press   **DEL**

Press   **RIGHT ARROW**

Type   3

to set the third field as the first key.

Press   **RIGHT ARROW** four times

Type   −1

to set the last word in the first field as the second key.

Press   **F7 Exit**

Now for the selection criterion:

Type   4 or s [Select]

Select Operators

WordPerfect positions the cursor in the select area and lists the select operators at the bottom of the screen. Most of them look vaguely mathematical, and they are, but you can also use them with text strings:

```
+(OR), *(AND), =, <>, >, <, >=, <=;   Press Exit when done
```

Table 33-1 describes how each operator works. Numeric comparisons are relatively straightforward. In alphabetic comparisons, however, the criterion is whether one word "comes before" or "comes after" in the alphabet, or is exactly equal.

For example, *Maine* comes before *Massachusetts* alphabetically, even though *Massachusetts* is longer than *Maine*. WordPerfect just compares each letter until it finds a tie-breaker. However, the postal code *ME* comes after *MA*. For two words to be equal, they have to contain the same letters in the same order. Thus, *Bernstein* is not equal to *Bernstien*, even though both words contain the same number of letters.

You select by *key number*, not by field:

Type   **key1=bernstein**

You don't have to use correct case, but you *do* have to type the entire name.

Press   **F7 Exit or RETURN**

to leave the select menu.

Table 33-1   Select Operators

Operator	Meaning
+	Contains either
*	Contains both
=	Is equal to (numerically)
	Is the same as (alphabetically)
<>	Is not equal to (numerically)
	Is not the same as (alphabetically)
>	Is greater than (numerically)
	Comes after (alphabetically)
<	Is less than (numerically)
	Comes before (alphabetically)
>=	Is greater than or equal to (numerically)
	Comes after or is equal to (alphabetically)
<=	Is less than or equal to (numerically)
	Comes before or is equal to (alphabetically)

Select and Sort

Note that the Action line now says Select and sort. If you didn't want to sort, you could type **5** or **a** [Action], and then **2** or **o** [Select Only]. WordPerfect would just extract the records in the order they appear in the input file. You'll soon learn a nifty use for this feature. Right now, though, leave the action as select and sort and perform the sort with the screen as both input and output.

Using Several Criteria

This time, you'll select two conductors, Bernstein and Barbirolli. Start the sort, but supply the file name, RECORDS, for the input file, because the screen no longer contains all the records. Leave the screen as the output file. Note that WordPerfect opens and displays the file for you. You'll change the selection criteria to add another qualifier:

Type   **4** or **s** [Select]

Press   **END**

Type   +barbirolli

so that the line reads key1=bernstein+barbirolli .

Press   **F7 Exit**

Oops! WordPerfect says:

ERROR: Incorrect format

That's because you have to include the key reference for each part of the selection. In addition, there must be spaces on either side of the + or * operators. Change the selection so that it looks like this:

key1=bernstein + key1=barbirolli

Note: You can't supply two words separated by a space in the select criterion. For example, if you were looking for all those records that feature von Karajan, you'd type Karajan alone.

Exit the select menu and perform the sort. A few cautionary notes about + and * are in order here. The + operator ("or") actually means "either ... or," but the * operator ("and") means "both ... and." Keep this in mind when you're setting up selection criteria. Also, you can use parentheses for grouping.

✔Clear the screen before you continue. Start the next sort, using REC-
ORDS as the input file and the screen as the output file.

Type   4 or s [Select]

Press   **END**

✔Use the **BACKSPACE** key to delete the second criterion. Then change
the criterion to this:

`key1=bernstein + key2=beethoven`

Exit the select menu and perform the sort. That's not what you wanted!
You wanted all recordings featuring Bernstein *and* Beethoven, not Bernstein
or Beethoven. Start the sort, but use the screen as the input file.

Type   4 or s [Select]

Change the + to an *. Then exit the select menu and perform the sort.
Next, you can do one that's more complicated.
✔Clear the screen and start the sort. Use RECORDS as the input file
and the screen as the output.

Type   4 or s [Select]

Now you want to select all records that contain Bernstein *and* Beethoven,
or any records that contain Barbirolli. Change the criteria so that they look
like this:

`(key1=bernstein * key2=beethoven) + key1=barbirolli`

Exit the select menu and perform the sort. Finally, to select only those
records with Barbirolli and Purcell as well as Bernstein and Beethoven, go
back into the sort, but use the screen as the input file this time. Change the
selection criteria so that they look like this:

`(key1=bernstein * key2=beethoven) + (key1=barbirolli * key2=purcell)`

Exit the select menu and perform the sort. A good rule to follow is: When
in doubt, use parentheses for grouping. I won't step you through these next
examples, but try them out if you wish. Clear the screen and start the sort
with RECORDS as the input file and the screen as the output. Use the same
keys, but delete the previous criteria with CTRL-END. Then change the sort
criterion to this:

```
key1<>bernstein
```

This sorts out records containing Bernstein and leaves the rest. Then do this one:

```
key1<>bernstein * key1<>barbirolli
```

Question: Would you get the same result if you tried the + operator instead of the * above? Try it! Finally, what does this one do?

```
key1>dorati
```

Oh, yes, you can have alphanumeric strings that are "greater than" other strings. This means that the sort will find all records for performers whose names come after *Dorati* in the alphabet.

Question: Would WordPerfect include *Donanyi? Answer:* No! Word-Perfect keeps comparing letters in the words until it breaks the tie. So, when it gets to the third letter of *Donanyi*, it realizes that *N* is "less than" *R* (that is, *N* comes before *R* alphabetically), so this name doesn't meet the select criterion.

✔When you're finished, clear the screen before you continue.

Global Selection

There's a special sort key—called the *global selection* key—that lets you select records without specifying a key number. WordPerfect will just look for whatever you type as the global criterion in *all* fields. That's what the "global" stands for. You can combine the global key with other keys, but you must enter the criterion as a complete word. To designate the global key, type **keyg**.

✔Clear the screen and start the sort, but use RECORDS as the input file and the screen as the output file. You want to find all records that contain the word *Symphony*.

Type   **4 or s** [S̲elect]

Press   **CTRL-END**

to delete the previous select criteria.

Type   **keyg=symphony**

Exit the select menu and perform the sort.

Caution: If you type a criterion incorrectly, you'll get incorrect results! For instance, I first typed the above line as **keyg=syphony** without the *m*. WordPerfect went "bananas"!

If you wish, try a combined global and regular selection. Change the select criteria to this and perform the sort again:

```
keyg=symphony * key3=bernstein
```

Creating Abstracts

Bibliophiles: The global key feature is especially useful when you want to extract paragraphs that contain a specific word or reference. For example, suppose you have a document with many notes on a book about food. Each note is a separate paragraph. You want to select only those paragraphs that have the word *sugar* in them and save them to a new file. Assume further that there are the same number of hard returns at the end of each note paragraph.

After you start the sort, to select only those paragraphs that contain the word *sugar*, first change the **7** [Type] choice to **3** [Paragraph]. Make sure the field setting is correct, too. Then type the global key like this: **keyg=sugar.**

Caution: You should also change the **5** [Action] choice to **2** [Select Only]. That way, WordPerfect won't sort the notes out of the order in which you've typed them! It just extracts those paragraphs that contain the word *sugar* in the order they appear in the original document.

Although you can combine a global key with another key number, you can't specify more than one criterion for the global key. What if you wanted only those paragraphs that contain *sugar* and *nonfattening?* Well, use the global selection routine to create a file for all those records that contain *sugar*. Then use the global selection on the new file, this time substituting *nonfattening* as the global criterion.

Here's another example. Your boss, a lawyer, has written a long brief. In it he's mentioned that notorious case, *Smudge & Smudge v. The State of California*, many times. He now wants to write an article, so he needs all references to this case. No problem! Just have sort and select make an abstract of the original brief. Neat!

Sorting Figures

Dear Reader, you've done enough typing! So, as an example of sorting columns of figures, you'll use a document from a previous chapter.

✔Clear the screen and retrieve the document MYMONEY.

First sort the monthly expenses by amount, smallest to largest. This must be a block, because you don't want to include the title in the sort.

Press   **DOWN ARROW** three times

The cursor should be at the left margin of line 4, and the Math On message appears. Yes, you *can* sort math sections, but always make sure that you don't include special math codes in a sort. If you reveal the codes, you'll notice that the cursor is directly past the math codes. However, you *do* want to include the [TAB] code in the sort, so that when WordPerfect rearranges the lines the columns are correctly aligned.

Press   **ALT-F4 Block** or **F12 Block**

Press   **DOWN ARROW** eleven times

Press   **END**

There's your block. Don't block out the extra hard return after the December line.

Press   **CTRL-F9 Merge/Sort**

Sort by Line should be showing at the top of the sort menu. If it isn't, type **7** or **t** [Type] and then **2** or **l** [Line]. Next, define the key field.

Type   **3** or **k** [Keys]

Press   **DEL** twice

This key will be for the second column (or so you think), which must be labeled as numeric.

Type   **n**

The cursor jumps to the Field column.

Type   **2**

for the second field in the document.

The rest of the definition is okay, so exit the key menu. Now, go into the select menu and delete the entire criteria line from the previous example. Then exit this menu and perform the sort. What happened? The sort didn't turn out as you expected. In fact, it's a mess! Why? Because WordPerfect assumes that the first *sort* column is at the left margin, so what looks distinctly like the second *math* column is actually the *third* sort column! Try again: Block out the text exactly as before and go into the sort menu.

Type   **3** or **k** [Keys]

Press   **RIGHT ARROW**

Type   **3**

for the third field.

Exit the key menu and perform the sort. That's better! Notice that WordPerfect didn't mind the dollar sign, although if you wanted to print the document, make sure to put the dollar sign at the top figure.

Sorting in Descending Order

Now try sorting in *descending* order, with the highest figure first. Block the text again, then go into the sort menu. Your field definition is correct, but there's one other thing to change:

Type   **6** or **o** [Order]

Type   **2** or **d** [Descending]

Type   **1** or **p** [Perform Action]

If you wish, try sorting out only those months with expenses greater than $2,000 and less than $3,000. How would your selection criteria look?

Sorting Secondary Merge Documents

I began this chapter with a brief mention of secondary merge documents, and I'll end with them, too. All you need to do to sort secondary documents is (1) as you would expect, refer to the field numbers from top to bottom and (2) change the sort type.

✔Clear the screen and retrieve the PATRONS document. Start the sort with the screen as both input and output files.

Type   **7** or **t** [Type]

Type   **1** or **m** [Merge]

The key definition setup changes slightly. Here, you've wisely set up your secondary document with different information in different fields, so you don't have to resort to negative numbers when you want to sort names. Say you'll sort alphabetically by last name, the fourth field in the document.

Type   **3** or **k** [Keys]

Type   **a**

Type   **4**

Press   **RIGHT ARROW** four times

Just to be on the safe side, you'll set a second key for first name, even though there aren't any ties in the document.

Type   **3**

Press   **F7 Exit**

If you're continuing from the previous lesson, make sure that there aren't any sort criteria before you perform the sort. Try sorting by zip code to take advantage of cheaper bulk mailing rates for your next form letter. Is this field, the eighth in the document, a numeric field? Here, yes, but if you use extended zip codes, be careful! Extended zip codes contain hyphens, so you'd have to tell WordPerfect that they are alphanumeric.

Second, and more important: Merge sort works by *line*, but there's a problem in this secondary document. Some address fields contain two lines, so if you set up the key to sort by zip code to be field 8 (the zip field), you won't get the right results. You must use a *negative* key, here, -1, and thus tell WordPerfect to count the fields backward.

If you wish, try sorting out certain records. This is helpful when you want to send letters to specific recipients. For example, if you want to "target" only those people who live in the three West Coast states, use a criterion such as **key1>90000** (assuming that the zip code field is the key). You may want to sort directly to a new output file if your secondary merge document is a large one.

Well, Dear Reader, sorting isn't *that* difficult—is it? You're almost finished exploring what WordPerfect has to offer, and there are just a few more topics to cover. The next two chapters take you back to the world of printing.

Graphics and Advanced Printing Features

In this chapter you'll learn the following new commands . . .

Function Key Commands

ALT-F9 Graphics   Insert or edit graphics elements

ALT-SHIFT-F9   "Hot key" for the GRAB utility

. . . you'll discover other uses of these commands . . .

SHIFT-F7 Print   (1) Change the graphics print quality, (2) perform type through printing, (3) "print" a document to a disk file

SHIFT-F8 Format   (1) Set up kerning instructions, (2) insert a printer command, (3) change the word and letter spacing, (4) change the word spacing justification limits

. . . you'll work with the following utility program . . .

GRAB   Capture and save a screen to a disk file

. . . and you'll learn some new codes:

[Box Num]   Caption in a graphics box

[Fig Opt]   Figure options change

[Figure]   Figure box

[HLine]   Horizontal line graphics element

[Just Lim]   Word spacing justification limits change

more . . .

[Kern:Off]	Kerning off
[Kern:On]	Kerning on
[New Fig Num]	Figure number change
[New Tab Num]	Table number change
[New Txt Num]	Text box number change
[New Usr Num]	User-defined box number change
[Ptr Cmnd]	Printer escape code or codes
[Table]	Table box
[Tbl Opt]	Table options change
[Text Box]	Text box
[Txt Opt]	Text box options change
[Usr Box]	User-defined box
[Usr Opt]	User-defined box options change
[VLine]	Vertical line graphics element
[Wrd/Ltr Spacing]	Word or letter spacing change

This chapter takes you back to printing techniques and forward to a new and exciting world. It introduces other operations on the SHIFT-F7 Print key that I didn't cover in Chapter 5, and it shows you how to insert, edit, and print graphics in your word processing documents. You'll also learn how to work with WordPerfect's advanced printing commands. Laser printer owners: Study this chapter before the next one.

> **DO WARM-UP**

The World of Graphics

I've already explained that the letters, numbers, and punctuation marks in your computer are part of a special character set (Chapter 15). Although the IBM and compatible computers have certain line, box, and shading characters in their character sets, these "graphics" characters don't represent true graphics elements at all. They are pre-established characters, just like the *a* or *!*.

Generally, a printer prints graphics as a series of little dots, because there couldn't possibly be any other way to represent all the various shapes in graphics elements. WordPerfect has to tell the printer when to print a character from the character set—a letter, number, or punctuation mark— and when to switch to graphics printing.

Note: Many conventional printers can't print graphics at all. I'm assuming that yours can! Some monitors may not be able to display graphics in the print view, but you'll see a box that indicates the size and location of the graphics.

If it just switched between character printing and graphics printing on the page, that would be a great convenience. But WordPerfect does much more! It lets you add text elements to graphics, for instance, a *caption* to a figure or table. You attach a graphics element to a paragraph, page, or character in the text, and WordPerfect move the graphics with the text. WordPerfect will even keep track of the figures and tables for you. Most graphics commands are on the **ALT-F9 Graphics** key, another key that has changed in Version 5.0.

WordPerfect's graphics features beg for a book of their own. Alas! My editor is admonishing me to get these last few chapters done, so I can just barely cover a couple examples of how to work with graphics. You should know, though, that here are five different types of graphics elements: (1) figures, (2) tables, (3) text boxes, (4) user-defined boxes, and (5) horizontal or vertical lines. WordPerfect can arrange the different graphics elements in separate lists.

Here's a consolation: The procedure for working with the first four graphics elements is essentially the same. I'll show you how to insert a figure, and you can experiment with the others at your leisure. For any of the first four types, the graphics element will be in a separate file. You tell WordPerfect the location of the graphics in the document, its file name, and other printing characteristics. WordPerfect will even "flow" the normal document text around graphics elements where necessary. When you print the document, Word-Perfect instructs the printer to print the graphics correctly.

A common use of the fifth type, horizontal or vertical lines, is as a visual divider between text columns. I'll step you through an example of how to set up a vertical line between two columns. WordPerfect does not keep graphics lines in separate files.

Note: Graphics lines are not the same as the lines you can draw with the line draw feature (Chapter 15), although in the finished product they may *look* about the same! For example, you can adjust the width or darkness of graphics lines, something you can't do with the standard line and box characters.

Tip: Rely on the print view feature a lot when you're setting up graphics. That way, you can quickly see whether the graphics element will print correctly.

The Basic Steps

In general, you follow these basics steps when you want to insert a graphics into a WordPerfect document:

1. Set up the graphics in its own file. A variety of "paint" programs let you create drawings and charts. WordPerfect can read most common paint program formats. WordPerfect also comes with a few example graphics files, all with the extension .WPG for "WordPerfect graphics format," and a utility program (GRAPHCNV.EXE) to convert other graphics files to WordPerfect graphics format.

2. Retrieve the document and position the cursor where you want to insert a graphics element. It will be a special code.

   Note: It's best to insert the graphics code at the left margin of the paragraph or page to which you want to attach the graphics. In a moment you'll see that you can tell WordPerfect where to print the graphics in relationship to the paragraph or page.

3. Insert the graphics.

4. Determine its size and other characteristics.

5. View the printout to make sure everything's correct.

6. Save your work!

Tip: You can also take a picture of a screen with WordPerfect's GRAB utility. As its name implies, GRAB "captures" a shot of the screen and saves it to a file. See The GRAB Utility later in the chapter.

Inserting a Figure

You'll work with one of the graphics files that come with WordPerfect, but I'm asking you to pretend that this is an actual figure in your Beethoven book. The graphics is in the file QUILL.WPG, and it displays—guess what?—Beethoven's famous quill pen! (Not really, but just pretend.)

✔Retrieve the document CHAPTER.2N now. If you didn't create this document in Chapter 22, use another document.

Press   **ALT-F9 Graphics**

WordPerfect presents the graphics menu:

`1 Figure; 2 Table; 3 Text Box; 4 User-defined Box; 5 Line: 0`

Type   1 or f [Figure]

WordPerfect presents the figure menu (the menus for tables, text boxes, and user-defined boxes are exactly the same):

`Figure: 1 Create; 2 Edit; 3 New Number; 4 Options: 0`

Type   1 or c [Create]

You see the definition: figure menu, shown in Figure 34-1. Again, the definition menus for the other graphics elements are virtually the same.

Type   **1** or **f** [Filename]

WordPerfect prompts:

```
Enter filename:
```

This means the file name that contains the graphics element. You must enter the entire file name with its extension if you don't now press F5 List Files and select file name from the directory.

Type   **quill.wpg**

```
Definition: Figure

    1 - Filename

    2 - Caption

    3 - Type                    Paragraph

    4 - Vertical Position       0"

    5 - Horizontal Position     Right

    6 - Size                    3.25" wide x 3.25" (high)

    7 - Wrap Text Around Box    Yes

    8 - Edit




Selection: 0
```

Figure 34-1   The Definition: Figure Menu

Caution: If the graphics files are on a different disk or in a different directory, supply the correct file name (for example, B:QUILL.WPG or \WP50\GRAPHICS\QUILL.WPG).

Press   **RETURN**

Type   **2** or **c** [Caption]

WordPerfect presents a caption setup area that's similar to the header and footer or note setup area. WordPerfect also numbers the figure correctly and displays Figure 1. If you reveal the codes, you'll see that this is a [Box Num] code, *not* real text! The cursor is directly past the code. You can add any other descriptive text:

Press   **SPACEBAR** twice

to add two spaces.

Type   `Beethoven's Famous Quill Pen`

That doesn't look too good, because it's not centered. Don't worry—WordPerfect will print the caption nicely. To alter how the caption prints, see Changing the Figure Number or Options later in the chapter. WordPerfect wraps caption text to fit within the width of the graphics box.

Note: To search for text in captions, use the extended search feature (Chapter 16).

Press   **F7 Exit**

to save the caption.

WordPerfect displays part of the caption and an ellipsis to tell you there's more. The Type option is okay, because you want the graphics to be tied to a paragraph. You can also tie a graphics to an entire page or to one character in the text. In general, follow these guidelines:

1. Tie the graphics to a paragraph when you want the graphics to stay with the text. That is, if the paragraph moves to another page, the graphics moves, too. WordPerfect will even break the page early if it can't fit the paragraph and the graphics on the same page.

2. Tie the graphics to a page when you want the graphics to stay in a fixed position on the current page. Make sure the graphics code is in front of any text that you might want to wrap around the graphics so that WordPerfect can make room for it on the page.

3. Tie the graphics to a character only if you want to insert graphics elements into headers, footers, footnotes, or endnotes.

The Vertical Position means the offset from the top of whatever you tie the graphics to—in this case, the first paragraph. Leave this setting at 0", which means that the graphics will print aligned with the first line of the paragraph. Now take a look at the Horizontal Position options:

Type   5 or h [Horizontal Position]

WordPerfect displays this menu:

Horizontal Position: 1 Left; 2 Right; 3 Center; 4 Both Left & Right: 0

WordPerfect "assumes" you want to position the graphics on the right side of the page, but you can choose left or center, too. The fourth choice, Both Left & Right, is for a *full-page* graphics. Leave the choice as right:

Press   **F1 Cancel** or **ESC**

to exit this menu.

WordPerfect also defaults to a specific size, but you can edit this size, too. You can either tell WordPerfect to size the graphics' width and height automatically or supply settings of your own. WordPerfect "assumes" that you want to wrap the paragraph text around the graphics. If you choose no, WordPerfect prints the graphics above the paragraph. In a moment you'll work with the Edit choice, because that brings up other possibilities.

You've successfully set up Figure 1, so now take a look at it:

Press   **F7 Exit**

Nothing has happened, but if you reveal the codes, you'll see a [Figure] code with the number and caption.

✔Now, to check how the graphics will look on the printed page, view the printout of the page. There's Beethoven's famous quill pen! Depending on your monitor, you'll see the actual picture or a box that indicates the size and location of the graphics item.

When you exit the print view, you'll see a box of broken lines and the tag FIG 1 to show where Figure 1 appears in the document. Because the text has changed to flow around the figure box, WordPerfect also adjusts the page breaks in the document. If you were to insert a graphics into a new document, WordPerfect would flow new text around the graphics as you type.

✔Save the document before you continue but leave it on the screen.

Scaling, Rotation, and Other Editing Niceties

To edit an existing figure, the cursor can be anywhere in the document. Here's where you learn about the various ways to change the look of a graphics.

✔Press **ALT-F9 Graphics**, type **1** or **f** [Figure], type **2** or **e** [Edit], type **1** for Figure 1, and press **RETURN**. Now type **8** or **e** [Edit] to bring up the graphics file itself and a special editing screen, the Figure Edit menu.

The various options here let you change the appearance of the graphics *within* the box. You can (1) *move* the picture left, right, up, or down; (2) *scale* the picture to flatten or widen it; (3) *rotate* it around at an angle; or (4) *invert* it, that is, turn it upside down!

You can use the menu at the bottom of the screen, or the special keys at the top. For instance, press ALT-F9 Graphics to bring up a rotation menu (certain types of graphics elements can't be rotated, however). A "hidden" option can save the graphics element to WordPerfect graphics format. Just press F10 Save and supply a new file name, but be sure to use the extension .WPG.

Tip: The keys at the top are more fun, because you can see what happens as you change the graphics. For instance, try the GRAY − and GRAY + keys to rotate the picture. Or press the various ARROW keys to move the picture around in the box. Go ahead!

✔Experiment with the various options to change the graphics within the box. If you want to save the changes, press **F7 Exit** when you're finished. To cancel the changes, press **F1 Cancel**. Make sure you save the document again if you change the figure.

Changing the Figure Number or Options

The last series of features lets you change the *starting number* for a figure, restart figure numbering, or fine-tune the *options* that determine how the figure and its caption print.

Tip: As with other numbering and options changes, make sure these changes appear in front of the first figure. Put them at the beginning of the document whenever possible.

The options include the border style, the amount of border space both around the figure and within it, the numbering method, the caption numbering style and position, and the amount of gray shading in the figure. Sheesh!

You won't do an example here but just follow these steps when you want to change the figure numbering or options (use the same basic steps for tables, text boxes, and user-defined boxes):

1. Position the cursor in front of the figure or figures.

2. Press **ALT-F9 Graphics**.

3. Type **1** or **f** [Figure] or select another graphics type.

4. To change the starting number or restart figure numbering, type **3** or **n** [New Number]. WordPerfect requests the number. Type it and press **RETURN**. You'll insert a [New Fig Num] code in the document.

5. To change the options, type **4** or **o** [Options]. WordPerfect presents the options: figure menu (Figure 34-2). There are quite a lot of choices! For instance, if you want to change the border style, you'll see this menu:

1 None; 2 Single; 3 Double; 4 Dashed; 5 Dotted; 6 Thick; 7 Extra Thick: 0

I can't delve any further into the myriad options. (If you're like me, sometimes you suffer from "WordPerfect Overload." Still, it's great to have all these capabilities.) After some trial and error, you'll get the exact look you want. Press **F7 Exit** to save your changes and insert a [Fig Opt] code into the document.

6. Save your work!

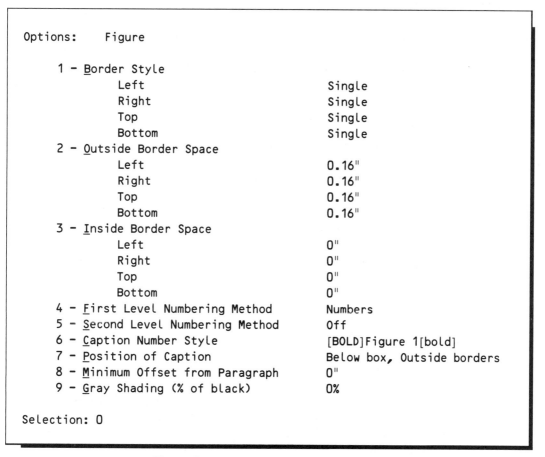

```
Options:     Figure

     1 - Border Style
              Left                      Single
              Right                     Single
              Top                       Single
              Bottom                    Single
     2 - Outside Border Space
              Left                      0.16"
              Right                     0.16"
              Top                       0.16"
              Bottom                    0.16"
     3 - Inside Border Space
              Left                      0"
              Right                     0"
              Top                       0"
              Bottom                    0"
     4 - First Level Numbering Method   Numbers
     5 - Second Level Numbering Method  Off
     6 - Caption Number Style           [BOLD]Figure 1[bold]
     7 - Position of Caption            Below box, Outside borders
     8 - Minimum Offset from Paragraph  0"
     9 - Gray Shading (% of black)      0%

Selection: 0
```

Figure 34-2   The Options: Figure Menu

Tables and Boxes

Follow the same steps to create or edit tables, text boxes, and user-defined boxes. Just substitute the choice you want. The codes you'll insert are similar: [Table], [New Tab Num], and [Tbl Opt] for tables; [Text Box], [New Txt Num], and [Txt Opt] for text boxes; [Usr Box], [New Usr Num], and [Usr Opt] for user-defined boxes.

Tips: You can use the **2** [Edit] choice to retrieve a WordPerfect text document into a box. WordPerfect can keep track of graphics elements in separate lists if you mark them with the following list numbers: 6 (figure boxes), 7 (table boxes), 8 (text boxes), 9 (user-defined boxes).

Graphics and Cross-References

This is just a reminder that you can tie cross-references to graphics elements, just as you can refer to pages, notes, and paragraph numbers. See Chapter 23 for the basic steps. When you set up a reference to a graphics element, you must supply the type of graphics: figure, table, text box, user-defined box, or line.

Drawing Lines Between Text Columns

The next example shows you how to draw a vertical line between two text columns. You can extrapolate the information to draw horizontal lines, too.

✔Clear the screen and retrieve the POULET document. Position the cursor on the first line of Column 1, then make sure the cursor is past the [Col On] code.

You don't want to start the vertical line at the top of the page, because it would print over the title line. Now, follow these steps:

Press   **ALT-F9 Graphics**

Type   **5** or l [Line]

Type   **2** or v [Vertical Line]

The graphics: vertical line menu appears (Figure 34-3). You'll accept the width and gray shading settings—you could change them if you wish—but you'll have to adjust the other settings. For example, horizontal position refers to the offset of the vertical line from the left edge of the page. You don't want the line at the left margin (the default), so:

Type   **1** or h [Horizontal Position]

WordPerfect presents this menu:

```
Graphics: Vertical Line

      1 - Horizontal Position            Left Margin

      2 - Vertical Position              Full Page

      3 - Length of Line

      4 - Width of Line                  0.01"

      5 - Gray Shading (% of black)      100%
```

```
Selection: 0
```

Figure 34-3   The Graphics: Vertical Line Menu

```
Horizontal Position: 1 Left; 2 Right; 3 Between Columns; 4 Set Position: 0
```

The fourth choice lets you set an absolute position on the page, but here you can use a predefined choice:

Type   **3 or b** [Between Columns]

WordPerfect prompts:

```
Place line to right of column: 1
```

That's exactly where you want the line, so:

Press   **RETURN**

WordPerfect shows Column 1 as the horizontal position. Now, you don't want the line to run down the full page; instead, you want it to run along the column text.

Type   **2** or **v** [Vertical Position]

WordPerfect presents this menu:

Vertical Position: 1 Full Page; 2 Top; 3 Center; 4 Bottom; 5 Set Position: 0

Type   **5** or **s** [Set Position]

WordPerfect displays **1.5"** as the top of the vertical line. That's exactly right!

Note: WordPerfect shows the vertical position as an offset in inches from the top edge of the page.

Press   **RETURN**

WordPerfect changes the length of the line to **8.5"**. As it turns out, you're finished, so:

Press   **F7 Exit**

WordPerfect inserts a [VLine] code here with the settings you've determined.

✔View the printout of this page to see the vertical line between the columns.

Note: If you want a vertical line between the columns on the *next* page, you must explicitly set one up. However, on the second page you'd also want the vertical line to run the length of the page, because there's no title line. Go ahead, try it!

If you were setting up a horizontal line between parallel columns, you'd go through similar steps.

Tip: You might have to add blank lines between parallel columns so that the horizontal line doesn't print too closely to a column. WordPerfect would insert a [HLine] code into the document. You can set up a vertical line in a header to have the line print on the entire page, for instance, in a legal brief. Remember that you can even print line numbers (Chapter 6) to the left of the vertical line!

✔Save the document as POULET.VER if you wish. Then clear the screen.

Printing Graphics

Just as you can change the text quality to draft, medium, or high (Chapter 5), you can determine the graphics print quality, too.

Note: Some printers can't work with all the different qualities. Press SHIFT-F7 Print, then use the **G** [Graphics Quality] option. If you have to print text and graphics separately, use the Do Not Print choice as I outlined in Chapter 5, first for graphics, then for text.

The GRAB Utility

The GRAB utility is in a separate program, GRAB.COM. This is a *memory resident* program that you must load *before* any other, including WordPerfect. To capture a screen to a file after GRAB is "resident" in your computer, you press a "hot key" sequence, ALT-SHIFT-F9. GRAB saves the current screen to a file called GRAB.WPG. If the file exists, GRAB uses the next file number, GRAB1.WPG, and so on. You can then use the files you create with GRAB as graphics elements in a WordPerfect document.

To start GRAB, exit WordPerfect, type **grab** and press **RETURN**. Then load WordPerfect if you want to capture a WordPerfect screen.

Tip: To get help with GRAB, type **grab/h** and press **RETURN**. Read the help screens for complete information on GRAB.

Other Print Operations

Because I didn't want to overwhelm you with all the many print functions that WordPerfect provides, I didn't cover certain, more esoteric, operations. Well, here are two more, type through printing and "printing" to a disk file. The final option on the print menu, 7 [Initialize Printer], relates to soft fonts (Chapter 35).

WordPerfect, the Typewriter

Sometimes you may have to fill in preprinted forms, a operation most word processors can't do too well. Or you may use an odd-size paper for memos, and you don't want the hassle of form and format changes. WordPerfect can pretend to be a typewriter. Press **SHIFT-F7 Print**, then type **5** or **y** [Type Through] to see the type through menu:

```
Type Through by: 1 Line; 2 Character
```

With the **1** [Line] choice, you type an entire line first before you actually send it to the printer. Don't worry if the print head moves as you type. You can still edit the line to correct typos before you press RETURN to send the line. Use this choice to print fast memos or short letters.

The **2** [Character] choice sends everything you type *directly* to the printer. Use this choice for filling in forms, but make sure that the print head is positioned where you want it. As on the typewriter, press the SPACEBAR and RETURN keys to move the print head over or down the paper before you type your text. You can type at most about 200 characters. If you type **1** or ι [Line], you'll see this (a similar menu appears for character type through):

```
Line Type Through printing

Function Key        Action

Move                Retrieve the previous line for editing
Format              Do a printer command
Enter               Print the line
Exit/Cancel         Exit without printing
```

Some printers can't use this option. If such is the case, WordPerfect presents this message:

```
Feature not available on this printer
```

You must select another printer resource file. Additionally, if there are jobs in the print queue, you'll see this message:

```
Printing in Progress
```

You can't use the type through feature when the print queue is not empty. Press **F7 Exit** or **F1 Cancel** when you're finished with type through.

"Printing" to Disk

As strange as it may seem, you can "print" a document to a disk file. WordPerfect saves a version of the document in its printed form. The disk file contains the text and all printer formatting instructions for the printer you select, just as if WordPerfect were sending the document to the actual printer. Why would you use this feature? When your printer is not available and you're in a rush, you can use the *DOS* PRINT command to print the document at another computer that doesn't have WordPerfect.

To print to a disk file, you must *temporarily* change the printer resources to tell WordPerfect that you want to use a different port. Follow the steps that you learned under Adding a Printer Resource File in Chapter 5 to edit the printer you've selected and bring up the select printer: edit menu. Then type **2** or **p** [Port]. Notice choice **8** [Other]. After you type **8** or **o**, WordPerfect prompts:

```
Device or Filename:
```

You must supply a *new* file name to print the document to that file. Type a new file name and press **RETURN**. Then press **F7 Exit** enough times to return to the print menu. Print the document as normal (you may have to issue a go once you've started the print job).

Caution: Make sure the file name is new. Otherwise, WordPerfect will blithely overwrite an existing file with the print file. Also, remember to change the port information back to the *real* port when you're finished printing to disk.

Tip: Select the standard printer to print a document to a disk file without formatting codes. There's also a DOS Text Printer that you can set up to print to a disk file. WordPerfect retains basic formatting like top and bottom margins and justification, but eliminates fonts and other special effects.

Use the same approach to print to another *device*, that is, printer on a local area network. Consult your network manual about how to supply the correct device name. To *convert* a WordPerfect file to a DOS text file without formatting, see Chapter 36.

The Advanced Printing Commands

In their attempt to enter—at least part of the way—into the world of desktop publishing, the designers of WordPerfect added a number of advanced printing commands to WordPerfect. These commands help you get the most polished results possible on a laser printer. However, some of them work on conventional printers, too.

For example, one command lets you send escape codes to the printer for various special printing effects, such as condensed or expanded printing. Another helps you overcome the "rivers" of white space that appear with justified right margins. To work with the advanced printing commands:

Press　　　**SHIFT-F8 Format**

Type　　　**4** or **o** [Other]

Type　　　**6** or **p** [Printer Functions]

The format: printer functions menu appears (Figure 34-4).

```
Format: Printer Functions

     1 - Kerning                              No

     2 - Printer Command

     3 - Word Spacing                         Optimal
         Letter Spacing                       Normal

     4 - Word Spacing Justification Limits
         Compressed to (0% - 100%)            75%
         Expanded to (100% - unlimited)       400%













Selection: 0
```

Figure 34-4   The Format: Printer Functions Menu

Kerning

The term *kerning* comes directly from the world of typesetting. It refers to the process of tightening up the spaces between certain pairs of letters, such as WA. The letter pairs that WordPerfect can kern are in the printer's resource file, for example, HPLASEII.PRS. You can turn kerning on and off throughout a document. Type **1** or **k** [Kerning], then type **y** or **n**. WordPerfect inserts [Kern:On] and [Kern:Off] codes in the document.

Tip: Set kerning on for large font sizes in headlines to reduce the space between letters.

Sending Printer Escape Codes

Every key you type has a decimal value, known as its *ASCII code* (Chapter 15). Many printers use special codes that begin with the ASCII value for the ESC key for such features as expanded or condensed printing. These special printer codes are, understandably, called *escape codes*. For example, a code might be ESC-F to turn expanded printing on and ESC-G to turn it off. As you know, WordPerfect has other uses for ESC, but you can still insert a printer escape code anywhere in a document.

First, refer to your printer's manual for the correct escape code. There are probably *two* codes: one for "on" and one for "off." Also, some printers may distinguish between upper- and lowercase letters, so be careful how you type the codes.

Tip: If you want to send several printer escape codes at once, set them up in a separate file. Set up the "off" codes in another file.

Next, determine how to enter the code in WordPerfect. You must use the decimal equivalent for the ESC key, which is 27. In addition, all decimal codes *less than 32* or *greater than 127* must be enclosed in angle brackets: < >. You can enter letters as is or as ASCII decimal values, once again enclosed in angle brackets. So the printer code ESC-F is either <27>F or <27><70>, because 70 is the ASCII value for *F*.

To insert a printer escape code or a file that contains several escape codes:

1. Position the cursor at the point in the document where you want the special printing to start.

2. Bring up the format: printer functions menu.

3. Type **2** or **p** [Printer Command]. WordPerfect prompts:

   1 Command; 2 Filename: 0

4. Type **1** or **c** [Command] to insert one escape code, or **2** or **f** [Filename] to insert several that are in a file.

   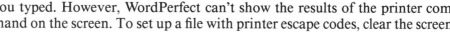

   Tip: You can set up the WordPerfect defaults to indicate another directory where printer commands are located (Appendix A).

5. Type the command or file name and press **RETURN**. For example, to insert ESC-F, you would type <27>F.

6. Press **F7 Exit** to return to the document.

WordPerfect inserts a [Ptr Cmnd] code with the command or file name you typed. However, WordPerfect can't show the results of the printer command on the screen. To set up a file with printer escape codes, clear the screen.

Then follow the above steps to insert each command individually. Save the file when you're done.

Word and Letter Spacing

Unlike kerning, which adjusts the spacing between certain letter pairs, *word and letter spacing* can adjust the space between adjacent words and letters throughout a document. Only trial printing will help you determine how much word and letter spacing, if any, you'll need.

When you type **3** or **w** [Word Spacing], WordPerfect prompts:

```
Word Spacing: 1 Normal; 2 Optimal; 3 Percent of Optimal; 4 Set Pitch: 2
```

Normal is the spacing that the printer's manufacturer recommends, while Optimal is the setting that WordPerfect Corporation considers best. You can enter a percentage of the optimal setting or insert a specific pitch of your own. (Recall that pitch refers to the number of characters per horizontal inch.) You can change both or either word or letter spacing, and WordPerfect inserts a [Wrd/Ltr Spacing] code into the document.

Word Spacing Justification Limits

The final choice, word spacing justification limits, lets you determine how WordPerfect inserts spaces to justify the right margin. Normally, WordPerfect inserts spaces between words only, but if you change these settings Word-Perfect will insert microspaces between letters when it has reached the limits you specified. Type **4** or **j** [Word Spacing Justification Limits], then supply new compression and expansion percentages. WordPerfect inserts a [Just Lim] code into the document.

Again, trial printing will be your guide with this setting. Don't change it unless there are too many "rivers" of white space that run down the printed page.

Dear Reader, WordPerfect has so many features! Little by little you'll get to learn and love them all. If you own a laser printer, you're now ready to study advanced ways to use it with WordPerfect.

Chapter

35

The Laser Revolution

In this chapter you'll discover new uses of this command . . .

SHIFT-F7 Print   (1) Mark soft fonts, (2) initialize the printer and download soft fonts

I mentioned, 'way back in Chapter 4, that the desktop publishing capabilities of the laser printer have altered WordPerfect's approach to typestyles and fonts. Although special software has emerged to tap the desktop publishing market, you don't have to buy and learn another program. With a little practice—and a lot of patience—you can produce some stunning documents with WordPerfect alone. This chapter starts you on your way.

Note: I use the Hewlett-Packard LaserJet Series II as the representative laser printer in this chapter. The Series II is similar to its predecessor, the LaserJet Plus. Even if you own another laser printer, the general remarks in the chapter still apply, and you can extrapolate the information you need from the examples.*

DO WARM-UP

---

*A useful publication for LaserJet owners is *LaserJet Journal.* You'll find good tips for using WordPerfect with any LaserJet printer. For subscription information, write to the journal at 1945 Techny Road, Northbrook, Illinois 60062.

Introduction

Refer to the general discussion of typestyles, fonts, and other desktop publishing terms in Chapter 4. Below are a few more points and terms you should be aware of before you work with the examples. Version 4.2 users: Changes there are aplenty. Make sure you upgrade to WordPerfect 5.0 before you study this chapter.

Laser Printer Fonts

Laser printers have three types of fonts: (1) internal fonts, (2) cartridge fonts, and (3) soft fonts. *Internal* fonts are built into the printer. Usually they're fixed-width fonts like Courier 10 pitch. After you add a laser printer to your list of printer resources, WordPerfect displays the internal fonts when you select or change the printer's base font. Indeed, WordPerfect probably chose an internal font as the default base font. You can use any internal font at any time because internal fonts are always available.

Cartridge fonts are on plug-in cartridges, and each cartridge has a number of fonts. Recall from Chapter 5 that you must tell WordPerfect which font cartridges you're using so that WordPerfect then "knows" what fonts are available. You *cannot* switch cartridges during a print job. They must be in the printer when you turn the printer on. That's why WordPerfect insists that you mark cartridges as initially present.

Soft fonts are software-based fonts. Because they're on disks, you must *load*—that is, copy—the fonts you want from the disk into the printer. This process is called *downloading*. Soft fonts normally remain in the printer's memory until you turn the printer off.

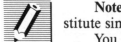

Note: The examples in this chapter use only soft fonts. You could substitute similar cartridge fonts if you wish.

You have to tell WordPerfect what soft fonts you want to use so that it can download the fonts for you. That is, you add the information about each font to your printer resource. This information may include proportional spacing tables, for example. Until now I've skirted the entire issue of soft fonts, so it will be one of the important topics of this chapter.

One big advantage to soft fonts over cartridge fonts is that you can choose exactly which fonts you want to use. You can't alter the configuration of a font cartridge. In addition, soft fonts last longer than cartridge fonts. For all intents and purposes, soft fonts last "forever," provided you always use copies of the font files. Usually, each font is in a separate file. Soft fonts are also cheaper than cartridges.

There's one big disadvantage to soft fonts: memory or, rather, the lack of same. Cartridge fonts contain their own internal memory that's separate from the printer's memory. Soft fonts take up the printer's memory, and quite a lot of it. Depending on the size of the fonts you plan to use and how much memory your printer has, you may be able to download only a few soft fonts.

You can, if you wish, add a memory expansion board to some laser printers, a costly but workable alternative.

Note: WordPerfect Corporation recommends that the printer have at least 1 megabyte of memory, but you *can* work with less.

Soft fonts also consume a great deal of disk space. If you don't have a hard disk, you'll be flipping a lot of floppies whenever you have to download soft fonts! **Tip:** If you have a hard disk, copy only the soft font files you need.

Portraits and Landscapes Again

Recall that every form has an *orientation*. Although you can manually insert paper into most conventional printers either vertically (portrait orientation) or horizontally (landscape orientation), you must explicitly tell a laser printer what orientation you need. That's because the paper enters the laser printer from a paper tray and can enter only one way. You can't shift the paper around yourself. I mentioned this when you set up an envelope form (Chapter 13).

Depending on the cartridges you're using, there may be far fewer fonts available in landscape orientation than in portrait orientation. Conversely, some fonts print only in landscape orientation. Usually soft fonts have a wider selection of landscape fonts.

How WordPerfect Selects Fonts

Normally WordPerfect switches to a different font when it sees a font change code in a document (Chapter 4). The change could be a [Font] code, which alters the base font and lists the font name. You can tell at a glance what base fonts you're using—should you forget.

Tip: I recommend that you insert comment boxes to remind you about the font requirements of a document. Many of the examples in this chapter contain comment boxes.

However, WordPerfect also selects different fonts depending on other font change codes that you've inserted with the F6 Bold, F8 Underline, or CTRL-F8 Font keys. That is, if there are size, appearance, or color font change codes in the document, WordPerfect tries to match the font.

For example, if you want text to print in italics, WordPerfect switches to the italic version of the base font *if it's available in the printer*. You don't have to select the font by name. If there's no italic font, WordPerfect continues to use the base font. Similarly, for a large font change WordPerfect will try to find the next larger font size, and so on (the automatic font change or AFC).

If WordPerfect can't find a soft font in the printer already, it will attempt to download the font from the disk. It can do this only if you've told it what soft fonts you plan to use and where the font files are located. You can also download the fonts before you start, a process that WordPerfect calls *initializing* the printer. The easiest way is to let WordPerfect do the downloading.

Symbol Sets and Default Fonts

A *symbol set* is merely a list of the characters that are available in a font. The problem with symbol sets is that they may not use the same codes as the ASCII character set of your computer (Chapter 15). The Hewlett-Packard LaserJet series, for instance, has Roman-8, USASCII, and LINEDRAW symbol sets, among others.

Virtually all text symbol sets contain the standard letters, numbers, and punctuation marks and, fortunately, use the same ASCII codes. That is, code numbers 32 through 127 are standard. However, many symbol sets can't print the "extended ASCII" characters—codes 1–31 and 128–255—or they may use different codes for the characters. You might have to determine what code, if any, represents the extended character you want.

On the LaserJet Series II, the *default internal font* is a 12 point Courier font. But it contains the Roman-8 symbol set, so the extended ASCII characters are different from what your computer displays. If you print the standard internal font test, you'll note that there are other, 12 point, internal Courier fonts with some—but not all—ASCII extended characters. You can select the font you want as the default internal font from the control panel. See the "Fonts" chapter in the printer manual for instructions.

Line and Page Formatting Issues

Laser printers can't print in the blank lines at the very top or bottom of the page. That means you should be careful about your top and bottom margin settings. Additionally, laser printers can't print at the exact left or right edges of the paper, so use a margin setting of zero (0) to have WordPerfect display the size of the unprintable region (page 115).

WordPerfect measures the line length in inches. The default line length is 6½ inches. So, no matter what different fonts you use on a line, WordPerfect still prints each line correctly.

Tip: If you don't like the way WordPerfect justifies lines in proportionally spaced fonts, change the word spacing justification limits (Chapter 34). WordPerfect also properly centers text in different fonts, even though the screen display of centered lines may not be exactly right. That's because WordPerfect wants to display the centered text on the screen so you can see it without having to scroll the display.

When you change fonts, WordPerfect adjusts the line height, or *leading*, automatically. Recall that you can change this setting to manual if WordPerfect's approach is not to your liking (Chapter 17).

"Wizzy Wig"

No matter what fonts you use with WordPerfect, you still won't achieve true *WYSIWYG* (pronounced "wizzy wig") on the screen. This term means "what you see is what you get." Depending on the type of monitor you have, the screen appearance of your document will differ a little or a lot from its final printout. On certain monitors you can see some fonts on the edit screen or in the print preview. That means, more than likely, that you'll probably print many "dry runs" of a document before you get the results you want.

Tip: View the printout often to see at least the overall look of the page.

The Setup

Before you get to the meat and potatoes of this chapter, you must tell WordPerfect about the fonts you plan to use. Basically, here's what you do:

1. Add the laser printer resource file to your list of printers as outlined in Chapter 5. Make sure you tell WordPerfect what font cartridges, if any, are present in your printer.

2. Determine the soft fonts you need before you work with them and whether the fonts are (1) initially present in the printer or (2) require downloading.

   Tip: It's a good idea to keep all soft font files in a special directory on your hard disk.

3. Mark the soft fonts in the printer resource file and tell WordPerfect their *location* on the disk. You can add or delete soft fonts at any time.

   What if WordPerfect tells you there's not enough memory to mark all the soft fonts you want? Apparently, the default is 360K (360 kilobytes). Just use the **2** [Change Quantity] choice on the Cartridges and Fonts screen to tell WordPerfect that you have more memory— even if technically you don't! Make sure that you've highlighted Soft Fonts first, as outlined in the next section. Then type 2 or q [Change Quantity], to which WordPerfect prompts Quantity:. Type a new amount in kilobytes, for example, 1024, and press RETURN. The new quantity appears at the top of the screen.

   Caution: If delete a font, WordPerfect displays an asterisk within the [Font*] code in a document that originally used the font. The asterisk indicates that the font is no longer available.

Once you've performed these steps, you can switch fonts as often as you like within a document—from internal to cartridge to soft, and back again. Before it prints a document WordPerfect downloads the soft fonts for you, or you can perform that step yourself. See Downloading Soft Fonts Yourself later in the chapter.

Version 4.2 users: You can convert your font files to WordPerfect 5.0 format with the FC utility (Chapter 36) if the fonts aren't on the 5.0 font list.

WordPerfect adds the fonts to the printer resources and displays them on the list.

Marking Soft Fonts

Dear Reader, I've done step 2 for you already! The examples in this chapter work with the default internal fonts and various Tms Rmn and Helv fonts from Hewlett-Packard's "AC" soft font package. If you have the "AD" package, the fonts are virtually the same. Later, you may want to try you hand at working with the marvelous Bitstream fonts that WordPerfect Corporation supplies for the asking.

Table 35-1 lists the sizes, styles, orientation, and file names of the "AC" fonts you'll be using. The rightmost column lists each font's name as WordPerfect displays it. By the way, *style* refers to regular (also known as *Roman*), italic, or bold. You'll note that various parts of Hewlett-Packard's font file names indicate the typeface (TR or HV), size, style (R, B, or I), symbol set (US), and orientation of the font (P or L). Hewlett-Packard and WordPerfect use *Tms Rmn* and *Helv*, because the real Times Roman and Helvetica fonts are registered trademarks of Allied Linotype Corporation.

Table 35-1   Hewlett-Packard "AC" Soft Fonts Used in the Examples

(All fonts except one are in portrait orientation.)

File Name	Font	What WordPerfect Displays
TR080RPN.USP	Tms Rmn 8-point regular	(AC) Tms Rmn 08pt
TR100RPN.USP	Tms Rmn 10-point regular	(AC) Tms Rmn 10pt
TR100IPN.USP	Tms Rmn 10-point italic	(AC) Tms Rmn 10pt Italic
TR120RPN.USP	Tms Rmn 12-point regular	(AC) Tms Rmn 12pt
TR120RPN.USL	Tms Rmn 12-point regular (landscape)	(AC) Tms Rmn 12pt (Land)
TR120BPN.USP	Tms Rmn 12-point boldface	(AC) Tms Rmn 12pt Bold
TR120IPN.USP	Tms Rms 12-point italic	(AC) Tms Rmn 12pt Italic
TR180BPN.USP	Tms Rmn 18-point boldface	(AC) Tms Rmn 18pt Bold
HV140BPN.USP	Helv 14-point boldface	(AC) Helv 14pt Bold

✔If you haven't added the Hewlett-Packard LaserJet Series II to your list of printers, do so now. Make sure you supply the correct port. Then from the select printer: edit menu, type **5** or **c** [Cartridges and Fonts] to bring up the select printer: cartridges and fonts screen.

To select and thus add soft fonts to this printer resource file:

Press   **DOWN ARROW**

to highlight Soft Fonts.

Type   **1** or **f** [Select Fonts]

WordPerfect presents a *long* list of fonts and tells you at the bottom of the screen:

```
Mark Fonts:  * Present when print job begins          Press Exit to save
             + Can be loaded during print job      Press Cancel to cancel
```

Which marker do you use? Normally, use the plus sign to indicate that the font may not be in the printer when a print job begins. That way, WordPerfect will download the font for you. Because of the printer's memory limitations, you might not be able to download all soft fonts at once, so WordPerfect will download only the ones you need in a particular document.

There is a disadvantage to this approach, though. WordPerfect will download the fonts every time you print a document that uses the soft fonts. If you work with the same soft fonts all the time, you may want to mark them with asterisks. Then you can download (initialize) the fonts at the beginning of the day. Keep in mind that your printer may have enough memory for only a few soft fonts.

Note: Don't use the GRAY + key for the plus sign. That key just scrolls down the font listing.

✔Highlight each font name that's listed in Table 35-1 and mark it with an asterisk (*) or a plus sign (+). If you mark the wrong font, press the marker again to "unmark." After you've marked all the fonts, press **F7 Exit** twice to return to the select printer: edit menu. WordPerfect tells you that it's updating the fonts.

Indicating the Location of Soft Fonts

From the select printer: edit menu, use choice **7** [Path for Downloadable Fonts and Printer Command Files] to tell WordPerfect where it can find the soft font files. For example, I keep my soft fonts in the FONTS subdirectory of the WP50 directory. So, my directory path is \WP50\FONTS.

Note: The directory must already exist before you indicate it here. If you *must* use floppy disks, supply the drive designator—for example, A:—as the path.

✔Set up the font file path. Then press **F7 Exit** enough times to return to the document. Make sure that you now copy all the font files listed in Table 35-1 to the directory where you plan to keep them on the hard disk. The files are not all on the same master disk, so do a directory listing of the disks to find the right files.

Some Examples

Well, after this lengthy introduction you're no doubt eager to try your hand at desktop publishing. I can (alas!) present only a few examples of ways to work with WordPerfect and laser printers. I hope that they give you "food for thought" and the inspiration to pursue your own needs. Later in the chapter are some tips on good page design.

Starting Simple

The first example shows how WordPerfect deals with a base font change from a fixed-width font to a proportionally spaced font. It also illustrates a common pitfall for the unwary.

✔Retrieve the document LAREST. Make sure the cursor is at the beginning of the document.

Your first order of business is to change the base font to Tms Rmn 12-point regular. No! Maybe your first order of business is to insert a comment to remind you which soft fonts this document uses.

✔With the CTRL-F5 Text In/Out key, insert the following comment at the top of the document:

```
Soft fonts used:
  Tms Rmn 12-point regular (base font)
  Tms Rmn 12-point italic
  Tms Rmn 18-point bold (very large font)
```

Now set up the base font at the beginning of the document:

Press   **CTRL-F8 Font**

Type   **4** or **f** [Base Font]

✔Highlight Tms Rmn 12pt and type **1** or **s** [Select], or just press **RETURN**.

When you move the cursor to the end of the document or rewrite the screen, WordPerfect reformats the text. A proportionally spaced font can print more characters on each line, so the line endings change.

Here's the common pitfall: Right now there are underline codes in the document, but you want italics instead. WordPerfect doesn't "know" that! So you have to replace the begin and end underline codes with begin and end italic codes:

✔Replace the begin underline codes with begin italics codes. Then replace the end underline codes with end italic codes.

(An aside: Purists might want to include the punctuation after words within the italics. For example, *Maya!* looks better than *Maya*!. That's what I did.)

✔When you're finished, save the document as LAREST.LAS and position the cursor at the beginning of the document. You're now ready to print the document, so prepare your printer and paper. Then tell WordPerfect to print the full document.

The results are impressive, but not impressive enough! You forgot to put the title in that larger, Tms Rmn 18-point type.

✔Position the cursor under the *T* of *The* in the title. Block the title, then:

Press   **CTRL-F8 Font**

Type   1 or **s** [S̲ize]

Type   6 or **v** [V̲ry Large]

The reason you used the very large font is because you wanted Tms Rmn 18-point. However, you've also marked the 14-point Tms Rmn font in the printer resources, so WordPerfect would consider that the large font. The moral here is to know what fonts are currently in the printer! Of course, one way to get around the confusion about large and extra large fonts is to put in a base font change that uses the font by name. Remember then to change the base font *back* to Tms Rmn 12-point at the end of the title line.

✔Print the first page. The results are in Figure 35-1. Save the document again, then clear the screen.

Tip: You could turn hyphenation on and hyphenate some words to "close up" some lines and avoid those rivers of white space (Chapter 20).

Mixing Fixed-Width and Proportional Fonts

WordPerfect always makes font changes according to whatever is the base font. In the previous example, WordPerfect switched to the large and italic versions of the base font automatically. When you want to alternate between fixed-width and proportionally spaced fonts, however, you must switch base

The Little Restaurants of Los Angeles

San Francisco, eat your heart out! Los Angeles has some of the *best* restaurants in the state, with more appearing all the time. I'm not talking big and fancy here. For the most part, these are smaller places, generally ethnic, but the food is great and the prices are right.

Certainly at the top of my list is *El Colmao,* purveyors of excellent Cuban food. If you don't like rice and beans, then skip this place, because rice and beans are the staple of the menu. But you'll be missing several treats, such as the *picadillo* (ground beef cooked in a sauce), or the *ropa vieja* (literally, "old clothes" -- shredded beef simmered in tomato sauce), or *boliche* (Cuban-style pot roast). The atmosphere is bouncy and unpretentious, and the portions are enormous. El Colmao is at 2328 West Pico Boulevard (closed Tuesdays).

Then there's *Palermo,* my choice for good Italian fare at very good prices. Palermo has had a faithful following for many years, so you'll probably have to wait for a table. The thin-crust pizzas are highly recommended, as is the *veal parmigiana.* Palermo has recently moved into bigger quarters at 1858 North Vermont Avenue and is now open every day.

Los Angeles has more Thai restaurants than you can shake a bamboo at, but the one I always find myself returning to is the *House of Chan Dara.* Here's another spot where you'll wait in line, and for good reason. The food is inexpensive and beautifully prepared. Try any of the meat and vegetable combinations, as well as the ubiquitous Thai iced tea or iced coffee. The ambience is definitely part of the fun at the Hollywood location (1511 Cahuenga Boulevard), while the Larchmont Village branch (310 N. Larchmont Boulevard) is more subdued.

Ah, *Maya!* No, this is not another taco joint, but rather the best Japanese restaurant in Los Angeles. No snooty sushi here, just well-prepared and delicious "country-style" food: *teriyaki, tempura, sukiyaki.* Small, intimate, reasonable -- maybe even the find of the century. I could never leave L.A. because I'd miss Maya (874 Virgil Avenue, closed Mondays).

"Good food, lousy parking" is what the sign says at the *Talpa.* That's exactly right, but don't let the lack of parking deter you. The Talpa has authentic Mexican food, a lively atmosphere, and rock-bottom prices. Any of the combination platters are good, as well as the *albondigas* soup. The Talpa is open every day except certain holidays, and you'll find it at 11751 West Pico Boulevard.

If you're on the east side, here's an equally good Mexican Restaurant near downtown. It's called *La Fuente,* and at it you'll enjoy excellent food from Mexico's state of Sonora. What you won't experience is a fancy decor, but who cares? La Fuente is at 5530 Monte Vista Street in Highland Park, and it's open every day.

Angelenos (yes, that's what they're called) love hamburgers, and people develop very strong loyalties to their favorite hamburger haven. Perhaps the place with the strongest following is *Tommy's,* open 24 hours a day to satisfy that urge. All Tommy's hamburgers come with tomato, pickle, mustard, onion, and chili sauce, but you can have it your way, too. It must be good, because no one minds the absence of french fries. Although there are several Tommy's locations throughout the city, the *only* one to go to is at 2575 Beverly Boulevard.

If, however, you want to have your cake and your burger, too, you should consider *Hampton's,* a pleasant place to experiment with a variety of different hamburger combinations, as well as salads and other, more "formal," entrees. Hampton's also has

Figure 35-1 Using Proportionally Spaced Fonts

In dBASE III PLUS, you can configure the *working environment* to suit your needs with the SET command. For example, dBASE's warning bell annoys you. Turn it off! At the dot prompt, type SET BELL OFF. Similarly, you don't want to see any menus on the screen. The command for that is SET MENU OFF. If you type just SET, the full-screen SET area appears. It lets you select all the SET options from pull-down menus.

Figure 35-2   Mixing Fixed-Width and Proportional Fonts

fonts. Take a look at Figure 35-2, which is the printout of the next example. It uses an internal font and two soft fonts.

✔Before you begin typing, insert the following comment at the top of the new document:

Base fonts used:
  Courier 12-point 10-pitch (fixed width)
  Tms Rmn 12-point regular (proportional)

✔Change the base font to Tms Rmn 12-point. Then type the example (remember to use the italic font for *working environment*), but when you get to the phrase *SET BELL OFF*, change the base font to Courier 12 point. At the end of the phrase, change the base font back to Tms Rmn. Finish the example, making the appropriate base font changes. Then save the document as DBASE.LAS and print the results. Clear the screen when you're finished.

Of course, you aren't limited to soft fonts and internal fonts. You can mix and match cartridge fonts, too. Dear Reader, WordPerfect's "intelligent" printing is impressive indeed!

Using a Landscape Font: Envelopes Again!

In Chapter 13 I showed you how to switch forms when you wanted to print on paper positioned horizontally in the printer—what typesetters call land-scape orientation. When it prints a form in landscape orientation, WordPerfect uses whatever is the landscape font that's the closest in size to the base font.

You can, of course, override WordPerfect's decision. Just insert a base font change that uses another landscape font. The next example shows you how and also what may happen if you're not careful.

✔Retrieve the ENV document that you created in Chapter 13. Recall that this document uses an envelope form. Make sure that the form's orientation is landscape.

You may have noticed that the cursor appears below the middle of the first return address line. If you reveal the codes, though, you'll see that the cursor is past the formatting codes. Earlier in the chapter you marked the "AC" Tms Rmn 12-point landscape font as one of the soft fonts. You'll now use this font as the base font.

✔Use the CTRL-F8 Font key to bring up the list of possible base fonts. Notice that WordPerfect has placed an asterisk next to a Courier landscape font to indicate that it's the base font. Highlight the Tms Rmn 12pt (Land) font and select it.

By the way, when you select a portrait font as the base font for a document that's in landscape orientation, WordPerfect tells you:

```
ERROR: Invalid printer file
```

Now, take a look at the page break. Did WordPerfect break the first page in the middle of the name and address lines? Originally you didn't change the bottom margin. You may have to change it to 0.5 inch, or whatever smaller setting works.

✔Save the document as ENV.LAS and print it if you wish. The printer may ask you to feed in the form. You can insert the envelope in the manual feed slot (the far left side of the slot) or use the envelope sheet feeder. Press the Continue button after you insert the envelope. Clear the screen when you're finished.

Printing Columns with Soft Fonts

You'll now print the POULET document with soft fonts. Along the way you'll change the base font a couple of times and learn a little more about WordPerfect's ways.

✔Retrieve the POULET document. Position the cursor under the *T* of *Texan's*, but make sure the cursor is past the begin center code. Then change the base font to 14-point Helv bold. At the end of the title line and past the end center code, change the base font to Tms Rmn 12-point regular. Save the document as POULET.LAS but leave it on the screen. (You could also insert a comment box that lists the soft fonts.)

Now take a look at the text. It's a visual mess! That's because more characters can fit on each line, so the appearance of the columns is screwy. To make the display more readable, you have two options: (1) turn the side-by-side display of columns off or (2) change the display width. Both options are topics of Appendix A. I chose to turn the side-by-side display off so that I could see each line. I then turned manual hyphenation on and moved the cursor through the document. WordPerfect didn't stop at any syllable breaks in this example, but you may need to hyphenate if the lines look too spaced out. Figure 35-3 shows printed page 1.

(Another aside for purists: You may want to use real typesetting open and close quotation marks to make this document appear printed. They're

Texan's Chili Conquers All

POULET, Texas. When he was a boy, Stanley Beburp dreamed of becoming the King of Chili. "Other boys wanted to be firemen and policemen. Not me! I wanted to be the world's expert on chili, the Reigning Monarch of the Red Hot."

Now it looks as if Beburp's dreams have come true. Not only did his "Buckaroo Chili" take first prize in the All-Texas Chili Round-Up, but it did so for the tenth consecutive year, a record that no one has ever come close to beating.

What's more, a large international food conglomerate has approached Beburp with an offer to mass produce and distribute his prize-winning chili as part of a new line of frozen food products emphasizing "regional American cuisine."

"It's like what I always knew would happen," he exclaimed. "Someday people everywhere would appreciate me for my true worth, would recognize the grandeur and majesty of good chili."

Beburp, or Stan, as he is most often known to virtually everyone in these parts, dipped a huge ladle into a steaming cauldron of -- what else? -- Buckaroo Chili, and offered it to the unsuspecting writer. Not being one to refuse a kind gesture, I took up the challenge. Thank goodness there was a pint of cold beer also readily available!

"It's hot, isn't it?" Stan asked, offering to help wipe the tears away from my eyes as I nearly swooned in what appeared to me to be a diabolical scheme to destroy my entire insides. "People who aren't used to chili, and especially to my chili, find it at first a bit hard to swallow. Get it? Hard to swallow. Hah!"

I smiled meekly, all the while trying to ascertain exactly where I was and what in heaven's name I was doing with the uncontrollable, burning sensation that writhed down my throat and ended in the pit of my stomach. The beer helped a little, but only a little, and only if I continued to down it like water. I was also thinking wistfully of quiche lorraine and other more, well, civilized food.

"Are you from New York?" he asked, as I politely refused another brimming ladleful. "I've found New Yorkers the most difficult to please. They never seem to enjoy my chili. I think their taste buds must have been destroyed in early childhood. Probably has something to do with the subways, I think."

(Little did Stan realize that the hottest of Hunan food, so much praised by residents of the Big Apple and elsewhere, couldn't come even close to the pinnacle of picantness that was and is Buckaroo Chili. As one who has always considered himself a relentless pursuer of the ultimate "hot trip," I felt that, at long last, I had met my match.)

Things were getting a bit befuddled and confused as I tried to listen to Stan recount his life story. My head was reeling, and my stomach was giving me notice that I would pay long and hard for my sins.

Meanwhile, Stan was blithely and rather rapidly rattling on about his childhood. All I could catch were snips and snatches here and there:

"Poor family ... never had enough to eat, it seemed ... father disappeared when he was 10 ... mother had to work and not the best of cooks anyway ... can't blame her ... neighbor's wife made chili for them every week ... it became an obsession, a craving that he couldn't satisfy ... he would spend hours over the pot ... she gave him the task of stirring the chili ... that was the real secret: in the stirring ..."

Soon the minor revolution that had begun in my stomach was turning into an event of major proportions, an uproar that swelled and took with it my sense of decorum and all my Eastern-bred reliance on the balance between the Inner and

Figure 35-3 Printing Text Columns with Soft Fonts

in the WordPerfect character set number 4, which contains the common type-setting symbols that aren't part of the ASCII character set. The left (open) double quote is 4,30; the right is 4,31. Use the CTRL-2 compose key to insert these characters. However, not all laser printer symbol sets contain the type-setting characters.)

✔Clear the screen before you continue.

Base Fonts Changes in Headers and Footers

If you're not attentive to the formatting of a particular document, you may not get the results you want. For example, suppose you set up headers and footers at the beginning of a document (Chapter 16). Later you retrieve the document and insert a base font change *past* the header and footer codes. WordPerfect will still print the headers and footers in the initial base font! The same is true for predefined page numbering. The moral? Make sure you insert a base font change in front of page numbering, header, and footer codes.

In the POULET document, for instance, your first base font change is to a large Helv font for the title, but that's not the real base font. If there were pagination, header, or footer codes in front of the title, you could insert a base font change for the Tms Rmn font ahead of the codes.

Tip: Another way to go is to set up the initial font for the document in the format: document menu (Appendix A).

A Fancy Letterhead*

The next example illustrates how to create your own typeset looking letterhead and thus save printing costs. The example includes a trick to cajole your laser printer into doing what *you* want it to do. This is slightly complicated, so be careful! Figure 35-4 shows the completed letterhead. What you want to do here is print three lines over another. The trick is to rely on the services of the *advance up* command (Chapter 15).

For the overall page formatting, I used a top margin of 0.75 inch and a bottom margin of 1 inch. I turned justification off and changed the left and right margins to 0.5 inch. That way, the letterhead extends across the page. I then changed the base font to Tms Rmn 18-point bold for the first line, Tms Rmn 14-point bold for the next four lines, and Tms Rmn 12-point italics for the *If It Meows* line.

I inserted four hard returns after the *If It Meows* line, because that's where the actual letter text will start. Then I used the advance up command to advance up about 0.75 inch. You'll have to experiment to get the right

---

*This section borrows heavily from an article by Lamont Wood, "Stepping Up to a Laser," in the April, 1986, issue of *Personal Computing* magazine, pp. 87–97.

Casa de Gato

A Boarding Hotel for Felines
11000 Venture Boulevard
Studio City, CA 91605
(818) 222-0000

R. Ramos, President
M. Ramos, Vice President
T. Ramos, Treasurer

"If It Meows, We Like It"

We Accept:
Visa, MasterCard,
American Express

<today's date>

Figure 35-4 A Sample Letterhead

advance. I switched to Tms Rmn 10-point for the officers' lines and used the ALT-F6 Flush Right command for the text at the right end of each line.

Finally, I returned the cursor to the end of the document, past those four hard returns, changed the left and right margins to 1 inch, and changed the base font to Courier 12-point (a fixed-width font) for the actual letter text. The phrase *<today's date>* shows this font.

You can retrieve this type of letterhead document as a boilerplate whenever you start a new letter or use it as part of a merge operation for form mailings or stock reply letters. Remember to save the entire letter document to a new file name so that you don't inadvertently overwrite the letterhead boilerplate.

✔If you wish, try to create a letterhead similar to this one. Save it as LHEAD.LAS.

WordPerfect Goes to 'Varsity!

This last example is the first page of a scholarly text. This document illustrates other techniques and provides more tips. You'll learn, for instance, how WordPerfect selects superscript fonts. The final printout is in Figure 35-5.

You don't have to type the example, but notice the numbers on the printout. They indicate points of interest that I'll cover in a moment. When I was setting up this document, I first inserted the following comment:

```
Soft fonts used:
  Tms Rmn 8-point  - Footnote references
  Tms Rmn 10-point - Indented quotes
```

Chapter 1

Descriptive Imagery and Metaphor

As a writer representative of his century, Charles Dickens filled his novels with a great deal of descriptive imagery. The author "sets the scene" not only to give the reader an idea of where the action is to take place, but also to present a feeling for the mood of the work. No example illustrates this more clearly than the opening pages of *Bleak House*.[1] The fog that is certainly part of many a London day becomes a metaphor for the obfuscating world of the law and of Chancery, the subjects of the novel:

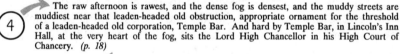

> Fog everywhere. Fog up the river, where it flows among green aits and meadows; fog down the river, where it rolls defiled among the tiers of shipping and the waterside pollutions of a great (and dirty) city. ... Fog in the eyes and throats of ancient Greenwich pensioners, wheezing by the firesides of their wards; fog in the stem and bowl of the afternoon pipe of the wrathful skipper, down in his close cabin; fog cruelly pinching the toes and fingers of his shivering little 'prentice boy on deck. ... *(p. 17)*

> The raw afternoon is rawest, and the dense fog is densest, and the muddy streets are muddiest near that leaden-headed old obstruction, appropriate ornament for the threshold of a leaden-headed old corporation, Temple Bar. And hard by Temple Bar, in Lincoln's Inn Hall, at the very heart of the fog, sits the Lord High Chancellor in his High Court of Chancery. *(p. 18)*

Dickens starts with a typical "mood" description of the London fog and slowly, but perceptibly, elaborates upon it until it becomes symbolic of the High Court of Chancery itself. Dickens, thus, starts with a general phenomenon and gradually gives it specific meaning. And in so doing he sets the stage for the entire novel, because *Bleak House* deals almost entirely with the "fog" of Chancery, how this fog "envelopes" the lives of many people and usually overcomes them.

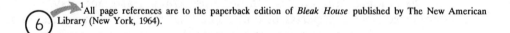

[1] All page references are to the paperback edition of *Bleak House* published by The New American Library (New York, 1964).

Figure 35-5   WordPerfect Goes to 'Varsity

```
Tms Rmn 12-point - Body text
Tms Rmn 14-point bold - Chapter heads
```

I changed the base font to Tms Rmn 14-point bold for the title, then changed the base font to Tms Rmn 12-point for the body text. I had to change the base font again to Tms Rmn 10-point for the indented quotes, because if I had used the small font WordPerfect would have printed the indented sections in Tms Rmn 8-point! I could, of course, have set up all the different formatting in styles (Chapter 26), but you get the idea.

Here's what the numbers mean:

1. I didn't have to insert a font change for the footnote reference. WordPerfect was "smart" enough to find the smallest font, Tms Rmn 8-point, and use it for the superscripted numbers. Keep in mind, though, that this font must be marked on the printer's font list.

2. To have WordPerfect set the correct leading for the single spaced indentations, I had to change line spacing to single here, rather than at the beginning of the indented section. It took me a long time to figure this one out!

3. I used the SHIFT-F4 ▶Indent◀ key for the indented sections, but I inserted the font change code in front of the first left and right indent code.

4. The default tab stops of every 0.5 inch made the tabs at the beginning of the indented paragraphs too wide. Instead of changing the tab stops, I used five *hard spaces* to begin each paragraph. Don't insert regular spaces, because WordPerfect then won't align the paragraphs correctly.

5. Here's where I changed the base font back to Tms Rmn 12-point.

6. I had to insert a base font change within the note itself to have the note print in Tms Rmn 10-point.

The point I'm trying to make in this example is that you have to be careful about the location of font change codes in relation to other formatting instructions. Only trial and error will help you in this regard, but I hope that my suggestions give you something to work with.

Downloading Soft Fonts Yourself

WordPerfect normally does all font downloading for you, but you should be aware of another way. Although you can download fonts individually, you'll soon find this a tedious—not to mention boring—process on a day-to-day basis if you use several fonts all the time. The easiest way to download font files yourself is to create a *setup file*. The setup file contains all the fonts you need. To create a setup file, you work with the PCLPak program that Hewlett-Packard supplies with soft fonts.

 Tip: Once you've created a setup file, you can delete the individual font files to make more directory space. The setup file contains a copy of each font file. You can have different setup files for different font requirements. WordPerfect will tell you that it can't find a font by its file name, but if the fonts are in the printer WordPerfect will still use them correctly. Use comments to remind you what fonts the document contains.

Using PCLPak

You first select soft fonts by file name, because each font is in a different file. Hewlett-Packard maintains a standard nomenclature that includes the abbreviated typestyle name, the point size, whether the font is regular, bold, or italic, and whether it's in portrait or landscape orientation. For example, the file TR120RPN.USP contains the Tms Rmn 12-point regular font for portrait orientation. Its landscape counterpart is TR120RPN.USL.

 Tip: *Before* you start PCLPak, jot down the file names you need so that you don't forget them.

Then load PCLPak at the DOS prompt. Type **pclpak** and press **RETURN**. Your next order of business—and the most important one—is to tell the program that the destination for fonts is to be a file. Normally, PCLPak sends soft fonts directly to the printer. You then go into the fonts menu and select each font by file name.

 Caution: You must set up all soft fonts as what Hewlett-Packard terms "permanent" fonts if you want to use them in more than one print job. WordPerfect won't clear the printer's memory of "permanent" fonts after each print job. Press **G** for "go" to send a copy of the font file to the destination file. The order in which you load the fonts in the setup file determines the order in which the printer receives them. Generally, try to load fonts in families, smallest to largest. That is, load all Tms Rmn fonts first before you load any Helv fonts.

Downloading the Setup File

You download a setup file from the DOS prompt. You can download different setup files at different times. See also Initializing the Printer.

 Tip: Before you download another setup file, turn the printer off and then on again to clear its memory of the last setup file. Version 4.2 users: There used to be a way to download fonts with a printer command that you insert into the document. This alternative seems to have disappeared in WordPerfect 5.0.

From the DOS prompt, you just copy the setup file to the printer. Do this *before* you print. If you're in WordPerfect, use the CTRL-F1 Shell key to go to DOS. Turn your printer on and make sure it's on-line. Then type copy <path/file name> lpt1:/b, and press **RETURN**. Substitute the correct path and file name for <path/file name> above.

This command copies the font setup file to the parallel printer port and, hence, to the printer itself. DOS likes to call the parallel printer port LPT1: (with a colon at the end). Substitute **com1:** (the first serial port) or **com2:** (the second serial port) for LPT1:, if necessary. The /B switch informs DOS that the file is in *binary* format. Normally the DOS COPY command stops copying a file when it sees a ^Z character (ASCII 26), but the /B switch overrides this default. That's all you have to know about binary, but do remember to use the /B switch!

To check whether the printer's memory could accommodate all the fonts in the setup file, run the printer's font test. If all the fonts print on the test, then they've loaded successfully. However, if the printer can't handle all the fonts in the file, it generally starts removing the first fonts that you loaded to accommodate a larger font. You may *think* you have five fonts available only to discover after you run the font test that you've only loaded one!

Initializing the Printer

The 7 [Initialize Printer] choice on the print menu sends all marked soft fonts to your printer before you begin a print job.

Caution: You *must* mark all soft fonts with an asterisk to tell WordPerfect that they are initially present in the printer. You can mark some soft fonts as initially present and others as "downloadable" with the plus sign. WordPerfect only downloads the fonts marked with an asterisk. Initialize Printer works correctly only if your printer has enough memory to load all the soft fonts that are marked as initially present in the printer definition.

Some Page Design Tips

Laser printers are either going to bring out the artist in us all or supply the psychiatrists and psychologists of this world with patients for years! It takes someone with a good "eye" to compose a page that is visually appealing to the reader. What was the old adage about silk purses and sows' ears? Still, there are some easy design do's and don'ts that can help you set up aesthetically pleasing laser generated printouts. I'll close this long and complicated chapter with them as an inspiration to you to continue where I'm leaving off.

- First and foremost, do *keep things simple.* Don't go overboard with a zillion fonts and sizes, graphics, and other doodahs. Simplicity doesn't mean superficiality.

- Do stick to one font family as much as possible. Rely on variations of the *same* family—such as different point sizes, boldface, or italics—instead of a different font family to vary the look of the page.

- Do use a lot of white space. That is, set up a good sized blank margin on all four sides of the page and adequate spacing between sections. Don't squeeze too many characters on a line. Maintain an adequate amount of leading—blank space—between printed lines. Too much type on the page is difficult to read!

- Don't go to extremes. It looks awful when a page has a wide range of point sizes. Stay within a limited range of font sizes, such as 12 to 18 points.

- Do show your printouts to others. Get a second opinion about how things look.

- Similarly, do take a look at what others have done. Open any book and try to determine what makes it visually appealing, or unappealing.

- Do consider printing in a large typesize and then photomechanically *reducing* the printout. This method produces an almost typeset quality look. It goes by the quaint name of *penny typesetting*.

- With the above considerations in mind, don't be afraid to experiment. Nothing ventured, nothing gained, you know.

And, oh yes, save scrap paper. You'll need it for the seemingly endless number of trial-and-error printings you'll have to do before you get that project "just right."

Dear Reader, the proof of the pudding is in the printout. With laser printers you'll have to spend considerably more time than usual to get the formatting correct, but once you do the results are great. Good luck!

36

A WordPerfect
Grab Bag

In this chapter you'll discover new uses of these commands . . .

CTRL-F2 Spell	Select a different main or supplemental dictionary
CTRL-F5 Text In/Out	Retrieve and save WordPerfect documents in DOS, generic word processing, or WordPerfect 4.2 formats
SHIFT-F8 Format	Select a different foreign language

. . . you'll look at some WordPerfect utility programs . . .

CONVERT	Convert documents to and from WordPerfect format
CURSOR	Change the size and shape of the cursor
FC	Convert WordPerfect 4.2 font files to WordPerfect 5.0 printer resource files
HYPHEN	Create or edit the hyphenation exception dictionary
PTR	Create, change, or delete printer resource files
SPELL	Create or edit dictionaries

. . . and you'll learn a new code:

[Lang]	Foreign language dictionary change

As incredible as it may seem, you *still* haven't covered all the many features of WordPerfect. My editor has finally given me an ultimatum to make this the last chapter. (I snuck in a few appendixes, too.) So, here you are: a mixed bag of topics like converting files, restoring deleted files, and using the WordPerfect utility programs. Dear Reader, once again—and for the last time—you have a long chapter on your hands. Just study the features you need as you need them!

> ## DO WARM-UP

Converting Documents

WordPerfect stores documents in its own format, which includes your text and the special codes the program needs to determine the formatting requirements of each document. You can convert document that you created in certain "foreign" programs (DOS, other word processors, data bases, or spreadsheets, for instance) to and from WordPerfect's format. Although WordPerfect 5.0 automatically converts WordPerfect 4.2 documents, you can also convert a 5.0 document back to 4.2 format.

Several conversions are on the CTRL-F5 Text In/Out key. The others require that you use the separate conversion utility, Convert. It's in the file CONVERT.EXE.

No matter what conversion you make, be prepared to *massage* both the input *and* the resulting output file. No two programs are alike, and although WordPerfect does a commendable job at converting text and many formatting codes (such as underlining), you'll still have to clean up the document when you work with it in the other program or in WordPerfect. And as one example below illustrates, you have to be very careful with certain formats (such as secondary merge documents) to get the results you want. Still, think of all the typing work you're avoiding!

Converting DOS (ASCII) Text Files

From within WordPerfect you can save and retrieve a document in "straight ASCII" format, without any codes, if need be. WordPerfect refers to this as a *DOS text file*. Use a DOS text file when you're writing programs for languages such a Pascal or C, or when you want to convert the file to a form that you can transfer over the telephone lines to someone who *doesn't* have Word-Perfect.

DOS text files have a hard return at the end of each line. These hard return codes translate into two printer instructions: a line feed to advance the paper up a line and a true carriage return to return the print head to the beginning of the line.

To *save* a file as a DOS text file, retrieve the file you want. Then press **CTRL-F5 Text In/Out** and type **1** or **t** [DOS Text]. WordPerfect prompts:

```
1 Save; 2 Retrieve (CR/LF to [HRt]); 3 Retrieve (CR/LF to [SRt] in HZone): 0
```

Type **1** or **s** [Save], then supply a new file name. To retrieve this type of file into WordPerfect and retain the hard returns at the ends of lines, use the **2** or **r** [Retrieve (CR/LF to [HRt])] choice. This is the choice you need when you want to create or change the AUTOEXEC.BAT file (discussed later) or the CONFIG.SYS file (see the Prelude).

There's an easy way to convert a DOS text file to WordPerfect document format with soft returns at the ends of lines and hard returns to signify the ends of paragraphs or blank lines. To convert a DOS text file to WordPerfect format, first make sure that the file is *single spaced* and has *at least two* hard returns between paragraphs. Then use the **3** [Retrieve (CR/LF to [SRt])] choice.

Type the file name and press **RETURN**. WordPerfect changes the hard returns within the hyphenation zone to its soft return codes, [SRt], but retains the hard returns at the ends of paragraphs. It also retains two or more hard returns, say, at the ends of paragraphs.

Caution: *Don't* use the **5** [Text In] choice from the F5 List Files command to convert a DOS text file, because WordPerfect retrieves the document with hard returns at the ends of lines.

There's another way to go. Retrieve the document as a DOS text file with CTRL-F5 Text In/Out. Then follow these steps:

1. At the beginning of the document, issue the Replace command to search for *two* hard return codes (press **RETURN** twice) and replace them with an unused character, such as |. Use the no confirm option for steps 2, 3, and 4 so that WordPerfect doesn't stop. Don't worry if the document looks like a mess at this point!

2. Start a backward replace. Replace all single hard returns (the hard returns at the end of each line) with a space.

3. Search for the unusual character you used in step 1 and replace all occurrences with two hard returns by pressing **RETURN** twice, thus reinstating hard returns between the paragraphs.

4. Go to the beginning of the document, thus having WordPerfect rewrite the screen as you go. Make any other formatting changes, then save the document.

Version 4.2 and the Generic Word Processing Format

The CTRL-F5 Text In/Out command includes an option, **4** or **w** [Save WP 4.2], to save a version 5.0 document in version 4.2 format. Option **3** or **g** [Save Generic] saves a WordPerfect document in a *generic* word processing format. WordPerfect converts paragraphs as one long text string that end in a hard return and substitutes eight spaces for tabs or indents. After you convert the document with WordPerfect and then call it up in the other word processing program, you align the paragraphs and massage the file as necessary.

The Convert Utility

To convert other document formats to and from WordPerfect, you'll have to work with the separate Convert utility. That is, you'd exit WordPerfect and insert the disk that contains CONVERT.EXE into the A drive (floppy disk users only). Hard disk users should find CONVERT.EXE in their WordPerfect directory. To start Convert:

Type   **a:convert** (for floppy disks)

or

Type   **convert** (for a hard disk)

Press   **RETURN**

WordPerfect asks for the input file name and then the output file name. For the latter, if you supply an existing file name or the same name as the input file, WordPerfect unceremoniously drops you back to DOS. Type each file name and press **RETURN**.

Tip: You can supply a file name *template*, such as *.TXT to convert all files with the extension .TXT. You'd then enter a corresponding template for the converted files, such as *.NEW.

A list of format conversion types appears. The sections below discuss all the choices on Convert's menu and some other important considerations. To cancel a conversion, press **CTRL-C** or **CTRL-BREAK** (the BREAK key is the SCROLL LOCK key).

Converting Other Word Processing Formats

To convert a WordPerfect document, type **1** [WordPerfect to another format]. The conversion program asks for the output format. If you select any type format except **1**, the conversion utility requests the "foreign" format and then converts the file to either WordPerfect document or secondary merge document format, as discussed in the next few sections.

The choices labeled WordStar and MultiMate convert documents from these popular word processing programs to WordPerfect. If you're using a word processing program that's not on the list, perhaps that program can convert files to *revisable form text (DCA)*, a standard adopted by IBM, or to WordStar or MultiMate format. Then you can convert to WordPerfect. For instance, Microsoft Word has a DCA conversion utility, so it's possible to convert Word documents to WordPerfect format even though there's no direct conversion choice from Word to WordPerfect.

If one of the above formats isn't what you're converting, you might be able to have the program convert to a "straight ASCII" file, or use the *generic word processing* format, as discussed previously.

Tip: If you need just part of a foreign document, use the other program to save that section to a new file before you convert it to WordPerfect format.

Converting DIF Format

Spreadsheet programs, like Lotus 1-2-3, store information in rows and columns. The choices labeled Navy DIF Standard and Spreadsheet DIF are confusing. They actually refer to *data base* information, where fields are columns and records are rows. The first choice converts a Navy DIF document into or from a standard WordPerfect document. The second choice converts a DIF document into a WordPerfect secondary merge document. For information about the Navy DIF or regular DIF format, see your spreadsheet program's documentation.

Some data base or spreadsheet programs don't save files in DIF format directly, but they may have their own utilities to convert files to DIF. You might have to do two conversions, one in the data base or spreadsheet program to convert to DIF and one for WordPerfect format, before you can use a file in WordPerfect. For instance, Figure 36-1 is part of a data base in a Lotus 1-2-3 spreadsheet. Note that the first row contains field names.

The Lotus Transfer utility can change this file to DIF format, but it will also include the field names from row one. (You can't convert a range that's been extracted to another file.) After you use the Transfer step, you can convert to WordPerfect secondary merge format with the Spreadsheet DIF choice. Then return to WordPerfect, retrieve the document, and delete the *first* record (the top row), which just contains the field names. That's one form of massaging.

Converting Lotus 1-2-3 Spreadsheets

Many spreadsheet programs, including Lotus 1-2-3, can "print" to an ASCII text file (Lotus 1-2-3 calls it an unformatted file). This might be your best bet, because WordPerfect can read those files directly. For example, say you have a Lotus 1-2-3 spreadsheet that contains contribution figures, part of which appears in Figure 36-2. You want to copy the contributions for the two companies into a report you've created in WordPerfect. It's best to set up the figures as a *range* and "print" this range to a DOS file. In Lotus 1-2-3, for instance, you include instructions from the Options Other Unformatted submenu of the Print menu. Here's how.

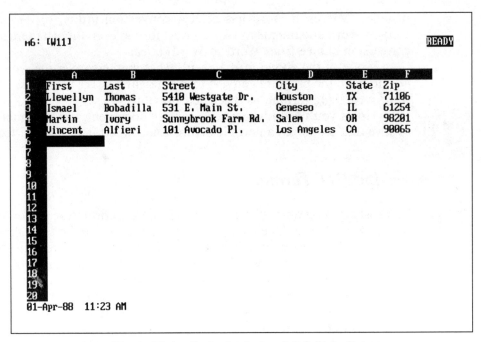

Figure 36-1   Part of a Lotus 1-2-3 Data Base

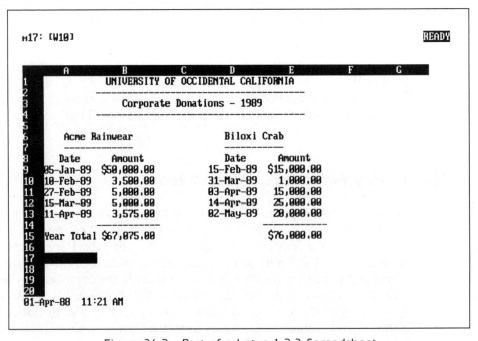

Figure 36-2   Part of a Lotus 1-2-3 Spreadsheet

In Lotus 1-2-3 you press / to enter a command, then press **P** (Print) to print. Press **F** (File), supply a file name, and press **RETURN**. Then indicate the range. Finally, press **O** (Options) **O** (Other) **U** (Unformatted) to tell Lotus that this is an unformatted disk file. Press **Q** (Quit) to leave this submenu and then **G** (Go) to print to disk. When you're finished, press **Q** (Quit) to leave the Print menu.

Lotus 1-2-3 gives the unformatted file the extension .PRN. The file, when you retrieve it as a DOS text file with CTRL-F5 Text In/Out from within WordPerfect, looks like this:

```
             UNIVERSITY OF OCCIDENTAL CALIFORNIA
             ----------------------------------------

                 Corporate Donations - 1989
             ----------------------------------------


        Acme Rainwear                   Biloxi Crab
        -------------                   -----------

        Date      Amount                Date      Amount
        05-Jan-89 $50,000.00            15-Feb-89 $15,000.00
        10-Feb-89  3,500.00             31-Mar-89  1,000.00
        27-Feb-89  5,000.00             03-Apr-89 15,000.00
        15-Mar-89  5,000.00             14-Apr-89 25,000.00
        11-Apr-89  3,575.00             02-May-89 20,000.00
                  -----------                     -----------

        Year Total $67,075.00                     $76,000.00
```

These are not real WordPerfect math columns with tab aligns. Only spaces separate the entries.

Converting WordPerfect Files for Telephone Transfer

The choice labeled Seven-bit transfer format is *only* useful if you want to set up WordPerfect documents for transfer over the telephone lines. You'll still need a modem and communications software to effect the actual transfer. The recipient would then use the same choice in the Convert program to put the document back into real WordPerfect format.

There's a way to avoid this double conversion routine entirely. If your communication software can send all eight bits of every byte, then you can transfer WordPerfect files without conversion. I don't want to go into "computerese" here, but trust my brief explanation. Most communications software by default transfer only seven bits in a byte and "drop" the eighth bit. You'll probably have to change just one *protocol* setting to get your program to send all eight bits correctly.

Converting from Mail Merge to WordPerfect

The choice called Mail Merge is also known as a *delimited* format in the computer world. Mail merge programs in some other word processors, such as those in WordStar and Microsoft Word, use delimiters between fields and records that are different from WordPerfect's ^R and ^E codes. Usually, but not always, fields end with commas, and records end with hard returns. Use this choice to convert a delimited "foreign" document to WordPerfect's secondary merge document format.

This choice is tricky, because you have to have the input file structure exactly the way WordPerfect expects it, and yet some things might still get in your way. For example, take a look at the following short document (you don't have to type it):

```
Llewellyn Thomas, 5410 Westgate Dr., Houston, TX, 77106
Ismael Bobadilla, 531 E. Main, Geneseo, IL, 61254
Martin Ivory, "Sunnybrook Farm Road, RR4", Salem, OR, 98201
Vincent Alfieri, 101 Avocado Place, Los Angeles, CA, 90065
```

Each field ends with a comma, and each record ends with a carriage return/line feed combination. The original merge program had no problem with the spaces after the comma delimiters (it would just ignore them), but Convert won't like them at all. What's more, the third record contains a comma *within* a field, so the field is enclosed in quotation marks to indicate to the original program not to consider that comma as a delimiter. (The quotation marks don't print.) Convert will have problems with the quotation marks, too.

After you start the conversion and select Mail Merge, Convert presents this message:

```
Enter Field delimiter characters or decimal ASCII values enclosed in {}
```

Technically, the delimiter is just a comma, but the utility won't convert this file correctly if you don't also tell it that there is a *space* following each comma. (Heaven help you if some commas are followed by spaces and others aren't!) Because you can't type a space in response to the prompt, you must provide the *ASCII codes* for the comma and the space, each code enclosed in curly braces. It turns out that the ASCII code for a comma is 44, and for a space, 32, so:

Type {44}{32}

Press **RETURN**

Now Convert wants to know the record terminator:

```
Enter Record delimiter characters or decimal ASCII values enclosed in ⁅
```

The hard return is actually a carriage return and line feed. To enter a carriage return/line feed combination, you would type their ASCII codes:

Type   {13}{10}

Press   **RETURN**

Convert now wants to know if there are any characters to be filtered out:

```
Enter Characters to be stripped from file or press Enter if none
```

Yes, there are: The quotation marks that tell the original program to disregard the embedded comma in the field. So:

Type   "

Press   **RETURN**

You can supply the actual character as long as you don't have to enter spaces or RETURN.

 Tip: If you really know what you're doing, you can bypass the prompts and enter all the information on the DOS command line. That is, you can start the Convert program, give it the two file names and all other information from the DOS prompt. For example, you want to convert the file OLD.TXT to NEW.WP using the same parameters as above. You would type at the DOS prompt (here, C>):

```
C> convert old.txt new.wp 7 , {13}{10} "
```

(notice the spaces between parameters), and then you would press **RETURN**. This sets up the files, chooses choice Mail Merge from the Convert menu, tells Convert that that comma is the delimiter, then informs Convert that the carriage return/line feed are the record delimiters and that Convert must strip out the quotation marks.

The conversion takes place. Now, if you entered WordPerfect and retrieved the file, here's what you'd see:

```
Llewellyn Thomas^R
5410 Westgate Dr.^R
Houston^R
TX^R
```

```
77106^E
Ismael Bobadilla^R
531 E. Main^R
Geneseo^R
IL^R
61254^E
Martin Ivory^R
Sunnybrook Farm Road^R
RR4^R
Salem^R
OR^R
98201^E
Vincent Alfieri^R
101 Avocado Place^R
Los Angeles^R
CA^R
90065^E
```

Everything seems okay, but is it? Take a look at the *third* record. The conversion utility dutifully removed the quotation marks, but because there was a comma within the field, the utility "thought" that this was a field. So, the third record contains one *extra* field, which you must correct by removing the superfluous ^R code and combining two lines, so that the entire record then has the same number of fields as the others. It would look like this when you're done:

```
Martin Ivory^R
Sunnybrook Farm Road, RR4^R
Salem^R
OR^R
98201^E
```

Whew! I think you understand that there are pitfalls associated with file conversions. Your biggest consolation is that probably most of the records will be okay, and if you convert a large file you'll save a lot of retyping. But always go over the converted file with a fine-tooth comb to make sure everything is exactly right.

Converting from dBASE to WordPerfect

If you're converting information in a data base file that you want to use as a WordPerfect secondary merge document, you'll first have to instruct the data base program to convert the file to a delimited format and *then* convert to WordPerfect's secondary merge format. A popular example concerns files that you've created in *any* of the dBASE products such as dBASE III PLUS (the procedure is the same for all dBASE programs, although I'm not sure about dBASE IV yet). That is, you first *copy* the information you need to what dBASE calls a "system data file." That's just a fancy term for an ASCII text file. Supply the correct *scope* to tell dBASE which fields and records you want to copy. You must use the DELIMITED option with the dBASE COPY command so that the program sets up a file with each field separated from the next by commas and enclosed in quotation marks.

For example, you want to copy out records for all teenage boys in Hollywood who have purple hair (half the current population of that city) to a file called HAIR. Open the data file in dBASE with the USE command. Then type the following command at the infamous "dot prompt." I've had it typeset on two lines, but you'd have to enter it all on one line:

```
.  COPY TO HAIR FOR CITY = "Hollywood" .AND. SEX = "M" .AND.
   (AGE > 12 .AND. AGE < 20) .AND. HAIR_COLOR = "Purple" DELIMITED
```

dBASE copies the information that fits the various conditions to a file called HAIR.TXT. dBASE always appends the file extension .TXT to system data files. Then you could convert the file to a WordPerfect secondary merge document, as outlined in the previous section.

To go in the opposite direction—from WordPerfect secondary merge format to dBASE—first convert the secondary merge document to delimited format. Then go into dBASE, open the file to which you want to copy the WordPerfect information, and use the APPEND command, again with the DELIMITED option.

You can also create a text file from a dBASE III PLUS report and then use CTRL-F5 Text In/Out to read the file into a WordPerfect document. This is *not* a delimited file, but merely a text file equivalent of a printed dBASE report, with columns and rows of information.

For example, suppose you've created a dBASE report form called NAMES and you want to save the report to an ASCII text file called NTEXT. After you open the data file and index file that the report uses, type **REPORT FORM NAMES TO FILE NTEXT**. dBASE appends the extension .TXT to the new NTEXT file, too. Include the report generator's PLAIN and NOEJECT options to make as "vanilla" a report as possible, if you wish. You'll note that dBASE still inserts form feeds between pages in the new text file. You can delete these form feeds later in WordPerfect.

Changing the Cursor

Use the separate program, CURSOR.COM, to change the size and shape of the cursor for the current work session. Do this before you load WordPerfect: Type **cursor** at the DOS prompt and press **RETURN**. Use the ARROW keys to select the cursor you want, then note the grid letters. Press **RETURN** to change the cursor. The new cursor stays in effect until you turn off or reboot your computer.

Tip: You can change the cursor from the DOS prompt and even put this change in your AUTOEXEC.BAT file (see the next section). Just type the first and second letters after a / on the command line. For example, to change the cursor to a large block, type `cursor/bf` and press **RETURN**.

The AUTOEXEC.BAT Batch File

A DOS *batch file* is a special file that contains a batch of commands that you want DOS to type for you in a certain order. The advantage to batch files is that you don't have to type the commands yourself every time you want to issue them. You set up a batch file once. Then whenever you want to run the commands in the batch file, type the file name and press **RETURN**. They represent your own personal DOS amanuensis!

Batch files are "straight ASCII" text files, and they must have the extension .BAT. In WordPerfect you save batch files as DOS text files with the CTRL-F5 Text In/Out command. Retrieve them with the **2** [Retrieve (CR/LF to [HRt])] choice.

The most important batch file is the *automatic executing file*. DOS always looks for this file when you turn on or reboot your computer. Its name *must* be AUTOEXEC.BAT, and it must be in the *root* directory. If the file exists, DOS executes the commands therein, thus saving you many keystrokes for those setup operations that you perform daily. A typical AUTOEXEC.BAT file might look like this:

```
ECHO=OFF
CLS
PATH=C:\;C:\WP50;C:\LIBRARY;C:\LOTUS
DATE
TIME
VERIFY ON
MODE LPT1:=COM1:
MODE COM1:=9600,n,8,1,P
SET WP=/R/M-START
CD \WP50
CURSOR/BF
WP
```

The first command turns off the echoing on the screen of each command as DOS executes the batch file. CLS just clears the screen.

A very useful DOS command is the next one, PATH. This command sets up the *file search path* so that if DOS can't find a command file in the current directory, it looks at the directories you've listed in the PATH statement. It continues to look in each directory in turn until it finds the command. Notice that semicolons separate the directory names. For example, if the current directory is \LOTUS and you type **wp**, DOS will look for the WordPerfect files in the other directories you've listed. Because the \WP50 is in the PATH statement, DOS can still load WordPerfect from the \LOTUS directory.

The next two commands request the date and time. The VERIFY ON command turns on the verification of all copying. Two MODE lines then redirect the printed output to a serial laser printer (COM1). The SET WP= /R/M-START line tells WordPerfect that you have expanded memory and that you want to run the macro called START.WPM. Use the SET command as here instead of individual switches if you wish.

The batch file then changes to the WP50 directory (CD \WP50), changes the cursor to a large block, and, finally, loads WordPerfect.

Note: Substitute the SHELL command for WP on the last line if you're using the WordPerfect Library.

Restoring Deleted Files

Even the most careful person will do this. I know, because I've done it scores of times: I've erased a file accidentally. Could DOS or WordPerfect bail me out of this predicament? Unfortunately, no. So I purchased what is known as a *utility package* for DOS. Most of these utility packages (some are even available free from public bulletin boards) contain an "unerase" program. They also can check a disk for bad sections and thus avoid the possibility of "trashing" files, among other things.

How can you unerase a deleted file once it's deleted? That sounds like magic, but it isn't. When you delete a file, you haven't deleted it at all. You've merely erased the file's *name* from the master directory of the disk. DOS won't touch the *contents* of the file until or unless it needs more disk space. So the file is there for a while. When you unerase a file, you put its name back in the directory, and then DOS can open the file again.

The trick to working with an unerase program is to restore an accidentally erased file *as soon as you can* after your boo-boo. If DOS needs the file's space, it will then truly erase the file (say, if you saved a large file on the diskette). But if you unerase a file directly after you erased it, you can generally get it back.

The FC and PTR Utilities

I'll mention *en passant*, as it were, that there are two printer utilities, FC and PTR. The former converts WordPerfect 4.2 font files to 5.0 printer resource files, while the latter adds, edits, renames, or copies printer resource files. This program was called Printer in WordPerfect 4.2. There may be files called FC.DOC and PTR.DOC that contain late breaking information about these programs.

To run either program, go to DOS, insert the disk that contains the utility program (floppy users only), type the file name—**fc** or **ptr**—and press **RETURN**.

Caution: Using the PTR program is a very advanced topic that's beyond the scope of this book. Unless you consider yourself a printer *guru* or seek adventure, don't change any printer files!

The Speller Utility

WordPerfect's spelling dictionary, WP{WP}US.LEX, contains a great many common English words "used everyday," as Groucho Marx and George Feniman used to say on *You Bet Your Life*. The dictionary also includes many proper nouns, such as some popular names and the names of cities and states, as well as some medical and legal words. Still, no dictionary could possibly contain all the words that you might use regularly.

You can customize the main dictionary to add your own words so that WordPerfect doesn't stop at these words every time you use the speller. Or you can set up separate, specialized dictionaries for specific subjects. To do this, you work with the Speller utility program. It's in a file called SPELL.EXE.

✔ Make sure you're at the DOS prompt, not within WordPerfect, before you attempt the following examples. Floppy disk users: Insert the Speller diskette in the A drive and any disk that contains supplementary files in the B drive, which should currently be the active drive. Then, with the DOS prompt on the screen:

Type   **a:spell** (for floppy disks)

or

Type   **spell** (for a hard disk)

Press   **RETURN**

The Speller utility's main menu appears. At the top right corner is the name of the main dictionary file, WP{WP}US.LEX. I'll take care of choices 9 and A right now: Choice 9 lets you convert your customized supplemental dictionaries from WordPerfect 4.2 to 5.0 format. Choice A combines all dictionaries that you've converted with choice 9 into a composite 5.0 dictionary.

Some Preliminaries: Locating Words in the Dictionary

Before you actually add words to the main dictionary or create a new dictionary, you should take a look at choices 5 through 8.

Type   **5** [Display common word list]

The common word list contains hundreds of the most frequently used words. When it checks a document, WordPerfect's speller first tries to find each word in the common word list before it tries the main dictionary. Press any cursor key, such as DOWN ARROW or PG DN, to view each screenful of common words. Press UP ARROW or PG UP to go back. Figure 36-3 shows the first screen of the list. When you're finished:

Press   **F1 Cancel**

to return to the main menu.

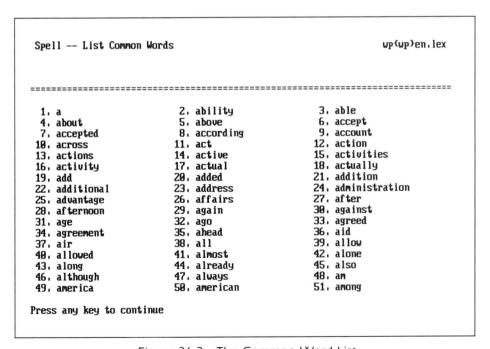

```
Spell -- List Common Words                              wp{wp}en.lex


==============================================================================

     1. a                 2. ability          3. able
     4. about             5. above            6. accept
     7. accepted          8. according        9. account
    10. across           11. act             12. action
    13. actions          14. active          15. activities
    16. activity         17. actual          18. actually
    19. add              20. added           21. addition
    22. additional       23. address         24. administration
    25. advantage        26. affairs         27. after
    28. afternoon        29. again           30. against
    31. age              32. ago             33. agreed
    34. agreement        35. ahead           36. aid
    37. air              38. all             39. allow
    40. allowed          41. almost          42. alone
    43. along            44. already         45. also
    46. although         47. always          48. am
    49. america          50. american        51. among

    Press any key to continue
```

Figure 36-3   The Common Word List

Because WordPerfect checks the common word list first, you may want to add your new words to this list. You can also add them to the main dictionary. In either case, you can ascertain the location of a word:

Type   **6** [Check location of a word]

WordPerfect asks for the word to check.

Type   [any word]

Press   **RETURN**

WordPerfect looks through the common word list and then the main dictionary to advise you where the word is located, if at all.
Note: WordPerfect does not look in the supplemental dictionary file.

Press   **F1 Cancel**

to return to the main menu.
Another way to view dictionary entries is to ask WordPerfect to display words that match a pattern.

Type   **7** [Look up]

WordPerfect asks for the word pattern. You can use the standard DOS **?** and ***** wildcards, as in the main spelling program. Here are two examples:

Type   **t?p**

Press   **RETURN**

WordPerfect shows all words in the dictionary that begin with *t* and end with *p*, no matter what the middle letter is.

Type   **top***

Press   **RETURN**

This time, WordPerfect shows many words that begin with the letters *top*. Press any key to see more. When you're finished:

Press   **F1 Cancel**

to return to the main menu.
Finally, you can look up words phonetically:

Type   **8** [Phonetic look up]

Type a phonetic representation of the word, such as:

Type   **tho**

Press   **RETURN**

WordPerfect shows words that sound like *tho*, and even some that don't (!). Figure 36-4 shows the process.

Press   **F1 Cancel**

to return to the main menu.

Adding Words to the Dictionary

When you add new words to your dictionary during a spelling check, WordPerfect adds the words to a supplemental dictionary file with the name WP{WP}US.SUP. Because the size of this file is limited, you may eventually get a message Dictionary full when you add too many words during a spelling check.

To avoid this problem, use the Speller utility to add your important words directly to the main dictionary or to the common word list. This procedure then frees the space that these words would take up in the supplemental dictionary.

```
 Spell -- Match Phonetic Pattern                               wp{wp}en.lex
 Word:

 ===========================================================================

      1. thai              2. thaw              3. the
      4. thee              5. they              6. thigh
      7. tho               8. thou              9. though
     10. thy
```

Figure 36-4   Sounding Out a Word

Sometimes you won't want all these skipped words in the dictionary, so it's a good idea to open this file and delete any unnecessary words before you add the remaining words to the dictionary from the file. Just retrieve the file in WordPerfect as any other and delete the words you don't want. Each word is on a separate line that ends in a hard return. You can also add words directly from the keyboard, or from another file.

Note: No matter how you choose to add words to the dictionary, WordPerfect has to update the entire dictionary, a procedure that takes a while. Here are some tips.

If you just need to add a few words, use the **6** [Check location of a word] choice *first* to ascertain whether the word isn't already in the dictionary. WordPerfect checks for duplicates anyway, but no use wasting time adding a word that's already there! For instance, it turned out that the dictionary contains my first name, but not the name I go by (*Vince*). Nor did it include my last name or some of my pets' names. So I added them to the dictionary like this (you should follow the same pattern):

Type   **2** [Add words to dictionary]

You can add new words to the common word list or the main dictionary.

Type   **1** [Add to common word list (from keyboard)]

WordPerfect prompts you to enter the word or words. You can separate words by spaces, and you don't have to use uppercase. Type your name and any other words that you want to add instead of the examples I've chosen, but make sure you spell them correctly!

Type   `vince alfieri hedda augie`

The last two entries are the sobriquets of my pets, except for Macho and Tux whose names are already in the dictionary!

Tip: Should you so desire, and if you consider yourself stylistically akin to Earnest Hemingway or James Jones, now would be an opportune time to add those "colorful" words that aren't in *any* dictionary!

Press   **RETURN**

You can continue to add more words from the keyboard or from a file. However, if you press F1 Cancel or type **0** [Cancel – do not add words], you return to the main menu. You must use the **5** [Exit] choice to update the dictionary, but when you do, it'll take WordPerfect a while to finish the operation.

Type   **5** [Exit]

WordPerfect tells you that it's updating the dictionary and asks you to wait. It first sorts the new words alphabetically and then updates the listings for each letter of the alphabet. Go have a cup of coffee!

Caution: Don't try to cancel this operation once it's started. You could damage the dictionary file.

Using a Word List Document

You may find it more helpful to create a *word list document* that contains all the words that you want to add to the dictionary. This will take a bit of time and planning on your part, but it pays off in the long run because you only do it once. What's more, if you plan to add or delete words later, you merely have to go into this word list document to see at a glance the words you've already added.

To add words from the supplemental dictionary or from another word list document file that you've created, for heaven's sake first make sure that each word is *correctly spelled!* Retrieve the document in WordPerfect and check to make sure that each word, including the last, is on a separate line that ends with a hard return. Then save the document, go into the Speller utility, type **2** [Add words to dictionary], and then use the **2** [Add to common word list (from a file)] or **4** [Add to main word list (from a file)] choices. WordPerfect requests the file name. Remember to type **5** [Exit] to finish the operation.

Deleting Words from the Dictionary

You can reverse the procedure and delete words either from the keyboard or from a word list document. Use the **3** [Delete words from dictionary] choice, and then type the correct choices, as for adding words. Supply the words from the keyboard or type the file name. Type **5** [Exit] to update the dictionary and give yourself another coffee break.

Creating a Dictionary

If you want to set up a separate dictionary with specialized words, the first step is to determine what words you need. Again, it might be best to keep the words in a special word list file. Suppose that you've set up a number of culinary terms and Los Angeles restaurant names in a file and you want to create a new dictionary and use it periodically when you're editing documents that pertain to food or L.A. eateries.

First, create the word list file and check that all words are spelled correctly. Then start the Speller utility and type **1** [Change/Create dictionary]. If you're working on a floppy disk system, exchange diskettes if necessary. Now, type the dictionary file name. If the file already exists, WordPerfect uses that dictionary for any further Speller operations. Here, suppose you're creating a new dictionary. It's best to give the dictionary file a name that identifies it as a dictionary. In this example, FOOD.DIC is the file name, so type **food.dic** and press **RETURN**. WordPerfect asks you to confirm that you want to create a new dictionary, so type **y**.

Now, you can add the words from the keyboard or from the word list file, delete words, or just check whether the dictionary contains certain words. However, when you're finished working with the new dictionary file, you must do one more thing: type **4** [Optimize dictionary]. This means that WordPerfect sets up the dictionary so that it will work as quickly as possible when you use it in a spelling check. It also arranges the words phonetically so that they appear on the list of alternates during spelling. After you start a spelling check with CTRL-F2 Spell, you would type **4** or **n** [New Sup. Dictionary] and supply the new dictionary name whenever you wanted to use this dictionary.

After you've added words to the main dictionary from the supplemental dictionary, make sure you delete the supplemental dictionary file so that the next time you use the speller WordPerfect starts with a clean slate. Also, make a copy of the new dictionary file, WP{WP}US.LEX, so that you don't have to go through this rigmarole again!

Choosing a Different Language Dictionary

WordPerfect Corporation provides dictionaries in many foreign languages, including British English (foreign enough to Americans!). You can tell WordPerfect that a document uses a different language. Here are the steps (I'm assuming that you want to keep the standard dictionary as the default):

1. Press **SHIFT-F8 Format**, then type **4** or **o** [Other].

2. Type **4** or **l** [Language], type the language abbreviation—an example would be FR for French—and press **RETURN**. To return to the normal American English dictionary, use the code EN. A list of language codes is in the WordPerfect documentation.

3. Press **F7 Exit** to return to the document.

WordPerfect inserts a [Lang] code that shows the language change. WordPerfect will now use the new language dictionary. WordPerfect also sets a different standard form (Chapter 13) for the country represented by the language. If the language has a different sort order, WordPerfect uses the new sort order for all sorting operations (Chapter 33).

 Tip: Because there's a code associated with a language change, it's best to insert this code at the beginning of the document so that it governs the entire document. You can also insert language codes around sections of a document that are in a different language. Then when you run a spelling check, WordPerfect will use the correct foreign language dictionary—provided you've purchased it from WordPerfect Corporation!

The Hyphenation Utility

During auto hyphenation, WordPerfect hyphenates words based on a set of hyphenation rules (algorithms) and a hyphenation dictionary. The hyphenation utility, a separate product available from WordPerfect Corporation, can create and maintain an *exception dictionary* of syllable breaks. You don't have to use the hyphenation utility at all if you're already satisfied with the way WordPerfect's automatic hyphenation works (Chapter 20).

The hyphenation rules are in the file WP{WP}US.HYC; the dictionary, in WP{WP}US.HYL. The hyphenation utility creates an exception dictionary file called WP{WP}US.HYD, but you can set up several different exception files. The exception files will contain the words for which WordPerfect can't figure out syllable breaks, or a list of preferred hyphenation spots. WordPerfect will honor your choice if the syllable break falls within the hyphenation zone. You can even designate priority levels for different syllable breaks!

Note: WordPerfect looks for the hyphenation files in a dictionary that you specify with the SHIFT-F1 Setup command (Appendix A). When hyphenation is on in a document WordPerfect first checks for the presence of an exception dictionary and uses it. If WordPerfect can't find an exception dictionary, it uses the hyphenation algorithms.

The easiest way to add or delete hyphenation exceptions is from a word list file, which is just a WordPerfect document that you create before you run the hyphen utility. (You saw a similar procedure for adding or deleting words from the supplemental spelling dictionary.) Type each word in lowercase on a separate line and end each line with a hard return. Include syllable breaks according to these guidelines:

- To designate one preferred syllable break, type a regular hyphen at the syllable break. For example: *pica-dillo.* WordPerfect won't hyphenate the word at any other syllable break.

- To designate several syllable breaks, mark the syllable break with the priority levels 3, 2, or 1. The highest priority is the hyphen itself, the same as level 3; the second highest is level 2; the lowest priority is level 1. For example, *mach1i2na-tion* tells WordPerfect that you'd prefer the break before the t. If that's not possible, the second choice is before the n, while the least favored spot is before the i. You could also have typed the word like this: *mach1i2na3tion.*

- To designate several breaks at equal levels, use the correct level for each. For example, the word *trans-porta-tion* contains two level-3 breaks. If both syllable breaks occur in the hyphenation zone, WordPerfect chooses the one that's closest to the right margin.

■ If you don't want WordPerfect to hyphenate the word at all, type the word with *no* marked syllable breaks. For example, to tell Word-Perfect not to hyphenate the proper noun Beethoven, just type that word as *beethoven*.

If you're deleting hyphenation exceptions with a word list file, just type each word as normal into the file, one word per line. You don't have to supply the syllable breaks. In either case, save the file correctly!

To start hyphenation utility, HYPHEN.EXE, exit WordPerfect and select the correct directory if the hyphenation files aren't in the WordPerfect program directory. Then type **hyphen** at the DOS prompt and press **RETURN**. If this is your first session with the utility (and there's no exception dictionary yet), or if the program can't find the exception dictionary, you'll see this message:

```
Exception dictionary wp{wp}us.hyd not found.
Create a new dictionary named wp{wp}us.hyd (Y/N)? No
```

Type y to create the exception dictionary. The hyphenation utility's main menu appears. Use choice **0** [Exit] to return to DOS. Here is a brief rundown of the other choices.

Select choice **2** [Add words to exception dictionary] or choice **3** [Delete words from exception dictionary]. Then enter the words from the keyboard—separate each word with a space—or use a word list file. If you're adding words, include the correct syllable break levels. When you're finished adding or deleting words, use choice **4** [Update exception dictionary] to save your changes. Then use menu choice **4** [Optimize exception dictionary] to reduce the size of the dictionary.

Choice **5** [Hyphenate words] shows where WordPerfect will hyphenate individual words or many words in a word list file. You can then decide whether to set up hyphenation exceptions. A nifty use for this choice is to hyphenate all words in a word list file first. You can then edit the file with WordPerfect to "filter out" unwanted or incorrect syllable breaks and set up hyphenation priorities. Finally, use the hyphenation utility to add the words to the exception dictionary.

Choices **6** and **7** [Look up] are essentially the same, except the former shows hyphen spots with hyphens while the latter displays the numerical priority levels. Type an individual word or a word pattern. **Tip:** To see all words in the exception dictionary, use the wildcard *.*. When you're finished, press RETURN alone, F1 Cancel, or F7 Exit to return to the main menu.

Dear Reader, thanks again for buying this book. Happy word processing!

Appendixes

Customizing WordPerfect

In this appendix you'll learn the following new commands . . .

Function Key Command
SHIFT-F1 Setup   Change WordPerfect defaults

Typewriter Keyboard Command
        CTRL-6   Return to the original keyboard
                  during editing

. . . and you'll discover other uses of this command:
    SHIFT-F8 Format   Change document format defaults

I've mentioned several times that if the WordPerfect formatting defaults aren't to your liking or useful for your document needs, you can change the defaults. Actually, you can customize many other aspects of WordPerfect, including the screen display and even how the program works with your keyboard. In fact, WordPerfect's keyboard layout feature is a very powerful extension of the macro language that you saw in Chapters 7 and 32.

DO WARM-UP

The SHIFT-F1 Setup Key

You change most defaults from the SHIFT-F1 Setup key. Once you've made your changes, they remain in effect until you change them again. There are no codes: WordPerfect stores the changes in the special setup file, WP{WP}.SET. Version 4.2 users: This key is new, although you'll recognize some options from 4.2.

Press   **SHIFT-F1 Setup**

    WordPerfect displays the setup menu, shown in Figure A-1. I'll cover each item in its turn, but just remember that you have to press SHIFT-F1 Setup first.

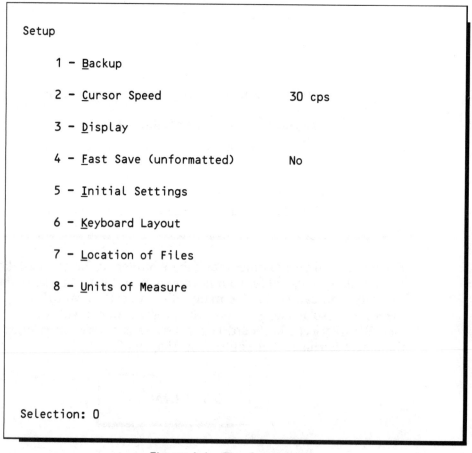

```
Setup

     1 - Backup

     2 - Cursor Speed            30 cps

     3 - Display

     4 - Fast Save (unformatted)    No

     5 - Initial Settings

     6 - Keyboard Layout

     7 - Location of Files

     8 - Units of Measure




Selection: 0
```

Figure A-1   The Setup Menu

Tip: Before you change the WordPerfect defaults, work with the program for a while and see if these defaults are satisfactory. Then, when you're familiar with WordPerfect, set the defaults to suit your needs.

Backup

Sometimes a power problem could "trash" a file while you're working on it. Fortunately, WordPerfect maintains overflow files on the disk, so the chances of your losing an entire file are small (Chapter 2). However, it's best to save your work regularly or configure WordPerfect with one or both of its automatic backup features. The default is for no backup. You'll see the setup: backup screen (Figure A-2).

The two backup types are distinctly different. The *timed backup* saves your document—while you're working—at a regular interval that you determine. For example, you could have WordPerfect save a document every 5

```
Setup: Backup

    Timed backup files are deleted when you exit WP normally.  If you
    have a power or machine failure, you will find the backup file in the
    backup directory indicated in Setup: Location of Files.

        Backup Directory

    1 - Timed Document Backup          No
        Minutes Between Backups        30


    Original backup will save the original document with a .BK! extension
    whenever you replace it during a Save or Exit.

    2 - Original Document Backup       No
```



```
Selection: 0
```

Figure A-2 The Setup: Backup Screen

minutes. WordPerfect stores the timed backup in temporary files WP{WP}.BK1 for Doc 1 and WP{WP}.BK2 for Doc 2. After it saves a document once, WordPerfect continues to save at regular intervals only if you've edited the document since the last timed save.

To set a timed backup: (1) type **1** or **t** [Timed Document Backup], (2) type **y**, (3) type an interval in minutes, (4) press **RETURN** to finish. To turn off the timed backup, repeat step (1), then type **n**. (I won't mention again how to turn a setting off—it's obvious!)

One disadvantage to this option is that WordPerfect will interrupt your train of thought and not let you continue for a few seconds until it's saved the document. The status line displays * Please Wait * when WordPerfect is saving the backup. Another disadvantage is that WordPerfect may save a new document to a file that you don't want to change, such as a format file that you've just retrieved. Be careful!

The *original backup* feature maintains the previous version of a document as a backup, with the extension .BK!, every time you save the document. That is, there are always two versions of a saved document: the most current, and the second-most-current versions. Be careful, however, when you're editing documents with the same file names but different extensions. For instance, WordPerfect would save only one backup, CHAPTER.BK!, for a document called CHAPTER.1 or one called CHAPTER.2, depending on which document you just edited. It would be best, then, to rename the backup document if there is a name conflict *before* you edit the next document with a similar name.

To set the original backup: (1) type **2** or **o** [Original Document Backup], (2) type **y**. You can retrieve a timed or original backup (.BK1) file, but you first have to rename it (Chapter 9).

Note: If you use a backup option and your machine goes "down," the next time you load WordPerfect the program will ask you to rename or delete the previous backup files before it can create new backups for the current work session.

Cursor Speed

Recall from Chapter 36 that you can change the size and shape of the cursor with the separate CURSOR.COM program. The **2** [Cursor Speed] option on the setup menu changes the speed from the default, 30 characters per second (cps), to another setting. You'll see this menu:

```
Characters Per Second: 1 15; 2 20; 3 30; 4 40; 5 50; 6 Normal: 0
```

Normal speed, by the way, is slower than 30 cps and nullifies WordPerfect's control of cursor speed.

Display

This option lets you determine various attributes that relate to how text status lines, messages, and menus appear on the screen as you work.

Note: Screen display does not affect the printout. Here you'll find many functions that were scattered over several keys in WordPerfect 4.2. When you use this option, WordPerfect displays the setup: display menu (Figure A-3). Your monitor type may be different. Here is a very brief run-down of the choices.

Automatically Format and Rewrite. When you set this option to no, WordPerfect will rewrite each line individually when you move the cursor down out of the current line. When you set the option to the default yes, WordPerfect rewrites the entire paragraph when you move the cursor up or down out of the line.

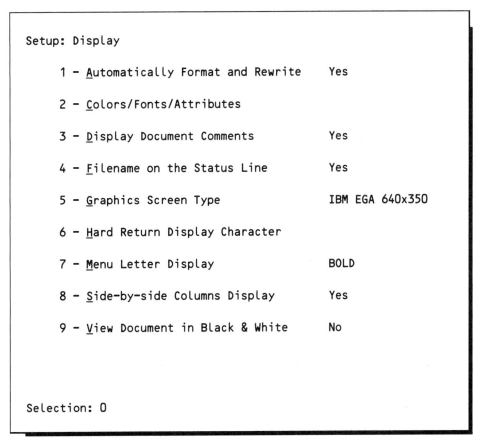

```
Setup: Display

    1 - Automatically Format and Rewrite    Yes

    2 - Colors/Fonts/Attributes

    3 - Display Document Comments           Yes

    4 - Filename on the Status Line         Yes

    5 - Graphics Screen Type                IBM EGA 640x350

    6 - Hard Return Display Character

    7 - Menu Letter Display                 BOLD

    8 - Side-by-side Columns Display         Yes

    9 - View Document in Black & White       No




Selection: 0
```

Figure A-3 The Setup: Display Menu

Colors/Fonts/Attributes. This choice brings up another menu to let you customize the colors that WordPerfect uses for various fonts or select a different font family for screen displays. What you can do depends on your monitor's capabilities. That is, WordPerfect may not let you change certain settings if your monitor can't work with the changes.

Display Document Comments. Normally, comment boxes display. When you set this option to no, you won't see the text of comments even if you reveal the codes.

Filename on the Status Line. Set to no if you don't want the file name to display.

Graphics Screen Type and View Document in Black & White. The term *graphics* here means both the graphics edit screen and the print preview, because they work in graphics mode instead of normal text mode. WordPerfect "senses" the video display card on your computer and uses the capabilities of this display automatically. Sometimes, however, the default settings may not be the most appropriate for your computer setup, so with this option you can tell WordPerfect to use a different display card type for the print preview. Even with a color monitor, you can view the graphics screen in black on white if you set choice **9** to yes.

Note: If you can't find your monitor on the list that WordPerfect supplies, do a directory listing of the graphics screen files on the original program disks. These files end in the extension .WPD. Then copy the file you need.

Hard Return Display Character. The default is to show hard returns as spaces. If you want hard returns to appear as another character (for example, >), type the character you want.

Menu Letter Display. This option lets you select a different font for the mnemonic letter display in all menus. In this book I show mnemonics with underlines.

Side-by-side Columns Display. You can have WordPerfect display text columns separately. If you're working with many columns, WordPerfect can then rewrite the screen more quickly. The default is yes.

Fast Save

Refer to Chapter 5 for my discussion of this feature. If you want WordPerfect to "fast save" all documents, set this option to yes.

```
Setup: Initial Settings

    1 - Beep Options

    2 - Date Format                3 1, 4

    3 - Document Summary

    4 - Initial Codes

    5 - Repeat Value               8

    6 - Table of Authorities

    7 - Print Options




Selection: 0
```

Figure A-4   The Setup: Initial Settings Menu

Initial Settings

Use this option to change the formatting defaults and a variety of other WordPerfect defaults. You'll see the setup: initial settings menu (Figure A-4).

Beep Options. You can have WordPerfect beep (1) when there's an error situation, (2) when WordPerfect stops and asks for a hyphenation decision (Chapter 20), or (3) when a search operation "fails," that is, WordPerfect can't find what you're searching for (Chapter 8).

Tip: Reduce noise pollution! Set all beep options to no!

Date Format. This brings up the date format menu (Chapter 15) to let you set a different default date or time format.

Document Summary. You can have WordPerfect request a document summary automatically when you save a *new* document the first time or when you exit the program and save a new document. You can also change the subject/account search string from *RE:* to something else (Chapter 9).

657

Initial Codes. Here's where you can supply formatting changes as codes that WordPerfect will use for every new document that you create. Just enter the codes as normal. Press **F7 Exit** when you're finished.

Tip: If you have a local area network, set up initial codes so that everyone on the network is working with the same document format. Set up footnote, outline, paragraph numbering, and other options here, too.

Note: Even if you reveal the codes, WordPerfect does *not* display initial codes at the beginning of the document. They're in the document prefix area (Chapter 1). You can override the initial codes for documents that require other formats. See Initial Settings later in the chapter.

Repeat Value. You can change the default ESC key repeat value from 8 to another value.

Table of Authorities. This choice governs how the table of authorities (Chapter 23) will *print*. You can set up dot leaders, underlining, and a blank line between each different authority.

Print Options. You can assign default binding, number of printed copies, graphics quality, and text quality option here.

Keyboard Layout

This choice brings up a new term: the *soft keyboard*. No, your keyboard won't turn to mush before your very eyes! Here, *soft* means that you can change or customize how each key operates in WordPerfect. You can even add key definitions or assign new and existing macros to keys. If, for example, you don't like the arrangement of the function keys or you want to use CTRL with the alphabet keys to mimic WordStar's cursor diamond, you can do it. Version 4.2 users: Here's a workable substitute for the Ctrl/Alt key feature that has disappeared in WordPerfect 5.0.

You'll see the setup: keyboard layout screen, which shows the available keyboard layout files. You may want to experiment with the files that WordPerfect Corporation supplies. Check the WordPerfect documentation to learn more about these layout files. Keyboard files end in the extension .WPK. At the bottom of the screen is this menu:

```
1 Select; 2 Delete; 3 Rename; 4 Create; 5 Edit; 6 Original; N Name Search: 1
```

By now you should be an old hand at working with these menu choices. For example, you can highlight an existing keyboard file and then edit, delete, or rename it. Here are just a couple tips for helping you create a different keyboard layout. When you type **4** or **c** [Create], WordPerfect requests a new file name to store the keyboard definitions. Type a name of up to eight characters, but don't use an extension. That way, WordPerfect can supply .WPK and list the keyboard file names on the setup: keyboard layout screen. WordPerfect then presents this menu:

```
Key: 1 Edit; 2 Delete; 3 Move; 4 Create;  Macro: 5 Save; 6 Retrieve: 1
```

When you create or edit a key, you press the key or keys as you would normally.

Note: WordPerfect won't let you change certain keys, such as NUM LOCK or CTRL. WordPerfect then puts you in the key: edit screen, which is just the macro editor in disguise! The key's original function is in the Action box. Follow the steps that I outlined in Chapter 7—remember the important CTRL-V—to change the key's function in the Action box. Then press **F7 Exit** enough times to save the key definition.

Caution: Make sure you assign the changed key's original function to another key. Otherwise, that function won't be available! For example, suppose you want F1 Cancel to be the help key, so it will take over the function of F3 Help. You'd then want to substitute another key—say ESC—for the original F1 Cancel key. You'd also substitute yet another key, maybe F3 Help, for the original ESC key. You can also have a key, say, CTRL-M, issue a macro. I don't recommend that you change CTRL-V or CTRL-B, because WordPerfect needs these keys.

For every key you create, WordPerfect adds it to the list on the screen. The **3** [Move] choice lets you move an existing key definition to another key. Highlight the key and type **3** or **m** [Move]. WordPerfect requests the new key. Press the key, and the definition changes to show that key.

You can define a new macro for a key or retrieve an existing macro by its file name. You don't have to type the .WPM extension, but recall that ALT key macros are in files like ALTA.WPM, ALTB.WPM, and so on. When you type **6** or **r** [Retrieve], WordPerfect first asks for the key to which you want to assign the macro. You can save a new key definition to a macro, too. Just highlight the definition, then type **5** [Save]. Again, WordPerfect requests the new macro's file name.

Tip: You can create different keyboard layouts with different ALT and CTRL key macros, then switch keyboards as often as you like. That way, you have unlimited macros!

When you're finished, press **F7 Exit** to return to the setup: keyboard layout screen. Then use the **1** or **s** [Select] choice to make your new keyboard definition file the default.

Note: Only those keys that you've added to your new keyboard layout file change. To return to the default keyboard layout, choose Original from the Keyboard Layout menu or press **CTRL-6** anytime while you're editing a document.

Location of Files

This option is most useful for hard disk users. There are a number of auxiliary files that WordPerfect needs to operate, such as the printer resource files (.PRS) and the main spelling dictionary (WP{WP}US.LEX). WordPerfect normally looks for its files in the program directory on your hard disk. You may want to set up ancillary files in separate directories so that you can keep track of them more easily. Use this option to tell WordPerfect where you've put the files. You'll see the setup: location of files menu.

Caution: Make sure you supply a complete directory path for each location. If you forgot how to work with paths, see Chapter 9. You can determine the location of the following files: backup files (.BK1), hyphenation files, macro files (.WPM), main and supplementary dictionaries, printer files (.PRS), the style library file if you've set one up (Chapter 26), and the thesaurus dictionary. For the style library file, supply a path *and* a file name.

Units of Measure

By default WordPerfect uses inches as the unit of measure for format settings and the current cursor position on the status line. You can, if you wish, go back to WordPerfect 4.2 units, where there are ten characters per horizontal inch and six lines per vertical inch. You can set the units of measure separately for (1) formats and (2) the status line display to inches, points (Chapter 4), centimeters, or WordPerfect 4.2 units. An undocumented choice is *w,* which stands for the internal unit of measurement that WordPerfect uses "behind the scenes." Settings are in 1/1200ths of an inch!

Document Format Settings

The format: document menu on the SHIFT-F8 Format key has a few more customization options that work for the *current* document only. To access the format: document menu, press **SHIFT-F8 Format**, then type **3** or **d** [Document]. WordPerfect saves the information in the document prefix, so you won't see any codes.

You've already learned how to create or edit a document summary (Chapter 9) and change the redline method (Chapter 24). Here in brief is what the other changes mean.

Display Pitch

WordPerfect normally displays ten characters per horizontal inch on the screen. Sometimes—especially when you're working with a complicated column setup that has proportional fonts—WordPerfect may overlap characters on the screen. They will print correctly, but you probably want to see them as you edit, too! Type **n** to turn automatic display pitch off, then supply a new width adjustment.

Initial Codes

This option lets you set the initial format settings for the current document only when you don't want to use whatever initial settings you determined with SHIFT-F1 Setup. Here's where you can see the initial codes that WordPerfect stores in the prefix. You can change the codes to other settings or delete them if you want to use WordPerfect's default formats.

Initial Font

This option assigns a base font that's different from the initial font in the printer resource file. Again, it works with the current document only. WordPerfect also uses this font for headers, footers, page numbering, and footnotes.

Tip: When you switch printers and the initial fonts of the two printers are different, WordPerfect may not reformat on the screen a document that you created with the first printer. That's because WordPerfect saves the original printer's initial font of the document in the prefix. However, WordPerfect will still pick a font on the new printer that matches or approximates the original font. You can change the initial font from this menu.

Note: To register your changes to a document's initial settings and initial font, retrieve the document first before you make the changes.

The Documents Used in This Book

Document Name	Created in Chapter	Used or Changed in Chapter
ACCEPT.LTR	30	
AGREE.DAT	29	
AGREE.FRM	29	
AGREE.1	29	
ARTICLE.OUT	10	11, 21
BAD.LTR	30	
BEGIN.LTR	30	
BOX.9	15	
CHAPTER.2	11	16, 22
CHAPTER.2N	22	32, 34
CHAPTER.3	26	
CHOICE.LTR	30	
CLOSING.LTR	30	
COFFEECK	10	
COURSE.OUT	21	
CUISINE	33	
DBASE.LAS	35	
DEPO.1	3	
DISQUAL.LTR	30	
DRAFT.STY	26	

Document Name	Created in Chapter	Used or Changed in Chapter
E	29	
ENV	13	35
ENV.LAS	35	
EQUATION	15	
FINAL.STY	26	
FORM.1	3	
FORMLET	30	
GOODBODY.ELT	13	14, 23
GRADES.RPT	31	
GRADES	31	
HARDSP.EX	20	
LAREST	11	12, 15, 16, 20, 22, 24, 32, 35
LAREST.2	24	
LAREST.BOX	15	
LAREST.CON	23	
LAREST.HY	20	
LAREST.LAS	35	
LAREST.NDX	23	
LAREST.NOT	22	23
LAREST.PAG	16	
LHEAD.LAS	35	
MACRO.MEN	31	
MAILING.1	27	
MAILING.ENV	28	29
MAILING.L2	28	
MAILING.LST	28	
MAILING.RL	28	
MEMO.1	4	8
MENU.NEW	31	
MINUTES	10	21
MINUTES.2	21	
MYMONEY	19	33
NAMES	13	
NEEDFORM.LTR	30	

Document Name	Created in Chapter	Used or Changed in Chapter
NEWS	1	2, 3, 8, 9, 15
NEWS.LN	15	
NOFORM.LTR	30	
NOTCLEAR.LTR	30	
PATRONS	27	
PATRONS.CMD	31	
PATRONS.C2	31	
PATRONS.HDR	31	
PATRONS.RPT	31	
PATRONS.R2	31	
PIES.1	10	
PIES.2	10	
POULET	18	20, 34, 35
POULET.HY	20	
POULET.LAS	35	
POULET.VER	34	
POULET.2	18	
RECORDS	33	
REJECT.LTR	30	
REPLY.DAT	29	
REPLY.FRM	29	
REPLY.1	29	30
REPLY.2	29	
REPLY.3	29	
RULES	33	
SALES.87	10	14, 17
SALES.HOR	19	
SPECIAL.BOX	15	
STATES	32	
SUDS.LTR	6	13
TEST.1	18	
TODAY	32	
TRYAGAIN.LTR	30	
WITNESS	14	
YES.LTR	30	

The WordPerfect Commands

This appendix presents a chart of the WordPerfect commands, arranged first by function key and then by other keys on the keyboard. You'll also find a list of some useful WordPerfect Library commands. Use the **F3 Help** key for more information about a specific command.

The numbers in brackets ([]) indicate the chapter where I *first* discuss the command. Any numbers in brackets after individual menu entries indicate where the specific menu item was introduced, if the item was not discussed in the same chapter as the command. Consult the index for more help.

The mnemonics for each menu choice appear in underlining. On your monitor they may display in a highlighting or color. The "new" icon will help you locate keys and commands that have changed in WordPerfect 5.0 from version 4.2. I also list separately the WordPerfect 4.2 commands that are no longer valid in WordPerfect 5.0.

The F1 *Key*

F1 Cancel [1]

No block: Cancels a command or displays the undelete menu [2]:

Undelete 1 Restore; 2 Previous Deletion

Block on: Cancels the block [2]

At the hyphenation prompt: Tells WordPerfect not to hyphenate the word [20]

ALT-F1 Thesaurus [12]

Displays the thesaurus menu (no mnemonics):

1 Replace Word; 2 View Doc; 3 Look Up Word; 4 Clear Column

SHIFT-F1 Setup [Appendix A]

Displays the setup menu:

Setup

    1 - <u>B</u>ackup

    2 - <u>C</u>ursor Speed

    3 - <u>D</u>isplay

    4 - <u>F</u>ast Save (unformatted)

    5 - <u>I</u>nitial Settings

    6 - <u>K</u>eyboard Layout

    7 - <u>L</u>ocation of Files

    8 - <u>U</u>nits of Measure

CTRL-F1 Shell [9]

Displays the shell menu:

Without the WordPerfect Library:

1 <u>G</u>o to DOS

With the WordPerfect Library:

1 <u>G</u>o to Shell; 2 <u>R</u>etrieve Clipboard [Appendix E]

The F2 *Key*

F2 ►Search [8]

Forward search

In the file listing: Starts a name search [9]

In macros: Sets up a repeating macro [32]

ALT-F2 Replace [8]

No block: Replaces in the entire document forward or backward from the cursor location

Block on: Replaces in the block only (no matter where the cursor is located)

SHIFT-F2 ◄Search [8]

Backward search

CTRL-F2 Spell [12]

No block: Displays the spell menu:

Check: 1 Word; 2 Page; 3 Document; 4 New Sup. Dictionary [36]; 5 Look Up; 6 Count

Block on: Checks the block immediately and gives a word count when finished

The F3 *Key*

F3 Help [1]

Provides help for commands, topics, and the keyboard template

ALT-F3 Reveal Codes [2] (same as **F11 Reveal Codes**)

Displays the formatting codes

SHIFT-F3 Switch [11]

No block: Switches to Doc 2 in the other window or on the other screen

Block on: Displays the case menu:

1 Uppercase [14]; 2 Lowercase [14]

Print view: Switches the foreground and background colors

CTRL-F3 Screen [6]

Displays the screen menu:

0 Rewrite; 1 Window [11]; 2 Line Draw [15]

The F4 *Key*

F4 ►Indent [10]

Indents text one tab stop to the right of the left margin

ALT-F4 Block [2] (same as **F12 Block**)

Turns the block on

SHIFT-F4 ►Indent◄ [10]

Indents text one tab stop to the right of the left margin and one tab stop to the left of the right margin

CTRL-F4 Move [3]

No block: Displays the move menu:

Move: 1 Sentence; 2 Paragraph; 3 Page; 4 Retrieve

Block on: Displays the block move menu:

Move: 1 Block; 2 Tabular Column [14]; 3 Rectangle [15]

The F5 Key

F5 List Files [9]

Works with the file directory

 ALT-F5 Mark Text [23]

No block: Displays the mark text menu:

1 Auto Ref; 2 Subdoc [25]; 3 Index; 4 ToA Short form; 5 Define; 6 Generate

Block on: Displays the block mark menu:

Mark for: 1 ToC; 2 List; 3 Index; 4 ToA

In the file listing: Marks or "unmarks" all files [9]

 SHIFT-F5 Date/Outline [6]

Displays the date/outline menu:

1 Date Text; 2 Date Code; 3 Date Format [15]; 4 Outline [10]; 5 Para Num [21]; 6 Define [21]

 CTRL-F5 Text In/Out [9]

No block: Displays the text in/out menu:

1 DOS Text [36]; 2 Password; 3 Save Generic [36]; 4 Save WP 4.2 [36]; 5 Comment

Block on: Changes the block to a comment

The F6 Key

F6 Bold [4]

No block: Bolds text as you type

Block on: Bolds the entire block

ALT-F6 Flush Right [14]

No block: Flushes right text as you type

Block on: Flushes right the entire block

SHIFT-F6 Center [2]

No block: Centers text as you type

Block on: Centers the entire block [14]

CTRL-F6 Tab Align [10]

Aligns characters around the alignment character (decimal point) at the next tab stop

The F7 Key

F7 Exit [1]

Clears the screen, saves the document, or exits WordPerfect

At the hyphenation prompt: Temporarily suspends hyphenation [20]

ALT-F7 Math/Columns [18]

Displays the math/column menu:

1 Math On [19]; 2 Math Def [19]; 3 Column On/Off; 4 Column Def

SHIFT-F7 Print [5]

No block: Displays the print menu:

```
Print

        1 - Full Document

        2 - Page

        3 - Document on Disk

        4 - Control Printer

        5 - Type Through [34]

        6 - View Document

        7 - Initialize Printer [36]


Options

        S - Select Printer

        B - Binding

        N - Number of Copies

        G - Graphics Quality [34]

        T - Text Quality
```

Block on: Prints the block after you confirm

CTRL-F7 Footnote [22]

Displays the note menu:

1 Footnote; 2 Endnote; 3 Endnote Placement

The **F8** *Key*

F8 Underline [4]

No block: Underlines text as you type

Block on: Underlines the entire block

ALT-F8 Style [26]

Displays the available styles and the style menu:

1 On; 2 Off; 3 Create; 4 Edit; 5 Delete; 6 Save; 7 Retrieve; 8 Update

SHIFT-F8 Format [6]

No block: Displays the format menu:

Format

    1 - Line

Hyphenation [20]	Line Spacing
Justification	Margins Left/Right
Line Height [17]	Tab Set
Line Numbering	Widow/Orphan Protection [17]

    2 - Page

Center Page (top to bottom)	New Page Number [16]
Force Odd/Even Page [16]	Page Number Position [16]
Headers and Footers [16]	Paper Size/Type [13]
Margins Top/Bottom	Suppress [16]

    3 - Document

Display Pitch [Appendix A]	Redline Method [24]
Initial Settings [Appendix A]	Summary [9]

    4 - Other

Advance [15]	Overstrike [15]

```
Conditional End of Page [17]    Printer Functions [34]
Decimal Characters [10]          Underline Spaces/Tabs
Language [36]
```

Block on: Protects the block to keep in on one page after you confirm [17]

CTRL-F8 Font [4]

No block: Displays the font menu:

1 Size; 2 Appearance; 3 Normal; 4 Base Font; 5 Print Color [15]

Block on: Displays the font attribute menu:

Attribute: 1 Size; 2 Appearance

The F9 Key

F9 Merge R [27]

Inserts a merge ^R code and hard return

ALT-F9 Graphics [34]

Displays the graphics menu:

1 Figure; 2 Table; 3 Text Box; 4 User Defined Box; 5 Line

ALT-SHIFT-F9 [34]

"Hot key" for the GRAB utility: Captures the screen to a graphics file (.WPG)

SHIFT-F9 Merge Codes [27]

Displays the merge codes menu:

^C [29]; ^D [29]; ^E; ^F; ^G [29]; ^N; ^O [29]; ^P; ^Q [28]; ^S [30]; ^T; ^U [30]; ^V [29]

CTRL-F9 Merge/Sort [27]

No block: Displays the merge/sort menu:

1 Merge; 2 Sort [33]; 3 Sort Order [33]

Block on: Sorts the block [33]

The **F10** *Key*

F10 Save [1]
No block: Saves the entire document
Block on: Saves the block to another file (boilerplate) [3]

ALT-F10 Macro [7]
Runs a macro by file name

SHIFT-F10 Retrieve [2]
Retrieves a document
Retrieves text from the move buffer [3]

CTRL-F10 Macro Define [7]
Begins and ends macro definition
In the macro editor: Toggles command tag insertion on/off

The **F11** *Key*

See **ALT-F3 Reveal Codes**

The **F12** *Key*

See **ALT-F4 Block**

Other Keys

ALT-⟨*letter*⟩ [7]
Runs a WordPerfect macro assigned to ⟨*letter*⟩

ALT-⟨*number*⟩ [15]
Enters an extended character whose code is ⟨*number*⟩ (use the numeric keypad only)

ARROW KEYS [Prelude]
Moves the cursor up, down, left, right
Cancels or backs out of a menu [1]
Additional functions:

DOWN ARROW

Indicates a forward search or replace [8]

UP ARROW

Indicates a backward search or replace [8]

ASTERISK (*) [9]

Marks or "unmarks" individual files in the file listing

BACKSPACE [1]

No block: (1) Deletes the character in front of the cursor (insert mode), (2) replaces the character to the left with a space (typeover mode)

Block on: Deletes the block (with confirm) [2]

CTRL-2 [15]

Composes a character, or inserts a character from a WordPerfect character set

CTRL-6 [Appendix A]

Restores the original keyboard layout

CTRL-BACKSPACE [1]

Deletes the word at the cursor

CAPS LOCK [Prelude]

Toggles the uppercase and lowercase alphabet keys

DEL [1]

No block: Deletes the character at the cursor position

Block on: Deletes the block (with confirm) [2]

In the file listing: Deletes the highlighted file or directory [9]

END [1]

Positions the cursor at the end of the line

CTRL-END [2]

Deletes from the cursor position to the end of the line

ESC [1]

Cancels most commands or repeats the next command, text, or macro a certain number of times [2]

At the hyphenation prompt: Inserts a soft hyphen [20]

GRAY − [1]

Positions the cursor at the top of the current screen or up by screenful ("screen up")

GRAY + [1]

Positions the cursor at the bottom of the current screen or down by screen-ful ("screen down")

HOME [1]

At times used with the arrow keys to position the cursor:

HOME,DOWN ARROW

To the bottom of the current screen or down by screenful

HOME,LEFT ARROW

To the left edge of the current screen

HOME,RIGHT ARROW

To the right edge of the current screen

HOME,UP ARROW

To the top of the current screen or up by screenful

HOME,HOME,DOWN ARROW

To the end of the document

HOME,HOME,LEFT ARROW [2]

To the left end of the line after any codes

HOME,HOME,RIGHT ARROW [2]

To the right end of the line

HOME,HOME,UP ARROW

To the beginning of the document past any codes

HOME,HOME,HOME,LEFT ARROW [2]

To the far left side of the line in front of any codes

HOME,HOME,HOME,UP ARROW [6]

To the beginning of the document in front of any codes

HOME,∗ [9]

Marks or "unmarks" all files in the file listing

HOME,/ [20]

Inserts a do not hyphenate code

HOME,BACKSPACE [1]

Deletes from the cursor position to the previous space character

HOME,DEL [1]

Deletes from the cursor position to and including the next space character

HOME,HYPHEN [20]

Inserts a hard hyphen (dash or minus sign)

HOME,INS [7]

Forces typeover mode on

HOME,HOME,INS [7]

Forces insert mode on

HOME,RETURN [20]

Inserts an invisible soft return

HOME,SPACEBAR [20]

Inserts a hard space

HOME,F2 ▶Search [16]

Extended forward search

HOME,ALT-F2 Replace [16]

Extended replace

HOME,SHIFT-F2 ◀Search [16]

Extended backward search

CTRL-HOME [2]

No block: Goes to a specific page or forward to a character (if the character is within the next page or so)

Block on: Goes to the beginning of the block [5]

CTRL-HOME,CTRL-HOME [3]

Cursor to the last "major motion" (block move or copy, search or replace [8], and so on)

ALT-F4 Block,CTRL-HOME,CTRL-HOME or **F12 Block,CTRL-HOME,CTRL-HOME** [3]

Rehighlight the last block

CTRL-HOME,ALT-F4 Block or **CTRL-HOME,F12 Block** [3]

Cursor to the beginning of the last marked block or to the beginning of the currently marked block

CTRL-HOME,DOWN ARROW

Cursor to the bottom of the current page [2] or text column [18]

CTRL-HOME,LEFT ARROW [18]

Cursor to the next text column to the left

CTRL-HOME,RIGHT ARROW [18]

Cursor to the next text column to the right

CTRL-HOME,UP ARROW

Cursor to the top of the current page [2] or text column [18]

CTRL-HOME,HOME,LEFT ARROW [18]

Cursor to the leftmost text column

CTRL-HOME,HOME,RIGHT ARROW [18]

Cursor to the rightmost text column

CTRL-HYPHEN [20]

Inserts a soft hyphen

INS [1]

Toggles insert and typeover modes

NUM LOCK [1]

Toggles the numeric keypad from cursor to numbers

PG UP and **PG DN** [2]

Moves the cursor to top of the previous or the next page, respectively

In the look screen: Scrolls quickly through the document [9]

 CTRL-PG UP (Macro Commands) [32]

Sets up a pause for keyboard input, displays menus as a macro runs, assigns a value to a variable, enters a comment, or accesses advanced macro programming commands

CTRL-PG DN [2]

Deletes from the cursor position to end of current page

PRT SC or * [9]

In the file listing: Marks or "unmarks" individual files

SHIFT-PRT SC [34]

Prints a screen dump

RETURN [1]

No command: Ends a paragraph or inserts blank line With some commands: Completes the command

CTRL-RETURN [13]

No parallel columns: Inserts a hard page code

With parallel columns: Positions the cursor at the top of the next column [18]

CTRL-S [9]

In the file listing: Scrolls the document down on the look screen

SPACEBAR [1]

Inserts a space

TAB [1]

Moves the cursor to the next tab stop and inserts a tab code (insert mode)

Moves the cursor to the next tab stop (typeover mode)

In the file directory: Moves the highlight to the next marked file [9]

In outline mode: Indents to the next outline level [10]

SHIFT-TAB [9]

Left margin rclease [10]

In the file directory: Moves the highlight to the previous marked file

In outline mode: Moves to the previous outline level [10]

CTRL-V [7]

Inserts an editing command in a macro definition, or accepts the next command or character literally

Inserts a WordPerfect character set character [15]

CTRL-V,CTRL-X [8]

Searches for pattern matches

WordPerfect Library Commands [Appendix E]

SHIFT-ALT-HYPHEN

Begins a block to copy to the Clipboard

SHIFT-ALT-+

"Pastes" a block from the Clipboard

SHIFT-ALT-F10 Macro

Runs a shell macro

SHIFT-CTRL-F10 Macro Define

Defines a shell macro

Commands That Are Different in WordPerfect 4.2

Function Key Commands

Here are the commands that have substantially changed. Below each command I refer you to the corresponding command in WordPerfect 5.0.

SHIFT-F1 Super/Subscript

No block: Displays this menu:

`1 Superscript; 2 Subscript; 3 Overstrike; 4 Adv Up; 5 Adv Dn; 6 Adv Ln`

Block on: Displays this menu:

`Block: 1 Superscript; 2 Subscript`

In WordPerfect 5.0:

> For superscripts and subscripts, see CTRL-F8 Font
>
> For overstrike and advance, see SHIFT-F8 Format

CTRL-F3 Screen

`0 Rewrite; 1 Window; 2 Line Draw; 3 Ctrl/Alt Keys; 4 Colors; 5 Auto Rewrite`

In WordPerfect 5.0:

> Ctrl/Alt keys are no longer in the product: use ALT with the numeric keypad, or set up CTRL keys with SHIFT-F1 Setup
>
> For screen colors and auto rewrite, see SHIFT-F1 Setup

CTRL-F4 Move

No block: Displays the move menu:

Move 1 Sentence; 2 Paragraph; 3 Page; Retrieve 4 Column; 5 Text; 6 Rectangle

Block on: Displays the block move menu:

1 Cut Block; 2 Copy Block; 3 Append; 4 Cut/Copy Column; 5 Cut/Copy Rectangle

In WordPerfect 5.0:

> For all functions see CTRL-F4 Move

ALT-F5 Mark Text

No block: Displays the mark text menu:

1 Outline; 2 Para #; 3 Redline; 4 Short Form; 5 Index; 6 Other Options

Block on: Displays the block mark menu:

Mark for: 1 ToC; 2 List; 3 Redline; 4 Strikeout; 5 Index; 6 ToA

In WordPerfect 5.0:

> For outlines, see SHIFT-F5 Date/Outline For redline and strikeout, see CTRL-F8 Font
>
> For all other functions, see ALT-F5 Mark Text

SHIFT-F5 Date

Displays the date menu:

Date 1 Insert Text; 2 Format; 3 Insert Function

In WordPerfect 5.0:

> This menu is SHIFT-F5 Date/Outline

CTRL-F5 Text In/Out

Displays the document conversion, summary and comments menu:

```
Document Conversion, Summary and Comments
     DOS Text File Format
          1 - Save
          2 - Retrieve  (CR/LF becomes [HRt])
          3 - Retrieve  (CR/LF in H-Zone becomes [SRt])
     Locked Document Format
          4 - Save
          5 - Retrieve
     Other Word Processor Formats
```

```
       6 - Save in a generic word processor format
       7 - Save in WordPerfect 4.1 format
Document Summary and Comments
       A - Create/Edit Summary
       B - Create Comment
       C - Edit Comment
       D - Display Summary and Comments
```

In WordPerfect 5.0:

For locked documents, see password on CTRL-F5 Text In/Out

For document summary, see SHIFT-F8 Format

WordPerfect 4.1 in no longer in the product

For all other functions, see CTRL-F5 Text In/Out

ALT-F7 Math/Columns

Displays the math/columns menu:

`1 Math On; 2 Math Def; 3 Column On/Off; 4 Column Def; 5 Column Display`

In WordPerfect 5.0:

For column display, see SHIFT-F1 Setup

For all other functions, see ALT-F7 Math/Columns

SHIFT-F7 Print

No block: Displays the print menu:

`1 Full Text; 2 Page; 3 Options; 4 Printer Control; 5 Type-thru; 6 Preview`

In WordPerfect 5.0:

For all functions, see SHIFT-F7 Print

CTRL-F7 Footnote

Displays the footnote menu:

`1 Create; 2 Edit; 3 New #; 4 Options; 5 Create Endnote; 6 Edit Endnote`

In WordPerfect 5.0:

For all functions, see CTRL-F7 Footnote

ALT-F8 Page Format

No block: Displays the page format menu:

`Page Format`

```
        1 - Page Number Position

        2 - New Page Number

        3 - Center Page Top to Bottom

        4 - Page Length

        5 - Top Margin

        6 - Headers or Footers

        7 - Page Number Column Positions

        8 - Suppress for Current page only

        9 - Conditional End of Page

        A - Widow/Orphan
```

Block on: Protects the block to keep it on one page after you confirm

In WordPerfect 5.0:

> For all functions, see SHIFT-F8 Format

SHIFT-F8 Line Format

Displays the line format menu:

`1 2 Tabs; 3 Margins; 4 Spacing; 5 Hyphenation; 6 Align Char`

In WordPerfect 5.0:

> For all functions, see SHIFT-F8 Format

CTRL-F8 Print Format

Displays the print format menu:

```
Print Format
        1 - Pitch

            Font

        2 - Lines per Inch

   Right Justification
        3 - Turn off

        4 - Turn on

   Underline Style
        5 - Non-continuous Single

        6 - Non-continuous Double

        7 - Continuous Single

        8 - Continuous Double

        9 - Sheet Feeder Bin Number
```

```
A - Insert Printer Command
B - Line Numbering
```

In WordPerfect 5.0:

    For pitch, font, and double underlines, see CTRL-F8 Font

    For all other functions, see SHIFT-F8 Format

ALT-F9 Merge Codes [20]

Displays the merge codes menu:

^C; ^D; ^F; ^G; ^N; ^O; ^P; ^Q; ^S; ^T; ^U; ^V

In WordPerfect 5.0:

    For all functions, see SHIFT-F9 Merge Codes

SHIFT-F9 Merge E [20]

Inserts a merge ^E code and hard return

In WordPerfect 5.0:

    See SHIFT-F9 Merge Codes

Alternate Keys in Version 4.2

Versions of WordPerfect before 4.0 used the keyboard differently. In those earlier versions, you would issue some commands by pressing the ALT or CTRL key together with one of the alphabet keys or a number key at the top of the keyboard. Most of these alternate commands are still in effect in version 4.2 only, *not* in version 5.0. You can, however, set up any of these keys on a new keyboard layout (Appendix A).

Alternate	*Regular*
ALT-1	F1 Cancel
ALT-2	SHIFT-F2 Super/Subscript, 2
CTRL-2	SHIFT-F2 Super/Subscript, 1
ALT-3	F5 List Files
ALT-4	CTRL-F8 Print Format
ALT-5	CTRL-F2 Spell
ALT-6	CTRL-F10 Macro Define
CTRL-6	ALT-F10 Macro
ALT-7	SHIFT-F10 Retrieve
ALT-8	F10 Save
ALT-9	CTRL-F4 Move
ALT-0	ALT-F4 Block

ALT-=	F7 Exit
CTRL-I	TAB
CTRL-J	RETURN
CTRL-K	CTRL-END
CTRL-L	CTRL-PG DN
CTRL-W	UP ARROW
CTRL-X	RIGHT ARROW
CTRL-Y	LEFT ARROW
CTRL-Z	DOWN ARROW

The WordPerfect Codes and Macro Command Tags

The numbers in brackets indicate in what chapter I introduce the code. The middle column shows how the code appears in WordPerfect version 4.2 if it's different.

Note: Someone please write to me if I've missed a code or two! For a general discussion of the macro editor's command tags, see Chapter 7.

The WordPerfect Codes

Code	4.2 Equivalent	Description
[ ]	[ ]	Hard space [20]
[-]	[-]	Regular hyphen [20]
-	-	Soft hyphen [20]
-	-	Hard hyphen [20]
/	/	Don't hyphenate this word [20]
!	!	Math formula to be calculated or recalculated [19]
?	?	(Merge) Suppress the printing of a blank line in the merge document [28]
??!	??!	Incorrect math calculation [19]

Code	4.2 Equivalent	Description
+	+	Subtotal of a column of numbers directly above the code [19]
*	*	Grand total of all totals above the code [19]
=	=	Total all subtotals above the code [19]
N	N	Subtract the number but don't display a minus sign [19]
		Extra subtotal entry [19]
T	T	Extra total entry [19]
^B	^B	Page number in a header or footer [16] (use extended search to look for this code)
^C	^C	(Merge) Wait for input from the keyboard [29]
^D	^D	(Merge) Print the current date in the merged document [29]
^E	^E	(Merge) End of record marker in the secondary document [27]
^F	^F	(Merge) Field number indicator in the primary document [27]
^G	^G	(Merge) Run the named macro after the merge is complete (two codes required) [29]
^N	^N	(Merge) Go to the next record in the secondary document [27]
	Not available	Identify fields by name in the secondary document [28]

Code	4.2 Equivalent	Description
^O	^O	(Merge) Display the enclosed prompt (two codes required) [29]
^P	^P	(Merge) Use the enclosed primary document (two codes required) [27]
^Q	^Q	(Merge) Stop the merge at this record in the secondary document [28]
^R	^R	(Merge) End of field marker in the secondary document [27]
^S	^S	(Merge) Use the enclosed secondary document (two codes required) [30]
^T	^T	(Merge) "Type" (print) the merged document and clear memory [27]
^U	^U	(Merge) Rewrite the screen [30]
^V	^V	(Merge) Insert the enclosed merge code into the merged document (two codes required) [29]
[AdvDn]	[Adv ▼]	Advance down [15]
[AdvLft]	None	Advance left [15]
[AdvRgt]	None	Advance right [15]
[AdvToCol]	None	Advance to a column [15]
[AdvToLn]	[AdvLn]	Advance to a line [15]
[AdvUp]	[Adv ▲]	Advance up [15]
[Align] and [C/A/Flrt]	[A] and [a]	Begin and end tab align [10]
[Block]		Beginning of the block when the codes are revealed [2]
[Block Pro:Off]	[BlockPro:Off]	Block protection off [17]
[Block Pro:On]	[BlockPro:On]	Block protection on [17]
[BOLD] and [bold]	[B] and [b]	Begin and end boldface [4]

689

Code	4.2 Equivalent	Description
[Box Num]	None	Caption in a graphics box [34]
[Center Pg]		Center text between the top and bottom of the page [6]
[Cntr] and [C/A/ Flrt]	[C] and [c]	Center a line [2]
[Cndl EOP]	[CndlEOP]	Conditional end of page [17]
[Col Def]	[Col Def]	Text column definition [18]
[Col Off]	[Col off]	Text column mode off [18]
[Col On]	[Col on]	Text column mode on [18]
[Color]	None	Print color change [15]
[Comment]	[Smry/Cmnt]	Document comment [9]
[Date]		Date code [6]
[DBL UND] and [dbl und]	None	Begin and end double underline [4]
[Decml/Algn Char]	[Align Char]	Decimal/align character or thousands' separator change [10]
[Def Mark:Index]	[DefMark:Index]	Location of index definition [23]
[Def Mark:List]	[DefMark:List]	Location of list definition [23]
[Def Mark:ToA]	[DefMark:ToA]	Location of table of authorities section definition [23]
[Def Mark:ToC]	[DefMark:ToC]	Location of table of contents definition [23]
[DSRt]	None	Deletable soft return [20]
[End Def]	[EndDef]	End of table, list, or index after generation [23]
[Endnote]	[Note:End]	Endnote [22]
[Endnote Placement]	None	Endnote location change [22]
[End Opt]	[FtnOpt]	Endnote style (options) change [22]
[EXT LARGE] and [ext large]	None	Begin and end extra large font [15]

Code	4.2 Equivalent	Description
[Figure]	None	Figure box [34]
[FINE] and [fine]	None	Begin and end fine font [15]
[Flsh Rt] and [C/A/Flrt]	[A] and [a]	Begin and end flush right alignment [14]
[Font]	[Font Change]	Base font change [4]
[Footer A]	[Hdr/Ftr]	Footer A change [16]
[Footer B]	[Hdr/Ftr]	Footer B change [16]
[Footnote]	[Note:Foot]	Footnote [22]
[Force]	None	Force odd or even page numbering [16]
[Ftn Opt]	[FtnOpt]	Footnote style (options) change [22]
[Header A]	[Hdr/Ftr]	Header A change [16]
[Header B]	[Hdr/Ftr]	Header B change [16]
[HLine]	None	Horizontal line graphics element [34]
[HPg]	[HPg]	Hard page [13]
[HRt]	[HRt]	Hard return [2]
[Hyph On]	[Hyph on]	Hyphenation on [20]
[Hyph Off]	[Hyph off]	Hyphenation off [20]
[HZone]	[HZone Set]	Hyphenation zone change [20]
[→Indent]	[->Indent]	Left indent [10]
[→Indent←]	[->Indent<-]	Both sides indent [10]
[Index]	[Index]	Index entry [23]
[ISRt]	None	Invisible soft return [20]
[ITALC] and [italc]	None	Begin and end italics [4]
[Just Lim]	None	Word spacing justification limits change [34]
[Just Off]	[Rt Just Off]	Right margin justification off [6]
[Just On]	[Rt Just On]	Right margin justification on [6]

Code	4.2 Equivalent	Description
[Kern:Off]	None	Kerning off [34]
[Kern:On]	None	Kerning on [34]
[Lang]	None	Foreign language dictionary change [36]
[LARGE] and [Large]	None	Begin and end large font [15]
[Ln Height]	[LPI]	Line height or leading change [17]
[Ln Num:Off]	[LnNum:Off]	Line numbering off [6]
[Ln Num:On]	[LnNum:On]	Line numbering on [6]
[Ln Spacing]	[Spacing Set]	Line spacing change [6]
[L/R Mar]	[Margin Set]	Left and right margin change [6]
[Mark:List] and [End Mark:List]	[Mark:List] and [EndMark:List]	Begin and end list entry [23]
[Mark:ToC] and [End Mark:ToC]	[Mark:ToC] and [EndMark:ToC]	Begin and end table of contents entry [23]
[←Mar Rel]	[<-Mar Rel]	Left margin release [10]
[Math Def]	[Math Def]	Math column definition change [19]
[Math Off]	[Math Off]	Math mode off [19]
[Math On]	[Math On]	Math mode on [19]
[New End Num]	[Set Note #]	Endnote number change [22]
[New Fig Num]	None	Figure number change [34]
[New Ftn Num]	[Set Note #]	Footnote number change [22]
[New Tab Num]	None	Table number change [34]
[New Txt Num]	None	Text box number change [34]
[New Usr Num]	None	User-defined box number change [34]
[Note Num]	[Note #]	Footnote or endnote number in the note text [22]
[Open Style]	None	Turn an open style on [26]

Code	4.2 Equivalent	Description
[OUTLN] and [outln]	None	Begin and end outline printing [4]
[Ovrstk]	[Ovrstk]	Overstrike [15]
[Paper Sz/Typ]	[Pg Lnth]	Paper size or type (form) change [13]
[Par Num]	[Par#]	Automatic or manual paragraph number [21]
[Par Num:Auto]	[Par#:Auto]	Outline entry [10]
[Par Num Def]	[Par#Def]	Outline or paragraph numbering style change [21]
[Pg Numbering]	[Pg#]	New starting page number or numbering style [15]
[Pg Num Pos]	[Pos Pg#] and [Pg# Col]	Page number position change (start page numbering or change the page number location) [16]
[Ptr Cmnd]	[Cmnd]	Printer escape code or codes [34]
[Ref]	None	Automatic reference (cross-reference) location [23]
[REDLN] and [redln]	[RedLn] and [r]	Begin and end redlining [24]
[SHADW] and [shadw]	None	Begin and end shadow printing ("doublestrike") [4]
[SM CAP] and [sm cap]	None	Begin and end small caps [4]
[SMALL] and [small]	None	Begin and end small font [13]
[SPg]	[SPg]	Soft page [13]
[SRt]		Soft return [2]
[STKOUT] and [stkout]	[StrkOut] and [s]	Begin and end strikeout [24]
[Style Off]	None	Turn a paired style off [26]
[Style On]	None	Turn a paired style on [26]

Code	4.2 Equivalent	Description
[Subdoc]	None	Location of a subdocument in a condensed master document [25]
[Subdoc End]	None	End of a subdocument in an expanded master document [25]
[Subdoc Start]	None	Start of a subdocument in an expanded master document [25]
[SUBSCPT] and [subscpt]	[SubScrpt]	Begin and end subscript [4]
[Suppress]	[Suppress]	Supress page format on the current page [16]
[SUPRSCPT] and [suprscpt]	[SuprScrpt]	Begin and end superscript [4]
[Tab]	[TAB]	Tab [2]
[Table]	None	Table box [34]
[Tab Set]		Tab set change [6]
[Target]	None	Target reference location [23]
[Tbl Opt]	None	Table options change [34]
[T/B Mar]	[Top Mar]	Top and bottom margin change [6]
[Text Box]	None	Text box [34]
[ToA]	[ToA]	Table of authorities long or short form entry [23]
[Txt Opt]	None	Text box options change [34]
[UND] and [und]	[U] and [u]	Begin and end underlining [4]
[Undrln]	[Undrl Style]	Underlining of spaces or tabs off [6]
[Undrln:Spaces]	[Undrl Style]	Underlining of spaces on [6]
[Undrl:Tabs]	[Undrl Style]	Underlining of tabs on [6]
[Usr Box]	None	User-defined box [34]

Code	4.2 Equivalent	Description
[Usr Opt]	None	User-defined box options change [34]
[VLine]	None	Vertical line graphics element [34]
[VRY LARGE] and [vry large]	None	Begin and end very large font [15]
[W/O Off]	[W/O Off]	Widow/orphan protection off [17]
[W/O On]	[W/O On]	Widow/orphan protection on [17]
[Wrd/Ltr Spacing]	None	Word or letter spacing change [34]

The Macro Editor Command Tags

WordPerfect Key	Command Tag
F1 Cancel	{Cancel}
ALT-F1 Thesaurus	{Thesaurus}
SHIFT-F1 Setup	{Setup}
CTRL-F1 Shell	{Shell}
F2 ▶Search	{Search}
ALT-F2 Replace	{Replace}
SHIFT-F2 ◀Search	{Search Left}
CTRL-F2 Spell	{Spell}
F3 Help	{Help}
ALT-F3 Reveal Codes	{Reveal Codes}
SHIFT-F3 Switch	{Switch}
CTRL-F3 Screen	{Screen}
F4 ▶Indent	{Indent}
ALT-F4 Block	{Block}
SHIFT-F4 ▶Indent◀	{L/R Indent}
CTRL-F4 Move	{Move}

WordPerfect Key	Command Tag
F5 List Files	{List Files}
ALT-F5 Mark Text	{Mark Text}
SHIFT-F5 Date/Outline	{Date/Outline}
CTRL-F5 Text In/Out	{Text In/Out}
F6 Bold	{Bold}
ALT-F6 Flush Right	{Flush Right}
SHIFT-F6 Center	{Center}
CTRL-F6 Tab Align	{Tab Align}
F7 Exit	{Exit}
ALT-F7 Math/Columns	{Math/Columns}
SHIFT-F7 Print	{Print}
CTRL-F7 Footnote	{Footnote}
F8 Underline	{Underline}
ALT-F8 Style	{Style}
SHIFT-F8 Format	{Format}
CTRL-F8 Font	{Font}
F9 Merge R	{Merge R}
ALT-F9 Graphics	{Graphics}
SHIFT-F9 Merge Codes	{Merge Codes}
CTRL-F9 Merge/Sort	{Merge/Sort}
F10 Save	{Save}
ALT-F10 Macro	{Macro}
SHIFT-F10 Retrieve	{Retrieve}
CTRL-F10 Macro Define	{Macro Define}
ESC	{Esc}
TAB	{Tab}
SHIFT-TAB	{Left Mar Rel}
BACKSPACE	{Backspace}
CTRL-BACKSPACE	{Del Word}
RETURN	{Enter}
CTRL-RETURN	{HPg}

WordPerfect Key	Command Tag
LEFT ARROW	{Left}
CTRL-LEFT ARROW	{Word Left}
RIGHT ARROW	{Right}
CTRL-RIGHT ARROW	{Word Right}
UP ARROW	{Up}
DOWN ARROW	{Down}
HOME	{Home}
CTRL-HOME	{Goto}
END	{End}
CTRL-END	{Del to EOL}
PG UP	{Page Up}
CTRL-PG UP	{Macro Commands}
PG DN	{Page Down}
CTRL-PG DN	{Del to EOP}
GRAY −	{Screen Up}
GRAY +	{Screen Down}
INS	{Typeover}
DEL	{Del}

E

The WordPerfect Library

In this appendix you'll learn these new WordPerfect Library commands:

SHIFT-ALT-HYPHEN	Begin a block to copy to the Clipboard
SHIFT-ALT-+	"Paste" a block from the Clipboard
SHIFT-ALT-F10 Macro	Run a Library macro
SHIFT-CTRL-F10 Shell Macro Def	Turn Library macro definition on/off

Here is a brief introduction to the WordPerfect Library, a separate program from WordPerfect Corporation. With the Library you can perform the following operations, among many others:

■ Load several programs at one time and switch between them with the press of just a few keys.

■ Transfer text and data between programs.

■ Manage files on your hard disk.

■ Do calculations on the fly and print or store the results.

■ Keep track of your appointments and sound an alarm to remind you about them.

■ Maintain a data base of names, addresses, and telephone numbers in WordPerfect secondary merge document format and have the Library dial telephone numbers from the data base for you.

■ Write computer programs and save them in ASCII text files with no word processing formatting.

■ Play a game when your boss isn't looking!

I can only discuss the basic features of the Library and some important commands. My version of the Library doesn't have mnemonics on the menus, but I'm assuming that they will appear in the next release (2.0). After you understand the Library's ways, refer to the documentation for more information. I won't show the little warm-up box, but make sure you've started the Library if you have it.

It's a Shell Game

In the world of computers, a *shell* is a program that serves as a conduit through which you access other programs and services. Generally, a shell presents a menu of programs, from which you choose by typing a letter or number instead of the program's actual name. When you're finished with one program, the shell reappears to let you choose another.

Besides the shell itself, the Library contains seven *utility* programs: a calculator, a calendar, a file manager, a data base manager called the Notebook, a program editor, a macro editor, and a game called Beast. The Library automatically displays on its menu two other WordPerfect Corporation programs, WordPerfect and *PlanPerfect* (originally MathPlan), but you must purchase these programs separately.

 Note: WordPerfect Corporation sells each of the Library utilities separately, and you can load them from the DOS prompt. See the manual for more information, or load a utility from the Library and press **F3 Help**.

The Library has a feature that most other shell programs don't: the ability to load several WordPerfect Corporation programs into memory at once. Provided you have enough memory, you can start both WordPerfect and PlanPerfect, for example, and then switch between them quickly. The Library supports expanded memory boards, too. These boards give your computer more memory than the standard DOS limit of 640 kb. As you might expect, the Library works best with WordPerfect Corporation programs. You *can* have the Library load other programs, but the Library can only work with these programs individually and can't keep them in memory. See Switching Between Programs.

Loading and Exiting the Library

To load the Library, follow the steps in the Prelude. The Library main menu appears. I'll call it just the main menu. Without starting another futile "chicken and egg" discussion, I can safely say that WordPerfect came before the Library. In fact, the designers of the Library set up three familiar keys to work in the Library exactly as they do in WordPerfect. Here are the "Big Three":

- The **F1 Cancel** key cancels whatever operation you just started.

- The **F3 Help** key gives you context-sensitive help for the Library programs.

- The **F7 Exit** key exits the current WordPerfect Corporation program, such as the Calculator, and returns to the Library's main menu. At the main menu, it exits the Library.

So, to exit the Library and return to DOS:

Press   **F7 Exit**

Notice that choice **1** [Go to DOS] does *not* exit the Library program. If you've loaded other WordPerfect Corporation programs within the Library, the Library reminds you that you might have other files open:

```
Save information in all programs? (Y/N) Y
```

If you type y, the Library closes all open files. Press **F7 Exit** a second time to exit the Library. If you type n, the Library then asks:

```
Exit shell? (Y/N) N
```

Type **y** to exit or **n** to stay in the Library.

Caution: Always save all files that you may have opened in non-WordPerfect Corporation programs *before* you exit the Library. The Library won't remind you to save these files.

Changing the Library Settings

All changes to the Library's default settings are in the Setup menu.

Type   **4** [Setup]

In the setup menu, when you press a menu letter you position the highlight on the program associated with that letter.

Note: You can't change the information for programs that are currently loaded into memory (* indicates these programs). Exit the programs first before you continue. See Removing Programs from Memory. If you accidentally delete programs, or make other changes to the setup that you don't want to keep, press **F1 Cancel**. The Library prompts:

```
Exit WITHOUT saving changes? (Y/N) N
```

Type **y** to return to the main menu and try again.

Screen Colors, Date and Time Formats, Menu Title

These items refer to how the Library appears on your monitor, that is, what colors you want for the various menus and prompts, how the date and time display on the main menu, and the title on the main menu.

Adding or Changing Program Information

The Library has to get some facts about each program you list on the main menu. It already "knows" certain things about WordPerfect Corporation products, but that information may not be complete. For example, if you have WordPerfect in another directory (such as \WP50), you have to tell that to the Library so it can find the program. After you select the program whose information you want to change, type **1** [Edit].

You can add a new program anywhere on the menu. Make sure the highlight is on the letter choice that will represent the new program. The Library pushes the other programs ahead. That is, if you want to add a program for the B choice, position the highlight there before you type **3** [Add]. If you want to add a new program for the next available letter on the menu, position the highlight on that letter and type **1** [Edit].

Use the RETURN or DOWN ARROW key to position the highlight on the item you want to change. For the last four entries, type **y** to change a NO answer to YES, or **n** to change a YES answer to NO.

Tip: You can press CTRL-END to delete an entry completely.

The `Menu Description` is how you want the program name to appear on the main menu. Make sure that you provide the *exact file name, including file extension* of the new program on the `Program Name` line, and its complete directory path on the `Default Directory` line. For example, suppose you're adding Lotus 1-2-3, which is in a directory called \LOTUS. For the program name, supply **b123.com**; for the directory, type **\lotus**.

Many programs let you specify startup options on the DOS command line. For example, if you load WordPerfect by typing **wp/r**, the program uses expanded memory. You can specify any startup options you wish on the `Startup options` line.

You can also have the Library pause while it's loading a program to ask you for any startup options or additional parameters. That way, you can use different options whenever you want. Change the NO answer to YES for the question `Prompt for startup options?` For example, suppose you're used to loading WordPerfect *and* opening a specific file at the same time. As you know, at the DOS prompt you can type **wp <filename>**. If you tell it to, the Library will stop and request startup options when it loads WordPerfect.

Tip: You can have the Library provide a prompt that reminds you what startup option to supply, for example, `?"What is the file name? "`. The first question mark indicates the location of information you'll supply in response to your prompt. Enclose the prompt in quotation marks. Supply the prompt on the `Startup options` line, but leave the `Prompt for startup options?` selection as NO.

The `Clipboard Filename` is discussed in Moving or Copying Text Between Programs. The two startup options lines are discussed in Changing Program Information. If your program is actually in a DOS batch file, answer YES to that option. Make sure you include the entire file name, such as **do.bat**, on the `Program Name` line. See also Automatic Program Loading.

Press **F7 Exit** when you're finished to return to the setup screen, or **F1 Cancel** to exit without making changes.

Note: There's space for 20 different programs on the main menu. You can have other programs in *submenus*. See the manual for more information.

Deleting Programs

When you highlight a program and type **4** [Delete], the Library asks you to confirm what you're doing:

`Delete this entry from shell menu? (Y/N) N`

Type **y** to confirm. The Library moves the other programs up to fill in the spot left by the deleted program. If you don't want the programs to be rearranged, press **CTRL-END** and type **y** to delete the highlighted program but leave the choice letter blank. You can then add another program for this choice.

Rearranging the Program List

Use the **5** [Move] choice to move a highlighted menu item. When you type **5**, the Library asks:

`Move entry to which letter?`

Type the letter when the entry is to go. You must then delete the original menu item, which no longer has an entry.

Caution: If you move a program to a spot that's currently occupied by another program, the Library deletes the second program.

Automatic Program Loading

You can have the Library automatically load programs that you know you'll be using. That way, you don't have to load the programs yourself each time you start the Library. Highlight each program and either press the GRAY + key on the far right side of the keyboard, or type a+ (SHIFT-=). A+appears next to the menu choice to remind you that the Library will load this program automatically.

If you decide to change your mind, or if you make a mistake and mark the wrong program, press the GRAY + key or type +again to toggle the mark off. You can also change the automatic program loading setting by editing the last entry on the program information screen.

Tip: To start the Library *without* having it load programs into memory automatically, at the DOS prompt type shell/n and press **RETURN**.

Manually Loading Programs from the Library

To load a program, merely type its menu letter. If you've instructed the Library to request startup options, type the options and press RETURN. You can load several WordPerfect Corporation programs into memory, one after the other, but you can have only one non-WordPerfect Corporation program running at a time.

Switching Between Programs

There are different methods for switching between programs depending on whether the programs are from WordPerfect Corporation or not. For non-WordPerfect Corporation programs, you must exit the program to return to the Library, then choose another program from the menu. For example, to exit Lotus 1-2-3, you select the Quit command by pressing /Q, then type y for yes.

Caution: Make sure you save all files that you may have opened in a non-WordPerfect Corporation program *before* you exit it! The Library can't save these files for you later.

From WordPerfect Corporation programs (such as WordPerfect or the PlanPerfect) that you've loaded from the Library, you can switch to another program in two ways:

1. If you don't remember the program's letter: Press **CTRL F1 Shell**. The Library presents this menu:

   `1 Go to shell; 2 Retrieve Clipboard: 0`

   Type **1** [Go to shell], then type the program's letter from the main menu.

2. If you *do* remember the program's letter: Press **SHIFT-ALT-‹letter›**, for example, **SHIFT-ALT-N** to select the Notebook. If the program isn't already loaded, the Library loads it for you.

In either case, the information currently showing in a program remains. That is, if you have some figures displaying on the Calculator's tape, they will still be there when you switch back to the Calculator.

Note: When you load WordPerfect from the Library, notice that the CTRL-F1 Shell key presents an expanded menu. You must go to the shell first before you can exit temporarily to DOS.

Removing Programs from Memory

When you exit a non-WordPerfect Corporation program, you've also removed it from memory. To remove WordPerfect Corporation programs from memory, select the program by typing its menu choice, then:

Press   **F7 Exit**

Some programs such as WordPerfect will ask you if you want to save a file. Type **n** if you don't want to save an open file, **y** if you do; follow the regular saving steps. Then type **y** to exit the program. Notice that the Library removes the * marker next to the program's name.

Caution: If you remove a program from memory and that program wasn't the last one you originally loaded, the Library *won't* release the memory until you exit the programs loaded after, or until you exit the Library. See Checking Available Memory.

Library Macros

Even though the Library was designed to save you a lot of keystrokes, you're probably *still* doing too much work! Take heart: The Library has a macro feature that's very similar to WordPerfect's. You can run Library macros from within any WordPerfect Corporation program that you've loaded from the Library, and even from some non-WordPerfect Corporation programs!

You can assign macros to files by name, or to any alphanumeric key (A-Z, 1-9, and 0). What distinguishes Library macros from WordPerfect macros is the required use of the SHIFT key. That is, instead of pressing ALT-F10 Macro, you press SHIFT-ALT-F10 Shell Macro, then type a file name and press RETURN to start a Library macro. When you want to start a Library macro assigned to an alphanumeric key, you press SHIFT-ALT-<key>, for example, SHIFT-ALT-G. You define macros as in WordPerfect by turning the macro definition on, issuing the keystrokes that the macro is to perform, and then turning macro definition off.

Caution: Because you normally press SHIFT-ALT-<letter> to move between programs in the Library, if you assign a macro to a letter key that already represents a program choice on the main menu, the macro takes precedence.

As an example of how to set up a Library macro, here's a simple one that just loads the Calendar and returns to the main menu. Presumably you'd issue this macro when you begin working in the Library each day. Because the Calendar is the E choice on the menu, you'll assign the macro to SHIFT-ALT-E.

Press   **SHIFT-CTRL-F10 Shell Macro Def**

to start the macro definition.

The Library prompts:

Define shell macro:

Press   **SHIFT-ALT-E**

The Library says:

* Starting shell macro *

Then you'll see this message:

* Macro def *

Type   **a** [Appointment Calendar]

The Calendar appears. Now, you just want to return to the main menu but leave the Calendar in memory:

Press   **CTRL-F1 Shell**

Type   **1** [Go to shell]

Press   **SHIFT-CTRL-F10 Shell Macro Def**

to end the macro definition.
The Library notes:

```
* Shell macro ended *
```

The Library stores the macro in a file called ALTSHFTE.SHM. All Library macros have the extension .SHM. So if you define a macro called WP, it's stored in a file called WP.SHM. To issue a macro like this one, you press **SHIFT-ALT-F0 Shell Macro**, type the file name, and press **RETURN**.
The next time you load the Library, to start the SHIFT-ALT-E macro:

Press   **SHIFT-ALT-E**

Here's a "generic go to shell" macro, SHIFT-ALT-S for "shell," that works in most programs. First, load WordPerfect and make sure you're in that program, *not* in at the Library main menu. Then:

Press   **SHIFT-CTRL-F10 Shell Macro Def**

to begin the macro definition.

Press   **SHIFT-ALT-S**

Press   **CTRL-F1 Shell**

Type   1 [Go to shell]

but don't use the mnemonic G, because not all WordPerfect programs have mnemonics.

Press   **SHIFT-CTRL-F10 Shell Macro Def**

to end the macro definition.
You'll get an "invalid macro name" error message if you attempt to define a WordPerfect-type macro, such as ALT-E. You can't press SHIFT-ALT-<letter> to switch between programs during a macro. A work-around is to press CTRL-F1 Shell, type 1 [Go to shell], then type the letter for the program you want to switch to.
The Library stores macro files in its own directory (usually \LIBRARY), no matter what directory you're currently in. If you attempt to redefine an existing macro, the Library asks you to confirm your decision by showing the

complete macro file name with directory path. Here's what you'd see if you try to redefine SHIFT-ALT-E:

```
Replace C:\LIBRARY\ALTSHFTE.SHM? (Y/N) N
```

Tip: You can set up Library macros that load non-WordPerfect Corporation programs and even end macro definitions while you're in the other programs, provided that the key combination SHIFT-CTRL-F10 isn't a command in the other program. For example, you could have a macro that loads Lotus 1-2-3, then starts the Lotus command to retrieve a file (**/File Retrieve**), pauses for you to enter a file name and press RETURN, then ends the macro. Because the command SHIFT-CTRL-F10 has no meaning to Lotus, you're okay.

Working with the Clipboard

One of the most useful applications of the Library is its ability to move or copy text between different WordPerfect Corporation programs. For example, you can copy part of a name-and-address list from the Notebook into a WordPerfect document, or copy figures that you've calculated in PlanPerfect into a WordPerfect report.

The Library's *Clipboard* is a reserved section of memory that serves as a holding zone for text that you want to transfer between programs. After you've marked or blocked information that you want to transfer to another program, you copy it to the Clipboard, switch to the other program, and then "paste" the text from the Clipboard into the second program. You can check the contents of the Clipboard, clear the Clipboard, save the contents of the Clipboard to a DOS text file for use at a later time, or retrieve a DOS text file into the Clipboard.

Note: Normally, when you copy new text to the Clipboard, you *overwrite* the Clipboard's previous contents. You can also *append* new text to the Clipboard. In any case, you can't selectively copy text from the Clipboard: you must copy the entire contents.

Moving or Copying Text Between Programs

There are two special Library commands that work in all WordPerfect Corporation programs running under the Library. These commands let you move or copy text quickly:

■ **SHIFT-ALT-HYPHEN** begins the Clipboard copy operation and is like the **ALT-F4 Block** command in WordPerfect. That is, you establish the beginning and ending limits of a block of text to copy.

■ **SHIFT-ALT-+** (just press the = sign key to get the +) pastes the contents of the Clipboard into the program you want. You can also press **CTRL-F1 Shell** and type **2** [Retrieve Clipboard].

The Library "assumes" that you don't want to format Clipboard text as a WordPerfect document. That is, the contents of the Clipboard are usually in DOS format, with hard returns at the ends of lines. This format is acceptable to other programs that don't use formatting codes, such as the Notebook or even the Calendar. You can also change the format to either paragraphs with soft returns or to WordPerfect secondary merge.

Note: When you block text for copying to the Clipboard, you delimit the block as a rectangle. That is, you establish the *upper left* and *lower right* corners of the block. With the two Clipboard commands just noted, you can only block text that's on the current screen; you can't scroll the screen. (There's a way to get around this restriction in WordPerfect only; see below.)

✔Load WordPerfect from the Library, then retrieve any document.

Suppose you want to copy a section of text to the Calendar. Here are the steps to take:

1. Position the cursor at the top left corner of the text.

2. Press **SHIFT-ALT-HYPHEN**. The cursor changes to a box.

3. Press **RETURN** to start the block. A line appears above the cursor.

4. Use the cursor movement keys to delimit the block to its lower right corner.

   Tip: Use the HOME extender keys to move the cursor quickly. The block appears highlighted or in a different color.

5. Press **RETURN** to establish the lower right corner of the block and bring up the Clipboard menu:

   `Clipboard:  1 Save; 2 Append; 3 Format: 1`

6. Most of the time, you'll want hard returns at the ends of lines, so you can proceed to step 7. To format the block with soft returns or in WordPerfect secondary merge format, type **3** [Format] *before* anything else. This menu appears:

   `Format:  1 Hard Return; 2 Soft Return; 3 Merge Return: 1`

   Type the appropriate choice. When you use format **2** [Soft Return], the Library inserts soft returns at the ends of each line except the last, which gets a hard return. Format **3** [Merge Return] may not do what you expect: It inserts an **^R** code at the end of each line. It does not insert any **^E** codes. After you've made your decision, the Clipboard menu reappears.

7. To overwrite the current Clipboard with your new block, type **1** [Save]. To append the block to the end of the Clipboard, type **2** [Append].

8. Go into the other program: press **SHIFT-ALT-\<letter\>**, where \<letter\> is the program's menu Library choice.

9. Position the cursor where the text is to go.

10. Press **SHIFT-ALT-+** (**SHIFT-ALT-=**) to paste the text from the Clipboard.

11. Save your work!

Tip: In WordPerfect you *can* block out more than a screenful of text with the standard ALT-F4 Block command. After you establish the limits of the block, press **CTRL-F1 Shell** to see this menu:

```
Clipboard: 1 Save; 2 Append: 0
```

Type your choice, but keep in mind that the Library formats the block with hard returns at the ends of all lines. Here are some additional guidelines about which format to use:

- From WordPerfect to PlanPerfect, or vice versa, use the normal Clipboard format with hard returns at the ends of lines.

- To move wordwrapped text from WordPerfect to the Macro Editor, use format **2** [Soft Return].

- To move records from WordPerfect secondary merge documents to the Notepad, use format **3** [Merge Return].

- To move text from WordPerfect to the Calendar, use either hard or soft returns.

- To move text from the Calendar into a WordPerfect paragraph format, use format **2** [Soft Return].

- Don't use the Clipboard to move text between WordPerfect secondary merge documents and the Notebook. Recall that the Notebook saves its information in secondary merge format anyway. If you just want to move Notebook text to include it in a report, then you can use the Clipboard.

- You can only move the contents of the Calculator's tape as text—*not* as real math operators—to other programs. To copy the current entry in the display register to the Clipboard, press **CTRL F1 Shell** and type either **2** [Save to clipboard] or **3** [Append to clipboard]. To copy the *entire tape* to the Clipboard, press **F5 Tape** or **CTRL-T** and type **5** [Save to Clipboard].

Managing the Clipboard

You can view or manage the contents of the Clipboard from the Library only, so you must first go back to the Library's main menu if you're in another program such as WordPerfect. Then type **2** [Clipboard] to see the present contents of the Clipboard at the top of the screen and this menu at the bottom:

```
1 Clear; 2 Save as text file; 3 Retrieve a text file: 0
```

To clear the present Clipboard contents and start with a fresh slate, type **1** [Clear]. To save the contents of the Clipboard to a file that you can use later, type **2** [Save as text file] and supply a new file name. To retrieve a text file into the Clipboard, type **3** [Retrieve a text file] and supply an existing file name. You can then paste the Clipboard text where you need it. Press **RETURN** or **F1 Cancel** to leave the Clipboard menu.

You can also retrieve a file into the Clipboard from the Library's File Manager. Highlight the file and press **CTRL-F1 Shell** to display this menu:

```
1 Go to Shell; 2 Save File to Clipboard: 0
```

Type **2** [Save File to Clipboard] to bring the file, once again with hard returns at the ends of line, into the Clipboard.

Caution: Use this feature for DOS text files *only*.

To *edit* the contents of the Clipboard—change parts of it, or delete or add sections—save it as a text file, switch to WordPerfect, use the CTRL-F5 Text In/Out command to retrieve the text file, edit it, save it again as a text file, press **SHIFT-ALT-2** to access the Clipboard menu, and type **3** [Retrieve a text file]. Enough said!

The Library and DOS

There are three ways to work with DOS commands within the Library:

1. To issue the DOS change directory command, CHDIR or CD, without going to DOS, type **3** [Change Dir], supply the complete directory path, and press **RETURN**.
2. To issue just one DOS command, type **d** [DOS Command]. After you enter the DOS command, the Library prompts:

   ```
   Press any key to continue ...
   ```
3. To stay in DOS and issue several DOS commands, type **1** [Go to DOS]. Notice that (shell) appears in front of the DOS prompt to remind you to type **exit** and press **RETURN** to return to the Library.

Tip: If you're in one of the utility programs, such as the Calculator, you can hold down the ALT and SHIFT keys and press the main menu choice. For example, to change directories, press **SHIFT-ALT-3**; to run a DOS command, press **SHIFT-ALT-D**. You can issue most file management commands, normally DOS operations, from the file listing in WordPerfect or the Library's File Manager.

Checking Available Memory

Use the **5** [Memory Map] choice to display the current memory usage and available memory. The Library lists the order in which you loaded each WordPerfect Corporation program and how much memory each requires. When you're finished viewing the memory map, press any key to return to the main menu.

If you've deleted a WordPerfect Corporation program from memory but that program wasn't the last one you originally loaded, you'll see an asterisk (*) next to the program's memory usage and this message:

```
* = Memory used by this program will remain allocated until programs
    loaded after this one are exited.
```

The Library can't reclaim the memory used by one program if you've loaded another program after the first. In computer terms, that would create a "hole" in memory. To reclaim memory, the Library would have to release the memory occupied by the second program.

Okay, there are the basic Library functions. Now it's your turn to work with the Library and discover its useful utilities. Have fun!

Index

! code for a math formula to be calculated or
recalculated, 339, 350
* (asterisk)
code to total all totals above the code, 339,
345, 351
contains both sort operator, 569
currently selected printer displayed in the
status line with a, 97
displayed next to each program loaded into
memory with the WordPerfect Library,
701
displayed next to each proportionally
spaced font name, 66
displayed next to paper size and type
settings WordPerfect does not "know,"
247
displayed with the [Font] code, 611
to mark or unmark individual files in the
file listing, 169, 180–81
marking a font with an, 105, 625
wildcard, DOS, 176–77
wildcard to look up a word with the
spelling checker, 230, 642
wildcard to restrict a file listing in
WordPerfect, 179–80, 184
+
code to subtotal a math column, 339
contains either sort operator, 569
sign to mark fonts in the select printer:
cartridges and fonts menu, 105
sign to mark soft fonts, 625
= code or = sign to total all subtotals above
the code, 339, 345, 351

?
merge code to suppress printing a blank
line in a merge document, 479
wildcard to look up a word with the
spelling checker, 230, 642
wildcard to restrict a file listing in
WordPerfect, 179–80
??! code for an incorrect calculation formula,
339

A

Abstracts, creating, 585
Addition operator, +, 339
to create a subtotal, 345
Advance menu, 276
[AdvDn] code to advance down, 269, 277
[AdvLft] code to advance left, 269, 277
[AdvRgt] code to advance right, 269, 277
[AdvToCol] code to advance to a column, 270,
277
[AdvToLn] code to advance to a line, 270, 277
[AdvUp] code to advance up, 270, 277
[Align] and [C/A/Flrt] codes to begin and
end tab align, 195
ALT key
and code number to enter an extended
(ASCII) character, 274
commands in WordPerfect version 4.2,
684–85
and a digit to store a temporary "macro,"
543
ALT-F1 to use thesaurus to find synonyms or
antonyms, 225, 232

[ITALC] and [italc] codes to begin and end
  italics, 63, 74

J

Justification
  fixing "rivers" that occur during, 91
  format: line menu option to toggle, 114,
    117
  [Just Off] code to turn off right margin,
    109
  [Just On] code to turn on right margin,
    109, 118
  word spacing limits for right, 117

K

Kerning
  defined, 604
  [Kern:Off] and [Kern:On] codes to turn off
    and on, 590, 604
  for large font sizes, 605
  SHIFT-F8 to set up instructions for, 589
Keyboard
  enhancer should not be loaded from within
    WordPerfect, 192
  "extended," xxx
  layout, customizing the, 658–59, 684
  soft, 658
  template, 20
  types of keys on the, xxx
Key(s)
  creating and editing, 658–59
  hot, 589, 601
  rules for pressing multiple, xxxi, 13–14
  sort, 570, 577–78
  in version 4.2, alternate, 684–85

L

[L/R Mar] code to change the side margins,
  109
Landscape orientation for printouts or
  envelopes, 241–42, 254, 481, 609, 617–
  18
[LARGE] and [large] codes to begin and end
  large font, 270–71
Laser printer, 607–26
  cartridge fonts for the, 608
  cartridges and soft fonts set for
    WordPerfect, 105
  examples of working with WordPerfect and
    the, 614–23
  fonts, 608–9
  evolution of the, 64
  initializing the, 625

internal fonts, 274, 608
letterheads created with the, 620–21
margins with the, 610
memory expansion board for a, 609
page design tips for a, 625–26
paper orientation for a, 241–42
printing mailing labels on plain paper in a,
  487
for scholarly text, 621–23
sheet feeders used with a, 103
SHIFT-F7 to initialize the printer and
  download soft fonts to the, 607
soft fonts for the, 608
unprintable regions, 115
LaserJet Journal, 607
Leaders, tabs with, 201–2
Leading
  adjusted automatically when you change
    fonts, 610
  maintaining an adequate amount of, 625
  SHIFT-F8 to change the, 311, 319–20. *See
    also* Line height
Legal paper size, option for using the, 249–50
Letter spacing
  SHIFT-F8 to change, 589
  [Wrd/Ltr Spacing] code to change, 590,
    606
Letterhead
  creating a typeset-looking, 620–21
  paper type, 240
Line(s)
  [AdvToLn] code to advance to a, 270
  centering a, 25, 43–44
  centering a, over a tab stop, 202
  between columns, drawing, 335
  CTRL-END to delete to the end of the, 25
  CTRL-F3 to draw a, 269
  deleting a, 38
  double, 281
  DOWN ARROW to move cursor down
    one, 3
  draw characters, changing, 282–83
  END key to position the cursor at the end
    of any length of, 37
  HOME,HOME,HOME,LEFT ARROW to
    move cursor in front of codes at the
    beginning of the, 25, 42
  HOME,HOME,LEFT ARROW to move
    cursor to the beginning of the, 25, 37
  HOME,HOME,RIGHT ARROW to move
    cursor to the end of the, 26, 37
  inserted in existing documents, 280–82

length of 6½ inches for text, default, 6
macro to delete a, 145–46
method WordPerfect uses to break, 360–61
SHIFT-F6 to center a, 25
SHIFT-F8 to advance the, 269
SHIFT-F8 to change the height (leading) of, 311, 319–20
sorting by, 576–77
"spaced-out," hyphenation feature to correct, 361
uncentering a, 44
UP ARROW to move cursor up one, 4
Line draw menu, 277–78, 283
Line height
adjusted automatically when you change fonts, 610
affected by font changes, 79
[Ln Height] code to change the, 311
[Ln Height:Auto] code to return to automatic, 320
Line number(s)
absolute, 276
format: line numbering menu options to print, 126
[Ln Num:Off] code to turn off the, 109, 127
[Ln Num:On] code to turn on the, 109, 126
where the cursor is located listed on the status line, 6
Line spacing
double spacing used on screen to represent line-and-a-half, 119
format: line menu option to change, 114, 116
[Ln Spacing] code to change, 109
macro to return to double, 221
List 1 definition menu, 407
Lists, 399, 401–10
ALT-F5 to mark text for, 399
[Def Mark:List] code for the definition location in, 399
generating, process for, 403–9
[Mark:List] and [End Mark:List] codes to begin and end an entry in, 399
marking entries for, 402–3
in a master document, generating, 442
Logical operators in word searches, semicolon, comma, and space as the, 184–85
Long lines, tips for working with, 249–55
Lotus 1-2-3 spreadsheets, converting unformatted files from, 631–33
Lotus Transfer utility, 631

LPT1 port for a parallel printer, WordPerfect assumes printer port is the, xxxv–xxxvi, 101, 624

M

Macro(s), 133–51, 541–67
to add a paragraph number, look for the next hard return code, and repeat itself to the end of the document, PN, 550–52
ALT-F10, 133, 138–39
ALT key, 136–38
assigned to CTRL keys, 134
backups of files containing, 135
to call up a menu of document formats, ALTM, 535
chaining, 547–54
to change the default margins, MA, 556–60
to change to secondary format (indented, single-spaced text), IN, 220, 222
to clear the screen, ALTC, 138
commands key, CTRL-PG UP, 542
conditional, 547, 564–67
CTRL-PG UP to display menus as a macro runs or access advanced programming commands for, 541–42
daisy chain of, 548–49
defined, 134
delays in, 562–64
to delete an entire line, ALTL, 145–46
to delete underlining codes, UN, 162
deleting a, 144, 187
directory for, using a special, 145
to display prompts and messages, 554–56
to display the tab ruler, ALTR, 147–48
editing a, 140–43
envelopes printed with two, SE and PE, 503–4
explanation of, 134–35
F1 to cancel a, 136
fill-ins handled with a, RE, 500–502
to force insert mode or typeover mode on, 145
to insert format documents, ALTI, 546–47
to insert italic codes, ALTI, 148
to insert the date and time as text, D1, 289–90
to insert the date as code, D2, 290–91
to insert your name and address, 138–39
invisible, 556–58
to join documents, ALTJ, 545
to list files, ALTF, 545–46
to look up state abbreviations, SC, 554–56

Hard Disk Management Techniques for the IBM®
Joseph-David Carrabis

This is a resource book of in-depth techniques on how to set up and manage a hard disk environment directed to the everyday "power user," not necessarily the DOS expert or programmer.

Each fundamental technique, based on the author's consulting experience with Fortune 500 companies, is emphasized to help the reader become a "power user." This tutorial highlights installation of utilities, hardware, software, and software applications for the experienced business professional working with a hard disk drive.

Topics covered include:

- Introduction to Hard Disks
- Hard Disks and DOS
- Backup and What You Need to Know
- Service and Maintenance
- Setting Up a Hard Disk
- Organizing a Hard Disk
- Hard Disk Managers
- Utilities to Manage Hard Disks, Find Files, UNERASE Files, Recover Damaged Files, Speed Up Disk Access, and Restore and Backup Disks
- Maintenance Utilities
- Security Utilities

372 Pages, 7½ x 9¾, Softbound
ISBN: 0-672-22580-8
No. 22580, $22.95

IBM® PC AT User's Reference Manual
Gilbert Held

Includes everything you need to know about operating your IBM PC AT—how to set the system up, write programs that fully use the AT's power, organize fixed-disk directories, and use IBM's multitasking TopView.

Includes a BASIC tutorial for beginners and includes several fixed disk organizer programs—all clearly described, explained, and illustrated.

Topics covered include:

- Hardware Overview
- System Setup
- Storage Media and Keyboard Operation
- The Disk Operating System
- Fixed Disk Organization
- BASIC Overview
- Basic BASIC
- BASIC Commands
- Advanced BASIC
- Data File Operation
- Text and Graphics Display Control
- Batch and Shell Processing
- Introduction to TopView
- Appendices: ASCII Code Representation, Extended Character Codes, BASIC Error Messages, Programming Tips and Techniques

453 Pages, 7 x 9¼, Softbound
ISBN: 0-8104-6394-6
No. 46394, $29.95

IBM® PC & PC XT User's Reference Manual, Second Edition
Gilbert Held

Expanded to include the more powerful PC XT, this second edition contains the most up-to-date information available on the IBM PC. From setup through applying and modifying the system, this book continues to provide users with clear, step-by-step explanations of IBM PC hardware and software—complete with numerous illustrations and examples.

Highlights of the second edition include instructions for using DOS 3.1 and upgrading a PC to an XT; information on the customized hardware configuration of the PC and XT; explanations on how to load programs on a fixed disk and how to organize directories; and material on available software, including compilers.

Topics covered include:

- Hardware Overview
- System Setup
- Storage Media and Keyboard Operation
- The Disk Operating System
- Fixed Disk Organization
- BASIC Overview
- BASIC Commands
- Data File Operations
- Text and Graphics Display Control
- Batch Processing and Fixed Disk Operations
- Audio and Data Communications
- Introduction to TopView

496 Pages, 7 x 9¼, Softbound
ISBN: 0-672-46427-6
No. 46427, $26.95

The Waite Group's Desktop Publishing Bible
James Stockford, Editor

Publish high-quality documents right on your desktop with this "bible" that tells you what you need to know—everything from print production, typography, and high-end typesetters, to copyright information, equipment, and software.

In this collection of essays, experts from virtually every field of desktop publishing share their tips, tricks, and techniques while explaining both traditional publishing concepts and the new desktop publishing hardware and software.

Topics covered include:

- Publishing Basics: Traditional Print Production, Conventional Typography, Case Studies in Selecting a Publishing System, and a Comparison of Costs for Desktop and Conventional Systems
- Systems: The Macintosh, PC, MS-DOS, An Overview of Microsoft Windows, Graphics Cards and Standards, Monitors, Dot and Laser Printers, UNIX, and High-End Work Stations
- Software: Graphics Software, Page Layout Software, Type Encoding Programs, PostScript, and JustText
- Applications: Newsletters, Magazines, Forms, Comics and Cartooning, and Music

480 Pages, 7½ x 9¾, Softbound
ISBN: 0-672-22524-7
No. 22524, $24.95

Visit your local book retailer or call
800-428-SAMS.

The Best Book of: Lotus® 1-2-3®, Second Edition

Alan Simpson

This is *the* book for beginning 1-2-3 users. Written as a tutorial, this book steps readers through the various functions of the program and shows them how to use Version 2.0 in today's business environment.

Divided into four sections—worksheets, graphics, database management, and macro—each chapter within a section is designed to allow newcomers to be productive right away. With each new chapter, the users' skills are honed for faster and more spontaneous use of the software.

Topics covered include:

■ Creating and Worksheet
■ Functions and Formulas
■ Formatting the Worksheet
■ Copying Ranges
■ Editing, Displaying, and Managing Worksheet Files
■ Practical Examples
■ Creating Graphs and Printing Graphs
■ Database Management and Sorting
■ Tables and Statistics
■ Macros
■ Custom Menus

350 Pages, 7½ x 9¾, Softbound
ISBN: 0-672-22563-8
No. 22563, $21.95

Lotus® 1-2-3® Financial Models

Tymes, Dowden, & Prael

With this book, Lotus 1-2-3 users will learn to create models for calculating and solving personal and business finance problems using Version 2.0! This book shows how to avoid frustration and delay in setting up individual formulas and allows users to perform any spreadsheet calculation in minutes.

This revision of the popular *1-2-3 from A to Z* includes numerous models or templates for the Lotus user, each preceded by a brief explanation of how the model works and how it can be altered. More advanced business models and an increased emphasis on macros as well as the inclusion of Version 2.0 make this book ideally suited to the business user.

Whether calculating a complex statistical analysis or a home heating analysis, readers can use this book as the one source for the guidance and tools needed to do spreadsheet calculations in the most efficient manner possible.

Topics covered include:

■ Personal Models
■ Business Models
■ Advanced Business Models

300 Pages, 7½ x 9¾, Softbound
ISBN: 0-672-48410-2
No. 48410, $19.95

The Best Book of: Microsoft® Works for the PC

Ruth K. Witkin

This step-by-step guide uses a combination of in-depth explanations and hands-on tutorials to show the business professional or home user how to apply the software to enhance both business and personal productivity.

Clearly written and easy to understand, this book explains how to use such varied applications as the word processor with mail merge, the spreadsheet with charting, the database with reporting, communications, and integration. For each application the author provides a detailed overview of the hows and whys followed by practical examples that guide the reader easily from idea to finished product.

Topics covered include:

■ Spreadsheet Essentials
■ Exploring the Spreadsheet Menus
■ About Formulas and Functions
■ Charting Your Spreadsheet
■ Exploring the Chart Menus
■ Database Essentials
■ Filling a Database
■ Exploring the Database Menus
■ Word Processor Essentials
■ Exploring the Word Processor Menus
■ Integration Essentials
■ Communications Essentials
■ Exploring the Communications Menus

350 Pages, 7½ x 9¾, Softbound
ISBN: 0-672-22626-X
No. 22626, $21.95

The Best Book of: WordStar® Features Release

Vincent Alfieri

With the release of WordStar Professional Release 5, this book will help word processors and computer operators access all of the more than 200 new features and improvements in this "classic" software package.

The book provides in-depth explanations of Professional Release 5 features such as the new advanced page preview, the ability to display font styles and sizes exactly as they appear, the new pull-down menus and additional information on font telecommunications, outlining, and merge printing.

Topics covered include:

■ Revisions
■ Print Effects, Page Preview and Printing
■ Formatting Essentials
■ Blocks and Windows
■ Finding and Replacing
■ Macros and Other Shortcuts
■ Working with DOS and File Management
■ Controlling the Page and the Printer
■ Boilerplates, Format Files, and Document Assembly
■ Conditional Printing
■ Working with Laser Printers
■ Appendices: The Files Used in This Book, Quick Reference Guide

768 Pages, 7½ x 9¾, Softbound
ISBN: 0-672-48434-X
No. 48434, $21.95

Visit your local book retailer or call
800-428-SAMS.